PENGUIN BOO

BBC BOOKS

THIS SCEPTREL

Christopher Lee was the first Quatercentenary Fellow in Contemporary History at Emmanuel College, Cambridge, and is the editor of the latest edition of Winston Churchill's *A History of the English–Speaking Peoples*. He specializes in contemporary political and military history and is the author and editor of eighteen books including *The Final Decade: Will We Survive the 1980s?* (1981) and *War in Space* (1986).

THIS
SCEPTRED
ISLE

❖

CHRISTOPHER LEE

PENGUIN BOOKS
BBC BOOKS

For Alexandra
a princess among researchers

PENGUIN BOOKS
BBC BOOKS

Published by the Penguin Group
Penguin Books Ltd, 80 Strand, London WC2R 0RL, England
Penguin Putnam Inc., 375 Hudson Street, New York, New York 10014, USA
Penguin Books Australia Ltd, 250 Camberwell Road, Camberwell, Victoria 3124, Australia
Penguin Books Canada Ltd, 10 Alcorn Avenue, Toronto, Ontario, Canada M4V 3B2
Penguin Books India (P) Ltd, 11 Community Centre, Panchsheel Park, New Delhi – 110 017, India
Penguin Books (NZ) Ltd, Cnr Rosedale and Airborne Roads, Albany, Auckland, New Zealand
Penguin Books (South Africa) (Pty) Ltd, 24 Sturdee Avenue, Rosebank 2196, South Africa

Penguin Books Ltd, Registered Offices: 80 Strand, London WC2R 0RL, England

www.penguin.com

First published in Great Britain by BBC Books 1997
Published in Penguin Books 1998
19

Extracts from *A History of the English-Speaking Peoples* by Sir Winston S. Churchill
reproduced with permission of Curtis Brown Group Ltd,
copyright © Sir Winston S. Churchill

C◆ precedes extracts taken from four volumes:
Vol 1 Cassell Publishers Limited 1956
Vol 2 Cassell Publishers Limited 1956
Vol 3 Cassell Publishers Limited 1957
Vol 4 Cassell Publishers Limited 1958

The moral right of the author has been asserted

Set in 9½/11¼ pt Monotype Bembo
Printed in England by Clays Ltd, St Ives plc

INTRODUCTION

The idea for this book, and for the preceding radio programmes, grew out of a study I began when I was Quatercentenary Fellow at Emmanuel College, Cambridge. I was looking at the way in which 2000 years of Britain's history influenced late twentieth-century political and diplomatic decision-making, and from that came the basis for *This Sceptred Isle* – the study of kingship and the development of what are now seen as the great institutions in our society.

The book itself is based on the original BBC Radio 4 series which was also called *This Sceptred Isle*. Some people have wondered why Churchill's *A History of the English-Speaking Peoples* was used in the scripts, especially as the programmes were not based on Churchill's text. In making the series we decided that we wanted 'another voice' and by quoting Churchill when we thought the scripts would benefit from an illustration, we could change the style without confusing the authority of the narrative. All Churchill extracts in the book are preceded by C❖. I have also quoted from several other literary sources, including *The Anglo-Saxon Chronicle*, and these extracts are preceded by v. Inevitably there are stylistic differences between the quoted extracts and my own text. I hope these won't be too distracting for the reader but I adopt the more formal spelling of older names, as in Æthelred. In the Churchill text it is Ethelred. I prefer Cnut. Churchill liked Canute. And so on.

This book is by no means a fully comprehensive history of these islands, but it does trace the story of the people who have lived in Britain since the Romans invaded in 55 BC, to the people who were alive when Queen Victoria died in 1901. It records the achievements and failures in the development of the laws which govern these islands, and it records the changing social and political conditions in which the people of these islands have lived through the centuries. And much more.

That the original idea for the programmes germinated into something broader than I imagined is an enormous encouragement for those working in radio during a period when there is a popular notion that television is all important. Michael Green, the then Controller of Radio 4, and his deputy Helen Wilson understood that if this story was to reach the widest possible audience, then the simple narrative form, uncomplicated by gimmicky production techniques, was the way to go about it. Those who were lucky enough to hear the original radio programmes, and the early tapes, will remember how the easy flowing style of the Churchill passages was captured by a master of the spoken word, Paul Eddington. Sadly, Paul died before the programmes were finished, yet he could have wished for no finer successor than Peter Jeffrey. With Anna Massey's intelligent understanding of the whole, and sometimes complex text, capturing just the right tempo as the narrator, the telling of British history can never have been such a joy to so many. The record number of letters received, and the BBC cassettes sold, told the story: hundreds of thousands of people wanted to, and did, listen day after day to their own history. So, there had to be a book.

The difficulty of producing a book of the radio series is that it could not begin to contain the more than half a million words of the original programmes. The cutting started easily enough by removing the repetition that is necessarily to be found in a programme series – the catching-up bits: the recapitulation that begins each new radio programme. A lot of this work was done by the producer, Pete Atkin, who had cleverly edited the original radio programmes into the cassette versions. Then followed the rewriting and further editing.

The success of *This Sceptred Isle* is largely due to the advice and encouragement I received from the Master and Fellows of Emmanuel College, whose Elizabethan founder Sir Walter Mildmay famously believed in the power of an acorn. If those programmes, the tapes and now this volume, inspire listeners and readers to dip into other more specialized works, then *This Sceptred Isle* will have indeed done Christian service and chivalry to the idea with which it started.

Christopher Lee
1997

CONTENTS

Cnut marries Emma (who was Æthelred's wife); 1035 Cnut dies; 1037 Harold I (Harold Harefoot) recognized as King; Harthacnut (son of Cnut and Emma) claims the throne on Harold's death; 1042 Harthacnut dies; 1043 Edward (son of Æthelred the Unready and Emma) is consecrated King, and later becomes the Confessor.

growth of the population and social changes; the Exchequer, the Chancery and the Wardrobe established; 1294 war with France; the Welsh revolt; Scotland makes an alliance with France; 1297 William Wallace defeats the English at Stirling Bridge; 1298 Wallace is beaten at Falkirk and escapes to France; 1299 Edward is forced to marry Margaret, daughter of the King of Castile; 1301 Prince Edward becomes the first Prince of Wales; 1305 Wallace is captured, tried and hanged at Tyburn; Robert the Bruce is crowned King of Scotland at Scone; 1306 Robert the Bruce flees to Rathlin Island, returns to Scotland and leads the rebellion against the English; 1307 King Edward dies.

1307 King Edward II; the Lords Ordainers; Piers Gaveston is made 'keeper of the realm'; the Barons force Piers Gaveston's banishment; Edward appoints Gaveston Lieutenant in Ireland; 1311 the Ordinances; Gaveston executed; 1314 Battle of Bannockburn; famine: cannibalism recorded; the Despensers head the Royalist party; 1321 Welsh Marcher Lords and Lancastrians join ranks against the Despensers; Lancaster beheaded; Isabella becomes Roger Mortimer's lover and together they invade England from France; the Despensers hanged; 1327 King Edward imprisoned in Berkeley Castle and slaughtered; the fourteen-year-old King Edward III crowned; Mortimer and Isabella rule; 1328 the 'Shameful Treaty of Northampton'; Edward III is married to Philippa of Hainault; Mortimer hanged and Isabella consigned to permanent captivity.

1331 Edward III drops his claim to the throne of France; 1332 Edward Balliol victorious at Dupplin Moor; Balliol crowned at Scone; 1333 Edward III besieges Berwick; 1334 David of Scotland flees to France; 1337 Philip of France confiscates Gascony; Edward resurrects his claim to the French throne; 1340 French and English navies fight off Sluys; the beginning of the Hundred Years' War; 1343 a parliamentary Speaker emerges for the first time; 1346 the Battle of Crécy and the Prince of Wales becomes known as the Black Prince; Calais becomes an English colony; the Staple is introduced; King David of Scotland is beaten at Neville's Cross and imprisoned in the Tower; Edward III founds the 'Order of St George of the Garter'; 1348 the Black Death; agriculture and livestock; social conditions; 1356 the Black Prince defeats the French at Poitiers and the French King, John, is imprisoned in the Tower; 1357 King David is

becomes a sober one; 1682 James, Duke of York, returns to England; 1683 the Rye House plot; Sidney and Russell executed; landowners move back into their old positions of social power; social conditions and population statistics; 1685 Charles II dies.

political definition of the role of Prime Minister; the rulebook of a workhouse; 1805 the Battle of Trafalgar; Addington resigns; Napoleon plans to invade England; Lord Nelson dies.

and Leader of the House of Commons; repeal of the Test Act; Huskisson resigns; 1829 Bill for Catholic Emancipation; Robert Peel and the Metropolitan Police Force; 1830 George IV dies; the July Revolution in France and Louis Philippe; William IV; Earl Grey becomes Prime Minister; Lord Melbourne is Home Secretary; 1831 the first Reform Bill; 1832 the Reform Act.

1834 Charles Darwin and the *Beagle*; Charles Dickens; 1833 slaves in the West Indies emancipated; 1834 the Poor Law amended; Melbourne becomes Prime Minister; Lord Palmerston becomes Foreign Secretary; organized labour; the Tolpuddle Martyrs; the Houses of Parliament burn down; William IV sacks Melbourne and Peel becomes Prime Minister; Lady Caroline Lamb; 1835 Melbourne becomes Prime Minister for the second time; the Municipal Corporations Act; 1837 William IV dies; Queen Victoria.

1837 Queen Victoria and Melbourne; Victoria's coronation; 1838 the Chartists; 1839 Melbourne resigns; Peel and the Ladies of the Bedchamber; Melbourne returns; the Chartism debate; the First Afghan War; the Opium Wars; the Treaty of Nanking and Hong Kong ceded to the British; 1840 Queen Victoria marries Prince Albert; 1841 the resignation of the Whig government.

1841 Sir Robert Peel becomes Prime Minister; William Gladstone at the Board of Trade; the repeal of the Corn Laws and the Anti-Corn Law League; 1843 Peel resigns; Russell refuses to form an administration; Benjamin Disraeli and Young England; Daniel O'Connell and Young Ireland; Drummond, Peel's Secretary, is assassinated; 1846 the Corn Laws are repealed; the potato famine in Ireland; the Coercion Bill; Peel resigns; the growth of Britain's industrial power; the beginnings of the Liberals; Lord John Russell becomes Prime Minister; social, political and constitutional reform; nineteenth-century writers; attempts on Queen Victoria's life; the Public Health Act; the penny post; the Great Exhibition; population statistics and social conditions; the state of Europe; Palmerston is fired by Russell.

THE RULERS OF BRITAIN

55 BC – AD 410
Roman Rule

AD 449
First invasions of Angles, Saxons and Jutes

c. AD 491
Aelle the Saxon becomes the first *bretwalda* of the southern English

There are seven English kingdoms (the heptarchy): Sussex, Wessex, Essex, Northumbria, East Anglia, Kent and Mercia

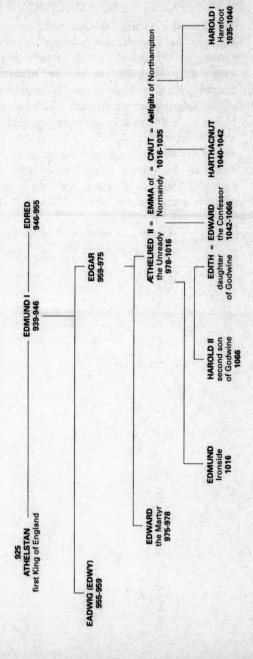

925
ATHELSTAN
first King of England

EDMUND I
939-946

EDRED
946-955

EADWIG (EDWY)
955-959

EDGAR
959-975

EDWARD
the Martyr
975-978

EDMUND
Ironside
1016

AETHELRED II = EMMA of = CNUT = Aelfgifu of Northampton
the Unready   Normandy 1016-1035
978-1016

HAROLD II
second son
of Godwine
1066

EDITH = EDWARD
daughter   the Confessor
of Godwine 1042-1066

HARTHACNUT
1040-1042

HAROLD I
Harefoot
1035-1040

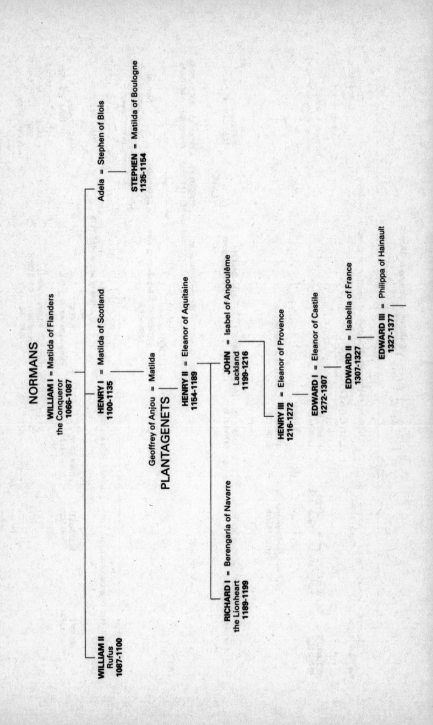

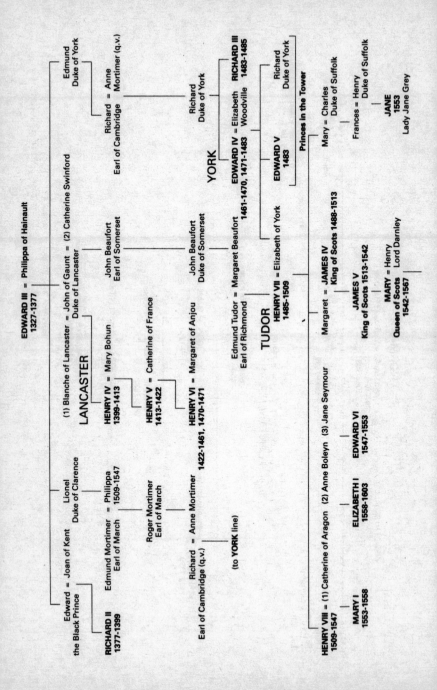

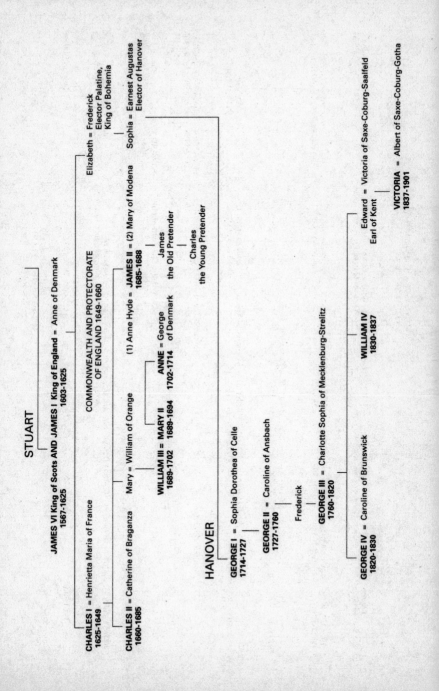

STUART

JAMES VI King of Scots AND JAMES I King of England = Anne of Denmark
1603-1625

CHARLES I = Henrietta Maria of France
1625-1649

COMMONWEALTH AND PROTECTORATE
OF ENGLAND 1649-1660

Elizabeth = Frederick
Elector Palatine,
King of Bohemia

Sophia = Earnest Augustas
Elector of Hanover

CHARLES II = Catherine of Braganza
1660-1685

Mary = William of Orange

(1) Anne Hyde = JAMES II = (2) Mary of Modena
1685-1688

James
the Old Pretender

Charles
the Young Pretender

WILLIAM III = MARY II
1689-1702   1689-1694

ANNE = George
1702-1714   of Denmark

HANOVER

GEORGE I = Sophia Dorothea of Celle
1714-1727

GEORGE II = Caroline of Ansbach
1727-1760

Frederick

GEORGE III = Charlotte Sophia of Mecklenburg-Strelitz
1760-1820

Edward = Victoria of Saxe-Coburg-Saalfeld
Earl of Kent

VICTORIA = Albert of Saxe-Coburg-Gotha
1837-1901

WILLIAM IV
1830-1837

GEORGE IV = Caroline of Brunswick
1820-1830

CHAPTER ONE

55 BC–AD 448

——— ❖ ———

O nce upon a time the British Isles were not islands. They were part of one great plain that spread from what we now call England to the Lowlands, so that the Thames and the Rhine were one. They remained one river until the plain was swamped, the chalk rocks split and great white cliffs were left bare. But that, in these islands, was once upon a time, a time without famous names.

Thomas Carlyle said that 'No great man lives in vain. The history of the world is but the biography of great men.' Perhaps he was right. And so this story begins with the first name in the history of these islands, Julius Caesar. And it begins also with the writings of Churchill who traced the history of this nation in his *A History of the English-Speaking Peoples*.

C❖In the summer of the Roman year 699, now described as the year 55 before the birth of Christ, the Proconsul of Gaul, Gaius Julius Caesar, turned his gaze upon Britain. . . . To Caesar, the Island now presented itself as an integral part of his task of subjugating the Northern barbarians to the rule and system of Rome. The land not covered by forest or marsh was verdant and fertile. The climate, though far from genial, was equable and healthy. The natives, though uncouth, had a certain value as slaves for rougher work on the land, in mines, and even about the house. There was talk of a pearl fishery, and also of gold.

By 56 BC Caesar had all but conquered Gaul. To stay above the law, he must continue to command, to defend and to conquer. Prosecutions for crimes were rarely pursued against victorious military heroes, thus Caesar remained above the law so long as he continued to conquer. So, Caesar plotted and planned. His power lay in his reputation and his generalship.

Caesar also kept a journal and the following extract describes the Britons he knew about, those in the southern part of the island.

❖The inland part of Britain is inhabited by tribes who, according to their own tradition, are native to the island, the coastal parts by tribes that crossed from Belgium for the sake of pillage and then stayed and started cultivating the land. Of all the people, much the most civilized are those who live in Kent, all of which is close to the sea; the life there is not much different from that in Gaul. Most of the inland peoples do not sow corn; they live on milk and flesh and dress themselves in skins. Notably, all the Britons dye themselves with woad, which produces a blue colour, and is used to give them a more frightening appearance in battle. They wear their hair long, and shave every part of the body except the head and upper lip. Groups of ten or twelve men hold wives in common, especially brothers together, and fathers with sons. But the children born from these groups are considered to belong to the group the woman was originally conducted to.

In Caesar's time the people of Britain were not the English. The English didn't arrive until hundreds of years later. These people were Celts. But historians still argue to this day over the precise definition of a Celt. One thing that is considered certain is that these people had a common language: Celtic. By the time Caesar arrived Celtic place names were so well established that the Romans often simply Romanized them. There were also Druids in pre-Roman Britain and Caesar had very definite views about them.

❖The whole Gaulish nation is to a great degree devoted to superstitious rites; and on this account those who are afflicted with several diseases, or who are engaged in battles and dangers, either sacrifice human beings for victims, or vow that they will immolate themselves. These employ Druids as ministers for such sacrifices, because they think that unless the life of man be repaid for the life of man, the will of the immortal gods cannot be appeased.

Tacitus, writing much later, gives an even more alarming picture of the Druids. By this time Caesar's invasion had taken place but the fearful sight of Druids on the island of Anglesey had not been forgotten.

❖The enemy was arrayed along the shore in a massive, dense and heavily armed line of battle, but it was a strangely mixed one. Women, dressed in black like the Furies, were thrusting their way about in it, their hair let down and streaming, and they were brandishing flaming torches. Around the enemy host were Druids, uttering prayers and curses, flinging their arms towards the sky. The Roman troops stopped as if their limbs were paralysed. Wounds were received while they stood frozen to the spot by this extraordinary and novel sight.

Britain in the year 55 BC had farms, hamlets and even villages. Hedges and boundaries suggest a form of regular and marked ownership of land and the river valleys were becoming more populated because of organized agriculture. The beginnings of industrial pottery, a common language and what are now called Gallo-Belgic coins suggest that Caesar was right when he said that the people in the lowland areas, broadly what are now called the South East and Midlands, were infiltrated by those from the Continent. Churchill describes Caesar's opinion of the Britons.

C❖Caesar saw the Britons as a tougher and coarser branch of the Celtic tribes whom he was subduing in Gaul. With an army of ten legions – less than 50,000 soldiers – he was striving against a brave, warlike race which certainly comprised half a million fighting men. . . . A raid upon Britannia seemed but a minor addition to his toils and risks. But at the seashore new problems arose. There were tides unknown in the Mediterranean; storms beat more often and more fiercely on the coasts.

By August 55 BC Gaius Julius Caesar was camped on the shores of what is now called Boulogne. Across the narrow seaway, the Britons knew he was there and what he was planning. These Britons had fought in Gaul *alongside* Caesar's men. They knew what he was capable of, and what he might do with that capability. Some of the tribes sent envoys to Caesar; they didn't want to fight. Also, many of the tribes were at war with each other so there was much to gain from making peace with the Roman. But that was for the future. Churchill describes what it was like at the time. There was a full moon.

C❖Caesar sailed . . . at midnight, and with the morning light saw the white cliffs of Dover crowned with armed men. He judged the place 'quite unsuitable for landing on', since it was possible to throw missiles from the cliffs onto the shore. He therefore anchored till the turn of the tide, sailed seven miles farther, and descended upon Albion on the low, shelving beach between Deal and Walmer. But the Britons, observing these movements, kept pace along the coast and were found ready to meet him. . . . The Islanders, with their chariots and horsemen, advanced into the surf to meet the invader. . . . Caesar brought his warships with their catapults and arrow fire upon the British flank. The Romans . . . leapt from their ships, and, forming as best they could, waded towards the enemy. There was a short, ferocious fight amid the waves, but the Romans reached the shore, and, once arrayed, forced the Britons to flight.

Caesar's cavalry had not done so well. They'd tried to get ashore during the first part of the invasion but the Romans were ignorant of tides and a full moon produces extreme tides.

There was also bad weather. At the first try they were blown far away and their ships were nearly wrecked. By the time they returned, Caesar had camped. As Churchill saw it, the plight of the Romans encouraged the Britons.

C❖The Britons had sued for peace after the battle on the beach, but now that they saw the plight of their assailants their hopes revived and they broke off the negotiations. In great numbers they attacked the Roman foragers. But the legion concerned had not neglected precautions, and discipline and armour once again told their tale. It shows how much food there was in the Island that two legions could live for a fortnight off the cornfields close to their camp. The British submitted. Their conqueror imposed only nominal terms. Breaking up many of his ships to repair the rest, he was glad to return with some hostages and captives to the mainland. He never even pretended that his expedition had been a success.

Caesar seems to have achieved two objectives. He now understood what it would take to beat the Britons and establish Roman rule and secondly, his expedition was seen in Rome as a great success. He returned to northern Italy and his men prepared a new fleet of specially designed warships and transports that could be sailed or pulled with great oars. Caesar had, in effect, designed the first landing craft – vessels that could be run right onto the beaches of Britannia and so make it simpler to get stores, men and horses ashore. The following year, 54 BC, Caesar returned to Britain. But the Britons, or some of them, had united under a leader called Cassivellaunus (who may have been the king of the Catuvellauni). The Catuvellauni were the strongest of the southern tribes and had settled in what is now Hertfordshire. They were resilient and inventive, especially in the way they deployed their chariots when fighting. Caesar wrote of the almost magical agility and inventiveness of these wild Britons.

❖The manner of fighting from chariots is as follows. First of all they drive in all directions and hurl missiles. When they have worked their way in between the troops of cavalry, they leap down from their chariots and fight on foot. Meanwhile the charioteers retire gradually from the combat, and dispose the chariots in such a fashion that, if the warriors are hard pressed by the host of the enemy, they may have ready means of retirement to their own side.

Cassivellaunus had many enemies. There were other tribes who hated his tribe; there were other leaders who hated him. It is thought that one of these tribes, the Trinovantes who lived in Essex, entered into a pact with Caesar. Other tribes joined this arrangement and so Cassivellaunus now fought Romans in front of him and treachery behind. Eventually peace was negotiated and Britons were taken hostage. But winter was approaching and there was a revolt in Gaul. So Caesar left Britain taking his British prisoners with him.

C❖In a dead calm 'he set sail late in the evening and brought all the fleet safely to land at dawn'. This time he proclaimed a conquest. Caesar had his triumph, and British captives trod their dreary path at his tail through the streets of Rome.

And that was it. The end of Caesar's flirtation with Britain. In ten years he would be murdered, and a century would pass before the Emperor Claudius would once more attempt to subjugate the tribes of Britain.

But the time between Caesar's withdrawal in 54 BC and the Roman return in AD 43 was not a dark age for the islanders. From the top of what is now Scotland south to the Kent coast there were more than twenty large tribes. Some of the names became famous. The Iceni in East Anglia, the Catuvellauni in the East Midlands and Essex, the Parisi in Yorkshire, the Silures in Wales and the Brigantes, probably in the Pennines. Strabo, writing in the first century BC in the fourth of his seventeen-volume *Geographica*, tells us that the Britons exported cattle, hides, grain, slaves, gold and silver and, apparently, hunting dogs. In return, they imported wine and oil and glass. And most of this trade was with the prosperous South East. So, even 2000 years ago, there was a north-south divide in Britain.

Some ninety years after Julius Caesar's departure, the Emperor Claudius was persuaded that it would be politically to his advantage to return to Britain by an exiled Briton. His name was Bericus. Cassius Dio, in his early third-century AD version of Roman history, describes what happened.

❖Plautius undertook this campaign, but had difficulty in inducing his army to advance beyond Gaul, for the soldiers were indignant at the thought of carrying on a campaign outside the limits of the known world and would not yield in obedience.

Even after 100 years and much trading beyond their shores, these islands were still at the edge of the 'known' world. But the Romans invaded once more and this time they found that the Britons weren't expecting them.

C❖The internal situation favoured the invaders. Cunobelinus [Shakespeare's Cymbeline] had established an overlordship over the South East of the Island, with his capital at Colchester. But in his old age dissensions had begun to impair his authority, and on his death the kingdom was ruled jointly by his sons Caractacus and Togodumnus. They were not every-where recognized, and they had no time to form a union of the tribal kingdom before the Roman commander, Plautius, and his legions arrived.

Tacitus wrote that although the Britons had many military strengths, they were not a cohesive force.

> ❖Once they owed obedience to kings; now they are distracted between the warring factions of rival chiefs. Indeed nothing has helped us more in fighting against their very powerful nations than their inability to co-operate. It is but seldom that two or three states unite to repel a common danger; thus, fighting in separate groups, all are conquered.

But the Britons did fight back. They had learned there wasn't much future in taking on the Romans at their own game. Instead, they hid in the forests and the swamps. And as Cassius Dio wrote, the Romans hadn't bargained on that.

> ❖. . . Plautius . . . had a great deal of trouble in searching them out; but when at last he did find them, he first defeated Caratacus and then Togodumnus . . . After the flight of these kings, he advanced farther and came to a river. The barbarians thought that the Romans would not be able to cross it without a bridge and bivouacked in rather careless fashion on the opposite bank; but he sent across a detachment of Germans who were accustomed to swim easily in full armour.

The following year Claudius joined the Roman legions on the banks of the Thames. Cassius Dio explains what happened after Claudius met up with his troops.

> ❖Taking command, and enjoining the barbarians who were gathered at his approach, he defeated them in a battle and captured Camulodunum [Colchester], the capital of Cynobellinus. He deprived the conquered of their arms and handed them to Plautius, bidding him also subjugate the remaining districts. Claudius now hastened back to Rome sending ahead news of his victory. The Senate on learning of his achievement gave him the title of Britannicus and granted him permission to celebrate a triumph.

But, Caratacus, or as Churchill and some others called him, Caractacus, resisted.

C❖Caractacus escaped to the Welsh border, and, rousing its tribes, maintained an indomitable resistance for more than six years. It was not till AD 50 that he was finally defeated by a new general, Ostorius, the successor of Plautius, who reduced to submission the whole of the more settled regions from the Wash to the Severn. Caractacus, escaping from the ruin of his forces in the West, sought to raise the Brigantes in the North. Their queen however handed him over to the Romans.

No one was to be trusted. But as Tacitus wrote, Caratacus had become a hero and not just amongst his own people.

❖His reputation had gone beyond the islands, had spread over the nearest provinces, and was familiar in Italy itself where there was curiosity to see what manner of man it was that had for so many years scorned our power. Then while the king's humble vassals filed past, ornaments and neck rings and prizes won in his foreign wars were borne in parade; next his brothers, wife and daughter were placed on view; finally, he himself. The rest stooped to unworthy entreaties dictated by fear; but on the part of Caratacus not a downcast look nor a word requested pity. Arrived at the tribunal, he spoke as follows: 'Had my lineage and my rank been matched by my moderation in success, I should have entered this city rather as a friend than as a captive. My present lot, if to me a degradation, is to you a glory. If I were dragged before you after surrendering without a blow, there would have been little heard either of my fall or your triumph: punishment of me will be followed by oblivion; but save me alive, and I shall be an everlasting memorial of your clemency.'

He was freed. The Romans struck his chains and those of his family but he was not to return to Britain. Caratacus, or so the chronicles tell us, remained in honourable captivity. Britain had been invaded but the most gruesome slaughter and the conquest was yet to come.

The centre of Roman Britain was Camulodunum, or Colchester. The idea was that Britain, or at least part of it, should become a province within the Roman Empire. But this was difficult to achieve. The Britons were warlike and because there were some twenty-three tribal regions, it was impossible to get overall agreement, or even an understanding, with more than a few of them.

The South and the East were the most easily controllable. The Romans had large forces there, they'd set up their capital at Colchester, there were good trade routes through Essex and Kent. The uplands of Britain presented a bigger problem. In AD 54 Claudius died and his stepson, Nero, became emperor. The death of another leader, this one in Britain, left a longer lasting impression upon British history and folklore.

C❖The king of the East Anglian Iceni had died. . . . 'his widow Boadicea (relished by the learned as Boudicca) was flogged and his daughters outraged . . .

Boadicea's tribe, at once the most powerful and hitherto the most submissive, was moved to frenzy against the Roman invaders. They flew to arms. Boadicea found herself at the head of a numerous army and nearly all the Britons within reach rallied to her standard.

The Romans had no more than 20,000 men in Britain in four legions: two were thirty days' march away on the farther side of Wales, one was not much closer in Gloucester, and the last was 120 miles away, at Lincoln. Churchill describes how Boudicca went for Colchester.

C❖There was neither mercy nor hope. . . . Everyone, Roman or Romanized, was massacred and everything destroyed. Meanwhile, the Ninth Legion [the one at Lincoln] was marching to the rescue. The victorious Britons advanced from the sack of Colchester to meet it. By sheer force of numbers they overcame the Roman infantry and slaughtered them to a man, and the Commander, Petilius Cerialis, was content to escape with his cavalry.

But when the Roman, Suetonius, whose job it was to defend London and its people, heard that Boudicca had chased Cerialis towards Lincoln and was now heading south, he abandoned London: he had not the numbers of soldiers he needed. Tacitus, in his *Annals*, tells us of the consequences of that harsh military decision on London and afterwards on Verulamium, or St Albans as it is now called.

❖He [Suetonius] decided to sacrifice the one town to save the general situation. Undeflected by the prayers and the tears of those who begged for his help he gave the signal to move, taking into his column any who could join it. Those [Romans] who were unfit for war because of their sex, or too aged to go, or too fond of the place to leave, were butchered by the enemy [the British]. The same massacre took place at the city of Verulamium, for the barbarian British, happiest when looting and unenthusiastic about real effort, by-passed the forts and the garrisons and headed for the spots where they knew the most undefended booty lay. Something like 70,000 Roman citizens and other friends of Rome died in the places I have mentioned. The British took no prisoners, sold no captives as slaves and went in for none of the usual trading of war. They wasted no time in getting down to the bloody business of hanging, burning and crucifying. It was as if they feared that retribution might catch up with them while their vengeance was only half-complete.

But for the Romans, and the reputation of Suetonius, all was not lost. Reinforced, he marched to the Midlands where Boudicca had amassed 230,000 troops. Suetonius had some 10,000 Romans but, as Tacitus records, that number would be sufficient for the Romans to succeed.

❖Selecting a position in a defile closed in behind a wood, and having made sure that there was no enemy but in front, where there was open flat unsuited for ambuscades, he [Suetonius] drew up his legions in close order, with the light-armed troops on the flanks, while the cavalry was massed at the extremities of the wings.

The Britons were successful against the Romans when they used hit and run tactics. Now, Boudicca was to fight on Roman terms, which was a foolish mistake. The Romans were at the top of a slope and they enticed the Britons on. When they came, the Romans launched their javelins, then charged with their legionaries and cavalry, then forced the Britons back on their carts and their families who were behind them. They slaughtered the cart horses so there was no escape and then massacred the Britons, the ancients, their women, their children.

C❖Boadicea poisoned herself. . . . Suetonius now thought only of vengeance, and indeed there was much to repay. Reinforcements of 4000—5000 men were sent by Nero from Germany, and all hostile or suspect tribes were harried with fire and sword. . . . The procurator, Julius Classicianus, whose tombstone is now in the British Museum, . . . pleaded vehemently for the pacification of the warrior bands, who still fought on without seeking truce or mercy, starving and perishing in the forests and the fens.

Diplomacy took over where military action had not always maintained the peace and the South never again rose against the Romans. There were battles to come, men to die and there were those Britons who preferred death to subjugation. But it was also true that Britain had embarked upon a civilized way of life that would last for 350 years.

The Romans ruled Britain for 500 years and they gave the Britons their first written historical descriptions. They recorded *their versions* of what was happening and the names of people who were making it happen. But when the Romans left Britain in AD 410, many of those who could write went with them, as did the imperial incentive to keep records, and so there were no further contemporary written accounts of what was going on in Britain for many years.

Exactly what followed the Roman exodus is very difficult to verify. There is a long period in the history of these islands that can never be accurately written. However there was a monk in the middle of the sixth century called Gildas the Wise. Most of what he wrote was a religious tract, but in it there are glimpses of history.

Gildas tells us of misery and the rising of a great tyrant, who was probably Vortigern – although Gildas did not name him. Vortigern was on the side of the Britons. He hired mercenaries to defend the Britons against the Anglo-Saxons who were led by Hengist and Horsa. There was a great victory at a place called Mons Badonicus. Gildas felt this victory was important because it brought peace for perhaps half a century. Churchill considers what the Saxon invaders wanted.

C❖Did the invaders exterminate the native population or did they superimpose
themselves upon them and become to some extent blended with them? . . .
The evidence of place names suggests that in Sussex extermination was the
rule. Farther west there are grounds for thinking that a substantial British
population survived. . . . Thus serious writers contend that the Anglo-
Saxon conquest was, for the bulk of the British community, mainly a
change of masters. The rich were slaughtered; the brave and proud fell back
in large numbers upon the Western mountains. Other numerous bands
escaped betimes to Brittany, whence their remote posterity were one day
to return.

In this period, the middle of the fifth century, there were great forests almost
everywhere. The Weald at that time ran from Kent to Hampshire: 120 miles
long and thirty miles deep. Where there wasn't forest, there were often
marshlands. There were roads, almost 5000 miles of them, left by the Romans
yet the towns were crumbling. It would be called urban decay today and it had
started before the Romans left. The Britons, and the Saxon invaders, weren't
stone masons; they didn't know how to repair the buildings and cared even less.
Churchill describes the languages they spoke.

C❖. . . the language of the valley settlers, living in compact groups, would be
dominant over that of the hill-cultivators, scattered in small and isolated
holdings. The study of modern English place-names has shown that hill,
wood, and stream names are often Celtic in origin, even in regions where
the village names are Anglo-Saxon. . . . Thus it came about that both Latin
and British yielded to the speech of the newcomers so completely that
hardly a trace of either is to be found in our earliest records.

But perhaps the most important clues to this period are to be found in *The Anglo-
Saxon Chronicle* and the *Historia Ecclesiastica Gentis Anglorum*, the Ecclesiastical
History of the English People by the Venerable Bede. Here, and among
archaeological records, are found the few traces of Saxon heritage and the names
that make up the history of these islands: Hengist, Horsa, Penda, Æthelberht
slaughtered by Offa, St Augustine, Eric Bloodaxe, Edward the Confessor, his
son Harold and, the greatest mystery of all Saxon history, King Arthur and
Camelot. There was a warrior king, or chieftain, who did great deeds but no
one is quite sure who he was. In the fifth century mercenaries came from
northern Europe, supposedly to help the Britons. But they started to help
themselves to Britain. Later, according to, among others, the ninth-century
Welsh scholar Nennius, they were sent packing. And it may have been Arthur
who defeated them. Arthur certainly appealed to the romantic knight in
Churchill's character.

C❖There looms large, uncertain, dim but glittering, the legend of King Arthur and the Knights of the Round Table. Somewhere in the Island a great captain gathered the forces of Roman Britain and fought the barbarian invaders to the death. . . . Twelve battles, all located in scenes untraceable, with foes unknown, except that they were heathen, are punctiliously set forth in the Latin of Nennius. Other authorities say, 'No Arthur; at least, no proof of any Arthur'. . . . Later these tales would be retold and embellished by the genius of Mallory, Spenser, and Tennyson. True or false, they have gained an immortal hold upon the thoughts of men. It is difficult to believe it was all the invention of a Welsh writer. If it was he must have been a marvellous inventor.

Writers usually relied upon hearsay. Even if Arthur was a minor king who fought twelve battles that defeated the barbarians, that may not have been so important in sixth-century Britain. In a country which accepted raiding, violence and its dreadful consequences as a matter of course, twelve battles over a couple of years would not have been remarkable.

C❖Modern research has not accepted the annihilation of Arthur. Timidly but resolutely the latest and best-informed writers unite to proclaim his reality. They cannot tell when in this dark period he lived, or where he held sway and fought his battles. They are ready to believe however that there was a great British warrior . . . Once Arthur is recognized as the commander of a mobile field army, moving from one part of the country to another and uniting with local forces in each district, the disputes about the scenes of his action explain themselves . . . If a chief like Arthur had gathered a band of mail-clad cavalry he could have moved freely about Britain, everywhere heading the local resistance to the invader and gaining repeated victories.

According to Nennius, Arthur's last battle took place on Mount Badon and although its location remains unknown, by cross-checking other events, including the birthdays and the deaths of chroniclers, it seems that this final – the twelfth – battle took place between 490 and 503. So it seems likely that a mighty knight did live and fight towards the end of the fifth century who defeated invaders and was seen as a chivalrous saviour. The Venerable Bede provides an exact date for another figure of the time: Columba, in his *Historia Ecclesiastica*.

❖In the year of our Lord 565, there came into Britain a famous priest and abbot, a monk by habit and life, whose name was Columba, to preach the word of God to the provinces of the northern Picts; who are separated from the southern parts by steep and rugged mountains.

Bede's steep and rugged mountains are the Grampians and Columba was sent to convert those who lived to the north of them. It seems that the southerners had already been converted by a Briton, Bishop Ninian, who had learned his theology in Rome. Columba's arrival coincided with the beginnings of what became the Ionan community. Bede is quite certain of Columba's origin.

❖Columba came into Britain in the ninth year of the reign of Bridius, who was the son of Meilochon, and the powerful king of the Pictish nation, and he converted that nation to the faith of Christ, by his preaching and example. It is true they followed uncertain rules in their observance of the great festival [Easter], wherefore they only practised such works of piety and chastity as they could learn from the prophetical, evangelical, and apostolical writings. The manner of keeping Easter continued among them for the space of 150 years, till the year of our Lord's incarnation 715.

So a simple religious journal gives us the dates of a Scottish king, Bride (Bridius), the son of Meilochon. Ninian and Columba measured men in their God's image and there were none who could not be saved and Easter, whether or not it was celebrated according to synodical decree, was the most important event in their year and preached the forgiveness of sins. Churchill's text describes the period in temporal terms.

C❖There was no crime committed which could not be compounded by a money payment. . . . An elaborate tariff prescribed in shillings the 'wergild' or exact value of every man. An atheling, or prince, was worth 1500 shillings, a shilling being the value of a cow in Kent, or a sheep elsewhere; an eorl, or nobleman, 300 shillings. A ceorl, . . . who was a yeoman farmer, was worth 100 shillings, a laet, or agricultural serf, forty to eighty shillings, and a slave nothing . . . The life of a slaughtered man could be compounded for cash. With money all was possible; without it only retribution or loss of liberty . . . Wergild at least, as Alfred said long afterwards, was better than the blood feud.

These then were the rules by which the Saxon Britons lived. A spiritual and temporal fairness was abroad in these islands but there was wickedness and violence too. There was also a new conflict that would end, once more, with the defeat of the Britons. This time, the English, who did not come from England, would be the victors.

CHAPTER TWO

449–884

———— ❖ ————

The Venerable Bede was taken into a monastery in Jarrow in the late seventh century, probably just before his tenth birthday, and it was in this monastery in the north-east of Britain that he wrote that book on which much of our knowledge of early England relies: the *Historia Ecclesiastica Gentis Anglorum*, the Ecclesiastical History of the English People.

❖In the year 449, Marcian being made emperor with Valentinian, ruled the empire for seven years. The nation of the Angles, or Saxons, being invited by the aforesaid king, arrived in Britain. . . . Those who came over were of the three most powerful nations of Germany: Saxons, Angles, and Jutes. From the Jutes are descended the people of Kent and of the Isle of Wight, and those in the province of the West-Saxons who are to this day called Jutes, seated opposite the Isle of Wight. From the Saxons, that is the country which is now called Old Saxony, came the East-Saxons, the South-Saxons and West-Saxons. From the Angles, that is the country which is called Anglia, are descended the East-Angles, the Middle-Angles, the Mercians, all the race of the Northumbrians, that is, of those nations that dwell on the north side of the river Humber, and the other nations of the English. The first two commanders are said to have been Hengist and Horsa.

In AD 449 no one spoke English in Britain. Churchill describes the population of the time.

C❖Of all the tribes of the Germanic race none was more cruel than the Saxons. Their very name, which spread to the whole confederacy of Northern tribes, was supposed to be derived from the use of a weapon, the seax, a short one-handed sword. Although tradition and the Venerable Bede assign the conquest of Britain to the Angles, Jutes and Saxons together, . . . it is probable that before their general exodus from Schleswig-Holstein the Saxons had virtually incorporated the other two strains.

According to Bede, Aelle was the first *bretwalda*, or ruler of Britain. *Bret* means Britain. *Walda* means ruler. So Aelle was the first of seven kings who claimed the kingdoms south of the Humber, probably in the final quarter of the fifth century.

C❖In Germany they had no kings. They developed them in Britain from leaders who claimed descent from the ancient gods. The position of the king continually increased in importance, and his supporters or companions gradually formed a new class in society, which carried with it the germ of feudalism, and was in the end to dominate all other conventions. But the lord was master; he must also be protector. He must stand by his people, must back them in the courts, feed them in time of famine, and they in return must work his land and follow him in war. . . . To make himself secure became his paramount desire. . . . But how was this to be achieved? Only by the king gathering round him a band of the most successful warriors and interesting them directly in the conquest and in the settlement. He had nothing to give them but land . . . The spoils of war were soon consumed, but the land remained for ever. . . . but to give individual warriors title to any particular tract was contrary to the whole tradition of the Germanic tribes. Now under the hard pressures of war and pioneering land increasingly became private property.

Here are the seeds of the landed gentry. Everything it had, including title and position, it owed to the monarch. This is the basis of aristocracy. But there was more than one king because, geographically, there had to be. There were limitations on the way fifth- and sixth-century people could travel. Also, no one now had an army that could be structured to subjugate the whole island race and the Saxons were migrating, not enlarging an existing empire. Nevertheless, it is warfare that propels nations, however fragmented. And it was war in the year 577 that expanded the hold of the Saxons over the defending Britons.

In the 570s and 580s, the southern Britons had been subjugated by the English – those who lived in the southern counties as they are now called – who made up the Sutangli, or Southern Angles, or Southern English. And this north-south divide affected the history of this island race. As the historian, Sir Frank Stenton, points out, 'From the age of the migrations down to the Danish wars of the ninth century, the peoples south of the Humber were normally subject to the authority of a common overlord'. The term 'common overlord' means that different parts were ruled by a sort of underlord or lesser king.

C❖. . . this new institution of personal leadership established in the divinely descended war chief sank deeply into the fibre of the Anglo-Saxon invaders.

. . . [but] they were never able to carry the evolution of kingship forward to a national throne.

Far away, another venture was in the making. The Pope understood what was happening in this once provincial holding of Rome. One hundred and fifty years had gone by since the Angles, the Saxons and the Jutes, in other words the English, had come to Britain. Britain was now being called England. Thirty years earlier, Columba had travelled from the land of the Scots, what is now called Ireland, to the highlands north of the Grampians and had become Abbot of Iona and the monastery had been built. But the Christian and heathen traditions sat uneasily side by side.

C❖The buildings, such as they were, were of wood, not stone. The people had lost entirely the art of writing. Some miserable runic scribblings were the only means by which they could convey their thoughts or wishes to one another at a distance. . . . The confusion and conflict of petty ruffians, sometimes called kings, racked the land. There was nothing worthy of the name nationhood, or even of tribalism. . . . For various reasons, including the spreading of the Gospel, it was decided in the closing decade of the sixth century that a guide and teacher should be sent to England to diffuse and stimulate the faith, to convert the heathen, and also to bring about an effective working union between the British Christians and the main body of the Church.

The Anglo-Saxon Chronicle tells what happened in the year 595. 'In this year', says the chronicler, 'Pope Gregory sent Augustine to Britain with very many monks who preached God's word to the English nation.' But they were nervous. They wanted to turn back. In fact Augustine did so. But Pope Gregory wrote to Augustine and his brethren.

❖Gregory, the servant of the servants of God, to the servants of our Lord. For as much as it had been better not to begin a good work than to think of desisting from that which has been begun, it behoves you, my beloved sons, to fulfil the good work which by the help of our Lord, you have undertaken. Let not, therefore, the toil of the journey nor the tongues of evil speaking men, deter you; but with all possible earnestness and zeal perform that which, by God's direction you have undertaken; God keep you in safety my most beloved sons.

Pope Gregory's letter worked. Augustine and his nervous monks trudged on and eventually crossed to the Isle of Thanet. But what they needed was protection and that could only come from the local king. And it did. The king was Æthelberht. Æthel means, more or less, nobly born. Æthelberht wasn't a Christian. In fact he worshipped Thor, the god of thunder. But he had thought of converting, not because he felt any spiritual need, but for a political reason. His wife, a Frankish princess, whose name was Bertha, was a Christian. Kent, recognized by the Romans as the most civilized part of the land of the Britons, was the one place where a revival would be most likely to take hold. Æthelberht sensed that it might not be such a bad idea to go with the mood of the people. And so Æthelberht became the first 'English' King to convert to Christianity. For Augustine it was, perhaps, a heaven-sent opportunity.

C❖With the aid of the Frankish princess he converted King Ethelbert. . . Upon the ruins of the ancient British church of St Martin he refounded the Christian life of Canterbury. . . . Ethelbert, as overlord of England, exercised an effective authority over the kingdoms of the South and West. His policy was at once skilful and ambitious; his conversion to Christianity, however sincere, was also in consonance with his secular aims. He was himself, as the only English Christian ruler, in a position where he might hold out the hand to the British princes, and, by using the Christian faith as a bond of union, establish his supremacy over the whole country. . . . Thus at the beginning of the seventh century Ethelbert and Augustine summoned a conference of the British Christian bishops. . . . It failed for two separate reasons: first, the sullen and jealous temper of the British bishops, and, secondly, the tactless arrogance of St Augustine.

There was a second conference. It failed as the first had. Worse than that, the gathering broke up with Augustine threatening war and making sure that the lot of Rome would be thrown in behind the English.

War never happened, but Augustine achieved the development of Christian belief in these islands. And he began the training of a clergy who would go out and achieve many of the things that this arrogant messenger from Rome had hoped for himself. But he was just one figure in the 2000-year saga of these islands.

C❖Except for the consecration of Mellitus as Bishop of the East Saxons in a church on the site of St Paul's, he [Augustine] had made little attempt to proselytize outside Kent. From the title loosely accorded him of 'Apostle of the English' he enjoyed for many centuries the credit of having re-converted the once-famous Roman province of Britannia to the Christian faith; and this halo has shone about him until comparatively recent times.

It was during this time that heathenism declined and Christianity prospered. But the question of whose version of Christianity should rule – Augustine's or the northern Celtic – divided the peoples of mid-seventh century England as much as the feud between the English and the Britons. The issues were quite basic: how should Easter be observed? Should the tonsure – a symbol of church doctrine – be worn?

C❖. . . Redwald, King of the East Angles, had established a wide dominion over the lands of Central England from the Dee to the Humber. With Redwald's aid the crown of Northumbria was gained by an exiled prince, Edwin [Æthelberht's son-in-law], who by his abilities won his way, step by step, to the foremost position in England. Even before the death of his ally, Redwald, Edwin was recognized as overlord of all the English kingdoms except Kent, and the isles of Anglesey and Man were also reduced by his ships. He not only established his personal primacy, but the confederation founded by him foreshadowed the kingdom of all England that was later to take shape under the kings of Mercia and Wessex. Edwin married a Christian princess of Kent, whose religion he had promised to respect. Consequently, in her train from Canterbury to Edwin's capital at York there rode in 625 the first Roman missionary to Northern England, Paulinus, an envoy who had first come to Britain in the days of St Augustine, twenty-four years before. . . . Paulinus converted Edwin, and the ample kingdom of Northumbria, shaped like England itself in miniature, became Christian.

Edwin wasn't simply an atheist. He worshipped idols. That meant he had courtiers, henchmen and priests who did the same. For the king to say, 'I give my life to Christ', is one thing; to carry with him these vital allies towards a religion that was relatively new in the kingdom was not only an act of faith, in early England it was also a political decision. He had to carry his realm with him. And that's exactly what he did. Churchill tells what happened next.

C❖. . . this blessed event brought with it swift and dire consequences. The overlordship of Northumbria was fiercely resented by King Penda of Mercia, or, as we should now say, of the Midlands. The drama unfolded with staggering changes of fortune. In 633 Penda, the heathen, made an unnatural alliance with Cadwallon, the Christian British King of North Wales, with the object of overthrowing the suzerainty of Edwin and breaking the Northumbrian power. Here for the first time noticed in history British and English fought side by side. Politics for once proved stronger than religion or race. In a savage battle near Doncaster, Edwin was defeated and slain, and his head – not the last – was exhibited on the ramparts of captured York. . . . This sudden destruction of the greatest king who had hitherto ruled in the Island brought in recoil an equally speedy vengeance

. . . upon their Saxon foes. . . . The name and fame of the slaughtered Edwin rang through the land. His successor . . . Oswald, of the house of Bernicia, had but to appear to find himself at the head of the newly Christianized and also infuriated Saxon warriors. Within a year of the death of Edwin, Oswald destroyed Cadwallon and his British forces. . . . This was the last pitched battle between the Britons and the Saxons and it must be admitted that the Britons fared as badly in conduct as in fortune. They had joined with the heathen Saxon Midlands to avenge their wrongs, and had exploited an English movement towards the disunity of the land. They had shattered this bright hope of the Christianity they professed, and now they were themselves overthrown and cast aside. The long story of their struggle with the invaders ended thus in no fine way; but what is important to our tale is that it had ended at last.

However, fundamental issues about Christianity, and which version to adopt, persisted. And, at this time in the island's history, any prolonging of differences could mean war.

C❖The celebrated and largely successful attempt to solve them took place at the Synod of Whitby in 663. There the hinging issue was whether British Christianity should conform to the general life-plan of Christendom, or whether it should be expressed by the monastic orders which had founded the Celtic Churches of the North. . . . in the end after much pious dissertation the decision was taken that the Church of Northumbria should be a definite part of the Church of Rome and of the Catholic system. Mercia soon afterwards conformed . . . The leadership of Saxon England passed to Mercia. For nearly eighty years two Mercian kings asserted or maintained their ascendancy over all England south of the Humber. Ethelbald and Offa reigned each for forty years. Ethelbald had been an exile before he became an autocrat. As a fugitive he consorted with monks, hermits, and holy men. On attaining power he did not discard his Christian piety, but he found himself much oppressed by the temptations of the flesh. . . . He showed charity to the poor; he preserved law and order . . . he took to styling himself 'King of the Southern English' and 'King of Britain'. South of the Humber these claims were made good.

Æthelbald actually called himself 'rex Britanniae' which was the Latin for the Saxon English title, *bretwalda*, ruler of Britain. But this wasn't an idle boast. *The Anglo-Saxon Chronicle*, for example, records that he was fighting, and winning, as far away as Somerton in Somerset. That meant that Æthelbald controlled a huge chunk of Wessex. One indication of that control was that he could buy and sell land as he wished. He was the strongest figure in southern Britain. In spite of his confessions of faith, he was barbaric and everyone, including the Church, knew that and could do little about it. No other king had ruled so masterfully and for so long. But then it came to an end. After forty-one years on his throne, Æthelbald was murdered, by his own bodyguard. The result was a civil war in the Midlands. It didn't last a full year and when it was done, the new king of the Mercians was Offa, one of the most famous names of this period.

C❖. . . the imprint of his power is visible not only throughout England but upon the Continent. Offa was the contemporary of Charlemagne. His policy interlaced with that of Europe; he was reputed to be the first 'King of the English' and he had the first quarrel since Roman times with the mainland.

Charlemagne wished one of his sons to marry one of Offa's daughters. Here we have an important proof of the esteem in which the Englishman was held. Offa stipulated that his son must simultaneously marry a daughter of Charlemagne. The founder of the Holy Roman Empire appeared at first incensed at this assumption of equality, but after a while he found it expedient to renew his friendship with Offa. It seems that the 'King of the English' had placed an embargo upon Continental merchandise, and the inconvenience of this retaliation speedily overcame all points of pride and sentiment. Very soon Offa was again the Emperor's 'dearest brother' and Charlemagne is seen agreeing to arrange that there should be reciprocity of royal protection in both countries for merchants, 'according to the ancient custom of trading'.

All this explains how powerful a king Offa was. What's more he saw himself as the defender of the faith. And it was here that a single incident that marked Offa as particularly relevant to our history occurred. Offa had his son *anointed* as King of Mercia. He was consecrated. And this is probably the first time that an English king was consecrated and, therefore, the moment that marked a religious dimension to the English throne. But for most people, Offa remains famous for one great work.

C❖We have a tangible monument of Offa in the immense dyke which he caused to be built between converted Saxon England and the still unconquered British. . . . This dyke, which runs over the hills and dales, leaving gaps for the impenetrable forests, from the mouth of the Severn to the neighbourhood of the Mersey, attests to our day the immense authority of the state over which Offa presided. . . . the fact that this extensive rampart could have been mainly the work of the lifetime and the will of a single man is startling. It conveys to us an idea of the magnitude and force of Offa's kingdom. . . . But 'Offa's Dyke' shows policy as well as manpower. In many sections it follows lines favourable to the British, and historians have concluded that it was a boundary rather than a fortification and resulted from an agreement reached for common advantage . . . the expression of a solemn treaty which for a long spell removed Offa's problem – the menace of a British incursion – and thus set him free with his back secure to parley and dispute with Europe.

The Venerable Bede, who died, peacefully, after Vespers on the Feast of the Ascension in AD 735, describes the land Offa inherited.

❖The Scots that inhabit Britain, satisfied with their own territories, meditate no hostilities against the nation of the English. The Britons, though they for the most part through innate hatred are adverse to the English nation, and wrongfully and from wicked custom oppose the anointed Easter of the whole Catholic Church; yet from both the divine and human power withstanding them can in no way prevail as they desire, for though in part they are their own master, yet elsewhere they are also brought under subjugation to the English. Such being the peaceable and calm disposition of the times, many of the Northumbrians as well of the nobility as private persons, laying aside their weapons, rather incline to dedicate both themselves and their children to the tonsure and monastic vows, than to study martial discipline. What will be the end hereof, the next age will show. This is for the present the state of all Britain; in the year since the coming of the English into Britain about 285.

By AD 796 Offa was dead, and the Vikings were about to arrive. The Romans had left at the start of the fifth century and the Angles, the Jutes and, of course, the Saxons, together became the English after the Romans left. At the end of the 700s the Vikings arrived from Scandinavia: Swedes, Norwegians and Danes. The first mention of them appears in *The Anglo-Saxon Chronicle*. The year was AD 789.

❖In this year Beorhtric took to wife Eadburh, daughter of King Offa. And in his days came first three ships of Norwegians from Horthaland; and then the reeve [sheriff] rode hither and tried to compel them to go to the royal manor, for he did not know what they were: and then they slew him. These were the first ships of the Danes to come to England.

C❖In the eighth century a vehement manifestation of conquering energy appeared in Scandinavia. Norway, Sweden and Denmark threw up bands of formidable fighting men, who, in addition to all their other martial qualities, were the hardy rovers of the sea. The causes which led to this racial ebullition were the spontaneous growth of their strength and population, the thirst for adventure, and the complications of dynastic quarrels. There was here no question of the Danes or Norsemen being driven westward by new pressures from the steppes of Asia. They moved of their own accord. Their prowess was amazing. . . . The relations between the Danes and the Norwegians were tangled and varying. Sometimes they raided in collusion; sometimes they fought each other in desperate battles; but to Saxon England they presented themselves in the common guise of a merciless scourge.

The Vikings arrived first in about 789 at Portland in Dorset. They killed many and then withdrew. A small incident, but important to the inhabitants of these islands, for this landing and these murders were the beginnings of the age of the Vikings. They returned in 793, as *The Anglo-Saxon Chronicle* records.

❖In this year terrible portents appeared over Northumbria and miserably frightened the people there; these were exceptional high winds and flashes of lightning and fiery dragons were seen flying in the air. A great famine soon followed these signs; and a little after that in the same year on the eighth day of January the harrying of the heathen miserably destroyed God's church in Lindisfarne.

C❖When the next year the raiders returned and landed near Jarrow they were stoutly attacked while harassed by bad weather. Many were killed. Their 'king' was captured and put to a cruel death, and the fugitives carried so grim a tale back to Denmark that for forty years the English coasts were unravaged.

This was probably a small group from a much larger fleet of long ships. They sailed on to the north of Scotland and landed. They set up encampments in Caithness and Sutherland, in the Orkneys and in Shetland. They went on to Ireland and eventually conquered a small community and it is thought that the Viking king, Olaf, founded what is now called Dublin.

In AD 865 the great invasion of the East coast of England started. And the pickings were great. England was proud of its Christianity, the Church had thrived. The people believed that all they had to do was to pay for the absolution of their many sins. And pay they did. So in church and monastery were stored great treasures and the Vikings were delighted. None more so than the one they called Ivar the Boneless. His father was Ragnar Lodbrok. Ragnar Lodbrok was captured by the King of Northumbria and thrown into a pit of poisonous adders to die. When the four sons of Ragnar Lodbrok heard this, each swore the vengeance known as Blood-Red Eagle. The killer of their father should be captured, his flesh and ribs cut and turned back so that the avenging son could tear out the living lungs – or so legend has it. However, whatever its form, no son took this oath of revenge more seriously than Ivar the Boneless.

C❖He it was who planned the great campaigns. . . . In the spring of 866 his powerful army . . . rode north along the old Roman road and was ferried across the Humber.

     He laid siege to York. And now – too late – the Northumbrians, who had been divided in their loyalties between the two rival kings, forgot their feuds and united in one final effort. They attacked the Danish army before York. At first they were successful; the heathens were driven back upon the city walls. The defenders sallied out and in the confusion the Vikings defeated them all with grievous slaughter, killing both their kings. . . This was the end of Northumbria. The North of England never recovered its ascendancy.

It is now the century of Alfred the Great. He lived for fifty years, born in 849, died in 899. Most people have heard of Alfred, but few are quite sure what he did, apart from burning some cakes. He tried to keep the Danes at bay by paying them not to fight him – which is where the expression 'Danegeld' comes from. And he has been called the father of the British navy. But he was far more than all these things. He was the grandson of King Egbert, the man who laid the foundations of resistance to the Danes, and younger brother of King Æthelred (not Æthelred the Unready). The two brothers fought the Vikings several times. On one occasion, Æthelred, a pious man, was still at his prayers when one of the battles was joined. But Alfred led the charge against Vikings, 'like a wild boar' according to Bishop Asser of Sherborne.

C❖The fight was long and hard. King Ethelred, his spiritual duty done, soon joined his brother. 'The heathens', said the Bishop, 'had seized the higher ground and the Christians had to advance uphill. There was in that place a single stunted thorn-tree which we have seen with our own eyes. Round about this tree, then, the opposing ranks met in conflict, with great shouting from all men – one side bent on evil, the other side fighting for life and their loved ones and their native land.' At last the Danes gave way, and, hotly pursued, fled back to Reading. They fled till nightfall; they fled through the night and the next day, and the whole breadth of Ashdown – meaning the Berkshire Hills – was strewn with their corpses, among which were found the body of one of the Viking kings and five of his earls. . . in a fortnight they were again in the field. But the Battle of Ashdown justly takes its place among historic encounters because of the greatness of the issue. If the West Saxons had been beaten all England would have sunk into heathen anarchy.

Since they were victorious the hope still burned for a civilized Christian existence in this Island. This was the first time the invaders had been beaten in the field. . . . Alfred had made the Saxons feel confidence in themselves again. They could hold their own in open fight.

Shortly after Easter 871, Æthelred died and was buried at Wimborne. Alfred became King but if he had indeed, as Winston Churchill writes, given the people of Wessex confidence, it didn't last. Within a month of becoming king, he was fighting the Danes just outside Salisbury, at Wilton. His losses were horrific. According to *The Anglo-Saxon Chronicle*, after that battle at Wilton, there were at least nine major campaigns against the Vikings in the south. And says the *Chronicle*, 'In the course of this year were slain nine jarls and one king; and this year the West Saxons made peace with the host.' In other words, Alfred bought them off with the Danegeld. The Vikings moved for the winter to London and it's here that coins with the Danish king, Halfdan, on one side and the monogram of London on the other first appeared. The Vikings were intent on staying, if not in London, in England.

C❖Alfred and the men of Wessex had proved too stubborn a foe for easy subjugation. Some of the Danes wished to settle on the lands they already held. . . . Henceforward they began to till the ground for a livelihood. Here was a great change. We must remember their discipline and organization. The ships' companies, acting together, had hitherto fought ashore as soldiers. . . . The sailors had turned soldiers, and the soldiers had turned yeomen. . . . The whole of the East of England thus received a class of cultivator who, except for purposes of common defence, owed allegiance to none; who had won his land with the sword, and was loyal only to the army organization which enabled him to keep it. From Yorkshire to Norfolk this sturdy, upstanding stock took root.

But this was not to be peace for the Saxons and the Danes. Certainly King Alfred didn't think so. True, he had bought some sort of peace, and he had started to build his famous navy. But *The Anglo-Saxon Chronicle* tells that in 875, Alfred 'sailed out to sea with a fleet and fought against seven ships' companies and captured one of them and put the others to flight'.

C❖Then in January 878 occurred the most surprising reversal of Alfred's fortunes. His headquarters and Court lay at Chippenham, in Wiltshire. It was Twelfth Night, and the Saxons . . . were off their guard, engaged in pious exercises, or perhaps even drunk. Down swept the ravaging foe. The whole army of Wessex, sole guarantee of England south of the Thames, was dashed into confusion. Many were killed. The most part stole away to their houses. A strong contingent fled overseas. Refugees arrived with futile appeals at the Court of France. Only a handful of officers and personal attendants hid themselves with Alfred in the marshes and forests of Somerset and the Isle of Athelney which rose from the quags. This was the darkest hour of Alfred's fortunes.

Alfred was on the run from the Danes. Some of his own people actually believed him to be dead, or even to have fled the country. But he was staying with a cowherd and his wife who, or so it is said, was baking bread. Alfred was sitting by the fire dreaming, perhaps, and sharpening his arrows in that dream. Then came the smell, the smoke and the burning. Up rushed the cowherd's wife, crying out, 'Alack, man, why have you not turned over the bread when you see that it is burning, especially as you so much like eating it hot.' Bishop Asser of Sherborne wrote this tale down and its importance, of course, is as proof of the fact that the king was in hiding. In today's terms, Alfred became a guerrilla fighter. And then came a massive and decisive engagement when Alfred gathered his Saxons together, filled with a new spirit.

C❖The Danes still lay upon their plunder at Chippenham. Alfred advanced to Ethandun – now Edington – and on the bare downs was fought the largest and culminating battle of Alfred's wars. . . . But the heathen had lost the favour of God through their violated oath, and eventually from this or other causes they fled from the cruel and clanging field. . . . Guthrum, king of the Viking army, so lately master of the one unconquered English kingdom, found himself penned in his camp. . . . But Alfred meant to make a lasting peace with Guthrum. He had him and his army in his power. He could have starved them into surrender and slaughtered them to a man. He wished instead to divide the land with them, and that the two races, in spite of fearful injuries given and received, should dwell together in amity. He received Guthrum, with thirty prominent buccaneers, in his camp. He stood godfather to Guthrum; he raised him from the font; he entertained him for twelve days; he presented him and his warriors with costly gifts; he called him his son.

The Danish army remained in camp at Chippenham for that summer of 878. Twelve months on they were gone to East Anglia. But a new Viking army sailed for England and camped at Fulham. By 886 the situation was so serious that Alfred and the West Saxons fought and took London. It is said that Alfred took London by burning and slaughter. He then rebuilt the town and for the first time London became the centre for resistance to England's enemies. It meant also that Alfred was now the Great, the great leader, obeyed, with the exception of the Dane lands (see Chapter Three), by all the English-speaking peoples.

CHAPTER THREE

885–1065

❖

Alfred the Great made an uneasy truce with the Vikings – or the Danes – in the late 800s, the last years of his life. The map of England, Scotland and Wales looked something like this: Wales was much as it is now. Wessex was a triangle with one corner in Land's End, another in North Foreland on the far Kent coast and the top corner on the north-west coast at about Liverpool. In that corner is what was called English Mercia. The rest, including East Anglia, was Danish, known as Danelaw. Danelaw's northern boundary was a squiggly line from the North Sea coast, about thirty miles south of Durham, across to the Cumbrian coast. The cauldron of peace bought in bribes (Danegeld), inter-marriages and baptisms was about to boil over. But the fire was lit, not in England, but on the Continent where, as Churchill wrote, the Viking raiders were at war.

C❖One final war awaited Alfred. It was a crisis in the Viking story. In 885 they had rowed up the Seine with hundreds of ships and an army of 40,000 men. . . . For six years they ravaged the interior of Northern France. Famine followed in their footsteps. The fairest regions had been devoured; where could they turn?. . . Such men make plans, and certainly their descent upon England was one of the most carefully considered and elaborately prepared villainies of that dark time.

Now here, the timing is important, because the Viking King, Guthrum, who lived in England, was about to die. It was the last decade of the ninth century. A few years earlier, in 878, Guthrum had been defeated by Alfred, but spared. What is more, Alfred had converted Guthrum to Christianity and was his godfather. Hence the uneasy peace. But *The Anglo-Saxon Chronicle* notes that that era was about to end.

❖And Guthrum, the northern King, whose baptismal name was Athelstan, passed away. In the year 892 the great host . . . went again from the kingdom of the east Franks westward to Boulogne and were there provided with ships, so that they crossed in one voyage, horses and all, and then they came up into the mouth of the Lympne with 250 ships. The river flows out from the forest; they rowed their ships up as far as the forest, four miles from the entrance to the estuary and there stormed a fort within the fen; occupying it were a few peasants and it was half built. Then soon after this, Haesten came with eighty ships into the mouth of the Thames and made himself a fort at Milton Regis.

Milton Regis is still there, just a couple of miles from Sittingbourne. But it is now flat, muddy creeked country, the village with some fine old houses and sometimes not so fine modern ones and there is no great forest. But back to the battle. Three fascinating points emerge:

First, Alfred once again offered gold to the invaders. This was a common practice. It was partly common sense, a recognition that if gold could buy peace then why not buy it. Second, Alfred, having paid up and so delayed the attack, persuaded the Viking King, Haesten, to have his two young sons baptized. And third, King Alfred was, perhaps, in failing health because he gave way to a younger leader, Edward, his twenty-two-year-old son. Alfred also had an ally, the young Mercian prince, Æthelred. The Vikings, as expected, broke their oaths of peace and Edward and Æthelred prepared for battle.

C❖In 893 . . . the young leaders struck hard. . . . They fell upon a column of the raiders near the modern Aldershot, routed them, and pursued them for twenty miles till they were glad to swim the Thames and shelter behind the Colne. . . . the enemy escaped.

The Danes had fortified themselves at Benfleet, on the Thames below London. . . . This the princes now assaulted . . . and put the army to flight. . . . In the captured stronghold the victors found Haesten's wife and his two sons. These were precious hostages, and King Alfred was much criticized at the time . . . because he restored them to Haesten.

The Danes, instead of attempting to take English Mercia, roamed and pillaged Wales before returning to the safety of East Anglia and then the Thames estuary. The long term result was a stalemate. Thanks to earlier Viking successes, the Danes were always going to be able to rely on support in Northumbria and East Anglia. Alfred was never going to get any more support than he had. Peace was impossible. And so it was that his kingdom was still at war when Alfred died in 899. He had ruled for almost twenty-nine years. His son, Edward, succeeded him.

C❖A quarrel arose between Edward and his cousin, Ethelwald, who fled to the Danelaw and aroused the Vikings of Northumbria and East Anglia to a renewed inroad upon his native land. In 902, Ethelwald and the Danish king crossed the upper reaches of the Thames at Cricklade and ravaged part of Wiltshire. Edward in retaliation ordered the invasion of East Anglia . . . but the Kentish contingent, being slow to withdraw, was overtaken and brought to battle by the infuriated Danes. The Danes were victorious, and made a great slaughter; but, as fate would have it, both Eric, the Danish king, and the renegade Ethelwald perished on the field, and the new king, Guthrum II, made peace with Edward on the basis of Alfred's treaty of 886. . . . In 910 this treaty was broken by the Danes and the war was renewed in Mercia. . . . in heavy fighting at Tettenhall in Staffordshire, the Danes were decisively defeated. This English victory was a milestone in the long conflict. The Danish armies in Northumbria never recovered from the battle, and the Danish Midlands and East Anglia thus lay open to English conquest. . . . now the tide had turned.

Edward's sister was Æthelfleda. It was she who married the Mercian leader, Æthelred. He died and she succeeded and so the legend of the Lady of the Mercians was born. Æthelfleda joined her Mercian warriors alongside her brother's men of Wessex. Together they set out, over the next ten years, to conquer the five boroughs of Danelaw. And they did. From *The Anglo-Saxon Chronicle* in the year 921:

❖King Edward marched to Stamford and had a fortress built on the south bank of the river. During the stay he made there his sister died at Tamworth, twelve days before midsummer; thereupon he took over the fortress at Tamworth and all the people of Mercia who had been under allegiance to his sister turned in submission to him.

Edward pressed north and the Danes knew there was little they could do to stop him. And they knew this in Wales too. These were the outposts of the Britons, not the English. The Welsh princes declared for Edward and soon the task started by Alfred the Great was completed. Then, in 924, Edward died and in 925, the year that St Dunstan was born, Edward's son, the remarkable Athelstan, came to the throne. If it is at all possible to say who the first King of *all* England was, then that person was Athelstan.

It is said that Alfred had known that, one day, his grandson would be king and that he had cloaked the child in scarlet and then invested him with the Royal Saxon sword with a golden hilt, the symbol of regal dignity. Athelstan was the first King of Wessex who was truly part of the Mercian aristocracy. His father wasn't. Certainly Alfred the Great wasn't. So Athelstan held a unique position, one of great respect, when he joined with the Mercians against Northumbria – still known as Danelaw and still an alien territory to the southern Kingdom.

C❖Athelstan, the third of the great West Saxon kings, sought at first, in accordance with the traditions of his house, peaceful relations with the unconquered parts of the Danelaw; but upon disputes arising he marched into Yorkshire in 926, and there established himself.

Northumbria submitted; the Kings of the Scots and of Strathclyde acknowledged him as their 'father and lord' and the Welsh princes agreed to pay tribute. There was an uneasy interlude; then in 933 came a general rebellion and renewed war, organized by all the hitherto defeated characters in the drama. The whole of North Britain, Celtic, Danish and Norwegian, pagan and Christian, together presented a hostile front under Constantine, King of the Scots, and Olaf of Dublin, with Viking reinforcements from Norway. On this occasion neither life nor time was wasted in manoeuvres. . . . and there was presently a fierce clash between the Northumbrian and the Icelandic Vikings on the one hand and a part of the English army on the other. In this, although the Northumbrian commander fled, the English were worsted. But on the following day the real trial of strength was staged. The rival hosts paraded in all the pomp of war and then in hearty goodwill fell on with spear, axe and sword. All day long the battle raged.

It was in praise of Athelstan's victory at Brunanburh in 937 that the first patriotic verse in the origins of our language was written. It is known as *Brunanburh*, written in Old English, and found in *The Anglo-Saxon Chronicle*.

C❖The victory of the English was overwhelming. Constantine, 'the perjured' as the victors claimed, fled back to the North and Olaf retired with his remnants to Dublin. Thus did King Alfred's grandson, the valiant Athelstan, become one of the first sovereigns of Western Europe. He styled himself on coin and charter, *Rex totius Britanniae*. These claims were accepted upon the Continent. His three sisters were wedded respectively to the Carolingian King, Charles the Simple, to the Capetian, Hugh the Great, and to Otto the Saxon, a future Holy Roman Emperor.

By marriage and political interest the house of Alfred, his son Edward the Elder, and Athelstan was bound up with events in mainland Europe. The first Saxon King of the Germans, Henry the Fowler, had attempted an alliance with Athelstan and it was as a result of this approach that Athelstan's sister, Edith, married Henry's eldest son Otto. As a result England and Germany became tied in all sorts of events, many of which had a direct influence on English ecclesiastical history and the reform of the monastery system. Small points perhaps, but reminders that history takes its time and doesn't only rest on the outcome of battles.

But Athelstan's great battle was not the end of Saxon troubles.

C❖... When Athelstan died, two years after [the battle of] Brunanburh, and was succeeded by his half brother, a youth of eighteen, the beaten forces welled up once more against him. Edmund, in the spirit of his race, held his own. He reigned only six years, but when he died in 946 he had not ceded an inch or an ell. Edmund was succeeded by his brother Edred, the youngest son of Alfred's son, Edward the Elder. He too maintained the realm against all comers, and, beating them down by force of arms, seemed to have quenched for ever the rebellious fires of Northumbria.

The legacy of Athelstan was a more united kingdom and an organization of courts and councils on a much wider basis. The result was that regional selfishness, while not disappearing, was at least tempered and therefore the unity of the land was more likely.

C❖A hundred and twenty years had passed since the impact of the Vikings had smitten the Island. For forty years English Christian society had struggled for life. For eighty years five warrior Kings – Alfred, Edward, Athelstan, Edmund and Edred – defeated the invaders. The English rule was now restored, though in a form changed by the passage of time, over the whole country. Yet underneath it there had grown up, deeply rooted in the soil, a Danish settlement covering the great eastern plain, in which Danish blood and Danish customs survived under the authority of the English King.

There now appeared the most fearsome Viking leader. And he had the name to go with it: Eric Bloodaxe. He was Norwegian and had been King until he was deposed and did what many of his luckless predecessors had done: sailed for England and the Northumbrian coast where his Viking countrymen lived, and where there was a desire to kick out the Saxons and join with the Vikings who lived in Dublin to establish one big Viking state.

The Northumbrian Vikings welcomed Eric. King Edred, of course, did not. He fought and burned his way through the region and instead of fighting Eric Bloodaxe, threatened the Northumbrians with earthly damnation. He meant to kill them all and burn their towns. So, the Northumbrians turned against Eric. But Eric Bloodaxe returned with stronger forces and once again called himself King. And for a time it worked. But Eric Bloodaxe was killed with his son and his brother at the Battle of Stainmore, on the heights overlooking what is now called Edendale. *The Anglo-Saxon Chronicle* dismisses it all in a single entry.

❖AD 954: In this year the Northumbrians drove out Eric, and Eadred succeeded to the Northumbrian Kingdom.

But Eric Bloodaxe had united the Vikings of Dublin and York, although he'd failed to establish a kingdom that could rival the English. And after he died it was no longer possible for a single invader, no matter how strong and resourceful, to begin a completely new dynasty to rule England.

In 955, a twelve-year-old boy, Edgar, became King of Mercia. His brother, Eadwig, was about three years older and he became King of Wessex. Wessex was the senior kingdom in England. But Eadwig died a couple of years later and Edgar, only just into his teens, also became King of Wessex, Mercia and Northumberland. Edgar's coronation was the first to have a written Order of Service, and it is the basis of the one used today.

Edgar's reign wasn't the record of slaughter and gore normally associated with kings of this period. One of the finest historians of the Saxons, Sir Frank Stenton, noted that 'It is a sign of Edgar's competence as a ruler that his reign is singularly devoid of recorded incident.' Churchill saw Edgar's reign as one of peaceful rebuilding of the sometimes very vulnerable mix of societies.

C❖The reconquest of England was accompanied step by step by a conscious administrative reconstruction which has governed the development of English institutions from that day to this. The shires were reorganized, each with its sheriff or reeve, a royal officer directly responsible to the Crown. The hundreds – subdivisions of the shire – were created, and the towns prepared for defence. An elaborate system of shire, hundred, and borough courts maintained law and order and pursued criminals. Taxation was reassessed. Finally, with this military and political revival marched a great re-birth of monastic life and learning and the beginning of our native English literature. The movement was slow and English in origin, but advanced with great strides from the middle of the century as it came in contact with the religious revival on the Continent.

The figure behind the crown at the time was the man who became St Dunstan. Dunstan was a nobleman born in 925. At the age of eighteen he was created Abbot of Glastonbury, for centuries past and centuries to come, an important church. It was from Glastonbury that Dunstan helped to rebuild English monastic orders. He had been banished from England by Edgar's eldest brother Eadwig (sometimes, Edwy). Eadwig was easily distracted and on his coronation day he left the anointing celebrations to amuse himself with a woman and her daughter. He was found, *in flagrante delicto*, by the bishop, Dunstan. The king was upset, the woman was upset, the daughter was upset and Dunstan ended up in exile, and the daughter ended up married to the king. But a couple of years later, when Edgar became King of Wessex, the historical partnership between Edgar and the now restored Dunstan began.

C❖The work of Dunstan, Archbishop of Canterbury . . . was to revive the strict observance of religion within the monasteries. Another and happy, if incidental, result was to promote learning and the production of splendid illuminated manuscripts. . . . Many of these . . . were written in English. The Catholic Homilies of Elfric, Abbot of Eynsham, mark, we are told, the first achievement of English as a literary language – the earliest vernacular to reach this eminence in the whole of Europe. . . . It must have seemed to contemporaries that with the magnificent coronation at Bath in 973, . . . the seal was set on the unity of the realm. Everywhere the courts are sitting regularly, in shire and borough and hundred; there is one coinage, and one system of weights and measures. The arts of building and decoration are reviving; learning begins to flourish again in the Church; there is a literary language, a King's English, which all educated men write. Civilization had been restored to the Island.

Edgar became King of Wessex in 959 but, perhaps for a religious reason, his coronation was not until 973. With Dunstan as his tutor, Edgar based his whole thinking on theology and so, under Edgar, the religious communities became important. This makes Edgar different from other men. And his authority was different. It came not from the crown he wore, but from the religious significance of anointment. After all, the kind of person who is anointed is a priest. Edgar became King of Wessex when he was sixteen, and in those days, a man could not be ordained priest until he was thirty. Edgar was thirty in 973, the year of his coronation, or anointment. But Edgar was not long for his throne. As one of the earliest poems in *The Anglo-Saxon Chronicle* tells us, he died in the seventh month of 975, and terrible times were to come.

❖His son, a stripling, succeeded then to the throne; the name of the prince of earls was Edward. Then the praise of the Ruler fell away everywhere throughout the length and breadth of Mercia, and many wise servants of God were expelled.

Edgar had married twice and Edward was his son by the first marriage. But Edward's mother died and in 964 Edgar married again. His new wife was a widow of the earldoman of East Anglia. Her name was Ælfthryth and the surviving son she bore Edgar was Æthelred who was to become known as the Unready. Not much is known about Edward's reign, but the *Chronicle* tells of his death.

❖In this year on 18 March, King Edward was murdered in the evening at Corfe. No worse deed for the English was ever done than this, since first they came to the land of Britain. Men murdered him but God exalted him; in life he was an earthly King, but after his death he is now a heavenly saint.

It was said that Edward was visiting his step-mother Ælfthryth and his half-brother Æthelred at their home, in Dorset. He arrived, dismounted, was surrounded by his step-mother's servants and held while he was repeatedly stabbed until he was dead. So the finger points to Ælfthryth, but nothing is known for certain. What is known is that within a month her son, Æthelred, was crowned in Edward's place.

C❖Now a child, a weakling, a vacillator, a faithless, feckless creature, succeeded to the warrior throne. . . . We have reached the days of Ethelred the Unready. But this expression, which conveys a truth, means literally Ethelred the Ill-counselled, or Ethelred the 'Redeless'.

In 980 serious raids began again. Chester was ravaged from Ireland. The people of Southampton were massacred by marauders from Scandinavia or Denmark. Thanet, Cornwall and Devon all suffered butchery and pillage.

At the epic Battle of Maldon in Essex, Danish Vikings on one side of the river met English Saxons on the other. The Vikings demanded gold, otherwise threatening the English with a storm of spears. The Essex alderman, a man called Byrhtnoth, refused. He pledged to defend the land of his prince, Æthelred. A writer of the time tells us that Byrhtnoth cried that 'The heathen shall fall in the war. Not so likely shall you come by the treasure: point and edge [in other words, spear and sword] shall first make atonement, grim warplay, before we pay tribute.'

C❖These high words were not made good by the event. As the tide was running out while these taunts were being exchanged, the causeway was now exposed and the English naively agreed to let the Vikings cross and form on the south bank in order that battle might be fairly drawn. No sooner had it begun than the English were worsted. Many of Byrhtnoth's men took to flight, but a group of his thanes, knowing that all was lost, fought on to the death. Then followed the most shameful period of Danegeld. . . . Alfred in his day had never hesitated to use money as well as arms. Ethelred used money instead of arms. He used it in ever-increasing quantities, with ever-diminishing returns. He paid as a bribe, in 991, 22,000 pounds of gold and silver, with rations for the invaders. In 994, with 16,000 pounds, he gained not only a brief respite, but the baptism of the raider, Olaf, thrown in as a compliment. In 1002 he bought a further truce for 24,000 pounds of silver, but on this occasion he was himself to break it [the truce]. In their ruin and decay the English had taken large numbers of Danish mercenaries into their service. Ethelred suspected these dangerous helpers of a plot against his life. Panic-stricken, he planned the slaughter of all Danes in the south of England. . . . This atrocious design was executed in 1002 on St Brice's Day.

Among the victims was Gunnhild, the wife of one of the principal Vikings, and sister of Sweyn, King of Denmark.

Sweyn systematically took revenge. The carnage and the massacres were without parallel. For four gruesome years, from Norwich and Thetford in East Anglia to the downs of Kent, to the upper reaches of the Thames, to Exeter in the west country, limbless, violated, sightless victims of Viking anger were piled high. The slaughter stopped only when, predictably, Æthelred paid more bribes. This time the price was 36,000 pounds of silver – probably three years of the national income. But it was not enough. Sweyn did leave but he returned. *The Anglo-Saxon Chronicle* tells what happened next. The year was 1011 and the host described by the chronicler was the Danish invader.

❖The King and his councillors sent to the host, and craved peace, promising them tribute and provisions on condition that they should cease their harrying. They had East Anglia, Middlesex, Oxfordshire, Hertfordshire, Buckinghamshire, Bedfordshire, Kent, Sussex, Surrey and Hampshire. . . . Then they besieged Canterbury. And there they seized the Archbishop and kept the Archbishop as their prisoner. Then the host became greatly incensed against the Bishop, because he was not willing to offer them more money and forbade any ransom to be given for him. Moreover they were very drunk. Then they took the Bishop and led him to their tribunal and pelted him to death with bones and the heads of cattle; and one of them smote him on the skull with the iron of an axe so that he sank down and his holy blood fell upon the earth and his holy soul was sent forth to God's Kingdom.

The difference between the times of King Alfred and those of Æthelred was that where Alfred used gold and the edge of his sword to bring about peace, Æthelred relied on the Danegeld. Consequently money was hard to come by. So much had been paid out that it probably took Æthelred's councillors a great deal of time before they could find enough to satisfy the invaders.

C❖In 1013 Sweyn, accompanied by his younger son, Canute, came again to England, subdued the Yorkshire Danes and the five boroughs in the Danelaw, was accepted as overlord of Northumbria and Danish Mercia, sacked Oxford and Winchester in a punitive foray, and, though repulsed from London, was proclaimed King of England, while Ethelred fled for refuge to the Duke of Normandy, whose sister he had married. On these triumphs Sweyn died at the beginning of 1014. There was another respite. The English turned again to Ethelred, 'declaring that no lord was dearer to them than their natural lord, if he would rule them better than he had done before'.

This was all about fifty years before the Battle of Hastings. Æthelred's bride was Emma, whom he married in 1002. As the sister of Richard, Duke of Normandy, she was an important link in Saxon history, one of the strands that would, a half century on, bring William to Hastings: Emma of Normandy was to be the mother of Edward the Confessor.

C❖. . . . soon the young Danish prince, Canute, set forth to claim the English crown. At this moment the flame of Alfred's line rose again in Ethelred's son, Edmund: Edmund Ironside, as he soon was called. At twenty he was famous. Although declared a rebel by his father, and acting in complete disobedience to him, he gathered forces and, in a brilliant campaign, struck a succession of heavy blows . . . the hearts of all men went out to him. New forces sprang from the ruined land. Ethelred died, and Edmund, last hope of the English, was acclaimed King. In spite of all odds and a heavy defeat he was strong enough to make a partition of the realm, and then set himself to rally his forces for the renewal of the struggle; but in 1016, at twenty-two years of age, Edmund Ironside died, and the whole realm abandoned itself to despair. . . .At Southampton, even while Edmund lived, the lay and spiritual chiefs of England agreed to abandon the descendants of Ethelred for ever and recognize Canute as King. . . .The family of Ethelred was excised from the royal line, and the last sons of the house of Wessex fled into exile. The young Danish prince received this general and abject submission in a good spirit, . . . and in 'an oath of his soul' endorsed by his chiefs, bound himself to rule for all.

So Cnut was King, but he had a problem. And this was where Emma of Normandy appeared once more. Æthelred was dead; Edmund Ironside was dead; but Emma's sons weren't. And their father was Æthelred – hence the agreement to strike the family from its royal line, in other words, its claim to the throne. But kings don't stay kings if they rely on paper agreements. So Cnut married Emma. But he already had a wife and a son so he packed her off; first to the north as his queen there, and then later he made her Regent of Norway. Emma and Æthelred's sons were not allowed to live in England. Nothing was left to chance. And by 1016 they were living in Normandy.

Cnut was not only King of Denmark, but conqueror of Norway. Soon he controlled everything from the entrance to the Baltic Sea down to the Bay of Biscay. And so Cnut's was a careful and wary reign of assurance and cajoling. But most interesting was that he did all this from England.

C❖. . . . of all his realms, Canute chose England for his home and capital. He liked, we are told, the Anglo-Saxon way of life. He wished to be considered the 'successor of Edgar', whose seventeen years of peace still shone by contrast with succeeding times. He ruled according to the laws, and he made it known that these were to be administered in austere detachment from his executive authority.

He built churches, he professed high devotion to the Christian faith and to the Papal diadem. He honoured the memory of St Edmund and St Alphege, whom his fellow countrymen had murdered, and brought their relics with pious pomp to Canterbury. . . . These remarkable achievements, under the blessing of God and the smiles of fortune, were in large measure due to his own personal qualities.

Cnut developed a system that we would now call devolved government. People had more responsibility for their affairs, but were not independent. Cnut didn't want England to go back to warlords, and so, for example, in Cnut's England a very real Danish relationship between the throne and the people who were in charge of the regions developed. And, in the English hierarchy, the Danish title of earl emerged. The earl was appointed by the King. So, the interests of the King would over-ride those of the region. This was a change in the way that England was governed.

But by the year 1030 or so, the Danish earls had disappeared. Cnut's chief advisers then seemed to be Godwine, Earl of Wessex, and Leofric, Earl of Mercia, both Anglo-Saxon. Here we have another important clue in the historical detective story. The rivalry of these two families, Godwine's and Leofric's, meant it was now quite impossible that England would be united against the Normans when they invaded in 1066.

C❖In 1035 Canute died, and his empire with him. He left three sons, two by a former wife and one, Hardicanute [or Harthacnut], by Emma. These sons were ignorant and boorish Vikings, and many thoughts were turned to the old West Saxon line, Alfred and Edward, sons of Ethelred and Emma, then living in exile in Normandy. The elder, Alfred, 'the innocent prince' as the Chronicler calls him, hastened to England in 1036, ostensibly to visit his again-widowed mother, the ex-Queen Emma. A Wessex earl, Godwin, was the leader of the Danish party in England. He possessed great abilities and exercised the highest political influence. The venturesome Alfred was arrested and his personal attendants slaughtered. The unfortunate prince himself was blinded, and in this condition soon ended his days in the monastery at Ely. The guilt of this crime was generally ascribed to Godwin. The succession being thus simplified, Canute's sons divided the paternal inheritance.

Cnut had wanted his son Harthacnut to succeed him as King of England and Denmark. But there was a war on Denmark's borders and he simply couldn't leave for England. Godwine and Emma said Harthacnut should be declared king, even if he stayed in Denmark. But Leofric, Godwine's rival, proposed that another son of the late king should be regent. (Leofric's teenage wife, by the way, was Lady Godiva.) His name was Harold. This was Harold I. The Saxons called him Harold Harefoot. By 1037, Harthacnut was still in Denmark, Harold Harefoot was recognized as King and Emma went into exile, in Flanders. Godwine, being Godwine, now supported Harold. But Harold didn't last long and as soon as he was dead Harthacnut arrived to claim the throne. But like all of Cnut's sons, he died at about the age of twenty-five. *The Anglo-Saxon Chronicle* records:

❖The year 1042: in this year Harthacnut died as he stood at his drink and he suddenly fell to the ground with a horrible convulsion; and those who were near thereto took hold of him, but he never spoke again, and passed away on June 8.

The year 1043: in this year Edward was consecrated King in Winchester on the first day of Easter with great ceremony. Soon in this same year the King had all the lands which his mother owned confiscated for his own use, and took from her all she possessed . . . because she had been too strict with the King her son in that she had done less for him than he wished both before and after his accession. Soon after, Stigand [the Archbishop of Canterbury] was deprived of his See, and all that he possessed was confiscated to the King, because he, Stigand, was his mother's confidant.

So Edward, not yet known as the Confessor, was crowned King of England.

C❖Edward was a quiet, pious person, without liking for war or much aptitude for administration. His Norman upbringing made him the willing, though gentle, agent of Norman influence, so far as Earl Godwin would allow. Norman prelates appeared in the English Church, Norman clerks in the royal household, and Norman landowners in the English shires. . . . According to tradition the King was a kindly, weak, chubby albino . . . and as he grew older his outlook was increasingly that of a monk. [Hence his name, the Confessor.]

Godwine grew more powerful with Edward on the throne, even though the King regarded him with great suspicion and still saw him as the man behind the death of his brother, Alfred. Alfred's elder sons became earls. One of them, Swein, stretched family loyalties when he seduced an abbess and murdered his cousin, one of the King's earls. Edward publicly declared him to be 'nithing', meaning 'a man without any honour'. Swein fled to Flanders.

C❖A crisis came in the year 1051, when the Norman party at Court succeeded in driving Godwin into exile. During Godwin's absence William of Normandy is said to have paid an official visit to the Confessor in England in quest of the succession to the Crown. Very likely King Edward promised that William should be his heir. But in the following year Godwin returned, backed by a force raised in Flanders, and with the active help of his son Harold [who was to become Harold of Hastings]. Together father and son obliged King Edward to take them back into power. . . . Seven months after his restoration Godwin died, in 1053. . . . Harold, his eldest surviving son, succeeded to his father's great estates . . . and for the next thirteen adventurous years was the virtual ruler of England.

The death of the official ruler is recorded in *The Anglo-Saxon Chronicle:*

❖King Edward came to Westminster towards Christmas [1065], and there had the abbey church consecrated which he himself had built to the glory of God, St Peter, and all God's saints; the consecration of the church was on Holy Innocents' Day. He passed away on the vigil of the Epiphany, and was buried on the Epiphany. Here in the world he dwelt for a time in royal majesty, sagacious in counsel; a gracious ruler for twenty-four years.

And so Edward died and with him the line of the Saxon Kings. The boy who should have been King on Edward's death was Edgar. He was the son of the King's nephew. But he was in no position to lead the nation, certainly not to defend it, especially as it was certain that Duke William of Normandy and the King of Norway would each claim the crown for himself. The English had to decide between a respect for the royal line and the need to be protected. Harold was unique. No one man, other than the King himself, had ever been so popular and so powerful throughout the land.

Yet one irony remained. On his deathbed, Edward warned of the great evil that was about to sweep his land. But the Archbishop encouraged Harold to ignore the warnings. This was nothing more, he said, than the ramblings of an ancient robbed of his wits. The Archbishop was that great ecclesiastical survivor, Stigand.

But the warnings were true and the spirit of Edward ruled English hearts for centuries, so much so that it wasn't until the fourteenth century that the people abandoned Edward as the nation's patron saint for the mythical St George.

And while England mourned, Duke William of Normandy made ready for sea.

CHAPTER FOUR

1066–1087

——— ❖ ———

E dward the Confessor died on 5 January 1066. The Battle of Hastings took place later that same year, on 14 October. But what happened in that ten-month gap before the Norman Conquest, the last successful invasion of these islands?

The first point to make is that the Normans weren't French in the way that the term is understood today. Their origins were in Scandinavia. Under a vigorous warrior king, called Rollo, the Vikings had settled in Northern France a century and a half before William the Conqueror was born. During the years before the invasion, Normandy, as Churchill describes, had become a land of ambitious, well-ordered, often uncompromising, peoples.

C❖. . . A class of knights and nobles arose who held their lands in return for military service, and sublet to inferior tenants upon the same basis. The Normans, with their craving for legality and logic, framed a general scheme for society, from which there soon emerged an excellent army. Order was strenuously enforced. No one but the Duke might build castles or fortify himself. . . . The Dukes of Normandy created relations with the Church which became a model for mediaeval Europe.

Now it may have been a structured society, but it wasn't as far advanced in statehood as England was at that time. Leaders in England were beginning to take quite seriously the business of government by bureaucracy rather than by battle axe.

C❖The King lived largely upon his private estates and governed as best he could through his household. The remaining powers of the monarchy were in practice severely restricted by a little group of Anglo-Danish notables. The main basis for support of the English kings had always been this select Council, never more than sixty, who in a vague manner regarded themselves as the representatives of the whole country. . . . But at this time this assembly of 'wise men' in no way embodied the life of the nation. . . . It tended to fall into the hands of the great families. . . . Feuds and disturbances were rife. The people, too, were hampered not only by the many conflicting petty authorities, but by the deep division of custom between the Saxon and the Danish districts.

The England of 1066 wasn't some peaceful pastoral canvas about to be slashed by a Norman vandal. Nor was it a state able to defend itself against a carefully planned invasion. There was no English fleet other than a few ships which the King could requisition. Also, gathering enough soldiers to reinforce his professional fighters was a complicated task. In general terms, a thegn held his land in return for military service. Peasants also had obligations, but it was often difficult to decide how far obligation went. And unlike the system across the Channel, England didn't have a complex of castles as defensive points in any county or region. The omens were not good for Harold, especially as he faced enemies on two fronts: his half-brother Tostig, who hated him, and William of Normandy who believed the English crown belonged to him.

C❖The successors of Canute in Norway determined to revive their traditions of English sovereignty . . . Tostig . . . arrived with full accounts of the crisis in the Island and of the weak state of its defences. King Harold Hardrada [the last of the great Viking hero kings] set forth to conquer the English crown. . . . With Tostig he wended towards the north-east coast of England with a large fleet and army in the late summer of 1066.

　　　Harold of England . . . heard that a Norwegian fleet . . . had sailed up the Humber, beaten the local levies under Earls Edwin and Morcar, and encamped near York at Stamford Bridge. . . . The news reached him in London. . . . At the head of his Danish household troops he hastened northwards up the Roman road to York, calling out the local levies as he went. His rapidity of movement took the Northern invaders completely by surprise. Within five days of the defeat of Edwin and Morcar, Harold reached York, and the same day marched to confront the Norwegian army ten miles from the city.

Hardrada was determined that the throne of England was rightfully his. *The Anglo-Saxon Chronicle* records:

❖Earl Edwin and Earl Morcar had gathered as great a force as they could; but a great number of the English were either slain or drowned or driven in flight, and the Norwegians had possession of the place of slaughter. After the battle King Harold of Norway and Earl Tostig entered York and received hostages from the borough and provisions. Then meanwhile came Harold the King of the English on the Sunday to Tadcaster and there drew up his household troops in battle order and on Monday marched through York. Harold King of Norway and Earl Tostig and their force had gone beyond York to Stamford Bridge. Then Harold, King of the English, came upon them unawares beyond the bridge. And that day no side gave quarter. There were slain Harold the Fairhead [Hardrada], the King of the Norwegians, and Earl Tostig and the remaining Norwegians were put to flight until some of them reached their ships, some were drowned, others burned to death and thus perished in various ways so many that there were few to survive. And the English had possession of the place of slaughter.

There were two battles, not one. In the first one, which the *Chronicle* states took place on the vigil of St Matthew – 20 September – Edwin and Morcar were defeated. In other words, when Harold King of the English arrived he was fighting a much reduced, weakened invader. And so he was in a good position to win, and he did. But Edwin and Morcar were so heavily beaten in the first battle, they were in no position to raise fresh forces and march with Harold to the Battle of Hastings.

Consequently Harold, the last King of the Old English, had now to march south with insufficient troops to repel the armies of William of Normandy. William, Duke of Normandy, had landed on a Sussex beach on the morning of Thursday 28 September, 1066. He had come to claim the throne of England for himself.

It is easy to see why William believed he had a right to the English throne. Emma of Normandy, who had been married to King Cnut, and also to Æthelred the Unready by whom she had the son who became Edward the Confessor, was also the sister of Robert, Duke of Normandy, William's father. In addition, Harold was not of the royal line, and he had agreed that when Edward died, he would support William's claim to the throne. It is this last part of the royal detective yarn that is depicted in the famous Bayeux Tapestry.

C❖. . . this story is told with irresistible charm in the tapestry chronicle . . . designed by English artists under the guidance of his [William's] half-brother, Odo, Bishop of Bayeux. It is of course the Norman version, and was for generations proclaimed by their historians as a full justification – and already even in those days aggressors needed justifications – of William's invasion of England. . . . It is probable however that Harold swore a solemn oath to William to renounce all rights or designs upon the English crown, and it is likely that if he had not done so he might never have seen either crown or England again. . . . Nevertheless it cannot be said that the bargain between the two men was unreasonable, and Harold probably at the time saw good prospects in it for himself.

But William was not secure as Duke of Normandy until he was twenty, in 1047. He was the bastard son of Duke Robert of Normandy and Arlette, a tanner's daughter, and his father died when he was seven. William had to fight for his inheritance and the experience hardened him.

It was also during this period, on the Continent, but not in Britain, that warfare began to change. The chain-mailed knight appeared and more thought was given to fortifications, to cavalry tactics (instead of simply using horses for transportation) and disciplined armies, which in some cases had not been seen since Roman times. William of Normandy emerged as a proper general, not just a general by right. He brought together disparate soldiery, including peasants and mercenaries, and welded them into formidable fighting units.

C❖In no part of the feudal world was the fighting quality of the new organization carried to a higher pitch than among the Normans. . . . William, like his father, was in close touch with the Saxon Court, and had watched every move on the part of the supporters of the Anglo-Danish party, headed by Godwin and his son Harold.

Fate played startlingly into the hands of the Norman Duke. On some visit of inspection, probably in 1064, Harold was driven by the winds onto the French coast. . . . A friendship sprang up between William and Harold. Politics apart, they liked each other well. . . . But the Duke looked forward to his future succession to the English crown. Here indeed was the prize to be won.

And so to the Battle of Hastings. The story is well known, but here are some graphic extracts from Churchill.

C❖ . . . Harold and his house-carls [the King's personal guild of fighting men], sadly depleted by the slaughter of Stamford Bridge . . . [marched] night and day to London. They covered the 200 miles in seven days. In London, the King gathered all the forces he could, and . . . marched out towards Pevensey and, in the evening of October 13, took up his position upon the slope of a hill which barred the direct march upon the capital.

And so, the night came. The fires were lit. On Senlac Hill in Sussex, Harold II of England waited for the reinforcements which he so desperately needed, but which he must have known would arrive too late, if at all. Eight miles away, the Normans made ready.

C❖The cavalry charges of William's mail-clad knights, cumbersome in manoeuvre, beat in vain upon the dense, ordered masses of the English. . . . William's left wing of cavalry was thrown into disorder, and retreated rapidly down the hill. On this the troops on Harold's right . . . broke their ranks in eager pursuit. William, in the centre, turned his disciplined squadrons upon them and cut them to pieces. The Normans then re-formed their ranks and began a second series of charges upon the English masses, subjecting them in the intervals to severe archery. . . . Never, it was said, had the Norman knights met foot-soldiers of this stubbornness. They were utterly unable to break through the shield walls and they suffered serious losses from the deft blows of the axe-men. . . . But the arrow showers took a cruel toll. So closely, it was said, were the English wedged that the wounded could not be removed, and the dead scarcely found room in which to sink upon the ground.

The Anglo-Saxon Chronicle concludes the story of the Battle of Hastings.

❖The King fought most resolutely with those men who wished to stand by him and there was great slaughter on both sides. King Harold was slain, and Leofwine, his brother, and Earl Gurth, his brother, and many good men. The French had possession of the place of slaughter, as God granted them because of the nation's sins.

Edward the Confessor's death-bed prophecy had come true. Harold was dead, according to the tapestry, from an arrow through the eye. William, who had three horses killed under him, survived and camped upon the battlefield.

It is said that the Battle of Hastings decided the fate of the English nation. And that's probably true. But on the night of 14 October 1066, when a purple robe was wrapped about King Harold's naked body, and William of Normandy began to count the cost of that day's slaughter, no one knew that for sure.

C❖William was a prime exponent of the doctrine . . . of mass terrorism through the spectacle of bloody and merciless examples. Now, with a compact force of Normans, French, and Bretons, he advanced through Kent upon the capital . . . The people of Romney had killed a band of Norman knights. Vengeance fell upon them. The news spread through the country, and the folk flocked 'like flies settling on a wound' to make their submission and avoid a similar fate. . . . When William arrived near London he marched round the city . . . isolating it by a belt of cruel desolation. From Southwark he moved to Wallingford, and thence through the Chilterns to Berkhamsted, where the leading Saxon notables and clergy came meekly to his tent to offer him the Crown.

The English still believed they could hold London and raise another army. But they needed a leader. They chose Edgar the Æthling. He managed to beat off

William, probably at London Bridge, and stopped him entering the town. This is why he went onward as Churchill records. (Incidentally, one of those who went to Wallingford to pledge his support was Archbishop Stigand – Stigand the great survivor.) But by now the English were fast waking from their dreams of saving themselves. And so the Earls Morcar and Edwin who had fought for Harold, the Bishop Ældred who had called for Edgar the Æthling to lead the uprising and Edgar himself, gave in. *The Anglo-Saxon Chronicle* notes that it was a shame they had not done so earlier.

❖They submitted from force of circumstance, but only when the plundering and pillaging was complete. It was great folly that they had not done so sooner. They gave him hostages and swore oaths of fealty, and he promised to be a gracious lord to them. But still his army harried everywhere they came. Then on Christmas Day Archbishop Ældred consecrated him King in Westminster and William gave a pledge on the gospels that he would govern this nation according to the best practice of his predecessors if they would be loyal to him.

A procedural complication arose with nearly catastrophic consequences and not a little black humour. William was there not because he was indisputably next in line for the throne. He was a conqueror. The people at the coronation had to show that they freely accepted him as King. But not all spoke English and not all spoke French. So the question was put to them in two languages. The commotion of their responses echoed about the building. Outside, William's guards could only hear roaring and shouting. They thought the crowd inside must have turned upon William. So they panicked and set fire to the surrounding buildings. But when all had calmed, and presumably the fires had been put out, the ceremony continued and the Crown of England was William's.

The physical legacy of the period is seen in castles and churches, but especially castles. One of the first was by the Thames, which was some indication of the importance of London and the fear that towns could be the centre of an uprising. Soon William replaced the castle with his lasting visible monument: the Tower. The castle of London and the taxes William imposed marked the start of his steady conquest of these islands.

But conquest does not necessarily mean control. It's true that six months after the Battle of Hastings, William felt confident enough to return to Normandy. But it was three years before Chester fell. And he had to make sure he wasn't going to be overthrown while he was away. So, he made Bishop Odo, his half-brother, Earl of Kent, installed him in Dover Castle and left him in charge along with William fitz Osbern who was his most trusted steward. Then, having decided to go, he took to Normandy the very people who might lead an uprising once his back was turned. But that didn't stop the whole nation being on the edge of rebellion.

C❖. . . whether William would retain the whole of his conquests unchallenged from without was not settled till his closing years. . . . For at least twenty years after the invasion the Normans were an army camped in a hostile country, holding the population down by castles at key points. The Saxon resistance died hard. Legends and chroniclers have painted for us the last stand of Hereward the Wake in the broad fens round Ely. Not until five years after Hastings . . . was Hereward put down. In his cause had fallen many of the Saxon thanage, the only class from whose ranks new leaders could spring. The building of Ely Castle symbolized the end of their order.

So little is known of Hereward that there's a temptation to think that he should hang in the same gallery as King Arthur and Robin Hood. But he was a real person. He came from Lincolnshire and he was one of the thegns: people who held land in return for military service. Today he'd probably be called a freedom fighter, or guerrilla. A modern day William would call him a terrorist. But he doesn't appear to have been a nobleman, which makes it hard to understand why so many followed him. There is, however, in a near contemporary document called *De Gestis Herwardi,* a description of the man. We're told he had yellow hair and large grey eyes, one of them slightly discoloured. He had great and sturdy limbs and none was his equal in daring and braveness. The most romantic of all ideas is that his mother might have been Lady Godiva and his father Leofric of Mercia.

It is known that for years Hereward led a rebellion in the southern part of East Anglia and that when Ely fell, he escaped into the fens. After that, like the less real figures of King Arthur and Robin Hood, Hereward's name became a symbol of resistance to evil authority. However, the King's next major rebellion came not from the English, but from his own people.

C❖In 1075, a serious revolt of disaffected Norman knights broke out in the Midlands, East Anglia, and on the Welsh border, and one surviving Saxon leader, Waltheof, who had previously made his peace with William, joined them. . . . The Saxon population supported the Conqueror against chaos. . . . Vengeance was reserved for Waltheof alone, and his execution upon a hill outside Winchester is told in moving scenes by the Saxon-hearted monkish chroniclers of the time.

It is thought that he was the only noble to be executed by King William. Yet, even in these cruel times, this death penalty of someone of such high rank, who had, incidentally, given himself up to William, was regarded as harsh, even unjust. The Saxon population may have wanted revenge (Waltheof was regarded as an Englishman), but not this.

Waltheof became a martyr. The mediaeval legend has it that the guilt of Waltheof's execution hovered over the King until his own death. William was King of England for twenty-one years and during that period it was clear that Saxon England would never be restored. Less obvious was the way life changed for almost everyone, conqueror and conquered.

C❖Norman castles guarded the towns, Norman lords held the land, and Norman churches protected men's souls. All England had a master, the conquest was complete . . .

Woe to the conquered!

William was a master of war, and thereby gave his small duchy some of the prestige which England had enjoyed thirty years before under the firm and clear-sighted government of Cnut.

C❖Everywhere castles arose. These were not at first the massive stone structures of a later century; they were simply fortified military posts consisting of an earthen rampart and a stockade, and a central keep made of logs. . . . In their early days the Normans borrowed no manners and few customs from the Islanders. The only culture was French. Surviving Saxon notables sent their sons to the monasteries of France for education . . . all who could, learnt French, as formerly the contemporaries of Boadicea had learnt Latin. At first the conquerors, who despised the uncouth English as louts and boors, ruled by the force of sharpened steel. But very soon, in true Norman fashion, they intermarried with the free population and identified themselves with their English past.

But if society was to live in some sort of harmony then it had to have basic rights. And these rights developed over long periods. There were laws for estate workers: a cowherd was, usually, entitled to the milk of an old cow after she was newly calved. A shepherd's due was twelve nights' dung at Christmas; he also got one lamb a year, a bell-wether's fleece and a bowl of buttermilk throughout the summer. And slaves, the lowest of all workers, were to be given food at Christmas and Easter and a strip of land they could plough and tend. A female slave was given three pence or one sheep for winter's food. There was also an indication that the Normans exacted clear penalties from those who offended this new society. An early twelfth-century document called *Textus Roffensis* gives some idea of what were known as the Laws of King William, particularly those to protect his Norman followers.

❖I will that all the men whom I have brought with me, or who have come after me, shall be protected by my peace and shall dwell in quiet. And if any one of they [sic] shall be slain, let the lord of his murderer seize him within five days; if he cannot, let him begin to pay me forty-six marks of silver so long as his substance avails. And when his substance is exhausted, let the whole hundred in which the murder took place pay what remains in common.

And if the murderer were caught, and if he were an Englishman, then the Laws of William the Conqueror were quite clear as to what happened next.

❖If a Frenchman shall charge an Englishman with perjury or murder or theft or homicide or 'ran', as the English call rapine, which cannot be denied, the Englishman may defend himself as he shall prefer, either by the ordeal of hot iron or by wager of battle. But if the Englishman be infirm let him find another who will take his place. If one of them shall be vanquished, he shall pay a fine of forty shillings to the King. If an Englishman shall charge a Norman and he be unwilling to prove his accusation either by ordeal or by wager of battle, I decree, nevertheless, that the Norman shall acquit himself by valid oath.

William ruled England for two decades. He was called William the Conqueror. He wanted to be known as King William. He wanted the English to accept him as Edward the Confessor's rightful heir. As King, he certainly adopted all the Old English powers. For example, he continued to impose taxes calculated to improve the state and not just his own coffers. But, further down the scale of nobility the Norman minority gradually overturned the power of the English.

C❖A military caste was imposed from above. A revolution not only in warfare, but also in the upper reaches of society, had taken place. . . . There were interminable controversies among the new masters of the country about the titles to their lands, and how these fitted the customs and laws of Anglo-Saxon England. . . . Finally in 1086 a vast sworn inquiry was made into the whole wealth of the King's feudal vassals, from whom he derived a large part of his own income. The inquest or description, as it was called, was carried through with a degree of minuteness and regularity unique in that age and unequalled for centuries later. The history of many an English village begins with an entry in Domesday Book.

A contemporary chronicler wrote that the book was to be called Domesday because 'It spared no man, but judged all men indifferently, as the Lord in that great day will do.'

The idea for Domesday came to William at Christmas in 1085. A writer of the time recorded that:

❖He sent his men all over England into every shire and caused them to ascertain how many hundred hides were in the shires, of what land and of cattle the King himself owned in this country or what dues he ought to receive every year from the shires. Also he caused them to write down how much land belonged to his archbishops and his suffragan bishops and his abbots and his earls. What and how much in land and in cattle each man possessed, who was occupier of land in England, and how much money it was worth. So very narrowly did he cause the survey to be made that there was not a single hide or rood of land, nor even was there an ox or a cow or a pig left that was not set down in his writing. And afterwards all these things were brought to him.

This was a time of great crisis in the reign of William of Normandy. There was talk of invaders from Scandinavia. So behind Domesday was the need to raise money as well as to find out who had the financial, and therefore political and military, power in England.

C❖The Norman garrison in England was threatened from abroad by other claimants. The rulers of Scandinavia still yearned for the Island, once the west of their empire. They had supported the rising in the North in 1069, and again in 1085 they threatened to intervene with greater vigour . . . and it was under the shadow of this menace that Domesday Book was compiled. In 1086, William called together at Salisbury 'all the land-holding men of any account throughout England, whosoever men they were'. The King had need of an assurance of loyalty from all his feudal tenants of substance, and this substantial body bound itself together by oath and fealty to his person.

Domesday was to be William's last great achievement. The survey, the great reckoning, was born out of crisis at home and abroad. But William of Normandy's influence was more lasting in England than anywhere else. He changed the way the English lived, the laws that governed them and the course of their history. He did so ruthlessly.

And, there was one particular aspect which made his rule different from any that had gone before. It determined the development of feudalism and, in some sense, it applies to this day. William said that whatever loyalty a person had to his immediate lord, his protector, that that person's allegiance to the monarch must always be greater. His reign was the more remarkable considering the conflicts in his own family and in particular, in Normandy, where his Queen, Matilda, ruled in his absence.

C❖Though England was a more valuable possession than Normandy, William and his sons were always more closely interested in their Continental lands. The French Kings, for their part, placed in the forefront of their policy the weakening of these Dukes of Normandy, now grown so powerful, and whose frontiers were little more than twenty miles from Paris. Hence arose a struggle that was solved only when King John lost Normandy in 1203. . . . Queen Matilda was a capable regent in Rouen, but plagued by the turbulence of her sons. The eldest, Robert, a Crusading knight, reckless and spendthrift, with his father's love of fighting and adventure but without his ruthless genius or solid practical aims, resented William's persistent hold on life and impatiently claimed his Norman inheritance. Many a time the father was called across the Channel to chastise rebellious towns and forestall the conspiracies of his son with the French Court. Robert, driven from his father's lands, found refuge in King Philip's castle of Gerberoi. William marched implacably upon him. Beneath the walls, two men, visors down, met in single combat, father and son. Robert wounded his father in the hand and unhorsed him, and would indeed have killed him but for the timely rescue by an Englishman, one Tokig of Wallingford, who remounted the overthrown Conqueror. Both were sobered by this chance encounter, and for a time there was reconciliation.

Robert also broke with his two brothers, William (who was to become known as William Rufus) and Henry, who one day would also be King. And, even when there was reconciliation it was never for long. All this meant that William spent more and more time away from England. It's difficult to track him down through contemporary documents, but it is known that for three years, between 1077 and 1080, William was not in England at all.

One writer of this time was William of Malmesbury.

❖They [the Normans] live with economy in large houses; they envy their equals; they wish to vie with their superiors; and they plunder their subjects though they protect them from others. They weigh treason by its chance of success, and change their opinions for money. They are the most polite of peoples; they consider strangers to merit the courtesy they extend to each other. After their coming to England they revived the rule of religion. You might see churches rise in every village and, in towns and cities, monasteries built after a style unknown before. They are exceedingly particular in their dress, and delicate in their food, but not to excess.

Normans, according to William of Malmesbury, are scheming, often brutal and at the same time civilized, whatever that might have meant at the time. In 1080, the Northumbrians killed the Bishop of Durham, a Norman and, we're told by one of the chroniclers, another 100 died with him. And in that same year, the Earl of Moray was killed by an army of Scots. The Scottish Kings had never accepted the lines drawn between England and Scotland. The Conqueror's knights had chased and fought the old northern Saxons who refused to give in to his rule. Among them had been Edgar the Æthling, a great survivor who indeed was to outlive William. He was now related by marriage to Malcolm the Bighead, the Scottish King. Malcolm had become King when he beat Macbeth (the real Macbeth) in 1057. He too outlived, and out-harried, William who found life even more difficult after the death of his wife, Matilda.

C❖Matilda died, and with increasing years William became fiercer in mood. Stung to fury by the forays of the French, he crossed the frontier, spreading fire and ruin till he reached the gates of Mantes. His Normans surprised the town, and amid the horrors of the sack, fire broke out. As William rode through the streets his horse stumbled among the burning ashes and he was thrown against the pommel of the saddle. He was carried in agony to the priory of St Gervase at Rouen. There, high above the town, he lay, through the summer heat of 1087, fighting his grievous injury. When death drew near, his sons William and Henry came to him. William, whose one virtue had been filial fidelity, was named to succeed the Conqueror in England. The graceless Robert would rule in Normandy at last. For the youngest, Henry, there was nothing but 5000 pounds of silver, and the prophecy that he would one day reign over a united Anglo-Norman nation. This proved no empty blessing.

The tidying of the family affairs was not such an easy matter as that makes it appear. At first the Conqueror refused to make his son, Robert, the Duke of Normandy. But the priests pressed the dying King to change his mind. One of the monks at the St Gervase Priory recorded William's words at the time. 'Since he has disdained to come here himself it is with your witness and the will of God that I shall act. With my testimony I declare that I forgive him all the sins he has committed against me and I grant him the whole Duchy of Normandy. He has learned to take advantage of my leniency and now he has brought down his father's grey hairs in sorrow to the grave.' William the Conqueror died on 9 September 1087.

So, the Conquest is done. For those who had lived under Edward the Confessor, then through the spring, summer and early autumn of 1066 under Harold and finally through the two decades of William, it had all been a terrible affair. Nothing but conflict, nothing but change. The last of the Saxon lords and landowners suffered more than the peasant class. All had to live beneath the rule of a foreign king. There could have been little consolation in the improved

CHAPTER FIVE

1087–1165

—— ❖ ——

It is 1087. The new King of England is William Rufus, or, as Churchill writes, William the Red.

C❖Under his son William, dubbed Rufus, the Red, it [the feudal system, based on land ownership] was not less harsh [than it had been under William the Conqueror], but also capricious. Moreover, the accession of the Conqueror's second surviving son to the throne of England did not pass without dispute. William I's decision to divide his English from his Norman lands brought new troubles in its train. The greater barons possessed property on both sides of the Channel. They therefore now owed feudal allegiance to two sovereign lords, and not unnaturally they sought to play one against the other. Both Duke Robert and William II were dissatisfied with the division, and their brotherly ties did not mitigate their covetous desires. During the thirteen years of the reign of William Rufus the Anglo-Norman realms were vexed by fratricidal strife and successive baronial revolts. The Saxon inhabitants of England, fearful of a relapse into the chaos of pre-Conquest days, stood by the King against all rebels.

William Rufus became king, partly because his dying father wished it and partly, and importantly, because one of the two most influential men in England, Archbishop Lanfranc, approved. Lanfranc was an Italian who had arrived in Normandy at the monastery of Bec in 1042. He had been responsible for the education of the Conqueror's sons so, more than anyone, Lanfranc understood William Rufus. Lanfranc's authority came from the Conqueror himself who made him Archbishop of Canterbury. It was he who rebuilt the great Kentish Cathedral. Almost no important political decision was taken in England without his approval. However, as *The Anglo-Saxon Chronicle* reports, although Lanfranc had his way, this was hardly an easy time for the new King.

❖In this year [1088] there was great commotion in this country and treason was everywhere, with the result that the most powerful Frenchmen in the land plotted to betray their lord and king, and make his brother Robert king, he who was Duke of Normandy. The leaders in this conspiracy were Bishop Odo, Bishop Geoffrey, and William Bishop of Durham. Earl Roger was also of that foolish conspiracy, and very many others too, all Frenchmen. As soon as Easter came, then they set out to harry and burn, and laid waste to the King's farms, and devastated the lands of all those men who owed allegiance to the King. Bishop Geoffrey and Robert of Mowbray went to Bristol, and harried, and brought the booty to the castle; thereafter they sallied forth and ravaged Bath and all the surrounding countryside. The chief men of Hereford, with the men of Shropshire and a great force from Wales came and burnt in Worcestershire . . . The Bishop of Durham did as much damage as he could everywhere in the north. Bishop Odo, who was the instigator of these troubles, went to his earldom in Kent and his men laid waste the lands of the King and the Archbishop, and all the spoil was taken into his castle at Rochester.

The King promised new and fair tax laws, he promised new hunting rights and almost anything else he could think of. Although there was no way he could, or would, keep these promises, he managed to get a large army on his side and he besieged Rochester Castle. But Odo had escaped, ironically to Pevensey where the Conqueror, his half-brother, had landed in 1066. But, eventually, the King won the day. Bishop Odo and the rest went into exile in Normandy. Odo never came back. He died at Palermo on his way to take part in a Crusade.

This English rebellion was not simply land grabbing, or the dislike of the King. It was just one episode in the conflict between the sons of the Conqueror. Robert fought William. William fought them all. And Henry was sometimes on one side, sometimes on the other.

England at this time was a society governed by ruthlessness, greed and poor kingship. When Lanfranc died, in 1089, there was no longer any restraint on the treacherous instincts of William Rufus. But the sons of the Conqueror deserved each other, even if the people deserved something better. This was a family so much at war that at one point, Robert and William joined against their young brother Henry. But events far from Normandy and Winchester were once more to divert the flow of rivalries.

In 1096 Robert decided to go on a Crusade, an expensive business. So William played pawnbroker and Robert hocked Normandy to him for 10,000 silver marks.

C❖The Crusading spirit had for some time stirred the minds of men all over Western Europe. The Christian kingdoms of Spain had led the way with their holy wars against the Arabs. Now, towards the end of the eleventh century, a new enemy of Christendom appeared 1500 miles to the east. The Seljuk Turks were pressing hard upon the Byzantine Empire in Asia Minor, and harassing devout pilgrims from Europe through Syria to the Holy Land. The Byzantine Emperor appealed to the West for help, and in 1095, Pope Urban II, who had long dreamt of recovering Jerusalem for Christendom, called on the chivalry of Europe to take the Cross. The response was immediate, overwhelming and at first, disastrous. An itinerant monk named Peter the Hermit took up the cry to arms. So powerful was his preaching that in 1096 an enthusiastic but undisciplined train of 20,000 men, most of them peasants, unskilled in war, set off from Cologne for the East under his leadership. Few of them ever reached the Holy Land. After marching through Hungary and the Balkans the majority perished by Turkish arrows amid the mountains of Asia Minor.

The so-called People's Crusade thus collapsed. But by now the magnates of Europe had rallied to the Cause: four armies, each numbering perhaps 10,000 men, and led by some of the greatest nobles of the age . . . The Byzantine Emperor was embarrassed. He had hoped for manageable mercenaries as reinforcements from the West. Instead he found, camped around his capital, four powerful and ambitious hosts.

Thirty-two years after the Battle of Hastings Robert of Normandy, one of the Conqueror's sons, and Edgar the Ætheling, the great-nephew of Edward the Confessor, joined forces against a common enemy: the Turks at Antioch. Robert led his warriors on land and Edgar commanded a grand fleet. This is really nothing more than an aside, but it is a reminder that history is not simply a string of dates: some characters, who at the time appear to have little more than a walk-on part can, and often do, turn up again later in pivotal parts.

C❖In August 1100 he [William Rufus] was mysteriously shot through the head by an arrow while hunting in the New Forest, leaving a memory of shameless exactions and infamous morals, but also a submissive realm to his successor. . . . While the rough hands of Rufus chafed and bruised the feudal relationship, they had also enforced the rights of a feudal king.

Prince Henry, the youngest of the royal brothers, had been a member of the fatal hunting party in the New Forest. There is no proof that he was implicated in the death of his brother, but he certainly wasted no time in mourning. He made straight for the royal treasury at Winchester . . .

William of Malmesbury wrote that the day before he died, Rufus dreamed that a surgeon was letting his blood and the stream flowed so high that it clouded out the daylight. A monk warned that he should not hunt the next day, but

Rufus, having drunk a great deal, did go into the forest. Then came the, apparent, accident. An attendant called Walter Tirel shot the King with an arrow. William of Malmesbury reported that a few countrymen recovered the body and took it on a cart to the cathedral at Winchester, the blood dripping from it all the way. Three days after the death of Rufus, Henry had himself crowned King.

C❖He set the precedent . . . of proclaiming a charter upon his accession. By this he sought to conciliate those powerful forces in Church and State which had been alienated by the rapacity and tactlessness of his predecessor. He guaranteed that the rights of the baronage and the Church should be respected. At the same time, having seen the value of Saxon loyalty in the reigns of his father and his brother, he promised the conquered race good justice and the laws of Edward the Confessor. . . . much to the suspicion of the Norman barons, [Henry made] a marriage with Matilda, niece of [David] the last surviving Saxon claimant to the [Northern] English throne and descendant of the old English line of kings. The barons, mollified by the charter, accepted this decisive step.

The new queen, who became known as Good Queen Maud, was the granddaughter of Edmund Ironside, the son of Æthelred the Unready who had been King of England before Cnut. But she wasn't English. Her father was Malcolm Canmore, King of the Scots, who had been killed in England. The marriage did two things: in theory at least, it gave Henry a respectability which was convenient and it neatly tied a knot with the Scottish kings. But for the moment, Henry had a family difficulty which was less easy to sort out. His brother, Robert, wanted Henry's blood.

C❖Henry was now ready to face Robert whenever he should return. In September 1100 this event occurred. Immediately the familiar incidents of feudal rebellion were renewed in England, and for the next six years the King had to fight to make good his title under his father's will. . . . in 1105, having consolidated his position in England, Henry crossed the Channel. In September 1106, the most important battle since Hastings was fought at Tinchebrai. King Henry's victory was complete. Duke Robert was carried to his perpetual prison in England. Normandy acknowledged Henry's authority and the control of Anglo-Norman policy passed from Rouen to London. The Saxons, who had fought heartily for Henry, regarded this battle as their military revenge for Hastings. . . . a certain broad measure of unity was re-established in the Island.

Henry introduced many long lasting reforms and he took nothing, certainly not unity, for granted, especially when tragedy settled on the family.

C❖The King had a son, his heir apparent, successor indisputable. On this young man of seventeen many hopes and assurances were founded. In the winter of 1120, he was coming back from a visit to France in the royal yacht called the *White Ship*. Off the coast of Normandy the vessel struck a rock . . . The Prince had indeed been embarked in a boat. He returned to rescue his sister. In this crisis . . . at the ship's side so many leaped into the boat that it sank. Two men remained afloat, the ship's butcher and a knight. 'Where is the Prince?' asked the knight above the waves. 'All are drowned . . .' replied the butcher. 'Then,' said the knight, 'all is lost for England.' . . . None dared tell it to the King. When at last he heard the tidings, 'he never smiled again'. This was more than the agony of parental grief for an only son. . . .The spectre of . . . disputed succession glared again upon England. The forces of anarchy grew, and every noble in his castle balanced his chances upon who would succeed to the Crown.

In the 1120s, the time of the *White Ship* disaster as it came to be called, the Scots claimed territory as far south as Lancashire. The King at the time was David. Under him Scotland reached the zenith of its powers. In 1124 David succeeded his brother, Alexander, as King of all Scotland. He became an important figure in the holding together of these islands from the north to the south. Until Alexander's death the two brothers had ruled jointly; Alexander ruled north of the Firth of Forth, David from the Lowlands south to Cumbria. As *The Anglo-Saxon Chronicle* records:

❖On 23 April, King Alexander of Scotland passed away, and David, his brother, who was Earl of Northamptonshire, succeeded to the kingdom, and held them both together, the kingdom of Scotland and the earldom in England. . . . In 1126, King Henry held his court at Christmas in Windsor. David, the King of the Scots, was present, and there he [Henry] obtained an oath from archbishops, bishops, abbots, earls and all those thanes present, that England and Normandy should pass after his death into the possession of his daughter.

Her name was Matilda, although the English later called her Maud. Her husband, the Holy Roman Emperor, was dead and now her father, Henry, the great English reformer, wanted her to be queen and, it seems, married. And after that Christmas at Windsor Matilda was remarried, as the *The Anglo-Saxon Chronicle* reports:

❖King Henry then sent her to Normandy, and with her went her brother Robert, Earl of Gloucester, and married her to Geoffrey Martel, he who was the son of the Count of Anjou. This marriage displeased all the French and all the English.

Geoffrey Martel was only fourteen and Matilda was twenty-five and, once again, two apparently lesser figures in history contributed significantly. Geoffrey and Matilda had three children. One of them, born on 5 March 1133, was baptized Henry. This child became Henry II, known in English history as Henry Plantagenet. But before his accession much happened, including the Laws of King Henry I. By later standards, these laws were hardly laws at all. Jurisprudence was not contained in an Act of Parliament, there was no such thing. These Laws of Henry I were simply passed to his judges by hand, or even by word of mouth. In them there was a clear statement that Edward the Confessor's memory would be honoured.

Henry didn't want to give any impression of breaking with the past, particularly with the ways and the image left by Edward the Confessor. The Confessor was so blessed in English memory, that it was in this, the twelfth century, that he was canonized. St Edward became the patron saint of the English peoples and remained so until St George, during the Hundred Years' War.

C❖There survived in medieval Europe a tradition of kingship more exalted than that of feudal overlord. The king was not merely the apex of the feudal pyramid, but the anointed Viceregent of God upon earth. . . . Henry [I] now set himself to inject this idea of kingship into the Anglo-Norman state; and in so doing he could not help reviving, whether consciously or not, the English conception of the King as the keeper of the peace and guardian of the people. . . . Henry realized that royal servants who were members of the minor baronage, if formed into a permanent nucleus, would act as a brake upon the turbulence of the greater feudatories. Here were the first beginnings, tentative, modest, but insinuating, of a civil administrative machinery, which, within its limits, was more efficient and persistent than anything yet known. These officials soon developed a vested interest of their own . . . and created what was in fact an official class.

. . . There was no distinction in feudal society between the private and public resources of the Crown. The King in feudal theory was only the greatest of the landowners of State. The sheriffs of counties collected not only the taxes and fines accruing to the Crown, but also the income from the royal estates, and they were responsible, when they appeared yearly at the royal treasury, for the exact payment of what was due from each of their counties. Henry's officials created a special organ to deal with the sheriffs, and the business the sheriffs transacted. This was the Exchequer ... It took its name from the chequered boards used for greater ease of calculation in Roman numerals, and its methods included the keeping of written records, among them the important documents called the Pipe Rolls because they were kept rolled up in the shape of a pipe. Thus the King gained a surer grip over the finances of the realm and the earliest specialized department of royal administration was born. ...

Henry [I] took care that the sheriffs of the counties were brought under an increasingly strict control, and several commissions were appointed during the reign to revise their personnel. In troublous times the office of sheriff tended to fall into the hands of powerful barons and to become hereditary. The King saw to it that whenever possible his own men held these key positions.

So for more than thirty years, under Henry I, England lived in relative peace and the Saxon population was largely reconciled to Norman rule. Towards the end of his life, Henry concerned himself with the succession. By now he was in his sixties, an old man for the times, and a happy grandfather. But in Normandy, his daughter and son-in-law, Matilda and Geoffrey, were at the centre of a rebellion against him.

C❖The English mood has never in later ages barred queens, and perhaps queens have served them best. But here at this time was a deep division, and a quarrel in which all parties and all interests could take sides. The gathered political arrays awaited the death of the King. The whole interest of the baronage, supported at this juncture by the balancing weight of the Church, was to limit the power of the Crown and regain their control of their own districts. ... Henry I expired on 1 December 1135, in the confident hope that his daughter Maud [Matilda] would carry on his work.

Henry's corpse was embalmed and carried to Reading where it was buried in the monastery church. For almost thirty-six years Henry had ruled England, and for twenty-nine of them, Normandy. But although he had managed to hold back his enemies, he had never satisfied them. Never brought them on his side. The barons had suffered because of what they saw as his dictatorial style. Yet it says something for his reign that he survived for so long, especially as the baronage was, on many occasions, at breaking point. *The Anglo-Saxon Chronicle* records that 'He was a good man, and was held in great awe. In his days no man dared to wrong another. He made peace for man and beast.' But after Henry's death there was to be little peace. Henry was barely embalmed when Stephen, his nephew and count of Blois, Champagne and Chartres, and, by his mother, a grandson of William the Conqueror, set out to claim the throne of England.

C❖The secular forces were divided and the judgment of the Church would be decisive. . . . Stephen made terms with the Church, and, thus sustained, was crowned and anointed King. . . . There was an additional complication. Henry I had a bastard son, Robert of Gloucester, a distinguished soldier and a powerful magnate in the West Country . . . Almost from the beginning he loyally supported his half-sister Maud [Matilda], and became one of Stephen's most determined opponents.

Stephen was consecrated on Chrismas Day, 1135. According to the twelfth-century chronicler, Walter Mapp, Stephen did not fit the template of his, often cruel, predecessors. Which is perhaps why the prospects for civil war and anarchy were so strong. One of Stephen's first decisions was to revive the holding of a court, a levee. King Henry had more or less abandoned these gatherings because he thought they were too costly. But this was Stephen's first chance to receive oaths of loyalty. And so the most important people in England gathered at the royal court. The *Constitutio Domus Regis,* the Establishment of the King's Household, describes a twelfth-century royal court and its attendant costs.

❖The chancellor shall receive five shillings a day, and one lord's simnel loaf, and two salted simnel loaves, and one sextary of clear wine, and one sextary of ordinary wine and one fat wax candle and forty pieces of candle. The cook of the King's kitchen shall receive three half pence a day for his man. The keeper of the vessels shall receive three half pence a day for his man and also a packhorse with its allowances. The porter of the King's bed shall receive three half pence a day for his man, and one packhorse with its allowances. The ewerer shall have double the customary food and when the King goes on a journey he shall receive a penny a day for drying the King's clothes and, when the King bathes, he shall have four pence except on the three feasts of the year. The watchmen shall have double food and three half pence for their men and four candles; and each of them shall receive in the morning two loaves and a tray of meat and a measure of beer. The stoker of the fire shall, from Michaelmas to Easter, have four pence a day for the fire. The usher of the chamber shall receive, on each day that the King travels, four pence for the King's bed. The keeper of the tents shall, when the tents have to be carried, receive an allowance for a man and a packhorse. . . . The four marshals who serve the men of the King's household – clerks and knights and serjeants – when they go billeting or when they stay outside on the King's business, shall each have eight pence a day and a gallon of ordinary wine and twelve pieces of candle.

This is only a fragment of the royal household, but already the titles that are familiar today, if now largely ceremonial, exist. At Easter 1136 those called to Stephen's Court were required publicly to display allegiance to the new King. However, a significant figure missing from that gathering was Robert of Gloucester, an important ally of Maud's (Matilda's).

Robert's support was so crucial to Stephen's future that the court was adjourned until Robert could be present. After considerable negotiations, Robert pledged his loyalty to the King. But he laid down conditions, and Stephen was forced to accept this qualified homage. For a while there was uneasy peace. There were small rebellions, but these were dealt with. Stephen crossed to Normandy where there were further uprisings. But when he got back, it was to face anarchy. The Scots were invading the northern counties, the Welsh were in rebellion but, most dangerously, Robert of Gloucester was preparing for war. The oath of homage was broken. In the early years of his reign Stephen lost the support of the three essential elements of his strength: the baronage, who were sure that this was the long-awaited moment to press their claims; the novel civil service now also began to stand aside from the new King; and much of the Church was against him. King David of Scotland, persuaded of the English decay, crossed the border and laid claim to Northumbria. The Archbishop of York advanced against him with the support of the northern counties and, in a murderous battle at Northallerton, the Archbishop and his forces repulsed and slaughtered the invaders. This reverse, far from discouraging the malcontents, was the prelude to civil war. An account of the battle by Richard of Hexham, probably written within living memory of the conflict, explains that King David had arrived at the fortress of Carham to reinforce his army which was already beaten back by the loyalist forces.

❖The King, perceiving the uselessness of his efforts, and the many and daily increasing losses to himself and his troops, at length raised the siege, and rushed with his whole force to devastate Northumberland, and murdered everywhere persons of both sexes, of every age and rank, and devastated towns, churches and houses. For the sick on their couches, women pregnant and in childbed, infants in the womb, innocents at the breast, or on the mother's knee, decrepit old men and worn-out old women, and by how much more horrible a death they could dispatch them, so much the more did they rejoice. About the Feast of the Purification of St Mary, Stephen, King of England, arrived with a great number of earls and barons and a large force of horse and foot. On hearing this the King of the Scots left Northumberland. But on the Friday of the week following the celebration of Easter, the King of the Scots once more returned and with no less ferocity and cruelty than he had previously exhibited, he devastated the sea-coast of the country, which on the former occasion had been left undisturbed.

Stephen could not control the rebellion. Certainly he was unable to bring together the forces of those who had sworn allegiance to him at court.

C❖In 1139, Maud [Matilda], freed from entanglements that had kept her in France, entered the kingdom to claim her rights. As Stephen had done, she found her chief support in the Church. . . . In 1141 a more or less general rebellion broke out against his rule, and he himself was taken prisoner at the Battle of Lincoln. . . . For nearly a year, Maud, uncrowned, was in control of England. . . . But the strain upon the system had been too great. The Island dissolved into confused civil war.

This was a war of many of the barons who had been dominated by the late king. It was also a chance for the Scots to reclaim territory in England which they believed to be theirs. As ever, the people suffered. Contemporary witnesses write that there was unspeakable cruelty. There was famine: dogs and horses were eaten, and thousands upon thousands starved to death. Stephen was incarcerated at Lincoln but within nine months he was released and was probably more popular than ever. Thanks to her often arrogant and unfeeling behaviour, Maud had made few friends among the English. So when, in 1145, Stephen's forces scored a great victory at Faringdon in Berkshire, everyone understood that Maud's fortunes had ebbed.

C❖It was realized how vital an institution a strong monarchy was for the security of life and property. . . . Men looked back with yearning to the efficient government of Henry I. But a greater than he was at hand.

In 1147 Robert of Gloucester died and the leadership of Maud's party devolved upon her son.

To the people of the time that son was called Henry Fitz-Empress: Fitz meaning son and empress from his mother Maud who had been an 'empress' by her first marriage. The emblem of his father's house was the Planta Genesta, the broom. And so Henry would become known as Henry Planta Genesta, Henry Plantagenet.

But in 1147 Henry was a teenager, just fifteen, and six weary years were to pass before he could claim the throne. By that time, the architects of anarchy as well as loyal opposition would be dead, so would King David of Scotland and so would Stephen's eldest son, Eustace. He died pillaging the abbey estates of Bury St Edmunds, and was hardly mourned. After this, the people, the bishops and magnates, tired of the war, persuaded Stephen to adopt Henry as his son and therefore his heir. Fourteen months later Stephen was dead and Henry Plantagenet arrived to claim his throne.

Henry's royal bloodline flowed from William the Conqueror and, on his grandmother's side, from the Anglo-Saxons. To the English people the young Henry Plantagenet represented a hope of strong, peaceful government. They'd suffered the consequences of anarchy while lords and masters had attempted to regain from Stephen the influence they'd lost during the reign of Henry I. There'd been famine, cruelty and uncertainty. And now there was a renewal of kingship and a reminder that the King of England was also the ruler of Normandy.

C❖The accession of Henry II began one of the most pregnant and decisive reigns in English history. The new sovereign ruled an empire and, as his subjects boasted, his warrant ran 'from the Arctic Ocean to the Pyrenees'. England to him was but one . . . of his provinces. . . . He was accepted by English and Norman as the ruler of both races and of the whole country. . . . Thus, though a Frenchman, with foreign speech and foreign modes, he shaped our country in a fashion of which the outline remains to the present day.

After 100 years of being the encampment of an invading army and the battleground of its quarrelsome officers and their descendants, England became finally and for all time a coherent kingdom, based upon Christianity and upon that Latin civilization which recalled the message of ancient Rome.

Walter Mapp, a clerk in the royal household, kept a record of the comings and goings at court. The record was called *Of Courtiers' Trifles*. Its tone was witty and sometimes satirical. Henry II is described:

❖He was a little over medium height, a man blessed with sound limbs and a handsome countenance, one upon whom men gazed closely a thousand times, yet took occasion to return. In physical capacity he was second to none, lacking no courtesy, well read to a degree both seemly and profitable, having a knowledge of all tongues spoken from the coasts of France to the river Jordan, but making use of only Latin and French. In making laws and in ordering the affairs of government he showed discrimination, and was clever in devising new and undiscovered legal procedure; he was easy of approach, modest and humble; though vexed by the importunity of suitors and litigants and provoked by injustice, he bore all in silence. Nevertheless he was ever on his travels, and in this respect he showed little mercy to his household which accompanied him. He had great experience of dogs and birds and was a very keen follower of hounds; in night-watches and labours he was unremitting.

Another writer describes Henry as having a red and freckled complexion, a large, round head and 'grey eyes which glowed fiercely and grew bloodshot in anger, a fiery countenance and a harsh, cracked voice'. And it was said that he never sat down unless it was to eat or ride.

C❖He journeyed hotfoot around his many dominions, arriving unexpectedly in England when he was thought to be in the South of France. He carried with him in his tours of each province wains loaded with ponderous rolls which represented the office files of his day. His Court and train gasped and panted behind him. . . . But this twelfth-century monarch . . . was no materialist; he was the Lord's Anointed, he commanded, with the Archbishop of Canterbury . . . the whole allegiance of his subjects. The offices of religion, the fear of eternal damnation, the hope of even greater realms beyond the grave, accompanied him from hour to hour. . . . He drew all possible delights and satisfaction from this world and the next.

Henry II was a confident, intelligent king, and a man full of energy. He needed to be. His first task was, naturally, to settle matters in England. After all, England provided him with a crown. His other lands did not. And he needed that symbol of his English throne to put him on a par with his continental overlord, the King of France. Henry might be Duke of Normandy, but Normandy was, supposedly, subservient to France's central control.

C❖The Battle of Hastings had made the greatest French subject, the Duke of Normandy, also King of England; but Henry II's accession to the Island throne in 1154 threatened France with far graver dangers. . . . The struggle between Anjou and Normandy in the eleventh century had rejoiced the French King, who saw two of his chief enemies at grips. But when in one hour Henry II was King of England, Duke of Normandy, Lord of Aquitaine, Brittany, Poitou, Anjou, Maine, and Guienne, ruler from the Somme to the Pyrenees of more than half France, all balance of power among the feudal lords was destroyed.

Louis VII found, instead of a dozen principalities, divided and jealous, one single Imperial power whose resources far surpassed his own. He was scarcely the man to face such a combination.

There was also a personal grudge against the English King. Eleanor of Aquitaine and Louis VII were married for fourteen years. She, beautiful, full of life. He, unbending, worthy, pious. Eleanor once said she was married to a monk, not a king. On one occasion, the Pope, Eugenius III, actually ordered them to sleep in the same bed. The result was, or seems to have been, the birth of a child. But even then there was disappointment. Eleanor gave birth to a daughter, while Louis longed for a male heir. In March 1152, Eleanor and Louis separated. He lost more than a wife: she was Eleanor of Aquitaine. He lost control of Aquitaine, at least half his kingdom. Two months later Eleanor married Henry. Her dowry was Aquitaine. But Henry's empire was far less impressive than it looked on the map.

C❖Henry had inherited vast estates; but with them also all their local and feudal discontents. Louis could no longer set the Count of Anjou against the Duke of Normandy, but he could still encourage both in Anjou and in Normandy those local feuds and petty wars which sapped the strength of the feudal potentates, in principle his vassals. Nor was the exploiting of family quarrels an unfruitful device. In the later years of his reign the sons of Henry II, eager, turbulent, and proud, allowed themselves to be used by Louis VII and by his successor, the wily and gifted Philip Augustus, against their father.

Henry realized he must re-establish central government rather than rely on the feudal system, with the power in the hands of the barons. And, apart from his continental empire, Henry inherited unresolved business closer to home. He needed to give some order to his relationship with Ireland, Scotland and Wales. The Scots had never regained the dominance achieved under King David I, who had died in 1153. They'd gained control of the northern counties from a weak king suffering civil war and David's successors could not hold them against a strong and well organized Henry.

The new King of Scotland, Malcolm, paid homage to Henry and Scotland did not regain her independence until Richard I came to the throne.

As for Ireland, Henry immediately considered an invasion. Probably the objection of his mother, who influenced many of his ideas, prevented this. But he did have one supporter for an expedition: the Pope. He saw it as a way of bringing Ireland under the direct influence of the Holy See. But that came later. Of immediate concern to Henry was Wales.

In 1157, Henry II launched an expedition against the Welsh prince, Owen Gwynedd. It was a disaster. A truce was agreed. Henry's attempts to subjugate north, and then south Wales continued to fail. And it wasn't until the peace of 1171 that he was content to leave the Welsh princes to get on with their own affairs. They visited England, they settled their nation's differences, they celebrated their peace with music and verse. And in 1176, at the festival of Christ's Mass, they gathered in the newly built Cardigan Castle for the first Eisteddfod. By then, and far away from bards and musicians, Henry's efforts to reform England were taking shape.

C❖He relaid the foundations of a central power, based upon the Exchequer and the judiciary, which was ultimately to supersede the feudal system of William the Conqueror. The King gathered up and cherished the Anglo-Saxon tradition of self-government under royal command in shire and borough; he developed and made permanent 'assizes' as they survive today. It is to him we owe the enduring fact that the English-speaking race all over the world is governed by the English Common Law rather than by the Roman. By his Constitutions of Clarendon he sought to fix the relationship of Church and State and to force the Church, in its temporal character, to submit itself to the life and law of the nation.

In this, Henry II was defeated. But these were the beginnings, of a remarkable reign that was to last more than three decades. It was a period of war, legal reform, the invasion of Ireland and the building of a palace in Dublin. A period of the break-up of his marriage, the rebellion of his sons, his own final anguish and the humiliation and the death of Thomas Becket.

CHAPTER SIX

1166–1189

❖

Henry II is usually remembered for three things: that he was the first Plantagenet king, that he developed the idea of the assizes and, of course, the martyrdom of Thomas Becket.

At the age of seventeen, three years before he became King of England, Henry became Duke of Normandy. His interests, responsibilities and complicated relationships with France dominated much of his private and public life. His education prepared him to rule with more than two strong arms and the courage of the double-handed swordsman. He was taught by the poet, Peter of Saintes. At the age of nine he began his studies in Bristol, where he was influenced by the scientist Adelard of Bath. He was instructed in ethics by William of Conches. Little wonder then, that as Henry II, he should be remembered more for his administrative genius and moral agonies rather than his military achievements and failures in France.

C❖How, may we ask, did all this affect the daily life of England and her history? A series of personal feudal struggles fought in distant lands, the quarrels of an alien ruling class, were little understood and less liked by the common folk. Yet these things long burdened their pilgrimage. For many generations their bravest and best were to fight and die by the marshes of the Loire or under the sun-baked hills of southern France in pursuit of the dream of English dominion over French soil. For this, two centuries later, Englishmen triumphed at Crécy, Poitiers and Agincourt, or starved in the terrible Limoges march of the Black Prince. . . . Throughout the mediaeval history of England, war with France is the interminable and often dominant theme. It groped and scraped into every reach of English life, moulding and fretting the shape of English society and institutions.

William fitz Stephen describes the London of Henry II in his *Materials for the Life of Thomas Becket*, as the capital of England and one which, he says, 'extends its glory farther than all the others and sends its wealth and merchandise more widely into distant lands.' He adds that, 'It is happy in the healthiness of its air; in its observance of Christian practice; in the honour of its citizens; in the modesty of its matrons.' He says that the Tower of London is fixed with mortar, 'tempered by the blood of animals'. He describes the Palace of Westminster as a 'building incomparable in its ramparts and bulwarks. Beyond the palace, [which is now called the Houses of Parliament], is the Thames, full of fish.' He goes on:

❖If the mildness of the climate of this place softens the character of its inhabitants, it does not make them corrupt in following Venus, but rather prevents them from being fierce and bestial, making them liberal and kind. Everywhere outside the houses in the suburbs are the spacious and beautiful gardens of the citizens. On the north side there are pastures and pleasant meadow lands through which flow streams wherein the turning of mill-wheels makes a cheerful sound. Very near lies a great forest in which there are the lairs of stags, fallow deer, wild boars and bulls. There are on the north side excellent suburban wells with sweet, wholesome water . . . among these are Holywell, Clerkenwell and St Clement's well. Those engaged in business of various kinds, sellers of merchandise, hirers of labour, are distributed every morning into their several localities according to their trade. By the river bank among the wines for sale in ships, and in the cellars, there is a public cook shop. I do not think there is a city with a better record for church-going, doing honour of God's ordinances, keeping feast days, giving alms and hospitality to strangers, and also, it may be added, in care for funerals and for the burial of the dead. The only plagues of London are the immoderate drinking of fools and the frequency of fires.

Obviously this picture of London, of which any tourist board would be proud, doesn't reflect that fact that England as a whole was less than well ordered. One aspect of twelfth-century society in need of reform was the law. Henry Plantagenet's chief justice, Rannulf Glanvill, supervised the setting out of the first comprehensive record of legal procedure: it was based on a new system of juries and writs. The assizes were developed.

Assize comes from the old French word for a sitting. A jury sat to assess. And the writ meant, in theory at least, that a man could appeal to the King to put right a wrong of that man's lord and master. The record of the Assize of Clarendon is the first big piece of Henry II's legislation, and the earliest document of his major administrative changes. The date is 1166, 100 years after the Norman Conquest:

❖And let anyone who shall be found accused or notoriously suspect of having been a robber or murderer or thief, or a receiver of them, since the lord King has been King, be taken and put to the ordeal of water.

'Notoriously suspect'. The law now attached great importance to a suspect criminal record.

❖And if the lord of the man who has been arrested shall claim him by pledge within the third day following his capture, let him be released on bail with his chattels until he himself shall stand trial . . . And when a robber or murderer or thief has been arrested, let the sheriffs send word to the nearest justice that they have arrested such men, and the justices shall send word back to the sheriffs informing them where they desire the men to be brought before them.

So bail may be set, and dates set for hearings.

❖And if anyone shall be taken in possession of the spoils of robbery or theft, if he be of evil repute and bears an evil testimony from the public and has no warrant, let him have no law. And if anyone shall confess to robbery or murder or theft, and afterwards he wish to deny it, let him not have his law.

This meant that anyone caught red-handed didn't get a trial. Nor did a person who admitted guilt, even if he denied it later. And there was an emphasis on previous convictions, or even local knowledge, that the accused was a villain.

❖The lord King wills that those who shall be tried by the law and absolved by the law, if they have been of ill repute and openly and disgracefully spoken of by the testimony of many, they shall abjure the King's lands, so that within eight days they shall cross the sea, and they shall not return to England again except by the mercy of the lord King.

These are just a few of the laws from the Assize of Clarendon. The law was set out so that no one could have any doubts. And the community was expected to maintain the law. In the Assize of Northampton, in 1176, for example:

❖Let no one in a borough or a vill [village] entertain in his house for more than one night any stranger for whom he is unwilling to be responsible, unless there be reasonable excuse for this hospitality, which the host of the house shall show to his neighbours. And when the guest shall depart, let him leave in the presence of the neighbours and by day.

If someone was found guilty the punishment was clear-cut and gruesome.

❖Let him go to the ordeal of the water. And if he fail let him lose one foot. And for the sake of stern justice he shall likewise lose his right hand with his foot, and he shall abjure the realm, and within forty days be banished from the kingdom.

Henry II was trying to make sure that the law was not simply legal memory. He wanted documents that could be referred to, and documents that could be amended. The law was becoming articulate and, therefore, an institution. And that other institution, the Church, watched with more than a little interest.

C❖The military state in feudal Christendom bowed to the Church in things spiritual; it never accepted the idea of the transference of secular power to priestly authority. But the Church, enriched continually by the bequests of hardy barons, anxious in the death agony about their life beyond the grave, became the greatest landlord and capitalist in the community. . . . But how was the government of the country to be carried on under two conflicting powers, each possessed of immense claims upon limited national resources? . . . It was the root question of the European world as it then existed.

Under William the Conqueror schism had been avoided in England by tact and compromise. Under Lanfranc, the Church worked with the Crown, and each power reinforced the other against the turbulent barons or the oppressed commonalty. But now a great personality stood at the head of the religious hierarchy.

That person was Thomas Becket.

The first sixteen years of Henry II's reign were dominated by the influence of this man. And, just as Henry was effecting secular reforms in his kingdom, so the Roman Church had been reinvigorated, often to its intense displeasure, by the late Pope Gregory VII. Pope Gregory believed that the King's single religious role was total obedience to the Church. Conflict between Church and State was inevitable.

C❖No episode opens to us a wider window upon the politics of the twelfth century in England than the quarrel of Henry II with his great subject and former friend, Thomas Becket, Archbishop of Canterbury. We have to realize the gravity of this conflict. . . . In a loose and undefined way Saxon England had foreshadowed the theory to which Elizabethan reformers long afterwards returned. Both thought of the monarch as appointed by God, not only to rule the State, but to protect and guide the Church. In the eleventh century however the Papacy had been reinvigorated under Pope Gregory VII and his successors. . . . The Gregorian movement held that the government of the Church ought to be in the hands of the clergy, under the supervision of the Pope. . . . By the reign of Henry II, the bishop was not only a spiritual officer: he was a great landowner, the secular equal of earls; he could put forces in the field; he could excommunicate his enemies, who might be the King's friends. Who, then, was to appoint the bishop? And, when once appointed, to whom, if the Pope commanded one thing and the King another, did he owe his duty? If the King and his counsellors agreed upon a law contrary to the law of the Church, to which authority was obedience due?

Thomas Becket was a month away from his thirty-sixth birthday when Henry II came to the throne in 1154. Henry was barely twenty-one. Thomas Becket was born in London, the son of a merchant from Rouen. As a student he had never excelled. In fact his Latin was so poor that on one occasion, at the Council of Tours, he refused to preach, so ashamed was he. Even as archbishop he had a tutor who would explain the complicated theology of the scriptures. But by the time he became a minister in Henry II's household, he was already Archdeacon of Canterbury and provost of Beverley. It was thanks to the then archbishop, and his mentor, Theobald, that Becket became Chancellor of the King's household. Theobald's hope was that Becket would guard the interests of the Church. Instead, he became the King's secretary, diplomat and even judge, and was won over by the glamour of court life so much that he often took the King's side rather than the Church's. No wonder then that when the archbishopric of Canterbury fell vacant, the King made every effort to have Becket elected. Henry believed that if his friend were chancellor and arch-bishop, then the ambitions of the Church in State affairs would be curbed.

C❖The Crown resented the claim of the Church to interfere in the State; but in the Middle Ages no king dared to challenge the Church outright, or, much as he might hope to limit its influence, thought of a decisive breach. It was not till the sixteenth century that an English king in conflict with the Papacy dared to repudiate the authority of Rome and nakedly declare the State supreme, even in spiritual matters. In the twelfth century, the only practicable course was compromise. But the Church at this time was in no mood for a bargain.

Some in the church were cautious about the appointment of Thomas Becket, and the King's emissary, Richard of Luce, tried to reassure the clergy that the friendship of King and Chancellor could only mean harmony, not division. Richard of Luce also reminded the gathered clergy of the consequences of not accepting the King's wishes:

❖The King is most zealous in everything which concerns the things of God and displays the utmost devotion towards holy Church, especially towards this Church of Canterbury, which he recognizes in all humility, loyalty and filial affection as his particular mother in the Lord. Wherefore that she be not in any way oppressed or thrown into disorder by remaining long bereft of a shepherd, be it known to you that the King accords you full freedom of election, provided however, that you choose a man worthy of so great an office and equal to the burden thereof. For it is not unknown to you that our lord, the King, is wont to endeavour nothing in such a matter save what he believes to be well-pleasing to God and profitable to his Church. For the rest, then, it is incumbent on you, and wholly expedient, to elect one under whose protection you may rejoice before God and men. For if king and archbishop be joined together in the bond of affection and cherish each other in all friendship, there is no doubt that the times will be happy and the Church will preserve her estate in joy and tranquillity. But if, which God forbid, things should turn out otherwise, the dangers and confusion, the labours and tumults, and, in the end, the loss of property and the peril of souls which may result therefrom, are not, I imagine, hidden from your reverences.

At last, with one dissenting opinion from Bishop Gilbert of London (who probably wanted to be archbishop himself), the clergy accepted Becket as the new Archbishop of Canterbury. And Becket made a prophetic warning to his king. From Richard of Luce:

❖I know of a truth that, should God so dispose it, you would speedily turn your face away from me, and the love which is now so great between us would be changed into the most bitter hatred. I know indeed that you would make many demands – for already you presume overmuch in ecclesiastical affairs – which I could never bear with equanimity. And so the envious would find occasion to stir up endless strife between us.

If Henry had hoped that Becket would be his envoy, he was to be disappointed. The new Archbishop threw away his credentials to the King's court.

C❖He now championed the Church against the Crown in every aspect of their innumerable interleaving functions. . . . After a tour upon the Continent, and a conclave with the religious dignitaries of France and Italy he returned to England imbued with the resolve to establish the independence of the Church from the hierarchy of the State as represented by the King. Thus he opened the conflict which the wise Lanfranc [William the Conqueror's archbishop] had, throughout his life, striven to avoid.

The open quarrel between the two former friends began as soon as Henry returned from Normandy in January 1163. Becket successfully opposed Henry's

demand for customary dues to be paid into the royal Exchequer. He excommunicated one William of Eynesford without consulting the King, as in theory
he should have done. He protected clerks and clergy from the full punishment
under the law even when some were charged with rape, murder and theft. The
King claimed, at the Council of Westminster, the right to punish clerks. The
bishops hesitated. Becket told them to stand firm. Henry then confiscated lands
owned by Becket from his days as chancellor. A meeting was arranged between
King and Archbishop. But what could have been reconciliation became
recrimination. And Becket did not have the full support of the clergy, nor of
the one person he expected to be sympathetic to his stand against the throne:
the Pope, Alexander III. The Pope did not wish to anger the King, nor could
he entirely ignore his archbishop. His decision was to advise Becket to give way
to Henry. Henry then made what appears to have been a mistake: he attempted
to revoke the promise made by King Stephen that the State should be
subservient to the Pope. He published this attempt to put back the state clock
in 1164, in what was called the Constitutions of Clarendon.

C❖In these Henry claimed, not without considerable truth, to be re-stating the
customs of the kingdom as they had been before the anarchy of Stephen's
reign. He sought to retrace thirty years and to annul the effects of Stephen's
surrender. But Becket resisted. He regarded Stephen's yieldings as irrevocable gains by the Church. . . . When, in October 1164, he was summoned
to appear before the Great Council and explain his conduct he haughtily
denied the King's authority and placed himself under the protection of the
Pope and God.

That Council was held at Northampton. Becket faced charges of contempt of
court, of wrongful use of money that had passed through his hands when he was
chancellor and of wrongfully borrowing money and using the King's name as
a guarantor. He was found guilty.

On the fourth day of the Council, the Archbishop offered the King 2000
marks in compensation. But Henry refused. He was determined to destroy his
former friend. The bishops divided. Becket was shamed and vilified and that
night he escaped, first from Northampton, and then from England, into exile.
Many churchmen were glad that he was gone. Confrontation with the monarch
was a dangerous game. Even the Pope found it hard to support Becket. But
Becket became vindictive. He wrote, from a monastery in France, to his former
friend the King:

❖The Church of God consists of two orders, clergy and people. And since
it is certain that kings receive their power from the Church, not the latter
hers from them but from Christ, so you have not the power to give orders

to bishops, nor to absolve or excommunicate anyone, nor to drag clerks before secular tribunals, nor to judge concerning churches or tithes, nor to forbid bishops to adjudge causes concerning breach of faith or oath, and many other things of this kind which are written among the customs of yours which you call ancient. . . .

This is a straight rejection of the Constitutions of Clarendon. And Becket also reminded Henry that if it weren't for the Church, then he wouldn't be King.

❖Restore then to the Church of Canterbury, from which you received your promotion and coronation, the rank and status it held in the time of your predecessors and mine, together with all its possessions. And, further, permit us to return freely and in peace and in all security to our See, there to perform the duties of our office, as we ought and as right commands. And we are ready faithfully and devotedly to serve you as our dearest lord and King with all our strength in whatsoever we are able, saving the honour of God and the Roman Church, and saving also our order. Otherwise you may know for certain that you will experience the divine severity and vengeance. . . .

On Whit Sunday, 1166, Becket excommunicated a whole bench of bishops. The bishops and clergy complained to the Pope and denounced Becket's declaration as uncanonical and unlawful. It was a quarrel that would have tested the powers of the cleverest diplomat. And here is the irony. Previously, Henry would have had the perfect envoy to resolve such a delicate matter: Becket himself.

But then, six years after his exile, something happened that would eventually bring them together: Henry wanted his son crowned as his successor, during his own lifetime. Becket, still Archbishop of Canterbury, should have been the person to officiate. Henry said that the Archbishop of York should stand in for him. The Pope said no. Henry ignored the Pope's ruling. To Becket this was an outrage. The Pope was bound to support him, and so was Louis VII of France, who was in a position to threaten Henry's French possessions. Henry relented. The two men met. Henry of Bosham witnessed the reconciliation.

❖The King and the Archbishop then turned their horses aside and rode together, talking to one another in private. The Archbishop craved the King's permission to punish by ecclesiastical censure his own suffragans for the injury they had inflicted upon him and the Church in Canterbury, in concert with the Archbishop of York, by crowning the King's son, Henry. To this the King assented, and the Archbishop, in all gratitude, forthwith dismounted and, in the sight of all there present, humbly prostrated himself at the King's feet.

That was on 22 July 1170. On 15 October the King issued a proclamation of reconciliation. The next month Becket, still in France and preparing to return to England, suspended the Archbishop of York and once again excommunicated the Bishops of London and Salisbury. On 1 December he landed at Sandwich in Kent, and rode to Canterbury. The excommunicated bishops sailed for Normandy, where the King was. William fitz Stephen, a friend of Becket, tells what happened in his *Materials for the Life of Thomas Becket*.

❖It was reported to the King that the Archbishop was about the kingdom at the head of a strong force of armed men. The King asked the bishops for their advice. At length, one of them said, 'My lord, while Thomas lives, you will not have peace or see good days.' At this, such fury, bitterness, and passion against the Archbishop took possession of the King that they appeared on his countenance and in his gestures. Perceiving his emotion, and eager to win his favour, four knights, Reginald fitz Urse, William de Traci, Hugh of Morville, and Richard Brito, having sworn, so it was said, to encompass the death of the Archbishop, quitted the Court.

It was 29 December 1170. The knights arrived at Canterbury and demanded to see Becket whom they accused of plotting to remove the crown from the King's son. Becket denied it and treated the knights with contempt. 'Cease your threats,' he said, 'and still your brawling. I put my trust in the King of Heaven. I have not come back to flee again. Here shall he who wants me find me.' Becket threatened to excommunicate all who disobeyed the Church. The knights sprang to their feet. One shouted at him, 'We declare that you have spoken in peril of your head.' The knights left but Becket knew they would be back. His clergy pleaded with him to escape. 'It is not meet to make a fortress of the house of prayer,' said Becket in reply. The knights returned and the clergy deserted Becket, hiding among the altars of the vast cathedral. But three remained, including Edward Grim, who wrote down what happened. This is a part of it.

❖The unconquered martyr, inclining his head as one in prayer and joining his hands and uplifting them, commended his cause, and that of the Church, to God. Scarce had he uttered the words than the wicked knight leapt suddenly upon him, cutting off the top of the crown which the unction of the sacred chrism had dedicated to God. Next he received a second blow on the head, but still he stood firm and immovable. At the third blow he fell on his knees and elbows, offering himself a living sacrifice, and saying in a low voice, 'For the name of Jesus and the protection of the Church, I am ready to embrace death.' But the third knight inflicted a terrible wound as he lay prostrate. By this stroke, the crown of his head was separated from the head in such a way that the blood white with the brain, and the brain no less red from the blood, dyed the floor of the cathedral. The same clerk who had entered with the knights placed his foot on the neck of the holy priest and precious martyr, and, horrible to relate, scattered the brains and blood about the pavements, crying to the others, 'Let us away, knights; this fellow will arise no more.'

The night passed in lamentation and mourning. The single most shocking event in the twelfth-century Christian world had occurred.

The Christian ruler of a Christian nation had ordered the assassination of his archbishop because that archbishop had stood up for his belief that no one, not even a king, was above the law of the Church and therefore, God. The rights and wrongs of the tale are irrelevant. That is how the event was seen by the majority. Becket was a martyr and within two years he was canonized. Churches were dedicated to his name. In the Holy Land the order of the knights of St Thomas of Acre was instituted. As far north as Iceland the life of the martyr appeared in sagas. He became the subject of iconography. Thomas Becket frescoes appeared in Rome. In his name antiphons were sung with psalms.

For two years Henry II was ostracized. But he recovered. He was, after all, a king.

C❖The immediately following years were spent in trying to recover what he had lost by a great parade of atonement for his guilt. He made pilgrimages to the shrine of the murdered Archbishop. He subjected himself to public penances. On several anniversaries, stripped to the waist and kneeling humbly, he submitted to be scourged by triumphant monks. We may however suppose that the corporal chastisement, which apparently from the contemporary pictures was administered with birch rods, was mainly symbolic. Under this display of contrition and submission, the King laboured perseveringly to regain the rights of the State. By the Compromise of Avranches in 1172 he made his peace with the Papacy on comparatively easy terms. . . . But Becket's sombre sacrifice had not been in vain. Until the Reformation, the Church retained the system of ecclesiastical courts independent of the royal authority, and the right of appeal to Rome, two of the major points upon which Becket had defied the King.

The penance of the King may have been 'mainly symbolic'. But it had to be done. Just as Henry had attempted to show that in his courts justice had to be seen to be done, so his own, self-inflicted, justice had to satisfy the public curiosity and sense of vengeance. There is a record of what happened at the great penance at the Cathedral in 1174. It comes from *The Chronicle of Gervase*.

❖He left the church of St Dunstan, which is sited a good distance outside the city, and walked barefoot and clad in a woollen smock all the way to the martyr's tomb. There he lay prostrate for a great while and in devout humility, and of his own free will was scourged by all the bishops and abbots there present and each individual monk of the church of Canterbury. There he remained constant in prayer before the holy martyr all that day and night. He neither took food nor went out to relieve nature, but, as he had come, so he remained, and would not permit a rug or anything of the kind to be provided for him. After lauds, he made a tour of the altars in the choir of the church and the bodies of the saints interred there, and then returned to the tomb of St Thomas in the crypt.

Besides forgiveness, Henry II had a particular ambition: to conquer Ireland, and he was certain that he had the Pope's support. The papacy disliked the way in which the monasteries dominated the Irish Church. The bishopric, the See of Armagh, was hereditary, and eight of the bishops appear to have been married, had children, and not even to have been ordained. No wonder Pope Alexander approved of Henry II's expedition.

The King landed at Waterford on 17 October 1171. He took with him nearly 5000 knights and archers. It took 400 ships from Bristol to transport men, stores, even siege towers. Only the kings of Tyrone and Tyrconnel refused to pay homage to Henry. This didn't bother him. He moved to Dublin, built a palace, entertained the princes and very soon the submission of the Irish Church followed. Within a year, Henry, supported by the Pope, was recognized as Lord of Ireland. The Pope made it clear to the bishops that they must support Henry in his work of subduing what he called, 'this barbarous and uncouth race, ignorant of divine law'.

But Henry failed to understand the triad of interests that existed. Anglo-Norman barons fought each other. The Irish fought among themselves and against the barons. And third, intermarriage founded a new class: the Anglo-Irish.

Despite this Henry Plantagenet, restored to papal favour after Becket's death, was one of the most powerful rulers in Europe.

C❖Eighteen years of life lay before the King after Becket's death. In a sense they were years of glory. All Europe marvelled at the extent of Henry's domains . . . Through the marriages of his daughters he was linked with the Norman King of Sicily, the King of Castile, and Henry the Lion of Saxony, who was the most powerful prince in Germany. Diplomatic agents spread his influence in the Lombard cities of Northern Italy. Both Emperor and Pope invited him in the name of Christ and all Europe to lead a new Crusade and to be King of Jerusalem. Indeed, after the Holy Roman Emperor, Frederick Barbarossa, Henry stood next in Christendom.

But Henry's success was dulled by the treachery and scheming of his own family. His sons, John, Henry, Geoffrey and Richard, wanted nothing less than his death.

C❖During these years he was confronted with no fewer than four rebellions by his sons. For the three eldest, he had provided glittering titles: Henry held Normandy, Maine, and Anjou; Richard was given Aquitaine, and to Geoffrey went Brittany. These boys were typical sprigs of the Angevin stock. They wanted power as well as titles, and they bore their father no respect. Urged on by their mother, Queen Eleanor, who now lived in Poitiers apart from her husband, between 1173 and 1186 they rose in revolt in various combinations. On each occasion they could count on the active support of the watchful King of France. Henry treated his ungrateful children with generosity, but he had no illusions. . . . [And eventually] John, whom he [Henry II] had striven to provide with an inheritance equal to that of his brothers, joined the final plot against him. In 1188 Richard, his eldest surviving son after the death of young Henry, was making war upon him in conjunction with King Philip of France. Already desperately ill, Henry was defeated at Le Mans and recoiled into Touraine. When he saw in the list of conspirators against him the name of his son, John, upon whom his affection had strangely rested, he abandoned the struggle with life. 'Let things go as they will,' he gasped. 'Shame, shame on a conquered king.'

The chronicler, Gerald of Wales, tells us that Henry, 'uttering words of dire calamity, the herald of his own confusion, passed away, overwhelmed and oppressed with grief rather than succumbing to a natural death'. At his burial, there was not, says Gerald, 'a ring for his finger, a sceptre for his hand or crown for his head; scarcely any insignia of royalty but what had been begged for the purpose'.

Henry II, the lawmaker, the gatherer of lands and riches, died on 6 July 1189. Only one son, Geoffrey, was at his deathbed. In cloisters and chancels, news of Henry's miserable end was recited and with it, the pronouncement that this was God's vengeance delivered upon Henry Plantagenet, murderer of Thomas Becket.

CHAPTER SEVEN

1189–1199

<hr>

❖

<hr>

Henry II's eldest son, Richard, succeeded Henry in 1189. Richard I was to rule for just ten years. But in that decade he built a naval town on the south coast, Portsmouth; drew up the first Articles of War; sold Scotland her independence; led a great Crusade and would be called Richard Coeur de Lion.

And yet this was the man who rejected the peace efforts of Pope and bishops and, with the King of France, defeated his own father in battle. The man who, once the campaign was done, forced the dying king, his father, into accepting humiliating terms and who wasted little time in mourning. And yet, Richard is popularly remembered as a man of great chivalry.

C❖Richard, with all his characteristic virtues and faults cast in a heroic mould, is one of the most fascinating mediaeval figures. He has been described as the creature and embodiment of the age of chivalry. . . . Little did the English people owe him for his services, and heavily did they pay for his adventures. He was in England only twice for a few months in his ten years' reign; yet his memory has always stirred English hearts . . . He was tall and delicately shaped; strong in nerve and sinew, and most dexterous in arms. He rejoiced in personal combat, and regarded his opponents without malice as necessary agents in his fame. He loved war, not so much for the sake of glory or political ends, but as other men love science or poetry, for the excitement of the struggle and the glow of victory. . . . Although a man of blood and violence, Richard was too impetuous to be either treacherous or habitually cruel. He was as ready to forgive as he was hasty to offend; he was open handed and munificent to profusion; in war circumspect in design and skilful in execution; in politics a child, lacking any subtlety and experience. . . . The advantages gained for him by military genius were thrown away through diplomatic ineptitude.

So Richard I was an absentee landlord. He freed his mother, Queen Eleanor, whom Henry II had imprisoned for encouraging Richard's and John's rebellion. Eleanor became Richard's representative in England. He also made peace with his late father's supporters, partly because it was in his nature to do so, but mainly because he didn't want a palace coup while he was away. He also intended to install himself as Duke of Normandy.

C❖During his rebellion against his father, Richard had pressed hard upon Henry's rout at Le Mans in the very forefront of the cavalry without even wearing his mail. In the rearguard of the beaten army stood Henry's faithful warrior, William the Marshal. He confronted Richard and had him at his mercy. 'Spare me!' cried Richard in his disadvantage; so the Marshal turned his lance against the prince's horse and killed it, saying with scorn, 'I will not slay you. The Devil may slay you.' This was humiliation and insult worse than death. It was not therefore without anxiety that the Marshal and his friends awaited their treatment at the hands of the sovereign to whom their loyalties must now be transferred. But King Richard rose at once above the past. . . . He confirmed his father's true servant in all his offices and honours . . . and at a stroke the Marshal became one of the most powerful of English barons. Indeed it was noted that the King's favour lighted upon those who had stood loyally by his father against him, even to the detriment of those who had been his fellow rebels.

Richard was also generous to his two surviving brothers who had not always shown loyalty to him. (The third brother, Henry, had died of dysentery.) To Geoffrey he gave the vacant archbishopric of York, and to the youngest son, John, he gave Isabel, the third daughter of the Earl of Gloucester. He was given lordships, castles and six entire counties: Devon and Cornwall, Dorset, Somerset, Nottingham and Derby. He was also Lord of Ireland.

When Richard finally arrived in England, in the summer of his father's death, he was received with great delight by the people. But within four months, and having been crowned at Westminster, he was gone again.

C❖The King's heart was set upon the new Crusade. This task seemed made for him. It appealed to every need of his nature. To rescue the Holy Land from the pollution of the infidel, to charge as a king at the head of knightly squadrons in a cause at once glorious to man and especially acceptable to God, was a completely satisfying inspiration. . . . the King, for the sake of Christ's sepulchre, virtually put the realm up for sale. Money he must have at all costs for his campaign in far-off Palestine. He sold and re-sold every office in the State. He made new and revolutionarily heavy demands for taxation. He called for 'scutage', the commutation of military service for a money payment, and later reintroduced 'carucage', a levy on every 100 acres of land. Thus he filled his chests for the Holy War.

Richard also sold Scotland. King William of Scotland and King Richard met at Canterbury. William was given back Berwick and Roxburgh; in return Richard received 10,000 silver marks.

C❖[Richard] started for the wars in the winter of 1189. He had promised Philip of France to marry his sister Alice, about whom, except for her looks, the tales were none too good. . . . after Richard had marched across France and sailed to Sicily, where he rested for the winter, his mother brought out to him Berengaria, daughter of the King of Navarre, whom he had known and admired and now resolved to marry. It was fitting that the 'Lion Heart' should marry for love and not for policy, but the rejection of Alice prevented a tie between the Kings of France and England which had been deemed essential to their comradeship in the Crusade. . . . The Christian kingdom founded at Jerusalem after the First Crusade had stood precariously for a century. . . . Its continued existence was largely due to the disunity that prevailed among the Moslem lands surrounding it. At length the rise of a great national leader of the Turks, or Saracens, united the Moslem power. In 1169 Saladin became Vizier of Egypt. . . . Soon his power was stretching out into Syria, encircling the Crusaders' principalities on the Levantine coast. . . .

But the quarrels of the Western princes prevented effective measures being taken in time. In 1186 Saladin in his turn proclaimed a Holy War. . . . The Christian army . . . perhaps 10,000 strong, was . . . cut to pieces by greatly superior numbers at Hattin. The King, [of Jerusalem, Guy of Lusignan] the Grand Master of the Templars, and many of the greatest nobles were taken prisoner.

The Pope sent emissaries throughout Europe pleading with princes and kings to stop fighting each other and turn their efforts towards Saladin. Richard's England responded to the Pope's call to 'Take the Cross', the expression used to go on the Crusade. And Richard, and Philip of France, although engaged in open conflict with each other, resolved to 'Take the Cross' together.

C❖All the chief princes of Europe were now in line around the doomed stronghold of Saladin, rivalling each other in prowess and jealousy. The sanctity of their cause was no bar to their quarrels and intrigues. King Richard dominated the scene. Fighting always in the most dangerous places, striking down the strongest foes, he negotiated all the time with Saladin. An agreement was in fact almost reached. To save his garrison, Saladin offered to surrender his Christian captives, to pay a large indemnity, and to give up the cross, captured by him in Jerusalem, on which Christ — though this after 1200 years was not certain — had suffered. But the negotiations failed, and Richard, in his fury, massacred in cold blood the 2000 Saracen hostages who had been delivered as guarantees. Within five weeks of his arrival he brought the two years' siege to a successful conclusion.

By the time Acre fell, King Richard's glory as a warrior and also his skill as a general were the talk of all nations. But the quarrels of the allies paralysed the campaign.

Richard pressed on. He led his army to within twelve miles of Jerusalem, but that was as close as he ever came to victory. Curiously, Richard became increasingly friendly with the man he was fighting, Saladin. They met and discussed ways in which Jerusalem might be partitioned. But nevertheless the Crusade was doomed, largely because of the disunity among its leaders. Richard set out for home, hurried by news that his own kingdom was in a state of near anarchy.

C❖William Longchamp, Bishop of Ely . . . had addressed himself with fidelity and zeal to the task of governing England, entrusted to him by Richard in 1189. Emulating the splendour of a monarch, he moved about the country with a pompous retinue and very soon drew upon himself the envy and then the active hatred of the whole nobility. As the King's faithful servant he saw that the chief danger lay in the over-mighty position of Prince John. The indulgence of Richard had allowed his brother to form a state within a state. . . . The return of Philip Augustus [of France] from the Crusade brought new opportunities to John's ambition. The French King saw in Richard's absence the chance of breaking up the Angevin power and driving the English out of France. In John he found a willing partner. It was agreed between them that Philip Augustus should attack Normandy, while John raised a revolt in England.

Early in 1193, at a moment already full of peril, the grave news reached England that the King was prisoner 'somewhere in Germany'.

Richard had sailed from Acre on 9 October 1192. But he was shipwrecked, and he tried to head home by land. This meant going through the region of Vienna controlled by Duke Leopold of Austria, a man with whom Richard had quarrelled during the Crusade. Leopold captured Richard in December and kept him prisoner until the following February and then sold him to the Holy Roman Emperor, Henry VI.

C❖The Holy Roman Emperor demanded the prodigious ransom of 150,000 marks, twice the annual revenue of the English Crown. . . . Richard approved and the English Council agreed. Meanwhile Philip and John . . .

offered the Emperor 80,000 marks to keep the English King under lock and key till Michaelmas 1194, or 150,000 marks to deliver him into their hands. But the Emperor felt that his blackmailing honour was engaged to Richard, with whom he had, perhaps precipitately, settled the figure.... It remained to collect the ransom. The charge staggered the kingdom. Yet nothing was more sacred than the feudal obligation to ransom the liege lord, above all when he enjoyed the sanctity of a Crusader.... The Church faced its duty. It was lawful to sacrifice even the most holy ornaments of the cathedrals for the ransom of a Christian lost in the Holy War.... Prince John of course set an example in collecting these taxes throughout his shires. His agents dwelt upon the sacred duty of all to pay, and he kept the proceeds of their faith and loyalty for himself.

Richard returned home on 13 March 1194. The ransom had all but impoverished his people, but they cheered him and his fame. Yet John made little secret of his treachery and attempts to raise another rebellion. However the war was now in France and Richard crossed the Channel to defend his possessions. He was never to return to England. The man who effectively ruled England in Richard's absence was the new Archbishop of Canterbury and chief justice, Hubert Walter. He had been a student at Bologna, a judicial and administrative clerk in the household of Henry II (whose system of law and government required the King's authority, but not necessarily his presence) and he now had a reputation as a clear-sighted and loyal servant of the absent King.

C❖With determination, knowledge and deft touch he developed the system of strong centralized government devised by Henry II. Hubert Walter stands out as one of the great mediaeval administrators. The royal authority was reasserted in the North ... A new machinery for keeping the peace was devised to which the origin of the Justices of the Peace can be traced, and the office of Coroner now emerged clearly for the first time. ... New assessments of land were begun, weights and measures were standardized. ... New concessions, involving the precious privilege of local self-government, were granted to London and the principal towns. ... The system of administration devised by Henry II – the Civil Service as we may call it – had stood the test and, undisturbed by royal interventions, consolidated itself to the general convenience and advantage.

Incidentally, this civic bureaucracy included the office of Mayor of London. The first 'Lord' Mayor of London appeared in about 1191, a man called Henry fitz Ailwin. The importance of this new machinery of administration is clear: the king was no longer the single guarantor of law and order.

But the law, the administration, and the genius of Hubert Walter could not lessen Richard's demands for funds to fight his war against Philip of France and his treacherous brother, John. And it was the need to finance this campaign that led to the death of the king.

C❖In 1199, when the difficulties of raising revenue for the endless war were at their height, good news was brought to King Richard. It was said that there had been dug up near the castle of Chaluz, on the lands of one of his vassals, a treasure of wonderful quality; a group of golden images . . . The King claimed this treasure as lord paramount. The lord of Chaluz resisted the demand, and the king laid siege to his small, weak castle. On the third day, as he rode daringly near the wall . . . a bolt from a cross-bow struck him in the left shoulder by the neck. The wound, already deep, was aggravated by the necessary cutting out of the arrow-head. Gangrene set in and Coeur de Lion knew that he must pay a soldier's debt. He prepared for death with fortitude and calm. . . . He declared John to be his heir, and made all present swear fealty to him. . . . [He] died in the forty-second year of his age on April 6, 1199.

Shortly before he died, Richard called the archer who had fired the fatal bolt to his deathbed. Publicly, he pardoned the man but once the King was dead the archer was taken outside and flayed alive. This was, after all, still the twelfth century.

CHAPTER EIGHT

1199–1216

❖

Richard the Lionheart's brother John became king.

C❖Monkish chroniclers have emphasized his [John's] violence, greed, malice, treachery, and lust. But other records show that he was often judicious, always extremely capable and, on occasions, even generous. He possessed an original and inquiring mind, and at the end of his life treasured his library of books. In him, the restless energy of the Plantagenet race was raised to a furious pitch of instability. . . . when the long tally is added, it will be seen that the British nation and the English-speaking world owed far more to the vices of John than to the labours of virtuous sovereigns; for it was through the union of many forces against him that the most famous milestone of our rights and freedom was in fact set up.

That milestone was Magna Carta, but it didn't appear until 1215. When John became King he immediately did what all heirs did in those days: he took control of the treasury. Then he rode to Rouen and his investiture as Duke of Normandy. Next, he crossed the Channel, and on Ascension Day John was crowned at Westminster, King of England. Not everyone applauded.

C❖Although Richard had declared John to be King, there were two views upon the succession. Geoffrey, his elder brother, had left behind him a son, Arthur, Prince of Brittany. . . . Queen Eleanor stood by her son against the grandson, whose mother she had never liked. John was accepted without demur in England. In the French provinces however, the opposite view prevailed. Brittany in particular adopted Arthur.

When John returned to the Continent he found less support than he would have liked. Constance, the mother of the teenage Arthur, had taken sides with the French King. Arthur was now in Paris under the protection of Philip of France.

King John was about to marry a Portuguese princess, then changed his mind and married Isabel of Angoulême. His first marriage to Isabel, daughter of the Earl of Gloucester, had been dissolved because they couldn't have children. But she was supposed to have married Hugh the Brown of Lusignan. In territorial terms, this was a good move, but the House of Lusignan was insulted and John was too arrogant to pay them off, which was the normal way of going about these matters in those days, and the family laid formal complaint at the court of Philip, who gleefully summoned John to court. John, through his French titles, was a vassal of the French King. So under French law he should have answered the summons. But he refused to go.

C❖John . . . was accordingly sentenced to be deprived of all the lands which he held in France because of his failure of service to his overlord. Thus armed with a legal right recognized by the jurists of the period, Philip invaded Normandy in the summer of 1202, capturing many towns with practically no resistance. The French king knighted Arthur, invested him with all the fiefs of which John had been deprived, except Normandy and Guienne, and betrothed him to his daughter Mary. Arthur was now sixteen.

King John then had to face Arthur of Brittany who now attempted to kidnap the King's mother, his own grandmother.

C❖Arthur, hearing that his grandmother Eleanor was at the castle of Mirabeau in Poitou with a scanty escort, surrounded the castle, stormed the outworks, and was about to gain custody of this important and hostile old Queen. Eleanor contrived, in the nick of time, to send word to John who was at Le Mans. Her son with ample forces covered the eighty miles between them in forty-eight hours, surprised Arthur and the besiegers at daybreak and, as he declared, 'By the favour of God' got the lot. Arthur and all who stood with him . . . fell at a stroke into John's power and his mother was delivered from her dangerous plight.

Arthur was imprisoned at Falaise and then at Rouen . . . All those barons of Brittany who were still loyal to John asked that the prince should be released, and on John's refusal went into immediate rebellion. John felt that he would never be safe so long as Arthur lived. . . . No one knows what happened to Arthur. The officer commanding the fortress [at Rouen] . . . gave out that upon the King's order he had delivered his prisoner at Easter, 1203, to the hands of agents sent by John to castrate him, and that Arthur had died of the shock.

The Bretons went into great revolt at the news of the murder of their duke. Philip of France watched as others withdrew their support from John. But Normandy was not ready to fall for the French King. It was rich, there were many loyal to John and reinforcements could be brought from England. But John wasn't an inspired leader. He appealed to Pope Innocent to rule against

Philip of France. It came to nothing and then in December, 1203, John returned to England and by midsummer's day, 1204, all that England had left of the Duchy of Normandy were the Channel Islands.

C❖The year 1205 brought a crisis. The loss of Normandy was followed by the death of John's mother, Eleanor, to whose influence he had owed so much of his position on the mainland. The death of Archbishop Hubert Walter, who for the last ten years had controlled the whole machinery of administration, deprived him of the only statesman whose advice he respected and whose authority stood between the Crown and the nation.

Pope Innocent III chose Cardinal Stephen Langton as the new Archbishop of Canterbury. King John, who wished John de Gray, Bishop of Norwich, to be the new Archbishop, retaliated against the decision by seizing Church lands. In 1208, the Pope responded by laying England under an interdict. An interdict meant that the whole country had been excommunicated. For six years, the churches remained closed. People couldn't be given a Christian baptism, marriage or burial. John seized more property. The Pope excommunicated him. Philip of France was delighted: he was all ready to invade England. After all, with England outside the Church, such an adventure would be regarded as a Crusade.

C❖John however was not at the end of his devices, and by a stroke of cunning choice, enough to be called political genius, he turned defeat into something very like triumph. . . . He offered to make England a fief of the Papacy and to do homage to the Pope as his feudal lord. Innocent leapt at this addition to his worldly dignities. He forgave the penitent King. . . . He accepted the sovereignty of England from the hands of John, and returned it to him as his vassal with his blessing.

This turned the tables upon John's secular enemies. He was now the darling of the Church. . . . Stephen Langton himself . . . foresaw the unbridled exploitation by Rome of the patronage of the English Church, and the wholesale engrossment of its benefices by Italian nominees. He became almost immediately an opposing force to the Pope. King John, who had lain at Dover, quaking but calculating, may have laughed while he pulled all these strings and threw his enemies into confusion.

But the barons and magnates – the constitutional grandchildren of Henry II's reforms – now felt the time had come to make sure that arbitrary rule by one king could never again usurp the custom and law of the land and its peoples, especially if those peoples included the barons.

C❖ [The barons] drew together under the leadership of Stephen Langton. The war with the French king was continued, and John's demands in money and service kept the barons' anger hot. . . . They formed plans to restrain the rule of a despotic and defeated King, and openly threatened revolt unless their terms were accepted. . . . But John had one final resource. Encouraged by the Pope, he took the vows of a Crusader and invoked sentence of excommunication upon his opponents. . . . In vain did John manoeuvre . . . to separate the clergy from the barons. Armed revolt seemed the only solution. Although in the final scene of the struggle, the Archbishop showed himself unwilling to go to the extreme of civil war, it was he who persuaded the barons to base their demands upon respect for ancient custom and law, and who gave them some principle to fight for besides their own class interests.

At St Paul's, Archbishop Langton produced the Charter itself and read it aloud to the barons. The barons took up the cry and promised they would enforce the liberties contained in that document. This was the start of the fight for what would be known as the Articles of the Barons, and eventually, Magna Carta.

C❖ In place of the King's arbitrary despotism they proposed . . . a system of checks and balances which would accord the monarchy its necessary strength, but would prevent its perversion by a tyrant or a fool. . . . Government must henceforward mean something more than the arbitrary rule of any man, and custom and the law must stand even above the King. It was this idea, perhaps only half understood, that gave unity and force to the barons' opposition and made the Charter, which they now demanded, imperishable.

On a Monday morning in June, between Staines and Windsor, the barons and churchmen . . . the King, the Papal Legate, the Archbishop of Canterbury, and several bishops [met at Runnymede]. . . . Someone, probably the Archbishop, stated briefly the terms that were suggested. The King declared at once that he agreed. He said the details should be arranged immediately in his chancery.

The short document that was drawn up after the meeting at Runnymede is perhaps the most momentous single document in the history of these islands. Without it, there would have been no Magna Carta, no Great Charter. And we have it still, the very parchment that was at Runnymede: there are two copies in the British Museum, one in Salisbury Cathedral and one in Lincoln Cathedral. The parchment of forty-nine Articles begins with the simple statement: 'These are the articles which the Barons ask for and the Lord King grants.' Here are a few of the Articles.

Article one: After the death of their predecessors, heirs who are of full age shall have their inheritance on the payment of the old relief, which is to be stated in the Charter.

Article six: The King shall not grant any baron the right to take an aid from his free men, except for ransoming his person, for making his eldest son a knight and for once marrying his eldest daughter, and this he shall do by a reasonable aid.

Article twelve: That the measure for wine, corn and widths of cloth and other things be improved; and so with weights.

Article twenty-one: That neither the King nor his bailiff shall take another man's timber for castles or other works of his, except with the agreement of him whose timber it is.

Article thirty-four: If anyone who has borrowed from the Jews any sum, great or small, dies before it is repaid, the debt shall not bear interest as long as the heir is under age, and if the debt falls into the hand of the King, the King shall not take anything except the principal.

Article forty-two: That the King make justices, constables, sheriffs and bailiffs of such as know the law of the land and mean to observe it well.

And the final article, Article forty-nine, is prefaced with these twenty famous words:

Article forty-nine: This is the form of security for the observance of the peace and liberties between the King and the kingdom.

From this, the Charter was produced; it reflects feudal law and feudal custom. The taxes (aids and scrutage) are feudal, so too are the ways of raising and paying debts. The assizes were to be held more often; the liberty of the Church was to be respected. Perhaps the most important clause was numbered as thirty-nine in the original.

Article thirty-nine: No free man shall be arrested or imprisoned or disseised [legally dispossessed of one's land] or outlawed or exiled or victimized in any other way, neither will we attack him or send anyone to attack him, except by the lawful judgment of his peers or by the law of the land.

On this Article alone rests much of the fame of Magna Carta. From it came what the moderate barons probably wanted most of all, and the long lasting concept that any man shall be entitled to trial by the due process of the law.

C❖. . . there is no mention in Magna Carta of Parliament or representation of any but the baronial class. The great watchwords of the future here find no place. The actual Charter is a redress of feudal grievances extorted from an unwilling king by a discontented ruling class insisting on its privileges, and it ignored some of the most important matters which the King and baronage had to settle, such as the terms of military service.

Magna Carta must not however be dismissed lightly. . . . If the thirteenth-century magnates understood little and cared less for popular liberties or Parliamentary democracy, they had, all the same, laid hold of a principle which was to be of prime importance for the future development of English society and English institutions. Throughout the document it is implied that here is a law which is above the King and which even he must not break.

In theory then, the Charter's great achievement was to establish that the King was not above the law. If he attempted to over-ride the law, there now existed a process, 'To distrain and distress him in every possible way.' Curiously, Magna Carta had little immediate constitutional significance. Some petty and cruel barons attacked officers of the royal household who tried to implement the Charter. What they wanted was to rid themselves of the King.

C❖The mis-government of his [John's] reign had brought against him what seemed to be an overwhelming combination. He was at war with the English barons who had forced him to grant the Charter. They had invited Louis, son of the implacable Philip, King of France, into the country to be their liege lord, and with him came foreign troops and hardy adventurers. The insurgent barons north of the Humber had the support of Alexander, King of Scots; in the West, the rebellion was sustained by Llewellyn, the powerful Prince of North Wales. The towns were mainly against the King; London was vehemently hostile. The Cinque Ports [Hastings, Sandwich, Dover, Romney and Hythe, and later Rye and Winchelsea also] were in enemy hands. Winchester, Worcester and Carlisle, separated by the great distances of those times, were united in opposition to the Crown.

On the other hand. . . A strong body of mercenaries, the only regular troops in the kingdom, were in John's pay. Some of the greatest warrior nobles, the venerable William the Marshal, and the famous romantic Ranulf, Earl of Chester, with a strong following of the aristocracy, adhered to his cause.

What we know of those terrible years, including the death of the King, mostly comes from John de Erley, the squire of William the Marshal. It was probably written down a decade after the events.

❖The barons, having collected at London, sent messengers to summon Louis the son of the King of France, whom they intended to make King of England. This was folly. Before Louis arrived, the King besieged Rochester. He spent a great deal of money there before he gained possession of it. He went to Dover by sea. Then he called in some Flemmings, knights and serjeants, who thought only of plunder and were less concerned with helping him in his war than with laying waste his land. In five weeks he had exhausted his treasure. The Londoners brought in Louis, who for a long time was master of the country. He captured Farnham, Winchester, Portchester and Southampton.

By Christmas 1215 John had reached Nottingham, by early January 1216 he was in York. By the middle of the month he was as far north as Berwick. The new Scottish King, Alexander II, encouraged by the northern barons, raided across the border. For nearly two weeks, John's troops struck into the lowlands, punishing the Scottish King by harrying his people. John then turned and marched south. John's foreign mercenaries plundered their way through Lincolnshire and then East Anglia. Also, local barons and squires used the war as an excuse to kill, maim, steal and landgrab. This was a chance for the King to replenish his stricken bank balance.

Instead of physically punishing wrong-doers, he imposed massive fines. One thousand pounds from York and Beverley. Eighty silver marks from Thirsk. Another 100 from Melton Mowbray. Within three months King John had reconquered the north of his country. And then came the end, as described by John de Erley.

❖Finally he, the King, made his way towards Lindsey. On the way he was seized by illness. He was forced to stop at Newark. With him were the Bishop of Winchester, John of Monmouth, Walter Clifford, sire Rogier, John Marshal and a number of other men of high rank. Feeling his illness growing worse, King John said to them: 'My lords, I must die; I cannot hold against this illness.'

The best evidence suggests that over-tiredness, too much food and too much wine left King John with dysentery. He died on 18 October 1216, exactly 150 years, almost to the day, after another king, Harold, had perished defending his realm against the invasion.

C❖The death of the King . . . changed the conditions of the conflict without ending it. . . . Louis was in the Island, and fighting. Many had plighted him their faith, already once forsworn. The rebel lords were deeply involved with their Scottish and Welsh allies; none was in the humour for peace. Yet the sole reason and justification for revolt died with John. Henry, a child of nine, was the undoubted heir to all the rights and loyalties of his grandfather's wide empire. . . . Upon what grounds could the oppressions of the father be visited upon his innocent son? . . . William the Marshal acted with honesty and decision. Had he failed in his duty to the Crown, the strong centralized monarchy which Henry II had created, and upon which the growing civilization of the realm depended, might have degenerated into a heptarchy of feudal princes, or even worse. The Papal Legate, sure of the unchanging policy of Rome, aided William the Marshal. The boy King was crowned at Gloucester, and began his reign of fifty-six years on October 28, 1216. John de Erley describes the scene.

❖The child was dressed in royal robes made to his size: he was a fine little knight. The great men carried him to the monastery. The Legate, Gualo, sang the mass and crowned him, assisted by the bishops. When he was anointed and consecrated, and the service was over, the knights carried the child in their arms to his chamber where he was dressed in other less heavy clothes. At this moment, just as the company was to sit at table, there came bad news. A messenger, more foolish than wise, told the Marshal that his castle of Goodrich had been besieged and that his constable was seeking his help. The Marshal immediately sent there knights, serjeants and cross-bowmen. Many of those present considered that this event, on the very day of the coronation, was a bad omen.

The dying king had called for William the Marshal to protect his heir. But William the Marshal was reluctant, as his squire, John de Erley, recounts.

❖They would never have overcome the resistance of the Marshal had the Legate not begged him to accept the Regency for the remission and pardon of his sins. 'In God's name,' said the Marshal, 'if at this price I am absolved of my sins, this office suits me, and I will take it, though it weighs heavily upon me.'

C❖William the Marshal, aged seventy, reluctantly undertook what we should now call the Regency. . . . The wisdom and the weakness of the new government were alike revealed in the reissue of the Charter . . . The religious character of the King's party had become predominant . . . The Church preached a virtual Crusade, and the chiefs of the opposing faction were excommunicated. . . . It was a reign of turmoil and distress, and yet the forces of progress moved doggedly forward.

In the winter of 1216 Louis returned to France for reinforcements and many of his English supporters deserted. On 20 May the following year, the barons and Louis were defeated in the narrow streets at the Battle of Lincoln or the Fair of Lincoln, as it became known. Three months later the reinforcements raised by Blanche of Castile, Louis's wife, put to sea under the command of the Royalist traitor, Eustace the Monk. Royalist sailors came alongside the French ships, threw quicklime into the eyes of the French crews, and seized the vessels. The intended invasion was over.

CHAPTER NINE

1217–1272

———— ❖ ————

Henry III was king for fifty-six years. For the first ten of them he was too young to rule. England was ruled by a Regency and was in need of firm government. When the nine-year-old Henry became King in 1216, England was still engaged in the Barons' War. After Louis's defeat (cushioned by 10,000 silver marks) all the King's men started to put Henry's house in order. Three of these were William the Marshal, Stephen Langton, the Archbishop of Canterbury, and Hubert de Burgh. However they didn't always support the Crown unquestioningly.

C❖ Stephen Langton, the great Archbishop, was the indomitable, unwearying builder of the rights of Englishmen against royal, baronial, and even ecclesiastical pretensions. He stood against King John; he stood against the Pope . . . The second personality which emerges from the restless scene is Hubert de Burgh. . . . Here is a soldier and a politician, armed with the practical wisdom which familiarity with courts and camps . . . may infuse into a man's conduct, and even nature. . . . Under [William] the Marshal . . . Hubert was an outstanding leader of resistance to the rebellion against the monarchy. At the same time, above the warring factions, he was a solid champion of the rights of England.

So we have the young king, formidably protected by Church, state, treasury and sword. At first, William the Marshal and Guala, the Papal Legate, managed the task. But within two years of Henry's coronation Guala left England. The following year, William the Marshal died. And so it was that Hubert de Burgh became the Justiciar, the chief officer of the realm. Hubert de Burgh had the full support and counsel of the Archbishop, Stephen Langton. And both led the young King to the point, in 1227, when he could confidently declare himself of age and rule his kingdom.

C❖ [Hubert] stood for doing the least possible to recover the King's French domains. . . . He hampered the preparation for fresh war; he stood firm against the incursions of foreign favourites and adventurers. He resisted the

Papacy in its efforts to draw money at all costs out of England for its large European schemes. He maintained order and, as the King grew up, he restrained the Court Party which was forming about him from making inroads upon the Charter. But . . . in 1232, he [Hubert] was driven from power by a small palace clique.

De Burgh's conduct had been far from blameless, but his fall had been deliberately engineered by men whose object was not to reform administration but to gain power. The leader of this intrigue was his former rival, Peter des Roches, the Bishop of Winchester. . . . De Burgh was the last of the great Justiciars who had wielded plenary and, at times, almost sovereign power. Henceforward the Household offices, like the Wardrobe, largely dependent on the royal will and favour, began to overshadow the great 'national' offices like the Justiciarship, filled by the baronial magnates. As they came to be occupied increasingly by foreign intruders, Poitevins, Savoyards, Provençals, the national feeling of the baronage became violently hostile. Under the leadership of Richard the Marshal, a second son of the faithful William, the barons began to growl against the foreigners. Des Roches retorted that the King had need of foreigners to protect him against the treachery of his natural subjects, and large numbers of Poitevin and Breton mercenaries were brought over to sustain this view. But the struggle was short. In alliance with Prince Llewellyn, the young Marshal drove the King among the Welsh Marches, sacked Shrewsbury, and harried des Roches's lands. In the spring of 1234, Henry was forced to accept terms . . . The Poitevin officials were dismissed, des Roches found it convenient to go on a journey to Italy, and de Burgh was honourably restored to his lands and possessions.

Henry III rebuilt Westminster in the name of Edward the Confessor: he wished to be seen as a devout King. But the next twenty-four years were uneasy years. The relationship between the young King and the barons was rarely anything but uneasy. When he was a child, Henry's Regency had to consult the barons. Once he became King, Henry, naturally, ruled in his own style and through the hand-picked servants of the Crown. The barons preferred the old way. Also, Henry had married Eleanor of Provence. The barons believed that her relations encouraged the King to think too much about his French claims. That meant spending money. It meant taxes and loans. And many of the barons no longer had direct interests in France. They also knew that Magna Carta, no matter how many times it was revised and re-issued (it wasn't a one-off document, more like a modern Act of Parliament which may be amended), wasn't enough to control the King and force him to consult them on important matters, not even through the Great Council.

In theory the Great Council was a sort of Privy Council. But because the

King could call anyone he liked to it, and therefore not call anyone he didn't like, it didn't have much power. So neither did the barons. In 1258 there was a constitutional confrontation, and it went on for seven years. The immediate result was the Provisions of Oxford.

The Provisions of Oxford were reforms rather than rules. They were issued by a Committee appointed by the Oxford Parliament in 1258. They were not contained in a single document. Neither were they a new Magna Carta. Power, instead of being in the hands of the monarch, was (in theory) invested in a Council of Fifteen and in the King. The key figure was the new Justiciar, Hugh Bigod.

And it was also in 1258 that the word Parliament entered the language. The word comes from the Norman French. It was a gathering to talk about important matters, to parley. It was a direct development of the curia regis, the royal court of the Norman kings.

The first Parliaments did not have a Speaker, a government party, an opposition front bench nor chief whips. The thirteenth-century Parliaments were the more important sessions of the Great Council. The Provisions of Oxford contain a series of oaths which illustrate something of the importance of the new Council of Fifteen and its Parliaments. For example:

❖There are to be three Parliaments a year. The first on the octave of Michaelmas. The second, the morrow of Candelmas [sic]. The third, the first [Holy] day of June, that is to say, three weeks before St John's day.

And the Provisions of Oxford began its conclusion with the fact that the Council, the Fifteen, shall be chosen, not by the King, but by the Earl Marshal, Hugh Bigod, John Mansel and the Earl of Warwick. And then:

❖And they are to have authority to advise the King in good faith on the government of the kingdom and all things pertaining to the King or to the kingdom, and authority to amend and redress all the things they see need to be redressed and amended. And authority over the chief Justiciar, and over all other people. And if they cannot all be present, what the majority does shall be firm and established.

The Provisions of Oxford were written in French, Latin and in English. There may seem little remarkable in that, but, for 100 years, English had not been used as an official language. So perhaps this tells us how important were the Provisions of Oxford: it must have the widest possible readership. In 1259 the Provisions of Oxford were reinforced by the Provisions of Westminster.

One of the names which appears in these Provisions, as representing the views of the earls and barons, was the Lord Simon, Earl of Leicester, more popularly remembered as Simon de Montfort.

C❖Simon had married the King's sister and had inherited the Earldom of Leicester. He had been governor of the English lands in Gascony for four years. Strong and energetic, he had aroused the jealousy and opposition of the King's favourites; and as a result of their intrigues had been brought to trial in 1252. The commission acquitted him; but in return for a sum of money from the King he unwillingly agreed to vacate his office. Friendship between him and the King was at an end; on the one side was contempt, on the other suspicion. In this way, from an unexpected quarter, appeared the leader whom the baronial and national opposition had long lacked . . . [He] was to become the brain and driving force of the English aristocracy. Behind him gradually ranged themselves most of the greater feudal chiefs, the whole strength of London as a corporate entity, all the lower clergy, and the goodwill of the nation.

Simon de Montfort has been called a man of great self-confidence, a man of clear imagination, a skilled soldier and an arrogant man. He was also foreign born without a partisan notion of what was going on in England. He didn't want to get rid of the throne; equally he was quite willing to lock up the King in order to achieve his aims. And, once he had achieved the limited success of the Provisions of Oxford and Westminster, he was not afraid to turn his attentions to the barons.

Simon de Montfort became increasingly powerful. He even struck up an understanding with the King's son, Edward, who was emerging as one of the first political princes in English history. Young men rallied to Edward. They knew that he'd be king one day and they believed him to be more trustworthy than his father. But the difference between Simon de Montfort and the young Prince Edward was this: Simon believed that through the Council – the Parliament – the King could be controlled. Edward saw the Council as a group of advisers, nothing more.

King Henry became suspicious of the alliance between his son and de Montfort, even though their differences were obvious. Henry sent Edward into exile, but wasn't a good enough king and leader to keep control of his kingdom as it headed for civil war. The death of Richard de Clare, Earl of Gloucester, in July 1262 was a blow for Henry. Gloucester did not subscribe to de Montfort's belief that the King could be over-ruled. But Gloucester, one of the King's closest supporters and the finest of Henry's generals in the Welsh Marches, was gone.

C❖. . . the baronial party rallied to de Montfort's drastic policy. Civil war broke out and Simon and his sons . . . a moiety of barons, the middle-class, so far as it had emerged, and powerful allies in Wales, together faced in redoubtable array the challenge of the Crown. . . . [But] by September 1263 a reaction against him [de Montfort] had become visible: he had succeeded only too well. Edward played upon the discontent among the barons, appealed to their feudal and selfish interest, fomented their jealousy of de Montfort, and so built up a strong royalist party. At the end of the year de Montfort had to agree to arbitration by Louis IX, the French king. The decision went against him.... Already however, the rival parties had taken up arms.... [At Lewes] in Sussex a fierce battle was fought [May 1264].... [Edward] conquered all before him, pursued incontinently, and returned to the battlefield only to find that all was lost. Simon had, with much craft and experience of war, laid a trap to which the peculiar conditions of the ground lent themselves, whereby when his centre had been pierced, his two wings of armoured cavalry fell upon the royal main body from both flanks and crushed all resistance.

This Battle of Lewes was the start of the Second Barons' War and the King and Edward were captured. De Montfort was, in effect, ruler of England. But he had no ambitions to replace Henry, nor Edward. With the Bishop of Chichester and Gilbert de Clare, the new Earl of Gloucester, Simon de Montfort governed England in the name of the King. But the alliance was short-lived because the new Earl of Gloucester had the same instincts as his father: he was a royalist. Throughout 1265 Simon de Montfort's position weakened. Gloucester's doubts were made more public, and in May, Prince Edward escaped from de Montfort. Gloucester went with him and Edward, singing the praises of Magna Carta, not the Oxford Provisions, raised an army in the Welsh Marches.

C❖By promising to uphold the Charters, to remedy grievances and to expel the foreigners, Edward succeeded in uniting the baronial party and in cutting away the ground from under de Montfort's feet. The Earl now appeared as no more than the leader of a personal faction ... Out-manoeuvred politically by Edward, he had also placed himself at a serious military disadvantage ... de Montfort was penned in, his retreat to the east cut off; and his forces driven back into south Wales. At the beginning of August he made another attempt to cross the river and to join the forces which his son, Simon, was bringing up from the South-East. He succeeded in passing by a ford in Worcester, but his son's forces were trapped by Edward near Kenilworth and routed. Unaware of this disaster, the Earl was caught in turn at Evesham; and here on August 4, the final battle took place.

It was fought in the rain and half-darkness of a sudden storm. The Welsh broke before Edward's heavy horse, and the small group around de Montfort were left to fight desperately until sheer weight of numbers overwhelmed them. De Montfort died a hero in the field.

After the Battle of Evesham in 1265, Simon de Montfort's followers were stripped of their properties and a guerrilla campaign began in England. Supporters of the dead de Montfort became known as the Disinherited. They became outlaws. They hid in hills and in forests including the great forest of Sherwood. Eventually, in 1267, the Statute of Marlborough was drawn up. The King could once again choose his own advisers, councillors and servants. Magna Carta was invoked. (Note how often this happened in English history: Magna Carta was the only authority for reform.) Regular Parliaments were to be held.

The great test of the new administrations came five years later. When Henry died, Edward was abroad on the Crusade. It took him nearly two years to return to England. Yet while he was away, the smooth governing of England continued, because although the reforms had led to civil war, they were nevertheless well-founded and well-respected.

And here is an irony. Simon de Montfort's reforms, or his ideas for them, would not die with him. And the person responsible for his death, the new King, Edward I, continued to implement them.

CHAPTER TEN

1272–1307

—— ❖ ——

Henry III was buried in the dearest object of his life, his new abbey at Westminster. He was sixty-five in November 1272, when he died, which was not a bad age for the Middle Ages. A man who reached sixty-five might well have mourned most of his childhood friends not because people naturally had short lives, but because many of the causes of death were not yet understood. Men knew how to wield swords but not scalpels. Science moved slowly but social change stepped up its pace. But with change came some sinister events.

After Henry's death the way land was administered and owned began to change.

C❖Land gradually . . . became, by successive steps, a commodity which could, in principle, like wool and mutton, be bought and sold. . . . The Jews had unseen and noiselessly lodged themselves in the social fabric of that fierce age. . . . The spectacle of land which could be acquired on rare but definite occasions by anyone with money led the English Jews into a course of shocking imprudence. . . . In a couple of decades, the erstwhile feudal lords were conscious that they had parted permanently – for fleeting lucre – with a portion of the English soil large enough to be noticed.

The Jews became objects of hate. They were said to be the biggest moneylenders in the state. William the Conqueror had brought Jewish moneylenders to England and under his, and William II's, protection, they settled. In 1189 there were widespread massacres. And during the second half of the thirteenth century feeling was so high against the Jews that, in 1275, the Statute of the Jewry was issued during the Michaelmas Parliament at Westminster:

❖The King has ordained and established that from now on no Jew shall lend anything at usury, either on land or rent or anything else, and that usuries shall not continue beyond the feast of St Edward last . . . And no distress for a debt owing to a Jew is to be made upon the heir of the debtor named in the Jew's deed or other person holding the land.

And that all Jews shall dwell in the King's own cities and boroughs, where the chirograph chests of the Jews [the boxes in which the money-lenders kept promissory notes] are wont to be: and that each Jew, after he is seven years old, shall wear a distinguishing mark on his outer garment, that is to say, in the form of two Tables joined, of yellow felt of the length of six inches and of the breadth of three inches. And that each one, after he is twelve years old, shall yearly at Easter pay to the King, whose serf he is, a tax of three pence, and this be understood to hold as well for a woman as for a man.

The King . . . grants them that they may live by lawful trade and by their labour and they may have intercourse with Christians in order to carry on lawful trade. But that no Christian for this cause or any other shall dwell among them.

C❖Edward saw himself able to conciliate powerful elements and escape from awkward debts by the simple and well trodden path of anti-Semitism. The propaganda of ritual murder and other dark tales . . . were at once invoked with general acclaim. . . . Exception was made for certain physicians without whose skill persons of consequence might have lacked due attention. Once again the sorrowful, wandering race, stripped to the skin, must seek asylum and begin afresh. To Spain or North Africa the melancholy caravan, now so familiar, must move on. . . . The bankers of Florence and Siena, who had taken the place of the Jews, were in their turn under Edward I's grandson to taste the equities of Christendom.

In the final quarter of the thirteenth century, Jews, accused of coin clipping (to steal the silver) in England, were publicly hanged.

This was a period of quickly changing political and constitutional fortune. Margaret was about to become Queen in Scotland, to be quickly followed by John Balliol. The Welsh, once more, revolted against the English. Llewellyn ap Gruffudd, Prince of Wales, was killed and Dafydd, who succeeded his brother Llewellyn, was captured and executed. And as the century drew to an end, William Wallace defeated the English at Stirling Bridge, only to be beaten the following year at Falkirk before escaping to France.

The population of England had doubled since the Conquest. By now it was probably about three million. The villages had grown, split into three or four communities, and the land that had been ravaged by the Conqueror was restored. Towns thrived. Newcastle became the centre of the only big coalfield of the time. Lynn became the port for the Fens, Hull for York. It was a land of exporters and importers: wool to Flanders, corn to Norway and to France, fish to the Continent. In return came timber, French and Italian wines, ginger, peppers, currants and jewels.

But this was not a wealthy and sophisticated society. Most people were peasants and while they were no worse off than at the time of Domesday, there's little evidence that their lot had much improved. Magna Carta and social and legal reform did not make people wealthier. The rich were richer and the divide between the haves and the have-nots was greater. Perhaps the biggest change came from the King himself. Edward I set out to remove as much corruption as was convenient so to do. But not, of course, by himself.

C❖Edward relied upon his Chancellor, Robert Burnell, Bishop of Bath and Wells, a man of humble birth, who had risen through the royal chancery and Household to his bishopric and, until his death in 1292, remained the King's principal adviser. . . . [Burnell] had not been Chancellor for more than three weeks, after Edward's return to England in 1274, before a searching inquiry into local administration was begun. Armed with a list of forty questions, commissioners were sent throughout the land to ask what were the rights and possessions of the King, what encroachments had been made upon them, which officials were negligent or corrupt, which sheriffs . . . concealed felonies, neglected their duties, were harsh or bribed. Similar inquests had been made before; none was so thorough or so fertile. . . . Edward I was remarkable among mediaeval kings for the seriousness with which he regarded the work of administration and good government. . . . By the end of the thirteenth century three departments of specialized administration were already at work. One was the Exchequer, established at Westminster, where most of the revenue was received and the accounts kept. The second was the Chancery, a general secretariat responsible for the writing and drafting of innumerable royal charters, writs, and letters. The third was the Wardrobe, with its separate secretariat, the Privy Seal, attached to the ever-moving royal household, and combining financial and secretarial functions, which might range from financing a Continental war to buying a pennyworth of pepper for the royal cook.

But Edward's personal world had changed for the worse. His wife, Eleanor of Castile, had died as had his mother, Eleanor of Provence, and his two eldest sons. The loss of his wife was particularly sad for him. He was clearly in love with her; theirs had not been a mediaeval marriage of convenience. Eleanor had been with Edward on his Crusade in 1270. In 1290 she died at Hadby in Nottinghamshire. Her body was brought to London and that last journey can be traced because everywhere the cortège stopped Edward built crosses. He built them at Lincoln, Grantham, Stamford, Geddington, Northampton, Stony Stratford, Woburn, Dunstable, St Albans, Waltham and, perhaps most famously, in London at Charing Cross.

Four years later and still in mourning, Edward had to go to war with France. He had come to an arrangement, a token surrender of the English garrisons in

Gascony, so that the French King, Philip the Fair, could show that his position of overlord was recognized. But the token surrender became absolute. Edward had to raise money for the campaign, and even needed to justify it. He did so by calling together a council, a Parliament.

C❖Parliament granted a heavy tax on all movable property. As the collection proceeded, a bitter and sullen discontent spread among all classes. In the winter of 1294, the Welsh revolted and when the King had suppressed them he returned to find that Scotland had allied itself with France. From 1296 onward, war with Scotland was either smouldering or flaring. . . . the French war degenerated into a series of truces. . . . Although the King did not hesitate to recall recurrent Parliaments to Westminster and explained the whole situation to them, he did not obtain the support which he needed. . . . The time was ripe for a revival of the baronial opposition which a generation before had defied Edward's father.

Records of the differences between the King and his earls were kept by Walter of Guisborough.

❖The King held his Parliament at Salisbury where he asked certain of the magnates to cross over to Gascony. They began to excuse themselves. And the King was very angry and threatened some of them, that either they went or he would give their lands to others who were willing to go. And many were offended at this and a split began to appear between them.

The Earl of Hereford and the Earl Marshal said they would gladly go if the King marched with them. But the King wanted them to march without him. A bitter argument flared up and the Earl Marshal walked out. Walter of Guisborough again:

❖The two Earls, Hereford and the Earl Marshal, joined by many magnates and more than thirty picked banners, grew into a multitude. They numbered 1500 men on armed horses ready for war and the King began to fear them. They went off to their own lands, where they would not allow the King's servants to take either wool or hides or anything whatever out of the ordinary or to exact anything from anyone against his will. Indeed they forbade them entry to their lands.

Edward sailed for Flanders but the earls and barons, instead of sailing for Gascony, rode with their forces into London and demanded that Magna Carta and extensions and protocols covering taxes on wool and hides (which Edward was exacting to pay for the war), liberties of the clergy and the people, and much more, should be accepted by the King. Edward was in Ghent. He accepted the principles, but acceptance and observance are different matters. Eventually, at another Parliament, this time held at Lincoln, solemn agreement was reached.

C❖By this crisis and its manner of resolution, two principles had been established from which important consequences flowed. One was that the King had no right to despatch the feudal host wherever he might choose. This limitation sounded the death-knell of the feudal levy and led, in the following century, to the rise of indentured armies serving for pay. The second point of principle now recognized was that the King could not plead 'urgent necessity' as a reason for imposing taxation without consent. Other English monarchs as late as the seventeenth century were to make the attempt. But by Edward's failure, a precedent had been set up, and a long stride had been taken towards the dependence of the Crown upon Parliamentary grants.

Since the end of the twelfth century, the English kings had fought their own clergy, barons and earls. The clergy refused to accept that, in matters spiritual, the King was above the church. The barons were protecting their own interests. But there was a constant in the conflict between monarch, people, church and baronage. It was this: the English kings were devoted to protecting their interests in France. It was, after all, where they came from. And their magnates had land, titles and families across the Channel. So for a long time after the Conquest it was easy for the King to convince his nobles, and therefore their exchequers, to fight for him in France. But as the decades went by fewer of the English magnates were directly tied to continental lands. The King's difficulty then was to persuade them to come up with the money, as well as the soldiers, for overseas expeditions.

By the closing years of the thirteenth century, successive kings had been so obsessed with their French campaigns that they had never properly dealt with the threat closer to home. It began in Scotland and, more immediately, in Wales.

C❖There had been fitful interference both in Wales and Scotland, but the task of keeping the frontiers safe had fallen mainly upon the shoulders of the local Marcher lords [the border lords]. . . . Edward I was the first of the English kings to put the whole weight of the Crown's resources behind the effort of national expansion in the West and North . . . He took the first great step towards the unification of the Island. . . . All assertions of Welsh independence were a vexation to Edward; but scarcely less obnoxious was a system of guarding the frontiers of England by a confederacy of robber barons who had more than once presumed to challenge the authority of the Crown.

As in Scotland, geography had a great deal to do with the character of the Welsh people and their relations with the English. Warring Welsh chieftains had long had the advantage of being able to withdraw to the hills and mountains, and even across the sea to Ireland. Furthermore, in Wales as in Scotland, there had never been, during this period, a national purpose. Local jealousies were always stronger than any claim of Welsh unity. Even when great Welsh lords such as Rhys or Owen Gwynedd commanded the country, family feuds dissolved any such unity once the lords were dead. So there could be no simple, single operation to gain control of Wales. By Edward's reign, Llewellyn II was ready for another attempt at independence.

C❖[Edward I] resolved, in the name of justice and progress, to subdue the unconquered refuge of petty princes and wild mountaineers in which barbaric freedom had dwelt since remote antiquity, and at the same time to curb the privileges of the Marcher lords.

[He] conquered Wales in several years of persistent warfare, coldly and carefully devised, by land and sea. The forces he employed were mainly Welsh levies in his pay, reinforced by regular troops from Gascony and by one of the last appearances of the feudal levy; but above all, it was by the terror of the winter campaigns that he broke the power of the valiant Ancient Britons.

Edward knew this was to be a drawn-out campaign. The first thing he did was to establish a base at Chester. Then, just as a modern general would have to do, Edward set up a communications line. He cut a road through the wooded coastline to Aberconway. He sent his fleet round to Anglesey and his Marcher lords in from the east and south. It took time, it was bloody, but it worked. Within two years of the signing of a treaty at Aberconway, much of the Welsh holdings were being organized on an English county system. All seemed settled but all was not.

On Palm Sunday, 1282, the Welsh attacked. Llewellyn's brother, Dafydd, invaded Cardigan and captured Aberystwyth. Early in December, Llewellyn left the North, where he was safe, for the Upper Wye valley. He was killed, not in some great battle, but at what might have been, except for his death, an insignificant skirmish close to Builth in 1282. Six months later, Dafydd was betrayed to the English and executed. A Statute, the Statute of Rhuddlan, was proclaimed on 19 March 1284, and Edward regarded himself as the conqueror of the Welsh.

C❖By Edward's Statute of Wales, the independent principality came to an end. The land of Llewellyn's Wales was transferred to the King's dominions and organized into the shires of Anglesey, Carnarvon, Merioneth, Cardigan and

Carmarthen. . . . The Welsh wars of Edward reveal to us the process by which the military system of England was transformed from the age-long Saxon and feudal basis of occasional service, to that of paid regular troops.

Even when the settlement was agreed, there were uprisings. And it took more than two centuries before Wales was incorporated into union with England, with representation in the Parliament. The methods of warfare also changed.

C❖A new type of infantry raised from the common people began to prove its dominating quality. This infantry operated, not by club or sword or spear, or even by hand-flung missiles, but by an archery which, after a long development, concealed from Europe, was very soon to make an astonishing entrance upon the military scene and gain a dramatic ascendancy upon the battlefields of the Continent. . . . In South Wales the practice of drawing the long-bow had already attained an astonishing efficiency, of which one of the Marcher lords has left a record. One of his knights had been hit by an arrow which pierced not only the skirts of his mailed shirt, but his mailed breeches, his thigh, and the wood of his saddle, and finally struck deep into his horse's flank. . . . For the first time, infantry possessed a weapon which could penetrate the armour of a clanking age, and which in range and rate of fire was superior to any method ever used before, or ever used again until the coming of the modern rifle.

It was in Carnavon Castle that the English King's son, Edward, was born, during the same year as the Statute of Rhuddlan was proclaimed, 1284. Seventeen years later, in 1301, this Edward became the first English Prince of Wales. One day he too would be King.

C❖The great quarrel of Edward [I]'s reign was with Scotland. For long years the two kingdoms had dwelt in amity. In the year 1286 Alexander III of Scotland, riding his horse over a cliff in the darkness, left as his heir Margaret, his granddaughter, known as the Maid of Norway. The Scottish magnates had been persuaded to recognize this three-year-old as his successor. Now the bright project arose that the Maid of Norway should at the same moment succeed to the Scottish throne and marry Edward, the [English] King's son. Thus would be achieved a union of royal families by which the antagonism of England and Scotland might be laid to rest. . . . It was a dream and it passed as a dream. The Maid of Norway embarked in 1290 upon stormy seas, only to die before reaching land, and Scotland was bequeathed the problem of a disputed succession, in the decision of which the English interest must be a heavy factor. The Scottish nobility were allied at many points with the English royal family, and from a dozen claimants, some of them bastards, two men stood clearly forth: John Balliol and Robert Bruce. Bruce asserted his aged father's closeness in relationship to the common royal ancestor; Balliol, a more distant descendant, the rights of primogeniture.

Ever since the ninth century and the conquests of the Picts by the Scots, the kings of the Scots had regarded a lot of what is now northern England as fair game. Had the Scots been less clannish, had they avoided their own internal jealousies, then perhaps the lands of the Scots might have expanded. But it was never to be. Under the true kingship of David I during the first half of the twelfth century, the Scots achieved recognition for his claims to the English northern counties. But by the time of Alexander II in 1237, those claims were abandoned by the Treaty of York, in return for yet more contrived family relations, payment in silver as compensation for English broken promises, and a few thousand acres of land.

But for the moment relations were sound: in fact they were so good that Edward I was called upon to arbitrate between the claims for the Scottish throne.

C❖King Edward, whose legal abilities were renowned . . . now imposed himself with considerable acceptance as arbitrator in the Scottish succession. Since the alternatives were the splitting of Scotland into rival kingships, or a civil war to decide the matter, the Scots were induced to seek Edward's judgment; and he, pursuing all the time a path of strict legality, consented to the task only upon the prior condition of the reaffirmation of his overlordship, betokened by the surrender of certain Scottish castles. . . . He [Edward] pronounced in 1292 in favour of John Balliol. . . . [But] John Balliol inevitably became not merely his [Edward's] choice but his puppet. . . . the Scottish baronage accepted King Edward's award, but they also furnished the new King John with an authoritative council of twelve great lords to overawe him and look after the rights of Scotland. Thus King Edward . . . [was] confronted . . . with an independent and not a subject Government, and with a hostile rather than a submissive nation.

At this very moment, the same argument of overlordship was pressed upon him by the formidable French King, Philip IV. Here Edward was the vassal, proudly defending feudal interests, and the French suzerain had the lawful advantage. . . . This double conflict imposed a strain upon the financial and military resources of the English monarchy which it could by no means meet. The rest of Edward's reign was spent in a two-fold struggle North and South, for the sake of which he had to tax his subjects beyond all endurance. . . . Thus . . . [Edward was] forced to drive his people beyond their strength, and in this process to rouse oppositions which darkened his life and clouded his fame.

And the Scots allied themselves with the French. Edward was furious. He demanded that Balliol meet him at Berwick. But the Scottish baronage told their King not to go. The time for consultations was over. Edward regarded the Scots' defiance and alignment with France as an act of war. He marched on Berwick and, in an act of savagery, sacked the once peaceful town. Thousands were slaughtered and the town surrendered. Edinburgh, Perth and Stirling followed. But Edward's victory was short-lived and William Wallace rose to lead the Scottish rebellion.

C❖Warenne, Earl of Surrey, was Edward's commander in the North. . . . At Stirling Bridge, in September 1297, he found himself in the presence of Wallace's army. Many Scotsmen were in the English service. One of these warned him of the dangers of trying to deploy beyond the long, narrow bridge and causeway which spanned the river. . . . He spoke of a ford higher up, by which at least a flanking force could cross. But Earl Warenne would have none of these things. Wallace watched with measuring eye the accumulation of the English troops across the bridge, and at the right moment hurled his full force upon them, seized the bridgehead, and slaughtered the vanguard of 5000 men. Warenne evacuated the greater part of Scotland. His fortress garrisons were reduced one after the other. The English could barely hold the line of the Tweed. . . . Wallace was now the ruler of Scotland, and the war was without truce or mercy. A hated English official, a tax-gatherer, had fallen at the bridge. His skin, cut into suitable strips, covered Wallace's sword-belt for the future. Edward, forced to quit his campaign in France, hastened to the scene of the disaster and, with the whole feudal levy of England, advanced against the Scots.

The deciding battle took place at Falkirk on 22 July 1298. Wallace made a simple and centuries-old mistake: instead of fighting the advancing forces in a series of disrupting skirmishes, he fought in open battle. His cavalry fled. Wallace had relied on his spearmen, but Edward had brought his longbow-men from Wales. They fired volley after volley at the Scottish schiltrons (circles of spearmen) until there were more dead and wounded than living.

C❖Into the gaps and over the carcasses, the knighthood of England forced their way. The slaughter ended only in the depths of the woods, and Wallace and the Scottish Army were once again fugutives . . . but still in arms. The Scots were unconquerable foes. It was not until 1305 that Wallace was captured, tried with full ceremonial in Westminster Hall, and hanged, drawn, and quartered at Tyburn.

Edward I now faced a new King, crowned at Scone, Robert the Bruce. In the summer of 1306, Bruce was defeated and fled to Rathlin Island off the Antrim coast, and the legend of the Bruce and the spider grew up. The legend claims that, on Rathlin Island, Robert the Bruce watched a spider trying, again and again, to climb a single slender strand, and that the spider's eventual success inspired the Bruce to return to Scotland and continue the fight. Robert the Bruce returned to Scotland and Edward, now too weak to ride, was carried to do battle once more against the rebellious Scots. But he died on the road as the rebellion continued.

CHAPTER ELEVEN

1307–1330

❖

The fourteenth century had hardly opened when Edward I died. In 1299 he was forced to marry Margaret, the daughter of the King of France, after the death of his great love, his wife Eleanor of Castile. This was yet another diplomatic marriage to signify some sort of peace between the two enemies. But Margaret sided against him.

Churchill called Edward 'a master-builder of British life, character, and fame'. It is true that he laid the basis of taxation through a parliament, established a documented and efficient administrative process and made clear the laws of his kingdom. And he did most of this without excessively offending his aristocracy which was becoming increasingly established and class conscious. But he left the country in debt because of his wars with Scotland. He left the matter of the monarch's standing as the Duke of Aquitaine unsettled. And this could, and would, threaten the peace of Europe.

He left also an heir, Edward II. A feckless prince whose love, whose obsession, for Piers Gaveston, a son of a Gascon knight, was to bring about anarchy and war.

C❖Edward II's reign may fairly be regarded as a melancholy appendix to his father's and the prelude to his son's ... He was addicted to rowing, swimming, and baths. He carried his friendship for his advisers beyond dignity and decency.... On the death of Edward I, the barons succeeded in gaining control of the mixed body of powerful magnates and competent Household officials [the Curia Regis]. They set up a committee called 'the Lords Ordainers', who represented the baronial and ecclesiastical interests of the State.

Scotland and France remained the external problems confronting these new masters of government, but their first anger was directed upon the favourite of the King. Piers Gaveston, a young, handsome Gascon, enjoyed his fullest confidence. His decisions made or marred. There was a temper which would submit to the rule of a King, but would not tolerate the pretensions of his personal cronies. The barons' party attacked Piers Gaveston.

As Prince of Wales, Edward had become infatuated with Gaveston. Immediately he became King, Edward made his young friend Earl of Cornwall. When the King went to France to marry Isabella, the twelve-year-old daughter of Philip IV, he left Gaveston as 'Keeper of the realm', effectively ruler of England. At the coronation on 25 February 1308, it was Gaveston who carried, in procession, the crown and the sword of St Edward. It was Gaveston who was described as being dressed more like the god Mars than a mere mortal. After the coronation, Isabella's kinsmen returned to France. They took with them a story that Edward loved Gaveston more than his Queen. The movement against Edward grew. At its head was Henry, the Earl of Lincoln. The barons would stand for no more of this domination by the King's favourite. An ordinance was presented to Edward, demanding that dignity be returned to the Crown. Indiscretion was one thing but allowing the object of that indiscretion to become a powerful figure in the governance of the realm was quite another. In other words, Gaveston must be banished.

At the April Parliament the barons forced the King to agree to their wishes. But Edward could not bear to lose his friend for so long. He appointed him his Lieutenant in Ireland and, when the time came for his sailing from Bristol, Edward was there to see him off. But even this temporary exile did not settle the aristocracy's long list of grievances. When that list was presented, in 1309, Edward agreed to reforms, but in return demanded the recall of Gaveston.

Lords Ordainers, a committee of twenty-one lay, ecclesiastical and lordly representatives, wrote the forty-one articles which have become known as the Ordinances of 1311. The Ordinances, among other things, declared that the King was not to leave the realm without the consent of the barons, was not to appoint a keeper of the realm (as he had Gaveston), was not to appoint whomsoever he wished as senior officials, and that all officials had to take an oath to uphold the Ordinances. Perhaps Gaveston was all the things the barons said he was. He was also a scapegoat for Edward's weaknesses and lack of kingship. Gaveston was exiled, yet again, this time to Flanders. And, yet again, he returned.

C❖Compelling him [Gaveston] to take refuge in the North, they [the Lords Ordainers] pursued him ... Besieged in the castle of Scarborough, Gaveston made terms with his foes. His life was to be spared; and on this they took him under guard. But other nobles, led by the Earl of Warwick, one of the foremost Ordainers, who had not been present at the agreement of Scarborough, violated these conditions. They overpowered the escort, seized the favourite at Deddington in Oxfordshire, and hewed off his head on Blacklow Hill, near Warwick.

The immediate effect of his execution was the utter distraction of Edward, and the break up of the group of Lords Ordainers who most wanted change. Nevertheless the barons had the changes they'd wanted.

But the King still possessed significant powers, and he was going to need them, for wars awaited him.

C❖In spite of these successes by the Ordainers, royal power remained formidable. Edward was still in control of Government, although he was under their restraint. Troubles in France and war in Scotland confronted him. To wipe out his setbacks at home he resolved upon the conquest of the northern kingdom. A general levy of the whole power of England was set on foot to beat the Scots. A great army crossed the Tweed in the summer of 1314. Twenty-five thousand men, hard to gather, harder still to feed in those days, with at least 3000 armoured knights and men-at-arms, under the nominal but none the less baffling command of Edward II, moved against the Scottish host. The new champion of Scotland, Robert the Bruce, now faced the vengeance of England. The Scottish army, of perhaps 10,000 men, was composed, as at Falkirk, mainly of the hard, unyielding spearmen who feared nought and, once set in position, had to be killed. But Bruce had pondered deeply upon the impotence of pikemen, however faithful, if exposed to the alternations of an arrow shower and an armoured charge. He therefore . . . took three precautions. First he chose a position where his flanks were secured by impenetrable woods; secondly, he dug upon his front a large number of small round holes, or 'pottes', . . . and covered them with branches and turfs as a trap for charging cavalry; thirdly, he kept in his own hand his small but highly trained force of mounted knights to break up any attempt at planting archers upon his flank to derange his schiltrons.

The story of what happened at Bannockburn has been told in verse and chronicle. There were 20,000 men and all their baggage trains. Many of them, such as the archers from Wales and the foot soldiers from the Midlands and the North-West, were experienced and in little hurry to get into battle with what they saw as a well-organized enemy. In fact the King's nephew, the Earl of Gloucester, wisely said that the troops should be rested for a day after their long march. Edward accused him of cowardice. The young Earl immediately led his cavalry against the massed schiltrons – those oblong hedges of Scottish shields and pikes – and was killed. It was 24 June 1314. The Battle of Bannockburn was on.

C❖. . . the English advanced, and a dense wave of steel-clad horsemen descended the slope, splashed and scrambled through the Bannock Burn, and charged uphill upon the schiltrons. Though much disordered by the 'pottes', they came to deadly grip with the Scottish spearmen. . . . As neither side would withdraw, the struggle was prolonged and covered the whole front. The strong corps of archers could not intervene. When they shot their arrows into the air, as William had done at Hastings, they hit more of their own men than of the Scottish infantry. At length, a detachment of archers was brought round the Scottish left flank. But for this Bruce had made effective provision. His small cavalry force charged them with the utmost promptitude, and drove them back into the great mass waiting to engage, and now already showing signs of disorder. Continuous reinforcements streamed forward towards the English fighting line. Confusion steadily increased. . . . The [English] retreat speedily became a rout. The Scottish schiltrons hurled themselves forward down the slope, inflicting immense carnage upon the English even before they could recross the Bannock Burn. No more grievous slaughter of English chivalry ever took place in a single day.

Bruce himself was a hero and sent his troops to raid, kill, and destroy great swathes of Northern England as far south as Yorkshire. Edward's own authority was reduced even further. After Bannockburn he was unpopular and very much reliant upon his closest officials. The growing aristocracy wanted control of the inner cabinet of the King's advisers – the King's Wardrobe – without either destroying the monarchy or bringing about the downfall of the bureaucracy so necessary for the running of state affairs. Edward very quickly found himself at the contemptuous mercy of his own people, particularly the group of Lords Ordainers led by Thomas of Lancaster.

C❖In the long story of a nation we often see that capable rulers, by their very virtues, sow the seeds of future evil, and weak or degenerate princes open the pathway of progress. . . . We have traced the ever growing influence, and at times authority, of the permanent officials of the royal Household. . . . The feudal baronage . . . could no more contemplate the abolition of these officials than their ancestors the destruction of the monarchy. The whole tendency of their movement was therefore, in this generation, to acquire control of an invaluable machine. . . . Thomas of Lancaster, nephew to Edward I, was [at] the forefront of the baronial opposition. Little is known to his credit. . . . Into the hands of Thomas and his fellow Ordainers, Edward was now thrown by the disaster of Bannockburn, and Thomas for a while became the most important man in the land. Within a few years, however, the moderates among the Ordainers became so disgusted with Lancaster's incompetence and with the weakness into which the process of Government had sunk, that they joined with the royalists to edge him from power.

It took some doing. From the autumn of 1315, Lancaster's authority had been unchallenged. He had control of the country's administration. He gave instructions to the chancellor, made appointments, and even issued pardons. He was Steward of England. And while all this was going on, the people were suffering a famine. For three years torrential rains ruined the harvests of Europe from as far north as Scotland and Russia, south to Italy. In England, men murdered for food. Cannibalism was recorded. Prices rose by as much as 800% in one year. Families fought each other. Counties were in rebellion, including Lancaster. Thomas not only had a revolt in his own county, but his wife, Alice Lacy, left him and hid with another earl, thus starting a private war with Yorkshire.

In all the disorganization of the King's realm, there emerged a new grouping, a middle party. It was led by the Earl of Pembroke who had fallen from favour after Bannockburn, and included the bishops. They appear to have been sincere in their aims for administrative reform.

C❖The victory of this middle party . . . did not please the King. Aiming to be more efficient than Lancaster, Pembroke and his friends tried to enforce the Ordinances more effectively, and carried out a great reform of the royal Household.

Edward, for his part, began to build up a royalist party, at the head of which were the Despensers, father and son, both named Hugh. These belonged to the nobility, and their power lay on the Welsh border. . . . Against both of them the hatreds grew, because of their self-seeking and the King's infatuation with the younger man.

But the Despensers were not favoured because the younger Hugh had taken the place of Piers Gaveston in the King's heart. Hugh the elder had long been a loyal royalist. He'd been a loyal servant of Edward I. Also, he'd been the only baron to support Gaveston during the move to get rid of him in 1308. He was by Edward's side at the retreat from Bannockburn. And Hugh the younger had been a member of Edward's household while he was still Prince of Wales. He'd married Eleanor, the King's niece. The Despensers were certainly no more opportunists than Lancaster and his supporters. But the clue to the great opposition to them is in their rank. The Despensers may have gained lands, titles and influence, but theirs was not one of the great families. In the mediaeval pecking order only the great landowning families had the right so clearly to influence the King.

C❖They were especially unpopular among the Marcher lords, who were disturbed by their restless ambitions in South Wales. In 1321, the Welsh Marcher lords and the Lancastrian party joined hands with intent to procure the exile of the Despensers. Edward soon recalled them, and for once showed energy and resolution. By speed of movement he defeated first the Marcher lords and then, in the next year, the Northern barons under Lancaster at Boroughbridge in Yorkshire. Lancaster was beheaded by the King.

But tragedy was waiting for Edward II. His wife, Isabella, disgusted by her husband's passion for Hugh Despenser, became the lover and confederate of Roger Mortimer, one of the chief Marcher lords, who had escaped to France. Isabella had gone to France to negotiate the restoration of Gascony – seized by her brother, Charles IV of France – to England.

In 1324, perhaps with Despenser's authority, Isabella's estates were sequestrated. There was also a rumour that the young Hugh was attempting an annulment of her marriage to the King.

C❖She hit on the stroke of having her son, Prince Edward, sent over from England to do homage for Gascony. As soon as the fourteen-year-old prince, who as heir to the throne [and] could be used to legitimatize opposition to King Edward, was in her possession, she and Mortimer staged an invasion of England at the head of a large band of exiles.

So unpopular and precarious was Edward's government, that Isabella's triumph was swift and complete, and she and Mortimer were emboldened to depose him. . . . the Despensers were seized and hanged. For the King, a more terrible death was reserved. He was imprisoned in Berkeley Castle, and there, by hideous methods which left no mark on his skin, was slaughtered. His screams, as his bowels were burnt out by red-hot irons passed into his body, were heard outside the prison walls.

Edward was murdered because of his foolishness. He was weak, without political imagination or intelligence. He lacked dignity, he lacked thoughtfulness. And, in reality, he was no longer king when he was imprisoned. He'd already been forced to abdicate and his young son was crowned in his place.

The English monarchy was now threatened by the most serious events since the Conquest. For three years after the hideous murder of Edward II in Berkeley Castle in 1327, England was effectively ruled by the Queen's lover, Roger Mortimer.

From 1324, they had plotted the King's downfall, from France. Isabella had betrothed her fourteen-year-old son, the heir to the throne, to the Count of Hainault's daughter, Philippa, in return for soldiers. And on 25 January 1327, Edward II's abdication became official. His son was crowned King and Mortimer and Isabella had seized power.

C❖The reign of King Edward III passed through several distinct phases. In the first he was a minor and the land was ruled by his mother and her lover. . . . This Government, founded upon unnatural murder and representing only a faction in the nobility . . . was marked by concession and surrender both in France and in Scotland. . . . The guilty couple paid their way by successive abandonments of English interests. . . . In May 1328 the 'Shameful Treaty of Northampton', as it was called at the time, recognized [Robert the] Bruce as King north of the Tweed, and implied the abandonment of all the claims of Edward I in Scotland.

The Treaty of Northampton was a ratification of the Edinburgh Treaty of March 1328 and was decided when, a few months earlier, 100 Scottish knights had been asked to a Parliament to talk peace. The Scots were probably ready for some understanding and the documents of the settlement had been written, or at least drafted, under the influence of Bruce himself at the abbey at Holyrood. But the young King Edward appears to have seen the treaty as a total humiliation. The Lanercost Chronicle of the time makes clear the belief that he really wanted nothing to do with the shameful document, especially as it committed future kings to acknowledge Scotland's independence. It was also yet another document to be blessed by royal intermarriage.

❖Acting on the pestilent advice of his mother and Sir Roger Mortimer (they being the chief controllers of the King, who was barely fifteen years of age), he was forced to release the Scots by his public deed from all exaction, right, claim or demand of the overlordship of the Kingdom of Scotland on his part, and from any homage to be done to the Kings of England. He restored to them also that piece of the Cross of Christ which the Scots call Black Rood. But the people of London would in no wise allow to be taken away the Stone of Scone, whereon the Kings of Scotland used to be set at their coronation at Scone. All these objects, the illustrious King Edward, son of Henry, had caused to be brought away from Scotland when he reduced the Scots to his rule. Also the aforesaid young King gave his younger sister, my lady Joan of the Tower, in marriage to David, son of Robert de Brus, King of Scotland, he then being a boy five years old. All this was arranged by the King's mother, the Queen of England, who at this time governed the realm. The nuptials were solemnly celebrated at Berwick on the Sunday before the feast of St Mary Magdalene.

The princess, Joan of the Tower, would have been about seven years old.

C❖The anger which these events excited was widespread. The regime might however have maintained itself for some time but for Mortimer's quarrel with the barons. After the fall of the Despensers, Mortimer had taken care to put himself in the advantageous position they had occupied on the Welsh border, where he could exercise the special powers of government appropriate to the Marches. This and his exorbitant authority drew upon him the jealousies of the barons he had so lately led. His desire to make his position permanent caused him to seek, from a Parliament convened in October at Salisbury, the title of Earl of March, in addition to the office he already held of Justice of Wales for life. Mortimer attended, backed by his armed retainers. But it then appeared that many of the leading nobles were absent, and among them Henry, Earl of Lancaster, brother of the executed Thomas and uncle of the king, who held a counter-meeting in London. From Salisbury Mortimer, taking with him the young King, set forth in 1328 to ravage the lands of Lancaster, and in the disorders which followed he succeeded in checking the revolt.

It was plain that the barons themselves were too much divided to overthrow an odious but ruthless government. But Mortimer made an overweening mistake. In 1330 the Earl of Kent was deceived into thinking that Edward II was still alive. Kent made an ineffective attempt to restore him to liberty and was executed in March of that year.

Kent had been a supporter of Mortimer and the Queen. But he was also a supporter of Lancaster. When Mortimer and his troops attacked Lancaster's lands and invaded the earldom of Leicester, Lancaster was deserted by Edmund of Kent. Isabella and Mortimer had long decided that Kent was dangerous. He had friends; he had influence; he was fickle. And Edmund Woodstock, Earl of Kent, was the late king's half brother.

There's evidence that Isabella and Mortimer instructed their agents to drop hints, to lay false evidence, which they knew Edmund would pick up. The opening lines of *Chronicon Galfridi le Baker de Swynbroke* describe how easily the ploy, an elaborate one, succeeded.

❖Certain men pretended that King Edward [II], lately murdered, was living magnificently in Corfe Castle, but never wished to be seen by day. Wherefore they caused dancing to take place on many nights on the walls and turrets of the castle, bearing before them tapers and torches so that they might be seen by the yokels of the countryside, as if they guarded within some great king. The news spread that the King's father was alive. The Earl of Kent therefore sent a Dominican friar to find the truth of the matter who, thinking that he had corrupted the doorkeeper of the castle by bribes, was himself deceived. He was let in to hide by day and to see by night the person whom he wished to see. At night he was brought into the hall and there he saw, as he thought, Edward the King's father, sitting splendidly at supper.

He told the Earl of Kent what he believed he had seen. The earl therefore swore, in the presence of some whom he ought not to have trusted, that he would work to release his brother from prison.

The young King was forced to hold a Parliament at Winchester and that was the end of Edmund. Lancaster and his supporters quickly realized that unless they seized some sort of initiative, then they too would be victims of the treachery of Isabella and her lover.

C❖They decided to get their blow in first by joining Edward III. All eyes therefore were turned to the young King. When fifteen, in 1328, he had been married to Philippa of Hainault. In June 1330, a son was born to him: he felt himself now a grown man who must do his duty by the realm. But effective power still rested with Mortimer and the Queen Mother. In October Parliament sat at Nottingham. Mortimer and Isabella, guarded by an ample force, were lodged in the castle. . . . Mortimer and Isabella did not know the secrets of the castle. An underground passage led into its heart. Through this, on an October night, a small band of resolute men entered, surprised Mortimer in his chamber, which as usual was next to the Queen's, and, dragging them both along the subterranean way, delivered them to the King's officers. Mortimer, conducted to London, was brought before the peers, accused of the murder in Berkeley Castle and other crimes, and, after condemnation by the Lords, hanged on 29 November. Isabella was consigned by her son to perpetual captivity. Three thousand pounds a year was provided for her maintenance at various country manors . . . She died nearly thirty years later.

Towards the end of her long life, Isabella became a nun and was buried in a Franciscan church at Newgate. But despite the undermining of the realm by Isabella and Mortimer, by the coming of the age of Edward III Parliament assumed a growing importance and the views of knights and burgers of the kingdom were listened to. Public opinion and the emergence of a Parliament which would – very slowly, but increasingly – represent the common view became important. Chroniclers began to write about 'the Commons'.

CHAPTER TWELVE

1331–1376

---❖---

E very so often there's a time in history when much happens in a relatively short space of time. The long and vigorous reign of Edward III, and several years after it, was one such time. The Hundred Years' War began. The Black Prince won his spurs at the battle of Crécy. The Order of the Garter was founded. The Black Death came and went. Langland's *Piers Plowman* was written. The first Stuart King of Scotland came to the throne. Richard II came to the English throne. The Peasants' Revolt took place. Wat Tyler died, John of Gaunt was born. The Scots beat the English at Otterburn. And Chaucer finished *The Canterbury Tales*. And all this happened in the sixty years between 1337 and 1397. Edward III reigned until 1377.

C❖The guiding spirit of the new King was to revive the policy, assert the claims, and restore the glories of his grandfather. The quarrel with Scotland was resumed. Since Bannockburn, Robert Bruce had reigned unchallenged in the North. . . . Edward, the son of John Balliol, the nominee of Edward I, had become a refugee at the English court. Large elements in Scotland after Bruce's death, in 1329, looked to a reversal of fortune . . . In 1332 . . . Edward Balliol rallied his adherents and . . . defeated the infant David's Regent at Dupplin Moor. Balliol . . . was crowned at Scone. . . . In 1333 therefore Edward III advanced to besiege Berwick and routed the Scots at Halidon Hill. . . . Balliol had to cede to the English King not only Berwickshire but the whole of south eastern Scotland. In exacting this concession, Edward III had overshot the mark; he had damned Balliol's cause in the eyes of all Scots.

David II of Scotland, who had come to throne in 1329 and was to rule for more than forty years, fled to France in 1334. He stayed there for seven years while the French court encouraged the Scots in rebellion against England. The English therefore were more than usually annoyed with the French. This is important because English kings had found it hard to get much support, especially financial help, from the barons, every time they wanted to fight the French. But something was about to happen that would encourage the English magnates to dig deeply into their pockets.

C❖The wool trade with the Low Countries was . . . almost the sole form of wealth which rose above the resources of agriculture. The Flemish towns had attained a high economic development . . . [and] they depended for their prosperity upon the wool of England. But the aristocracy under the Counts of Flanders nursed French sympathies. . . . Repeated obstructions were placed by the Counts of Flanders upon the wool trade . . . The mercantile element in the English Parliament . . . pleaded vehemently for action.

In 1336 Edward . . . decreed an embargo on all exports of English wool, thus producing a furious crisis in the Netherlands. The townspeople rose against the feudal aristocracy. . . . The victorious burghers, threatened by aristocratic and French revenge, looked to England for aid, and their appeals met with a hearty and deeply interested response.

Edward had to show that there was more to the dispute than the price of wool. And indeed there was. Edward had made a claim to the throne of France after the death of the heirless Charles IV. In 1331 he dropped the claim, or rather, he laid it aside. But when, in 1337, Philip of France confiscated Gascony, Edward dusted off his claim to the French throne. And to keep people and Parliament on his side, Edward III published his manifesto, telling everyone the reasons for the coming war.

❖These are the offers made to the King of France by the King of England, to avoid war. First the King sent to the King of France various solemn messages, begging him to return to him lands which he is withholding from him; but the King of France did nothing, until, at last, he promised that if the King of England would come in his own person, he would do him justice, grace and favour.

Philip at first refused to see Edward, then took even more of Edward's possessions. Edward then claimed that he made the ultimate offers to the French monarch, offers which even casual students of this period will find familiar.

❖First, the marriage of his eldest son, now Duke of Cornwall, with the daughter of the King of France, without taking anything for the marriage. The marriage of his sister, now Countess of Guelders, with his son, together with a very great sum of money. The marriage of his brother, the Earl of Cornwall, with any lady of the royal blood. Because the King of England was given to understand that the King of France wished to undertake a Crusade to the Holy Land, and wished to have him in his company, the King of England offered to go with a large force with him in the Crusade; provided that, however, before he set off, the French King should make him full restitution of all his lands. Then he offered to go with him on condition that, before he went, the French King should restore half, or a certain part of his lands. Then that he would go with the French King if he would make such restitution on his return from the Holy Land. But the King of France would accept none of these offers; but, seeking his opportunities, busied himself in aid and maintenance of the Scots, the enemies of the King of England, attempting to delay him by the Scottish war, so that he would have no power to pursue his rights elsewhere.

This manifesto was given to the most important men in the land.

C❖Philip VI looked first to the sea. . . . All the resources of the French marine were strained to produce a fleet; even hired Genoese galleys appeared in the French harbours. In Normandy, plans were mooted for a counter-invasion which should repeat the exploits of William the Conqueror. But Edward had not neglected the sea-power. His interest in the Navy won him from Parliament early in his reign the title of 'King of the Sea'. He was able to marshal a fleet equal in vessels and superior in men. A great sea battle was necessary before the transport of the English army to France and its maintenance there was feasible. In the summer of 1340, the hostile navies met off Sluys, and a struggle of nine hours ensued.

The chronicler, Geoffrey le Baker, reports what happened.

❖After nine o'clock, when he [Edward III] had the wind and the sun at his back and the flow of the tide with him, with his [260] ships in three columns, he gave his enemy the challenge they wished for. An iron shower of quarrels from crossbows and arrows from long bows brought death to thousands of people. Stones hurled from the turrets of masts dashed out the brains of many. The first and second squadrons were captured, and dusk was falling, so the English lay off until morning because the night was so dark and they were so weary. During the night thirty ships of the third squadron fled and one great ship called the *James of Dieppe* tried to take with it a certain ship of Sandwich, which belonged to the prior of Christ Church, Canterbury. The crew of that ship defended themselves manfully and their fight lasted throughout the night. In the morning, the Normans were defeated and the Englishmen found in the captured ship more than 400 slain. The number of the enemy killed and drowned exceeded 25,000. Of the English, 4000 were slain.

It was the prelude to a grisly war that would preoccupy Kings of England and France for more than its 'hundred' years. And the first great land battle was at

Crécy. The Battle of Crécy took place in 1346, in the first decade of the Hundred Years' War.

The English beat the French at Crécy, but Crécy was important for two other reasons. It cleared Edward III's way to Calais and the result was that Calais became an English colony for 200 years. Secondly, it proved that with the tactical use of longbow-men, mounted knights would no longer be the force they had been throughout the feudal era. And there's an aside. Edward III decreed that wool could only be exported through certain ports so that his officials could tax it. He needed the taxes to finance the war. These ports, and the system of control itself, were known as the Staple. It's from this system that we derive the modern expressions 'staple' and 'staple export', etc.

C❖By taxing the wool exports which passed through his [Edward III's] hands at the Staple port, he was assured of an important revenue independent of Parliament. Moreover the wool merchants who held the monopoly formed a corporation interested in the war, dependent on the King, and capable of lending him money in return for considerate treatment. This development was not welcomed by Parliament, where the smaller wool merchants were increasingly represented.

On 12 July 1346 the English had reached the walls of Paris. Philip of France, perhaps thinking that Edward intended to by-pass Paris and head on to Gascony, had an uncertain start, but he had superior forces, and the English withdrew. The war then continued in country which became grimly familiar in the early years of the twentieth century – Amiens, the Somme, Picardy, Abbeville – until the two armies fought themselves to a standstill, the English lucky to escape defeat. But they still could not get back to the Channel coast without another fight: Crécy.

C❖The King gathered his chiefs to supper and afterwards to prayer. . . . No other resolve was open than to fight at enormous odds. The King, and the Prince of Wales, afterwards famous as the Black Prince, received all the offices of religion, and Edward prayed that the impending battle should at least leave him unstripped of honour. With the daylight, he marshalled about 11,000 men in three divisions. Mounted upon a small palfrey, with a white wand in his hand, with his splendid surcoat of crimson and gold above his armour, he rode along the ranks, 'encouraging and entreating the army that they would guard his honour and defend his right'. . . . Their position on the open rolling downs enjoyed few advantages, but the forest of Crécy on their flanks afforded protection and the means of a final stand.

On the French side, which included kings and princes, the King of Bohemia, who incidentally was blind, claimed the right to command the first division and even prophesied that he would be killed in battle. He was. The King of Majorca, so confident of victory for the French, claimed that when the battle was over, he had the right to Edward III as his prisoner. But when others took up this demand for selective prisoners, Philip of France was worried that they were over-confident. He ordered that the great banner of Oriflamme should be flown. This was the banner of St Denis, traditionally blessed by the abbot of St Denis before a war. Once flown, no prisoners were to be taken. Edward responded by unfurling his banner of the Dragon to remind everyone, especially the French, that the English under his command would give no quarter. The chronicler, Geoffrey le Baker, has left us an account of the battle. A few extracts imply something of its atmosphere and ferocity.

❖The . . . impressive multitude of the French [were] continually increased by fresh arrivals. About sundown, the first charge was made by the French with resounding trumpets, drums, and kettle-drums with strident clarions; and with shouting almost like thunder, the crossbow-men of the French advanced, but none of their quarrels reached the English. At the tremendous clamour of the crossbow-men, the English archers were called forth and riddled their adversaries with arrows. When they saw that their crossbow-men were not harming the English, the French men-at-arms mounted on warhorses, rode down the crossbow-men, standing to the number of 7000 between them and the English, crushing them under the feet of their horses, rushing forward to show . . . how brave they were. So anguished were the cries of pain from the trampled that those in the rear of the French thought it was the English who were being slain. Upon hearing all this, the French pressed forward on the heels of those in front; in this ill-considered ardour, the most conspicuous were raw young knights, in whom the army abounded, all panting for the great honour of capturing the King of England.

Edward was not going to make the same mistake as the French. His archers, superior to the French crossbow-men, were set along the flanks so that they shot across from the sides of his army. And perhaps remembering the experience of the Scottish campaigns, when English knights tumbled and were slain in pits, the English now quickly dug holes in front of their positions.

❖A great outcry rose to the stars from the miserable and trampled crossbow-men and from the horses pierced by the arrows. The French became confused. Fighting with the English men-at-arms, they were beaten down with battle-axes, lances and swords, and in the middle many Frenchmen were crushed to death without any wound but by the weight of numbers.

In such a woeful encounter, Edward of Woodstock, the King's eldest son, being then sixteen years old, showed his valour to the French, piercing horses, laying low the riders, shattering helmets and breaking spears, helping his men, and showing an example to all. The French repeatedly changed their front line, bringing up fresh hordes. These continual accessions of strength kept the Prince and his companions so closely engaged that the great mass of the enemy compelled him to fight on his knees. Then someone rode to the King, his father, imploring help. He was sent with twenty knights to help the Prince, and found him and his men leaning on spears and swords, and taking breath and resting quietly on long mounds of corpses. . . . The total number of knights and men of superior dignity killed in this battle exceeded 4000. No one troubled to count the others who were slain.

In the morning King Philip of France and a small retinue escaped to Amiens. They left behind them the bodies of the King of Bohemia, the Counts of Blois, Flanders, Alençon, Harcourt, Auxerre, Aumale, Savoy, Moreuil, Nevers and many more. And Geoffrey le Baker recounts, if his word can be relied upon, that only forty English died in the two days of fighting. Edward reached Calais by the beginning of September, and laid siege to the city.

C❖Calais presented itself to English eyes as the hive of that swarm of privateers who were the endless curse of the Channel. Here on the nearest point of the Continent, England had long felt a festering sore. . . . The siege lasted for nearly a year. Every new art of war was practised by land; the bombards flung cannon balls against the ramparts with terrifying noise. By sea, elaborate barriers of piles stopped the French light craft, which sought to evade the sea blockade by creeping along the coast. All reliefs by sea and land failed. But the effort of maintaining the siege strained the resources of the King to an extent we can hardly conceive. When the winter came, his soldiers demanded to go home, and the fleet was on the verge of mutiny. In England everyone complained, and Parliament was morose in demeanour and reluctant in supply. . . . Calais held out for eleven months, but famine left no choice to the besieged. They sued for terms. . . . Calais, then, was the fruit, and the sole territorial fruit so far, of the exertions . . . of the whole power of England in the war with France.

King David of Scotland attempted to help his allies, the French, but, in 1346, two months after the Battle of Crécy, he was beaten at Neville's Cross, captured and imprisoned in the Tower. This English victory removed the Scottish threat for a generation.

When Edward returned from France, he officially founded what has been called the 'most brilliant inspiration of the Age of Chivalry', the Order, the Garter. The idea seems to have come to him at the end of a grand tournament at Windsor in 1344, two years before Crécy. He's said to have been so inspired by the occasion that he swore to set up if not a new Camelot, then his own Round Table of his closest knights. How the garter became the symbol of this order is disputed. But it may well have had something to do with the Countess of Salisbury and the siege of Calais. Edward was in love with the countess and, at a celebration ball at the end of the siege of Calais, the countess is said to have dropped her garter. The King picked it up and bound it to his knee. The whole court knew of his love for the countess and there was much 'sniggering and tittering'. The King is said to have rebuked them with 'Honi soit qui mal y pense'. The Garter became the symbol, the French became the motto. Geoffrey le Baker recorded the Order's purpose.

❖A fellowship, a college of knights to represent how they ought to be united in all Chances and various Turns of Fortune; co-partners in both peace and war, assistant to one another in all serious and dangerous exploits: and thro' the whole course of their lives to shew fidelity and friendliness to one another.

And he describes these chivalrous knights, twenty-six only including the King, as they gathered at Windsor.

❖All were clad in gowns of russet . . . wearing the . . . garters on their right legs, and wearing mantels of blue with escutcheons of St George . . . in honour of the holy martyr, to whom they specially dedicated their noble fraternity, [they called] their company that of St George of the Garter.

St George had replaced the saintly Edward the Confessor as patron saint of England. But no saint could protect the people from a catastrophe in that same year, 1348. The Black Death reached England and for twenty or so years, it came, went, returned, retreated, returned again and went. It was terrible.

C❖Christendom has no catastrophe equal to the Black Death. . . . The plague entered Europe through the Crimea, and in the course of twenty years destroyed at least one third of its entire population. The privations of the people, resulting from ceaseless baronial and dynastic wars, presented an easy conquest to disease. The records in England tell more by their silence than by the shocking figures which confront us wherever records were kept. We read of lawsuits where all parties died before the cases could be heard; of monasteries where half the inmates perished; of dioceses where the surviving clergy could scarcely perform the last offices for their flocks and for their brethren; of the Goldsmiths' Company, which had four Masters in a year. . . . The character of the pestilence was appalling. The disease itself, with its frightful symptoms, the swift onset, the blotches, the hardening of the glands under the armpit or in the groin, these swellings which no poultice could resolve, these tumours which, when lanced, gave no relief, the horde of virulent carbuncles which followed the dread harbingers of death, the delirium, the insanity which attended its triumph, the blank spaces which opened on all sides in human society, stunned and for a time destroyed the life and faith of the world.

This England to which the plague arrived, was a changing but not always happy land. It was a land of wood, corn and beasts. Wood was used as the main source of fuel, building and manufacturing. There were great hardwood forests throughout the kingdom and there were corn belts in East Anglia and the South Midlands even then. There were large herds and flocks of livestock. Large beasts were needed to cart goods and to plough. Dairy farming was increasing and sheep, apart from their value in the lucrative wool trade, were invaluable as a source of manure for grain cultivation. But this was not an idyllic rural England. Floods, which had covered much of Europe, brought famine to a peasantry already weakened by indifferent nutrition and the demands of war. Sheep were drowned in their thousands. Crops, in spite of efforts of improve yields, were often poorly grown and disappeared. Prices dropped.

One result was that big landlords rented off parcels of farms, therefore tenant farming increased even if it was at subsistence level. The people lived in small groupings. Towns were small. Probably only London and York had populations of more than 10,000. Yet hamlets and villages were so well established that all the rural communities that exist today, existed in the fourteenth century.

But the conditions in which people lived, their general constitution, their ignorance of preventative medicine, the entire lack of antidotes, and, most of all, the viciousness of the plague, all meant that life for many in the middle of the fourteenth century was miserable. The effects of the plague were devastating and the consequences far reaching. The *Chronicon Henrici Knighton* reports other, non-human, disasters.

❖There was a great murrain of sheep everywhere in the realm, so that in one place more than 5000 died in a single pasture. They rotted so much that neither beast nor bird would approach them. And there was great cheapness of everything for fear of death. . . . A man could have a horse which was formerly worth forty shillings for half a mark, that is one sixth of that amount. A big fat ox he could have for four shillings, a heifer for six pence, a sheep for three pence, a large pig for five pence, and a stone of wool for nine pence. Sheep and oxen strayed through the fields and among the crops, and there was none to drive them off and none to collect them. They perished in unaccounted numbers for lack of shepherds. There was no recollection of such severe mortality since the time of Vortigern, King of the Romans, in whose day, as Bede testifies, the living did not suffice to bury the dead.

While this was happening south of the border those north of the border, who had been looking for an opportunity to raid the weakening kingdom, believed their time had come. They believed the plague was on their side, as the *Chronicon Henrici Knighton* records.

❖The Scots, hearing of the cruel pestilence in England, imagined that it had come about at the hand of an avenging God, and gathered at Selkirk forest with the intention of invading the kingdom of England. There the horrible death overtook them, and their ranks were thinned by sudden and terrible mortality, so that in a short time 5000 had perished. . . . At this time there was so great a scarcity of priests that many churches were left destitute, lacking divine offices, masses, matins, vespers, and sacraments. A chaplain could scarcely be obtained to serve in any parish for less than ten pounds or ten marks, whereas when there was an abundance of priests, a chaplain could be obtained for four or five marks, or even two marks.

Half the clergy in Winchester, Norwich, Ely and Exeter died. Many of the houses and mansions of England became uninhabited and fell into ruin. Villages emptied. Labourers and servants, those most vulnerable to the plague, died in such great numbers that the estates could not be worked. Landlords had to give up rents from tenants and waive penalties for non-payment. There was no one to pay. There was also a feeling among the people that their Church and their God had betrayed them.

C❖The Church . . . was wounded grievously in spiritual power. If a God of Mercy ruled the world, what sort of rule was this? Such was the challenging thought that swept upon the survivors. Weird sects sprang into existence, and plague-haunted cities saw the gruesome procession of flagellants, each lashing his forerunner to a dismal dirge, and ghoulish practices glare at us from the broken annals. It seemed to be the death rattle of the race.

But of course it was not. When the Black Death struck for the first time, in 1348, survivors remarried and had children. But, in 1360, when the plague returned – albeit in a weaker form – those very children would have been the most vulnerable. Indeed this plague's main victims appear to have been children. Eight years later there was a further outbreak, and a decade later yet another, this time mainly in the north of the country.

C❖But at length the plague abated its force. The tumours yielded to fomentations.
Recoveries became more frequent; the resistant faculties of life revived. . . .
The calamity which fell upon mankind reduced their numbers and
darkened their existence without abating their quarrels. The war between
England and France continued in a broken fashion, and the Black Prince,
the most renowned warrior in Europe, became a freebooter.

By 1355, the war with France was back in full swing. The Black Prince defeated
the French at Poitiers the following year, and captured a rather foolhardy John
II of France. In 1357, the King of Scotland, David II, who had been under arrest
in the Tower for ten years, was released. And around 1362 Long Will, or
William Langland as he was known, produced the first version of *Piers Plowman*.
It is full of high towers of truth, dungeons of wrong, bribery, reason and
conscience. It was, probably, an accurate reflection of fourteenth-century
England.

One of the grander victims of plague was Edward III's wife, Philippa. She
died in 1369 in what would have been the third of the plagues or the Black
Death. Philippa wasn't an Isabella or an Eleanor of Aquitaine, both evil and
therefore much recorded. She was brought from Hainault and married off to
Prince Edward when he was fifteen and she was just a child. But Philippa grew
into a loving and loyal regal figure, who was committed to her husband and
the family. She bore her husband fourteen children, two of whom died in
infancy. The seven surviving sons and five daughters were married off, and
well. Of the sons, all seemingly as warlike and sporting as their father, the two
most famous are Edward the Black Prince, who had commanded with such
distinction at Crécy, and John, Earl of Leicester, Lincoln and Derby, Duke of
Lancaster and born in Ghent and thus known as John of Gaunt. And so when
the Hundred Years' War resumed, it was no surprise to find these two princes
in the line.

C❖In 1335 King Edward obtained from Parliament substantial grants for the
renewal of active war. An ambitious strategy was adopted. The Black Prince
would advance northward from the English territories of Gascony and
Aquitaine towards the Loire. His young brother, John of Gaunt . . . struck
in from Brittany. The two forces were to join for a main decision. But all
this miscarried and the Black Prince found himself, with forces shrunk to
about 4000 men, of whom however nearly a half were the dreaded archers,
forced to retire with growing urgency before the advance of a French army
20,000 strong. . . . At Poitiers, the Prince was brought to bay. . . . King John
of France was resolved to avenge Crécy and finish the war at a stroke. Forced
against all reason and all odds to fight, the haggard band of English
marauders who had carried pillage and arson far and wide, were drawn up

in array and position chosen with consummate insight. The flanks were secured by forests; the archers lined a hedgerow and commanded the only practicable passage.

The English may have been outnumbered, but the terrain, wooded, hedged, and amongst hills of vines, was on the side of defenders. And the French King helped the English cause. He attacked the hedge. Or to be more exact, he sent in cavalry to make a break in it.

C❖The French nobility left their horses at the rear. The Black Prince had all his knights mounted. . . . The French chivalry encumbered by their mail, plodded ponderously forward amid vineyards and scrub. Many fell before the arrows, but the arrows would not have been enough at the crisis. It was the English spear and axe men who charged in the old style upon ranks disordered by their fatigue of movement and the accidents of the ground. At the same time, in admirable concert, a strong detachment of mounted knights, riding round the French left flank, struck in upon the harassed and already disordered attack. The result was slaughter as large and a victory as complete as Crécy, but with even greater gains. The whole French army was driven into ruin. King John and the flower of his nobility were captured or slain. . . . [He himself] was carried to London. Like King David of Scotland before him, he was placed in the Tower . . . in May 1360, the Treaty of Brétigny was concluded. England acquired, in addition to her old possession of Gascony, the whole of Henry II's possessions in Aquitaine in full sovereignty, Edward I's inheritance of Ponthieu, and the famous port and city of Calais, which last was held for nearly 200 years. A ransom was fixed for King John at three million gold crowns . . . This was eight times the annual revenue of the English Crown in time of peace.

But this all sounds much better than it actually was. The Battle of Poitiers was in 1356. The Treaty of Brétigny was not agreed until four years later. Edward III had probably expected the French crown for himself, and although he still had the French King in the Tower, he could no longer bargain from such strength as he once thought. And the French never did come up with the three million gold crowns. The French King was released, but when the arrangements for his regal bail went awry, he insisted on returning to London. And that's where he died, in 1364.

C❖The years of the war with France are important in the history of Parliament. The need for money drove the Crown and its officials to summoning it frequently. This led to rapid and important developments. One of the main functions of the representatives of the shires and boroughs was to petition for the redress of grievances, local and national, and to draw the attention of the King and his Council to urgent matters. The stress of war forced the government to take notice of these petitions of the Commons of England, and during the reign of Edward III, the procedure of collective petition, which had started under Edward II, made progress. The fact that the Commons now petitioned as a body in a formal way . . . distinguishes the lower House from the rest of Parliament. Under Edward I, the Commons were not an essential element in a Parliament, but under Edward III they assumed a position distinct, vital, and permanent. They had their own clerk who drafted their petitions and their rejoinders to the Crown's replies. The separation of the Houses now appears.

So the Houses of Parliament, Lords and Commons, date from the fourteenth century. And in Edward III's time many of those Parliamentary offices which would be recognized at Westminster today had their origins.

C❖The Lords had come to regard themselves not only as the natural counsellors of the Crown, but as enjoying the right of separate consultation within the framework of Parliament itself. In 1343 the prelates and magnates met in the White Chamber at Westminster, and the knights and the burgesses adjourned to the Painted Chamber to discuss the business of the day. Here, in this Parliament, for the first time, the figure of a Speaker emerged. He was not on this occasion a Member of the House, and for some time to come the Commons generally spoke through an appointed deputation. But by the end of the reign, the role of the Speaker was recognized, and the Crown became anxious to secure its own nominees for this important and prominent office.

In 1377 Sir Thomas Hungerford became the first Speaker designate, but this still wasn't a Parliament fully established and meeting Monday to Friday in the Palace of Westminster. This Parliament still had to be called together, summoned. And it didn't have to be in London, and frequently wasn't. It was often an expensive and elaborate business to attend. Eyre & Spottiswoode's *English Historical Documents* includes a record of the expenses of four representatives who travelled from London to a Parliament at Cambridge. It details the sorts of comforts politicians of the day expected.

❖Expenses incurred in attending Parliament by Adam Bamme, Henry Vanner, William Tonge, and John Clenhound:
    In the first place: for timber and carpentry, tilers and daubers, in preparing the house for their lodging, as well the chambers as the hall, buttery, kitchen, and stables; and for making stools and forms throughout,

and for carting out the rubbish, such house being quite ruinous; for payment made good to the man of the house for the said lodging, six pounds nine shillings.

Also for firewood, charcoal, turf, and sedge, five pounds thirteen shillings.

Also, for the hire of horses, and for hay and oats, and for straw for the beds, as well as for litter for the horses; and for horse shoeing, twelve pounds fifteen shillings and seven pence.

Also for expenses incurred in riding on horseback to Cambridge, and back; and for carriage of wine and all harness thither and back, seven pounds sixteen shillings and eight pence.

Also, two pipes of red wine taken thither from London, and for other wine bought at Cambridge, nine pounds two shillings. Also, for clothes for them and their servants, arrayed in like suit, twenty-two pounds and fifteen shillings.

Also expended at Cambridge throughout the time of the Parliament on bread, ale, flesh-meat, fish, candles, sauce, the laundry man, and in gifts to minstrels of the King and of other lords, together with divers other outlayes [sic] made, twenty-three pounds, five shillings and nine pence.

In the same year that Queen Philippa died, 1369, English society appeared exhausted. The effects of the Black Death lingered. The Pope was established in Avignon and was seen as anti-English, or at least pro-French. The Church was corrupt, and the Oxford theologian, John Wyclif, emerged as the man who led the renewal of Christianity. Wyclif committed the unthinkable act: the translation of the Bible into English. And within less than a decade England had changed step. The Black Prince, the heir to the throne, died, a sad, broken figure, no longer the dashing prince in black armour. The King, in his widowhood and approaching his dotage, took up with Alice Perrers, a former lady-in-waiting to Queen Philippa, and a political intriguer.

C❖The long reign had reached its dusk. The glories of Crécy and Poitiers had faded. The warlike King, whose ruling passions were power and fame . . . was now, in old age, a debtor to time and fortune. . . . He saw the wide conquests which his sword had made in France melt like snow at Easter. . . . The King, at length worn down by war, business, and pleasure, subsided into senility. He had reached the allotted span. . . . In 1376 the Black Prince expired, leaving a son not ten years old as heir apparent to the throne. King Edward III's large share of life narrowed sharply at its end. Mortally stricken, he retired to Sheen Lodge where Alice . . . encouraged him to dwell on tournaments, the chase and wide plans when he should recover. But hostile chroniclers have it that when the stupor preceding death engulfed the King, she took the rings from his fingers and other moveable property and departed. . . . All accounts, alas! confirm that King Edward died deserted by all, and that only the charity of a local priest procured him the protection and warrant of the Church in his final expedition.

Edward III had been King for more than fifty years. He's said to have been an adventurer, unscrupulous and vain. He was certainly dissipated, and maybe his pre-senile dementia was the price he paid. Yet he honoured the chivalrous and warrior hopes of his country. He built a military reputation for England and he balanced Church and Parliament, often not very well, but he corrupted neither. Fourteenth-century English men and women liked him. His wife was devoted to him. His sons did not intrigue against him. He may have died alone but the people of England mourned his passing.

CHAPTER THIRTEEN

1377–1399

——— ❖ ———

Richard II came to the throne in 1377. He was just ten years old, and the eleventh King of England since William the Conqueror, almost 300 years earlier. Richard wasn't supposed to be King at all. The Black Prince, Edward III's eldest son, should have been King, but he died before his father and Richard was the Black Prince's eldest son. And so it was the ten-year-old Richard who swore, with childlike firmness, that he would solemnly preserve the laws and customs conceded by ancient and devout kings before him. It was John of Gaunt, Duke of Lancaster, and the King's uncle, who carried the sword, *Curtana*, at the coronation. As a symbol, *Curtana* was, and has remained, all-important in the coronation procession. It is a blunted sword, the sword of mercy. Therefore the bearer of *Curtana* also carried the authority of the King's highest prerogative, mercy. The importance was not lost on those gathered at the coronation. It was John of Gaunt who became Steward of England and ran the Regency for the boy-King. But John of Gaunt was unpopular with the businessmen of the City of London, the hierarchy of the clergy, and the Commoners of Parliament.

John of Gaunt led the anti-clerical party in England. Fundamentally, he was trying to re-establish the authority of the crown and the Royal Family. In 1371, six years before Edward III's death, John of Gaunt managed the removal of both the chancellor and the treasurer: the charge was maladministration. Their replacements were less efficient and even more corrupt.

Five years later, Parliament – since called the Good Parliament of 1376 – attacked the government and, in particular, Gaunt's cronies. But Gaunt had another Parliament called, fixed it by packing it with his supporters, and reversed all the decisions of the Good Parliament. John of Gaunt was able to use Parliament for his own purposes because, in the fourteenth century, parliaments were councils, meetings that were called only by the monarch, usually to get money. So the England of the late 1370s and early 1380s was leaderless, overtaxed and at war, and not very successfully so.

C❖Throughout the summer of 1381 there was a general ferment. . . . In May the violence broke out in Essex. It was started by an attempt to make a second and more stringent collection of the poll-tax which had been levied in the previous year.

The poll tax had been levied 150 years earlier. It comes from the mediaeval word 'polle' or head. The fourteenth-century poll tax had traumatic effects. People avoided paying for every member of the family and when the returns showed that less had been collected than anticipated, household assessments were made: a sort of fourteenth-century means test. Furthermore, since 1351, the Statute of Labourers had frozen wages to pre-Black Death rates. This Statute and the new poll tax were the root causes of what is now called the Peasants' Revolt which occurred in 1381.

C❖In Kent . . . the peasants marched through Rochester and Maidstone, burning manorial and taxation records on their way. At Maidstone they released the agitator, John Ball, from the episcopal prison, and were joined by a military adventurer with gifts and experience of leadership, Wat Tyler.
  The royal Council was bewildered and inactive. Early in June the main body of rebels from Essex and Kent moved on London. Here they found support . . . the alderman in charge of London Bridge did nothing to defend it, and Aldgate was opened treacherously to a band of Essex rioters. For three days the city was in confusion. Foreigners were murdered; two members of the council, Simon Sudbury, the Archbishop of Canterbury and Chancellor, and Sir Robert Hales, the Treasurer, were dragged from the Tower beheaded on Tower Hill; the Savoy palace of John of Gaunt was burnt; Lambeth and Southwark were sacked. . . . But the loyal citizen body rallied round the mayor and at Smithfield the young King faced the rebel leaders. Among the insurgents there seems to have been general loyalty to the sovereign. Their demands were reasonable but disconcerting. They asked for the repeal of oppressive statutes, for the abolition of villeinage, and for the division of Church property. In particular, they asserted that no man ought to be a serf or do labour services to a *seigneur*, but pay four pence an acre a year for his land and not have to serve any man against his will, but only by agreement.

King Richard, who was just fourteen, called everyone together at Smithfield, or Smooth-field, as it was. And by St Bartholomew's, a house of church canons, he stopped. In front of him on the east side were the people, the Commoners, the Commons. A chronicler of the time reports what happened.

❖And when he was called by the mayor of London, William Walworth, Wat Tyler of Maidstone came to the King in haughty fashion, mounted on a little horse so that he could be seen by the Commons. And when he had dismounted, he half bent his knee and took the King by the hand, and shook his arm forcibly and roughly saying to him, 'Brother, be of good comfort and joyful, for you shall have within the next fortnight 40,000 more of the Commons than you have now and we shall be good companions.' And the King said to Wat, 'Why will you not go back to your country?'

Wat Tyler (whose name was also spelled Tyghler) listed their demands and the King appears to have said that, within reason, everything they wanted would be granted. He then told Tyler to go home to Kent and to lead his revolutionaries out of London.

❖At this time, a yeoman of Kent, who was among the King's retinue, asked to see Wat, the leader of the Commons; and when Wat was pointed out, he said openly that he was the greatest thief and robber in all Kent. Wat heard these words and commanded him to come out to him, shaking his head at him in a sign of malice. Wat would have run him through with his dagger and killed him in the King's presence.

Because of this, the mayor of London, William Walworth by name, reasoned with the said Wat for his violent behaviour and contempt done in the King's presence, and arrested him. And the said Wat struck the mayor with his dagger in the stomach with great anger, but as God would have it, the mayor was wearing armour. The said mayor drew his cutlass and struck back at the said Wat and gave him a deep cut on the neck and then a great cut on the head. A yeoman of the King's household drew his sword and ran Wat two or three times through, mortally wounding him. And the said Wat spurred his horse, crying to the Commons to avenge him, and the horse carried him four score paces, and there he fell to the ground half dead.

The Commons did not come to Wat's help and meanwhile the mayor took to his horse and to the City. The City of London was, even then, split into twenty-four wards. Each had a watch commander, and each commander was instructed to tell everyone to arm themselves and rush to the King's side at Smithfield.

❖And when the lord mayor came to Smithfield, he could not find the said Wat Tyler. He was told that Tyler had been carried to the hospital of the poorfolks near St Bartholomew's and was put to bed in the chamber of the master of the hospital. And the mayor went thither and found him and had him carried to Smithfield in the presence of his fellows, and there he was beheaded. And the mayor caused his head to be set upon a pole and carried before him to the King. And when the Commons saw their leader, Wat Tyler, was dead in such a manner, they fell like men discomforted, crying to the King for mercy.

Tyler received such support in London only partly because of his own cause. The jealousies between trade guilds within the City meant that many Londoners supported him. But the King cancelled the promised reforms, by proclamation, so the Peasants' Revolt failed to achieve its objectives, although it did kill the poll tax. But the uprisings of 1381 showed just how much the people had lost confidence in those who governed them, and in John of Gaunt in particular.

At the same time the influence of a new aristocracy – one that had been developing for at least a generation – was growing. A handful of families, all connected by blood with the throne: the Lancasters, the Yorks, the Gloucesters, Cornwall and Clarence, were beginning to make their mark. Yet it was still the King's Court and royal judges who restored order when the feudal classes lost their nerve and, by 1389, the King was in his early twenties and, at last, had begun to rule for himself.

John of Gaunt left England to pursue his claim to the kingdom of Castile, a claim he thought himself entitled to through his second wife, Constance of Castile, the heiress daughter of Pedro the Cruel. He left his son, Henry Bolingbroke, in charge of his English estates, estates inherited when his first wife, Blanche of Lancaster, died.

C❖It was not till he was twenty that Richard determined to be complete master of his Council, and in particular to escape the control of his uncles. . . . His Household and Court around it were deeply interested in his assumption of power. . . . Its chiefs were the Chancellor, Michael de la Pole, Chief Justice Tresilian, and Alexander Neville, Archbishop of York. Behind them Simon Burley, Richard's tutor and close intimate, was probably the guide. A group of younger nobles threw in their fortunes with the Court. Of these the head was Robert de Vere, Earl of Oxford, who now played a part resembling that of Gaveston under Edward II. The King . . . spread his favours among his adherents and de Vere was soon created Duke of Ireland. This was plainly a political challenge to the magnates of the Council. Ireland was a reservoir of men and supplies, beyond the control of Parliament and the nobility, which could be used for the mastery of England.

The accumulation of Household and Government offices by the clique around the King and his effeminate favourite affronted the feudal party, and to some extent the national spirit. . . . A purge of the Civil Service, supposed to be the source alike of the King's errors and of his strength, was instituted; and we may note that Geoffrey Chaucer, his equerry, but famous for other reasons, lost his two posts in the Customs.

When the commissioners presently compelled the King to dismiss his personal friends, Richard, in deep distress, withdrew from London. . . . He sought to marshal his forces for civil war . . .

And so it was that Thomas of Woodstock, Duke of Gloucester, the youngest and most ambitious brother of the absent John of Gaunt, joined forces with the young Henry Bolingbroke, and with Mowbray of Nottingham and the Earls of Arundel and Warwick, and marched on London. They called themselves the Lords Appellant and accused Richard's closest advisers of treason.

One of those accused, de Vere, the King's favourite, raised an army in Cheshire and marched to the King's rescue. They didn't get very far. Just before Christmas Day, 1387, troops led by Gloucester and Bolingbroke scattered them at Radcot Bridge in Oxfordshire. The Lords Appellant were in command and, in February 1388, they summoned what became known as the Merciless Parliament. It was a good name. The King's friends, Tresilian, Burley and Brember, were executed: hanged, drawn and quartered.

C❖Only the person of the King was respected, and that by the narrowest of margins. . . . We must suppose that this treatment produced a marked impression upon his [Richard's] mind. . . . He brooded upon his wrongs, and also upon his past mistakes. . . . He laid his plans for revenge and for his own rights with far more craft than before. For a year there was a sinister lull.

That lull was, according to Thomas Walsingham's *Historia Anglicana*, broken in the month of May 1389.

❖The King, led by the advice of certain whisperers, convoked the magnates and many worthy men of the realm together, and suddenly entered the council house, where his magnates were awaiting him. Seating himself, he asked them how old he was. They replied that he was now twenty-two years old. 'Then,' he said, 'I am full age to govern my house and household and also my kingdom. It seems to me unjust that my state should be worse than that of the last person in the kingdom. Surely any heir of my kingdom, when he has reached the age of twenty-one years and his parent is dead, is permitted to conduct his own affairs freely. Why therefore should this be denied to me when it is conceded by law to anyone of lower rank?'

The astonished barons replied that nothing ought to be subtracted from his rights, and that he ought to have the rule of his kingdom, which was due to him as his right. At this the King exclaimed: 'Well! Know that I have for long been ruled by tutors; and it was not possible for me to act at all, or almost at all, without them. Now henceforth, I will remove those from my council, and, as heir of lawful age, I will appoint whom I will to my council and conduct my own affairs. And I order that in the first place, the chancellor should resign to me his seal.'

For the next eight years, England was well and quietly governed. John of Gaunt returned from Castile and perhaps his still-great presence reduced the influence of the Lords Appellant. In 1394, John of Gaunt went to Ireland. The English domain, known as the Pale, was yet again under threat. The 1366 Statute of Kilkenny forbade English settlers to intermarry, or adopt Irish customs or language. But the English authority ran only around Dublin, including Meath, Louth and Kilkenny. Certainly by the sixteenth century, this area was commonly known as the Pale, as was the English area around Calais. Hence anything outside the domain was 'beyond the Pale'.

For all his weaknesses, Richard saw that the difficulties of Ireland had as much to do with the English administration as with the eccentric and sometimes barbarous behaviour of the Irish themselves. He also saw Ireland as a source of support.

In the same year, 1394, Richard's wife, Anne of Bohemia, died. Two years later he married Isabella, the seven-year-old daughter of the French King, Charles VI. This political marriage sealed a thirty-year truce with France, and a secret clause meant that, should Richard be opposed at home, France would come to his aid.

C❖The Irish expedition had been the first stage towards the establishment of a despotism; the alliance with France was the second. . . . In January 1397, Richard decided at last to strike.

Arundel and Gloucester . . . saw the King advancing upon them in cold hatred . . . Arundel and some others of his associates were declared traitors and accorded only the courtesy of decapitation. Warwick was exiled to the Isle of Man. Gloucester, arrested and taken to Calais, was there murdered by Richard's agents . . .

Parliament was called only to legalize these events. It was found to be so packed and so minded that there was nothing it would not do for the King . . . it suspended almost every constitutional right and privilege gained in the preceding century. . . .

The relations between Gaunt's son, Henry, the King's cousin and contemporary, passed through drama into tragedy. . . . A quarrel arose between Henry and Thomas Mowbray, now Duke of Norfolk. . . . Henry accused Mowbray of treasonable language. . . . Each, when challenged, gave lie to the other. Trial by battle appeared the correct solution . . . but the King, exasperating the spectators of all classes who had gathered in high expectation to see the sport, . . . forbade the combat, and exiled Mowbray for life and Henry for a decade. . . . Mowbray soon died; but Henry, astounded by what he deemed ingratitude and injustice, lived and schemed in France.

And then, it seems, Richard lost his reason. John of Gaunt died in February 1399 and instead of allowing Henry Bolingbroke to inherit his father's vast estates by proxy, Richard took them over. And then, totally oblivious to the probable consequences, Richard set off on an expedition to Ireland, leaving his kingdom unguarded.

C❖In July Henry of Lancaster, as he had now become, landed in Yorkshire, declaring that he had only come to claim his lawful rights as heir to his venerated father. He was immediately surrounded by adherents, particularly from the Lancaster estates, and the all-powerful Northern lords, led by the Earl of Northumberland. . . . It took some time for the news . . . to reach Richard in the depths of Ireland. . . . Having landed in England on 27 July he made a rapid three weeks' march through north Wales in an attempt to gather forces. What he saw convinced him that all was over. The whole structure of his power, so patiently and subtly built up, had vanished as if by enchantment. The Welsh, who would have stood by him, could not face the advancing power of what was now all England. At Flint Castle he [Richard] submitted to Henry . . . He rode through London as a captive. . . . His abdication was extorted; his death had become inevitable.

Many still mourn Richard II as a romantic figure, but it was the job of the King to stand between oppression and the people. Between 1389 and 1397 Richard protected his people well, but later he hounded them for revenge and corrupted the role of Parliament. He usurped the judiciary and he acted in the belief that the very lives of his people were subject to his every whim. That was not kingship. That was tyranny.

CHAPTER FOURTEEN

1399–1454

❖

By the end of the fourteenth century, the Plantagenets had ruled England for almost 250 years. There had been eight kings, beginning with Henry II and ending, in 1399, with Richard II. But now the dynasty, although still Plantagenet, was to splinter. First the House of Lancaster, then the House of York, each tracing its line to the original Plantagenet monarch, Henry II. For the next sixty or so years, England was ruled by the House of Lancaster, the three Henrys, beginning with Richard's successor Henry Bolingbroke, who was to be Henry IV and would rule for fourteen years. In that time Owen Glyndwr began the war for Welsh independence and defeated the English at Pilleth and then mysteriously disappeared; the King crushed a rebellion led by Richard Scrope, the Archbishop of York, and then had him executed; the first James became King of the Scots and the first Lollard religious reformer was martyred by burning at Smithfield.

From the first day of his reign, Henry IV had to accommodate his supporters. After all, to attempt to overthrow a king is high treason. To fail, is death. Therefore his backers demanded their rewards and Henry needed their continuing support. It was by no means an easy succession for the House of Lancaster and its complications clouded the reigns of all three Lancastrian Kings. Also, when Henry came to the throne Richard II was not dead, he was merely in prison.

C❖As each change of power had been attended by capital vengence upon the vanquished there arose in the Commons a very solid and enduring desire to let the great lords cut each other's throats if they were so minded. . . . During this time therefore Parliamentary power over finance was greatly strengthened. Not only did the Estates supply the money by voting the taxes, but they began to follow its expenditure, and to require and to receive accounts from the high officers of the State. Nothing like this had been tolerated by any of the Kings before. They had always condemned it as a presumptuous inroad upon their prerogative. These great advances in the polity of England were the characteristics of Lancastrian rule, and followed naturally from the need the house of Lancaster had to buttress its title by public opinion and constitutional authority.

Richard II was a prisoner in Pontefract Castle and as the general bitterness towards him began to wilt, the weakness of Henry's government became more obvious. In January 1400 some of the nobles tried to rise in favour of the imprisoned Richard. They failed, but as long as Richard remained alive, the greater the chance of him becoming a rallying figure. It is generally said that he was starved to death, but one contemporary writer believed that Henry sent one of his knights, Sir Peter Exton, to kill Richard. But even then it was necessary to display Richard's body at St Paul's Cathedral to convince the people that he was really dead.

Henry was now faced with demands from the Church to restrain the excesses of the Lollards. The Lollards, who got their name from a mediaeval Dutch word meaning 'mutter', as in praying, were religious reformers, followers of the late John Wyclif. They did not believe in transubstantiation, and they believed the clergy indulged in excesses. John Wyclif had translated the Bible into English; he believed that everyone who wanted to read the Testaments should be able to. The simplest way to deal with the Lollards, said the Church, was officially to declare them heretics. And so, in 1401, a Statute of enormous significance was published, written to deal with what its draughtsmen called 'the innovations and excesses of the Lollards'. The *Statute De Heretico Comburendo* made it legal in England to take anyone convicted of heresy and burn him, or her, at the stake.

❖ And if any person refuses to abjure his heresy so that according to the holy canons he ought to be handed over to the secular court, then the sheriff shall receive the said persons, all of them, after such sentence has been promulgated, and cause them to be burned in a high place, so that such punishment may strike with fear the minds of others, and by this no such wicked doctrine and heretical and erroneous opinions shall be sustained or in any way suffered.

In 1401 the burning began. It would seem that Henry IV supported the Statute only partly from his religious orthodoxy; the greater pressure was political. Henry's loyalty debts were still being paid.

Henry also faced war with both Scotland and Wales. The Scots had renewed their alliance with France and, led by the Earl of Douglas, had destroyed the English force and captured young Hotspur, Henry Percy, the son of the first Earl of Northumberland. Henry IV advanced north as far as Edinburgh and then had to return south. The Welsh were on the move. Adam of Usk's Chronicle of autumn 1401 tells the story.

❖ Owen Glyndwr, all north Wales and Cardigan and Powys siding with him, sorely harried with fire and sword the English who dwelt in those parts, and their towns. Wherefore the English, invading those parts with a strong power, and utterly laying them waste and ravaging them with fire, famine and sword, left them a desert, not even sparing children or churches, and they carried away into England more than 1000 small children of both sexes to be their servants. Yet the same Owen did no small hurt to the English, slaying many of them, and carrying off the arms, horses, and the tents of the King's eldest son, the Prince of Wales, which he bore away for his own use to the mountain fastness of Snowdon.

C❖[But] Henry's most serious conflict was with the Percys. These lords of the Northern Marches, the old Earl of Northumberland and his fiery son Hotspur, had for nearly three years carried on the defence of England against the Scots unaided and almost entirely at their own expense. . . . They could no longer bear the burden. . . . The King in bitter poverty could offer but £40,000. . . . The Percys had played a great part in placing Henry on the throne. But Edmund Mortimer, Hotspur's brother-in-law, had joined Glendower in rebellion, and the family were now under suspicion. . . . Hotspur raised the standard of revolt. But at Shrewsbury on July 21, 1403 Henry [IV] overcame him and slew him . . . The old Earl, who was marching to his aid, was forced to submit, and pardon was freely extended to him. . . . But two years later, with his son's death at heart, he rebelled again and this time the conspiracy was far-reaching. Archbishop Scrope of York and Thomas Mowbray, Earl of Nottingham, were his principal confederates. . . . Once again Henry marched north, and once again he was successful. Northumberland was driven across the border . . . Scrope and Mowbray [were] beheaded after a summary trial. Scrope's execution caused a profound shock throughout the land, and many compared it with the murder of Thomas Becket.

If there had only been one pope at the time, Henry IV would probably have been excommunicated for Scrope's execution. But the schism in the Church had left a pope in Rome and a pope in Avignon. Henry supported the Roman pope, and if he punished Henry, Henry might defect to Avignon. So, although the Church protested, Henry remained its child.

By 1408 the Earl of Northumberland was dead, killed in battle against the King's men at Bramham Moor, and Henry's England was free from uprising if not from malcontents. But the King was ill, as Adam of Usk's Chronicle records.

❖In that same year, 1413, an agreement was made between Prince Henry, first born son of the King, Henry, Bishop of Winchester, and almost all the lords of England, that they should ask the King to give up the crown of England, and permit his first-born to be crowned, because he was so horribly afflicted with leprosy. When this advice was given, he was unwilling to agree to this counsel but returning to London, he died at Westminster in the abbot's lodging in a certain low chamber, called the Jerusalem Chamber, about the feast of St Cuthbert.

Henry IV's heart gave out and he left behind a country lacking unity and woefully in debt, and therefore dependent upon the goodwill and mercy of its magnates. The new King, the young man of twenty-five, almost immediately led his country towards the one thing that would bring order and, even, unity: war with France. Henry V and his archers were on the road to Agincourt.

C❖He [Henry V] came to the throne at a moment when England was wearied of feuds and brawl and yearned for unity and fame. He led the nation away from internal discord to foreign conquest; and he had the dream, and perhaps the prospect, of leading all Western Europe into the high championship of a Crusade. Council and Parliament alike suddenly showed themselves bent on war with France. . . . The Commons were thereupon liberal with supply. The King on his part declared that no law should be passed without their assent. A wave of reconciliation swept the land. The King declared a general pardon. He sought to assuage the past. He negotiated with the Scots for the release of Hotspur's son and reinstated him in the Earldom of Northumberland. He brought the body, or the reputed body, of Richard II to London and reinterred it in Westminster Abbey with pageantry and solemn ceremonial. A plot formed against him on the eve of his setting out for the wars was suppressed, by all appearance with ease and national approval, and with only a handful of executions. In particular he spared his cousin, the young Edmund Mortimer, Earl of March, who had been named as the rival King, and through whose family much that was merciless was to follow later.

So in 1415, Henry V set out for France. Even in the mediaeval age, national unity tended to be a consequence of foreign war. But only as long as the foreign war was won and didn't cost too much in gold or in lives. Also, in this particular case, the English King had lucrative, and family, possessions and titles in France, and, like his forebears, he wished to fight to maintain or increase them. Moreover, the French had aligned themselves with the Scots, and even with the Welsh. And Henry V appeared to believe in a sense of divine support, if not right. He seemed convinced that it was his task to conquer France and then lead soldiers from both nations on the great Crusade to recover Jerusalem.

And so Henry claimed his right to the throne of France. The French were weak from civil conflict between the Burgundians and the Orleanists, the Royalists. The latter offered Henry a large part of Aquitaine, 850,000 crowns and Catherine, the daughter of King Charles VI. Henry was also negotiating with the Burgundians to let him enter France in safety, and he promised that he would take their side against the Orleanists if they would support his claim to the throne.

C❖The English army of about 10,000 fighting men sailed to France on August 11, 1415 . . . and landed without opposition at the mouth of the Seine. Harfleur was besieged and taken by the middle of September. . . . He [Henry V] now invited the Dauphin to end the war by single combat. The challenge was declined. The attrition of the siege, and disease, which levied its unceasing toll on these mediaeval camps, had already wrought havoc in the English expedition. The main power of France was now in the field. The Council of War, on October 5, advised returning home by sea.

But the King, leaving a garrison in Harfleur, and sending home several thousand sick and wounded, resolved, with about 1000 knights and men-at-arms and 4000 archers, to traverse the French coast in a 100-mile march to his fortress at Calais, where his ships were to await him. All the circumstances of this decision show that his design was to tempt the enemy to battle.

When the two sides came face to face, it was at a field called Agincourt. The English saw the terrible odds: Facing them were perhaps 20,000 French cavalry and footsoldiers. One chronicler says there were, eventually, 60,000 French soldiers, but it would not have been possible to organize them all as a fighting force in that small area.

Henry tried to negotiate a withdrawal at one point. He offered to give back Harfleur and the considerable numbers of French prisoners he'd taken. The French wanted one more concession: Henry would have to renounce his claim to the French throne. He refused. And so, on the feast of St Crispinian and St Crispin, the brotherly patron saints of shoe-makers, Henry V led the advance to the French lines. To his right, his vanguard was commanded by the Duke of York; to his left, his rearguard was led by Lord Camoys.

C❖The French . . . stood in three dense lines, and neither their crossbowmen nor their battery of cannon could fire effectively. Under the [English] arrow storm they in turn moved forward down the slope, plodding heavily through a ploughed field already trampled into a quagmire. Still at thirty deep, they felt sure of breaking the line. But once again the long bow destroyed all before it. Horse and foot alike went down; a long heap of armoured dead and wounded lay upon the ground, over which reinforcements struggled bravely, but in vain. . . . Now occurred a terrible episode. The French third line, still intact, covered the entire front, and the English were no longer in regular array. At this moment the French camp-followers and peasantry, who had wandered round the English rear, broke pillaging into the camp and stole the King's crown, wardrobe, and Great Seal. The King, believing himself attacked from behind . . . issued the dread order to slaughter the prisoners. Then perished the flower of the French nobility, many of whom had yielded themselves to easy hopes of ransom. Only the most illustrious were spared. The desperate character of this act . . . supplies what defence can be found for its ferocity. . . . The alarm in the rear was soon relieved, but not before the massacre was almost finished.

The English lost perhaps fewer than 300, the French, maybe 6000, including slaughtered prisoners. The English army was so weakened by the campaign that it struggled to reach the safety of Calais. By the following month, November, Henry V returned to England. He was the hero the nation had longed for. The account given in *Henrici Quinti Regis Gesta* describes his triumphant progress.

❖He took his journey by way of the sacred thresholds of the churches of Canterbury and of St Augustine's Canterbury, to his manor at Eltham, proposing to honour the City of London on the following Saturday. The citizens, hearing with the greatest joy the news of his approach, prepared themselves and the City. And when the desired day dawned, the citizens went out to meet the King at the brow of Blackheath. The mayor and twenty-four aldermen in scarlet, and the rest of the lesser citizens in red cloaks with red and white hoods, to the number of about 20,000 horsemen. And when the King came through the midst of them at about ten o'clock, and the citizens had given glory and honour to God, the citizens rode before the King towards the city and the King followed.

But Henry's own ambitions were not realized and for the next two years he set out to overcome Normandy by siege and steady attrition. An agreement was reached that Henry would marry Catherine, the daughter of the mad Charles VI, and on Charles's death, Henry would become King of France. Henry and Catherine were married in June 1420.

But by now Henry was desperate for a conclusion to the war. He took just one day's honeymoon before he returned to the conflict. Exhausted, and vulnerable to disease, he was dead two years later. The hero, the wise and true Englishman, Henry V, left a united England and a miserable France. But the cost of victory had to be paid long after the bells finished chiming, and the new King, Henry VI, was but nine months old.

Physically, Henry VI was weak. Mentally, he was probably simple; on some occasions, obviously so. He never much changed during his forty or so years on the throne. And when he was fifty, he was murdered.

Henry V had wanted his brother, the good Duke Humphrey of Gloucester, to be Regent of England but the magnates of England had other ideas. They wanted the chance to run the country without a king, without a strong leader. Gloucester was given the title, Protector, but the country was really in the hands of an aristocratic council and the seemingly inevitable struggle for influence. Henry VI never had the measure of this council.

C❖At the time of [Henry V's] death, the ascendancy of the English arms in France was established. In his brother John, Duke of Bedford, who went to France as Regent and Commander in Chief, a successor of the highest military quality was found. The alliance with Burgundy, carrying with it the allegiance and sympathies of Paris, persisted. . . . The war continued bitterly. . . . Many sieges and much ravaging distressed the countryside. In 1421 the French and their Scottish allies, under the Earl of Buchan, defeated the English at Baugé . . . These Scotsmen were animated by a hatred of the English which stood out beyond the ordinary feuds. . . . Buchan, who had been made Constable of France after Baugé, had induced his father-in-law, the Earl of Douglas, to bring over a new Scots army and to become Constable himself. The French, having had some success, were inclined to retire behind the Loire, but the rage of the Scots, of whom there were no fewer than 5000 under Douglas, was uncontrollable. They forced a battle, and were nearly all destroyed by the arrow storm. Douglas, Buchan, and other Scottish chieftains fell upon the field, and so grievous was the slaughter of their followers that it was never again possible to form, in these wars, a separate Scottish brigade.

In England, the modest success of the army in France was not much of an occasion for joy. The Parliaments were reluctant to pour more money into wars. The longer the war, the more campaigns to finance. The more territory gained, the more to administer, the greater the costs. And because the territories were so ravaged by war, they were quite incapable of generating anything for their own upkeep, never mind supporting the English forces and camp followers.

The infant Henry VI knew little of this. Seven years later he was thought old enough to be crowned King of England. There was nothing special about the coronation. The English were used to boy-kings. And, it would seem, huge feasts. The menu of the coronation feast has survived.

❖The first course: frumenty with venison. Meat royal, planted with lozenges of gold. Boars' heads in castles armed with gold. Beef. Mutton. Cygnet. Stewed capon. Heron. Great pike. A red leach of sliced meats, eggs, fruits and spices, with lions carved therein in white. Custard royal with a leopard of gold sitting therein. Fritter like a sun, with a fleur-de-lis therein.

And those were only the starters. There were two more enormous and varied courses to come, with sorbets of minstrels and poets to follow. But when the feasting was done, the business of intrigue and defending lands continued. The English were being held up on the southward march through France by the Armagnac possession of Orleans. Under the Earl of Salisbury they laid siege to the town. It wasn't much of a siege. The English force was weak, badly supplied and in bad mood when the Earl himself was killed.

It was at this siege that Joan of Arc made her famous appearance. She had, so it was said, a vision and she heard voices. And in March 1429, Joan of Arc went to the court of the Dauphin and told him of those voices and the message that he would be crowned King in Rheims. But first she had to deal with the English who, depleted and war-weary, fell back at Orleans. Joan of Arc then led the still sceptical Dauphin through Champagne, took Troyes and Chalons, and on 17 July, as the voices had promised, the Dauphin was crowned King Charles VII in Rheims cathedral.

The Maid of Orleans believed her mission completed. She wanted no more of war. She wanted to go home but the court wouldn't let her. In May 1430 she was captured by the Burgundians and sold to the English for 10,000 gold francs. The French King made no attempt to rescue her.

C❖Joan of Arc perished on May 30,1431, and thereafter the tides of war flowed remorselessly against the English. . . . The whole spirit of the country was against the English claim. . . . Bedford died and was succeeded by lesser captains. . . . The French artillery now became the finest in the world. Seven hundred engineers . . . [fired] gigantic stone balls against the numberless castles which the English still held. Places which, in the days of Henry V, could be reduced only by famine, now fell in a few days to smashing bombardment. All Northern France, except Calais, was reconquered.

The Hundred Years' War was effectively at an end. But by now the English were at war with themselves: on one side the Beaufort family, bastard descendants of John of Gaunt and therefore Lancastrians (as was the King). On the other side the King, Henry VI: kindly, soft, soon to be judged insane, and his new bride, Margaret. She was the seventeen-year-old Margaret of Anjou, married to Henry in a two-year truce with France. Margaret was a remarkable woman. She championed the Beauforts, set herself against the Duke of Gloucester, had him arrested and, so many believe, arranged his death.

The politics were complex but the ambitions were simple. The factions that had, at the start of the King's reign, fought for control of government, now fought for the throne. Against this background, the country was in turmoil for another reason. In 1450 the Kentish rebellion led by Jack Cade was protesting against the government's incompetence and oppressive taxes. But in his published demands, taken from *Stow's Memoranda* Cade was careful to honour the King.

> ❖Thus our Sovereign Lord shall reign and rule with great honour, and have the love of God and of his people. For he shall have such great love of his people that he shall, with God's help, conquer where he will. As for us, we shall always be ready to defend our country from all nations with our own goods, and to go with our Sovereign Lord, as his true liegemen, where he will command.

But this peaceful and reasonable declaration is misleading. Cade, styled as Captain of the Kentish rebels, entered and took over London for three days. There were, in that time, some unseemly, certainly unreasonable, scenes.

> ❖Arrived in the City, Cade sent to the Tower for Lord Say, who was fetched and brought to the Guildhall. There with others he [Say] was indicted for treason. They took him out and brought him to the Standard in Cheapside and there smote off his head. The same day, Crowmer was beheaded in Mile End. Afterwards they brought the heads of the Lord Say and of Crowmer on two poles and at various places in the city they put the heads together making them seem to kiss each other.

Cade's uprising was a simple, violent illustration of the breaking down of law and order. The anger towards those who governed was great enough to spark violence and a belief that demands would be met. Cade's rebellion began on the day William Aiscough, Bishop of Salisbury, was murdered by his own parishioners. Another bishop, Adam Moleyns, Bishop of Chichester, was murdered by sailors in Portsmouth when he arrived to give them their backpay. The sailors were angry because the Bishop confessed to another's crime. He admitted (or so they said) that the late Duke of Suffolk had plotted for a French invasion, and that he had sold the French details of English defences and had been bribed to prevent English armies going to France. The navy, or possibly a pirate, caught up with Suffolk and beheaded him in a long boat. As for Cade, he was eventually chased off and killed during a skirmish at Heathfield in Sussex in 1450. During the next three years the English were thrown out of Normandy and, with the French victory at Castillon, the Hundred Years' War was at an end.

And then, in 1453, the King went mad.

> C❖He had gone down to Wiltshire to spend July and August. Suddenly his memory failed. He recognized no one, not even the Queen. He could eat

and drink, but his speech was childish or incoherent. He could not walk. For another fifteen months he remained entirely without comprehension. . . . When these terrible facts became known, Queen Margaret aspired to be Protector. But the adverse forces were too strong for the Lancastrian party to make the challenge. Moreover . . . on October 13, she gave birth to a son. . . . Now it seemed there would be a Lancastrian ascendancy for ever.

But there were suspicions that the new prince, Edward, Prince of Wales, was not the King's son. However, it was also clear that the King was incapable of ruling. The power of the Duke of York – father of the future Richard III – in the Council was sufficient that, in March 1454, he was declared Protector. For more than a year, he was monarch in all but title. But then, in 1455, the King recovered his wits. Queen Margaret was ready to do battle. So was York. By May of that year the Queen's closest ally, Edmund, Duke of Somerset, was killed, and the King was taken prisoner. Margaret's screams for revenge echoed about the House of Lancaster. The Wars of the Roses had started.

CHAPTER FIFTEEN

1455–1485

❖

The Wars of the Roses spread over thirty years. But they weren't, as is sometimes imagined, one long war. On one side was the House of Lancaster; on the other, the House of York; but the houses of York and Lancaster came from the same dynasty, the same family tree: the Plantagenets. And just because there were Yorkists and Lancastrians, that doesn't mean that the wars were between Yorkshire and Lancashire. Just as in modern times, noble titles had little to do with places.

The Lancastrians were in power because Henry VI was a Lancaster. His wife, Margaret, was French, and the Lancasters commanded the Crown lands, for example, the Duchy of Cornwall. And they had all the Lancastrian earldoms: Lancaster itself, Derby, Lincoln, Leicester, Hereford and Nottingham. The other families who supported them gave them Somerset, Surrey, East Anglia and Devon. Then, with the Percys and the *elder* Nevilles in the Lancastrian camp, they had control of the northern strongholds.

The Yorkist strength was in the Mortimer family, and their lands were mainly on the Welsh borders, the Marches. They had strong support in Kent, some in Norfolk, and, because of the *younger* Nevilles, they had the Earl of Warwick and Salisbury, and the estates of Wiltshire and the southern Midlands.

Because the King had come to the throne when he was only nine months old, the barons who ran the country on his behalf had, inevitably, become very powerful and factious. Maladministration, corruption and incompetent government were rife in England and all the main players had personal ambitions. None of these reasons, by themselves, account for the Wars of the Roses. But put them together and civil war seemed inevitable.

C❖The four years from 1456 to 1459 were a period of uneasy truce. . . . War began in earnest in July 1460 . . . the Yorkist lords under Warwick . . . confronted the Lancastrians and the Crown at Northampton. Henry VI stood entrenched and new cannon guarded his line. But when the Yorkists attacked, Lord Grey of Ruthven, who commanded a wing, deserted him and helped the Yorkists over the breastworks. The royal forces fled in panic. King Henry VI remained in his tent . . . The victors presented themselves to him, bowing to the ground . . . They carried him to London, and having him in their power once more, ruled in his name. . . . Henry was to be King for life; York was to conduct the government and succeed him at his death. . . . But the settlement defied the fact that Queen Margaret, with her son, the Prince of Wales, was at liberty at Harlech Castle, in Wales. . . . The Queen fought on.

With her army of the North and North Wales, Margaret advanced to assert the birthright of her son. The Duke of York . . . marched against her. At Wakefield, on December 30, 1460, the first considerable battle of the war was fought. The Lancastrians, with superior forces, caught the Yorkists by surprise . . . and a frightful rout and massacre ensued. . . . No quarter was given. The Duke of York was killed; . . . the old Earl of Salisbury, caught during the night, was beheaded immediately by Lord Exeter . . . The heads of the three Yorkist nobles were exposed over the gates and walls of York. The great Duke's head, with a paper crown, grinned upon the landscape, summoning the avengers.

The Queen's army marched south, beat Warwick on the way, and recaptured the King. That should have been that: the House of Lancaster was back on the throne and the Yorkists were humiliated. But it wasn't. Edward, the Earl of March and the late Duke of York's eldest son, hoisted his father's banner, and joined with the bruised Warwick in Oxfordshire. Together they entered London in triumph.

A week after he arrived in London, the Earl of March was ruling England, and the Queen was heading north. Edward caught up with her at Towton Field in Yorkshire and, in a snow blizzard, slaughtered hundreds of Lancastrians. Henry VI escaped with his life, but not his throne. The twenty-year-old Duke of York was crowned Edward IV, and one-third of the estates in England changed hands.

C❖After Towton, the Lancastrian cause was sustained by the unconquerable will of Queen Margaret. . . . [She] herself besieged the castle at Norham, on the Tweed near Berwick. Once again Edward and the Yorkists took the field and the redoubtable new artillery . . . was carried north. The great guns blew chunks off the castles. Margaret fled to France, while [King] Henry buried himself amid the valleys and the pious foundations of Cumberland. This was the final parting of King Henry VI and his Queen. . . . Poor King Henry was at length tracked down near Clitheroe in Lancashire and conveyed to London. . . . [He] was led three times round the pillory and finally hustled to the Tower . . .

It was 1465. The Queen was penniless in France. The King was in the Tower. But the new King, Edward IV, was mysteriously reluctant to commit himself to his kingmaker's marriage plans for him. Richard Neville, the Earl of Warwick – of the Neville family who were more or less running the country at the time – was Edward's kingmaker, and he could see the political advantages of marrying the King to a French princess. He made all the diplomatic arrangements only to discover, belatedly, that his King was already married. Warwick was outraged. Edward had married Elizabeth Woodville, the widow of the Lancastrian, Lord Grey. And Edward was a Yorkist. Inevitably Warwick and Edward IV clashed.

In the summer of 1469 a rebellion broke out in the north. The contrived complaint was high taxes and favouritism. While this was going on, the marriage between Clarence (the King's brother) and Isabella (Warwick's daughter), which had been forbidden by the King, took place at Calais. Clarence and Warwick returned to England, and Royalists and rebels met at the Battle of Edgecote. The King, trying to rally his scattered forces, was captured. Warwick now had two Kings at his mercy: Henry VI was still a prisoner.

C❖Warwick had struck with suddenness and, for a while, no one realized what had happened. As the truth became known, the Yorkist nobility viewed with astonishment and anger the detention of their brave, victorious sovereign, and the Lancastrians everywhere raised their heads in the hopes of profiting by the Yorkist feud. The King found it convenient to dissemble. . . . He undertook to mend his ways, and after he had signed free pardons to all who had been in arms against him, he was liberated.

But within a few months, there was another rising, this one in Lincolnshire. This time the King survived and Warwick and Clarence, who were now exposed, left England. In France, Louis XI forced Warwick to negotiate with the exiled queen, Margaret of Anjou. She agreed to a marriage between her son, Prince Edward, and Warwick's daughter, Anne Neville. Their plan was that Margaret's son would one day be king and Warwick's daughter queen. But first they had to get rid of Edward and restore the imprisoned Henry VI to the throne.

Richard Neville, Earl of Warwick, and the Duke of Clarence, the King's brother, landed at Dartmouth. Much of southern England welcomed Warwick who marched on London and freed Henry VI from the Tower, where he had been imprisoned for five years, and restored him to the throne. Edward IV fled the country.

But Warwick had made a serious mistake. He'd promised Clarence that he would be the next king. But a freed Henry, and the real chance of an heir, greatly lessened Clarence's chances. When Warwick had made Clarence this promise he'd deserted his brother, Edward IV, and now when Edward IV returned to fight Warwick, Clarence deserted Warwick, rejoined his brother, fought Warwick's army, defeated it and that was the end of the kingmaker, Warwick. He was killed along with his brother, Lord Montague. As Warwick was dying, Queen Margaret was landing with her army and the young Prince of Wales at Weymouth. The two sides met at Tewksbury. Margaret's army was defeated. Out came the axe, off came the heads of the Prince of Wales and Margaret's supporter, Edmund, Duke of Somerset. Edward IV then returned to London, dragged out the hapless King Henry and beheaded him. A fifteenth-century royal soap opera perhaps, but the Wars of the Roses were still not yet done.

C❖Queen Elizabeth [Elizabeth Woodville] . . . had produced not only five daughters, but two fine boys who were growing up. In 1483 one was twelve and the other nine. The succession to the Crown seemed plain and secure. The King himself was only forty. . . . His main thought was set on securing the Crown to his son, the unfledged Edward V; but in April 1483 death came so suddenly upon him that he had no time to take the necessary precautions. After only ten days' illness, this strong King was cut down in his prime. . . . A Protectorate was inevitable. . . . Richard [of Gloucester, the King's faithful brother] stood forth without compare and had been nominated by the late King himself.

At what point Richard planned to be King is uncertain. But within a few weeks he was. He first arrested Earl Rivers and Sir Richard Grey, accusing them of plotting. They were the young prince's minders. Grey was his half-brother. Two weeks later, doubting the support of Lord Hastings and the Archbishop of York and the Treasurer, the Bishop of Ely, Richard imprisoned the two bishops and beheaded Hastings. Meanwhile he'd lodged the twelve-year-old Edward V in the Tower. Shortly afterwards, Elizabeth, the Queen Mother, was persuaded to part with her other son, the nine-year-old Duke of York. Now both princes were in the Tower.

All Richard had to do now was convince Parliament, and the people, that the late King's marriage to Elizabeth Woodville was invalid and therefore their heirs had no right to the throne. Richard's chaplain was sent to St Paul's Cross in London to preach the sermon that would explain the Church's view. As this extract from *The Great Chronicle of London* shows, it didn't quite work as Richard had intended.

❖On the second Sunday after Lord Hastings' execution, there being present the Lord Protector, the Duke of Buckingham, and a large audience of laity and clergy, Doctor Ralph Shaa declared, and proved by reasons as he devised there and then, that the children of King Edward were not the rightful heirs of the crown, and that King Edward was not the legitimate son of the Duke of York, as the Lord Protector was. He then alleged that the Lord Protector was most worthy to be King, and none other. Which sermon offended so greatly the greater part of that audience that whereas before that time the said doctor was held to be most famous and holy in the minds of the common people, after this day he was held in little repute or regard. Then on the Tuesday after this Sunday, the Duke of Buckingham came to the Guildhall. The Duke made an oration which lasted a good half hour, recounting the excellence of the Lord Protector, the many virtues [with] which God had endowed him, and the rightful title he had to the throne. When he had finished, and well exhorted the assembly to accept the Lord Protector to be their liege lord and King, a small number of his listeners cried 'Yea!' to satisfy his mind, and more for fear than for love.

But Richard was not unduly put out by this lack of spontaneous approval. Parliament was the important body, not the people. Two days later, Richard, Duke of Gloucester, was proclaimed King Richard III. However from the day of his coronation, there is a sense that the new King was not trusted by his people, nor by many of his magnates.

C❖ . . . during these first three months of Richard's reign, Buckingham, from being his chief supporter, became his mortal foe. His motives are not clear. Perhaps he shrank from becoming the accomplice in what he foresaw would be the closing act of the usurpation. . . . So we come to the principal crime ever afterwards associated with Richard's name. . . . According to Sir Thomas More's story, Richard resolved, in July, to extirpate the menace to his peace and sovereignty presented by the princes. He sent a special messenger, by name John Green, to Brackenbury, the Constable of the Tower, with orders to make an end of them. Brackenbury refused to obey. 'Whom should a man trust,' exclaimed the King . . . 'when those who I thought would most surely serve at my command will do nothing for me?' A page who heard this outburst reminded his master that Sir James Tyrell, one of Richard's former companions in arms, was capable of anything. Tyrell was sent to London with a warrant authorizing Brackenbury to deliver to him for one night all the keys of the Tower. Tyrell discharged his fell commission with all dispatch. One of the four gaolers in charge of the princes, Forest by name, was found willing, and with Dighton, Tyrell's own groom, did the deed. When the princes were asleep the two assassins pressed pillows hard down upon their faces till they were suffocated . . . it was not until Henry VII's reign, when Tyrell was lying in the Tower under sentence of death for quite a separate crime, that he is alleged to have made a confession upon which, with much other circumstantial evidence, the story as we know it rests.

Meanwhile the Duke of Buckingham was conspiring with the Countess of Richmond who, as a Beaufort, was a descendant of John of Gaunt and therefore in the Lancastrian line of Edward III. She'd married the Earl of Richmond, who was now dead. Their son, Henry Tudor, was now Earl of Richmond and in exile in Brittany after a previous Lancastrian loss.

C❖All Buckingham's preparations were for a general rising on October 18, . . . But the anger of the people at the rumoured murder of the princes deranged [the] plan. In Kent, Wiltshire, Sussex and Devonshire there were risings ten days before the appointed date . . . King Richard . . . marched against rebellion. . . . Buckingham's forces melted away . . . Buckingham, with a high price on his head, was betrayed to Richard, who lost not an hour in having him slaughtered. The usual crop of executions followed. Order was restored throughout the land, and the King seemed to have established himself securely upon his throne. . . .

A terrible blow now fell upon the King. In April 1484 his only son, the Prince of Wales, died . . . and his wife, whose health was broken, could bear no more children. Henry Tudor, Earl of Richmond, now became obviously the rival claimant and successor to the throne. . . . As the months passed, many prominent Englishmen, both Yorkist and Lancastrian, withdrew themselves from Richard's baleful presence, and made their way to Richmond, who from this time forth stood at the head of a combination which might well unite all England.

On 17 August 1485 the King, with 10,000 well-disciplined troops, set forth towards Leicester at the head of his army. Richmond's forces were rebels and the wild card, or unknown factor, was Lord Stanley's forces. The King, doubtful of him, had held his son and threatened to behead him if his father failed to support the royal standard. But Stanley, at the last moment, joined Richmond.

Richard's fate is described by Polydore Vergil in his *Anglica Historia* which chronicled the reign of Henry VII.

❖When Earl Henry [Tudor] was drawing nearer, King Richard knew it perfectly by evident signs and tokens that it was Henry. Wherefore, all inflamed with ire, he struck his horse with spurs, and ran against him out of his own army ahead of the vanguard. King Richard, at the first brunt, killed some men and overthrew Henry's standard, together with William Brandon the standard bearer. Then he matched himself against John Cheney, a man of such strength, far exceeding the common sort, who strove with him as he came; but the King with great force drove him to the ground, making way with his weapon on every side. But yet Henry abode the brunt longer than even his own soldiers would have thought, who were almost out of hope of victory, when suddenly William Stanley, with 3000 men, came to the rescue. Then, truly in a moment, the remainder fled and King Richard was killed in the thickest press of his enemies. Many forbore to fight who came to the field with King Richard for awe, and for no goodwill, and departed without any danger, as men who desired not the safety but destruction of that prince whom they hated. The body of King Richard, naked of all clothing, and laid upon a horse's back, with arms and legs hanging down both sides was brought to the abbey at Leicester, a miserable spectacle in good truth, and was buried there two days afterwards without any pomp or solemn funeral.

And that was the Battle of Bosworth. It was 1485 and the end of the Wars of the Roses, wars that had made little difference to the daily lives of the peoples of England. Incidentally no one, at the time, called them the Wars of the Roses. It seems that the first person to refer to them by that name was Sir Walter Scott in his novel, *Anne of Geierstein*, and that wasn't until 1829.

CHAPTER SIXTEEN

1485–1515

❖

The story of Tudor England began in 1485, when Henry Tudor was crowned Henry VII at the Battle of Bosworth, and the deformed and naked dead body of Richard III symbolized the end of the Wars of the Roses.

Henry VII was Welsh, and when he came to the throne he was twenty-eight years old. His late father was Edmund Tudor, the Earl of Richmond, and his mother, Margaret Beaufort, was a direct descendant of John of Gaunt. Polydore Vergil, who became Archdeacon of Wells, was a tax collector of the time. Here is his description of Henry, from in his *Anglica Historia*.

❖Henry [VII] reigned twenty-three years and seven months. By his wife Elizabeth he had eight children: four boys and the same number of girls. His figure was slim, but well-built and strong. In height he was above average. Extremely attractive in appearance, his face was cheerful, especially when he was speaking. He had small blue eyes; a few poor, black-stained teeth. His hair was thin and white. He had a most tenacious memory, and was, in addition, not devoid of scholarship. Further, in government he was shrewd and far-seeing, so that none dared to get the better of him by deceit or sharp practice. Above all else he cherished justice; and he punished with the utmost vigour robberies, murders, and every other kind of crime. He was a most zealous supporter of religion, daily taking part, with great devotion, in divine service. But in his later days, all these virtues were obscured by avarice, from which he suffered.

And what of the people and the country? England had yet to recover from the Black Death which reached these islands nearly a century and a half earlier. Before the plague the population was between four and five million. Yet now it was not much more than two-and-a-quarter million. A stagnant population gives a false prosperity. Food prices are kept low, or even fall, because there's little or no increase in demand. Also, if population is slow to recover, then so is whatever industrial life it supports.

The England now ruled by the first Tudor was sluggish and tired. It was slow to recover from the plagues and from famines and war. An Italian, Andreas

Franciscius, came to England in 1497 and wrote a long letter to his friend
Jacobus Sansonus. It describes Henry VII's England.

❖They dress in the French fashion, except their suits are more full and,
accordingly, more out of shape. They show no trace of schooling (I am
talking of the common people) but they delight in banquets. They eat very
frequently, at times more than is suitable, and are particularly fond of young
swans, rabbits, deer, and sea birds. The farmers are so lazy and slow that they
do not bother to sow more wheat than is necessary for their own
consumption; they prefer to let the ground be transformed into pasture for
the use of the sheep that they breed in large numbers.

Now I must write about the town of London, since it is the capital of the
whole kingdom. First of all, its position is so delightful that it would be hard
to find one more convenient and attractive. The town stretches from east to
west and is three miles in circumference. However, its suburbs are so large
that they greatly increase its circuit. It is defended by handsome walls,
especially on the northern side. Within these stands a very strongly defended
castle on the banks of the river, where the King of England and his Queen
sometimes have their residence. There are also other great buildings, and
especially a beautiful bridge over the Thames, of many marble arches, which
has on it many shops built of stone, and mansions, and even a church of
considerable size. Nowhere have I seen a finer or more richly built bridge.
Throughout the town are to be seen many workshops of craftsmen in all sorts
of mechanical arts. The working in wrought silver, tin, or white lead is very
expert here, and perhaps the finest I have ever seen. All the streets are so badly
paved that they get wet at the slightest quantity of water, and this happens
very frequently owing to large numbers of cattle carrying water, as well as on
account of the rain, of which there seems a great deal in this island.

Henry VII was preoccupied with the uncertainty of his own position. He knew
that he was King partly because Richard III had got rid of most other contenders
for the throne. Henry had also been smart enough to declare himself King
before the Battle of Bosworth began. So all the losers were easily branded as
traitors. When Parliament confirmed his right to the crown, he married
Elizabeth of York, Edward IV's daughter. Henry was a member of the House
of Lancaster but this marriage satisfied most of those Yorkists who had joined
Henry against Richard, not for Henry's sake, but because of their hatred of
Richard. So a new dynasty, the Tudors, had begun.

C❖Henry had to keep ceaseless watch for the invasion of pretenders supported
by foreign aid. . . . The Court at Burgundy was a centre of plots against him,
the Duchess being the sister of Richard III, and twice she launched pretenders

against the Tudor regime. The first was Lambert Simnel, who finished
ingloriously as a scullion in the royal kitchens. The second and more
formidable was Perkin Warbeck, . . . put forward as the younger of the princes
murdered in the Tower. Backed by discontented Yorkist nobles in Ireland,
by Burgundian money, Austrian and Flemish troops, and Scottish sympathy,
Warbeck remained at large for seven years, plotting openly. . . . But the classes
who had backed the King since Bosworth were staunch. . . . he [Warbeck]
was executed, after confessing his guilt, on the scaffold at Tyburn. The affair
ended in ignominy and ridicule, but the danger had been a real one.

Churchill's point about the discontented nobles in Ireland is a reminder that
both Lancastrian and Yorkist sympathies were to be found within the important
Anglo-Irish families. Who controlled Ireland was important to England. And
controlling Ireland meant controlling more factions than there were in England
and not taking their loyalties for granted.

C❖The Butler family, under its hereditary chief, the Earl of Ormonde, was
Lancastrian because it had always been more loyal to the King of England
than the rival house of Fitzgerald. The Fitzgeralds, led by the Earl of Kildare
in Leinster and the Earl of Desmond in Munster, . . .were Yorkist in
sympathy, because they thus hoped to promote their own aggrandisement.
   In Munster, the Desmond Fitzgeralds were already 'more Irish than the
Irish'. In the Pale, Kildare . . . might perform his feudal duties and lead the
English, but on the remoter lands on the Shannon a different rule prevailed.
. . . Power in Ireland still rested on the ability to call out and command a
sufficiency of armed men. In this the English King exercised a potent and
personal influence. . . . This precarious and shifting balance was for a while
the only road to establishing a central Government. No English king had
yet found how to make his title of 'Lord of Ireland' any more real than his
title of 'King of France'.

The key to English control over Irish affairs, for a time, was the English ability,
and the Irish inability, to make cannons. But for Henry Tudor, relations with
Scotland could not be tempered by cannon balls and were more immediately
threatening. Mediaeval England seemed to be in a state of perpetual warfare
with the Scots, and the alliance between Scotland and France was always seen
as a threat to the security of England. So Henry tried to resolve the differences
between Scotland and England before he tackled Ireland.

C❖Henry took the first steps to unite England and Scotland by marrying his
daughter Margaret to James IV in 1502, and there was peace in the North
until after his death.

With France too his policy was eminently successful. He realized that more could be gained by the threat of war than by war itself. Henry summoned Parliament to consent to taxation for a war against France, and proceeded to gather together a small army, which crossed to Calais and besieged Boulogne. At the same time he entered into negotiations with the French King who, unable to face Spain, the Holy Roman Emperor, and England simultaneously, was compelled to buy him off. . . . when Henry's eldest son, Arthur, was betrothed to . . . the Infanta Catherine [the daughter of Ferdinand and Isabella of Spain], England and Spain worked steadily together to secure booty from France – Spain in the form of territory, Henry as an annual tribute in cash, which amounted in the earlier year, to about a fifth of the regular revenues of the Crown.

Henry VII was doing what many of his predecessors failed to do: putting the state books in order. Polydore Vergil said he was avaricious, but the St Andrews historian, John Guy, described Henry as the best businessman ever to sit on the English throne. Perhaps the two go together. Certainly the first Tudor monarch should be remembered as a king who, instead of introducing revolutionary systems into the administration of the state, made the old ones work better.

C❖His achievement was indeed massive and durable. . . . He thriftily and carefully gathered what seemed in those days a vast reserve of liquid wealth. He trained a body of efficient servants. He magnified the Crown without losing the co-operation of the Commons. He identified prosperity with monarchy.

Henry also used wealth, and others' lack of it, to control officials, sometimes the courts, and often the nobility itself. But then he felt he had to. The seventeenth-century idea that government was based on its army, or the nation's nobility, was true for Henry VII. He had no permanent army but he certainly had a ruling aristocracy, and he knew how to control it, and therefore steady his country and keep his crown, and his head.

Henry VII ruled for twenty-four years. In that time he formed the Yeomen of the Guard (1485); Christopher Columbus 'discovered' America (1492); King's College, Aberdeen, was founded (1494); Cabot received the Royal Licence to explore the other side of the Atlantic (1496); and weights and measures were standardized (1496). Erasmus visited England (1499); building work started on Holyrood House (1500); the heir to the throne, Prince Arthur, married Catherine of Aragon (1501) then died the following year; and the year after that (1503) Catherine was engaged to marry the new heir to the throne, Prince Arthur's brother, Prince Henry. In 1509, Henry VII died and Prince

Henry, therefore, became Henry VIII and immediately married Catherine. He was just eighteen years old; his bride was twenty-four.

Henry VIII quickly revealed himself to be boisterous, vindictive and brooding, and at the same time keen to be grand and imperial, wanting victories and fanfares for his every deed. However, if Arthur had lived to be king, Henry would probably have become a priest.

C❖Deeply religious, Henry regularly listened to sermons lasting between one and two hours, and wrote more than one theological treatise of a high standard. . . . His zeal in theological controversy earned him from the Pope the title of 'Defender of the Faith'. An indefatigable worker, he digested a mass of dispatches, memoranda, and plans each day without the help of his secretary. He wrote verses and composed music. Profoundly secretive in public business, he chose as his advisers men for the most part of the meanest origin: Thomas Wolsey, the son of a poor and rascally butcher of Ipswich, whose name appears on the borough records for selling meat unfit for human consumption; Thomas Cromwell, a small attorney; Thomas Cranmer, an obscure lecturer in divinity. Like his father he distrusted the hereditary nobility, preferring the discreet counsel of men without a wide circle of friends.

Considering what happened to some of them, at Henry's instigation, perhaps they'd have been better off with a wider, or at least a different, circle of friends. Henry VIII cared very much for the trappings of monarchy. There was, certainly in his earlier years, something about him that would have been at home in ancient Rome. And the new King was aware of the European Renaissance which was now reaching northern Europe. But most of all, especially given his temperament, Henry was aware of exploration. This, after all, was the time of Columbus and Cabot. Yet the new King could hardly afford to become a merchant venturer and may not have had the commercial vision of his father.

C❖It was nearly 100 years [after Columbus] before England began to exert her potential sea-power. Her achievements during this period were by comparison meagre. The merchants of Bristol tried to seek a north-west passage beyond the Atlantic to the Far East, but they had little success or encouragement. Their colleagues in London and Eastern England were more concerned with the solid profits from trade with the Netherlands. Henry Tudor, however, appreciated private enterprise, provided it did not involve him in disputes with Spain. He financed an expedition by John Cabot, who was a Genoese like Columbus, and lived in Bristol. In 1497, Cabot struck land near Cape Breton Island. But there was little prospect of trade and an immense forbidding continent seemed to block further advance. On a second voyage Cabot sailed down the coast of America in the direction of Florida, but this was too near the region of Spanish efforts. Upon Cabot's death, the cautious Henry [VII] abandoned his Atlantic enterprise.

In the year Columbus sailed for the Americas, 1492, the future Henry VIII was one year old. When Cabot landed at Cape Breton Island, he was six. Now, as King, his ambitions could lie not so much with the new world, but within the old.

C❖Henry VII had only once sent English levies abroad, preferring to hire mercenaries who fought alongside foreign armies. Henry VIII now determined that this policy should be reversed. . . . Henry planned to reconquer Bordeaux, lost sixty years before, while King Ferdinand invaded Navarre, . . . and the Pope and the republic of Venice operated against the French armies in Italy. The year was 1512. . . . The English expedition to Gascony failed. Ferdinand took the whole of Navarre . . . But the English found that the style of warfare . . . with longbows and ponderously armed mounted men, had become obsolete on the Continent. . . . [The Marquess of] Dorset's army, as unaccustomed to Gascon wine as to French tactics, and ravaged by dysentery, disintegrated. The troops refused to obey their officers and boarded the transports for home. . . . After negotiations lasting throughout the winter of 1512–13, Ferdinand and the Venetians deserted Henry and the Pope, and made peace with France. . . . [Henry] arranged to hire the Emperor Maximilian, with the Imperial artillery and the greater part of the Austrian army. . . .These arrangements, though costly, were brilliantly successful. Under Henry's command, the English, with the Austrian mercenaries, routed the French in August 1513 at the Battle of the Spurs, so called because of the rapidity of the French retreat. . . . To crown all, Queen Catherine, who had been left behind as Regent of England, sent great news from the North.

It was not, however, great news for the Scots. In the late summer of 1513 50,000 Scots warriors invaded England. Henry had but one experienced general left in England. He was the Earl of Surrey whose father, the Duke of Norfolk, had been killed at the Battle of Bosworth by Henry's father. Ironically, out-of-date warfare that had failed Henry in France succeeded at home.

C❖This skillful veteran . . . knowing every inch of the ground, did not hesitate to march round the Scottish army, and, although outnumbered by two to one, placed himself between the enemy and Edinburgh. At Flodden Field, a bloody battle was fought on September 9, 1513. Both armies faced their homeland. The whole of Scotland, Highland and Lowland alike, drew out with their retainers in the traditional schiltrons, or circles of spearmen, and around the standard of their King. The English archers once again directed upon these redoubtable masses a long, intense, and murderous arrow storm. . . . When night fell the flower of the Scottish chivalry lay in their ranks where they had fought, and among them King James IV. . . . In Scotland, a year-old child succeeded to the throne as James V. His mother, the Regent, was Henry's sister Margaret, and peace now descended on the northern Border for the greater part of the reign.

An important figure in the organization of Henry's success in the French wars was Thomas Wolsey. He had been in royal service with Henry's father, had been master of Magdalen College Oxford, and had been made almoner to Henry's Royal Household. Henry VIII needed someone who would carry out his wishes in such an uncompromising way that Henry would be allowed to get on with his pastimes, his music, his hunting, his pleasures. But not until he was satisfied with Wolsey did he allow his back to be turned by these distractions.

Henry persuaded the Pope to create Wolsey Papal Legate in England. That done, the Cardinal sat above all ecclesiastical authority in the land. The English Church, therefore, was controlled by one of its number, who was a royal servant.

C❖Wolsey was richly rewarded for the foreign successes. He received the Bishopric of Lincoln during the course of the negotiations [with the French]; then, after the peace terms were settled, the Archbishopric of York; and a year later, after long negotiation by the King on his behalf, a cardinal's hat. This shower of ecclesiastical honours did not, however, give Wolsey sufficient civil authority, and in December 1515, Henry created him Lord Chancellor . . .

For fourteen years, Wolsey, in the King's name, was the effective ruler of the realm. He owed his position not only to his great capacity for business, but to his considerable personal charm. . . . All this commended him to his young master. Other would-be counsellors of Henry's saw a different side of the Cardinal's character. They resented being scornfully overborne by him in debate; they detested his arrogance, and envied his ever-growing wealth and extensive patronage. At the height of his influence, Wolsey . . . successfully held in his grasp an accumulation of power that has probably never been equalled in England.

Once he had been appointed Lord Chancellor and Chief Councillor, Wolsey's powers were absolute. Parliament rarely met and under his instigation the Court of Star Chamber (so named because it sat in the Star Chamber at the Palace of

CHAPTER SEVENTEEN

1516–1546

———— ❖ ————

It is worth pausing at this stage of Henry VIII's reign, to see him through the eyes of a foreign visitor. On St George's Day 1515 – Henry was just two months short of his twenty-fifth birthday – a Venetian diplomat, by the name of Pasqualigo, was given audience at the anniversary of the institution of the Order of the Garter. Pasqualigo's dispatches from that time paint a vivid picture of the King and the way he lived.

> ❖They led us into a sort of hall [at the Palace of Richmond], and though it was before mass, they made us breakfast, for fear we should faint; after which we were conducted to the presence, through sundry chambers all hung with most beautiful tapestry, figured in gold and silver, and in silk, passing down the ranks of the bodyguard, which consists of 300 halberdiers in silver breastplates and pikes in their hands; and, by God, they were all as big as giants. . . . We at length reached the King, who was under a canopy of cloth of gold, embroidered in Florence, the most costly thing I have ever witnessed. He was leaning against his gilt throne, on which there was a large gold brocade cushion, where the long gold sword of state lay. He wore a cap of crimson velvet, in the French fashion, and the brim was looped up all around with lacets, which had gold enamelled tags. His doublet was in the Swiss fashion, striped alternately with white and crimson satin, and his hose were scarlet and slashed from the knee upwards. Very close round his neck he had a gold collar, from which there hung a round cut diamond, the size of the largest walnut I ever saw, and to this was suspended a most beautiful and very large round pearl. His mantle was of purple velvet, lined with white satin, the sleeves being open, and with a train verily more than four Venetian yards in length.

This was the period of the European Renaissance, the revival of art and letters based on classical forms and classical models. It had begun in Italy and was now spreading into northern Europe. One of the first effects in England was Christian humanism. The humanists offered biblical piety and the study of the Greek New Testament. As Pasqualigo was being overwhelmed by the splendour at Richmond, Desiderius Erasmus was finishing his *Novum Instrumentum*, a new version of the New Testament. He published tracts against the superstitions of Catholicism and thus the Pope.

Having escaped the frustrations and considerable anger of the church in Amsterdam, Erasmus came to the comparative freedom of Cambridge to finish his New Testament and, as part of the 'new learning', indeed an important figure in it, he was embraced by the new scholars of England, including Thomas More and John Colet. John Colet, the Dean of St Paul's (now there was a humourless man) had been to Italy, had mastered Greek, wrote of divine truths and the importance of original texts and preached church reform from within, and spiritual revival. Thomas More's *Utopia*, published in 1516, presented an imaginary society of pagans and suggested that Christians could learn from such wretches. More, of course, was to go to the Tower eventually and his head would be hung over London Bridge.

Perhaps the first open signs of the changes of fortunes of those trusted by Henry came with the slide of Wolsey. Already doubted by Henry because of his part in the failure of further policies towards the French, Wolsey now found himself vulnerable to the King's ambition to get rid of his wife, Catherine of Aragon.

C❖In 1525 she was aged forty. . . . A typical Spanish princess, she had matured and aged rapidly; it was clear that she would bear Henry no male heir. Either the King's illegitimate son, the Duke of Richmond, now aged six, would have to be appointed by Act of Parliament, or perhaps England might accept Catherine's child, Mary, now aged nine, as the first Queen of England in her own right since Matilda. . . . The first step, clearly, was to get rid of Catherine. In May 1527 Cardinal Wolsey, acting as Papal Legate, and with the collusion of the King, held a secret ecclesiastical court at his house in Westminster. He summoned Henry to appear before him, charged him with having married his deceased brother's wife within the degrees of affinity prohibited by the laws of the Church. Henry's authority had been a Bull of Dispensation . . . which said in effect that since the marriage between Catherine and Arthur had not been consummated, Catherine was not legally Henry's deceased brother's wife and Henry could marry Catherine. Although Catherine . . . maintained to her dying day that her marriage with Arthur had not been consummated, nobody was convinced. . . . the court decided that the point should be submitted to a number of the most learned bishops in England. Several bishops replied, however, that provided Papal dispensation had been secured such a marriage was perfectly lawful.

But Henry was, by now, determined to marry Anne Boleyn, the young sister of his sometime mistress, Mary Carey. Opposition came from very powerful people other than the learned bishops of England. They included Charles V, the Emperor of the Habsburgs. Italy had fallen to the Habsburgs so the Pope, although he needed Henry on his side, had more or less to do what Charles V wanted him to. And Charles V's aunt was Catherine of Aragon. Wolsey's attempts to negotiate failed and his stock fell further.

C❖New counsellors were called in. . . . Dr Cranmer, a young lecturer in divinity at Cambridge and a friend of the Boleyns, made a . . . suggestion . . . that the question whether the King had ever been legally married should be . . . submitted to the universities of Europe. The King at once took up the idea. Cranmer was sent for and complimented. Letters and messengers were dispatched to all the universities in Europe. . . . Wolsey retired in disgrace to his Diocese of York, which he had never visited.

Eventually Wolsey was arrested for high treason. He died at Leicester Abbey on his way to the Tower of London.

C❖Cranmer's idea of an appeal to the universities . . . proved a great success. . . . The King had known all along that he was right and here, it seemed, was the final proof. He determined to mark his displeasure with the Pope by some striking measure against the power of the Church of England. . . . The King would ask his learned Commons to propose reforms. . . . A committee was formed of all the lawyers in the House, and they drafted the necessary Bills in record time. . . . On February 7, 1531, the clergy acknowledged that the King was 'their especial Protector, one and supreme lord and, as far as the law of Christ allows, even supreme head'. Throughout these proceedings, Queen Catherine remained at Court. The King, although he rode and talked openly with Anne, left Catherine in charge of his personal wardrobe, including supervision of the laundry and the making of his linen. . . . Anne was furiously jealous, but for months the King refused to abandon his old routine. . . . Finally, about the middle of July [1531], Anne took the King on a long hunting expedition . . . Catherine waited day after day . . . At last the messenger came: the King would come back. But His Majesty did not wish to see the Queen; she was commanded to retire instantly to Wolsey's former palace at Moor, in Hertfordshire. Henceforward she, and her daughter Mary, were banished from Court.

Inevitably the popular story of Henry VIII is also the story of six wives: Catherine of Aragon, Anne Boleyn, Jane Seymour, Anne of Cleves and the last two Catherines, Catherine Howard and Catherine Parr. But the two who mattered historically were Catherine of Aragon and Anne Boleyn. The divorce of the first to marry the second brought about the break with Rome and the position of the English monarch as head of the Church of England. And Anne Boleyn was the mother of Elizabeth I. When Henry VIII and Anne Boleyn married in secrecy she was already pregnant and on 7 September 1533 the future Queen Elizabeth was born.

After all the agonies, the diplomatic and military risks, Henry had, not the male heir he so desperately wanted, but another daughter. It is said that in his anger he went to stay at the house of Sir John Seymour. There he fell in love with Sir John's daughter, Jane. Anne Boleyn's days were numbered, and before their daughter Elizabeth reached her third birthday, Anne was accused (perhaps falsely so) of treasonous adultery and was beheaded with a double-edged sword at the Tower.

The decision to abandon Catherine of Aragon was followed by a whirlwind of legislation. The Acts of Appeals discarded the Pope's right to rule in English Church law suits. The Act of Supremacy made the English monarch the supreme head of the Church of England. And the Treasons Act made it a high treasonable offence, that is punishable by execution, to deny the monarch's supremacy. The Act against the Pope's authority, the Act of Reformation, was to come.

The administrative and constitutional revolution was led by Henry, but with the help of Thomas More and against the doubts of John Fisher, the Bishop of Rochester. When they rebelled and refused to swear to the supremacy of the King they fell, and then Cranmer and Thomas Cromwell stood by the King.

C❖To publish or pronounce maliciously by express words that the King was a tyrant or heretic was made high treason. As the brutality of the reign increased many hundreds were to be hanged, disembowelled and quartered on these grounds. . . . While Fisher was in the Tower, the Pope created seven cardinals, of whom one was 'John, Bishop of Rochester, kept in Prison by the King of England'. Directly Henry heard the news he declared in anger several times that he would send Fisher's head to Rome for the Cardinal's hat. Fisher was executed in June 1535 and More in July.

By the following year Henry was married to Jane Seymour, perhaps the truest love of his life. The marriage lasted but eighteen months. The new Queen died apparently under crude surgery, after the birth of their son, the future Edward VI. For the moment Henry's grief had to be set aside. Other affairs, affairs of State, were calling. The need to replenish his Treasury was uppermost in his mind and the obvious source was the fount of the greatest wealth in the land: the Church.

Henry VIII wished to suppress the 400 or so small monasteries which were, anyway, in decline, and whose endowments were, in Henry's view, wasted on intellectually shabby monks.

So the Dissolution of the Monasteries really follows on from the dissolution of the so-called Alien Priories a century earlier. This wording, from the 1536 Act of Parliament, makes very clear that there was not much regard for the smaller houses, as the monasteries were known.

❖Forasmuch as manifest sin, vicious, carnal and abominable living is daily used and committed amongst the little and small abbeys, priories, and other religious houses of monks, canons, and nuns, where the congregation of such religious persons is under the number of twelve persons, whereby the governors of such religious houses and their convents, spoil, destroy, consume, and utterly waste as well their churches, monasteries, priories, principal houses, farms, granges, lands, tenements, and hereditaments, as the ornaments of their churches and their goods and chattels to the high displeasure of Almighty God, slander of good religion, and to the greater infamy of the King's Highness and realm, if redress should not be had thereof, and albeit that many continual visitations hath been heretofore had by the space of 200 years and more, for an honest and charitable reformation of such unthrifty, carnal, and abominable living, yet nevertheless little or none amendment, and by cursed custom so rooted, and infested, that a great number of the religious persons in such small houses do choose to rove abroad in apostasy than to conform to the observation of good religion, so that without such small houses be utterly suppressed and the religious persons therein committed to great and honorable monasteries of religion in this realm, where they may be compelled to live religiously for reformation of their lives . . . there can else be no reformation in this behalf . . .

And so it goes on and very much on. If ever there was an Act that disgraced the reputations of the lawmakers then this document was the template. And the man who was instrumental in making sure the template fitted the King's wishes was his new first minister, Thomas Cromwell.

C❖Thomas Cromwell . . . had served his apprenticeship in statecraft under Wolsey, but he had also learned the lessons of his master's downfall. Ruthless, cynical, Machiavellian, Cromwell was a man of the New Age. His ambition was matched by his energy and served by a penetrating intelligence. When he succeeded Wolsey as the King's principal Minister, he made no effort to inherit the pomp and glory of the fallen Cardinal. Nevertheless his were more solid achievements in both State and Church. . . . Before his day Government policy had for centuries been both made and implemented in the royal household. Though Henry VII had improved the system, he had remained in a sense a mediaeval king. Thomas Cromwell thoroughly reformed it during his ten years of power and, when he fell in 1540, policy was already carried out by Government departments, operating outside the household. Perhaps his greatest accomplishment, though not so dramatic as his other work, was his inception of the Government service of modern England. Cromwell is the uncommemorated architect of our great departments of state.

In 1536 the Privy Council replaced the King's Council as a sort of executive board of advisers and governors. It enforced policy, made sure the law courts worked – or tried to – and managed the economy. Through this system Cromwell began the financial reforms of England which eventually distanced the financing of royalty – what is now called the Civil List – from that of government.

But his main task was to oversee the break up of the monasteries, the Dissolution. Monasteries often owed their allegiance to institutions outside England but this now contravened Henry's supreme power over the Church. More-over, if Henry were to keep the nobility on his side, he had to make sure, with Cromwell's help, that they'd be looked after. The best way to do that was with patronage and money.

C❖. . . Cromwell handled the Dissolution of the monasteries with conspicuous, cold-blooded efficiency. . . . The high nobility and country gentry acquired on favourable terms all kinds of fine estates. . . . Many local squires had long been stewards of monastic lands, and now bought properties which they had managed for generations. Throughout the middle classes there was great irritation at the privileges and wealth of the Church. They resented the undue proportion of the national income engrossed by those who rendered no economic service. The King was assured of the support of Parliament and the prosperous classes. Most of the displaced monks, nearly 10,000 in all, faced their lot with relief or fortitude, assisted by substantial pensions. Some even married nuns, and many became respectable parish clergy. The Dissolution brought lands into the Crown's possession worth at the time over £100,000 a year, and by the sale or lease of the rest of the former monastic properties, the Crown gained a million and a half – a huge sum in those days, though probably much less than the properties were worth. The main result of this transaction was, in effect if not intention, to commit the landed and mercantile classes to the Reformation settlement and the Tudor dynasty.

The events of the 1530s had a profound effect on the practice of religion: England was still a Catholic nation.

C❖The Bible now acquired a new and far-reaching authority. The older generation considered that Holy Writ was dangerous in the hands of the unlearned and should only be read by priests. . . . But complete printed Bibles, translated into English by Tyndale and Coverdale, had appeared for the first time late in the autumn of 1535, and were now running through several editions. The Government enjoined the clergy to encourage Bible-reading . . . and, in August 1536, Cromwell ordered the Paternoster and Commandments to be taught in the mother tongue instead of in Latin. . . . The country folk were deeply agitated, particularly in the fiercely Catholic and economically backward North.

In the autumn, when the new taxes came to be assessed after Michaelmas, farmers and yokels collected in large numbers throughout the North of England and Lincolnshire, swearing to resist the taxes and maintain the old order in the Church. The revolt, which took the name of 'The Pilgrimage of Grace', was spontaneous.

The rebels captured the King's Tax Commissioners. He responded with a threat to 'burn, spoil and destroy their goods, wives, and children with all extremity'.

C❖In early 1537 the rebellion collapsed as quickly as it had arisen, but Henry determined to make examples of the ringleaders. . . . Altogether some 250 of the insurgents were put to death. . . . Henry now . . . began suppressing the larger monasteries . . . As a further blow to the old school, the Government commissioned, in Paris, a great printing of English Bibles . . . and, in September 1538, directed that every parish in the country should purchase a Bible of the largest volume in English to be set up in each church, where the parishioners might most commodiously resort to the same and read it. . . . This Bible has remained the basis of all later editions, including the Authorized Version prepared in the reign of James I.

There was little holy in what remained of the reign of this Henry, once trained in priesthood. His plundering of the institutions of the monasteries, 560 of them, continued until there was no booty left. The cost of wars that followed in the 1540s probably wiped out the financial gains and the material losses were obvious: the melting of fine jewellery and ornaments, the wanton destruction of Gothic buildings, and the shredding of libraries. Cromwell did much to ease the consequence of constitutional and philosophical vandalism, but even he was eventually thrown to his enemies and to execution. Anne of Cleves, Henry's fourth wife, was indirectly responsible for Cromwell's death. Cromwell had encouraged the marriage as a means of creating a union with the North German Lutheran princes, the best hope of alliance on the Continent. But the marriage was never consummated – Henry thought Anne plain and uninteresting – and the failure of Cromwell's match-making made him vulnerable.

C❖The Duke of Norfolk headed the reaction [against Cromwell] . . . One of Norfolk's nieces, Catherine Howard, was presented to Henry and captured his affections at first sight. . . . In June 1540, the King was persuaded to get rid of Cromwell and Anne together. Cromwell was condemned under a Bill of Attainder charging him principally with heresy and 'broadcasting' erroneous books and, implicitly, with treason. . . . A few days after Cromwell was executed, on July 28, Henry was privately married to his fifth wife, Catherine Howard.

Catherine, about twenty-two, with auburn hair and hazel eyes, was the prettiest of Henry's wives. . . . But wild, tempestuous Catherine was not long content with a husband nearly thirty years older than herself. Her reckless love for her cousin, Thomas Culpeper, was discovered . . .

Henry had her head chopped off. The basket, or so it was said, rested on the same spot upon which it had caught the head of Anne Boleyn. Eighteen months later, Catherine Parr was Queen and nurse to Henry. Henry had long suffered from an enormous ulcer in his leg. Even his largely ceremonial armour had to be shaped to cope with the increasing pain. Craftsmen and tailors were not, however, able to cope with his increasing rages, perhaps gingered by his illness. Nor was it possible to calm his antagonism against Scotland and France.

Henry wanted war with France. But he understood that given the long alliance with Scotland, France would always be in a strong position to encourage the Scots to raid England should Henry's army cross the Channel in any great numbers. Indeed, Henry understood, even if he resisted, the notion that bringing England, Scotland, Ireland, and Wales into some form of reasonable co-existence was a foremost responsibility of any King of England. The easiest part of this task, to some extent set in motion by Cromwell, was to achieve unity with Wales. In 1543, the year of Henry's marriage to Catherine Parr, the Act for the Government of Wales was passed. This meant that Wales was now under English law, including the system of administration by counties. From that date, twenty-four Welsh parliamentary representatives would be sent to Westminster, and new Courts of Great Session were established to oversee the judiciary. It is from this date that the Welsh language began its decline. And the war with Scotland and France had already started.

C❖Reviving the obsolete claim to suzerainty, Henry [VIII] denounced the Scots as rebels and pressed them to relinquish their alliance with France . . . in the autumn of 1542, an expedition under Norfolk had to turn back at Kelso . . . and the Scots proceeded to carry the war into the enemy's country. Their decision proved disastrous. Badly led and imperfectly organized, they lost more than half their army of 10,000 men in Solway Moss and were utterly routed. The news of this second Flodden killed James V, who died leaving the kingdom to an infant of one week, Mary, the famous Queen of Scots.

At once the child became the focus of the struggle for Scotland. Henry claimed her for the bride of his own son and heir. But the Scots Queen Mother was a French princess, Mary of Guise. The pro-French Catholic party . . . began negotiations for marrying Mary to a French prince. Such a marriage could never be accepted by England. . . . Once again, England and the Empire made common cause against the French and, in May 1543, a secret treaty was ratified between Charles V [the Emperor] and Henry. . . the King himself was to cross the Channel and lead an army against Francis [the French King] in co-operation with an Imperial force from the north east.

The plan was excellent, but the execution failed.

Henry captured Boulogne. The Emperor, his supposed ally, was at the same time making a separate treaty with King Francis. The outcome for Henry was a treaty of sorts which allowed Boulogne to remain English for eight years, but then to be handed back, complete with new fortifications. The cost of this war to England was enormous. At the same time, everything was going wrong for Henry in Scotland. Raids by English forces, and in particular the attack on Edinburgh by the English, united the Scots against Henry. So now Henry had exactly what he'd tried so hard to avoid: war with Scotland and France at the same time.

C❖Without a single ally, the nation faced the possibility of invasion from both France and Scotland. The crisis called for unexampled sacrifices from the English people; never had they been called upon to pay so many loans, subsidies, and benevolences. . . . At Portsmouth he [Henry] prepared for the threatened invasion in person. A French fleet penetrated the Solent and landed troops in the Isle of Wight; but they were soon driven off, and the crisis gradually passed.

During the previous six years, Henry, perhaps arrogantly, believed that he could be his own chief minister, leaving the everyday running of the country to the Privy Council. Henry, who was increasingly ill, seemed satisfied that he could hold apart the rival factions – the radicals of Thomas Cranmer, and the old guard of his Secretary Stephen Gardiner, the Bishop of Winchester, and the Duke of Norfolk. All three supported Henry, but for different reasons. But the question in the minds of everyone at Court was simple: who would became Protector to the young King Edward when Henry VIII died? Many thought the Norfolks. But would that be so?

C❖A sudden and unexpected answer was given. On December 12, 1546 Norfolk and his son Surrey, the poet, were arrested for treason and sent to the Tower. . . . The King remembered that years before, Norfolk had been put forward as a possible heir to the throne, and Surrey had been suggested as a husband for Princess Mary. His suspicions aroused, he acted swiftly; in mid-January, Surrey was executed.

Parliament assembled to pass a Bill of Attainder against Norfolk. On [27 December] the royal assent was given and Norfolk was condemned to death. But that same evening, the King himself was dying. The physicians dared not tell him so, for prophesying the King's death was treason by Act of Parliament. Then as the long hours slowly passed, Sir Anthony Denny, 'boldly coming to the King, told him what case he was in, to man's judgment not like to live; and therefore exhorted him to prepare himself for death.' . . . Shortly before midnight, the King awoke. He sent for Cranmer. When he came Henry was too weak to speak; he could only stretch out his hand to Cranmer. In a few minutes, the Supreme Head had ceased to breathe.

It was the year 1547: Henry VIII had ruled since 1509. Henry's reign is remembered as the time of the break with Rome, of six wives, of savage persecution, torture, and execution. Yet the English church was in need of reform, and throughout Europe there was a revolt against papal authority. The Reformation, the new thinking, Erasmus and Luther, would have meant change whoever ruled England.

And with Henry gone, England needed a strong man at the centre of power to fend off the threat of constitutional and political implosion. Instead, the nation now had a weakling nine-year-old King and the vacillating Hertford, Duke of Somerset, as his Protector.

CHAPTER EIGHTEEN

1547–1557

❖

Between the death of Henry VIII, in 1547, and the coming of the first Elizabethans, in 1558, Edward VI came to the throne; the Book of Common Prayer came into existence; the Royal Protector, the Duke of Somerset, was executed; Lady Jane Grey was proclaimed Queen, then executed; Queen Mary came to the throne; first Catholics, then hundreds of Protestants including Ridley and Latimer and Cranmer, were executed; and another Anglo–French war began. And those, as a modern newsreader might say, are only the headlines.

C❖The English Reformation under Henry VIII had received its guiding impulse from the King's passions and his desire for power. He still deemed himself a good Catholic. However, none of his Catholic wives had borne him a son. Catherine of Aragon had given birth to the future Queen Mary, Anne Boleyn to the future Queen Elizabeth; but it was Jane, daughter of the Protestant house of Seymour, who had produced the future Edward VI. . . . Nevertheless, the Catholic Norfolks retained much of their power and influence. . . . [But] with the new reign, a deeper and more powerful tide began to flow. The guardian and chief counsellor of the child-King was his uncle, Edward Seymour, now Duke of Somerset. He and Cranmer proceeded to transform the political reformation of Henry VIII into a religious revolution.

The intrigues and ambitions of Somerset, of Dudley, who became Duke of Northumberland, and, of course, of Cranmer have tended to overshadow the young Edward VI. He inherited a kingdom that, for the first two of his six years on the throne, was unsettled. There were disturbances in East Anglia where Robert Ket led a rebellion against land enclosures, and in the West Country where rioters attacked Exeter. It was Somerset's inability to control these crises that made him so vulnerable to the other plotters at court. But the unrest was largely to do with the county administrators' inability to control local injustice and social disorder; it wasn't an attack on the monarchy.

C❖Warfare had been going on for decades between landowner and peasantry. Slowly and surely the rights and privileges of the village communities were infringed and removed. Common land was seized, enclosed, and turned to pasture for flocks. . . . In some counties as much as one-third of the arable land was turned over to grass, and the people looked in anger upon the new nobility, fat with sacrilegious spoil, but greedy still.

[The Duke of] Somerset had thus to face one of the worst economic crises that England has endured. Not only was there widespread unemployment, but also hardship caused by Henry's debasement of the coinage. The popular preachers were loud in denunciation. The Sermon of the Plough, preached by Hugh Latimer at Paul's Cross in 1548, is a notable piece of Tudor invective.

'In times past men were full of pity and compassion; but now there is no pity; for in London their brother shall die in the streets for cold; he shall lie sick at the door between stock and stock [that is, between the door-posts], and then perish for hunger. In times past, when any rich man died in London, they . . . would bequeath great sums of money toward the relief of the poor. . . . Charity is waxen cold . . .'

Edward's successor, Queen Mary, had Latimer burned at the stake in 1555. But the social unrest was as great in both reigns. The population increase (which had, by the 1550s, gained on what it had been before the Black Death) meant there was more labour available than land, and inflation meant that the cost of food had trebled. So it was greed and economic survival that sent landlords in the direction of enclosure.

Somerset, the Protector, appointed commissions to enquire into the enclosures.

C❖But this increased the discontent . . . in Norfolk . . . a tannery owner named Robert Ket took the lead. He established his headquarters outside Norwich, where about 16,000 peasants gathered in a camp of turf huts roofed with boughs. . . . Ket, day after day, tried country gentlemen charged with robbing the poor. No blood was shed, but property acquired by enclosing common land was restored to the public, and the rebels lived upon the flocks and herds of the landowners. The local authorities were powerless.

John Dudley, Earl of Warwick, marched to Ket's camp to suppress the uprising, but when a small urchin spoke and gestured rudely at his followers the urchin was immediately shot. The murder enraged Ket's followers and fighting began. Three thousand five hundred peasants were killed and there were no wounded. Ket was hanged at Norwich Castle. Warwick, strengthened by his management of the incident, became the leader of the Opposition and his party, the Lords in London, met to take measures against the Protector. No one supported Somerset and in January, 1552, he was executed.

Warwick created himself Duke of Northumberland, restructured the Privy Council and, instead of calling himself Protector, he became Lord President of the Council. He returned Boulogne to the French and withdrew English soldiers from Scotland. He aligned himself with the Protestant cause and this decision had long-lasting results. For when Cranmer published the second edition of his Book of Common Prayer in 1552, it had to be approved by Parliament and supported by the Acts of Uniformity. It was from this point that the authority of the Church of England became reliant upon Parliament.

So the laity triumphed over the church. But Northumberland (Warwick) had an immediate constitutional crisis to resolve. Edward VI, always a sickly youth, was dying. Mary, the daughter of Henry VIII's first wife, Catherine of Aragon, was the constitutional successor. But Mary was a Catholic. Northumberland persuaded the dying Edward VI to disinherit Mary and Elizabeth in favour of Lady Jane Grey, the daughter of the Marquess of Dorset and the granddaughter of Henry VIII's sister, Mary.

C❖On July 6, 1553, Edward VI expired, and Lady Jane Grey was proclaimed Queen in London. The only response to this announcement was gathering resistance . . . The common people flocked to Mary's support. The Privy Councillors and the City authorities swam with the tide. Northumberland was left without an ally. In August, Mary entered London with Elizabeth at her side. Lady Jane and her husband were consigned to the Tower. In vain, Northumberland grovelled. . . . But nothing could save him from an ignominious death.

Northumberland was executed. And now little could save the Protestants from Mary's revenge and the revenge of those closest to her. She released the deposed Bishop of Winchester, Stephen Gardiner, from the Tower and made him Lord Chancellor. Even allowing for the biased record writing of a later time, between them, Gardiner – and after him the Papal Legate, Cardinal Pole – and the Queen were probably responsible for more than 200 people being burned at the stake, including Archbishop Cranmer. The Queen's single ambition was reunion with Rome.

C❖In Stephen Gardiner . . . she found an able and ardent servant. The religious legislation of the Reformation Parliament was repealed. But one thing Mary could not do. She could not restore to the Church the lands parcelled out among the nobility. The Tudor magnates were willing to go to Mass, but not to lose their new property. . . . There was rioting in the capital. Gardiner's life was threatened. He wore a mail shirt throughout the day and was guarded by 100 men at night. A dead dog was flung through the window of the Queen's chamber, a halter round its neck, its ears cropped, and bearing a label saying that all the [Catholic] priests in England should be hanged.

Mary married her cousin the future Philip II of Spain. But before there was any agreement to his marriage to Mary, he, or his advisers, demanded the execution of the young Elizabeth. She was, they pointed out, in line to the throne and therefore a threat. Mary refused and they had to make do with Elizabeth's imprisonment.

Gardiner died in 1555 and Cardinal Pole became Archbishop of Canterbury. Reginald Pole was an exiled Catholic who had been forced to leave England in 1532. He published an attack on Henry's anti-papal ideas in 1536 and, because he was out of the country, his mother, the Countess of Salisbury (and a one-time governess to Mary), was executed in his place.

The new King, Philip, was feared (the Inquisition was in everyone's mind) and Simon Renard, the Holy Roman Emperor's ambassador, described the situation in a letter to his Emperor, dated 3 September 1554.

❖The Spaniards are hated, as I have seen in the past and expect to see in the future. There was trouble at the last session of Parliament, and disagreeable incidents are of daily occurrence. Only ten days ago, the heretics tried to burn a church in Suffolk with the entire congregation that was hearing Mass inside. On examining the brief sent hither by the Cardinal and intended to dispense those who hold Church property, I have noticed that it is not drawn up in a suitable manner. The Pope intends to grant the dispensations to those for whom the King and Queen intercede, though with a restrictive clause binding them to consult the Pope on cases that appear to be of importance. Another feature of this document is that the King is mentioned, though it was dated last June when the marriage had not been consummated. It is my duty to inform your majesty that the Catholics hold more Church property than do the heretics, and unless they obtain general dispensation to satisfy them that their titles will never be contested they will not allow the Cardinal to execute his commission. The Holy See's contention is naturally that if it grants a dispensation for Church property before an obeisance is offered, it will seem as if the same obeisance is being bought, and an evil and scandalous precedent would be created; but the loftier aims of religion ought to be considered in preference to a mere question of Church property, especially in this realm where the abbeys have all been destroyed and overthrown by the King's authority.

When Cardinal Pole arrived, he stood by his Queen to bring about the reconversion of the land to Catholicism. Or so he hoped.

C❖Mary has been for ever odious in the minds of a Protestant nation as the Bloody Queen who martyred her noblest subjects. These stories have become part of the common memory of the people – the famous scenes at Oxford in 1555, the faggots which consumed the Protestant bishops, Latimer and Ridley, the pitiful recantation and final heroic end, in March 1556, of the frail, aged Archbishop Cranmer. Their martyrdom rallied to the Protestant faith many who till now had shown indifference.

These martyrs saw in vision that their deaths were not in vain, and, standing at the stake, pronounced immortal words. 'Be of good comfort, Master Ridley,' Latimer cried at the crackling of the flames. 'Play the man. We shall this day light such a candle, by God's Grace, in England, as I trust shall never be put out.'

Cranmer's end was no more pitiful than that of the other martyrs. He was, with Ridley, one of the most important theologians of the Reformation. It was Cranmer who insisted that the people should understand that Christ exists in faith, not in material symbols, even such as bread and wine. His original arrest would seem to have been as much to do with Queen Mary's need to avenge Cranmer's part in the divorce of her mother, Catherine of Aragon. But he had to be shown as a traitor to the throne or better still as a heretic. There followed long months of interrogation to prove his heresy. Eventually Cranmer appears to have lost his nerve – a crude summary perhaps of the interminable questioning, humiliation and continuing threat of death he was subjected to. The wording of the document which Cranmer signed has been called a recantation of all that in which he believed.

❖I, Thomas Cranmer, do renounce, abhor, and detest all manners of heresies and errors of Luther and Zwinglius, and all other teachings which be contrary to true sound doctrine. And I believe most sincerely in my heart, and with my mouth I confess, in one Holy and Catholic Church visible, without the which there is no salvation; and therefore I acknowledge the Bishop of Rome to be supreme head on earth, unto whom all Christian people ought to be subject. I believe and worship in the Sacrament of the Altar the very body and blood of Christ, being contained most truly under the forms of bread and wine.

The document was published. But it had been witnessed by a Spanish friar and the feelings towards the Spanish at the time caused many to doubt its authenticity. Another document was prepared, this time to disgrace the old

Reformation movement. Cranmer, by now old and broken, signed it. He was led from his room in Oxford, in procession to St Mary's, where a great crowd had gathered to hear the sermon of execution preached by the Provost of Eton.

Cranmer knelt in prayer, and then, to the audience, hardly a congregation in the liturgical sense, he rejected all the documents he had signed, all the statements made in his name. And as he reached the end of his last sermon it began to dawn on the crowd that they were witnessing Cranmer's most defiant statement of his faith.

❖I renounce and refuse as things written with my hand contrary to the truth which I thought in my heart, and written in fear of death and to save my life if it might be; and that is, all such bills which I have written or signed with mine own hand since my degradation: wherein I have written many things untrue. And forasmuch as my hand offended in writing contrary to my heart, therefore my hand shall be first punished; for if I may come to the fire, it shall be first burned. And as for the Pope, I refuse him as Christ's enemy and anti-Christ, with all his false doctrine. And as for the Sacrament. . . .

Cranmer never finished his last, perhaps his greatest, sermon. He was dragged away along Brasenose Lane to the site in front of Balliol where Latimer and Ridley had been executed. One hundred and fifty faggots of furze and a hundred faggots of wood were stacked, and Cranmer was stripped to his long white shirt and bound by the waist to the stake. As the flames grew Cranmer stretched his arm into the fire and cried, 'This hand hath offended.' It was 21 March 1556.

Queen Mary had wanted Cranmer a Catholic or no Cranmer at all. She had had her way.

CHAPTER NINETEEN

1558–1587

⎯⎯⎯ ❖ ⎯⎯⎯

I n 1558, Mary I, known as Bloody Mary, died. She had reigned for five
tempestuous years and tried to reverse the Reformation. She failed. She also
could not prevent another war with France and in her last year she lost the
English possession across the Channel, Calais.

And so, in 1558, Queen Elizabeth I came to the throne. There's hardly a
town in England without a pub or street named after a character from her reign.
The roll call of the famous from her forty-five-year reign has produced libraries
of study for each individual character. There was Elizabeth herself, and Cecil,
Walsingham, Essex, Mary Queen of Scots, Darnley, Knox, Gresham, Dudley,
Hawkins, Raleigh, Drake, Frobisher, Sydney, Cavendish, Whitgift, Spenser,
Marlowe, Shakespeare, Byrd, Jonson. And many more.

Churchill described the England which the twenty-five-year-old Elizabeth
knew when she came to the throne on 17 November 1558.

C❖Few sovereigns ever succeeded to a more hazardous inheritance than she.
England's link with Spain had brought the hostility of France and the loss
of Calais. Tudor policy in Scotland had broken down. The old military
danger of the Middle Ages, a Franco-Scottish alliance, again threatened. In
the eyes of Catholic Europe Mary, the Queen of Scots,. . . had a better claim
to the English throne than Elizabeth, and with the power of France behind
her, she stood a good chance of gaining it. . . . Even before the death of
Henry VIII, England's finances had been growing desperate. English credit
at Antwerp, the centre of the European money market, was so weak that
the Government had to pay 14% for its loans. The coinage, which had been
debased yet further under Edward VI, was now chaotic. England's only
official ally, Spain, suspected the new regime for religious reasons.

So there were many in 1558 who thought that Elizabeth wouldn't last very long.
But Elizabeth took after her father, Henry VIII. She was experienced enough
– perhaps sharpened is a better description – to understand the dangers of
dogmatism, from whichever side of the religious divide it appeared. She had
been threatened with beheading, had been locked in the Tower and was then

made prisoner at Woodstock. Her mother had been executed and, for at least the past five years, Elizabeth had been seen as a direct threat to Queen Mary Tudor.

C❖Around her had gathered some of the ablest Protestant minds: Matthew Parker, who was to be her Archbishop of Canterbury; Nicholas Bacon, whom she appointed Lord Keeper of the Great Seal; Roger Ascham, the foremost scholar of the day; and most important of all, William Cecil, the adaptable civil servant who had already held office as Secretary under Somerset and Northumberland. Of sixteenth-century statesmen, Cecil was undoubtedly the greatest. He possessed a consuming thirst for information about the affairs of the realm and immense industry in the business of office. Cautious good judgment marked all his actions. Their [Cecil's and the Queen's] close and daily collaboration was to last, in spite of shocks and jars, until Cecil's death, forty years later.

Religious peace at home and safety from Scotland were the foremost needs of the realm. England became Protestant by law, Queen Mary's Catholic legislation was repealed, and the sovereign was declared supreme Governor of the English Church.

But it wasn't simply a matter of course for England to become a Protestant state after the death of Mary I. All the bishops, and probably most of the people, were still Catholics. It's quite possible that if some arrangement could have been made with Rome that would have proved a better security for England and its monarch, then it would have been seriously pursued. But the then Pope, Paul IV, believed that princes and kings should grovel to papal authority.

C❖It is at this point that the party known as the Puritans, who were to play so great a role in the next 100 years, first enter English history. Democratic in theory and organization, intolerant in practice of all who differed from their views, the Puritans challenged the Queen's authority in Church and State, and although she sought freedom of conscience and could maintain with sincerity that she 'made no windows into men's souls', she dared not let them organize cells in the body religious or the body politic. A discordant and vigorous minority could rupture the delicate harmony that she was patiently weaving. Protestantism must be saved from its friends. . . . she realized that unless the Government controlled the Church, it would be too weak to survive the Counter Reformation now gathering head in Catholic Europe. So Elizabeth had soon to confront not only the Catholic danger from abroad, but Puritan attack at home, led by the fanatical exiles of Mary's reign who now streamed back from Geneva and from the Rhineland towns.

... All the novel questions agitating the world – the relation of the National Church to Rome on one side and to the national sovereign on the other; its future organization; its articles of religion; the disposal of its property and the property of its monasteries – could only be determined in Parliament where the Puritans soon formed a growing and outspoken Opposition. The gentry in Parliament . . . fell into two great divisions: those who thought things had gone far enough, and those who wanted to go a step farther. It was the future distinction of Cavalier and Puritan, Churchman and Dissenter, Tory and Whig.

It isn't possible to identify an exact Puritan theology. As with many similar groupings, describing what it was against, rather than precisely what it was for, is an easier way of defining Puritanism. Puritans were the extreme Protestants. Their theology was largely based on Calvinism. Puritans wanted a sparer, less ritualistic Church of England.

In 1558 the Continent was dominated by two opposing Catholic powers: the Valois monarchy of France and the Habsburg Empire, with Philip of Spain at its head. But there were signs of a truce, and if that were to happen, then the Pope might encourage them both to join in a Crusade – against the English. After all, in Catholic eyes, the English throne was now occupied by the daughter of the two people who caused the break with Rome. She represented a serious threat to Catholicism.

So for Elizabeth to maintain her religious balancing act, whatever measures were taken to defend the throne must also reflect what was going on elsewhere in Europe. And Elizabeth's own view was that she mustn't be seen to be fanatically Protestant because of the threat from Rome, and because of the disquiet of some of her own people who were still mostly Catholics. At the same time, she mustn't be seen to be leaning towards Rome, or she would not be able to contain the Protestant and Puritan opposition.

In 1559 the Acts of Supremacy and Uniformity were passed. The Act of Uniformity laid down the use of common prayer, divine service and the administration of the sacraments. It was, in some senses, a compromise. For the Protestants it didn't go far enough. It implied, to take just one example, the wearing of Catholic vestments. As the Scottish reformer John Knox remarked, 'She that now reigneth over them is neither good Protestant nor yet resolute Papist.' The important section of the Statute was the one which made the use of the Book of Common Prayer compulsory, and the penalties imposed for not using it. Here's one part of the document which is far from being a compromise.

❖If any manner of parson, vicar or other whatsoever minister that ought to sing or say common prayer or minister the sacraments refuse to use the said common prayers, or shall wilfully or obstinately use any other rite, ceremony, order, form, or manner of celebrating of the Lord's Supper openly or privily, and shall be lawfully convicted according to the laws of this realm, he shall suffer penalties as follows: first offence, forfeiture of one year's profit of his spiritual benefices or promotions and six months' imprisonment; second offence, one year's imprisonment and deprivation; third offence, deprivation and imprisonment for life.

The two Bills were passed by Parliament, significantly without the consent of any of the churchmen, the first demonstration of William Cecil's abilities which might best be described in modern terms as those of the most robust government chief whip. The whole matter was concluded in 1563 with the definition of church doctrine: the Thirty-Nine Articles, which were based on Cranmer's first draft completed as long ago as Edward VI's time. Eight years later, the Subscription Act made it unlawful for clergy not to subscribe to the Articles.

Elizabeth's Establishing of the Church in Law – that is, the Established Church – prevented a religious civil war similar to the one running through France at the time. It also set the course for what is now called the Anglican Church, as the mainstay of the Elizabethan State. That settled, the court turned its attention to the next important matter: the continuation of the dynasty. In other words, finding a husband for the Queen.

C❖The security of the English State depended in the last resort on an assured succession. . . . The country was well aware of the responsibility which lay upon her. If she married an Englishman, her authority might be weakened, and there would be fighting among the suitors. The perils of such a course were borne in on her as she watched the reactions of her Court to her long and deep affection for the handsome, ambitious Robert Dudley, a younger son of Northumberland, whom she made Earl of Leicester. This was no way out. During the first months of her reign she had also to consider the claims of her brother-in-law, Philip II of Spain. A Spanish marriage had brought disaster to her sister, but marriage to Philip might buy a powerful friend; refusal might drive his religious animosity into the open. But by 1560, she had achieved temporary security and could wait her time. Marriage into one of the reigning houses of Europe would mean entangling herself in its European policy and facing the hostility of her husband's rivals. In vain, the Houses of Parliament begged their Virgin Queen to marry and produce an heir. Elizabeth was angry. She would admit no discussion. Her policy was to . . . [use] her potential value as a match to divide a European combination against her.

And then, in October 1562, when Elizabeth seemed to by dying of smallpox, the Protestants feared, once more, a Catholic succession. When she recovered, the Commons again said she had a duty to marry and she must carry out that duty. If not abroad, then at home.

But unlike Mary Stuart, Elizabeth knew the dangers of choosing a husband from her Court.

C❖Mary Stuart was a very different personality from Elizabeth, though in some ways her position was similar. She was a descendant of Henry VII, she held a throne; she lived in an age when it was a novelty for a woman to be the head of a state; and she was now unmarried. [She was the widow of Francis II of France.] . . . The Catholic English nobility, particularly in the North, were not indifferent to Mary's claims. Some of them dreamed of winning her hand. But Elizabeth knew her rival. She knew that Mary was incapable of separating her emotions from her politics. The Queen of Scots lacked the vigilant self-control which Elizabeth had learned in the bitter years of childhood. . . . Mary had only been a few years in Scotland when she married her cousin, Henry Stuart, Lord Darnley, a weak, conceited youth, who had both Tudor and Stuart blood in his veins. The result was disaster. The old feudal factions, now sharpened by religious conflict, seized Scotland in their grip. Mary's power melted slowly and steadily away.. . . Her husband became a tool of her opponents. In desperation she connived at his murder, and in 1567 married his murderer, a warlike Border lord, James Hepburn, Earl of Bothwell, whose unruly sword might yet save her throne and happiness. But defeat and imprisonment followed, and in 1568, she escaped into England and threw herself upon the mercy of the waiting Elizabeth.

Mary had inherited the title of Queen of the Scots as a baby when her father James V died shortly after the Battle of Solway Moss in 1542. Yet since the age of six she had lived in France, spoke French and Latin but probably could not understand the native Scots. But they most certainly understood what she represented. So when she fled to England, Elizabeth and her advisers felt more threatened than welcoming. Elizabeth imprisoned Mary in Tutbury Castle.

C❖Mary in England proved even more dangerous than Mary in Scotland. She became the focus of plots and conspiracies against Elizabeth's life. The survival of Protestant England was menaced by her existence. Secret emissaries of Spain crept into the country to nourish rebellion and claim the allegiance of Elizabeth's Catholic subjects. The whole force of the Counter-Reformation was unloosed against the one united Protestant country in Europe. If England were destroyed it seemed that Protestantism could be stamped out in every other land. Assassination was to be the first step. But Elizabeth was well served. Francis Walsingham, Cecil's assistant and later his rival in the government, tracked down Spanish agents and English traitors. This subtle intellectual and ardent Protestant, who had remained abroad throughout the reign of Mary Tudor, and whose knowledge of European politics surpassed that of anyone in Elizabeth's counsel, created the best secret service of any government of the time. But there was always a chance that someone would slip through; there was always a danger, so long as Mary lived, that public discontent or private ambition would use her and her claims to destroy Elizabeth.

The northern part of England was mainly Catholic, the south mainly Protestant; and, in 1569, the Northern Rebellion began. It was the start of some seven years of instability in Elizabethan England. And England's relationship with Spain was strained almost to the point of war, partly because Cecil had ordered the seizure of Spanish treasure ships on their way to the Netherlands.

At the same time the Pope, tired of what he saw as English disobedience, excommunicated Elizabeth in 1570 and issued an order that loyal Catholics should get rid of her. The conflict between the Netherlands and Spain became a rallying banner for Englishmen against Catholicism and Spain, and they volunteered to defend the Netherlands, the Lowlands.

In Elizabeth's government, there were strong differences of opinion. The cause was accepted, but not England's military commitment to it. But when the leader of the Dutch Protestants was assassinated the cause was revived. This was followed, in 1585, by Philip II of Spain seizing all the English ships in his ports and making plans to invade England.

So the rapidly evolving differences between Spain and Europe and England were inevitably leading to war, and encouraged the ever-present threat of internal plotting on behalf of Mary Stuart against Elizabeth Tudor.

C❖A voluntary association of Protestant gentry was formed in 1585 for the defence of Elizabeth's life. In the following year, evidence of a conspiracy, engineered by one Anthony Babington, an English Catholic, was laid before the council by Walsingham. One of his agents had mingled with the conspirators for over a year. Mary's connivance was undeniable. Elizabeth was at last persuaded that her death was a political necessity. After a formal trial Mary was pronounced guilty of treason. Parliament petitioned for her execution and, at last, Elizabeth signed the death warrant. Within twenty-four hours she regretted it and tried, too late, to stop the execution.

. . . In the early morning of February 8, 1587, Mary was summoned to the great hall of Fotheringay Castle. . . . [She] had arrayed herself superbly for the final scene. As she disrobed for the headsman's act, her garments of black satin, removed by the weeping handmaids, revealed a bodice and petticoat of crimson velvet. . . . Thus the unhappy Queen halted, for one last moment, standing blood-red from head to foot against the black background of the scaffold. . . . She knelt, and at the second stroke the fatal blow was delivered. The awed assembly had fulfilled its task. In death, the majestic illusion was shattered. The head of an ageing woman with false hair was held up by the executioner. A lapdog crept out from beneath the clothes of the bleeding trunk.

It is said there were bonfires in the streets. And dancing. And the Queen wept. But the head of Mary Stuart did not bring peace to England. Eighteen months later the Spanish Armada was sighted off the Scilly Isles.

CHAPTER TWENTY

1587–1602

———— ❖ ————

The English often see themselves as great explorers. Elizabethan England, with its Drakes, Raleighs, Gilberts and Hawkinses, is portrayed as a period when the senses of curiosity are slaked by the thirst for knowledge. But the real reasons for this wonderful period of English maritime exploration, perhaps the greatest in her history, were trade, the slave trade in particular, and piracy. And, of course, that Elizabethan patriotic pastime: robbing the Spaniards. There was, however, a real need to broaden trade. England was poor, the standards of living low, expertise insignificant to the extent that, without German help, even something as elementary as mining was unproductive. Only a quarter of the land was used for valuable grain. The one area in which England led the world was wool production: about 80% of the nation's exports were in cloths. And although the Muscovy Company had been formed in 1545, most of England's overseas trade was with continental Europe or Africa.

C❖Spain was deliberately blocking the commercial enterprise of other nations in the New World so far as it was then known. A Devon gentleman, Humphrey Gilbert, began to look elsewhere and was the first to interest the Queen in finding a route to China, or Cathay as it was called, by the north-west. . . . His ideas inspired the voyages of Martin Frobisher, to whom the Queen granted a licence to explore. . . . [Gilbert] was the first Englishman who realized that the value of these voyages did not lie only in finding precious metals. There were too many people in England. Perhaps they could settle in the new lands. . . . With six ships, manned by gentlemen adventurers, including his own half-brother, Walter Raleigh, he made several hopeful voyages, but none met with success.

In 1583, Gilbert took possession of Newfoundland in the Queen's name, but no permanent settlement was made.

In the following year Gilbert perished when, in high seas, his ship, the *Squirrel*, foundered. Raleigh continued and, in 1585, Roanoke Island, off the American coast, was named Virginia. There was little commercial success, but the English had gained a decade of seamanship – invaluable experience when few understood deep-sea voyaging and survival.

C❖[John] Hawkins had learned his seamanship in slave-running on the West African coast and in shipping negroes to the Spanish colonies. . . . He had moreover educated an apt pupil, a young adventurer from Devon, Francis Drake.

   This 'Master Thief of the unknown world', as his Spanish contemporaries called Drake, became the terror of their ports and crews. His avowed object was to force England into open conflict with Spain, and his attacks on the Spanish treasure ships, his plundering of Spanish possessions on the western coast of the South American continent on his voyage round the world in 1577, and raids on Spanish harbours in Europe, all played their part in driving Spain to war.

   . . . The Spaniards had long contemplated an enterprise against England. . . . Troops were not the difficulty. . . . the assembly of a fleet was a more formidable undertaking. . . . Every available vessel was summoned into Western Spanish waters. . . . in May 1588, the Armada was ready. One hundred and thirty ships were assembled, carrying 2500 guns and more than 30,000 men . . . Their aim was to sail up the Channel, embark the expeditionary corps of 16,000 veterans from the Netherlands under Alexander of Parma and land it on the south coast of England.

   . . . The nation was united in the face of the Spanish preparations. . . . An army was assembled at Tilbury which reached 20,000 men, under the command of Lord Leicester. . . . While the Armada was still off the coasts of England, Queen Elizabeth reviewed the army at Tilbury and addressed them in these stirring words:

'My loving people, we have been persuaded by some that are careful for our safety to take heed how we commit ourselves to armed multitudes, for fear of treachery. But I assure you, I do not desire to live to distrust my faithful and loving people. Let tyrants fear. . . . and therefore I am come amongst you, as you see, resolved, in the midst and heat of the battle, to live or die amongst you all, to lay down for my God, and for my Kingdom, and for my people, my honour and my blood, even in the dust. I know I have the body of a weak and feeble woman, but I have the heart and stomach of a King, and of a King of England too, and think foul scorn that Parma or Spain or any prince of Europe should dare to invade the borders of my realm; to which, rather than any dishonour shall grow by me, I myself will take up arms, I myself will be your general, judge and rewarder of every one of your

> virtues in the field. I know already for your forwardness you have
> deserved rewards and crowns; and we do assure you, in the word of
> a prince, they shall be duly paid you.'

Philip II envisaged a land battle. The Armada was simply the armed transport for the Duke of Parma's forces. Towards the end of July, 1588 the Armada appeared off the Lizard. In a crescent-shaped flotilla, the Armada headed up the Channel. Drake attacked the Armada from astern, but the Spanish fleet maintained its discipline and made for the French coast opposite Dover. The Armada was supposed to make a rendezvous with the Duke of Parma's forces from the Netherlands. The fleet anchored, but couldn't get its ships into port. No one had worked out the depth of water against the deep draft of the vessels.

During the nights of 28 July and 7 August, the English sent in fireships – small, old vessels loaded with explosives and burning barrels on their bows, sixteenth-century maritime petrol bombs. The Armada scattered. The English fleet pounded it, sinking four ships, but damaging many more. A south-west gale drove the survivors into the North Sea, to escape as best they could around the north of Scotland.

C❖. . . to the English people as a whole, the defeat of the Armada came as a
miracle. . . . One of the medals struck to commemorate the victory bears
the inscription 'Afflavit Deus et dissipantur' – 'God blew and they were
scattered'. . . .

Elizabeth and her seamen knew how true this was. The Armada had
indeed been bruised in battle, but it was demoralized and set on the run by
the weather. Yet the event was decisive. . . .

With 1588, the crisis of the reign was past. England had emerged from
the Armada as a first-class Power. . . . the last years of Elizabeth's reign saw
a welling up of national energy and enthusiasm focusing upon the person
of the Queen. In the year following the Armada, the first three books were
published of Spenser's *Faerie Queene*, in which Elizabeth is hymned as
Gloriana. . . . Elizabeth had schooled a generation of Englishmen.

So, the Armada was one of the most decisive battles of our history. But it didn't decide the war between Spain and England. It didn't, as Drake had dreamed it would, bring down the Spaniards, or cut off their fleets from the riches in the Americas. And neither Catholicism nor Protestantism was any stronger for this decisive battle. The result was that here was proof, in this naval tournament, that the ambitions of one power to impose religious dogma on another could not rely on force to achieve it. That was the legacy of the engagement in the Channel in 1588.

C❖By now, the men who had governed England since the 1550s were passing from power and success to their graves. . . . Young and eager men like Walter Raleigh and Robert Devereux, Earl of Essex, quarrelled for permission to lead enterprises against the Spaniards. The Queen hesitated. She knew that the security she had striven for all her life was very fragile. She knew the danger of provoking the might of Spain, backed as it was by all the wealth of the Indies. She was growing old and out of touch with the younger generation, and her quarrel with Essex marked and revealed her changing mood.

Elizabeth was moody and she was cautious to the point of indecisiveness. And, she could not shed her three great burdens: the security of her nation, the constantly emptying Treasury, and her succession. Moreover, she was not helped by the rivalry amongst her courtiers.

In the late 1590s, Walter Raleigh and Robert Devereux, the Earl of Essex, were rivals, adventurers, and heroes who first charmed the Queen, then didn't. Essex was the younger, the brasher one, who, having been given his head, lost it – for ever. Raleigh was the Queen's favourite when Essex arrived but Essex very soon replaced Raleigh in that role. They both went to fight the Spaniards at Cadiz and they were both successful, but they came home with not much booty. And only booty pays for victories. Nevertheless, Essex was now seen as an heroic figure which was fine for his reputation, but not entirely good for his plans to woo his sovereign: the Queen feared he would become more popular than she. However, he was promoted and, with Raleigh in a subordinate position, Essex was given command of a fleet sent to fight a new Armada in the Azores.

Only the weather appears to have saved Essex's ships from defeat and all that that would have meant for England. The only good news to reach Elizabeth after that event was the death of the man who sent the first Armada, Philip of Spain. Essex was forced to leave the Court. His letters and pleas did little to restore his standing. And then came a chance for his redemption, or so he thought.

C❖Troubles in Ireland, which now came to a head, seemed to offer him the chance of recovering both the Queen's goodwill and his own prestige. Throughout the reign, Ireland had presented an intractable problem. Henry VIII had assumed the title of King of Ireland, but this involved no real extension of his authority. Though Irish chiefs were given English titles . . . they still clung to their ancient feuding clan-life, and largely ignored the commands of the Lord-Lieutenants in Dublin. The Counter-Reformation revived and reanimated opposition to Protestant England. For the Queen's Government in London this meant strategic anxieties, since any Power hostile to England could readily take advantage of Irish discontents. . . . In the first thirty years of Elizabeth's reign, Ireland was shaken by three major rebellions. Now, in the 1590s, a fourth rising had erupted into a wearing and expensive war.

With Spanish backing, Hugh O'Neill, Earl of Tyrone, was threatening the whole English dominance of Ireland. If Essex became Lord Deputy and destroyed the rebellion he might recover his power in England. It was a perilous gamble. In April 1599, Essex was allowed to go to Ireland at the head of the largest army that England had ever sent there.

Essex wasn't Elizabeth's first choice; she wanted Lord Mountjoy to go, but Essex was persuaded to make a case for himself. The young lord may not have been very bright in everything he did, and he may have spent too much time seeking glory (which success in Ireland was hardly likely to bring), but there's evidence that he wasn't altogether sure of his chances. Shortly after being appointed to lead the army, Essex wrote to Lord Southampton. The text of that letter, written in January 1599, has survived, and it reveals his doubts.

❖Unto Ireland I go. The Queen hath irrevocably decreed it; the council do passionately urge it, and I am tied to my reputation to use no tergiversation. And, as it were indecorum to slip the collar now, so were Ireland to be lost. . . . I am not ignorant what are the disadvantages of absence: the opportunities of practising enemies when they are neither encountered nor overlooked: the construction of princes under whom a great reputation is more dangerous than an evil one, and success of less account than no success: the difficulties of a war where the rebel that hath been hitherto ever victorious is the least enemy that I shall have against me; for without an enemy, the disease of that country consumes our armies, and if they live, yet famine and nakedness make them lose both heart and strength. All these things which I am like to see, I do foresee.

Essex's orders were to subdue Ulster and the Earl of Tyrone, Hugh O'Neill. But Essex turned south, to Leinster. He needed time to gather his forces together, for the weather to improve, and to try to find sufficient packhorses, as a further extract from his letter to Southampton shows.

❖There is not means to carry competent provisions of dry victuals by reason of the country is not able to supply half so many carriage horses as is requisite for the necessary use of the army, though ready money should be paid for them; and touching garrons [packhorses], which the country is bound by their tenures to answer to, they will hardly be able to supply half their numbers. As for the carriage horses levied in England, they are not yet here by reason of the contrariety of the wind.

Essex's decision to go to Leinster was dismissed by his enemies in London as nothing but a parade, which it most certainly was not. Apart from knocking his troops into a fighting force that was to his liking in conditions that were not, the march south allowed Essex to assess what was needed for the greater campaign.

Foolishly, he sent his assessment to Elizabeth and added that the war would take a great deal of expensive time. He then added – and this was double foolishness – that the Queen was wrong to confer special favour on his old rival, Raleigh. The Queen was furious. Essex's enemies – including the powerful Robert Cecil – were delighted.

A furious exchange of letters shuttled across the Irish Sea between Essex and his sovereign. Rumours of Essex giving away knighthoods by the helmet-full, pocketing spoils but not getting on with the task of subduing Tyrone, only added to the Queen's fury. Eventually she told Essex that he had to remain in Ireland until the north was put down. But Essex's army was in no state to take Tyrone.

At the Lagan river, the two men, Essex and Tyrone, met. A fortnight's truce was agreed. It gave Tyrone fourteen days to regroup and Essex thought that with this agreement, he was free to return to London. He was desperate to get back there because he knew that only his pleading, only his presence, would satisfy his Queen that he was her champion and her loyal subject.

C❖Robert Cecil had quietly waited for his rival to over-reach himself. Angry scenes followed between Essex and the Queen, and the Earl was confined to his house. Weeks dragged by, and a desperate plot was made by Essex and his younger companions, including Shakespeare's patron, the Earl of Southampton. There was to be a rising in the City, a concentration upon Whitehall, and a seizure of the Queen's person. . . .

The scheme failed, and the end came in February 1601, with Essex's death within the Tower. . . . Essex had been not simply a courtier soliciting, and even fighting for, the affections of his Queen. He was the leader of a bid for power by a faction of her Court. . . . This was not yet an age of party politics, but of patronage and clientage. . . . The spoils of office, power, and influence were at stake, and victorious Essex would have dispensed appointments throughout England, and perhaps even have dictated terms to the Queen. . . . in destroying Essex, she saved England from the consumption of civil war.

But on the streets and in the countryside, the people had a more everyday worry: poverty. There was increased wealth in late Elizabethan England, but the beneficiaries were the middle men, the merchants. It's been estimated that as many as 40% of the population survived at below subsistence level; thousands of families were 'on the Parish', that is, in need of support. And there was starvation, especially in the remoter parts of the country. As early as 1536 Poor Laws had been introduced. They offered relief, but with an insistence that the so-called 'sturdy' beggars should be made to work and whipped to do so. There was genuine pity; there was also a very real fear of beggars. 'Hark, hark, the dogs do bark, the beggars are coming to town', warned the rhyme. Some made begging their profession. In great places, notably Ipswich and London, a sixteenth-century workless traveller might be better off living on handouts than looking for work.

CHAPTER TWENTY-ONE

1603–1624

❖

On 24 March 1603, before dawn, Elizabeth I died. James VI of Scotland was to become James I of England. It was the end of the Tudor dynasty. But people don't go to bed Elizabethans and wake up Stuarts in the sense that their circumstances are any different. The larder is just as full or empty as it was the night before. Society evolves. It does not suddenly change. A nation wears the same clothes, washes the same dishes and cheers the new monarch from the same rooftops as the ones from which it mourned the last. So why was a Scottish King now King of England?

James I was the son of Mary Queen of Scots and her second husband, Darnley. He became James I of England as a result of the Treaty of Berwick, which he and Elizabeth had signed, in 1586, after almost four years of plot and counter-plot and rebellion. The two monarchs agreed that they'd respect each other's religions, be allies and help if the other were to be invaded and, more important from Elizabeth's point of view, neither side would help anyone who threatened the other. So Elizabeth signed the treaty because it meant that Scotland wouldn't help France, which was of immense importance to England. James got £4000 a year out of it from the English, plus an understanding that Elizabeth would block any move in the English Parliament to oppose James's claim to the English throne, as long he waited until after her death. If Elizabeth had chosen to, she could have easily, and with considerable support, broken that understanding, but she didn't. James did nothing to spoil the arrangement. Even the year following the treaty's signing, when his mother was executed by Elizabeth, he said nothing. So James VI of Scotland travelled to England to become King.

C❖[Robert] Cecil was his ally and skilful manager in the tense days after the Queen died. James was proclaimed King James I of England without opposition, and in April 1603 began a leisurely journey from Holyrood to London.

He was a stranger and an alien, and . . . detested the political ideas of his Calvinist mentors. He had fixed ideas about kingship and the divine right of monarchs to rule. He was a scholar with pretensions to being a philosopher, and in the course of his life published numerous tracts and treatises, ranging from denunciations of witchcraft and tobacco to abstract political theory. He came to England with a closed mind, and a weakness for lecturing. But England was changing. The habit of obedience to a dynasty had died with the last of the Tudors.

One of James's tracts, published anonymously five years before he became King of England, gives some idea of what he thought of the one thing he apparently valued above all else – being a king. Certainly his views on the relationship between Parliament and the monarch were not the same as the new thinking in England, as the following extract demonstrates.

❖The King makes daily statutes and ordinances, enjoining such pains thereto as he thinks meet, without any advice of Parliament or Estates, yet it lies in the power of no Parliament to make any kind of law or statute without his sceptre be to it for giving it the force of law. And as ye see it manifest that the King is overlord of the whole land, so he is master over every person that inhabiteth the same, having power over life and death of every one of them. For although a just prince will not take the life of any of his subjects without a clear law, yet the same laws whereby he taketh them are made by himself or his predecessors, and so the power flows always from himself . . . the King is above the law as both the author and giver of strength thereto, yet a good king will not only delight to rule his subjects by the law, but even will conform himself in his own actions thereunto; always keeping that ground that the health of the commonwealth be his chief law.

The England to which James I came, in 1603, was a land of about four million people. The combined population of Scotland, Ireland, and Wales was probably about half that. The birthrate might have been greater but for crude contraception, simple celibacy, and a trend towards later marriages and therefore fewer child-bearing years. But in spite of this social change, the population survival rate in the first half of the seventeenth century was greater than the previous 100 years. The impact of disease and starvation lessened, and increased population demanded growth in agricultural production, but that never really kept up with consumption with the result that food prices rose at almost double the rate of wage rises. More people now bought their food than grew it, and therefore more of their income went on basic needs than before. The result was a decline in living standards. There was also greater pressure on government to look after its people. Yet government wasn't always able, or competent, to do so. Such new ideas meant raising funds. And it wasn't a good time for that.

C❖. . . there loomed a fiscal crisis of the first magnitude. The importation of precious metals from the New World had swelled the rise in prices, and throughout Europe inflation reigned; every year the fixed revenues of the Crown were worth less and less. By extreme frugality, Elizabeth had postponed a conflict. But it could not be averted, and bound up with it was a formidable constitutional problem. Who was to have the last word in the matter of taxation? Hitherto, everyone had accepted the mediaeval doctrine that 'The King may not rule his people by other laws than they assent unto, and therefore he may set upon them no imposition [that is, tax] without their assent.' But no one had analysed it, or traced out its implications in any detail. . . . Relief at an undisputed succession gave the new sovereign a loyal, and even enthusiastic reception. But James and his subjects were soon at odds about this and other topics.

. . . In dutiful but firm language, the Commons drew up an Apology, reminding the King that their liberties included free elections, free speech, and freedom from arrest during Parliamentary sessions. . . . James, like his son after him, treated these expressions of national grievance contemptuously, brushing them aside as personal insults to himself and mere breaches of good manners.

The confrontation with Parliament was postponed until the winter of 1604 because of a plague. But when James I's first Parliament met it went on until the end of 1610, more than six years. After that, it didn't meet again for three years. James often reminded his Parliament that it had been established after kings and that he didn't depend on its members for his authority. But if James was to get the funds he needed, Parliament was his only way. This in turn gave its members the chance to tackle him on greater subjects, and that is what annoyed him, especially as he wasn't as good as Elizabeth had been at using his ministers to manipulate the political system.

But at the heart of Parliament's role were the two functions: law-making and sorting grievances. The two could go together and to give an idea of the influence of Parliament, more than half the laws came, not from the King's ministers, but from the members. But still the King's main interest was the ways in which he could get money out of Parliament. And the Lord Treasurer's speech (what would now be called the Expenditure White Paper) of 1610 spells out the cost of running England. (Elizabeth had committed large amounts to the Irish expedition and the obsequies – the cost of Elizabeth's funeral – are lumped into coronation and state visits.)

❖Queen Elizabeth entered into the Irish wars having £700,000 in her coffers. From 1598 until her death, the charge of Ireland cost £1,600,000. When the King came to the crown he could not possibly dissolve the army upon a sudden so that the charge of Ireland in his time hath cost £600,000. Besides which he hath redeemed the lands mortgaged by the late Queen, hath taken away the copper money, the exchange of Ireland, and paid divers debts of the Queen's; all amounting to £300,000.

The Low Countries hath cost him £250,000. The obsequies of the Queen; the King's entrance; the entrance of the Queen and her children; the coronation; the entertainment of the King of Denmark; embassages and gratulations sent and received: £500,000. In tertio Jacobi [in the third year of the reign of King James], when the last Lord Treasurer accompted, the gross debt of the King was £700,000, since which time his majesty hath been at great charge in the rebellion of Sir Cahir O'Dogharty. In maintaining the charge of the Prince, in building ships, and paying interest for money borrowed; so that at Michaelmas 1603, he owed, in toto, £1,400,000 . . . since that time there hath been an alleviation of his debt and charge, so that the King's debt is now down to £300,000.

Parliament may have been the King's source of funds, but James I had little but contempt for Parliament. In that first gathering there were 467 Members in the House of Commons. Many of them were inexperienced, had no understanding of what they were trying to do, other than to do it as noisily as possible. The King described one session as a gathering without any control that 'voted without order, nothing being heard but cries, shouts, and confusion'. And for good measure, he noted that the real problem was the gaggle of lawyers who tried to dominate everything. He wanted rid of them. It was a popular view. Just a few years before James came to the throne, Shakespeare wrote: 'The first thing we do, let's kill all the lawyers.'

But James I had greater problems than the cost of law. One of the legacies of the Elizabethan reign was the Roman Catholic conundrum. When James became King there were, or so it's thought, about 40,000 Catholics in England. He told his closest adviser, Robert Cecil, that he would 'never allow in my conscience that the blood of any man shall be shed for diversity of opinions in religion'. Which is not quite what he meant.

James I accepted that some people were Catholics, and that as long as they didn't grow in numbers and cause trouble, they should remain so. But their priests, especially the Jesuits, he called 'firebrands of sedition', and in February, 1604, he ordered them out of England. He had a similar attitude towards the Puritans. The general people were fine; it was the zealots among them whom he refused to tolerate.

This, on the face of it, was a more relaxed attitude to different religious persuasions in England, and Catholics started to be more public about their beliefs. The Archbishop of York, Matthew Hutton, had no doubts of the danger when he told Cecil that the Catholics (Papists he called them), 'have grown mightily in number, courage, and influence. 'Tis high time to look unto them.'

Cecil took note and spoke to the King, and a year later James claimed that he disliked Catholics so much that he'd rather be childless than risk his son becoming one. The differences might have been left at that and the Catholics would have been safe, had it not been for a group of the very zealots James feared.

C❖Disappointment and despair led a small group of Catholic gentry to an infernal design for blowing up James and his whole Parliament by gunpowder while they were in session at Westminster. They hoped that this would be followed by a Catholic rising and that in the confusion a Catholic regime might be established with Spanish help. The chief plotter was Robert Catesby, assisted by Guy Fawkes, a veteran of the Spanish wars against the Dutch. One of their followers warned a relative who was a Catholic peer. The story reached Cecil, and the cellars of Parliament were searched. Fawkes was taken on the spot, and there was a storm of excitement in the City. James went down to open Parliament and made an emotional speech upon what an honourable end it would have been to die with his faithful Commons. Kings, he said, were exposed to perils beyond those of ordinary mortals; only his own cleverness had saved them from destruction. The House displayed an incomprehensible indifference and, turning to the business of the day, discussed the petition of a Member who had asked to be relieved of his Parliamentary duties owing to an attack of gout.

The indifference was but a passing moment. The plot confirmed everything their harshest critics had believed about Catholics. By the next year, Parliament, apparently having settled the matter of gouty members, banned Catholics from living anywhere near London, from holding public or official office, and allowed James to take over two-thirds of the lands owned by Catholics. Most important of all, Catholics were to swear an oath of allegiance to the crown.

There was one part of this oath that had been drafted by James himself. The Powder Traitors, as they were called, had to publicly swear that neither the Pope, nor his agents, had any right to try to depose the King or invade his territories. But what happened if the Pope, in his supreme position, gave Catholics absolution from this declaration? James, or his advisers, had thought of that, and added an almost impossible provision, impossible if you happened to be a Catholic.

❖I do from my heart abhor, detest and abjure, as impious and heretical, this damnable doctrine and position, that princes which be excommunicated or deprived by the Pope, may be deposed or murdered by their subjects or any other whosoever. And I do believe, and in my conscience am resolved, that neither Pope nor any person whatsoever hath power to absolve me of this oath or any part thereof.

James believed, or said he believed, that as the earth hadn't a single monarch, then even though he was willing to accept that the Pope was the Prince of Bishops, *Princeps Episcoporum*, he was no more than that. Rome was not the holder of the only truth.

As early as January 1604 the Protestants, led by Bishop Bancroft, and the Puritans met the King at a special conference at Hampton Court. James had been brought up by Calvinists, and he disliked them. Nevertheless, the Puritans saw what they thought was an opportunity to persuade the King of the merits of their case.

The Puritans consisted of the so-called 'low church', clergy who wanted to be rid of the more ceremonial features of Rome. Apart from vestments, they objected also to genuflexion, to making the sign of the cross over a child at its baptism, to confirmation, and even to wedding rings. They also wanted competent priests who were learned and who lived in the parishes, instead of the long-time practice of giving livings to men who never went near the parish, yet collected a stipend and often an income from glebe lands.

The bishops, fearful that the Puritan leaders would have their way with the new King, came up with a plan to load the forthcoming conference with moderate Puritan speakers rather than zealots. The result was a few changes with which the bishops could agree, certain disappointments for the Puritan leaders, but most of all, a declaration that brought non-conformist ministers into some sort of line. There were few moments of accord in that conference; but the leader of the Puritan delegation, Dr John Reynolds, came up with a suggestion that particularly gained the King's attention, and whose results have had a lasting effect.

C❖. . . Reynolds, President of the Oxford College of Corpus Christi, had asked, seemingly on the spur of the moment, if a new version of the Bible could be produced. The idea appealed to James. Till now, the clergy and laity had relied on a number of different translations – Tyndale's, Coverdale's, the Geneva Bible, the 'Bishop's Bible' of Queen Elizabeth. . . . Each party and sect used the version which best suited its own views and doctrines. . . . Within a few months, committees or 'companies' were set up, two each in Oxford, Cambridge, and Westminster, comprising in all about fifty scholars and divines. . . . Each committee was assigned a portion of the text, and their draft was to be scrutinized by all the other committees and finally revised by a committee of twelve. Tendentious renderings were forbidden, and marginal notes or glosses were prohibited except for cross references or to explain the meaning of Greek or Hebrew words which were difficult to translate. About three years passed in preliminary research, and the main work did not get under way till 1607, but it was then accomplished with remarkable swiftness. In an age without an official postal service or mechanical methods of copying and duplicating texts, the committees, though separated by considerable distances, finished their task in 1609. Nine months sufficed for the scrutiny of the supervisory committee, and in 1611, the Authorized Version of the Bible was produced by the King's Printer.

It won an immediate and lasting triumph. . . . No new version was deemed necessary for nearly 300 years. . . . This may be deemed James's greatest achievement, for the impulse was largely his.

The Puritans continued to press their cause in and out of Parliament and eventually James made compromises, promises, and even threats. He made it clear also that the conflict reminded him too much of the rebellion in the Netherlands and the way the troubles had started in his native Scotland. In his view, Puritans were Presbyterian subversives. It wasn't a tactful comparison, nor, come to that, wise. The eventual outcome was that the Church remained much as it had been when he became King: a Puritan church with the King and bishops in charge, the Protestant Church in England.

But within a decade, the Puritan ethic had spread. Certain plays, including Ben Jonson's celebrated *Masque of the Metamorphosed Gipsies*, were seen as too free-thinking. And this spirit spread to the administration of local justice. In the records of the churchwardens of Windsor, between 1618 and 1625, disapproval, and fines, for offences which, a few years earlier, would have hardly come to anyone's notice are listed.

For example:

❖Item of Edward Browne for drunkenness, five shillings.
Item of Christopher Coleston and Robert Barlo for absence from church, two shillings.
Nicholas Whyte for abuse in his house in service tyme, one shilling.
Vidua Bebe, for tippling in service tyme, one shilling.
Widow Thirkittle, for swearing, two shillings.

But for many at the beginning of the seventeenth century, the thing that mattered most was the fact that a Scottish King ruled England. James was descended from both Tudors and Stuarts, and his mother had always believed that he would be the king to unite the two thrones. But the question was how to make Union official?

The debate in Parliament was long and, at times, acrimonious. James could be King of each country, but if they were to be joined, if there were to be Union, then the new country needed a name. In the spring of 1604, the House of Lords made a proposal that took until October to discuss. By then, the King had become impatient with the Members. He issued his own proclamation. He knew what he wanted the united country to be called.

> ❖Seeing that there is but one head of both peoples, which is Ourself, We have thought good to discontinue the divided names of England and Scotland out of Our regal style, and do intend and resolve to take and resume unto Us the name and style of King of Great Britain.

It was 20 October 1604 and, for the first time, the name Great Britain was used, officially, by a monarch. But, in spite of his every effort, James would never see Parliament pass an Act of the Union. That didn't happen for another century.

Since 1603, when James came to the throne, Walter Raleigh, and many other prominent Elizabethans, had been in prison. Raleigh was accused of plotting with Spain to put the King's cousin, Arabella Stuart, on the throne. There's some evidence to suggest that he was set up by yet another rival, Salisbury. There's little evidence to suggest that Raleigh was guilty. But at Winchester, the court decided he was and he was sentenced to death, reprieved, and then locked up in the Tower. And in 1616, the year Shakespeare died, he was still there.

Raleigh was a poet and historian as well as an adventurer, and it was in the Tower that he wrote his *History of the World*. Raleigh was perhaps more of a romantic than he was a political manipulator. He'd allowed himself to be outwitted by Essex, although he had survived him. He'd fallen out with Salisbury, Robert Cecil, which was probably why he was in the Tower. And there he might have stayed if it hadn't been for George Villiers. Villiers was charming, handsome, apparently witty, and young. He was a dear favourite of James I, who disturbed some of his advisers by his attentions to young men. Villiers gained Raleigh's release to lead an expedition to Guiana in search of El Dorado, a place both believed existed. But without approval, Raleigh's men attacked and destroyed the Spanish settlement of San Thomé. The Spanish government protested in the strongest terms and, because of James's passion for relations with Spain (which was not to last), Raleigh had to pay. When he returned to England, inevitably without gold, he was re-arrested and beheaded at Westminster, not for the attack on the Spanish settlement, but for his original alleged crime. The Spanish, for the moment, were satisfied.

Raleigh's execution was part political in as much as it had been demanded by the new relationship with Spain. Churchill's view is that this didn't impress the English people.

C❖His death, on October 29, 1618, was intended to mark the new policy of appeasement and prepare the way for good relations with Spain. This deed of shame sets a barrier for ever between King James and the English people.

James's view of Europe was complicated by two factors: one personal, the other political. King James's daughter, Elizabeth, had married the Elector Palatine of the Rhine in 1613. The Elector was a Protestant zealot – one of the very people James feared the most. Secondly, this was also the age of Louis XIII and the rise of that most forbidding of French political figures, Armand Jean du Plessis de Richelieu, Cardinal Richelieu.

C❖When he [James] came to the throne, England was still technically at war with Spain. With Cecil's support, hostilities were concluded and diplomatic relations renewed. . . .The house of Habsburg, at the head of the Holy Roman Empire, still dominated the Continent from Vienna. The territories of the Emperor and of his cousin, the King of Spain, now stretched from Portugal to Poland . . . The Commons and the country remained vehemently hostile to Spain, and viewed with alarm and anxiety the march of the Counter-Reformation. But James was unmoved. He regarded the Dutch as rebels against the Divine Right of Kings. . . . His daughter however was already in the opposite camp . . . and Frederick [her husband] was soon projected into violent revolt against the Habsburg Emperor Ferdinand. . . . The storm centre was Bohemia where a haughty, resolute Czech nobility obstructed the centralizing policy of Vienna, both in religion and politics. . . . In 1618, their leaders flung the Imperial envoys from the windows of the royal palace in Prague. This action, later known as the Defenestration, started a war which was to ravage Germany for thirty years. The Czechs offered Frederick the throne of Bohemia. Frederick accepted and became the recognized leader of the Protestant revolt.

Although his daughter was now Queen of Bohemia, James showed no wish to intervene on her behalf. He was resolved to keep out of the conflict in Europe at all costs, and judged he could best help his son-in-law's cause through friendship with Spain. Parliament was indignant and alarmed. He [James] reminded them that these matters were beyond their scope. No taunts of personal timidity moved him. He stuck to his convictions and kept the peace. . . .

The Elector Frederick was soon driven out of Bohemia, and his hereditary lands were occupied by Habsburg troops. So short had been his reign, that he is known to history as 'the Winter King'. The House of Commons clamoured for war. Private subscriptions and bands of volunteers were raised for the defence of the Protestants. James . . . ignored the demand for intervention, and continued his negotiations for the Spanish match.

Yet another political marriage was thought an advantage between two countries who had been at each other's throats until recently. And at home the old order was once more changing, and not necessarily to the King's advantage.

C❖James was much addicted to favourites, and his attention to handsome young men resulted in a noticeable loss of respect for the monarchy. After the death of his wise counsellor, Robert Cecil, the Court had been afflicted by a number of odious scandals. One of his favourites, Robert Carr, created Earl of Somerset by the King's caprice, was implicated in a murder by poison, of which his wife was undoubtedly guilty. James . . . at first paid little attention to the storm raised by this crime; but even he found it impossible to maintain him in high office. Carr was succeeded in the King's regard by the good-looking, quick-witted, extravagant youth, George Villiers, soon ennobled as Duke of Buckingham. This young man quickly became all-powerful at Court, and in the affections of James. He formed a deep and honourable friendship with Charles, Prince of Wales. He accepted unhesitatingly the royal policy of a Spanish marriage, and in 1623 staged a romantic journey to Madrid for the Prince and himself to view the bride.

The Prince, with Villiers at his side, rode incognito to Madrid and, quite unannounced, claimed the Infanta of Spain as his bride.

C❖Their unorthodox behaviour failed to impress the formal and ceremonious Court of Spain. Moreover, the Spaniards demanded concessions for the English Catholics, which James knew Parliament would never grant. . . .

Contrary winds delayed the return of the Prince of Wales and his companion, now disenchanted with all things Spanish. The English fleet which was to escort him remained weather-bound at Santander. England waited in a tremor; and when the news spread through the country that he was safely back at Portsmouth, unwedded to the Infanta, unseduced from the Protestant faith, a surge of joy arose among all classes. . . . But Buckingham and Prince Charles were now eager for war. James at first wavered. . . .

Buckingham, with remarkable agility . . . using all his personal address to over-persuade the sovereign . . . sought and obtained the support of Parliament and people. He took a number of steps which recognized, in a manner unknown since the days of the house of Lancaster, Parliamentary rights and power. Whereas all interference by Parliament in foreign affairs had been repelled by the Tudors, and hitherto by James, the Minister-Favourite now invited Lords and Commons to give their opinion.

Parliament wanted war. James, if he agreed at all, wanted war in Europe, on the land. His daughter wanted him to rescue Frederick's lands: the Palatinate. Parliament wanted a naval conflict. The easiest way for Parliament to control the matter was to restrict funds. And that is what it did. Buckingham then suggested involving France. If Charles couldn't marry the Spanish Infanta, perhaps he could marry Henrietta Maria, Louis XIII's sister, the thirteen-year-old daughter of King Henry IV and Marie de' Medici. Then there could be a land army.

France agreed to supply 3000 cavalry under the command of a mercenary, Count Mansfeld. The idea was that the combined force would fight their way to the Palatinate. But James was cautious. He thought the French were devious. So James demanded that Louis give, in writing, faith of his support for the operation. The French thought this was English deviousness, and a prelude to James's planned agreement with Spain. It wasn't, but that didn't matter. It was what the French thought that mattered. The result of this mutual suspicion was a disaster. Louis refused to let the English land in France; they had to go to the Netherlands, where they froze or fell foul of disease. As they died by the dozen a day, Mansfeld's great force was isolated. And as the winter dragged on and the English soldiers perished, James became ill, and then too ill to recover. James, the first King of Great Britain, died on 27 March 1625.

CHAPTER TWENTY-TWO

1625–1639

❖

Charles I came to the throne, at the age of twenty-five. His father was James I, his mother, Anne of Denmark. The court in which he was brought up was a place of crudeness, immorality and harsh debate. Charles, apparently, was shy, artistic and he stammered.

Towards the end of his father's life, Charles virtually ruled with George Villiers, the Duke of Buckingham. It was Buckingham who arranged the entrance of Charles into the French royal family, with his marriage to Henrietta Maria. Charles and his wife were happy. They had seven children, including the future Charles II, and James II. Maryland in America was named after Queen Henrietta Maria. And when he became King, Charles was welcomed by the people and by Parliament. But not for long.

C❖A great political and religious crisis was overhanging England. Already, in King James's time, Parliament had begun to take the lead, not only in levying taxes, but increasingly in the conduct of affairs, and especially in foreign policy. The furious winds of religious strife carried men's thoughts afar. . . .The English people felt that their survival and their salvation were bound up for ever with the victory of the Reformed Faith, and they watched with straining, vigilant eyes every episode which marked its advance or misfortune. . . .

The secular issues were nevertheless themselves of enormous weight. . . . Men looked back to earlier times. Great lawyers like Coke and Selden had directed their gaze to the rights which they thought Parliament possessed under the Lancastrian kings. Ranging farther, they spoke with pride of the work of Simon de Montfort, of Magna Carta, and even of still more ancient rights in the mists of Anglo-Saxon monarchy. . . . The past seemed to them to provide almost a written Constitution, from which the Crown was threatening to depart. But the Crown also looked back, and found many precedents of a contrary character, especially in the last 100 years, for the most thorough exercise of the Royal Prerogative. Both King and Parliament had a body of doctrine upon which they dwelt with sincere conviction.

The confrontation that was to come wasn't simply a case of a new king not understanding what Parliament wanted and how much it might be given. Charles was not a stranger to Parliament. James I had sent his son to the Lords in 1621 as part of his education. The Prince was there to learn the ways of the House so that when he became King, he would understand its workings and its importance and protect it.

And certainly, when he did become King, Parliament was generous towards him. But in one particular matter, it was ungenerous. Parliament wanted rid of George Villiers, Duke of Buckingham, the King's closest adviser. Perhaps most frustrating for Buckingham's critics – and they stretched across every corridor, every courtyard, every bench of the agitated Parliament – was Charles's belief that Buckingham had the good of the state at heart as well as their friendship. So Parliament blocked the supply of money to the King until he agreed to get rid of Buckingham.

Charles regarded this as an affront – which it probably was – and dissolved Parliament, but not before Parliament had impeached his friend. Within twelve months of being on the throne, Charles had moved from being a liked and informed member of the Lords, to being a King on a terrible collision course with that same institution.

The King blamed what he called the 'violent and ill-advised passions of a few members of the House'. Sir Dudley Carleton, Secretary of State and Member of the Commons, said that in other countries, monarchs had started to get rid of their elected bodies when they saw 'the turbulent spirits of their Parliaments'. The implication was clear: for the King to support Parliament, then Parliament had to be worthwhile for the King. If it wasn't, then the King would look elsewhere for counsels.

But first he had to look elsewhere for money. He and his Council tried to insist on what was called 'a Forced Loan' – a tax without Parliament's approval. Charles went to law for approval but the judges turned him down and many very senior people in the land refused to pay this illegal tax.

C❖. . . having secured a promise that the impeachment of Buckingham would not be pursued, the King agreed to summon Parliament. The country was now in a ferment. The election returned men pledged to resist arbitrary exactions [such as Forced Loans]. The Parliament which assembled in March 1628 embodied the will of the natural leaders of the nation. It wished to support the war [with France over the fate of the French Huguenots], but it would not grant money to a King and Minister it distrusted. . . .

Parliament, which had approved the wars, was playing a hard game with the King. . . . They offered no fewer than five subsidies, amounting to £300,000, all to be paid within twelve months. Here was enough to carry on the war; but before they would confirm this in a Bill, they demanded their price.

Parliament passed four resolutions.

- That no freeman ought to be restrained or imprisoned unless some lawful cause is expressed.
- That the writ of habeas corpus ought to be granted to every man imprisoned or restrained, even though it might be at the command of the King or of the Privy Council.
- That if no legal cause for imprisonment is shown, that party ought to be set free or bailed.
- That it is the ancient and undoubted right of every freeman to have a full and absolute property in his goods and estate, and no tax, loan, or benevolence ought to be levied by the King or his Ministers without common consent by Act of Parliament.

Charles appears to have believed that the way Parliament had behaved, and the way he had responded, would win the affection of the people. But Sir Edward Coke, the man who been responsible for the prosecutions of Elizabeth's one-time favourites, Essex and then Raleigh, and who had prosecuted the Gunpowder Plotters, urged the House to frame the Petition of Right. The King knew exactly what this meant.

This 1628 Petition threatened the Royal Prerogative. It emphasized the common freedoms of the people and started by citing the law from Edward I's time by which no tallage or aid shall be laid or levied by the King without the consent of magnates and freemen. Nor did the Petition miss a point of great vexation in seventeenth-century England. The militia and sailors were often billeted on civilians. Civilians didn't like it. Also, there were times when soldiers, usually a motley lot, many of them mercenaries, were guilty of the cruellest misdemeanours, but escaped the law because they claimed the protection of martial law. Here's part of the Petition of Right.

❖They do therefore humbly pray your Most Excellent Majesty, that no man hereafter be compelled to make or yield any gift, loan, benevolence, tax, or such like charge, without common consent by Act of Parliament; and that none be called to make answer, or take such oath, or to give attendance, or be confined, or otherwise molested or disquieted concerning the same, or for refusal thereof; and that no freeman, in any such manner as is beforementioned, be imprisoned or detained; and that your Majesty will be refused to remove the said soldiers and mariners, and that your people may not be so burdened in time to come; and that the foresaid commissions for proceeding by martial law, may be revoked and annulled; and that hereafter no commissions of like nature may issue forth to any person or persons whatsoever, to be executed as aforesaid, lest by colour of them and of your Majesty's subjects be destroyed or put to death, contrary to the laws and franchise of the land.

C❖Unless the King accepted the Petition he would have no subsidies . . . [so] Charles, resorting to manoeuvre, secretly consulted the judges, who assured him that even his consent to these liberties would not affect his ultimate Prerogative. He was none too sure of this; and when his first evasive answer was delivered in the House of Lords, a howl went up, not only from the Commons, but from the great majority of all assembled. He therefore fell back upon the opinion of the judges and gave full consent . . . The Commons voted all the subsidies, and believed that a definite bargain had been struck.

We reach here, amid much confusion, the main foundation of English freedom. The right of the Executive Government to imprison a man, high or low, for reasons of State, was denied. . . . The King, having got his money, dwelt unduly upon the assurances he had received from the judges that his Prerogative was intact.

Charles dismissed the Houses and, with Buckingham, planned an expedition to La Rochelle where Protestant Huguenots were besieged. They planned a seventeenth-century Crusade, led by Buckingham, to rescue the Protestants. At least that was the plan. But Buckingham was assassinated by one of his own men before his ship ever left Portsmouth harbour.

In 1640 Charles, under enormous pressure, summoned another Parliament. It was called the Long Parliament. Throughout this time Charles battled for the preservation of the Royal Prerogative. He also had to find other ways of getting money, but his Parliament was becoming increasingly recalcitrant. And the Puritans continued their struggle against the High Churchmen.

It was at this point that William Laud emerged as a major influence on Charles. He had been Archbishop of Canterbury since 1633. Perhaps Charles should have listened to James I, who had a sceptical opinion of the clergyman. He was a restless spirit and, said James, one who 'cannot see when matters are well, but loves to bring things to a pitch of reformation floating in his brain'.

C❖Here emerges the figure of [Laud] who, of all others, was Charles's evil genius . . . He was a convinced Anglican, whole-hearted in his opposition both to Rome and to Geneva, and a leader in the movement away from Calvinism. But he had an itch for politics, had been a confidant of Buckingham, was indeed the reputed author of his most successful speeches. He stepped with agility from an academic career at Oxford into national politics and the King's Council at a time when religious affairs were considered paramount. The Elizabethan settlement was dependent on the State. By itself, the Church had not the strength to bear the strain. An informal compact therefore grew up between the secular and spiritual aspects of government, whereby the State sustained the Church in its property and the Church preached the duty of obedience and the Divine Right of Kings.

From this point alone, it can be seen why there were those who believed the Church would be for the King in any civil conflict.

C❖Laud by no means initiated this compact, but he set himself with untimely vigour to enforce it. Among his innovations was the railing off of the altar, and a new emphasis on ceremony and the dignity of the clergy. The gulf between clergy and congregation was widened and the role of authority visibly enhanced. . . . Laud now found a new source of revenue for the Crown. Under the statutes of Elizabeth, everyone was obliged to go to church; they might think as they liked, but they must conform in public worship. This practice had fallen into widespread disuse. . . . Now all over England, men and women found themselves haled before the justices for not attending church, and fined one shilling a time. Here indeed was something that ordinary men and women could understand. . . . The Puritans, already chafed, regarded it as persecution . . . it is by no means certain that, left to herself, England would have broken into revolt. It was in Scotland, the home of the Stuarts, and Charles's birthplace, that the torch was lighted which began the vast conflagration. Laud was dissatisfied with the spiritual conditions prevailing in the Northern kingdom, and he moved the King to make some effort to improve them. The Scots must adopt the English Prayer Book, and enter broadly into communion with their English brethren.

Laud's insistence that the Scots use the English Prayer Book was the first mistake. The Scots took one look at it, and believed it to be the work of the Pope. The second mistake – and there were three – was that Charles planned to confiscate Scottish church lands taken by Scottish nobles since the Reformation. The result was predictable: the nobility turned against him.

Charles probably had no idea that what had started out as a simple idea of Laud's would end in open revolt, but the leaders of the revolt either believed, or found it convenient to believe, that what was happening was an attempt to impose Popery on Scotland.

C❖Nothing of this sort had ever been intended or dreamed of by the King. The Marquess of Hamilton, an experienced Scottish statesman, who was to follow his King to the scaffold, was sent to the North as a lay commissioner, with the supreme aim of making friends again. . . . The King was confronted with a hostile and organized Assembly, gathered to adjust religious differences, but now led by armed lay elders, whose aims were definitely political and whose demand was the actual and virtual abolition of the Episcopacy. He [Hamilton] ordered the dissolution of the Assembly. That body declared itself resolved to continue in permanent session. . . . The refusal of the General Assembly of Scotland, in November 1638, to dissolve upon the demand of the King's commissioner has been compared to that of the French National Assembly in 1789, when for the first time they resisted the royal will. The facts and circumstances no doubt were different; but both events led by unbroken chains of causation to the same end, namely, the solemn beheading of a King.

And the third mistake, with Parliament still not yet called, was made by Hamilton.

C❖Hamilton . . . now declared himself in favour of drastic measures. The matter was long debated in the King's Council. On the one hand, it was asked, why draw the sword upon a whole people who still proclaimed their love and reverence for the Crown? And how levy war on them without money or armed forces and without the support of a united England?

If Charles was going to fight the Scots, he needed money for an army (the monarchy didn't have an army of its own) so he also needed official backing from the people. And there was only one place to acquire official backing: Parliament. However, the Scots weren't about to wait to see what Charles would or wouldn't do. The supporters of the Assembly were known as Covenanters, and in the powerful lowlands there was a strong Covenanters' army and, more important than that, it had been reinforced by reserves of war-hardened warriors from Scottish soldiers fighting for the Protestant cause in Germany.

C❖Alexander Leslie had risen in the Thirty Years' War to the rank of Field-Marshal. He felt himself called upon to return and fight the same quarrel on his native soil. To him it was but a flanking operation in the vast conflict of the Protestants with the Catholic Church. The appeal of Scotland to her warriors abroad was not in vain. Back they flowed in thousands . . . The nobles of Scotland bowed to Leslie's military reputation. . . . In a few months Scotland had the strongest armed force in the Island. It . . . was inspired with earnest, slowly roused, and now fanatical religious passion. . . . In May 1639 this army, about 20,000 strong, stood upon the Scottish Border opposite the wea!.er, ill-disciplined, and uncertain forces which Charles and his advisers had gathered. [This was the first Bishops' War].

It was clear from the first that in the King's camp there was no united desire to make war upon the Scots . . . and on June 18, the so-called 'Pacification of Berwick' was agreed. The Scots promised to disband their army . . . The King agreed to the summoning in the following August both of a General Assembly and of a Parliament . . . Charles, however, thought of the Pacification as a device to gain time, and the Covenanters were soon convinced of this. . . . The Scottish Parliament claimed . . . forthwith that the King's Privy Council should be responsible to it. . . . They repudiated the jurisdiction of the Treasury . . . they even required that honours and dignities should be bestowed in accordance with their wishes. . . . Before the Assembly dispersed, it left in full authority a powerful and representative committee, which was in fact the Government of Scotland.

The inevitable outcome of that third mistake was the use of force. The result was that Scotland saw how strong it was and capitalized on its alliance with France.

Sir Thomas Wentworth, the soon-to-be-created first Earl of Strafford, advised the King that war with Scotland was the way forward. Sir Thomas was an autocrat, quite ruthless, a crony of Archbishop Laud and, in 1632, as Lord Deputy of Ireland, had sought to make Ireland English in all its forms. More important to Charles, Wentworth had an Irish army of 8000 men.

And so, after nearly eleven years of believing he could do without Parliament, Charles was forced to issue writs for elections to a new session: he needed money to raise and pay troops. And his chances of avoiding confrontation with Parliament were not helped by his loving, devoted, but Catholic, Queen.

Henrietta Maria's closest adviser was, ironically, a Scotsman called George Con. Con had been sent by the Pope to act as Papal Legate to the Queen's court. Henrietta Maria and Con made it clear they believed that Catholics were the natural supporters of the King. They even tried to raise Catholic troops from the Spanish enclaves of the Netherlands. The Catholic Earl of Nithsdale raised Scottish Roman Catholics for the King and, in Ireland, the Earl of Antrim said he too would raise an army. Many believed that Charles was too influenced by Rome, and that that was his greatest single weakness.

Whatever the truth, all the help promised by Scottish Catholics and Irish peers did not save Charles. The Scots crossed the border. They were in possession of Northumberland and of Durham. And their great allies, the Parliamentary and Puritan party, watched and encouraged them, from London.

C❖Only Parliament could save the land from what had become an act of Scottish aggression. At this moment, King Charles's moral position was at its worst. He had plumbed the depths of personal failure.

The King, whether or not he liked it, was being led towards the most historically important Parliament ever faced by an English monarch. And as England, in 1640, prepared for what would later be known as the Long Parliament, the public axeman numbered the days of Wentworth, and then of Archbishop Laud.

CHAPTER TWENTY-THREE

1640–1649

❖

Until King Charles I was forced to call a Parliament in 1640, he had governed England himself for eleven years, and he was constitutionally within his rights. Charles governed through his King's Council, a sort of Cabinet, and the period became known as the Personal Rule. But Parliament had to be assembled because Charles needed money to put down the Scottish Rebellion. The first Parliament of 1640 became known as the Short Parliament. It lasted for three weeks in April. But under the leadership of a Puritan called John Pym, who had encouraged the Scots in their war, Parliament wanted to discuss eleven years of grievances before giving Charles his money. And then John Pym pressed for a petition to the Lords to rid England of the 'most decrepit age of Popery'. He then attacked the King's demands for money. And Charles, in frustration, or anger, or both, and against Strafford's advice, dissolved Parliament.

But by November 1640, and because he was defeated in the second Bishops' War, Charles was forced to summon another Parliament. This became known as the Long Parliament. It was the fifth Parliament of Charles's reign, and his last. It was also the last for some of his closest friends.

C❖[John] Pym and [John] Hampden, the leading figures in the new House of Commons, were immediately in command of a large and indignant majority. The Crown now made no resistance to the principle that redress of grievances should precede supply; but the grievances of the Commons could be satisfied only by vengeance. Strafford possessed convincing proofs of the correspondence carried on by Pym and others with the invading Scots. This was plain treason if the King's writ ran. It was believed that Strafford meant to open this formidable case; but Pym struck first. All the rage of the Parliamentary party . . . concentrated upon 'the wicked Earl' a blast of fury such as was never recorded in England before or since. On the morning of November 11, the doors of St Stephen's Chapel were locked; the key placed upon the table; no strangers might enter, no Member might leave. Late in the afternoon, Pym and Hampden, attended by 300 Members, carried the articles of Strafford's impeachment up to the House of Lords. At the King's request Strafford had come to London. In the morning he had been greeted with respect by the peers. Hearing what was afoot, he returned to the Chamber. But now all was changed . . . . Shouts were raised that he should withdraw while the issue was being debated. . . . In less than an hour, the powerful minister saw himself transformed into an accused prisoner. He found himself . . . kneeling at the Bar to receive the directions of his peers. He was deprived of his sword and taken into custody by Black Rod.

Pym was very clever with the impeachment of Strafford. Strafford was charged with treason. But treason is a crime against the Crown, and he'd been working on behalf of Charles. Pym simply produced an idea of constructive treason, which he described as 'against the being of the law' as opposed to the rule of law.

Parliament nearly accepted the Pym version, but many peers felt uneasy that they were being asked to commit one of their number for a crime which was not recognized as a crime. And there were a few at least who saw that what was happening to Strafford could easily happen to them. The speech which Strafford gave in his defence touched the very hearts of the doubters. It was the speech of a man fighting for his life, who but days earlier had decided the lives of others.

❖My lords, the shedding of my blood may make a way for the tracing of yours. If every word, intention, circumstance of yours be alleged as treasonable, not because of statute, but a consequence, a construction, heaved up in a high rhetorical strain [then] I leave it to your lordships' consideration to foresee what may be the issue of so dangerous, so recent precedencies. These gentlemen tell me they speak in defence of the Commonweal against my arbitrary laws. Give me leave to say it, I speak in defence of the Commonweal against their arbitrary treason; for if this latitude be admitted, what prejudice shall follow to the King, to the country, if you and your posterity be disabled by the same from the greatest affairs of the Kingdom.

There may have been some in the Lords moved by Strafford's plea, but not in the Commons. Seeing the difficulty before them, the Commons continued with an Act of Attainder. In simple terms, this meant that any allegation could be declared without the need for a formal trial. By this time, many Members had gone home – perhaps because they wanted no part in what was happening. The Act was passed and Charles – with enormous misgivings – gave his royal assent.

Strafford was executed, the first of Charles's ministers to fall victim to Parliament's – and Pym's – revenge. Laud was also impeached in 1640, but then he was inconveniently found not guilty by the Lords, which meant another Bill of Attainder in the Commons. He was eventually executed. The Lord Keeper and the Secretary of State both escaped death by fleeing to the Continent.

The Commons passed a Bill banning bishops from Parliament. The Lords resented this, not so much for the loss of bishops, but more because the House of Commons was telling them what to do. The Lords threw out the Bill. Then Parliament, after much discussion, presented a Bill which guaranteed that there couldn't be more than a three-year gap between Parliaments. This second of three Triennial Acts of that time, was a direct challenge to the King who considered that he alone decided when Parliament should be called.

C❖The King perforce subscribed to this. . . . It was in fact a law making this Parliament . . . perpetual. Many other changes necessary to the times and remedial to the discontents were made [although not in the Triennial Acts]. . . . The Court of Star Chamber . . . was abolished. So was the Court of High Commission, which had striven to impose religious uniformity. The jurisdiction of the Privy Council was strictly and narrowly defined. The principles of the Petition of Right about personal liberty, particularly freedom from arbitrary arrest, were now finally established. . . . The whole Tudor system which the Stuarts had inherited was shaken from its base. . . .

Upon this melancholy scene, a hideous apparition now appeared. The execution of Strafford liberated all the elemental forces in Ireland which his system had so successfully held in restraint. . . . The passions of the original inhabitants and of the hungry, downtrodden masses, bursting from all control, were directed upon the gentry, the landowners, and the Protestants, both within and without the Pale. . . . Cruelties unspeakable were reported on all sides, and the Government, under the Lords Justices, struck back without mercy. A general slaughter of males and a policy of devastation were proclaimed. . . . It was deeply harmful to the King's interests. The Puritan party saw, or declared they saw, in the Irish outrage the fate to which they would be consigned if the Popish tendencies of the bishops were armed with the sword of an absolute sovereign. They regarded the native Irish as wild beasts to be slain at sight, and the cruelties which they in their turn were to wreak in their hour of triumph took their impulse from this moment.

So, anyone who thinks the Civil War started simply because Parliament argued with the King is right, but that's just the simple picture. The more complicated picture is an amalgamation of the Scots invading England, the King needing money to fight them, Parliament having to be called to get that money; Parliament, led by Pym, seeing an opportunity to put right eleven years of dissatisfaction; the destruction of the King's inner cabinet by the zealous Pym (who, incidentally was mixed up in some shady commercial deals, so was hardly the Puritan goody some pretended him to be), and then the Irish rebellion.

The story is further complicated because by the autumn of 1641, Pym's support was not as strong as it had been at the start of the Parliament. And the

King's supporters were gathering their strength. A document called the Grand Remonstrance, which told the King where Parliament stood, and where the Parliamentarians thought he should stand, was put to the vote. Pym and his colleagues thought that would sort the Parliamentarians from the Royalists. And the document, with more than 200 articles, was quite explicit in its allegations of constitutional corruption. Here is one extract.

❖The root of this mischief we find to be a malignant and pernicious design of subverting the fundamental laws and principals of government, upon which the religion and justice of this kingdom are firmly established. The actors and promoters hereof have been:

One: the Jesuited Papists, who hate the laws, as the obstacles of that change and subversion of religion which they so much long for.

Two: the Bishops, and the corrupt part of the clergy, who cherish formality and superstition as the natural effects and, more probably, supports of their own ecclesiastical tyranny and usurpation [sic].

Three: such Councillors and Courtiers as for private ends have engaged themselves to further the interests of some foreign princes or states to the prejudice of his Majesty and the State at home.

On 22 November 1641, the Grand Remonstrance was put to the vote. The debate was furious. As one Member remarked, 'We had like to have sheathed our swords in each other's bowels.' In the Commons, the Member for Cambridge, Oliver Cromwell, the future Lord Protector of England, awaited the outcome. It is said that he told a friend that if Parliament lost the vote, then he would leave England for ever. The Parliamentarians won, but only just. They secured 159 votes; the Royalists, 148. The King's supporters had stood by him, but a majority of 11 was not sufficiently convincing for the Parliamentarians.

Charles offered Pym the job of Chancellor of the Exchequer. Pym turned it down. Charles made Opposition Lords members of his Privy Council. Pym's people accused them of becoming closet Royalists. And so by the end of 1641, the Parliamentarians – the Pymites – and the Royalists were quietly getting their forces together. And then the King lost his nerve. Taunted and goaded by Queen Henrietta, he decided to prosecute five of his principal opponents: Pym, Hampden, Holles, Hazelrigg and Strode, for high treason. It was 4 January 1642 and the King, and 300–400 swordsmen, later known as the Cavaliers, went down to the House of Commons to demand the surrender of the five. But Pym and his colleagues had been warned, and they were not in the Commons.

When Londoners heard what had happened they gathered and, as Churchill puts it, 'bellowed outside the Palace, [and] caused Charles and his Court to escape from the capital to Hampton Court'.

The London mobs were well organized, probably by Pym's City supporters. They included the Guild and Trade apprentices. It was their pudding basin
haircuts that later gave the Parliamentary forces their name: the Roundheads.

In the early months of 1642 the King and Parliament negotiated, but their
differences were great. Parliament wanted the King to surrender his sovereignty
over Church and State.

C❖But underlying the apparently clear-cut constitutional issue was a religious
and class conflict. The Puritans were predominant in Parliament, High
Churchmen at Court. . . . When the alignment of the parties on the outbreak of the Civil War is surveyed, no simple divisions are to be found.
Brother fought against brother, father against son. . . . The greater part of
the nobility gradually rallied to the Royalist cause; the tradesmen and
merchants generally inclined to the Parliament; but a substantial section of
the aristocracy were behind Pym, and many boroughs were devotedly
Royalist. The gentry and yeomen in the counties were deeply divided.
Those nearer London generally inclined to Parliament, while the North
and West remained largely Royalist. Both sides fought in the name of the
King and both upheld the Parliamentary institution. The Roundheads
always spoke of 'King and Parliament'.

And so, by the summer of 1642, a league for, and a league against, the King were
beginning to take shape. In late August of that year, the King raised his royal
standard in Nottingham. This was the formal declaration of war.

C❖By the end of September he [the King] had with him 2000 horse and 6000
foot. A few weeks later their numbers were more than doubled . . . The
Queen, who had found refuge in Holland, sent arms and trained officers,
procured by the sale of the Crown jewels. But the Navy, which Charles had
quarrelled with his subjects to sustain, adhered to Parliament and the
blockade was hard to run. The great nobles supplied the King with money.
. . . The University of Oxford melted their plate . . . When Cambridge
University was found in the same mood, Cromwell intervened with armed
force. Meanwhile the Roundheads, sustained by ample funds from the
wealth and regular taxation of London, levied and trained an army of 25,000
men under [the third Earl of] Essex.

At this early point in the Civil War, Oliver Cromwell was not the leader of the
Parliamentary Army. At the beginning, he was a colonel who methodically
organized the cavalry of the Army of the Eastern Association commanded by
the second Earl of Manchester. Only later did Cromwell become supreme

commander. And, in the opening months it's clear, from letters he wrote to sympathizers, that, like every commander, he needed money to pay his troops and to find their food and weapons. He wrote to the people of Fen Drayton 'in the Hundred of Papworth':

❖Whereas we have been enforced, by apparent grounds of approaching danger, to begin to fortify the Town of Cambridge for preventing the Enemy's inroad, and the better to maintain the peace of this county:

> Having in part seen your good affections to the Cause, and now standing in need of your further assistance to the perfecting of the said fortifications, which will cost at least £2000, we are encouraged as well as necessitated to desire a Freewill Offering of a Liberal Contribution from you, for the better enabling of us to attain our desired ends – viz., The Preservation of our County – knowing that every honest and well affected man, considering the vast expenses we have already been at, and our willingness to do according to our ability, will be ready to contribute his best assistance to a work of so high concernment and so good an end.

> Yours ready to serve,
> Oliver Cromwell,
> Cambridge, March 8, 1642.

Oliver Cromwell was, just, related to the famous Thomas Cromwell, Henry VIII's chief minister: his great-grandfather was a nephew of Thomas Cromwell. Oliver Cromwell was born on 25 April 1599; he was about eighteen months older than the King. He was born in Huntingdon and his parents were local gentry who'd done quite well when monastery lands had been taken from the Church. He spent a year at Sidney Sussex, Cambridge, which was a Puritan college. He probably only left because his father died. Oliver had been the MP for Cambridge in Charles's third Parliament, then again in the Short Parliament, and then again in the Long Parliament. He supported John Pym and he condemned Strafford and Laud. He spoke vigorously, sometimes cruelly, against the suppression of the rights of the common man. He appeared against Anglicans and (of course) Catholics. But it's difficult to label Cromwell simply as a Puritan, because of his own contradictions. As he said, 'I can tell you what I would not have, though I cannot, what I would.' What is clear, is that once he decided that he was doing 'God's work', then he did so tirelessly and single-mindedly. And perhaps that was one of the secrets of his military success. He believed that a soldier who prayed best fought best.

At the outset the Parliamentary rebellion claimed to fight for the King, and their commanders had instructions to rescue the King from his malicious advisers and counsellors. But by the autumn, the Parliamentary forces, instructed by German officers, were full of the passion of their cause.

Charles had been joined by his two nephews, Prince Rupert of the Rhine and his younger brother, Prince Maurice. The two sides were about to meet. And on 23 October 1642, at Edgehill in Warwickshire, the first major battle of the English Civil War began. It was, in sporting terms, a draw; but, naturally, both sides claimed victory. After that, apart from some skirmishes rather than full-blooded battles, the year closed without the decisive engagement and the consequent peace that many had hoped for.

C❖From the beginning of 1643 the war became general. Classes and interests as well as parties and creeds did their best against one another. The ports and towns, the manufacturing centres, mostly adhered to the Parliament; what might be called Old England rallied to Charles. In the two great areas of the North and the West, the King's cause prospered. In the North, Queen Henrietta Maria arrived from Holland. Braving the blockade, she brought a considerable shipload of cannon and munitions to Bridlington, on the Yorkshire coast. . . . [But] at first the decisive action was not in the North.

As Churchill noted earlier, the Civil War split families, and friendships: the Roundhead commander, Sir William Waller, and the Royalist general, Sir Ralph Hopton, were very close friends. But the outcome of the battle they were about to fight would decide who held the West Country: King or Parliament.

C❖At Lansdowne, outside Bath, Hopton's Cornishmen stormed Waller's position. The feature of Waller's army was the London cavalry. These were so completely encased in armour that they looked like 'moving fortresses' and were called by both sides 'the Lobsters'. The Lobsters were charged uphill by the Royalists, who wrought great havoc among them. Waller was defeated, but Hopton's losses were so severe that he took refuge in Devizes. Hopton himself was wounded . . . His horsemen, under Prince Maurice [the King's nephew], ran away. But the Prince, returning . . . with fresh cavalry from Oxford, found Waller drawn up to receive him on Roundway Down. The Royalists attacked and drove the Lobsters headlong down the steep slopes, while Hopton moved out from the town and completed the victory with his infantry.

Fired with these successes, [Prince] Rupert, with the Oxford army joined to Hopton's forces, summoned, assaulted, and procured the surrender of the city of Bristol. This was the second city in the kingdom, and on the whole its inhabitants were Royalist. They had undermined the resistance of the Parliamentary garrison; they looked upon Rupert as a deliverer. The warships in the port declared for the King, and hope dawned of a royal squadron which could command the Bristol Channel. King Charles was master in the West.

Parliament doubted the capacity of Essex as a general. He was a strange man. He apparently went to war believing himself to be doomed: he took his coffin and shroud with him. But he was rich and an aristocrat, and so he was a valuable Parliamentary ally at the start of the war. He became the first Commander of the Parliamentary forces. He was at Edgehill and Newbury, but after his defeat at Lostwithiel in 1644 he resigned.

In the North, thanks to the whitecoats, the retainers of another aristocrat, the corpulent Marquess of Newcastle, York was held for the King. Hull, for a long time a Parliamentary stronghold, went over to the Royalists. In Wales, the clergy and the nobles and the gentry were Royalists. It is said that not a single document was written in Welsh to explain the Parliamentary cause.

And so, a map of England and Wales at the time would look something like this: a line going up the country from Southampton to a few miles south of Northampton which then branches off at ten o'clock as far as the coast at Liverpool. Everything to the left, to the west, of that line, is for the King. Then, except for a wide corridor between Wales and the Dales, the country from the Scottish borders south to the Wash is also the King's.

Everything else – that northern corridor, the south east and the whole of East Anglia – belongs to the Parliamentarians. This leads back to the man who was at the centre of the rebellion in Parliament, John Pym, and – a definite sign that there were many who wanted no war at all – the Peace party.

C❖. . . in London Pym, the master of the Parliament, the heart and soul of the Roundhead war, was in grievous straits. . . . As head of the Government he was obliged to raise money for an increasingly unpopular war by methods as little conformable to the principles he championed as those which Charles had used against the Scots in 1640. . . . Strong currents of Royalism now flowed in the capital. These joined themselves to the peace movement. The Common Council of the City was unyielding; but Royalist opinion was too strong to be silenced. At one time, seventy merchants were in prison for refusing to pay taxes which they judged illegal. On another occasion, hundreds of women crowded to Westminster to present a petition for peace. When the troopers rode in among them, the frantic women tried to drag them from their saddles. . . . the soldiers drew their swords and slashed the women with extreme brutality, chasing them round Palace Yard . . . The House of Lords, consisting now of fewer than twenty sitting peers, carried a precise and solemn resolution for peace negotiations. Even the Commons, by a narrow majority in a thin House, agreed to the Lords' propositions.

If the war ended the King would be back in London. Pym was ill with cancer and his greatest colleague, Hampden, had died of wounds sustained after a clash with Rupert's cavalry at Chalgrove Field. It is possible that these events helped to stiffen the Parliamentary resolve.

C❖All the Puritan forces in London were roused to repudiate peace. The preachers exhorted their congregations, and warlike crowds beset Westminster. The House of Commons rescinded their conciliatory resolution. . . . Both armies headed for London, and on September 20, they [the armies] clashed at Newbury in Berkshire. There was a long and bitter conflict. Once again, Rupert's cavalry beat their opponents; but they could make no impression on the London pikemen and musketeers. A third of the troops were casualties and, on the Royalist side, many nobles fell . . . the King withdrew, stricken by the loss of so many personal friends. . . .

On both sides, men's thoughts turned to peace. Not so the thoughts of Pym; he looked to the Scots . . . He led Parliament, on September 25, into signing a Solemn League and Covenant among themselves and with the Scots to wage war with untiring zeal. It was a military alliance expressed in terms of a religious manifesto. Then on December 8 [1643], Pym died, uncheered by success, but unwearied by misfortune.

Charles became bolder. He declared Parliament to be undemocratic and called a Counter-Assembly to his headquarters at Oxford. Two hundred and fifty-eight members of the Lords and Commons went to the King. But as the Royalists gathered, the news from the north was gloomy. An army of 21,000 Scots had crossed the Tweed into England. But this was not simply an invasion on Parliament's behalf. The origins of the Scots' involvement in the war could be traced to the time when Charles and his Aarchbishop, Laud, tried to impose the English Prayer Book on Scotland. The Scots now fancied they could force Presbyterian Church government on the English.

The Scottish army advanced southwards and dominated the northern Royalist counties. When their Commissioners arrived in London they made three principal demands. They wanted the imposition of Presbyterianism throughout England; a share in the government; and the maintenance of the monarchy.

The Scots wanted to keep one of their own (Charles I was a Stuart) on the throne. At Westminster, few, including the increasingly important figure of Oliver Cromwell, accepted the Scottish demands, especially the insistence on Presbyterianism. For the King, the debate over religious alliance, while important, was not so demanding as the military presence of the Scots. Furthermore, his strongest ally in the north, the Marquess of Newcastle, was besieged in York. Charles sent Prince Rupert to York. On the way he plundered Stockport and stormed Bolton. On 1 June Lord Goring and 5000 cavalry joined Prince Rupert and together they took Liverpool and saved York.

The Scots and the Roundheads joined forces under Lord Manchester and Cromwell and the three combined Puritan armies numbered 20,000 foot and 7000 horse. Their outposts were on Marston Moor. The united forces of Prince Rupert and the Marquess of Newcastle reached 11,000 foot and 7000 horse and on 2 July found themselves near the Roundheads' encampments at Marston Moor. This was the bloodiest battle of the Civil War. It was a disaster for the Royalist cause: 4150 of them killed, 1500 taken prisoner. Cromwell's nephew, also Oliver, had been killed by a cannon shot, possibly at Marston Moor. Cromwell wrote to his brother:

❖To my loving brother,

It's our duty to sympathize in all mercies; and to praise the Lord together in chastisements or trials, that so we may sorrow together. Truly England and the Church of God hath had a great favour from the Lord, in this great victory given unto us, such as the like never was since those wars began. It had all the evidences of an absolute victory obtained by the Lord's blessing upon the Godly Party principally. We never charged but we routed the enemy. The Left Wing, which I commanded, being our own horse, saving a few Scots in our rear, beat all the Prince's horse. God made them as stubble to our swords. We charged their regiments of foot with our horse, and routed all we charged. The particulars I cannot relate now; but I believe, of 20,000, the Prince hath not 4000 left. Give Glory, all the Glory to God.

Sir, God hath taken away your eldest son by a cannon shot. It brake his leg. We were necessitated to have it cut off, whereof he died. At his fall, his horse being killed with a bullet, and as I am informed three horses more, I am told he bid them, open to the right and left, that he might see the rogues run. You have cause to bless the Lord. He is a glorious saint in heaven, wherein you ought exceedingly to rejoice. The Lord be your strength so prays,

your truly faithful and loving brother, Oliver Cromwell, July 5, 1644.

By the autumn the two armies had met once more – this time at Newbury – but without any conclusion. Charles returned to Oxford; Cromwell, now Lieutenant-General Cromwell, to Westminster. And at Westminster Cromwell tried to convince the Parliamentarians of the need to change the way the army was organized. In the House of Commons on Monday 25 November 1644, Cromwell attacked the army's leader, the Earl of Manchester.

❖That the said Earl hath always been indisposed and backward to engagements and the ending of the war by the sword. Since the taking of York, as if the Parliament had now advantage fully enough, he hath declined whatsoever tended to farther [sic] advantage upon the enemy; hath neglected and studiously shifted off opportunities to that purpose, as if he thought the King too low, and Parliament too high.

The Earl's response, a week later, was heavy-handed and confused. On the second Wednesday in November, 1644, Cromwell addressed the Grand Committee in the House.

❖The important occasion now is no less than to Save the Nation, out of a bleeding, nay, a dying condition, which the long continuance of this war hath already brought it into, so that without a more speedy, vigorous and effectual prosecution of the war, we shall make the Kingdom weary of us, and hate the name of Parliament. Members of both Houses have got great places and commands, and the sword in their hands; and will perpetually continue themselves in grandeur, and not permit the war speedily to end, lest their own power should determine with it. I know the worth of those commanders. But if I may speak my conscience without reflection upon any, I do conceive if the army be not put into another method, and the war more vigorously prosecuted, the people can bear the war no longer and will enforce you to dishonourable peace.

These are the beginnings of what became the famous New Model Army. On 21 January 1645 Sir Thomas Fairfax was appointed General, with instructions to form the New Model Army. Incidentally, it was this army which produced a uniform which, at least in its ceremonial form, survives to this day – the red coats.

But it was at about this time that Parliament introduced something called the Self-Denying Ordinance. This effectively banned Members of either House from military service, which explains why Cromwell could not command the New Model Army himself. Eventually, Cromwell was made an exception to this Ordinance, because, if the war was to be speedily concluded, his generalship was needed.

In June 1645, Cromwell was made General of the Horse, and on 14 June the New Model Army met the Royalists in Northamptonshire.

C❖. . . the last trial of strength was made. Charles, having taken Leicester, which was sacked, met Fairfax and Cromwell in the fine hunting country about Naseby. The Cavaliers had so often saved themselves by the offensive spirit, which Rupert embodied to the eclipse of other military qualities, that they did not hesitate to attack, uphill, the Roundhead army of twice their numbers. The action followed what had almost become the usual course. Rupert shattered the Parliamentary left, and though, as at Edgehill, his troopers were attracted by the Parliamentary baggage column, he returned to strike heavily at the central Roundhead infantry. But Cromwell on the other flank drove all before him, and also took control of the Roundhead reserves. The royal foot, beset on all sides by overwhelming numbers, fought with devotion. The King wished himself to charge to their rescue with the last reserve which stood about his person. He actually gave the order; but prudent hands were laid upon his bridle . . . and the royal reserves wheeled to the right and retreated above a mile.

Fairfax, who had himself cut down the King's colour bearer, gathered his infantry to sweep up the Royalist infantry. They shot at the Royalists and when they fled many of them died, cut to pieces by Cromwell's Ironsides. (The Ironsides got their name at the Battle of Marston Moor in 1644 when the Royalist, Prince Rupert, called Oliver Cromwell Ironside. They were a Parliamentary regiment raised from East Anglian farmers without whom the Parliamentarians would not have beaten the King.) But it was the Earl of Lichfield who made the stand that threw off the seemingly superior force. Naseby should be remembered as the conclusion of the 'first' Civil War, the first real success for the New Model Army and the beginning of the end of Charles I.

The King and Rupert escaped to Leicester. But Cromwell was to find a greater prize. His infantry attacked the Royalist headquarters. There they discovered secret correspondence with the Queen. Those letters showed that Charles had tried to get help from abroad. He had hoped for forces from the Irish papists. It was these letters which were eventually published and used to disgrace the King.

The Civil War was really two wars. The first lasted from 1642 until 1646, the second one from 1648 to 1649. For the people who lived through those times the wars were often devastating. Just as today there are civilian victims of conflict, so it was in mid-seventeenth-century England. In Sussex, for instance, there were hundreds of letters and petitions from the parishes to Parliament. Here are three of them.

❖To Speaker Lenthall,

Wee heare there are both foote and horse come from the King into the citty . . . divers houses are threatened to be plundered within and without the city, the sherife being abetted by the gentlemen is extreme violent.

We are, Edward Higgins, William Cawley and Henry Chitty, Chichester, November 1642.

Humblie showeth that which your eyes have herefore seene, and your ears heard, the sad and distressed estate of us, the poore, plundered, robbed and spoyled inhabitants of the said burrough, who were driven by the King's forces from house and habitation, to secure our lives and, in our absence, robbed and spoyled of all outward comforts to mayntayne a livelyhood; some of our houses, being burnte, and others made stables of, and some pulled downe, and all our goods imbeasled, and taken away, to our great impoverishing.

We, the merchants of Arundel, to the Committee at Billingshurst, in the year 1645.

We doe humbly pray that our sad differences and divisions may be happily composed, all misunderstandings between princes and people timely removed, his majestie according to our solemne engagement rendered glorious.

Rendered glorious. The King wasn't at all sure about that. And as ever, when there was war, people paid not only with their misery. War costs money. So, there'd been increases in taxation: between 15–20% taxes on the rich and the middle classes. Taxes on beer touched everyone because, at that time, men, women and children drank ale every day as a matter of course. Taxes also came in other forms. Money had to be paid to the municipality, or for sheriffs and bailiffs. This tax, known as the scot, was keenly avoided. If you didn't have to pay, then you got off: scot-free.

But not many got off scot-free when it came to billeting. Both sides demanded that their troops be taken in free of charge. Others, probably thousands, had their estates confiscated and 80% of the revenues were taken for the war effort. And as if all that wasn't enough, in the second half of the 1640s, treacherous weather all but wiped out harvests. Small wonder that towards the end of the war Parliament was considered even more despotic than had been the King.

After the Battle of Naseby in June 1645, the King fled first to Leicester and then, ironically, he turned to the Scots, who had been brought and bought by the Parliamentarians to help defeat the King. But the King had his reasons.

C◆He [King Charles] saw the deep division which was now open between Scotland and the Ironsides. He had no physical resources, but he hoped that . . . though stripped of power, [he] might yet raise, from what seemed a most adverse quarter, a new resource for his unquenchable purpose. He also had expectations of aid from France, where Queen Henrietta Maria had taken refuge. In the event, all her efforts on his behalf came to nothing, and she never saw her husband again . . . in the end, he resolved to place himself in the hands of the Scots. A French agent obtained from them a verbal promise that the King should be secure in his person and in his honour . . . but he soon found he was a prisoner . . . he entered upon nearly a year's tenacious bargainings on the national issues at stake. . . . Parliament's plan was to keep Charles captive till they had built him a constitutional and religious cage, and meanwhile to use his name . . . for all that they wished to do in their party interest.

In theory, Parliament couldn't do anything without the King, or at least without his name. Also, in his own mind, Charles hadn't given up being King. But if he thought himself safe with his Scottish friends in their stronghold on the banks of the Tyne, he was wrong.

C❖In February 1647, the Scots, having been paid an instalment of half the sum due to them for their services in England, handed over Charles under guarantee for his safety to Parliamentary Commissioners and returned to their own country. . . . Charles was led with the greatest deference to Holmby House in Northamptonshire by his new owners. His popularity became at once manifest. From Newcastle southwards the journey was a progress of cheering crowds and clashing bells. . . . Completely broken in the field, Charles was still incomparably the most important figure in England. . . . But a third and new partner had appeared on the English scene. The Ironside Army, 22,000 strong, was not yet the master, but was no longer the servant, of those who had created it. At its head stood its renowned and trusted generals: Thomas Fairfax . . . Oliver Cromwell . . . Henry Ireton. . . . Now that the war was won, most Members of Parliament and their leaders had no more need of the Army. It must be reduced to modest proportions. The civil power must reign. The expenses must be curtailed.

But the army wasn't going to be that easy to dismiss. To start with, some of its members hadn't been paid for ten months. There was also the instinctive support for the Crown (or a mistrust of the Parliament – whichever). And here Charles must have been in a strong position. His plan was to keep Parliament talking, not to agree to its demands and to watch its powers crumble. Parliament wanted the King to agree to its demands, wanted to disband as much of the army as possible, wanted to retain the power it believed it had won in battle.

And there was another faction to contend with: the Levellers. The Levellers were a group led by a man called John Lilburne who had been imprisoned in the 1630s for smuggling Puritan pamphlets into England. The Levellers, as might be guessed from their name, wanted social distinctions removed – levelled – in English society. Probably the instinct of many in the army was to follow the Levellers. The army began to lean on Parliament. The result was the second Civil War.

C❖King, Lords and Commons, landlords and merchants, the City and the countryside, bishops and presbyters, the Scottish army, the Welsh people, and the English Fleet, all now turned against the New Model Army. The Army beat the lot. And at their head was Cromwell. . . . A mere detachment sufficed to quell a general rising in Cornwall and the West. They broke the Royalist forces at Colchester . . . Cromwell, having subdued the Welsh rising, moved swiftly to the North, picked up his forces, and fell on the Scottish army as it was marching through Lancashire. . . . By the end of 1648, all was over. Cromwell was Dictator. The Royalists were crushed; Parliament was a tool; the Constitution was a figment; the Scots were rebuffed, the Welsh back in their mountains; the Fleet was reorganized, London overawed. . . . It was the triumph of some 20,000 resolute, ruthless, disciplined, military fanatics over all that England has ever willed or ever wished.

It may have been a triumph, but the army still hadn't been paid, agreement with the King was not forthcoming; little had actually been solved. The King himself hadn't even taken an active part in the second Civil War. In November the previous year, he'd escaped the mainland and taken refuge on the Isle of Wight at Carisbrooke.

On 30 November 1648 the army went to Carisbrooke and, although they didn't actually arrest him, took the King to the mainland. They had him where they wanted him, under lock and key. Seven days later, a detachment locked Parliament. This became known as Pride's Purge after Colonel Thomas Pride who led the force. He stopped all but about sixty members, radical Independents, sitting in the Commons. This group became known as the Rump. That was in early December. The following month, Charles was brought before a High Court that called 'Charles Stuart, that man of blood, to account for the blood he had shed and mischief he had done to his utmost against the Lord's cause and the people in these poor nations'. Charles refused to recognize the court. He refused to speak in his own defence but it would have made little difference. His death warrant was already written and was simply waiting for signature. It read:

❖To Colonel Francis Hacker, Colonel Huncks, and Lieutenant Colonel Phayr, and to every of them [sic], At the High Court of Justice for the Trying and Judging of Charles Stuart, King of England, January 29, 1648.
    Whereas Charles Stuart, King of England, is and standeth convicted, attained and condemned of High Treason and other high crimes; and sentence upon Saturday last was pronounced against him by this court, to be put to death by the severing of his head from his body; of which sentence execution yet remaineth to be done: These are therefore to will and require you to see the said Sentence executed, in the open street before Whitehall, upon the morrow, being the thirtieth day of this instant month of January,

between the hours of ten in the morning and five in the afternoon, with full effect. And for so doing, this shall be your warrant.

Given under our hands and seals, John Bradshaw, Thomas Grey, Lord Groby, Oliver Cromwell.

It was snowing when Charles Stuart was beheaded in front of the Banqueting House which his father, James I, had commissioned Inigo Jones to build.

CHAPTER TWENTY-FOUR

1649–1660

❖

England became a Republic in January, 1649. The monarchy, the House of Lords, and the Anglican Church were all abolished. The great seal of England was thrown aside and a new one minted: on one face, a map of England; on the other, the House of Commons. Scotland was integrated, Ireland savaged. Adultery became punishable by death. War was declared on the Dutch. The Sergeant at Arms, Edward Dendy, with his trumpeters and outriders, went about the city proclaiming that whosoever shall proclaim a new King in this nation of England shall be a traitor and suffer death.

Parliament had taken the legal murder of the King (for that's what some believed it to have been) most seriously, and understood perfectly that its authority would have to be enforced by the sternest of means. Cromwell's name had been on the King's death warrant but at this stage in 1649 he wasn't what would now be called the President of the Republic.

C❖The country was now to be governed by a Council of State . . . Its forty-one members included peers, judges and Members of Parliament, among them most of the principal regicides. It was found to be fearless, diligent, and incorrupt. The judiciary hung for a time in the balance. Six of the twelve judges refused to continue, but the rest, their oath of allegiance being formally abrogated, agreed to serve the Commonwealth.

The highly conservative elements at the head of the Army held firmly to the maintenance of the Common Law and the unbroken administration of justice in all non-political issues. The accession of the lawyers to the new regime was deemed essential for the defence of privilege and property against the assaults of the Levellers, agitators, and extremists. This had now become the crucial issue. Fierce and furious as was the effort of the Levellers, there was no hesitation among the men in power to put them down. . . . It was essential to divide and disperse the Army, and Cromwell was willing to lead the larger part of it to a war of retribution in the name of the Lord Jehovah against the idolatrous and bloodstained Papists of Ireland.

A group which became known as the Diggers thought that the Republic should expand its principles to include equal rights in property, so they set up a commune of farmers. Hence Diggers. But the idea didn't last because too many were against them. Their leader, Gerard Winstanley, announced the colony in a notice published on 26 April 1649. And he wrote an appeal to the House of Commons. Here's a part of it.

❖Sirs, you know the land of England is the land of our nativity, both yours and ours, and all of us by the righteous law of our creation ought to have food and raiment freely by our righteous labouring of the earth, without working for hire or paying rent one to another. England you know hath been conquered and enslaved divers times, and the best laws that England hath (viz. Magna Carta) were got by our forefathers' importunate petitioning unto Kings, that still were the task masters; and yet these best laws are yokes and manacles, tying one sort of people to be slaves to another. Clergy and gentry have got their freedom, but the common people still are left servants to work for them, like the Israelites under the Egyptian taskmasters.

You and we cried for a Parliament, and a Parliament was called. We looked upon you to be our chief council, to agitate business for us. You saw the dangers so great that without a war, England was like to be more enslaved, therefore you called upon us to assist you with plate, taxes, freequarters and our persons; and you promised us, in the name of the Almighty, to make us free people.

In page after page, the appeal to the Commons claims that the people, having paid with their money, in kind, and with their lives, remained enslaved. Winstanley wanted to get rid of the landlords. But, more generally, this half-forgotten radical and pamphleteer expressed what many, including some of the lower ranks of the army, felt, but few voiced.

They had rid themselves of what the Diggers called 'the descendants of William the Conqueror', only to be discarded by the very Parliament in which they'd had so much hope. Their main demand – that the common land should be just that, common to all – was not what Parliament had in mind. To them the Diggers, the Levellers of John Lilburne, and any other extremists, could not be tolerated, especially since many of them were soldiers.

C❖No one was more shocked than Cromwell. He cared almost as much for private property as for religious liberty. . . . The Council of State chased the would-be cultivators off the common land, and hunted the mutinous officers and soldiers to death without mercy. Cromwell again quelled a mutiny in person, and by his orders Trooper William Thompson, a follower of Lilburne, was shot in an Oxfordshire churchyard. ... [He] also discharged from the army, without their arrears of pay, all men who would not volunteer for the Irish war. ... He joined the Puritan divines in preaching a holy war upon the Irish, and made a religious progress to Charing Cross in a coach drawn by six Flemish horses. All this was done as part of a profound calculated policy in the face of military and social dangers which, if not strangled, would have opened a new ferocious and measureless social war in England.

Cromwell's campaign of 1649 in Ireland was equally cold-blooded, and equally imbued with those Old Testament sentiments which dominated the minds of the Puritans.

Cromwell was determined that not only would he crush the Irish leaders in the military sense, but he would do it so bloodily that it would send shivers of submission through the consciousness of the remainder of the people. And Ireland wasn't united: there were factions and creeds, families for the Crown, families against, families against each other.

The Protestant Royalists led by the Marquess of Ormonde were once a well-organized troop of perhaps 12,000 men. But when Cromwell arrived in Ireland, Ormonde was weak yet ready to defend the towns of Wexford and Drogheda.

After the battle (or was it a massacre?) in the early autumn of September 1649, Cromwell wrote to the President of the Council of State, John Bradshaw.

❖Sir,

It hath pleased God to bless our endeavours at Drogheda. After battle we stormed it. The enemy were about 3000 strong in the town. We refused them quarter. I believe we put to the sword the whole number of the defendants. I do not think thirty of the whole number escaped with their lives. This hath been a marvellous great mercy. I do not believe that any officer escaped with his life, save only one lieutenant, who I hear, going to the enemy, said that he was the only man that escaped of all the garrison. The enemy upon this were filled with much terror. And truly I believe this bitterness will save much effusion of blood, through the goodness of God,

Your most Humble Servant, Oliver Cromwell, Dublin, September 16, 1649.

Cromwell wrote once more to London. Here he gave more details, but, most important to an understanding of Cromwell, he gave thanks to God for everything that had happened, according to his belief that a soldier who prayed fiercely, fought fiercely. Here's a small part of that long explanation.

❖For the Honourable William Lenthall, Esquire, Speaker of the Parliament of England.

Sir,
That which caused your men to storm so courageously, it was the Spirit of God who gave your men courage, and took it away again; and gave the enemy courage, and took it away again; and gave your men courage again, and therewith this happy success. And therefore it is good that God alone have all the glory.

Meanwhile the late King's eldest son had been proclaimed King of Great Britain, France and Ireland, in Scotland. One of the conditions of support for the Royalist cause was that the newly proclaimed King, Charles II, should support the Presbyterian cause. This was a terrible condition, especially as it tacitly condemned his mother, a devout Catholic, as an idolater. But the Scottish Commissioners, who demanded of the King more than he could give in his heart, were determined to succeed, and they did. And it was from this moment that Cromwell understood that once he was done with Ireland, he would have to fight on the Scottish borders.

Just twelve months on from the massacre of Drogheda, Cromwell's forces left 3000 Scots dead at the Battle of Dunbar. The remainder fled. The Scots rallied under Charles II's banner. At Scone they crowned him King, and followed him across the border. Cromwell let them. He watched their supply columns stretch, and he knew that the English Royalists would be of little use.

One year on from Dunbar, and two years on from Drogheda, Cromwell defeated the Scots at Worcester. The King escaped and hid in a tree, and so spawned hundreds of public houses called the Royal Oak. Eventually he made his escape to Holland.

By now, Cromwell, the commander of the army but not yet of the country, saw the signs that the army's coming battle was with neither Royalist nor Irish opponents, but with Parliament itself. The army was no longer the servant militia of the great families and princes. It had, since Naseby, been a standing army, a national army. Cromwell understood the power it represented and the potential danger in its leaders.

From the moment the Rump Parliament, (the group of Long Parliamentarians who kept their seats and announced that England was to be a Commonwealth), ordered the execution of Charles I, its actions, unwittingly and with hindsight, led to the restoration of the monarchy. Instead of taking bold decisions, Parliament, in its incompetence, became reactionary. The law, local administration, and financial management were largely unchanged, and the weaknesses in them were never overcome. And so the Republic was run by committee. Cromwell, the most powerful personality of the time, was seeking Parliament's revenge in Ireland, putting down the rebellion in Scotland, defeating the royalists at Worcester. It was the Rump Parliament that struggled ineffectively with the day-to-day conundrums of government.

Cromwell wanted a God-fearing reform of society. Parliament was incapable of delivering so Cromwell called together an assembly of 140 like-minded, supposedly saintly, souls who became known as members of the Barebones Parliament after one of its members, a preacher called Praisegod Barbon. For five months they pontificated, sniped and sneered. They swept aside legislation and replaced it with little that was practicable and even less that was popular, especially with the Church, property owners, and the army. Eventually the army decided to get rid of the Saints.

C❖The Army leaders . . . persuaded or compelled the more moderate Saints to get up very early one morning before the others were awake and pass a resolution yielding back their power to the Lord General from whom it had come. Cromwell did not waste his strength wrestling against their wish. . . . His high place, for all its apparent strength, depended on the precarious balance of Parliament and Army. . . . The executive office of Lord Protector conferred upon Cromwell was checked and balanced by a Council of State, nominated for life, consisting of seven Army leaders and eight civilians. A single Chamber was also set up, elected upon a new property qualification. . . . [And] all those who had fought against Parliament were disqualified from voting.

It didn't work. The hard-headed Republicans wanted to rip the Constitution apart. But Cromwell fiercely protected the principle of the 1653 Instrument of Government – the only written Constitution Britain has ever had – and determined that the Republicans should go. The Instrument of Government was designed to establish a Protectorate and to create a balance between the Army and Parliament. Cromwell was declared Lord Protector on 16 December 1653, but he found, having rid himself of the Republican zealots, that he still didn't have the control he wanted so he dissolved Parliament.

A series of Royalist plots were attempted, including a popular one known as Penruddock's Rising. None was successful, but in 1655 Cromwell decided to split England and Wales into eleven districts, each to be run by a Major-General, a rank devised in the New Model Army in 1642. The Major-Generals policed, taxed and administered with a Puritan zeal that Cromwell respected.

C❖None dared withstand the Major-Generals; but the war with Spain [in 1655] was costly and the taxes insufficient. Like Charles I, Cromwell was driven again to summon a Parliament. The Major-Generals assured him of their ability to pack a compliant House. But Levellers, Republicans, and

Royalists were able to exploit the discontent against the military dictatorship, and a large number of Members who were known enemies of the Protector were returned. By a strained use of a clause in the Instrument of Government, Cromwell managed to exclude 100 of his opponents from the House, while another fifty or sixty voluntarily withdrew in protest. Even after this purge, his attempt to obtain a confirmation of the local rule of the Major-Generals met with such vehement opposition that he was compelled to do without it. . . . It was at this stage that a group of lawyers and gentry decided to offer Cromwell the Crown.

By 1657 Cromwell had a clearly more agreeable, although not an entirely satisfactory, Parliament which produced an amended constitution called A Humble Petition and Advice. This allowed Cromwell to name his successor and to choose his own council of rulers. (So much for the starting point of modern democracy.)

The Humble Petition and Advice also offered Cromwell the crown, and there's some evidence that he liked the idea of becoming King to continue what he saw as the Lord's work. But Cromwell, who had such distinct views on how society should behave, who could be ruthless (as the Irish had discovered at the massacre at Drogheda), who could bend and break the Constitution when it suited, was incapable of taking that final step to the throne. For weeks and weeks, in conference after conference, the Lord Protector produced little more than page after page after page of speeches imperfectly punctuated with indecision, with references to the apostles, to the Psalmist, and always to God's will. But it was not until one Friday afternoon in May 1657, that Cromwell could bring himself to give Parliament his answer to their question: would he be King, or wouldn't he?

❖Mr Speaker,

I come hither to answer that that [sic] was in your last paper to your committee, which was in relation to the Desires that were offered me by the House in that they call their Petition. I confess that Business hath put the House, the Parliament, to a great deal of trouble. I am very sorry for that. It hath cost me some too and some thoughts: and because I have been the unhappy occasion of the expense of so much time, I shall spend little of it now. . . . I think it my duty, only I could have wished I had done it sooner, for the sake of the House, who have laid such infinite obligations on me; I wish I had done it sooner for your sake, and for saving time and trouble; and for the Committee's sake, to whom I must acknowledge I have been unreasonably troublesome. I should not be an honest man if I did not tell you that I cannot accept of the Government. . . . I say I am persuaded to return this answer to you, that I cannot undertake this Government with the title of King. And that is mine answer to the great and weighty business.

That was probably the shortest speech Oliver Cromwell made on the subject. But behind his refusal was, as ever, the army. Particularly the lower orders who did not like the regalia of monarchy. It is doubtful that Cromwell could have held the army's loyalty if he had accepted the crown. Thanks to Cromwell, there was now a well-trained army and if it turned on anyone, it could, should it wish, devour them, and there was no other institution in the land capable of stopping it from doing so.

But the important point here is not so much that Cromwell did or did not become king, but that a large and important group understood that kingship once more mattered to the survival of society. Cromwell understood it clearly. This offer of the crown to Cromwell was, therefore, an admission that at some stage the monarchy would be restored. It was also a recognition that Cromwell's weakness was partly based on the decision to execute Charles I. It may be an over-simplification, but Parliament, in its unsophisticated practice of politics and constitution, didn't know how to exercise lasting power. Hence the irony: the real reason for offering Cromwell the crown was to curb the very power that he had used to enforce his vision.

C❖Although Cromwell easily convinced himself that he had been chosen the Supreme Ruler of the State, he was ever ready to share his power with others, provided of course that they agreed with him. He was willing, indeed anxious, to govern through a Parliament, if that Parliament would carry the laws and taxes he required. But neither his fondlings nor his purges induced his Parliaments to do his will. Again and again he was forced to use or threaten the power of the sword, and the rule which he sought to make a constitutional alternative to absolutism or anarchy became in practice a military autocracy.

But then, on 3 September 1658, it came to an end. On the anniversaries of the terrible massacre at Drogheda, of the Battle of Dunbar, and of the Battle of Worcester, the Lord Protector died.

The great experiment, the Commonwealth, the Republic, died with Cromwell. Officially it didn't die, but without Oliver Cromwell it ran out of steam. Cromwell's son, Richard, took over as Lord Protector, but within eighteen months, Charles II was heading for the throne.

The momentous and revolutionary abolition of the monarchy in the middle of the seventeenth century failed because, in spite of the constitutional revolution, there was no structured party system. There was no machinery that could control jealousies, or at least contain them beneath a recognized label. And where Oliver Cromwell had understood and coped with the jealousies of the army commanders, his son, Richard, didn't, couldn't, and simply fell victim to them.

C❖'Tumbledown Dick', as his enemies nicknamed him, was a respectable person with good intentions, but without the force and capacity required by the severity of the times. He was at first accepted by the Army and duly installed in his father's seat; but when he attempted to exercise authority he found he had but the form. The first appointment Richard Cromwell sought to make in the Army, of which his own brother-in-law, Charles Fleetwood, was Commander in Chief, was objected to by the Council of Officers. Richard was made aware alike that the command of the Army was not hereditary, and also that it could not remain unfilled. His brother, Henry, who was both able and energetic, strove like Richard to strengthen the civil power even at the expense of the monarchical attributes of the Protector's office. Upon Henry Cromwell's advice Parliament was summoned.

Parliament was not yet a permanent body. It was called when the head of state either considered, or was forced to consider, that it had to be consulted. And although Cromwell, the Republic, and Parliament are often lumped together, they were not one and the same. Cromwell fought Parliament just as earlier monarchs had done. Parliament fought the powers of the Protector, just as earlier Parliaments had fought the monarchs. Parliament was rather like an elected extraordinary general meeting of a corporation. And it was up to the Commons to grab back all those powers which it believed Oliver Cromwell had taken over.

C❖They questioned the validity of all Acts since the [Cromwell's] purge of 1657 had robbed Parliament of its representative integrity. They sought to transfer the allegiance of the army from the Protector to themselves. The Army leaders were, however, determined to preserve their independent power. . . . The Commons thought it unbearable that the Army should establish itself as a separate Estate of the Realm. They called upon the assembled officers to return to their military duties. . . . They resolved that every officer should pledge himself in writing not to interrupt the sittings and debates of Parliament.

   . . . Both sides marshalled their forces; but . . . the will of the inferior officers and the rank and file prevailed over all. Within four months of succeeding to his august office Richard Cromwell found himself deserted even by his personal guard. The immediate dissolution of Parliament was demanded and a Committee of Officers waited all night for compliance. . . . the spirit of the troops had become hostile to the Protectorate. They were resolved upon a pure republic, in which their military interest and sectarian and Anabaptist doctrines should hold the chief place.

Anabaptists believed in rebaptism, born-again baptism for adults, and religious suspicions remained the cause of many confrontations, sometimes manifested in very basic ways. For example, Catholics weren't allowed to travel more than five miles from their own homes, especially to the capital. One William Blundell, a Catholic with Cavalier sympathies, needed to escort his daughter to London. She was to go to France to become a nun. To take her to London Blundell had first to write a grovelling letter to the man who was his virtual jailer.

❖To Colonel Gilbert Ireland

Honoured Sir,

I do earnestly beg you will be pleased to let me know by my servant (the bearer hereof) whether the humble suit I lately made unto you for a licence to travel to London may now be granted. I shall forbear to plead the importance of those occasions that call me thither, lest I may seem to urge a favour whereof I may haply prove incapable. Sir, I shall hope for your favourable answer, and will remain ever and however,

Your most humble and faithful servant,

Will Blundell, August 16, 1658.

Blundell, under what was almost house arrest, had to take stock of his assets. His notebook gives us some idea of the value, and also of the size of stock and goods in a less than modest household in 1658.

My Goods and Money at August 1658

Horses, nine:	£37
Oxen and steers feeding, eight:	£40
Bulls, two:	£8
Heifers, nine:	£30
Sheep and lambs, 113:	£26
Malt:	£6
Groats and oat meal:	£1.15s
Bed frames, twenty-five:	£11
Trunks, Chests, Boxes, Desks and Presses:	£11
Tables, chairs, forms and cupboards:	£19
A lead cistern:	£4
Featherbeds, sixteen:	£48
Chaff beds, six:	£1.4s
Bolsters and pillows, blankets and coverings, curtains, cushions, counterparts [soft furnishings] with other things suitable:	£51
Linens for the housewife:	£48
Jewels, a watch and odd knacks:	£9.15s

I have so far paid my debts that the value of my goods exceeds them by £64.14s not reckoning new corn and hay. But reckoning new corn and hay, I am worth £208.14s.4d.

Richard Cromwell was overthrown and the army resurrected the old guard of the long rejected and ridiculed Rump Parliament. But these were the death days of the great experiment in constitutional reform. The army was once more dividing, but for reasons of powerful ambition rather than monarchist and Republican dogma. The rift at the top of the army grew and this sent shivers of disunity throughout the senior ranks who, to a man, started to have doubts about their hard-line actions against Parliament. It was December 1659.

C❖The schism in the rank and file was beginning to destroy the self-confidence of the troops and put an end to the rule of the sword in England. At Christmas, the Army resolved to be reconciled with Parliament. 'Let us live and die with Parliament,' they shouted. They marched to Chancery Lane and drew up before the house of Speaker Lenthall. Instead of the disrespect with which they had so recently treated him, the soldiers now expressed their penitence for having suspended the sittings of the House. They submitted themselves to the authority of Parliament and hailed the Speaker as their general and the father of their country.

George Monck, Commander in Chief of the army, had been one of the parliamentary commanders in Ireland. His secret neutrality agreement with the Ulster Irish had made Cromwell's suppression of Ireland that much simpler. Now, he marched south from Coldstream in the Scottish borders to London. But he marched with no personal ambition; Monck opposed the notion of army rule. He therefore accepted the need for free parliamentary elections and free elections meant that back into both Houses of Parliament came those who had never really wanted a Republic. This didn't mean they accepted without question the rule of the king or queen, but they did accept, on reasonable terms, the institution of monarchy. So it was from this point that the Restoration of the monarchy was inevitable.

Imagine the excitement that an ordinary change of government causes in our modern society and then imagine what it might have been like in 1660 when the news spread of Monck's arrival and the introduction of free elections. Perhaps these stirring months were the encouragement for the young man who now began to keep a diary that became one of the most famous London journals. The diaries of Samuel Pepys open in January 1660. Here are some entries from February, 1660.

February 3
I and Joyce [Pepys's cousin] went walking all over Whitehall, whither General Monck was newly come and we saw all his forces march by in very good plight and stout officers.

February 7
Boys do now cry 'Kiss my Parliament' instead of 'Kiss my Arse' so great and a general contempt is the Rump come to among all men, good and bad.

February 11
I walked in Westminster Hall, where I heard the news of a letter from Monck, who was now gone into the city again, and did resolve to stand for the sudden filling up of the House; and it was very strange how the countenance of men in the Hall was all changed with joy.

The big debate in the 1650s may have been for the Republic, the Commonwealth, to have or not to have a king, to be Roman Catholic or Puritan, but at the same time as the political and social upheaval, a scientific and artistic revolution, which frightened the political leaders, was under way.

By the end of the Republic, with Cromwell gone and Charles II about to ascend the throne, a different style of writing began to appear. It may be that people were adjusting to the new freedoms, trying to see who they were, rather than being told who they were and what they ought to be. Certainly the Restoration writers, for all their scalliwag style, described what they saw around them and they had long abandoned the so-called metaphysical seriousness of their Elizabethan predecessors.

Literature was constantly debated, and scientists were starting to prove that accepted ideas were bunkum. John Donne, in *An Anatomy of the World*, published in 1611, grappled with the new ideas.

The new philosophy calls all in doubt,
The element of fire is quite put out;
The sun is lost and the earth, and no man's wit
Can well direct him where to look for it.
And freely men confess that this world's spent,
When in the planets and the firmament
They seek so many new; they see that this
Is crumbled out again to his atomies.
'Tis all in pieces, all coherence gone;
All just supply, and all relation:
Prince, subject, father, son, are things forgot,
For every man alone thinks he hath got

To be a phoenix, and that there can be
None of that kind, of which he is, but he.
This the world's condition now . . .

And even when Donne had taken holy orders, his poetry still reflected what the Oxford scholar, Maurice Ashley, called 'an awareness of the mighty riddles of human life'.

The seventeenth century was a century when writers and poets were categorized by their religious persuasions. Taylor, Vaughan and of course Donne were seen as Church of Englanders. Dryden and Richard Crashaw were Roman Catholics and Bunyan and Milton, Puritans. It was also a century that saw the introduction of a new industry.

Until now something like 80% of the population had worked in agriculture. The biggest industry was cloth, but the dark satanic mills were yet to come; the cloth industry was still a cottage industry. So imagine the consequences of the Civil War. The land had been ravaged and therefore so had the staple industry.

But by the Restoration, the second half of the seventeenth century, the new industry that took root was coal. In the sixteenth century coal was a poor man's fuel but in the first half of the 1600s there was a thirteen-fold – perhaps as high as a fifteen-fold – increase in coal production.

Coal was not a cottage industry, it needed organized gangs of fit men to mine it. This is the beginning of private enterprise industry, industry that produced collective, structured employment.

By the end of the seventeenth century, the population of England and Wales stood at 5.25 million. London had doubled its size from 200,000 to 400,000. The next biggest town was Norwich, followed by Bristol and York and then Newcastle. The poor continued to be poor and the well off lived very well indeed. Here's a typical noble's household account for a week's groceries.

Meat: twenty-seven stone two pounds of beef. One breast of veal. A side and a neck and breast of mutton. One pork. Two gammons of bacon. Tripe. Sheep's feet. One neat's [ox's or cow's] tongue.	£4.15s.10d.
Poultry: five tame pigeons. Eighteen wild pigeons. Three pullets. Seven chickens. Four hens. Two capons. A cock, for broth.	£1.14s. 5d.
Fish: three lobsters. Four salt fishes. Six flounders.	8s. 6d.
Fruit and vegetables: six oranges and three lemons.	6d.
Asparagus. Onions. Herbs.	5s.10d.

And when the Earl of Bedford paid a visit to Cambridge, a six-day jaunt, it was all carefully accounted for. The account is rendered at Royston:

October 12	The bill at Royston for meat and drink, and to the servants of the house of the poor.	£1. 8s. 6d.
October 13	Coachman and groom's bill.	£1.12s. 6d.
October 15	To the ringers.	10s.
	To the harpers.	5s.
October 16	Music morning and dinner at Trinity college. Mr Herring's servants. To the town clerk. To the sergeants. Crier, bellman, beadle, housekeeper. And to the poor box and prisoners' box. The ostler's bill. To the poor at inn when your lordship took coach. The bill at inn for two dinners and supper. For oil of bitter almonds by Mr Collas. To the servants. Shoeing a horse by the way and at Mr Brown's. To porters that fetched the wine. The bill for wine and glasses broke. Total £74.16s. 5d.	

An expensive, and perhaps noisy time. And there was one additional item.

Given to a mad woman at Royston	6d.

Eating, for those who could afford it, was a pastime as well as a necessity. Here is Samuel Pepys in 1663 entertaining in his London house:

❖My poor wife rose by five o'clock in the morning, before day, and went to market and bought fowle and many other things for dinner – with which I was highly pleased. Things being put in order and the cooke come, I went to the office, where we sat till noon; and then broke up and I home – whither by comes Dr Clerke and his lady, his sister and a she-cosen, and Mr Pierce and his wife, which was all my guests. I had for them, after oysters at first course, a hash of rabbits and lamb, and a rare chine of beef; next a great dish of roasted fowl, cost me about thirty shillings, and a tart; and then fruit and cheese. My dinner was noble and enough. At night to supper; had a good sack posset and cold meat and sent my guests away about ten o'clock at night both of them and myself highly pleased with our management of this day. I believe this day's feast will cost me near five pounds.

He may have enjoyed spending his money on such a feast, but generosity was not always shown towards the servants should they interfere with a mere bowl of common whey. Here is the great diarist once more.

❖*June 12*

I having from my wife and the maids complaints made of the boy, I called him up and with my whip did whip him till I was not able to stir, and yet I could not make him confess any of the lies that they tax him with. At last, not willing to let him go away a conqueror, I took him in task again and pulled off his frock to his shirt, and whipped him till he did confess that he did drink the whey, which he hath denied.

I confess it is one of the greatest wonders that I have met with, that such a little boy as he could be able to suffer half so much as he did to maintain a lie. But I think I must be forced to put him away. So to bed, with my arm very weary.

The servant boy's treatment was common enough, but when the common people complained about their lot they were rarely listened to; and there was no one to represent them. At least no one they wanted to be represented by.

They certainly wouldn't have chosen Thomas Hobbes as their representative. In *Leviathan*, Hobbes's treatise on political thought, published in 1651, he argued against all the doctrinal notions that people were good and had the right to much better things. Hobbes argued that people weren't at all good. They were, he thought, purely selfish creatures, out for what they could get, not for others, but for themselves.

And Hobbes thought that notions of 'right and wrong, justice and injustice, have there no place'. The only way to maintain society, he said, was to establish a total ruler, a dictator, and make everyone obedient. Hobbes argued that the extent of that obedience should be subject to various conditions, one of which was that the people should obey only as long as the sovereign was able to protect them.

And so, according to Hobbes, the price of sovereignty was protection. And, in the year 1660, that concept was about to be tested once more. Across the water in Holland, King Charles II waited and drafted his promise that on his return he would grant 'liberty to tender consciences'. By the end of May he entered London, and unlike his father, he did so in triumph and little fear for his life.

The barely begun Republic was discarded and the people lined the streets to welcome the restoration of the monarchy and Charles II for his coronation.

CHAPTER TWENTY-FIVE

1660–1681

———— ❖ ————

Before Charles II could return to England from his exile in Holland, one significant announcement, a concession almost, was needed. And it had to come from Charles himself, because it had to do with the fear of revenge and the settlement of old scores, and something dear to the army's heart, back pay.

If the returning monarch demanded retribution for all the acts committed against the Crown during the Civil War it would be a catastrophe. So a document, which became known as the Declaration of Breda, was drawn up. It was a finely drafted balance between what Parliament wanted and what Charles was willing to concede, and it began with the pomp and courtly style that had been missing from proclamations and decrees for more than a decade. It reminded the people that the Crown was the King's as God's anointed.

❖Charles, by the grace of God, King of England, Scotland, France and Ireland, Defender of the Faith, to all our loving subjects, of what degree or quality soever, greeting. If the general distraction and confusion which is spread over the whole Kingdom doeth [sic] not awaken all men to a desire and longing that those wounds which have so many years together been kept bleeding may be bound up, all we can say will be to no purpose.

However, after this long silence we have thought it our duty to declare how much we desire to contribute thereunto, and that as we can never give over the hope in good time to gain the possession of that right which God, and nature, hath made our due, so we do make it our daily suit to the Divine Providence that he will, in compassion to us and our subjects after so long misery and suffering, remit and put us into a quiet and peaceable possession of that our right, with as little blood and damage to our people as is possible. Nor do we desire more to enjoy what is ours than that all our subjects may enjoy what by law is theirs, by a full and entire administration of justice throughout the land, and by extending our mercy where it is wanted and deserved.

And now the important point, that revenge may be the Lord's but not the King's.

❖And to the end that the fear of punishment may not engage any, conscious to themselves what is past, to a perseverance in guilt for the future . . . we do declare that we do grant a free and general pardon, which we are ready upon demand to pass under our great seal of England, to all our subjects, of what degree or quality or soever, who within forty days after the publishing hereof shall lay hold upon this our grace and favour, and shall by any public act declare their doing so, and that they return to the loyalty and obedience of good subjects (excepting only such persons as shall hereafter be excepted by Parliament). Those only excepted, let all our loving subjects, how fault soever, rely upon the word of a King, solemnly given by this declaration, that no crime whatsoever committed against us or our royal father before the publication of this shall ever rise in judgment or be brought in question against any of them, to the least endamagement of them, either their lives, liberties, or estates, or (as far forth as lies in our power) so much as to the prejudice of their reputations by any reproach or term of distinction from the rest of our best subjects; we desiring and ordaining henceforward all notes of discord, separation and difference of parties be utterly abolished among all our subjects, whom we invite and conjure to a perfect union among themselves, under our protection, for the resettlement of our just rights and theirs in a free Parliament, by which, upon the word of a King, we will be advised. And because the passion and uncharitableness of the times have produced several opinions in religion, by which men are engaged in parties and animosities against each other, which, when they shall hereafter unite in a freedom of conversation, will be composed or better understood, we do declare a liberty to tender consciences, and that no man shall be disquieted or called in question for differences of opinion in matter of religion which do not disturb the peace of the kingdom; and that we shall be ready to consent to such an Act of Parliament as upon mature deliberation shall be offered to us for the full granting of this indulgence.

This, the Declaration of Breda, might well be subtitled the Declaration of Let Bygones be Bygones. These are the words to which Charles II put his name and it's this document, probably written by his Chancellor Edward Hyde (whose granddaughter incidentally would one day become Queen Anne) which meant that he could and would return to England. The constitutional tidying up could begin.

C❖While the negotiations reached their final form, the elections for a new Parliament were held. Nominally, those who had borne arms against the Republic were excluded, but the Royalist tide flowed so strongly that this ban had no effect. Presbyterians and Royalists found themselves in a great majority, and the Republicans and Anabaptists went down before them in every county. In vain did they rise in arms; in vain did they propose to recall Richard Cromwell who was about to seek refuge in France. They were reminded that they themselves had cast him out. Lambert [who helped to install Cromwell as Protector] escaping from the Tower . . . prepared to dispute the quarrel in the field. His men deserted him, and he was recaptured without bloodshed. This fiasco sealed the Restoration. Monk, the bulk of his army, the City militia, the Royalists throughout the land, the great majority of the newly elected House of Commons, the peers, who assembled again as if nothing had happened, were all banded together and knew that they had the power. The Lords and Commons were restored. It remained only to complete the three estates of the Realm by the recall of the King.

Parliament hastened to send the exiled Charles a large sum of money for his convenience, and soon concerned itself with the crimson velvet furniture of his coaches of State. The Fleet, once so hostile, was sent to conduct him to his native shores.

On board the significantly named *Naseby*, one of the vessels that sailed to Holland to return with the King, was Edward Montagu, one of the men responsible for restoring Charles to his throne, and Samuel Pepys. Montagu was to become the first Earl of Sandwich. Pepys was in his twenties and had two masters at the time. He was a clerk in the Exchequer where he was employed by George Downing (from whom Downing Street takes is name) and he also served Edward Montagu.

Pepys described the first glimpse of the King as he prepared to leave the Netherlands. With Charles were his brothers the Dukes of York and Glouces-ter, his aunt Elizabeth, who was the Queen of Bohemia, his sister Mary who was now the Princess Royal and her son, William, who was the Prince of Orange and who would one day be King of England himself.

May 23
The King, with the two Dukes, the Queen of Bohemia, Princess Royal and Prince Orange, came on board where I, in their coming in, kissed the King's, Queen's and Princess's hands, having done the other before. Infinite shooting off of the guns, and that in a disorder on purpose, which was better than if it had been otherwise. Dined in great state, the royal company by themselves in the coach, which was a blessed sight to see.

We weighed anchor, and with a fresh gale and most happy weather we set sail for England – all the afternoon the King walking here and there, up and down (quite contrary to what I thought him to have been, very active and stirring). Upon the quarter-deck he fell in discourse of his escape from

Worcester. It made me ready to weep to hear the stories that he told of his difficulties that he had passed through. As his travelling four days and three nights on foot, every step up to his knees in dirt, with nothing but a green coat and a pair of country breeches on and a pair of country shoes, that made him so sore all over his feet that he could scarce stir.

May 25

By the morning we were come close to the land and everybody made ready to get on shore. The King and the two Dukes did eat their breakfast before they went, and there being set some ships diet before them, only to show them the manner of the ships diet, they eat of nothing else but pease and pork and boiled beef. I spoke with the Duke of York about business, who called me Pepys by name, and upon my desire did promise me his future favour. I went, and Mr Mansell and one of the King's footmen, with a dog that the King loved (which shit in the boat, which made us laugh and me think that a king and all that belong to him are but just as others are) went in boats by ourselves.

The casualness of the short voyage from Holland evaporated as their boats came alongside at Dover. The people who had once chased the King and his followers from England, now lined the coast to wave him ashore.

C❖Immense crowds awaited him at Dover. There on May 25, 1660, General Monk received him with profound reverence. . . . Charles must have wondered whether he slept or waked when on Blackheath he saw the dark, glistening columns of the Ironside Army drawn up in stately array and dutiful obedience. It was but eight years since he had hidden from its patrols in the branches of the Boscobel oak. It was but a few months since they had driven his adherents into rout at Winnington Bridge. The entry to the City was a blaze of thanksgiving. The Lord Mayor and Councillors of rebel London led the festival. The Presbyterian divines obstructed his passage only to have the honour of presenting the Bible amid their fervent salutations. Both Houses of Parliament acknowledged their devotion to his rights and person. And all around, the masses, rich and poor, Cavalier and Roundhead, Episcopalian, Presbyterian, and Independent, framed a scene of reconciliation and rejoicing without compare in history. . . .

   The wheel had not, however, swung a full circle, as many might have thought. This was not only the restoration of the monarchy; it was the restoration of Parliament. Indeed, it was the greatest hour in Parliamentary history. The House of Commons had broken the Crown in the field; it had at length mastered the terrible Army it had created for that purpose. It had purged itself of its own excesses, and now stood forth beyond all challenge,

or even need of argument, as the dominant institution of the realm . . .
Above all, everyone now took it for granted that the Crown was the
instrument of Parliament and the King the servant of his people.

At this stage it would be wrong to believe that Parliament had a revolutionary
role in government. In many ways, Parliament had no more effective powers
than it had under the previous three monarchs. Power was certainly shifting
from the centre which meant that the shires had more authority. But that didn't
necessarily bring about a universal improvement of the people's lot. Parliament
still suffered the weaknesses of the Republican legislators and the open
disagreement between Lords and Commons hardly helped. And it was still the
King, and no one else, who summoned Parliament.

But what is clear in 1660, with the start of the Restoration, that is the
restoration of the monarchy, is that the first signs of a democratic system of
government were emerging and before the century was done, the first political
parties appeared. Monarchy was supposed to be supreme, but it has been argued
that when the monarchy returned, it did so with few powers. And the conflict
of the past decade had begun because Parliament believed that the King had too
many powers – or at least claimed them – and that the King saw himself above
the rule of Parliament. Churchill argues that the change in the relationship
between King and Parliament, on Charles II's return, was total.

C❖If the doctrine of Divine Right was again proclaimed, that of Absolute
Power had been abandoned. The criminal jurisdiction of the Privy
Council, the Star Chamber, and the High Commission Court were gone.
The idea of the Crown levying taxes without the consent of Parliament or
by ingenious and questionable devices had vanished. All legislation hence–
forward stood upon the majority of legally elected Parliaments, and no royal
ordinance could resist or replace it. The Restoration achieved what Pym
and Hampden had originally sought, and rejected the excesses into which
they were drawn by the stress of conflict and the crimes and follies of war
and dictatorship.

It is said that Charles II's Restoration was conditional. But his reign did not start
in 1660. It was declared that it started at the exact moment of his father's
beheading, in 1649. And so all the Parliamentary acts that Charles I had agreed
were now legal under Charles II. Everything else was illegal and therefore
dropped. Take, for example, the Cromwellian practice of selling off the Church
and Royal estates: they were all restored. And Parliament didn't have any
greater role in the governing of the land than it had had before the rebellion.

However the power of the King and his advisers was contained, even
reduced, by increasing regional and local responsibilities. More people would

take part in the governing of the realm – it was the beginning of what is now called power sharing. But in the early days of the Restoration, one fundamental difficulty remained: money and how to get it. And the first person to want money was, as ever, the King himself. This wasn't simply the usual demands of the monarch, he wanted Parliament to pay his debts. And since the agreement was that he'd been King since his father had died, Parliament must pay, and pay a great deal, because the debts included those of his father, King Charles I, which he, as monarch, was obliged to clear. The bill was dropped onto the dispatch box within four months of the King's return. And the sums mentioned are not converted into twentieth-century pounds sterling. This is the actual cost, nearly 340 years ago.

❖The Committee for public debts, 3 September 1660.

It be reported to the House as the opinion of this committee, that the debts hereafter mentioned are such as Parliament is bound to honour to take care of, which now stand charged as underwritten:

There is charged upon his Majesty's Exchequer and was charged thereupon by his late Majesty during the late troubles, the sum of £65,000.

Tallies struck for the same, for money lent to his late Majesty by divers of the nobility and gentry, £50,000.

There was charged by the Lords and Commons, on 22 April 1646, for the yearly support of the Queen of Bohemia, his Majesty's aunt, £50,000.

For wares and commodities about the years 1641 and 1642, £60,000.

There is due to the old farmers of the customs, for which they had tallies struck, £253,000.

Due to the Princess Royal for her portion, for which his present Majesty is engaged, £40,000.

Due to his Majesty to the late Tin Farmers, certified as aforesaid, £11,600.

The total being, £529,600.

The aforementioned debts were all charged by his late Majesty, and for which his present Majesty is engaged in honour to see satisfied, and are humbly offered to the Parliament by this committee as debts which in honour they are bound to take care of.

Memorandum. No part of the debts of his present Majesty, either in England or elsewhere, are brought into this account.

The present King's debts were yet to come. Charles and his secretary, Edward Hyde, recognized that they would have to come to a compromise over the amount Parliament could afford to pay their King.

C❖Finance at the Restoration was, as ever, an immediate and thorny subject.

Large sums were needed, apart from the ordinary charges of paying off the Army and the debts contracted by the King in exile. The debts of the Protectorate were heartily repudiated. The King relinquished his feudal dues from wardships, knight service and other mediaeval survivals. Parliament granted him instead revenues for life which, with his hereditary property, were calculated to yield about £1,200,000 . . . in fact the figure proved optimistic, but he and his advisers professed themselves content. The country was impoverished by the ordeal through which it had passed; the process of tax-collecting was grievously deranged; a settlement for life was not to be disdained. For all extra-ordinary expenditure the King was dependent upon Parliament . . . The Crown was not to be free of Parliament [but both] were to be free of the Army. That force, which had grown to 40,000 men, unequalled in fighting quality in the world, was to be dispersed . . .

But not all debts were settled in gold. Although many escaped what the Cavaliers thought should have been the most terrible punishment for their part in the war against the monarchy, others most certainly did not. Pepys, who had, as a teenage lad, seen Charles I beheaded, was witness to the death of one of those who had signed Charles's death warrant.

> October 13
> I went out to Charing Cross, to see Major General Harrison hanged, drawn, and quartered – which was done there – he looked as cheerful as any man could do in that condition. He was presently cut down and his head and his heart shown to the people, at which there [were] great shouts of joy. It is said that he said that he was sure to come shortly at the right hand of Christ to judge them that now have judged him, and that his wife doth expect his coming again. Thus it was my chance to see the King beheaded at Whitehall and to see the first blood shed in revenge for the blood of the King at Charing Cross

One wonders at Pepys's inner feelings that day in Charing Cross. After all this diarist who, but six months earlier, had kissed the monarch's hand, had been at the execution of Charles I because he, Pepys, had then been a Roundhead. Times and loyalties had changed.

C❖Of about sixty men who had signed the late King's death warrant, a third were dead, a third had fled, and a bare twenty remained. King Charles strove against his loyal Parliament to save as many as possible. Feeling ran high. The King fought for clemency for his father's murderers, and Parliament, many of whose members had abetted their action, clamoured for retribution. In the end, nine suffered the extreme penalty of treason. They were the scapegoats of the collective crime. Nearly all of them glorified in their deed. Harrison and other officers stepped upon the scaffold with the conviction that posterity would salute their sacrifice. Hugh Peters, the fiery preacher, alone showed weakness, but the example of his comrades and a strong cordial sustained him, and when the executioner, knife in hand, covered with blood, met him in the shambles [meat markets or slaughter houses] with 'How does that suit you, Dr Peters?' he answered steadfastly that it suited him well enough.

The numbers of those executed fell so far short of the public demand that an addition was made to the bloody scene which at any rate cost no more life. The corpses of Cromwell, Ireton, and Bradshaw were pulled out of their coffins in Westminster Abbey, where they had been buried a few years earlier in solemn state, drawn through the streets on hurdles to Tyburn, hanged upon the three-cornered gibbet for twenty-four hours, their heads spiked up in prominent places, and the remains cast upon the dunghill. Pym and twenty other Parliamentarians were also disinterred and buried in a pit. . . .

Only two other persons in England were condemned to death, General Lambert and Sir Harry Vane. Lambert had a wild career behind him, and in the last year of the Republic might at any moment have laid his hands upon supreme power. . . . Now, the Ironside general, hero of a dozen fields, humbled himself before his judges. He sought mercy from the King. He found in the King's brother, the Duke of York, a powerful advocate. He was pardoned, and lived the rest of his life in Guernsey . . . and later in Plymouth, consoling himself with painting and botany.

Vane was of tougher quality. He scorned to sue for mercy, and so spirited was his defence, so searching his law and logic, that he might well have been indulged. But there was one incident in his past which now proved fatal to him. It was remembered that twenty years before he had purloined and disclosed to Pym his father's notes of the Privy Council meeting alleging that Strafford had advised the bringing of an Irish army into England, thus sealing Strafford's fate. . . . Charles showed no desire to spare him.

The blood-letting done, Charles and his Parliament got on with the governing of the realm. And it was Charles's Parliament: he, after all, could say when it should and should not be called. The Triennial Act meant little and, in truth, Parliament meant not much more. There was no great bureaucratic reformer as Thomas Cromwell had been in Henry VIII's time. But Charles felt safe with his Parliament of Cavaliers. He judged that they would be as loyal as any other group and so for eighteen years they governed together, although, it must be said, not very well and sometimes with little clear idea of who was in charge.

It was a period when the King was not inclined to champion causes, to take on political commitments, to depart from an instinct of compromise (all this so typical of people who have been in exile for long periods).

Certainly the King appears to have been someone who didn't want anything to happen; anything, that is, that would disturb what he considered to be a very agreeable lifestyle. Charles II was, by all accounts, charming, considerably lazy and passionate. A man of pastimes, he was known as the Merry Monarch. He was tall, dark, handsome and athletic. He was also, in the romantic sense, a rogue. He took many mistresses (Nell Gwyn was only one of them), and fathered at least fourteen bastards.

C❖Court life was one unceasing flagrant and brazen scandal. His two principal mistresses, Barbara Villiers, created Countess of Castlemaine, and Louise de Kérouaille – ('Madame Carwell', as the English called her) – created Duchess of Portsmouth, beguiled his leisure and amused themselves with foreign affairs. His marriage with Catherine of Braganza . . . in no way interrupted these dissipations. His treatment of his wife was cruel to an extreme degree; he forced her to accept Barbara as her Lady-in-Waiting. . . . It was with relief that the public learned that the King had taken a mistress from the people, the transcendently beautiful and good-natured Nell Gwyn, who was lustily cheered in the streets as 'the Protestant whore'. . . . The Commonwealth had punished adultery by death; Charles scourged chastity and faithfulness with ridicule. . . . The people . . . descended with thankfulness from the superhuman levels to which they had been painfully hoisted. The heroic age of the constitutional conflict and of the Civil Wars and the grim manifestation of the Puritan Empire were no more.

Perhaps this explanation puts into context some of the more saucy extracts of seventeenth-century life that have been left us by the Restoration writers and, of course, by the diaries of the time written by Samuel Pepys.

July 23

Being in an idle and wanton humour, walked through Fleet Alley, and there stood a most pretty wench at one of the doors. So I took a turn or two; but what by sense of honour and conscience, I would not go in. But much against my will, took coach and away to Westminster Hall, and there light of Mrs Lane and plotted with her to go over the water; so met at White Stairs in Channel Row, and over to the old house at Lambeth Marsh and there eat and drank and had my pleasure of her twice – she being the strangest woman in talk, of love to her husband sometimes, and sometimes again she doth not care for him – and yet willing enough to allow me a liberty of doing what I would with her. So spending five or six shillings upon her, I could do what I would; and after an hour's stay and more, back again and set her ashore there again, and I forward to Fleetstreet [sic] and called at Fleet Alley, not knowing how to command myself; and went in and there saw what formerly I have been acquainted with, the wickedness of those houses and the forcing a man to present expense. The woman indeed is a most lovely woman; but I had not courage to meddle with her, for fear of her not being wholesome, and so counterfeited that I had not money enough.

Presumably Pepys was certain that Mrs Lane, with whom he had often dallied, was wholesome. And Pepys suspected his wife was dallying with her dancing master; this was, after all, the Restoration. It is not surprising perhaps that in this 'merry' climate, Charles II's chief minister was, by contrast, a very serious man. Edward Hyde, created Earl of Clarendon by Charles, was austere. He had been a member of the Short Parliament, served the King's father during the start of the Civil War (although he was never quite trusted) and then he worked diligently as Charles II's adviser in exile. Clarendon's daughter, Anne, married the King's brother, the Duke of York, who was to become James II. Hyde (Clarendon) was, therefore, a figure of considerable power and, hardly surprisingly, often openly disliked.

Charles II at first ruled through his Privy Council. This Council, or inner government of the King, made policy at one private meeting, and unmade it at another. However it was soon made less effectual when all important matters were first discussed through Privy Council committees, the most powerful of which was probably the origin of Cabinet government. From 1668, five men assumed the most important portfolio. They were: Clifford, Arlington, Buckingham, Ashley and Lauderdale, known as the Cabal. Parliament itself was ill-tempered, with the Lords and Commons at odds and with much time spent talking about what to talk about. Yet this was the longest of Parliaments. It lasted eighteen years, from 1661 to 1679, and was known as the Cavalier Parliament.

C❖From the moment when it first met, it showed itself more Royalist in theory than in practice. It rendered all honour to the King. It had no intention of being governed by him. . . . Thus from the Restoration there emerged no national settlement, but rather two Englands, each with its different background, interests, culture and outlook. . . . As Macaulay wrote. . . , 'There was a great line which separated the official men and their friends and dependants, who were sometimes called the Court party, from those who were sometimes honoured with the appellation of the Country party.'

The Cabal was swayed by two forceful personalities, Clarendon who was powerful but not a member, and Ashley, later the Earl of Shaftesbury, who was.

C❖Shaftesbury had plunged into the revolution in the Short Parliament when he was but eighteen. . . . He had fought on the Roundhead side. . . . As a leader of the Presbyterians he had influenced and aided Monk in bringing about the Restoration. . . . Shaftesbury was the most powerful representative of the vanished domination . . .

For the first seven years of the reign, Clarendon continued [as] First Minister. This wise, venerable statesman wrestled stoutly with the licentiousness of the King and Court, with the intrigues of the royal mistresses, with the inadequacy of the revenue, and with the intolerance of the House of Commons. He was also confronted with the intrigues of Henry Bennett, Charles's favourite, who was made Secretary of State and Earl of Arlington. An important and sometimes sinister part in the politics of the reign was played by this flamboyant figure.

But Clarendon, for all his authority (he was now father-in-law to the future King), could not survive. For all of what Churchill insists was his statesmanship, he was not a match for the intrigues of the King's mistresses, nor for Shaftesbury, and particularly not for Arlington (although he would fall). He never understood the complexities and the importance of managing Parliament, and the need to build a political base among the old guard of Parliamentarians and Royalists. He'd been blamed when the Thames froze over during the winter following the Great Fire of London. And so when the Dutch sailed up the Medway to draw to an end the disastrously managed war with them in 1667, it may not have been Clarendon's fault, but he took the blame.

C❖. . . recriminations began. The Court asked how the country could be defended when Parliament kept the King so short of money. Parliament retorted that he had spent too much on his mistresses and luxuries. Clarendon . . . was assailed by all. He had fallen out with Parliament, rebuked the mistresses, and, worst of all, bored the King. An impeachment was launched against him, and he went into exile. . . . After Clarendon's fall, the King was for a while guided chiefly by Arlington, and in his lighter moods by his boon companion Buckingham, son of James I's murdered favourite, a gay, witty, dissolute nobleman, whose sword was stained with the blood of an injured husband whom he had slain in a duel.

What could not be slain was the dragon of suspicion that Catholicism was attempting to gain hold of the King and country. It wasn't just continuing paranoia. Charles clearly believed that if a gentleman wanted to be religious, then Rome was a more satisfying persuasion than most. And his wife, Catherine of Braganza, was a Portuguese Princess and a Catholic. His brother James, the

Duke of York, was a convert to Catholicism, and because Catherine had not given birth, James was next in line for the throne.

But there was also a Treaty negotiated in secret with Louis XIV of France. It was called the Treaty of Dover. It provided England with much-needed cash, and Louis with a promise that England would help him in a third war against the Dutch. Within that Treaty there was a secret clause which was not published at the time. That clause was the most damning. It said: 'The King of Great Britain, being convinced of the truth of the Catholic faith, is determined to declare himself a Catholic as soon as the welfare of his realm will permit.'

C❖Whispers ran afoot through London that the King and his Ministers had been bribed by France to betray the freedom and the faith of the Island. . . . The growing antagonism of the Commons to France, the fear of the returning tides of Popery, . . . the conversion of the Duke of York to Rome, all stirred a deep and dangerous agitation throughout the country, in which the dominant Anglican forces were in full accord with Presbyterian and Puritan feeling . . . pamphlets circulated; by-elections were scenes of uproar. A Bill was forced upon the King for a Test. No man could hold office or a King's commission, afloat or ashore, who would not solemnly declare his disbelief in the doctrine of Transubstantiation.

A declaration of disbelief was, obviously, a total denial of Rome. This 1673 Test Act went a great way towards destroying the Cabal of senior ministers. But what about the Duke of York? His wife Anne, the daughter of the Earl of Clarendon, and a Protestant, was dead, and the Duke, a Catholic convert, had married a Catholic.

C❖His marriage, after the death of his first wife, Anne Hyde, to the Catholic princess Mary of Modena had rendered him suspect. . . . Very soon it was known that the heir to the throne had laid down his post of Lord High Admiral rather than submit to the Test. This event staggered the nation. The Queen was unlikely to give Charles an heir. The Crown would therefore pass to a papist King, who showed that for conscience' sake he would not hesitate to sacrifice every material advantage. The strength of the forces now moving against the King and his policy rose from the virtual unanimity which prevailed between the Anglicans and Dissenters. . . . They were all on the same side now, and at their head was the second great Parliamentary tactician of the century, Shaftesbury.

It is important to remember that religious conflict wasn't simply something which started with the Puritans and the Royalists. Who was and who wasn't a

Catholic, for example, had tormented political reformers for at least five monarchs and one dictator.

In the late 1670s there had been allegations of a papist plot to kill the King. Charles's Catholic wife was vulnerable to the charge that she was involved against him, but she was not. The plotters planned to replace Charles with his Catholic brother, James, Duke of York.

C♣A renegade priest of disreputable character, Dr Titus Oates, presented himself as the Protestant champion. He had acquired letters written by Catholics in England to their co-religionists in St Omer and other French Catholic centres. From these materials, he accused the Duchess of York's private secretary, Coleman, of a conspiracy to murder the King, bring about a French invasion, and cause a general massacre of Protestants. Many responsible men in both Houses of Parliament believed Oates's accusations, or pretended that they did. An order was issued for Coleman's arrest. It is certain that he had no intent against Charles, but he was a centre of Catholic activity and correspondence. He succeeded in burning the bulk of his papers; but those that were seized contained indiscreet references to the restoration of the Old Faith, and to the Catholic disappointment at Charles's attitude, which in the rage of the hour gave colour to Oates's accusations. Coleman was examined in October 1678 before a magistrate, Sir Edmund Berry Godfrey, and while the case was proceeding, Godfrey was found dead one night at the foot of Greenberry Hill.

But the plot, even if it came to nothing, or wasn't even true, was important for the emotions it rallied. Behind the affair lay the continuing fear of Roman Catholicism, which extended beyond religious matters to continuing suspicions that the Catholic French would attempt to unseat the monarch. On top of this was the failure of Charles's Court to produce a great statesman, a wise administrator.

And because of this lack, the pervading fear of Catholicism and the argument about whether the monarch should or should not be a Catholic, there was an attempt to control the rights of the monarch, and a confrontation between two political opponents.

On one side was the first Earl of Danby who had been the King's minister and who used his influence (and bribes) to build the Court party. On the other was Shaftesbury, a sometime Cromwellian, and also, separately, Lord Chancellor to Charles. Shaftesbury believed there should be a free Parliament, free that is, from the Crown. He was against standing armies, which he rightly feared could take over the country. He also wanted religious tolerance without which, he said, there could be little chance of political stability.

In 1679 Shaftesbury led the fight to get Parliament to pass an Act of

Exclusion, an Act which would exclude James from succeeding Charles.

Between 1679 and 1681 Shaftesbury and his Country supporters organized petitions and fought three elections. The campaign was intense and the Parliamentary grouping was well organized. And this organization changed the nature of politics completely. Shaftesbury had, in effect, started the first political party in English history: the Whigs. And the gentry, the opposition to the Whigs, became known as the Tories.

C❖If petitions for the exclusion of the Duke of York were signed by many thousands in the cities and the towns, so also abhorrence of these demands upon the Crown was widespread in the country. But no parties could live under such labels as Petitioners and Abhorrers. Instead of naming themselves, they named each other. The term 'Whig' had described a sour, bigoted, canting, money-grubbing Scots Presbyterian.

Whiggamores were the Scots who'd marched on Edinburgh just a few years earlier. One hundred years later Samuel Johnson remarked that he'd always thought the first Whig was the devil.

C❖Irish papist bandits ravaging estates and manor houses had been called Tories [Irish: *Toraidhe*]. Neither side was lacking in power of abuse. [It was said that], 'A Tory is a monster with an English face, a French heart, and an Irish conscience. A creature of a large forehead, prodigious mouth, supple hams, and no brains. They are a sort of wild boars, that would root out the Constitution, . . . that with dark lanthorn policies would at once blow up the bulwarks of our freedom, Parliaments and juries; making the first only a Parliament of Paris, and the latter but mere tools to echo back the pleasure of the judge.' The Whig, on the other hand, 'talks of nothing but new light and prophecy, spiritual incomes, indwellings, emanations, manifestations, sealings. . . . He prays for the King, but with more distinctions and mental reservations than an honest man would in taking the Covenant.'

Churchill is quoting from David Ogg's *England in the Reign of Charles II*.

For the first time, Parliament was divided into political parties. The Whigs and the Tories had arrived. Shaftesbury's Whigs were formed to get the Exclusion Bill through the House. But the Whigs lost their first battle partly because some Members took up violent tactics, and partly because of their inability to agree on who should rule if not James. Some wanted James's daughter Mary, who was, in spite of her father's conversion, a Protestant; others wanted Charles's bastard son, Monmouth.

And thirdly, and this was still the most important power of the King, Parliament could be dissolved and summoned more or less at the King's pleasure. This, and Charles's in-built majority in the Lords, meant that the Exclusion Bill was never likely to get through.

But the most important personal mistake made by Shaftesbury and his Whigs was their inability to understand that Charles would never give in on what he thought was a point of principle: the principle that he ruled by Divine Right. And in this the country supported the King and not Shaftesbury. But the King's senior advisor had fallen. For the man Charles had come to rely upon, Danby, was a schemer who relied on bribery and patronage, rather than an innate sense of chancellorship.

C❖Sir Thomas Osborne [Danby], a Yorkshire landowner, had gathered great influence in the Commons, and was to a large extent forced upon the King for his own salvation. His policy was the union into one strong party with a popular programme of all those elements which had stood by the monarchy in the Civil War and were now deeply angered with the Court. Economy, Anglicanism, and independence from France were the principal ideals of this party. Osborne . . . was very soon raised to the peerage as Earl of Danby and began an administration which was based on a party organization possessing a small but effective majority in the House of Commons.

In foreign affairs, the new minister publicly differed from his master. He opposed French ascendancy and interference, and gained general support thereby; but he was forced to become privy to the King's secret intrigues with Louis XIV, and, holding strongly to the Cavalier idea that the King should have considerable personal power, he was lured into asking the French monarch for money on Charles's behalf. The height of his precarious popularity was reached when he contrived a marriage between Mary, the Duke of York's daughter by his first wife, and the now famous Protestant hero, William of Orange.

Danby was probably quite corrupt; he was often found out but he was also a survivor. He eventually became chief minister to King William of Orange. But as Charles II's minister Danby was about to take his first tumble.

C❖Montagu, a former ambassador to France, in collusion with the Whig and Puritan leaders, had exposed letters written by Danby in which there was mention of six million livres as the price of English assent to the proposed Treaty of Nimwegen between the French and the Dutch, and also the King's desire to be independent of Parliamentary grants. . . . Charles, wishing to stay the capital proceedings instituted against his minister, partly unjustly, and anyhow for actions which Danby had taken only to please the King, at length, in December 1678, dissolved the Cavalier Parliament. . . .

He hoped that a new set of Members would be less rigid. . . . He supposed that the country was more friendly to him than the London hive in which Shaftesbury was now supreme. But this was an illusion. . . . The trusty followers of the Court, who hitherto had mustered 150, now returned barely thirty.

So Danby had to be sacrificed and he was sent to the Tower. Nearly a decade of high drama, but what of the rest of the King's country?

While all this was going on, many ordinary people's lives were sacrificed to the plague. In one week in 1665, more than 7000 people died in London. Most of those people, including their physicians, died of bubonic plague. Twelve months later, to the very week, almost 14,000 houses burned to the ground. The Great Plague and the Great Fire have often been linked. It is said that the fire destroyed the plague – or its source – and so saved further misery. It is a convenient hypothesis, but it's one that doesn't stand up.

Of course London knew all about plagues. It had suffered them for more than three centuries since the Black Death had killed perhaps one-third of the population of England. The plague had simply never gone away. During the Civil War of the 1640s, nearly one-third of the people of Chester died. It was said that the carriers were not rats but soldiers, whose dirty coats and linen were infested with the plague flea.

But London, in 1665, had all but forgotten the disease by the time it returned. A letter from Samuel Pepys to the wife of the Treasurer of the Navy has survived.

❖Woolwich, September 4, 1665

The absence of the court and emptiness of the city takes away all occasion of news, save only such melancholy stories as would rather sadden than find your ladyship any divertissement in the hearing. I have stayed in the city till above 7400 died in one week, and of them, above 6000 of the Plague, and little noise heard day or night but tolling of bells; till I could walk Lombard Street and not meet twenty persons from one end to the other, and not fifty on the Exchange, till whole families, ten and twelve together, have been swept away; till my very physician, Dr Burnett, who undertook to secure me from infection, having survived the month of his own house being shut up, died himself of the Plague; till the nights, though much lengthened, are grown too short to conceal the burials of those that died the day before, people thereby constrained to borrow daylight for that service; lastly, till I could find neither meat nor drink safe, the butcheries being everywhere visited, my brewer's house shut up, and my baker, with his whole family, dead of the Plague.

Pepys wasn't the only diarist of the period. One of the founders of the Royal Society, which had been set up in 1662, was John Evelyn. Evelyn kept a diary for sixty years, and so left records ten times the length of Pepys's.

Evelyn was in London on 3 September, the night the fire started.

September 3
The Fire continuing, after dinner I took coach with my wife and son, and went to the bank side in Southwark, where we beheld that dismal spectacle, the whole city in dreadful flames near the water side; all the houses from the bridge, all Thames Street and upwards towards Cheapside, down to the Three Cranes, were now consumed; and so returned exceeding astonished what would become of the rest.

The conflagration was so universal, and the people so astonished, that from the beginning, I know not by what despondency or fate, they hardly stirred to quench it, so that there was nothing heard or seen but crying out and lamentation, running about like distracted creatures without at all attempting to save even their goods, such a strange consternation there was upon them; so as it burned both in breadth and length the churches, public halls, Exchange, hospitals, monuments and ornaments, leaping after a prodigious manner from house to house and street to street, at great distances from one from the other, for the heat with a long set of fair and warm weather had even ignited the air, and prepared the materials to conceive the fire, which devoured after an incredible manner, houses, furniture and everything. All the sky was of a fiery aspect, like the top of a burning oven, and the light seen above forty miles round about for many nights. God grant mine eyes may never behold the like, who now saw above 10,000 houses all in one flame.

In less than five days the City of London, between the Tower and the Temple, was destroyed. And the bubonic plague died out. But it is unlikely that the fire destroyed the plague because, by 1665, the epidemic was almost played out. The breeding ground was the slum area beyond the city walls and this wasn't much touched by the fire, therefore wasn't rebuilt. Undoubtedly the change in building style that followed the fire (from wood to brick and from straw floors to carpets) helped, although there's no evidence of any radical change in hygiene. It seems very likely that it was a simple quirk of nature. The plague, which had originated in the Far East, was carried by flea-ridden black rats. When the fleas jumped, so did the plague. At about this time the black rat began to be overcome, not by man but by brown rats. And the brown rat seems to have been less likely to have carried the fleas. Simple as that.

What the fire most certainly did, apart from destroying eighty-eight churches and St Paul's, was to give Londoners the chance to change the shape of their city. It was a maze of crooked streets and alleys with more twists and turns than the mind of the most devious courtier. But, despite the fact that this was the age of Christopher Wren, the city remained unchanged. Wren planned a new City of London but London didn't want to be replanned. So Wren and centuries of his admirers had to be satisfied with a commission to build fifty-one churches and, of course, the great cathedral of St Paul's.

Wren didn't start his professional life as an architect. He was born in the year the painter Van Dyck came to live in England, 1632. He first studied mathematics, which led to astronomy, and by the time he was twenty-eight he was Professor of Astronomy at Oxford. The inscription over the north door at St Paul's is said to have been written by his son. *Si monumentum requiris, circumspice*: If you would see his monument, look around.

And as the great cubes of Portland stone began to be shipped from the Dorset quarries for Wren's buildings, so there was an even more urgent sort of construction taking place: ship building. While London had struggled with the plague and then with the fire, Charles II and his ministers had sent England to war. As London buried its dead, the admirals and sea generals fought the Dutch.

C❖The rivalry of England and Holland upon the seas in fishery and in trade had become intense, and the strength of the Dutch had revived since Cromwell's war. The commerce of the East Indies flowed to Amsterdam, that of the West Indies to Flushing; that of England and Scotland passed to the Continent through Dort and Rotterdam. . . . The Dutch East India Company gathered the wealth of the Orient. . . . great Dutch fleets, heavily laden, doubled the Cape of Good Hope several times a year. On the West African coast, the Dutch also prospered, and their colonies and trading stations grew continually. They had a settlement on the Hudson, thrust among the colonies of New England. It was too much. Parliament was moved by the merchants; the King was roused to patriotic ardour, the Duke of York thirsted for naval glory. The great sum of over £2,500,000 was voted. War at sea began off the West African coast in 1664, and spread to home waters in the following year.

In June, the English fleet of more than 150 ships, manned by 25,000 men and mounting 5000 guns, met the Dutch in equal strength off Lowestoft, and a long fierce battle was fought, in which many of the leaders on both sides perished. . . . [But] the English artillery was markedly superior in weight and skill, and the Dutch withdrew worsted though undismayed. . . .

. . . An even greater battle was fought in June 1666. . . . For four days the English and Dutch fleets battled off the North Foreland. . . . The sound of the guns was heard in London . . .

This time the Dutch were the victors but within two months the English fleet was refitted, put to sea and triumphed. But the war was not at an end. The French joined in, and it became clear that the once-superior English navy could not protect the islands. It was time to sue for peace.

C❖Want of money prevented the English battle fleet from keeping the sea and, while the negotiations lingered, the Dutch, to spur them, sailed up the Medway under Admiral De Ruyter, victor at the battle of North Foreland in the previous year, broke the boom which guarded Chatham harbour, burnt four ships of the line, and towed away the battleship *Royal Charles*.

There is an irony in this: the *Royal Charles* was the very ship sent to Holland to bring Charles II back from exile in 1660. It was then called the *Naseby* after the famous Roundhead victory.

C❖The sound of enemy cannon, this time loud and near, rolled up the Thames. In the general indignation and alarm, even Cavaliers remarked that nothing like this had happened under Cromwell. Among the Puritans, the plague, the fire, and the disaster at sea were regarded as direct visitations by which the Almighty chastised the immorality of the age, and especially of the Court.

But peace came and with it a new city: one laid out by the Dutch who ceded to Charles one of their New World territories. It was called New Amsterdam and Charles renamed it after his brother, the Duke of York.

CHAPTER TWENTY-SIX

1682–1684

❖

The Restoration period is for many summed up in the often saucy scenes from Restoration Comedy. The men powdered and beauty-spotted, the women flighty and full-bosomed. And if, as seems likely, Restoration Comedy reflected Merry Monarch life, how are two of the most important works of the time, *Paradise Lost* and *Pilgrim's Progress*, explained?

In the early years of the century, writers saw Godliness as a text. Political writers referred to God's involvement in everyday life. But by the closing years of the century, the Church of England was no longer able to make people members by the force of law. The Church of England came to be regarded as spiritually impotent and literature, especially the literature of political thought, reflected this.

During the seventeenth century thinkers, intellectuals, became preoccupied with the question of the boundaries of Church and the State. John Milton saw God leading his people through the conflicts of the 1650s and then abandoning them in the 1660s – the Restoration. In 1658, the year Cromwell died, Milton started to write *Paradise Lost* in which the common man is allowed to fall to evil. By the time he wrote *Samson Agonistes*, he was preoccupied with man's failure to use his God-given gifts. The Republicans were Samsons, distracted and failing to do God's good works. And when Bunyan's *Pilgrim's Progress* – the search for salvation – appeared in 1678, there was an emerging belief in a God whose text was less mysterious. Preachers searched the congregations more for goodliness, for kindliness and for tolerance and less for transformation.

But when Charles returned to England, he wanted to settle the religious question. He wanted to restore the Church of England. Charles had no theological conviction, simply a sense of history, and in order to achieve religious tolerance he offered to make some of the moderate Puritans bishops. In October 1660, his Worcester House Declaration was a stopgap arrangement which weakened the power of the bishops and made some of the Book of Common Prayer optional – a sort of early Alternative Service Book. For eighteen months Charles tried to convince the Anglican majority in the Cavalier Parliament. But Charles's religious reformation appeared doomed.

The King's hope now rested with his closest adviser, Edward Hyde, the Earl of Clarendon.

C❖Since Clarendon as Lord Chancellor was chief Minister . . . his name is identified with the group of Acts [the Clarendon Code] which re-established the Anglican Church and drove the Protestant sects into enduring opposition. Charles would have preferred to take the way of toleration, Clarendon that of comprehension. But the zeal of the Cavalier Parliament . . . and of some recalcitrant Presbyterian leaders, baffled them both. Parliament recognized that there were religious bodies definitely outside the National Church, and determined, if not to extirpate them, at least to leave them outside under grievous disabilities. In so doing, it consolidated Nonconformity as a political force . . .

. . . the Clarendon Code was a parting of the ways. It destroyed all chance of a United National Church. . . . The Cavalier Parliament accepted the schism, and rejoiced in belonging to the larger, richer, and more favoured section. . . . The Clarendon Code of 1662 . . . consisted of a series of statutes: the Corporation Act . . . was to confine municipal office, closely connected with the election of Members of Parliament, to Royalist Anglicans. The Act of Uniformity . . . imposed upon the clergy the Prayer Book of Queen Elizabeth, with some excisions . . . and additions. . . . One-fifth of the clergy, nearly 2000 ministers, refusing to comply, were deprived of their livings. The Conventicle Act sought to prevent the ejected clergy from preaching to audiences of their own, and the Five-Mile Act of 1665 'forbade them to go within five miles of any City or Town Corporate, or Borough or any parish or place where they had preached or held a living'.

The Prayer Book Act left nothing to chance. Its draughtsmanship was a model of uncompromising recognition of an established Church which left no room for dissenters to remain within the Anglican communion. There could be no excuse allowed. Furthermore, the Act ordered the parishioners themselves to be responsible for making sure that the Prayer Book was available, and paid for, in every church – including the church in Wales. And here, champions of the Welsh language must surely grind their teeth at the way in which the Prayer Book was to be used to promote English as the tongue of the Welsh people.

Article Twenty-Two
A true printed copy of the said book entituled [sic] the Book of Common Prayer, shall at the cost and charges of the parishioners of every parish church and chapelry, cathedral church, college and hall, be attained and gotten before the Feast Day of Saint Bartholomew in the year of our Lord,

1662, upon pain of forfeiture of £3 by the month for so long time as they shall then after be unproved thereof by every parish or chapelry, cathedral church, college and hall remain default therein.

Article Twenty-Three

The bishops of Hereford, Saint David's, Aspah, Bangor, and Llandaff and their successors shall take such order among themselves for the souls' health of the flocks committed to their charge within Wales that the book hereunto annexed be truly and exactly translated into the British or Welsh tongue, and that the same translated, and being by them or any three of them at the least viewed, perused and allowed, be imprinted to such number at least . . . so that one of the said books so translated and imprinted may be had for every cathedral, collegiate and parish church and chapel of ease in the said respective dioceses and places in Wales where the Welsh is commonly spoken or used . . . and one other Book of Common Prayer in the English tongue shall be bought and had in every church throughout Wales in which the Book of Common Prayer in Welsh is said to be had . . . that such as understand them may resort at all convenient times to read and peruse the same, and also such as do not understand the said language may be conferring both tongues together the sooner to attain to the knowledge of the English tongue.

Behind Charles's hope for religious tolerance was his need to protect himself politically. Whereas the Puritans in his father's time were protected by Parliament, the Non-Conformists now needed protection from Parliament, and the King was the person to do that. Clarendon was not happy with the legislation, even though it was drafted in his name. It upset religious groupings which upset political stability. Furthermore, Charles didn't have a political agenda. Consequently his ambition, perhaps very simply put, was for a quiet life. Also, although not a Catholic, he was inclined to Catholicism. Imagine the political upheaval if he'd converted to Rome during his reign, instead of during his final hours. It was this combination of a King without vision, yet with a belief in his Divine Right to rule, that produced an outward appearance of tolerance. It was a curious combination in a century full of anything but tolerant political systems, institutions and professions.

In the mid-seventeenth century a triad of professions, the priests, the physicians and the lawyers, kept their knowledge firmly under lock and key. The Latin of their text books helped maintain the mystery. But Nicholas Culpeper, who remarked, 'The liberty of our Commonwealth is most impaired by three sorts of men, priests, physicians, lawyers,' was determined to change things. Culpeper was a radical and a Republican and his translation of one of the medical mysteries, the *Pharmacopoeia Londinensis*, was made in protest against the withholding of knowledge. In a random set of his thoughts, his reasoning becomes clear.

❖ The Papists and the College of Physicians will not suffer divinity and physic to be printed in our mother tongue, both on one and the same ground. . . . Time was when he would have been accounted a monster that should have attempted to hide the rules of physic from the vulgar in an unknown tongue. I am resolved not to give over, until I have published, in English, whatsoever shall be necessary to make an understanding, diligent, rational man a knowing physician. . . . My aim is not to make fools of physicians, but to help those that are ingenious, rational and industrious, though they have not the knowledge of tongues that were to be desired. . . . The works of God are common for everyone to view and for everyone to receive benefit by, and it is a sin in man to impropriate what God hath left common. If God hath left the medicine common, who gave man commission to impropriate?

Culpeper and many like-minded men were reflecting a suspicion, even a hostility, that existed in the lower classes of British society. The physicians especially were protected by monarchs and so when, during the Republic, Culpeper feared the return of the monarchy, it is likely that his ideas had much support among those of the same persuasion. And just imagine how easy it was for people, without the tongue of learning, Latin, to believe Culpeper's view that this language was the mark of a conspiracy much deeper and more sinister than even the mark of breeding, which he loathed.

❖ They have imposed such multiplicity of needless rules in the learning of the Latin tongue that unless a man have gotten a very large estate, he is not able to bring up his son to understand Latin; a dozen years expense of time will hardly do it as they have ordered the matter, in which time, by whipping and cruel usage, the brains of many are made so stupid that they are unfit for study, but are fain to pin their faith upon the sleeve of that monster, Tradition. The poor commonality of England is deprived of their birthright by this means.

One consequence of Culpeper's translation of the *Pharmacopoeia Londinensis* was the growth of physicians without professional qualification – something that was illegal before 1640 but encouraged in the atmosphere of Republican revolution. As one critic remarked, by the Restoration, 'Stocking weavers, shoemakers, millers, masons, carpenters, bricklayers, gunsmiths, porters, butlers etc., are admitted to teach and write physic.' And George Fox, the founder of the Quakers, reflected 'whether I should practise physic for the good of mankind, seeing the nature and virtues of things.' Yet Fox had no medical training, simply inspiration. And Fox is a good enough example of the many who were attempting to do for religion what Culpeper had tried to do for medicine. Fox, who when imprisoned for blasphemy, told the judge to 'quake at the word of the Lord' (so giving the Quakers their name) wanted medicine and religion to shake off their mysteries.

The closed shop of the medical profession was controlled by the College of Physicians. In London, the college licensed just fifty physicians. In the countryside some boroughs paid for physicians but others, especially the poorer ones, turned to the apothecaries and white witches. Quacks they may have been, according to the College of Physicians, but cures they did make, with one exception. Surgery remained a mystery that could not be solved by the translation of a Latin text.

And what of the third member of the triad, the lawyers? The common law was rewritten in the seventeenth century. Relative peace meant that people had time to settle disputes, to trade, and to make claims of land and riches plundered in more violent times. And every claimant, every negotiator, needed a new style of contract and therefore a lawyer, and the rewritten common law often favoured commercial interests. Also delays and obfuscation favoured the rich and, of course, the lawyers. And there was no police force, so everything had to be proved by the lawyers and the official informer, the forerunner of the private detective.

The law became such a lucrative profession that a father was quite willing to spend £40 a year to send his son to one of the Inns of Court. As few had £40 a year, 90% of law students were sons of gentlemen and peers.

So, in the closing years of Charles II's reign, there was a clamouring for the reform of the practice of medicine, the law and the Church. Science soon reformed medicine but the law and the Church held their ground against reformation. However the important point here is the rebellion itself.

And what of education? In the seventeenth century the two great universities were, largely, theological colleges and finishing schools for gentlemen. Yet the rebellion came because more people were thinking, writing, being read, followed and not so easily written off as eccentrics. However frightening to some, it is clear that Cromwell's decade made certain that the intellectual radical was here to stay. Furthermore, the gay atmosphere of Restoration England was changing. Even the mood of the King himself was changing. The lazy, sometimes detached Charles became the protector of his great belief, the Divine Right of his dynasty to rule. It was a sober Charles II who emerged from the fear of another Civil War which followed the papist plot and the downfall of Danby. And while the King fought the anti-Catholic rising at home, his brother watched from a distance, in exile.

C❖The Duke retired to the Low Countries, carrying with him on his staff a very young captain in the British Army, John Churchill, his trusted aide-de-camp and man of business. Charles, thus relieved at home, faced the fury of the anti-Popish hurricane. . . . Not for mean motives he endured the horrible ordeal, which his subjects imposed upon him, of signing the death warrants of men he knew were guiltless. But there was a great change in his conduct. He abandoned his easy, indolent detachment from politics. He saw that his life and dynasty were at stake, he set himself, with all his resources and statecraft, to recover the ground that had been lost. The last five years of his reign are the most honourable to his memory.

However nothing would induce the King to betray the succession. He conceived it his sacred duty to pass the crown to a brother whose virtues and whose vices alike rendered him, of all others, the man, as the King knew well, least fitted to wear it. Men voted against James, the Duke of York, becoming King as the Protestant tide again swept the country. Earnest and venerable divines tried to induce James to return to the Church of his fathers and his future subjects, but he remained obdurate. He possessed the zeal of a convert and preferred exile to the surrender of his faith. But his exile was short. In May 1682 James returned to England and the whole nation feared the coming to the throne of a Catholic monarch.

The following year another plot was discovered, real or otherwise, to assassinate the King. The story told was that the King and his brother, the Duke of York, loved horse racing. They planned to go to the races at Newmarket (followers of the turf will of course know that by 1683 Newmarket was well established as a racecourse). The royal party would travel along the Newmarket Road and pass Rye House in Hertfordshire.

Either on their way there or on their way back (it's not quite clear which) the bodyguard would be overpowered and the King done to death. But – and here's another of history's critical buts – there was a fire at Newmarket, and the royal racegoers left earlier than expected for London and arrived safely. The person who lived in Rye House was Hannibal Rumbold, a former Roundhead officer. Immediately suspects among the Whigs were arrested. One of them, Lord Howard, confessed. Another, the Earl of Essex (a title often found in court intrigue), committed suicide. Two other Whig leaders, Lord Russell and a prominent opponent of the monarchy, Algernon Sidney, were put on trial.

C❖Hitherto, the Whigs had exploited the Popish Plot and made common folk believe that the King was about to be butchered by the Roman Catholics. Here was the antidote. Here was a Whig or Puritan plot from the other side to kill the King. All the veneration which Englishmen had for the monarchy, and the high personal popularity of Charles, with his graceful manners and dangerously attractive vices, were reinforced by the dread that his death would make his Papist brother King. From this moment Charles's triumph was complete. . . . Neither William Lord Russell nor Algernon Sidney had sought the King's life; but Russell had been privy to preparations for revolt, and Sidney had been found with an unpublished paper, scholarly in character, justifying resistance to the royal authority. . . . After public trial, both went to the scaffold. Russell refused to attempt the purchase of his life by bowing to the principle of non-resistance. Sidney affirmed with his last breath the fundamental doctrines of what had now become the Whig Party. Intense discussion was held by Church and State with both these indomitable men. Nothing was yielded by them. . . . These executions were of lasting significance. Martyrs for religion there had been in plenty. . . . Great Ministers of State and public men had fallen in the ruin of their policies; the Regicides had faced the last extremity with pride. But here were the first martyrs for the sake of a Party.

So Charles was triumphant and for the final two years of his reign, lived seemingly contented with his lot at home.

This period also saw the restoration of the gentry as the social leaders of the nation. The Commonwealth had set aside the upper class system of hereditary right to a position in society. When the Restoration came along, the landowners, the gentry, moved easily back into their old positions of benevolent and social power. Through this comfortable merging of gentry and parish responsibilities, came the social structure of English Church life and often that of a whole community which would survive as an obvious parochial pecking order into the twentieth century.

How the other half lived, we can generally guess. According to one observer at the time, 20% of the nation occasionally needed parish help. At the same time, modern critics of the social welfare system may or may not take comfort from the fact that seventeenth-century spongers were just as capable of fiddling the system as their twentieth-century descendants.

At the time of the Restoration, not much short of £1 million (in seventeenth-century money) a year was needed for parish handouts – and the figure was rising. On the parish or not, the staple diet of a less-than-well-off family was meat, bread and beer and very few vegetables. Meat was eaten at least twice a week, even for the one million on poor relief. For a comfortable family the main meal was at midday and it was enormous. Lots of meat and fish every day.

At the time of Charles II's death, the population was more than five million. Part of the breakdown of the population is provided by figures produced from taxes. For example, there were probably about 7000 lords, temporal and spiritual; 7800 knights; 70,000 lawyers; 52,000 clergymen; and 250,000 shopkeepers. There were 750,000 farmers; two and a half million labourers, outservants, cottagers, and paupers. And, as the record tells us, 30,000 vagrants described variously as gypsies, thieves and beggars.

The end of the reign of the restored monarchy came in February 1685.

C❖. . . an apoplectic stroke laid him low. The doctors of the day inflicted their tormenting remedies upon him in vain. With that air of superiority to death for which all mortals should be grateful, he apologized for being 'so unconscionable a time in dying'.

His brother James was at hand to save his soul. Old Father Huddleston, the priest who had helped him in the days of the Boscobel oak, was brought up the backstairs to rally him to Rome and give him the last sacrament. Apart from hereditary monarchy, there was not much in which Charles believed in this world or another. He wanted to be King, as was his right, and have a pleasant life.

Here is John Evelyn's verdict.

❖Thus died King Charles II, of a vigorous and robust constitution, and in all appearance promising a long life. He was a prince of many virtues, and many great imperfections; debonair, easy of access, not bloody nor cruel; his countenance fierce, his voice great, proper of person, every motion became him; a lover of the sea, and skilful in shipping; not affecting other studies, yet he had a laboratory, and knew of many empirical medicines, and the easier mechanical mathematics.

He loved planting and building, and brought in a politer way of living, which passed to luxury and intolerable expense. . . . He took delight in having a number of little spaniels follow him and lie in his bedchamber, where he often suffered the bitches to puppy and give suck, which rendered it very offensive, and indeed make the whole court nasty and stinking.

He would doubtless have been an excellent prince had he been less addicted to women. . . . He frequently and easily changed favourites, to his great prejudice.

As to the other public transactions and unhappy miscarriages, it is not here I intend to number them; but certainly never had King more glorious opportunities to have made himself, his people and all Europe happy, and prevented innumerable mischiefs, had not his easy nature resigned him to be managed by crafty men, and some abandoned and profane wretches who corrupted his otherwise sufficient parts.

King Charles II died, from natural causes, in 1685. His reign had been a period in which the emergence of party politics became apparent, and a period when to be in an opposing party wasn't necessarily revolutionary, and certainly not treasonable. Charles had been an unconscionable time in dying, although perhaps not in the way he meant. Maybe the Restoration would have been better served by a shorter reign, if not by a more reforming governance. Yet he left behind a people who shared his over-riding belief in the Divine Right of Kings.

CHAPTER TWENTY-SEVEN

1685–1686

——— ❖ ———

The year is 1685, the new King of Great Britain and Ireland is James II, the first Catholic monarch of England since Bloody Mary, more than a century earlier. James reigned for three eventful years in which Protestant fears of Catholic domination and autocratic government led to Revolution.

James was the second son of Charles I and Henrietta Maria so he was Charles II's brother. By his first marriage, to the Earl of Clarendon's daughter, he had two daughters, Mary and Anne. James was humourless and he had the uncompromising belief of the convert. And the society over which he had just became King mistrusted Catholics so much that there were laws to control them. Little wonder that the memory of regicide lingered in the Court of King James II.

C❖His accession to the throne seemed to him to be the vindication of the downright conceptions for which he had always stood. All he thought he needed to make him a real King, on the model now established in Europe by Louis XIV, was a loyal Fleet and a standing Army, well trained and well equipped. . . . Here was the key by which all doors might be opened. Prating Parliaments, a proud, politically minded nobility, the restored, triumphant Episcopacy, the blatant Whigs, the sullen, brooding Puritans, all would have to take their place once the King of England possessed a heavy, tempered, sharpened sword. Everyone was awestruck or spellbound by the splendour of France under absolute monarchy. The power of the French nation, now that its quarrels were stilled and its force united under the great King, was the main fact of the age. Why should not the British Islands rise to equal grandeur by adopting similar methods?

But behind this, there swelled in the King's breast the hope that he might reconcile all his people to the old faith and heal the schism which had rent Christendom for so many generations. . . . It is one of the disputes of history whether toleration was all he sought. . . . He was a bigot, and there was no sacrifice he would not make for his faith.

In the countryside there were matters of everyday living to concern the largely yeoman and farming population. Whatever the grand reputation of Louis XIV, or the thoughts of English rebels, a farmer's concern was likely to be the one and six pence he had to pay for every acre of grass to be mowed, or the three shillings to cut and bind an acre of wheat. In the seventeenth-century account books of the housekeeper to Sir Harbottle and Sir Samuel Grimston, there's not only an idea of the cost of living for a country gentleman, but also the style, including a reasonable amount to be paid for a volume first published twenty-three centuries earlier.

January

Mr Howard for tuning Miss Betty Grimston's harpsicals:		5s.
Mr Barking, for drawing my master's tooth:		10s.
Silk to make Miss Mary a coat:	£ 1. 12s.	

February and March

For a looking glass for Miss Elizabeth Grimston:	£ 1. 10s.	
For cutting both the children's hair:		10s.
For cutting the page's hair:		6d.

April

The huntsman's board-wages, ten weeks and a half:	£ 2. 2s.	
Miss Grimston's singing master for a month:	£ 2.	
For corsets to Miss Mary:	£ 6. 9s.	

July

A dancing book for the page, the page's stockings with green tops:	£ 1. 12s.	
For a bathing tub:	£ 1. 5s.	
For a French Grammar:		2s. 6d.
Aesop's Fables:		4s.
A fiddler for Miss Grimston's birthday:		5s.
Mr Isaac, for teaching the two ladies to dance:	£12.	
Mr Pesgrave, for setting Mary's arm:	£ 2.	

Even Miss Grimston's singing master would have been aware of the constitutional discord surrounding the new monarch. The tea-house gossips insisted that there would be an uprising, perhaps led by Monmouth, one of the late King's Protestant bastards, against King James. (Incidentally, tea was becoming popular. Twenty years earlier, Pepys wrote that it was being drunk, although it was not so common then; certainly he'd not tried it.) But the King ruled with considerable authority. During Charles II's closing years he had ruled without Parliament therefore there was no challenge in the House from the Whigs. Furthermore the Whigs had been politically and commercially hounded.

The Crown and its supporters still had the power to clean out the places where the Whigs could build powerful committees and alliances. And this wasn't confined to Parliament: the local corporations were cleared, so were the powerful livery companies in the City, and the bench of judges. Also many of the Whigs capable of mustering support were now gone. Algernon Sidney and William Lord Russell had been executed. The Earl of Essex had committed suicide in the Tower (or was he pushed?) and Shaftesbury had died in exile. So, when Parliament did come together, in May 1685, it was not a balanced political group. It was dominated by the Tories (although James hardly cared for them).

There were 513 MPs of whom only fifty-seven were Whigs, which didn't make for much of an opposition. However there was a genuine celebration at the arrival of James on the throne in spite of the fears of some at Westminster. Bonfires were lit, church bells rung and parties were held everywhere when James was crowned on, of course, St George's Day. And when, six months later, James celebrated his fifty-second birthday on 14 October (the anniversary of the Battle of Hastings), the bells rang out once more, fresh bonfires were lit and parties started all over again. James had put down the great rebellion of Monmouth that summer, so there was little doubting his strength, if not his popularity, for the time being anyway.

C❖He took every measure which forethought could enjoin to grasp the royal power, and his earliest declarations carried comfort to an anxious land. He tried to dispel the belief that he was vindictive or inclined to arbitrary rule. 'I have often heretofore [he said] ventured my life in defence of this nation, and I shall go as far as any man in preserving it in all its just rights and liberties.' He declared himself resolved to maintain, both in State and Church, a system of government established by law. 'The laws of England,' he said, 'are sufficient to make the King a great monarch.' He would maintain the rights and prerogative of the Crown, and would not invade any man's property. . . . Nevertheless, from the moment he felt himself effectively King, on the second Sunday after his accession, he went publicly to Mass in his chapel. . . .

His public practice of the Roman faith immediately disquieted the Anglican clergy; but its effects did not reach the country for some time. . . . [The House of Commons] voted him a revenue for life which, with the growth of trade, amounted to nearly £2 million a year. Sir Edward Seymour, High Tory, who was out of temper with the management of the elections in his own West Country, alone warned the House of its imprudence and urged delay. Encouraged by the attitude of Parliament, James decided at first to pursue constitutional methods. He knew what he meant to have, and he hoped it might be given him by agreement.

But if constitutional methods would not work, there were other means. James began to break his word. He ordered the release of imprisoned Catholics who were in gaol for not going to church. He even had their fines repaid. And when more than 300 MPs asked him to enforce the laws against dissenters from the Church of England, he refused. Of course he refused because dissenters included Catholics.

The first real challenge to James II came with the Monmouth Rebellion. It was named after James, Duke of Monmouth, whose mother was Lucy Walter, one of Charles II's mistresses, and whom Charles had always believed was his son. He certainly treated him as one. There was even a claim that Charles II and Lucy Walter had married in secret. Monmouth was thirty-six and married to the rich Countess of Buccleuch. He was handsome, dashing, had fought in the third of the wars with the Dutch, and in 1679 had overcome a Scottish Presbyterian rebellion on the Clyde. Most important of all, Monmouth was a Protestant and during the protest against the succession of James II (while Charles II was still alive) Monmouth had been an alternative choice as King. But for the moment he was in exile in Protestant Holland.

In the summer of 1685, James's first summer as King, Monmouth was persuaded that the time was right for him to mount a rebellion. He was encouraged by, among others, a fellow exile, Archibald Campbell, the Earl of Argyll, who promised to invade Scotland in support of him. So, hardly had James been crowned, than Monmouth decided the time for rebellion was right. But the young Duke wasn't very bright. In June he landed at Lyme Regis, with a motley crew of eighty or so followers and picked up an army of 7000 poorly led, untrained peasants and yeomen. He had a cavalry of sorts mounted not on chargers, but carthorses. He headed towards Taunton, not east towards the capital, where he denounced James as a usurper and accused him of having murdered Charles II.

C❖But when the messengers brought the news at a gallop to Whitehall, James was found in the first flush of his power. He had no large army; but there were the Household Cavalry and a regiment of Dragoons under his long-trusted officer and agent, Lord Churchill. There were also two regiments of regular infantry under Colonel Kirke ... All the ruling forces rallied round the Crown ... the Earl of Feversham was placed in command of the royal troops; but Churchill by forced marches had already reached the spot. Monmouth and his rebels ... made a long march through Taunton and Bridgwater towards Bristol, which closed its gates against him, then circled back by Bath and Frome, and finally, a month after his landing, reached Bridgwater again. Churchill, now joined by Kirke, hung close upon him from day to day, while the Royal army approached. . . . the unhappy Duke knew that he was doomed. He had learned that Argyll, landing in Scotland, had been overpowered and captured. . . . One last chance remained – a sudden night attack upon the royal army. Feversham was surprised in his camp at Sedgemoor; but an unforeseen deep ditch, called the Bussex Rhine, prevented a hand-to-hand struggle. Churchill . . . took control. The West Country peasantry and miners . . . fought with Ironside tenacity. They were slaughtered where they stood, and a merciless pursuit, with wholesale executions, ended their forlorn endeavour. Monmouth escaped the field only to be hunted down a few days later. He could claim no mercy and none did he receive.

To say Monmouth escaped the field is one way of looking at it. In truth, he abandoned his men to the butchery. It is said that he proclaimed himself King so that, by a statute of Henry VII, his followers might be sheltered because they had obeyed a King *de facto*. This did not much impress the King's Chief Justice Jeffreys.

Monmouth's stupidity was his timing. James was enjoying what today would be called his political honeymoon. If Monmouth had waited, even a year, he might have had more support. One person in particular watched the goings-on in England with more than passing interest. And he watched from the Netherlands. William of Orange knew well the imperfections of Monmouth's plan. He knew also that, with the Protestant Monmouth executed, he, William, was, through his wife Mary, now closer to the English throne.

Monmouth was captured and executed; and so were more than 200 of his followers. Another 800 were sent off to Barbados as slaves. It is said that the ladies (the Royal mistresses and those in-waiting) of James's court made a handsome profit out of it: white slaves commanded good prices in the seventeenth century. The man who sent these men to the gallows, or to the West Indies, depending on his interpretation of their offence, was George Jeffreys, first Baron of Wem, better known as Judge Jeffreys.

One of the most vivid records was written by Gilbert Burnet. He'd been educated in Scotland, appointed chaplain to King Charles II and then dismissed when he criticized Charles for his social behaviour. Burnet understood well the stupidity of Monmouth for attempting a rebellion while James was at the height of his popularity, in the first months of his reign. But Burnet also believed that had James shown mercy, then his popularity might have lasted.

❖But his own temper, and the fury of his ministers, and the maxims of the priests, who fancied that nothing could now stand before him: all these concurred to make him lose advantages that were never to be recovered. The army was kept for some time in the western counties, which both officers and soldiers lived in as in an enemy's country, and treated all that were believed to be ill-affected to the King with great rudeness and violence. Kirke [Colonel Kirke who, with Churchill and Feversham, had defeated Monmouth] ordered several of the prisoners to be hanged up at Taunton, without so much as the form of law, he and his company looking on from an entertainment they were at. At every new health [where one took the waters], another prisoner was hanged up. And they were so brutal that observing the shaking of the legs of those whom they hanged, it was said among them that they were dancing; and upon that, music was called for.

Judge Jeffreys was sent to the Western Assizes to dispense justice. Burnet has his own view of what happened.

❖His behaviour was beyond anything that was ever heard of in a civilized nation. He was perpetually either drunk or in a rage, more like a fury than the zeal of a judge. He required the prisoners to plead guilty. And in that case he gave them some hope of favour, if they gave him no trouble; otherwise he told them he would execute the letter of the law upon them in its utmost severity. This made many plead guilty, who had a great defence in law. But he shewed no mercy. He ordered a great many to be hanged up immediately without allowing them a minute's time to say their prayers. The impieties with which he treated them, and his behaviour towards some of the nobility and gentry that came and pleaded in favour of some prisoners, would have amazed one, if done by a bashaw in Turkey. England had never known anything like it.

Burnet's next point, if true, explains something more about the character of the King.

❖That which brought all his excesses to be imputed to the King himself, was that the King had a particular account of all his proceedings writ to him every day. And he took pleasure to relate them in the drawing room to foreign ministers and at his table, calling it 'Jeffreys' campaign', speaking of all he had done in a style that neither became the majesty nor the mercifulness of a great prince.

C❖The defeat of the rebels and the prevention of another civil war had procured a nation-wide rally to the Crown. Of this, he [James] took immediate advantage. . . . he proposed to his council the repeal of the Test Act and the Habeas Corpus Act. These two hated relics of his brother's reign seemed to him the main objects of assault. In the emergency he had given many commissions to Catholic officers. He was determined to retain them in his new, tripled army. Halifax, as Lord President of the Council, pointed to the statutes which this would affront; Lord Keeper North warned his master of the dangers he was incurring. Halifax was removed, not only from the Presidency of the Council, but from the Privy Council altogether; and when North died soon after, Chief Justice Jeffreys, red-handed from 'the Bloody Assize', was made Lord Chancellor in his stead. Robert Spencer, Earl of Sunderland, later in the year became Lord President in the place of Halifax, as well as Secretary of State, and was henceforward James's Chief Minister.

James was shifting his political chessmen. He believed – rightly – that his honeymoon with the people continued. (These were still the early months of his reign.) He felt confident after the crushing of Monmouth, even though – and this is important – the King's militia had nearly failed him. He was content with the Church of England's policy of non-resistance. Now he sought to gather about him like-minded souls, and then to make his move against the one institution he couldn't rely upon: Parliament. The year was 1685, the month, November.

C❖Parliament met for its second session on November 9, and the King laid his immediate purpose before it. In his blunt way he declared, with admitted reason, that the militia was useless. They had twice run away before Monmouth's half-armed peasantry. A strong standing Army was indispensable to the peace and order of the realm. He also made it plain that he would not dismiss his Catholic officers on the morrow of their faithful services. These two demands shook the friendly Parliament to its foundations. It was deeply and predominantly imbued with the Cavalier spirit. Its most hideous nightmare was a standing Army, its dearest treasure the Established Church. Fear and perplexity disturbed all Members, assaulted both in their secular and religious feelings; and beneath their agitation, anger grew. . . .

In the House of Lords, Devonshire, the hardy Whig; Halifax, the renowned ex-Minister; Bridgewater and Nottingham, actually members of the Privy Council; and, not the least, Henry Compton, Bishop of London, son of a father who had died for Charles I at Newbury, asserted the rights of the nation. A day was fixed for further discussion and the judges were invited to pronounce upon the lawfulness of the King's proceedings. . . . On November 20, he suddenly appeared in the House of Lords, summoned the Commons to the Bar, and prorogued Parliament. It never met again while he was King.

It was now the Church, the Anglican Church, which led the opposition. The Church opposed the King's policies, but did not make a downright attempt to dethrone him. But this was the beginning of that end. Sermons and pamphlets and slim books started to appear – all opposing Roman Catholicism. The centre for the opposition was London, led by its bishop, Henry Compton. He was a thoughtful, powerful man, much respected by his clergy. He had voted for James when the Lords had debated the Bill of Exclusion, but now he and his clergy preached against popery. James issued his famous 'Directions to Preachers' which told the clergy to stick to less contentious matters. They refused. James set up his Commission for Ecclesiastical Causes, which immediately suspended Bishop Compton. Two years later, Compton's signature appeared on a secret letter sent to Prince William of Orange, inviting him to bring his army to England.

C❖By the end of [1686], James had driven away many of his most faithful friends and disquieted everybody. Halifax, who had saved him from the Exclusion Bill, was brooding in the country. Danby, only liberated from the Tower in 1684, had perforce abandoned his dream of Church and King. He saw it could never be realized with a Papist sovereign. Albemarle, son of General Monk, who had brought about the Restoration of the monarchy, had quitted the royal service. . . . It was plain that the King, with all the downright resolution of his nature, was actively and of set purpose subverting the faith and the Constitution of the land.

One by one, more famous names fell. Clarendon and Rochester went, to be replaced by Catholics. The eighteen-year-old Duke of Berwick, the son of James II and his mistress, Anne Hyde, found himself Governor of Portsmouth. The King still had supporters who were not Catholics. Some of them such unlikely characters – Whigs even – that they were seen as collaborators. But, of course, the inevitable was happening. Only a few years before, the first political parties in British history had been formed. On one side, the Tories who had supported James's right of succession. On the other, the Whigs, who had been founded to oppose the Catholic succession. James was now uniting the party that was responsible for his being on the throne with the party which had been against him. Now they were on the same side – against him.

And across the sea, the thin, asthmatic, hump-backed Prince William of Orange watched. He was son-in-law to the King of England and should James fall, his wife would have a right to the English throne.

CHAPTER TWENTY-EIGHT

1687–1688

———— ❖ ————

It's a truism that there's no believer so dogmatic, so intolerant, so narrow-minded as a convert, perhaps particularly a religious convert. But James II had crossed the line between devotion and unbending evangelism. Many Catholics understood this and some of them saw that the King would bring about catastrophe rather than the return of the nation to Rome. Now there would be open rebellion, and James would be the last Catholic King of Britain.

His people believed that what was happening in England was part of the wider return of Catholicism, and that it was a symptom of the advance of France's Catholic Louis XIV. Indeed, Charles II had made secret agreements with Louis, and he had been converted to Rome – albeit on his deathbed and with a sincerity that was doubted even at the time. Louis's power had grown in less than a decade and the way he had demonstrated that power gave many Protestants in England cause to believe that what they saw taking place on the Continent could spread to England.

C❖England, rent by her domestic quarrels, had ceased to be a factor in European affairs. The Habsburg Empire was equally paralysed for action in the West by the Ottoman invasion and Hungarian revolts. Louis, conscious of his dominating power, sought to revive the empire of Charlemagne on a vaster scale. . . . His neighbours cowered beneath his unrelenting scourge in pain and fear. His flail fell upon the Huguenots, but he also engaged in a most grievous quarrel with the Papacy. He marshalled and disciplined the French clergy with the same thoroughness as his armies. He grasped all ecclesiastical revenues and patronage. He claimed not only temporal but in many directions spiritual control. The Gallican Church yielded itself with patriotic adulation to his commands. All who diverged fell under the same heavy hand which had destroyed the Huguenots.

There were those in England and beyond who saw in James the same uncompromising determination. This was the James, once Duke of York, whose succession to the throne had been opposed, but who when the Whigs were routed, had been cheered in the streets. This was a King who had been crowned with vows of religious tolerance and who now swept them away. And so by 1688, Britain was once more on the brink of civil war. But this was not the sort of war that so divided the people in 1642. Military science had come a long way in forty years or so.

C❖The King had a large, well-equipped regular army, with a powerful artillery. He believed himself master of the best, if not at the moment the largest, navy afloat. He could call for powerful armed aid from Ireland and from France. He held the principal sea-ports and arsenals under trusty Catholic governors. He enjoyed substantial revenues. He assumed that the Church of England was paralysed by its doctrine of non-resistance, and he had been careful not to allow any Parliament to assemble for collective action. Ranged against him on the other hand were not only the Whigs, but almost all the old friends of the Crown. The men who had made the Restoration, the sons of the men who had fought and died for his father at Marston Moor and Naseby, the Church whose bishops and ministers had so long faced persecution for the principle of Divine Right, the universities which had melted their plate for King Charles I's coffers and sent their young scholars to his armies, the nobility and landed gentry whose interests had seemed so bound up with the monarchy – all, with bent heads and burning hearts, must now prepare themselves to outface their King in arms. Never did the aristocracy or the Established Church face a sterner test . . . than in 1688.

During the previous twelve months, sides had been taken. In April 1687 James had made a Declaration of Indulgence. This was a decree which suspended the laws against dissenters and Roman Catholics. He was probably quite successful in taking some, perhaps many, dissenters into his camp. Even the Quakers, who had refused to acknowledge a similar Indulgence of Charles II, were among the eighty or so groups which proposed formal addresses of thanks to the King. Even Whigs supported the King, including James Vernon, Francis Winnington, Lord Brandon and William Sacheverell who had opposed his right to succeed his brother. Others had good reason to give thanks to their monarch. William Williams, for example, had been made Solicitor General. Thomas Cartwright and Samuel Parker had been made bishops. But they were exceptional. Archbishop William Sancroft attacked the Indulgence; he believed it would lead to a law which could never be repealed.

There was also a strong group of moderates, led by the Marquess of Halifax and the Earl of Nottingham. Halifax was known as the Trimmer, so great was his reputation as a moderate. He was obviously good at balancing political weights because later he became Lord Privy Seal and the chief minister.

The impatient group was headed by Charles II's former chief minister, the

Earl of Danby. This was the very man who had been impeached for his part in negotiations with, of all people, Louis XIV, and sent to the Tower. Danby joined the conspiracy to bring Prince William and an army to England.

James II believed he had the army on his side. But did he? What about Churchill, his general and agent? Or Kirke, who had been with Churchill when Monmouth's rebellion had been put down in the West Country?

C❖The supreme object of all the conspirators, civil or military, was to coerce the King without using physical force. This was certainly Churchill's long-formed intention. With him in secret consultation were the colonels of the two Tangier regiments, Kirke and Trelawny, the Duke of Grafton, commanding the Guards, the Duke of Ormonde, and a number of other officers. . . .

At the end of April James had issued a second Declaration of Indulgence. He ordered that the Declaration should be read in all the churches. On May 18 seven bishops, headed by the Primate, the Venerable William Sancroft, protested against this use of dispensing power . . . the Declaration was left unread.

James was furious and demanded that the bishops should be sent for trial on the grounds of seditious libel. But even Judge Jeffreys thought that trying bishops was going too far. James would not listen and the bishops were sent to the Tower.

And then, on 10 June 1688, an event occurred which Danby and his friends believed was the moment they'd been waiting for. The Queen gave birth to a son who later became known as the Old Pretender. The significance was obvious: the Catholic line would be continued.

It was now that Danby and his group of conspirators wrote to Prince William of Orange. With this document, British history twisted in another direction. And it was a letter that didn't shrink from explaining the considerable risks involved.

❖We have great reason to believe we shall be every day in a worse condition than we are, and less able to defend ourselves. . . . the people are so generally dissatisfied with the present conduct of the government in relation to their religion, liberties and properties and they are in such expectation of their prospects being daily worse, that your Highness may be assured there are nineteen parts of twenty of the people throughout the kingdom who are desirous of change, and who, we believe, would willingly contribute to it if they had such a protection to countenance their rising as would secure them from being destroyed before they could get to be in a posture able to defend themselves. It is no less certain that much the greatest part of the nobility and gentry are as much dissatisfied, although it be not safe to speak to many of them beforehand; and there is no doubt but that some of the most considerable of them would venture themselves with your highness at your first landing . . . this is a season in which we may more probably contribute to our own safeties than hereafter (although we must own to your Highness there are some judgments differing from ours in this particular) . . . We must also lay our difficulties before your Highness, which are, chiefly, that we know not what alarm your preparations for this expedition may give, or what notice it will be necessary for you to give the States [the States-General: the Dutch Parliament] beforehand, by either of which means their intelligence or suspicions here may be such as may cause us to be secured before you landing.

The next part of the letter tells of the suspicions, real or contrived, about the Queen of England. She was Mary of Modena, forty years old by then, and a devout Catholic.

❖ And we must presume to inform your Highness that your compliment upon the birth of the child (which not one in a thousand here believes to be the Queen's) hath done you some injury, the false imposing of that upon the Princess and the nation being not only an infinite exasperation of people's minds here, but being certainly one of the chief causes upon which the declaration of your entering the kingdom in a hostile manner must be founded on your part, although many other reasons are to be given on ours. If on due consideration of all these circumstances your Highness shall think fit to adventure upon the attempt, or at least to make such preparations for it as are necessary (which we wish you may), there must be no more time lost in letting us know your resolution concerning it.

For William of Orange to plan, or to agree to a plan, to usurp the throne of his wife's father was not to be taken lightly. But William of Orange was a Protestant and Protestant desperation was high.

The Protestants really did believe that the newborn Prince was not the son of the King and Queen. It was even suggested, and believed for many a year after, that the baby had been smuggled into St James's Palace in a warming pan. James, it was said, must have an heir, by any means.

Danby's letter to William of Orange was signed by, among others, Shrewsbury, Devonshire, Russell, Sidney and the Bishop of London. And it was written on the day that the seven bishops who'd been taken from the Tower to Westminster Hall were found not guilty. The people cheered the news.

C❖The letter was conveyed to The Hague by Admiral Herbert, disguised as a common sailor, and its signatories spread throughout the Island for the purpose of levying war upon the King. Shrewsbury, a former Catholic, converted Protestant, after mortgaging his estates to raise £40,000, crossed the sea to join William. Danby undertook to raise Yorkshire . . . Devonshire, who had lain since 1685 in obscurity at Chatsworth, formed his tenantry into a regiment of horse. William, stricken in his ambition by the birth of a male Stuart heir, exclaimed 'Now or never!' and began to prepare his expedition.

But William's own lands were threatened by the French. If they gave sign of attacking, there was no way in which William's Parliament, the States-General, would allow him to sail for England.

C❖At a moment when the whole of the French Army was massed and ready for immediate advance, it was not easy to persuade the anxious burghers of Holland or the threatened princes of Germany that their best chance of safety lay in sending a Dutch Army into England. However, William convinced Frederick III of Brandenburg, and received from him a contingent under Marshal Schomberg. The other German princes acquiesced in the Prussian view. Most of Catholic Spain set political above religious considerations and made no difficulty about attempting to dethrone a Catholic King. The Emperor's religious scruples were removed by the Pope. All these diverse interests and creeds were united in a strategy so farseeing and broad-minded as is only produced by an overpowering sense of common danger.

Imagine what it must have been like at the time. Most people could remember back forty years or so, or they had parents who could. In that time alone, they'd have seen Charles I have his head chopped off in Whitehall (or at least heard about it); Cromwell's Roundheads ruling the country in the name of a Republic, a Commonwealth; and then they'd seen, and cheered, the return of the monarchy in the form of Charles II. They'd have heard all sorts of stories about papist plots to kill that King and then they'd celebrated the arrival of a new one, James II, even though he was a Catholic. And now the country was about to be pulled apart by yet another civil war and the King was trying to make his kingdom a Catholic state. He wasn't trying to hide what he was doing. He'd put Catholics in prominent positions, including in the army and the navy.

Thus the chessmen of Europe had to be in exactly the right positions before William had the clear line he needed to take the King, and everything depended upon the French. If Louis decided to strike at the German coalition, then that freed William.

Ironically, the solution to the dilemma was in James's hands, not Louis's. The French, if they were to invade Holland, would need the English on their side. If James had aligned himself with Louis, then he might have saved himself, because then William would probably not have left Holland. But James did nothing.

By now there was so much dissent and uncertainty, together with rumour of war, that by the late autumn of 1688, even the unbending Judge Jeffreys tried to persuade James to reverse his reforms. The country was on the edge of panic and James had no option but to back down.

C❖On October 3, James agreed to abolish the Ecclesiastical Commission, to close the Roman Catholic schools, to restore the Protestant Fellows of Magdalen College, Oxford, to put the Act of Uniformity into force against Catholics and Dissenters. The dismissed Lord-Lieutenants were invited to resume their functions in the counties. Their charters were restored to the recalcitrant municipalities. The bishops were begged to let bygones be bygones. The Tory squires were urged to take their old places in the magistracy. In the last few months of his reign, James was compelled to desert the standard he had himself set up and to try . . . by the sacrifice of all his objectives to placate the furies he had aroused. But it was too late.

The signatories to the invitation to William had tried to protect themselves from implication in any plot (still a treasonable matter), but the King's men knew perfectly well what was happening, hence the efforts to change. Intelligence reports had been flooding from the Continent ever since September. They had reported troops being gathered, ships being stored, anchorages being cleared. This was an armada: sixty warships; 500 smaller vessels; 14,000 men made up of Dutch, Scandinavians, six Scottish and English regiments, and displaced Huguenots. By the third week in October, William of Orange had put to sea.

William planned to land in the north of England but the elements took control. A gale blew up and the fleet had to sail through the Dover Straits and then west, not so far from where Monmouth had made his landing three years before. The fleet got as far west as Torbay before putting its army ashore. Even then, James had hoped to stop his son-in-law, not by diplomatic persuasion – he knew it was too late for that – but by sheer force. James had a large army, perhaps 40,000 men, but they were in different parts of the country. Also, the London garrison had to stay where it was to protect the capital but that still left the King with approximately 25,000 men.

By 19 November, two weeks after William's landing, James joined his army at Salisbury. But many officers, already seeing the way the military wind was blowing, began to move towards William's camp. Churchill, at whose home the young Princess Anne, the future Queen, had been staying, had already pledged his intentions to William. In a letter written to the Prince in Holland, he made clear his treasonable intent.

> ❖Mr Sidney will let you know how I intend to behave myself; I think it is what I owe to God and my country. My honour I take leave to put into your Royal Highness's hands, in which I think it safe. If you think there is anything else that I ought to do, you have but to command me, and I shall pay an entire obedience to it, being resolved to die in that religion that it has pleased God to give you both the will and the power to protect.

Churchill wasn't a major player in what followed but he was typical, and clearly influential. James might have followed his instincts and had him arrested but he didn't. In any case, by this time, it would have made little difference to the outcome.

C❖Lord Cornbury, eldest son of the Earl of Clarendon, [and] an officer of the Royal Dragoons, endeavoured to carry three regiments of horse to William's camp. James, warned from many quarters, meditated Churchill's arrest. On the night of November 23, having failed to carry any large part of the Army with them, Churchill and the Duke of Grafton, with about 400 officers and troopers, quitted the royal camp. At the same time the Princess Anne, attended by Sarah Churchill, and guided by Bishop Compton, fled . . . northwards. And now revolt broke out all over the country. Danby was in arms in Yorkshire, Devonshire in Derbyshire, Delamere in Cheshire. Lord Bath delivered Plymouth to William. Byng, later an admiral, representing the captains of the Fleet, arrived at his headquarters to inform him that the Navy and Portsmouth were at his disposal. City after city rose in rebellion. By one spontaneous, tremendous convulsion, the English nation repudiated James.

By the end of the year it was all over. James had been allowed to escape from England: they didn't want him. He was still King, for the moment, and there was no question of another regicide. Two years later James landed in Ireland with French troops and laid seige to Londonderry. About 30,000 Protestants were trapped, but they held out for three months until rescued, an occasion still celebrated in Ulster. Later James was defeated at the Battle of the Boyne(see Chapter Twenty-Nine) and retreated to France where he became a pen-sioner of Louis XIV's. He died in France on 6 September 1701. It is Bishop Burnet, not at all a friend of James, who left a complete picture of this humourless King.

❖He was a Prince that seemed made for greater things than will be found in the course of his life, more particularly of his reign. He was esteemed in the former parts of his life a man of great courage. He had no vivacity of thought, invention of expression; but he had a good judgment where his religion or his education gave him not a bias, which it did very often. He was bred with strange notions of the obedience due to princes, and came to take up as strange ones of the submissions due to priests. He was naturally a man of truth, fidelity and justice; but his religion was so infused in him, and he was so managed in it by his priests, that the principles which nature had laid in him had little power over him when the concern of his Church stood in the way. In a word, if it had not been for his popery, he would have been, if not great, yet a good Prince.

But that was not, of course, a Catholic view of James II. The Earl of Nottingham, for example, said any invitation to William to become King was in violation of the law. He called it high treason and a violation of the oath he'd taken to his sovereign. However there is no evidence from William, nor from his supporters, that he intended to be anything but Regent. After all his wife was Mary, James II's daughter, and she was a Protestant. It was Mary who would be monarch, not William, unless of course she insisted that he shared her throne.

When William of Orange landed in England in 1688 not everyone intended that he should be King even though he had been in the thick of the conspiracy to remove James. The Whigs, the party formed to fight for the exclusion of James, as a Catholic, from his right to the crown, were not unexpectedly on William's side. The Tories were the party of the Crown. But even the Anglican Tories were not all for William's accession, although they welcomed his invasion.

But once William had arrived in London, and once James had escaped (probably with William's help: he needed his father-in-law out of the way, but not as an assassinated or executed martyr) there seems little doubt that William wanted to be King – he certainly wanted the English Army to help fight his own battles. And the solution was obvious: William's wife, Mary, would be Queen and William could be Regent. Better still, Mary could insist that they should rule together: King and Queen. Perhaps that had been the Dutchman's idea all along. For all his weak appearance, humped back and sickly nature, William of Orange was a prince of considerable cunning.

C❖From his earliest years, the extraordinary Prince who . . . robbed his father-in-law of the British throne had dwelt under harsh and stern conditions. William of Orange was fatherless and childless. His life was loveless. His marriage was dictated by reasons of State. He was brought up by a termagant grandmother, and in his youth was regulated by one Dutch committee after another. His childhood was unhappy and his health bad. . . . But within this emaciated and defective frame there burned a remorseless fire, fanned by the storms of Europe, and intensified by the grim compression of his surroundings. His greatest actions began before he was twenty-one. From that age he had fought constantly in the field, and toiled through every intrigue of Dutch domestic politics and of the European scene. For four years, he had been the head of the English conspiracy against the Catholic King James II.

William was a Calvinist but he wasn't single-minded. He was on good terms with the Pope. He took advice from Catholics. He's said to have hated the French Catholics, but perhaps not because they were Catholics but because they were French. And here is a clue to William's determination to be King: the one reason why he might not have invaded England was Louis XIV of France. If Louis had decided to invade the Netherlands that year, as well he might have, then William would have been forced to stay in Holland. Louis in fact moved on Germany. Besides, William could very well say that what he was doing, he was doing for his wife. After all, he would hardly do it for the English, the Irish, the Welsh and the Scots. He didn't like any of them.

C❖William was cold, but not personally cruel. He wasted no time on minor revenges. His sole quarrel was with Louis XIV. For all his experience from a youth spent at the head of armies, and for all his dauntless heart, he was never a great commander. . . . He was no more than a resolute man of good common sense whom the accident of birth had carried to the conduct of war. His inspiration lay in the sphere of diplomacy. He has rarely been surpassed in the sagacity, patience, and discretion of his statecraft. The combinations he made, the difficulties he surmounted, the adroitness with which he used the time factor, or played upon the weakness of others, his unerring sense of proportion and power of assigning to objectives their true priorities, all mark him for the highest repute.

William's adroitness and timing were very obvious during the first few weeks after he arrived in England. Conspirators against King James II implied to William that he could be king (although some of them, including Danby, denied this). What they really wanted was a compliant and Protestant monarch. William worked quickly: James left England on 23 December and arrived in France on Christmas Day. On Boxing Day William called a meeting in London. In front of him were some of the surviving members of Charles II's last Parliament. Joining them were the aldermen, the Lord Mayor of London and men from the common council of London. William didn't invite the Tories from James II's Parliament, which meant that the group was dominated by Whigs – the people who didn't want James to be king in the first place.

One month later a Declaration of Rights was made which offered the Crown to William and Mary. And twelve months after that the Declaration became an Act of Parliament. But what about lawful succession? During the winter of 1688 and 1689, the Tory Anglicans had tried to stop the transfer of the Crown. The bishops didn't mind James being King as long as he was legally bound to the Church. But in January 1689 the Tories decided that they wanted William's wife, Mary, to rule as Regent, but on James's behalf, so that James remained King. That proposal was defeated, but only just. Then the Tories said that James's flight from the country amounted to abdication and since too many people believed that James and Mary of Modena's son was not actually theirs, that the baby had been smuggled into St James's Palace to maintain the Catholic line of succession, then James's daughter Mary was the obvious successor. It was then that William showed his intentions. He didn't want to be, as he called it, 'a gentleman usher' to his wife. The Declaration of Rights provided the form of words for Mary to declare that she wished to rule as Queen with her husband, William, as King.

❖The late King James II, by the assistance of divers evil counsellors, judges, and ministers employed by him, did endeavour to subvert and extirpate the Protestant religion, and the laws and liberties of this kingdom.

Twelve paragraphs follow, all short, all condemning James for, among other things . . .

❖By assuming and exercising a power of dispensing with and suspending of laws, and the execution of laws, without consent of Parliament . . .

He certainly wasn't the first king to do that.

❖By raising and keeping a standing army within this kingdom in time of peace, without consent of Parliament . . .

Not that it did him much good. He was hiding in France when this was being written. And then came the big decision. First a Parliament, then the crown.

❖And whereas the said late King James II having abdicated the government, and the throne being thereby vacant, his Highness the Prince of Orange (whom it hath pleased the Almighty God to make the glorious instrument of delivering this kingdom from popery and arbitrary powers) did (by the advice of the lords spiritual and temporal, and divers principal persons of the Commons) cause letters to be written to the lords temporal, being

Protestants; and other letters to the several counties, cities, universities, boroughs, and Cinque ports, for the choosing of such persons to represent them, as were of right to be sent to Parliament, to meet and sit at Westminster upon January 22, in this year 1689, in order to such [sic] an establishment, as that their religion, laws, and liberties might not again be in danger of being subverted: upon which letters, elections have been accordingly made.

Thirteen paragraphs putting right all the wrongs they believed James had inflicted follow. Then, after a preamble which is so full of seventeenth-century obsequiousness (still used today) that William appears all but godlike, the offer came which the Prince of Orange had no intention of refusing.

❖The said lords spiritual and temporal, and commons assembled at Westminster, do resolve, that William and Mary, Prince and Princess of Orange, be and be declared, King and Queen of England, France and Ireland, and the dominions thereunto belonging, to hold the crown and royal dignity of the said kingdoms and dominions to them the said Prince and Princess during their lives, and the life of the survivor of them; and after their decease, the said crown and royal dignity of the said kingdoms and dominions to be to the heirs of the body of the said Princess; and for default of such issue to the Princess Anne of Denmark and heirs of her body; and for default of such issue to the heirs of the body of the said Prince of Orange.

So the succession was arranged and the Princess's heir was next in line to the throne because, whatever the feelings towards James, his daughter was still next in line. But there was something else to be resolved: perhaps, just perhaps, the most important section of the Declaration of Rights. It declared that, in future, no Catholic could be monarch. The issue remains sensitive to this day, even when it does not involve a Catholic. When Lieutenant Philip Mountbatten became engaged to Princess Elizabeth, the Archbishop of Canterbury advised that although the future husband of the future Queen was Greek Orthodox, it would be better if he were received into the Church of England. Just two weeks before the wedding, in 1947, he was.

So William, who had little regard for these islands and their peoples was to be King of England, Ireland and France. But William had an even greater dislike for Louis XIV.

C❖His paramount interest was in the great war now begun throughout Europe, and the immense confederacy he had brought into being. He had regarded the English adventure as a divagation, a duty necessary but tiresome, which had to be accomplished for a larger purpose. . . . He required the wealth and power of England by land and sea for the European war. He had come in person to enlist her. He used the English public men who had been his confederates for his own ends, and rewarded them for their services, but as a race he regarded them as inferior in fibre and fidelity to his Dutchmen.

It would seem that William accepted, indeed wanted, the crown for two reasons. One: as his wife, Mary, the beautiful daughter of James II, had a hereditary claim on England, then she (and he) should exercise it. Two: England's wealth and military power would be an invaluable weapon in his real ambition: the submission of France.

King William was regarded as an oaf, a bore, an uncouth King. Yet he was well educated, could speak six languages, including fluent Latin, and bewildered London society by his artistic learning. As William of Orange, he had used a mixture of cunning, astute diplomacy and military nous; rid his country of the French by 1674, formed an Alliance with Lorraine, Brandenburg and Spain to deter the French, and had become the head of what was then called the United Provinces. But the steady march of Louis XIV was yet to be checked.

Seventeenth-century London didn't really understand the dangers as William saw them. Given the character of the new King and what he regarded as his special sense of vision it was inevitable that William thought so little of his new people. And just imagine how this new regime went down with a society that still remembered, with some fondness perhaps, the easy going times of the Merry Monarch, Charles II. And also, think what it must have been like to see armed Dutch infantry around the capital of England, not English soldiers.

C❖Once securely seated on the English throne, he scarcely troubled to disguise these sentiments. It was not surprising that such manners, and still more the mood from which they evidently arose, gave deep offence. For the English, although submissive to the new authority of which they had felt the need, were as proud as any race in Europe. No one relishes being an object of aversion and contempt, especially when these affronts are unstudied, spontaneous and sincere. . . . William's unsociable disposition, his greediness at table, his silence and surliness in company, his indifference to women, his dislike of London, all prejudiced him with polite society. The ladies voted him 'a low Dutch bear'. The English Army too was troubled in its soul. Neither officers nor men could dwell without a sense of humiliation upon the military aspects of the Revolution. They did not like to see all the most important commands entrusted to Dutchmen. They eyed sourly the Dutch infantry who paced incessantly the sentry-beats of Whitehall and St James's, and contrasted their shabby blue uniforms with the scarlet pomp of the First Guards and Coldstreamers, now banished from London. As long as the Irish war continued, or whenever a French invasion threatened, these sentiments were repressed; but at all other times they broke forth with pent-up anger.

Apart from a general mistrust of the French, James II was still alive and in France, hoping to regain his throne with French help. And there was an uneasy relationship between William and the people of London.

The diarist John Evelyn writes that in the early months of 1689, when William and Mary accepted the kingdom as theirs, there was a sense that England had been taken over by the Prince and Princess of Orange: not everyone was happy with the manner of their deliverance from popery. There is even a feeling in Evelyn's diary of the time that England had been the subject of a *coup d'état*.

❖I saw the new Queen and King proclaimed the very next day after her coming to Whitehall, Wednesday February 13, with great acclamation and general good reception. Bonfires, bells, guns, etc. It was believed that both, especially the Princess, should have shew'd some (seeming) reluctance at least, of assuming her father's crown, and made some apology, testifying by her regret that he should by his mismanagement necessitate the Nation to so extraordinary a proceeding, which should have shew'd very handsomely to the world, and according to the character given of her piety; consonant also to her husband's first declaration, that there was no intention of deposing the King, but of succoring the Nation.

But nothing of all this appear'd. She came into White Hall laughing and jolly, as to a wedding, so as to seem quite transported. She rose early the next morning, and in her undress, as it was reported, before her women were up, went about from room to room to see the convenience of White Hall, lay in the same bed and apartment where the late Queen lay, and within a night or two sat downe to play at basset as the Queen her predecessor used to do.

Basset was a card game in which players bet on the order in which cards, especially court cards, would appear from the pack: somehow appropriate for the time. A later entry in John Evelyn's diary refers to the King, James, not William.

❖Divers bishops and noblemen are not at all satisfied with this so sudden assumption of the Crown, without offering some conditions to the absent King.

March 8

Dr Tillotson, Dean of Canterbury, made an excellent discourse on five Matthew, verse forty-four, exhorting to charity and forgiveness of enemies; I suppose purposely, the new Parliament being furious about impeaching those who were obnoxious, and, as their custom has ever been, going on violently without reserve or moderation, whilst wise men were of the opinion that the most notorious offenders being named and excepted, an Act of Amnesty would be more seasonable, to pacify the minds of men in so general a discontent of the nation, especially of those who did not expect to see the government assumed without any regard to the absent King.

It is interesting that there was still concern that the King, whatever the state of his popularity, should not be dumped. A nation which remembers the execution of one monarch, and the removal of the monarchy altogether, is not a nation easily at peace with itself. It was also an unsophisticated nation; a suspicious, credulous and easily frightened nation. One chronicler, Sir John Reresby, was sufficiently moved to record a witch's trial at the Assizes of York.

❖A poor old woman had the hard fate to be condemned for a witch. Some, that were more apt to believe those things than me, thought the evidence strong against her. The boy said he was bewitched, falling into fits before the bench, to see her. But in all this it was observed that the boy had no distortion, no foaming at the mouth, nor did his fits leave him gradually, but all of a sudden, so that the judge thought for to reprieve her. However, it is just to relate this odd story. One of my soldiers, being upon the guard at eleven o'clock at night at Clifford Tower Gate the night the witch was arraigned, hearing a great noise in the castle, came to the porch, and being there saw a scroll of paper creep from under the door, which, as he imagined by moonshine, turned first into the shape of a monkey, then a turkeycock, which moved to and fro by him. Whereupon he went to the gaol and called the under-gaoler, who came and see [sic] the scroll dance up and down and creep under the door, where there was scarce the room of the thickness of half a crown. This I had from the mouth of both the soldier and gaoler.

It wasn't until the next century that Parliament repealed the death penalty for witchcraft. The point of all this is to illustrate that the people as a whole were inevitably involved in the grander designs of King William, because they had still to pay taxes, fight his wars, pay his penalties; but they remained ill-educated, and struggled to live day by day. A gentleman like Sir John Reresby would expect to have an income of about £880 a year, a lord bishop at least £1200 and a well-bred nobleman, about £3000 or more a year.

At the same time, the figures from the records of two counties, Somerset and Worcestershire, of the wages paid to ordinary workers show how low they were by comparison.

A maid servant by the year:	£1. 10s.
A dairy maid by the year:	£2
A labourer by the day, without meat and drink from the feast of All Saints until Candelmas [sic]:	7d.
and with meat and drink:	3d.
A mower by the day, without meat and drink:	1s.
with meat and drink:	4d.
A reaper, as like as a mower.	
Sawyers by the hundred, without meat and drink:	2s. 4d.
with meat and drink:	1s. 2d.
A thatcher:	1s.
A carpenter:	1s.
A mason the like wages as a carpenter.	
Men making hay, finding themselves:	10d.
Women making hay, finding themselves:	7d.

Somerset and Worcestershire were among the poorer counties but the wages probably didn't vary a great deal in the richer shires. The richest county of all was probably Middlesex and close to it was Surrey – the expansion of London had started, even in the seventeenth century. Next came Buckinghamshire, Bedfordshire and Hertfordshire, then Oxfordshire and Northamptonshire. Sussex and Kent were not rich, nor were they specially poor. They were close enough to the capital, were well placed on the trade route to the Channel and had constant demand for their downland sheep and fruit. The poverty of the north was made worse by the continuing instability of the region. The poorest counties in England were Cheshire, Lancashire, Yorkshire, Durham and Derbyshire, and the poorest of all was Cumberland.

The modern demographer and economist would probably recognize the social and fiscal structure of the seventeenth century as a template for late twentieth-century counties.

This then was the kingdom of William and Mary. The King however was preoccupied not with the circumstances of a mower or a thatcher finding for themselves, but with the doings of a French King. Planning a war with France was meat and drink to William. But first he would have to turn his mind and his soldiers to a more immediate matter – the coming of the Jacobites.

CHAPTER TWENTY-NINE

1689–1701

———— ❖ ————

Continuing battles and skirmishes between the Scots and the English discouraged the hopes that many, including James, had had for a proper union. But by the seventeenth century, Scotland was ruled by London. As Trevelyan noted, 'The smaller of the two kingdoms was governed in accordance with plans concocted in London by bishops, courtiers or Parliament men, who knew nothing of Scotland's needs and habits' (and, he might have added, cared even less and sought only to make her serve some English partisan policy of the hour).

There was a Privy Council in Scotland, in Edinburgh. But it did as it was told and so no English leader, from James I to William III, could ever take Scotland's support for granted – as the new monarch was about to understand.

C❖The British Islands now entered upon a most dangerous war crisis. The exiled James was received by Louis with every mark of consideration and sympathy which the pride and policy of the Great King could devise. Ireland presented itself as the obvious immediate centre of action. James, sustained by a disciplined French contingent, many French officers, and large supplies of French munitions and money, had landed in Ireland in March [1689]. He was welcomed as a deliverer. He reigned in Dublin, aided by an Irish Parliament, and was soon defended by a Catholic army which may have reached 100,000 men. The whole island, except the Protestant settlements in the North, passed under the control of the Jacobites, as they were henceforth called.

The Jacobites took their name from Jacobus, the Latin for James, and they continued to support the descendants of James II, well into the eighteenth century. It's hard to trace the deeper thoughts of the Jacobites because their leaders rarely trusted their plans and ideas to letters – often the best source of who thought what about what in the seventeenth and early eighteenth centuries. One of the best sources of Jacobite documents was in Paris – and that was destroyed during the French Revolution. So whether they were just a bunch of dissidents, or a real force that could have brought down the monarchy, it is probably true that the Jacobites were joined by people who were disillusioned rather than impassioned. The most widespread support for Jacobitism was in Scotland.

Thomas Morer wrote a journal, *A Short Account of Scotland*, which gives his impression of the Kingdom of Scotland in 1689 and of how it was governed.

❖The government of Scotland is monarchical, and has been for above 2000 years. The authorities of their princes was [sic] heretofore very much eclipsed by the power of their nobles, but upon the union with England the prerogative began to receive some lustre, and was at length screwed to such a pitch as to be obeyed without reserve. The Kings of Scotland, as of England, govern by Parliaments made out of three estates, Lords Spiritual, Lords Temporal and Commons, which are called by the royal writ to treat of arduous matters, yet are not left to their own heads concerning the points to be debated at their sessions, but are bounded and guided by a certain number of their fellow peers commissioned by the King, according to the usage and constitution of that kingdom.

William's arrogance (insensitivity would be a charitable description) towards the Scots did not help his cause. And in 1689, the year William and Mary came to the throne, the Jacobites mounted a rebellion.

On 27 July, John Graeme of Claverhouse, Viscount Dundee, led his Jacobites against William's men at the Pass of Killiecrankie. The King's men retreated, but Dundee, a veteran of Charles II's army, was wounded and later died. It was this soldier who was remembered in song and poetry as Bonny Dundee. This Jacobite Rebellion was important for what *didn't* happen. Few rallied to Claverhouse's standard, the Jacobite cause, because it wasn't until William showed that he was willing to massacre the Scots to get his way that the Jacobite cause grew. But two decades later, after an Act of Union between England and Scotland had been passed, the Jacobite determination to continue their fight would not be dampened. The battle at the Pass of Killiecrankie would not be the last.

Thomas Morer also described the people of Scotland and the way they lived. In this passage the raw animosities between the Scots illustrate that lack of Scottish unity that made warfare easier for Scotland's enemies.

❖Once or twice a year, great numbers of them [Highlanders] get together and make a descent into the lowlands, where they plunder the inhabitants and so return back and disperse themselves. The Lowlanders have plenty of most sorts of grain, especially oats and barley; and as for cattle, though they have herds and lags of their own, yet their plenty of this kind depends much on the yearly descent of the Highlanders. Orchards they have few, and their apples, pears and plums are not the best kind. They have excellent pit-coal, so bituminous and pitchy that it burns like a candle. But this chiefly for their gentry and boroughs. The common people deal in peat and turf, cut and dried in the summer, and would be no bad fuel but that at first kindling it makes a very thick and offensive smother.

Their habit is mostly English, saving that the meaner sort of men wear bonnets instead of hats and plaids instead of cloaks; and those plaids the women also use in their ordinary dress when they go abroad either to market or church. They cover their head and body with them, and are so contrived as to be at once both a scarf and hood. The quality [the gentry] go thus attired when they would be disguised.

Their quarrels and animosities between their great ones made it always necessary in elder times to be very well armed, and the custom continues to this day, so that you shall seldom see them, though only taking the air, without a sword and dirk.

Their language is generally English, but they have many words derived from the French, and some peculiar to themselves. They are great critics in pronunciation, and often upbraid us for not giving every word its due sound.

Meanwhile, in the south the French were beginning to dominate the sea-lanes in the English Channel which, of course, the French did not regard as English at all. So just as William was preparing to fight James in Ireland, the French fleet was putting to sea.

C❖Had William used his whole strength in Ireland in 1689, he would have been free to carry it to the Continent in 1690; but in the new year he found himself compelled to go in person with his main force to Ireland, and by the summer, he took the field at the head of 36,000 men. Thus the whole power of England was diverted from the main theatre of the war [on the Continent]. The Prince of Waldeck, William's Commander in the Low Countries, suffered a crushing defeat at the skilful hands of Marshal Luxembourg in the Battle of Fleurus. At the same time, the French Fleet gained a victory over the combined fleets of England and Holland off Beachy Head. It was said in London that 'the Dutch had the honour, the French had the advantage, and the English the shame'. The command of the Channel temporarily passed to the French under Admiral Tourville, and it seemed that they could at the same time land an invading army in England and stop William returning from Ireland.

Queen Mary's Council, of which Marlborough [John Churchill who had changed his allegiance from James II to William and was now an earl] was a member, had to face an alarming prospect. They were sustained by the loyalty and spirit of the nation.

The whole country took up what arms they could find. With a nucleus of about 6000 regular troops and a hastily improvised militia and yeomanry, Marlborough stood ready to receive the invasion.

But the French didn't come because when James II landed in Ireland from France he, naturally, brought French soldiers with him, and when he lost the Battle of the Boyne he ordered the French frigates lying off the Irish coast to escort him back to France. So the French were distracted from their real intention. If James hadn't commandeered the French vessels to escort him to France, those frigates would have caused havoc with the English supply lines and William would have had to stay longer in England.

Before recounting the Battle of the Boyne, here is a glimpse of seventeenth-century Ireland from the diary of a soldier called John Stevens. Stevens gives a soldier's somewhat scornful opinion of the people and their conditions; a gloomy picture of the people among whom the Catholic James and the Protestant William fought.

❖Orders were given to march miles to the westward of Limerick to a village called Carrick O'Gunnel and the adjacent places. We had plenty of meat and barley bread baked in cakes over or before the fire, and abundance of milk and butter, but no sort of drink. Yet this is counted the best of quarters, the people generally being the greatest lovers of milk I ever saw, which they eat and drink about twenty several sorts of ways, and what is strangest, for the most part love it best when sourest.

None but the best sort of inhabitants of great towns eat wheat, or bread baked in an oven, or ground in a mill. The meaner people content themselves with little bread, but instead thereof eat potatoes, which with sour milk is the chief part of their diet. Beer or ale they seldom taste, unless they sell something considerable in a market town.

They all smoke, women as well as men, and a pipe an inch long serves the whole family several years, and though never so black and foul is never suffered to be burnt. Seven or eight will gather to the smoking of a pipe, and each taking two or three whiffs gives it to his neighbour, commonly holding his mouth full of smoke till the pipe comes to him again. Very little clothing serves them, and as for shoes and stockings, much less. In the better sort of cabins there is commonly one flock bed, seldom more, feathers being too costly. This serves the man and his wife. The rest all lie on straw, some with one sheet and blanket, only their clothes and blanket to cover them. The cabins have seldom any floor but the earth, or rarely so much as a loft. They say it is of late years that chimneys are used, yet the house is never free from smoke. That they have no locks to their doors is not because there are not thieves but because there is nothing to steal . . . whether nastiness of the air be the cause of it I know not, but all the kingdom, especially the north, is infected with the perpetual plague of the itch.

John Stevens makes the point that the condition of the Irish is in part due to the terrible conditions imposed by the English.

❖It is not through prejudice I give this account, but of love to truth, for few strangers love them better or pity them [more] than I do. And therefore to do them justice, I cannot but say it is not to be admired they should be so poor, having been so long under the heavy yoke of the Oliverian English party, whose study it was always to oppress and if possible extirpate them. Poverty enervates the spirits and makes them dull and slothful, and so from race to race they grow more and more degenerate, wanting the improvements of a free and ingenuous education, and being still brought up in a sort of slavery and bondage.

Stevens was sympathetic to the Irish cause and he hoped that James would free them from the Protestant English. But the Battle of the Boyne set William's rule over Ireland not James's. James had considerable support in Ireland but support is not enough to win battles.

There's an account of the battle, fought just north of Dublin, in some documents left by one George Clarke who was there. He tells something of the almost casual way in which the battle took place and also of the flight of James. Bit by bit, William's guards and cannon scared the Jacobites away, rather than the great slaughter of many earlier royal encounters. But first to a small incident just before the main fighting. It's the point when William himself might have been killed and just imagine the change in history if that had happened. Because even at this stage, there were those in very important positions in the English court who secretly wished that William had not been crowned. They'd have been happier with his widow as monarch.

❖The day before the battle as the army marched up to the Boyne and drew up upon a rise that sloped towards the river as fast as they came to their ground, the King rode along the line with intent to view the river he intended to pass and the enemy on the other side of it. He had not rode half a quarter of a mile before the Irish fired two field-pieces.

The company that followed the King rode up the rising from the river in some disorder upon the firing of these two pieces, which were immediately after pointed against the horse guards, who upon that were ordered to dismount that they might be less exposed to the shot that flew pretty thick and had done mischief among the horses.

Upon the movement made by the company that attended the King, the enemy gave a great shout and when we were told a little after that the King was wounded on the shoulder with a cannon ball, but not dangerously, I could not bring myself to believe that he was still alive. But to my great satisfaction I saw him soon after riding towards that place where he received his hurt. But no one except the Marshal Schomberg was allowed to ride with him, that he might not be again exposed to their shot from his quality being discovered by the number of his attendants.

The battle the next day was unremarkable, as George Clarke records. By the late part of the day, it was all but done.

❖Some cornets of horse made a little stand by the advantage of a small river and stone bridge, so that the cannon were sent for, and in the meantime we could see their foot making the best of their way without any manner of order towards Dublin. I think too their horse quitted Duleek before the cannon came. Our horse and cannon pursued them till dusk of the evening, but they got through a defile before we could come up with them and made another stand, so that our dragoons drew up in line to face them, and stayed for the cannon that were coming up. By this time it was dark and the King went back to Duleek where the foot were ordered to halt and His Majesty lay that night in the Prince of Denmark's coach, for the baggage was not come up. We slept very heartily upon the ground. In the night the enemy's horse that faced our dragoons marched away, and we heard no more of them.

We were told that King James went off with a good body of horse soon after the action began, for the general officers had addressed to him the night before in a council of war not to expose his person.

William went on to take Dublin and to establish his rule over Ireland, and was now free to take Britain to war in Europe.

C❖No sooner had King William set out upon the Continental war than the imminent menace of invasion fell upon the Island he had left denuded of troops. Louis XIV now planned a descent upon England. King James was to be given his chance of regaining the throne. The exiled Jacobite court . . . had for two years oppressed the French War Office with their assertion that England was ripe and ready for a restoration. An army of 10,000 desperate Irishmen and 10,000 French regulars was assembled around Cherbourg. The whole French Fleet . . . was concentrated in the Norman and Breton ports.

It was not until the middle of April 1692 that the French designs became known to the English government. Fevered but rigorous preparations were made for defence by land and sea . . . everything turned upon the Admiral [Edward Russell]. Russell, like Marlborough, had talked with the Jacobite agents: William and Mary feared, and James fervently believed, that he would play the traitor to his country and his profession. Jacobite sources admit, however, that Russell plainly told their agent that, much as he loved James and loathed William's government, if he met the French Fleet he would do his best to destroy it, 'even though King James himself were on board'. . . .

On May 19 and 20, the English and Dutch fleets met Tourville [Admiral Tourville, the commander of the French Channel Fleet] off Cape La Hogue. Russell's armada, which carried 40,000 men and 7000 guns, was the stronger by ninety-nine ships to forty-four. . . . Tourville was decisively beaten. Russell and his admirals, all of whom were counted on the Jacobite lists as pledged and faithful adherents of King James, followed the beaten navy into its harbours. During five successive days, the fugitive warships were cut out under the shore batteries by flotillas of English row boats. The whole apparatus of invasion was destroyed under the very eyes of the former King whom it was to have borne to his native shore.

The Battle of Cape La Hogue, with its consequential actions, . . . was the Trafalgar of the seventeenth century.

The Nine Years' War, also known as the War of the League of Augsburg, was fought by a coalition of, among others, German princes who were determined that Louis's march through Europe should cease. William III's determination was second to none, and so with his British and Dutch troops in a not altogether happy alliance, he led the charge. But William was lacking one of his most able commanders, one who was eventually called genius: Marlborough. William had replaced him partly because he wanted his Dutchmen to direct the campaign, and partly because he didn't trust Marlborough's links with James. The result was disastrous.

C❖On land the campaign of 1692 unrolled in the Spanish Netherlands, which we now know as Belgium. . . . Namur fell to the French armies. But worse was to follow. In August, William marched by night . . . to attack Marshal Luxembourg. The French were surprised near Steinkirk in the early morning. Their advanced troops were overwhelmed and routed . . . But Luxembourg . . . managed to draw out an ordered line of battle. The British infantry formed the forefront of the Allied attack. Eight splendid regiments under General Mackay charged . . . Luxembourg now launched the Household troops of France upon the British division, already strained by its exertions, and after a furious struggle, fought mostly with cold steel, beat it back. . . . Count Solms, the Dutch officer and William's relation, who had replaced Marlborough in command of the British contingent . . . refused to send Mackay the help for which he begged. The British lost two of their best generals and half their numbers [were] killed or wounded . . . By noon, the whole of the Allied army was in retreat, and although the losses of 7000–8000 men on either side were equal, the French proclaimed their victory throughout Europe.

Parliament proclaimed its disgust. Never again, said the Lords, should a Dutchman command the English contingent. King William's contempt for the English was endorsed when the Commons accepted, nevertheless, the argument that Count Solms had been the best man available and even voted more money for more war.

C❖In July 1693 was fought the great Battle of Landen, unmatched in Europe for its slaughter except by Malplaquet and Borodino for over 200 years. The French were in greatly superior strength. . . . After an heroic resistance the Allies were driven from their position by the French with a loss of nearly 20,000 men, the attackers losing less than half this total. William rallied the remnants of his army, gathered reinforcements, and, since Luxembourg neglected to pursue his victory, was able to maintain himself in the field. In 1694, he planned an expedition upon Brest . . . Tollemache, the British commander on land, was received by heavy fire from prepared positions, was driven back to his ships with great loss, and presently died of his wounds.

Now, how many times in the hundreds and hundreds of years of the history of these islands have there been accounts of wars, quickly followed by anxious Kings trying to find the money to pay for them? Sometimes the only reason Parliament was called was to raise taxes to finance a monarch's armoured excursion across the Channel. And with William's determination to continue his campaign against the French, the crown had reached yet another financial crisis. The war chests were all but empty. Two years earlier one of the Lords of the Treasury had proposed a government loan of £1 million which was accepted and became known as the National Debt. That same financier had another idea, but one for which an altogether more complicated arrangement was needed: a company was set up. It had 1268 shareholders and together they raised £1,200,000 which they then loaned to the government. They charged the government 8% interest a year and for good measure charged another £100,000 a year to administer the loan. But it was illegal to lend the King money without the agreement of Parliament so it was decided to pass an Act that would give these moneylenders a legitimate charter.

That year, 1694, a Royal Charter was issued. Its title was 'The Governor and Company of the Bank of England', which is why we have a Bank of England today and why its director is called its Governor. The man who invented the National Debt and the Bank of England was a Whig by the name of Charles Montagu.

The throne at this time was supported, financially anyway, by Parliament as well as by the private landings and rents of the Royal Household. This is what is commonly known as the Civil List. Although an Act of Parliament for the Civil List was not passed until 1697, it had, in practice, existed for some time. It was always controversial. For example, a speech by Sir Charles Sedley in the Commons, six years earlier, made it clear that the debate sometimes heard today is little different from the one taking place 300 years ago. He said the Commons provided for the navy, for the army and now for the Civil List. 'Truly, Mr Speaker,' bemoaned Sir Charles, 'it is a sad reflection that some men should wallow in wealth and places [large houses], whilst others pay away in taxes the fourth part of their incomes.'

Much of the money went not to royalty but to the senior officers of the Crown. The first Great Officer was the Lord High Steward of England, or Viceroy, then the Lord High Chancellor, then came the Lord High Treasurer; the Lord President of the King's Privy Council, an office dating back to King John; the Lord Privy Seal; the Lord Great Chamberlain, then the Constable, the Earl Marshal and the last of the Great Officers of the crown, the Lord High Admiral, so trusted that the holder was often the King's son or near kinsman. And they, and theirs, were always well paid. Here is the list of some of their wages at the time of King William III.

❖His Majesty's Household officers and servants attending in the several offices below stairs, under the command of William, Earl of Devonshire.

The Board of Greencloth

William, Earl of Devonshire, Lord Steward, board-wages:	£1360.		
Francis, Viscount Newport, Treasurer and Cofferer of the Household:	£1092.	2s.	6d.
Thomas Wharton, esquire, Comptroller:	£1092.	2s.	6d.
Thomas Felton, esquire, Master of the Household:	£ 433.	6s.	8d.
Sir William Forrester, knight, Clerk of the Greencloth:	£ 455.	13s.	4d.

His Majesty's officers and servants in ordinary above stairs

Lord Chamberlain, the Right Honourable, Charles, Earl of Dorset and Middlesex:	£1100.	
Vice Chamberlain, Sir John Lowther, Baronet:	£ 492.	15s.

Gentlemen of the Bedchamber are nine, whereof the first is Groom of the Stole, that is groom or servant of the long robe or vestment, he having the office and honour to present and put on His Majesty's first garment or shirt every morning, and to order the things of the bedchamber. The Gentlemen of the Bedchamber consist usually of the prime nobility of England, whose office in general is, each one in his turn, to wait one week in every nine weeks in the King's bedchamber, there to lie by the King on a pallet all night, and in the absence of the Groom of the Stole to supply his place.

William's inner circle was a chain of remarkable men, mostly unremarked in history. Apart from a couple of great deeds, Godolphin, gambler, racehorse breeder at Newmarket and the man who would become Lord Treasurer, is barely remembered. Likewise Wharton the Comptroller of the Household, Shrewsbury who was William's Secretary of State, and even John Churchill, the Earl of Marlborough, is hardly known until later when he became perhaps the most remarkable general in English history. Yet for example, Robert Spencer, Earl of Sunderland, made a contribution to the way in which English government works, which has survived to this very day.

Sunderland was an opportunist and like many who swayed periously on the upper boughs of the tree of state, he was a survivor, a man who could change religious and courtly allegiance with remarkable dexterity. He was born in 1641 and he understood court politics and, most usefully, European politics. He became an ambassador and then Charles II's Secretary of State. Then he supported the attempt to exclude James, Duke of York, from succeeding Charles, and promoted the Protestant cause of William of Orange.

When James became King, Sunderland claimed that he too was a Roman Catholic and he was soon appointed Secretary of State, and helped James in his attempt to establish Catholicism in England. When James was chased out of the country Sunderland came back, abandoned Catholicism, reverted to Protestantism, became William's closest adviser and through his own skills of intrigue and political management, convinced the King that it was possible to govern with a small inner group. Sunderland's idea of a small inner group has had an influence that has lasted to this day. The Earl of Sunderland, an all but forgotten figure, was in fact creating what is now called Cabinet Government. Churchill describes its members.

C❖. . . the Jacobites held the Earl [Sunderland] mainly responsible for the Revolution. Sunderland was henceforth bound to William's interest, and his knowledge of the European political scene was invaluable to his sovereign's designs. . . . The actual government was entrusted to the statesmen of the middle view: the Duke of Shrewsbury, Sidney Godolphin, and Marlborough, and, though now, as always, he stood slightly aloof from all parties, Halifax. All had served King James. Their notion of party was to use both or either of the factions to keep themselves above water and to further the royal service. Each drew in others. 'Shrewsbury was usually hand-in-glove with Wharton; Godolphin and Marlborough shared confidences with Admiral Russell'. [Churchill is quoted from KG Feilin's *A History of the Tory Party 1640-1714*]. Of these men it was Godolphin during the next twenty years who stood closest to Marlborough. Great political dexterity was combined in him with a scrupulous detachment. He never thrust forward for power, but he was seldom out of office. He served under four sovereigns, and with various colleagues, but no one questioned his loyalty.

Here then was the small group who would influence not only the King, but would set the basis for English government. And incidentally, it was probably Thomas Wharton (and not Purcell as some think) who wrote the ballad 'Lilliburlero'. It is for this ballad, rather than his political skill, that Wharton's name lives on. The words are Irish, the song was contemptuous of the papists and, among the soldiers of the time, was as popular as, say, 'It's a Long Way To Tipperary' has been among twentieth-century troops.

By now these gentlemen and comptrollers of the monarchy were worried about the succession: William and Mary were childless. And then, shortly after Christmas, 1694, Queen Mary died. Apart from being the daughter of the deposed James II, she is rarely mentioned for doing anything at all. It's almost as if the monarch had a hyphenated name: William-and-Mary. And yet if it hadn't have been for Mary, William would probably not have been King.

Mary was considered beautiful and graceful in contrast to her husband who was not a physically appealing character. They married for political reasons and it was only later that William appears to have recognized the importance of his wife in much that he did, and they grew to love each other.

Bishop Burnet, in his memoir of the times, says Mary was gracious, modest and gentle. But this ignores the determined way in which she broke with her sister, Princess Anne, and Anne's confidante, Sarah Churchill, the wife of the Earl of Marlborough, when William fell out with Anne's husband, Prince George of Denmark. However on 28 December 1694, all thoughts of reconciliation between the daughters of James II disappeared. The Queen was dead – just thirty-two and a victim of smallpox.

C❖Hitherto, the natural expectation had been that Mary would long survive her husband. . . . Instead of this, the crown now lay with William alone for life, and thereafter it must come to Anne. This altered the whole position of the Princess, and with it that of the redoubtable Churchills, who were her devoted intimates and champions. From the moment that the Queen had breathed her last, Marlborough's interests no longer diverged from William's. He shared William's resolve to break the power of France; he agreed with the whole character and purpose of his foreign policy. A formal reconciliation was effected between William and Anne. Marlborough remained excluded for four more years from all employment, military or civil, at the front or at home; but with his profound gift of patience and foresight upon the drift of events, he now gave a steady support to William.

In 1695, the King gained his only success. He recovered Namur in the teeth of the French armies. This event enabled the war to be brought to an inconclusive end in 1696. It had lasted for over seven years. England and Holland – the Maritime Powers as they were called – and Germany had defended themselves successfully, but were weary of the struggle. . . . The Grand Alliance began to fall to pieces, and Louis, who had long felt the weight of a struggle upon so many fronts, was now disposed to peace. William was unable to resist the peace movement of both his friends and foes. He saw that the quarrel was still unassuaged; his only wish was to prolong it. But he could not fight alone.

The end, if that's what it was, came on 20 September 1697. France conceded that the war must end and signed, with England, the Holy Roman Empire, Spain, and the Netherlands, the Treaty of Ryswick. But the Peace of Ryswick was not an end to war in Europe, more of a truce. What happened in England is what always happens at the end of a long confrontation; nowadays the term is 'peace dividend'. At the end of the seventeenth century, the jargon was different, but the sentiment the same: cut back the numbers of troops, save money. It was perfectly understandable. As ever on these occasions, the nation was fed up with paying taxes for a war not everyone was convinced was in the people's interest. Taxes had been raised in the easiest ways, including a levy on births, marriages and funerals:

❖ An Act for Granting to His Majesty certain rates and duties upon Marriages, Births and Burials, and upon bachelors and widowers, for the term of five years, for carrying on the war against France with vigour . . .

We, your Majesty's most dutiful and loyal subjects the Commons in Parliament assembled, have cheerfully and unanimously given and granted unto your Majesty as an additional supply and aid, the rates, duties, impositions and sums hereinafter mentioned . . .

Duke or Archbishop – Wife or widow shall pay £50; eldest son, £30; other child, £25.

Marquess, wife or widow, £40; eldest son, £25.

Earl, wife or widow, £30; Knight bachelor or dean, wife or widow shall pay, £5; eldest son £5; youngest son, £1.

Similar sums were to be paid on the birth or marriage of an eldest son and any other child. And the government knew exactly how to make sure that no one should escape this early form of death duty.

❖Be it further enacted for the better levying and collecting the duties granted by this Act, that all persons in Holy Orders, deans, parsons, deacons, vicars, curates, or any of their substitutes, do within their respective parishes, precincts and places take an exact and true account, and keep a register in writing, of all and every person or persons married, buried, christened or born.

The reason why parish registers are so detailed is, in part, that King William needed the money to finance a war. But now, in 1697, the seventeenth-century peace dividend had to be paid. The army of nearly 90,000 men was to be reduced to fewer than 10,000. The navy was be reduced to a point where it could hardly defend the shores. And this in a society which didn't have a system for coping with sudden change. Demobbing tens of thousands of troops presented a social conundrum to a government and a country which was poor from paying for war and which had nothing approaching a seventeenth-century social security system. One result was a large increase in crime: many soldiers became footpads and highwaymen. Even before the war an Act of Parliament described these outlaws as an infestation. The Act was not simply to put robbers outside the law – that is, to declare them out-laws – but to encourage the population to catch them. This was necessary because it was believed – with good reason – that many of the people supported them.

❖Whereas the highways and roads within the Kingdom of England and dominion of Wales have been of late times more infested with thieves and robbers than formerly, whereby so many murders and robberies have been committed that it is become dangerous in many parts of the nation for travellers to pass on their lawful occasions. For remedy whereof be it enacted that every person who shall apprehend and take one or more such thieves or robbers, and prosecute them until they be convicted of any robbery committed in or upon any highway, passage, field or open place, shall have and receive from the sheriffs of the county for every such offender so convicted the sum of £40 within one month after such conviction. And if any person or persons being out of prison shall afterwards discover two or three more persons who already hath or hereafter shall commit any robbery, [he] is hereby entitled to the gracious pardon of their Majesties, their heirs and successors, for all robberies which he or they have committed at any times before such discovery be made.

So there's nothing much new in the idea of grassing and plea-bargaining.

At the end of the war with Louis, England became isolationist. Not that William wanted it to, it was simply that Parliament and the people were fed up with paying for a war that by and large they didn't want. There had been fears of a French invasion and it might even have happened while James II was still trying to get his throne back, but it didn't.

Perhaps William did realize that if, instead of showing his contempt for the English and their ruling classes, he'd tried to use the political system, then he'd have had the support he wanted for his crusade against the French. But he didn't and in the end, the two parties, the Whigs and the Tories, proved that they were now far more powerful than he'd ever believed they could be.

C❖The Whigs were sensitive to the danger of the French aggression in Europe. . . . The Tories, on the other hand, resented the country being involved in Continental commitments and voiced the traditional isolationism of the people. . . . The landed gentry, the class which largely financed the war through the land tax, . . . foresaw [in the foundation of the Bank of England] the advent of a serious rival for political influence in the merchant classes, now enhanced by a formidable credit institution. The Bank had been a Whig creation. The Bank supported Government loans and drew profit from the war. . . . In 1697, the Whig Administration was driven from office upon such themes and, Robert Harley, now the rising hope of Toryism, created his power and position in the House of Commons. . . . He it was who conducted the reckless movement for the reduction of the armed forces. He it was who sought to rival the Whig Bank of England with a Tory Land Bank. All the time, however, he dreamed of a day when he could step above Parliamentary manoeuvrings and play a part upon the great world stage of war and diplomacy. Harley was supported by Sir Edward Seymour . . . who marshalled the powerful Tories of Cornwall and the West. In the Lords he was aided by Nottingham and the Earl of Rochester. Together these four men . . . froze out and hunted into poverty the veteran soldiery and faithful Huguenot officers. They forced William to send away his Dutch Guards. They did all they could to belittle and undermine the strength of their country. In the name of peace, economy and isolation they prepared the ground for a far more terrible renewal of the war. . . .

William's distresses led him to look again to Marlborough, with whom the future already seemed in a great measure to rest. The King's life and strength were ebbing, Anne would certainly succeed, and with the accession of Anne the virtual reign of Marlborough must begin.

Marlborough, although instinctively a soldier, was now determined that he would, in the last years of William's time, pull together the Tory party, the strongest force in England. And Parliament was now determined to take an even stronger hold on the powers of the English monarchy. For a start, there was the matter of who would succeed not only William, but also Anne. The Act of Settlement declared that through a line descending from the daughter of James, the throne should pass to the House of Hanover. More importantly, it declared that every sovereign had to be a member of the Church of England. Furthermore, and after the experience of William, the Act stated that no foreign-born monarch could go to war without Parliament's absolute permission.

The next test came while William was still alive. And it started, not because of the ambitions of William, but because of a crisis in the future of the Spanish monarchy. This was not some simple domestic dispute: Spain had an empire. But more important to Europe than the Spanish possessions in the so-called New World was that part of the Spanish empire that included parts of Italy and the southern Netherlands – what is now called Belgium.

The King of Spain was Charles II. The reason for the dispute was that Charles was childless. There were three claimants to his throne: France, through either the Dauphin or his second son, Philip the Duke of Anjou, Louis XIV's grandson. The second claimant was the Emperor of Austria, Leopold, who had visions of reviving the grander days of the Habsburgs. And the third claimant was the emperor's grandson, the Electoral Prince of Bavaria.

William and Louis produced a plan, the Partition Treaty of 1698, to partition the empire. They said they would recognize the Prince of Bavaria. But the young Prince of Bavaria died, suddenly. Another Treaty was produced. The Emperor's second son, the Archduke Charles, was selected by William and Louis, but not by the King of Spain. A decision had to be reached. However, on 1 November 1700 Charles died and his will stated that his throne was to go to the Duke of Anjou.

C❖Louis XIV had now reached one of the great turning points in the history of France. Should he reject the will, stand by the treaty, and join with England and Holland in enforcing it? But would England stir? On the other hand, should he repudiate the treaty, endorse the will, and defend his grandson's claims in the field against all comers? Would England oppose him? . . . It was decided to repudiate the treaty and stand upon the will. . . .

But now a series of ugly incidents broke from outside upon the fevered complacency of English politics. A letter from Melfort, the Jacobite Secretary of State at Saint-Germain, was discovered in the English mail-bags, dis-closing a plan for the immediate French invasion of England in the Jacobite cause.

James II was still alive, just, and his Jacobite court was at St Germain.

C❖ William hastened to present this to Parliament as proof of perfidy. . . . But the supreme event which roused all England to an understanding of what had actually happened in the virtual union of the Crowns of France and Spain was a tremendous military operation effected under the guise of brazen legality.

Philip V [the Duke of Anjou] had been acclaimed in Madrid. The Spanish Netherlands rejoiced in his accession. . . . During the month of February 1701, French forces arrived before all the Belgian cities. . . . The Dutch garrisons, overawed by force, and no one daring to break the peace, were interned. . . . All that the Grand Alliance of 1689 had defended in the Low Countries in seven years of war, melted like snow at Easter. . . . Europe was roused, and at last England was staggered [surprised]. . . . William felt the tide had set in his favour. By the middle of the year, the parties in opposition to him in his two realms, the Tory majority in the House of Commons and the powerful burgesses of Amsterdam, were both begging him to do everything that he 'thought needful for the preservation of the peace of Europe' – that is to say, for war.

War was inevitable. But there was one final event which made even the English Parliament recognize this: James II died. This mattered because James II's son, James Edward Stuart, was proclaimed by his father's court as James III of England and VIII of Scotland. That was no surprise, of course, but the significant point is that Louis XIV of France announced that he recognized the son, the Old Pretender as he became known, as King of England.

C❖ Whigs and Tories vied with one another in Parliament in resenting the affront. The whole nation became resolute for war. . . . supplies were tendered to the Crown. King William was able to sever diplomatic relations with France. The Emperor had already begun the war, and his famous general, Prince Eugene of Savoy, was fighting in the North of Italy.

William was never to see the war through. On 20 February 1702, he fell from his horse and broke his collar-bone. He was a tired, weak man and in this second year of the eighteenth century medicine had no remedy.

So Anne became Queen and the long term significance of England's involvement in the War of Spanish Succession was that because of it, England was led, a reluctant player, into a decade of war. It was a war which brought ruthless battles, and a war which gave Britain the island of Minorca and also a tiny colony: Gibraltar.

CHAPTER THIRTY

1702–1706

——— ❖ ———

Queen Anne, the last of the Stuart monarchs, came to the throne in 1702. She was the daughter of James II; her mother was his mistress, Anne Hyde, whom he married. Anne married Prince George of Denmark and although she was pregnant eighteen times, they had no surviving child. She has been described as unhealthy, dull-witted and, like her father, a bigot, although Anne was a Protestant whereas James was, of course, a Roman Catholic. Her connection with and affection for John Churchill, whom she made Duke of Marlborough, developed while she was still Princess Anne. Marlborough's wife, Sarah Churchill, was her lady of the bedchamber – her closest confidant. Anne, like her sister Mary, was quite disloyal to her father. During the 1688 revolution, Anne joined the Rebellion at Nottingham. Yet if this all sounds like disaster for England, it wasn't. Close to the throne were some of the most able people of the new century.

C❖The Age of Anne is rightly regarded as the greatest manifestation of the power of England which had till then been known. . . . Sarah Churchill managed the Queen, Marlborough managed the war, and Godolphin managed the Parliament.

This was Sidney Godolphin, who had served Charles II and James II and who was, for the first five years at least, Anne's closest political adviser.

C❖There was at that time an extraordinary wealth of capacity in the English governing class. . . . It was also the Augustan Age of English letters. Addison, Defoe, Pope, Steele, Swift . . . There was a vehement outpouring of books, poems, and pamphlets. Art and science flourished. The work of the Royal Society, founded in Charles II's reign, now bore a largesse of fruit. Sir Isaac Newton in mathematics, physics, and astronomy completed the revolution of ideas which had begun with the Renaissance. Architecture was led to noble achievements by Wren, and to massive monuments by Vanbrugh.

Wren is usually thought of as a seventeenth-century figure, with the rebuilding of the City of London after the Great Fire, but he was a prodigious worker, very much a favourite of the court, and he didn't die until 1723.

C❖The beginning of Queen Anne's reign seemed to open a period of Tory prosperity. All King William's Whig Ministers were banished from power. . . . But from the very outset a deep division opened between Marlborough, to whom Godolphin was inseparably bound, and their Tory colleagues. The traditional Tory view was that England should not aspire to play a leading part in the Continental struggle.

That is, the War of Spanish Succession, which England was partially responsible for starting.

C❖Her true policy was to intervene only by sea-power, and amid the conflicts of Europe to gain many territories overseas in the outer world. The Tories regarded with aversion the sending of large armies to the Continent. . . . The Whigs, on the other hand, though banished from office, were ardent advocates of the greatest military efforts. They supported Marlborough in all his courses. . . . This clash of opinion . . . governed the politics of the reign.

Marlborough believed that if England didn't join the war, Louis would win it. There was too another matter: Marlborough (and the Whigs were with him on this) believed that whichever power had military domination of Europe could, or even would, have control of the distant colonies. Trade with far away Newfoundland was well established; smuggling from continental Europe was already big business and the Royal Navy was already deploying squadrons in Canadian waters. The Board of Trade was moved to write a formal notice to the Privy Council.

March 26, 1702
The season of the year approaching for the usual convoys to be sent to Newfoundland, we humbly take leave to lay before your Majesty such account of the state of that place as we conceive necessary for the further security and advantage thereof. The importance of that trade and fishery being very great to this kingdom, and several provisions having been made by a late Act of Parliament for the better regulating the same, we did in pursuance thereof prepare particular heads of inquiry and directions, which were accordingly given by the Lords Commissioners of the Admiralty to Captain Graydon, Commander in Chief of the squadron sent thither the last year, unto which we received answers; and humbly offer to your Majesty that it does appear to us:

> That the admirals and masters of ships do not exactly observe the rules prescribed by Act of Parliament.

> That European commodities are carried directly from France, Spain, and Portugal to Newfoundland in English ships, contrary to law, and sold or trucked . . .

Trucked in this context doesn't mean carted. It's the seventeenth-century word for 'dealing' – hence refusing to have any truck with someone.

> . . . with the traders from New England for tobacco, sugar and other of the enumerated commodities, and carried to foreign parts; so that at the latter end of the year, the masters are wholly taken up in the management of that illegal trade, which might in some measure be prevented had the officer or officers commanding your Majesty's ships power like that of a custom house officer to seize such goods.

The concerns of the Whigs were realistic and the commercial defence of England's interests did indeed start in Europe.

The new Queen's mind was occupied with far more than a strategic understanding of what war might mean for her people. Having lived through one rebellion and even taken part in it against her own father, she was well aware of the possibility of another such rebellion.

C❖. . . there was a religious complication. Queen Anne, Marlborough, and Godolphin were all Tories born and bred, and all were Anglicans. Anne had long ago abandoned the conviction that her father's son, the exiled Prince of Wales, was not her brother. The Prince lived under French protection. He is known to British history as the 'Old Pretender', but more gallantly in French annals as the Chevalier of St George. Queen Anne felt herself in her inmost conscience a usurper, and she was also gnawed by the feeling that she had treated her dead father ill. Her one justification against these self-questionings was her absolute faith in the Church of England. It was her duty to guard and cherish at all costs this sacred institution, the maintenance of which was bound up with her own title and the peace of her realm.

But now the effort was concentrated on the war in Europe. In 1702 Louis believed that the death of King William, his one-time enemy, had weakened the English resolve to join the Grand Alliance against him.

C❖He counted upon a period of hesitation and loss of contact which, if turned to good account by military action, might break the Dutch and scare off the English. He regarded Marlborough as a favoured Court personage, able no doubt, and busy with intrigue, but owing his influence entirely to the Queen's affection for his wife. The French High Command therefore did not hesitate to place their main army, as soon as the campaign season began, within twenty miles of Nimwegen . . .

In May, Marlborough made for Nimwegen. He found widespread despondency among the Allied troops and jealousy among the generals. But when his hand was felt upon the Army and its operations, a different mood prevailed. . . . In a brilliant campaign, the new Captain–General conquered all the fortresses of the Meuse, and thus the whole river channel was freed. When . . . Marlborough . . . returned to The Hague, he was received with intense public joy by the Dutch, and on his arrival in England, he was created Duke by the Queen. In his very first year, the tide of the war was set flowing in the opposite direction, and the whole Alliance, which had seemed about to collapse, was knit together by new bonds of constancy and hope.

This war was crucial to the history of these islands. If Marlborough could command the Grand Alliance against Louis XIV and beat him, then the threat to Europe of dangerous domination by one nation would recede. Also, while Louis remained uncurbed, there continued to be a real threat of invasion. There is little doubt that one of France's ambitions during the War of Spanish Succession was to invade Britain on behalf of the Catholic Pretender to the throne, James Edward Stuart.

In May 1702 the Grand Alliance of England, the Dutch Republic and the Holy Roman Empire in support of the Habsburg, Charles III, declared war on the Franco-Spanish Alliance. In September Bavaria joined the French. Later, the Portuguese and the Germans, or some German States, since Germany wasn't united then, joined the Grand Alliance. But by 1703 (the year Samuel Pepys died), in spite of initial success, the Grand Alliance was losing ground to the French.

C❖Both at home and abroad the fortunes of the Grand Allies sank to a low ebb in the winter of 1703. . . . Marlborough during the winter months planned the supreme stroke of strategy which turned the whole fortune of the war.

But before he could proceed to the Continent, it was essential to reconstitute the Government of the High Tories. . . . [Robert] Harley, whom we have seen so active in reducing the armed forces and opposing King William's foreign policy, had been Speaker, leader of the moderate Tories, and virtually Leader of the House of Commons. He was now invited to become a Secretary of State, and the inner circle of the Government was widened to admit him. The combination became Marlborough, Godolphin, and Harley, with the Queen and Sarah [Churchill,

Marlborough's wife] as before. In Harley's train, Henry St John, a young Member who had made himself conspicuous by his brilliant speeches . . . and was in high favour with the Tories, became Secretary at War, a post which brought him into close contact with Marlborough. All this being arranged, and a Parliamentary majority composed of the moderate Tories and the Whigs being procured, the Duke sailed for Holland.

Or as they were then known, the United Provinces. This journey was the start of one of the most famous land battles in English history. French and Spanish forces advanced on Vienna. The English and Dutch armies were on the defensive in the Netherlands. Many of the Alliance leaders grumbled that Austria was too far away for them to worry about. Marlborough didn't think so, he saw the survival of Austria as essential to the Alliance, and its fall as the main ambition of the French.

Marborough began secret preparations to move part of his army away from the Netherlands towards the Danube. He didn't want the French to know what he was doing, but more than that, he didn't want the Dutch to realize what he was doing: they would not have agreed. They would have seen it as leaving them undefended. But the Danube was a 250-mile march across Europe, with French troops heavily entrenched west of the Rhine. Marlborough had 21,000 men, a very obvious force and difficult to hide. On 20 May he left Bedburg, saying that he was going to fight on the Moselle, which he wasn't. He picked up 5000 Hanoverians at Koblenz and 14,000 Danish and Germans at Mainz, eleven days later.

The marvel of this march was Marlborough's logistical planning. The weather was appalling: rain and mud. He marched his men for four days, then rested for one. Fresh boots and equipment were pre-positioned. Marlborough was a calculating tactician, marshal, and quartermaster-general rolled into one man. By the end of June, Marlborough had 40,000 men, had lost only 900, and had Prince Eugene of Savoy at his side.

C❖The twin captains – 'one soul in two bodies' as they were described – fell upon the French and Bavarian army at Höchstädt, on the Danube, early in the morning of August 13. . . . The battle was fought with the greatest fury on both sides. Eugene commanded the right and Marlborough the left and centre. The English attack upon the village of Blindheim – or Blenheim as it has been called in history – was repulsed, and for several hours the issue hung in the balance; but Marlborough, [at] about half-past five in the afternoon, after a series of intricate manoeuvres, crossed the Nebel and concentrated an overwhelming force of cavalry, supported by infantry and guns, against the French centre, which had gradually been denuded to withstand the attacks on either wing. At the head of eighty squadrons

[Marlborough] broke the centre, routed the French cavalry, drove many thousands to death in the Danube, cut to pieces the remaining squares of French infantry, surrounded the great mass of French troops crowded into the village of Blenheim and, as dusk fell on this memorable day, was able to write his famous letter to his wife: 'I have not time to say more, but to beg you will give my duty to the Queen, and let her know her army has had a glorious victory. Monsieur Tallard and the two other Generals are in my coach and I am following the rest.'

The victory of Blenheim almost destroyed the French and Bavarian armies on the Danube. Over 40,000 men were killed, wounded, captured or dispersed. . . . One-third of both armies lay stricken on the field.

This wasn't simply a terrible battle. Before it, there had been a sense that France was invincible. Now there was shock in the court of Louis XIV. Blenheim was more than a defeat, it was the ruin of a greater part of Louis XIV's army. And there was more to come. In May 1704, the English admiral George Rooke arrived in the Mediterranean with his Anglo-Dutch fleet. In July, he was joined by a squadron commanded by Sir Cloudesley Shovell. Reinforced by a land assault, Rooke bombarded a garrison at the mouth of the Mediterranean. This was the prelude to the famous battle for Gibraltar. And, after mixed fortunes, an event occurred in 1706 that was to have even greater consequences than Blenheim. The arena this time was the Low Countries, what is now called Belgium.

C❖Louis XIV had convinced himself . . . that a defensive war could not be maintained against such an opponent. In robust mood he authorized [his commander] Marshal Villeroy to seek battle . . . and furnished him with the best-equipped army of France, all clothed in new uniforms and in perfect order. On May 18, Marlborough's Intelligence Service reported . . . that the French army had crossed the Dyle and advanced to within four miles of Tirlemont. . . .

At dawn on May 23 [1706], the two armies were in presence near the village of Ramillies. Marlborough, having deployed about noon, began a heavy but feigned attack upon the French right with the British troops. Availing himself of the undulations of the ground, he hurled the whole mass of the Dutch, British, and Danish cavalry, over 25,000 strong, upon the French horse between the villages of Taviers and Ramillies. Here stood the finest cavalry of France, including the famous Household troops. . . . After furious fighting, in which 40,000 horsemen were engaged, he broke the French line, drove their right from the field, and compromised their centre.

This battle won for the Alliance the whole of Belgium. Yet there was, for

Marlborough, a harder campaign to come. It would not take place in Flanders but in a bloodier cockpit: the trenches, defiles and ramparts of Whitehall and Westminster. Marlborough's honeymoon with the Queen's inner circle was coming to an end.

CHAPTER THIRTY-ONE

1707–1713

———— ❖ ————

It is now 1707. The war against France and Spain continued, but an event whose consequences have lasted to the present day occurred in these islands. 1707 was the year the Act of Union with England and Scotland became law; or, more accurately, the Act linked Scotland with the 1536 union of England and Wales. Although James I had styled himself King of Great Britain, it had taken a full century for Great Britain to become a legal fact.

Churchill touches on some of the reasons why union happened at this point, and he seems to suggest that the War of Spanish Succession played its part.

C❖Britain's military prowess and the sense of the Island being at the head of mighty Europe now bore lasting fruit. The Union with Scotland was approaching its closing stage. It had been debated, sometimes acrimoniously, ever since the Queen's accession. At last England was prepared to show some financial generosity to the Scots, and they in turn were willing to accept the Hanoverian succession. Marlborough . . . regarded the measure as vital to the strength of the realm. Not only the two nations but their Parliaments were joined together. If Scotland, on the death of Queen Anne, were to choose a different dynasty from England, all the old enmities of the Middle Ages might revive. Both sides judged it well worth some sacrifices to avoid such a breach between the two kingdoms.

There are two separate union events which can be confused: the union of the crowns and the Union itself. In 1603 James VI of Scotland became James I of England. That was the union of the crowns, and anyone born in Scotland after James came to the throne was also English – a full English citizen.

The Act of Union, 104 years later, united the two Parliaments. As long as Scotland and England had separate parliaments it was always possible that the Scottish Parliament could follow, for instance, a totally different foreign policy. And, at the time of the War of the Spanish Succession, this was important. Imagine the difficulties if Scotland chose to support a different side.

Also, and perhaps more significant, the Scottish Parliament could choose a different monarch if it so wished – and it might well. In 1701, the Act of

Settlement promised the throne to the Hanoverians once Queen Anne was dead. (Elizabeth, daughter of James I and Anne of Denmark, married Frederick, Elector Palatine. Their daughter married Ernest-Augustus of Hanover; George – later George I – a Protestant, was their son.) But the Scottish Parliament didn't accept that at all and many in the English Parliament thought that the Scots might support Anne's half-brother, James Edward Stuart, the Old Pretender, even though he was a Catholic, because first and foremost he was a Stuart.

However, before the Act of Union could become law, there were many differences to resolve. For the Scots, the massacre at Glencoe, which took place in 1692, had done little to convince them that anything much would be gained by union. Campbell of Glenlyon had slaughtered nearly forty MacDonalds, including the Jacobite chieftain, Alexander MacDonald. The Scots believed the Glencoe massacre was carried out on the orders of King William and so union was impossible under him.

The English Parliament was dominated by High Church Tories to whom the Scottish Presbyterian Church was beyond the Pale. The Tories didn't want them, nor their followers in the English, or single, Parliament. So they didn't want the union. Equally the Scottish Assembly was dominated by the Country party and the extreme views of the Episcopalians, who were Jacobites, and the Presbyterians.

The Scottish Parliament forced through four Acts which the Queen's men could never accept. The first Act more or less outlawed the Episcopalians. The second stopped the Queen going to war without the Scottish Parliament's agreement. The third allowed French wines to be imported, thus breaking the trade embargo on the French with whom England was at war. The fourth was the ultimate hold over England – in theory at least. It said that if the Queen died without an heir, then Parliament could appoint her successor. Queen Anne was told to veto the fourth Act, the Act of Security. She was advised that if she didn't, there could be two monarchs after her death. A few lines from the Act of Security make this clear:

❖Upon the said death of her Majesty, without heirs of her body, or a successor lawfully designed and appointed, the foresaid estates of Parliament convened or meeting are hereby authorized and empowerd [sic] to nominat [sic] and declare the successor to the Imperial Crown of this Realm, and to settle the succession thereof upon the heirs of the said successor's body, the said successor and the heirs of the successor's body, being always of the Royal Line of Scotland and of the true Protestant religion.

After Queen Anne's veto, the Scottish Parliament was adjourned for a month but in the following year, 1704, the Act came up again, and the Scots refused to pay taxes unless it went through. For hundreds of years English monarchs had paid lip-service to the crudest forms of democracy for the simple reason that monarchs need money for war. And at the point when the Scots were refusing to pay taxes unless the Act of Security was passed, Marlborough was planning his great campaign against the French. So the Queen, and her advisers, backed down. The Act was passed just as Marlborough was beating the French at Blenheim. However in 1705 the English Parliament passed the Alien Act. It was described as:

❖An Act for the effectual securing [of] the kingdom [of] England from the apparent dangers that may arise from several Acts lately passed by the Parliament of Scotland.

The Alien Act stated precisely what would happen if the Scottish Parliament refused to pass its own Act along the lines of the English Act of Settlement: the one nation, one monarch, law. It said that a commissioner would be appointed to negotiate a union of Scotland and England and unless the Scots produced such a law, then, after Christmas Day 1705, Scots would become aliens in England with all that meant for citizenship and trade. The success of this Act was helped by the disunity among the Scots themselves. The English government agent in Scotland was the man who, fifteen years later, would win lasting memory as the author of *Robinson Crusoe*, Daniel Defoe.

Defoe reported back that he thought the Act would succeed. 'There is,' he reported cynically, 'an entire harmony in this country, consisting in universal discords.' Very simply, the Presbyterians and Episcopalians may have disliked union with England and Wales, but they disliked each other even more. However, when a Bill was passed which secured the Protestant religion and Presbyterian Church government within the kingdom of Scotland, the Scottish Parliament agreed to the Act of Union.

Many believed that unless the differences between the two kingdoms were sorted out, then there could be another war, not with France and Spain, but between England and Scotland. And so it was that on 16 January 1707 the Scottish Parliament, as EN Williams, the historian, wrote, 'signed its own death warrant by passing the Treaty of Union'. Scotland was to be united with England and Wales. After Anne's death, the throne was to descend to the Hanoverians. There was to be but one Parliament in which the Scots were to be represented by forty-five Members (only one more than Cornwall) and sixteen peers. The Scots would keep their own legal system, including the feudal private law courts and, most attractive to many in Scotland, the Scots would now have the freedom to trade on equal terms with England and the colonies. And in June, 1707, a famous proclamation was issued.

❖ *Anne Regina*

Whereas in pursuance of the two and twentieth article of the Treaty of Union, as the same hath been ratified and confirmed by two Acts of Parliament, the one passed by the Parliament of England and the other in the Parliament of Scotland, we, for many weighty reasons, have thought fit to declare by our royal proclamation . . . we do by this our royal proclamation under the Great Seal of Great Britain, with the advice of our Privy Council, declare and publish our will and pleasure to be, and do hereby appoint, that our first Parliament of Great Britain shall meet and be holden at our City of Westminster on Thursday the twenty-third day of October next, whereof the Lords Spiritual and Temporal, and knights, citizens and burgesses, and the commissioners for shires and burghs of our said first Parliament of Great Britain, and all others whom it may concern, are hereby required to take notice.

Given at our Court at St James's, the fifth day of June 1707, in the sixth year of our reign.

And so they did. On 23 October 1707, the first ever Parliament of Great Britain met at Westminster. The Act of Union brought together churches, politics and religion, albeit shakily.

In that year, 1707, the War of Spanish Succession rumbled across Europe until it officially ended when the nine Treaties of Utrecht were agreed. But for the moment, Marlborough was a national hero. The nation gave him his own palace, Blenheim, at Woodstock in Oxfordshire. Later, Capability Brown designed the gardens to resemble the layout of the troops, their regiments and squadrons, as they formed up for the Battle of Blenheim itself.

Meanwhile the British had captured Gibraltar and the Earl of Peterborough had captured Barcelona. Families were leaving for the New World to join the children of the Pilgrim Fathers who sailed for America more than eighty years earlier. Daniel Defoe was now editing his own newspaper, the *Review*, and masons were working on Vanbrugh's Castle Howard in Yorkshire. A treaty had been signed with Portugal to allow port wine to be brought into England at reduced customs rates. Commerce had expanded and harvests were good. Trade was gaining an importance that had not always been there. Trade was uniting people's interests even if religion split them. Rivers were deepened, widened and locks were built, which suggests that roads were poor and trade good, although the first canal, the Bridgewater, was not cut until 1761.

The people lived much as before: the north tended to be poor, the south prosperous. Defoe thought the Lake District wild, barren and frightful. People lived in buildings little better than cowsheds, yet this was changing. Cloth weaving was bringing a new prosperity to the region and child labour was not seen as a disgrace, but a sign of industry. Defoe wrote about one town where,

'There was not a child in the town or in the villages round it of about five years old, but, if it was not neglected by its parents and untaught, could earn its bread.'

And poverty shouldn't be confused with early eighteenth-century ignorance. Further north, in Northumberland for example, more of the population could read than in the financially secure south. The Scots produced more books and, not surprisingly, the Lowlands had more in common with the north than did the southern counties.

Wherever the traveller went in the kingdom, the one thing to be found was beer. It was certainly safer than the water and drunkenness was commonplace. The more prosperous of London had other pastimes. Since Charles II, the fashionable had taken coffee and tea and, later, chocolate. By Queen Anne's time it was possible to pick and choose company at the different houses in St James's. Whigs were to be found at the St James's Coffee House, Tories at the Cocoa Tree, the clergy went to Truby's, the very smart to White's. Here then was the beginning of the London gentlemen's club. And there was one chocolate house that was to become greater than them all; it was run for the commercially, the financially, minded in Lombard Street by a man called Edward Lloyd.

London may have been fashionable, but it was disgusting to some, including the monarch. The population of England was about five million, nearly 700,000 of whom lived in London. And London, with its huge coal fires was a hell-hole for almost every invalid. Anne suffered from gout, she preferred Bath or Windsor. She certainly avoided having every sore joint shaken by official carriage rides through London's roughly laid streets. John Macadam, although born in the eighteenth century, wouldn't be laying his smooth roads for another 100 years – and then he chose Bristol anyway.

Whitehall itself was in a sorry state; almost every building had been burned to a shell in 1698; only the Banqueting House had survived. But Parliament had grown stronger, power had shifted and the monarchy was weaker. The result was that the power of the Court (but not yet of the monarchy) was waning.

Marlborough, for example, still put great store in his influence with the Queen, which was exercised through his wife, Sarah Churchill. But now, because of the new influences at Westminster, especially the re-emergence of the Whigs, that was changing. By 1707 the arrangement was under considerable strain.

C❖About this time, Sarah's relations with the Queen entered on a long perilous phase. She had to bear the brunt of her mistress's repugnance to a Whig infusion in the Cabinet. Anne loathed the Whigs from the bottom of her heart . . .

Queen Anne was pious and she regarded the Whigs as irreligious. Marlborough did not share his monarch's distaste, if only for very practical reasons.

C❖. . . her ministers could not see how it was possible to carry on the war without the Whigs and with only half the Tory Party at their back. Sarah wore out her friendship with the Queen in her duty of urging upon her an administration in harmony with Parliament. At the same time, an interloper appeared. As Sarah grew older and as all the affairs of a great lady with much more than the power of a Cabinet Minister pressed upon her, she sought some relief from the constant strain of personal attendance upon the Queen, which had been her life for so many years. Anne's feminine friendships were exacting. She wanted her companion to be with her all day long and playing cards far into the night. Gradually, Sarah sought to lighten the burden of this perpetual intercourse. In a poor relation, Abigail Hill, she found an understudy. She brought her into the Queen's life as a 'dresser', or lady's maid. The Queen, after a while, took kindly to her new attendant. Sarah experienced relief, went more to the country and lived her family life. Abigail, by the beginning of 1707, had acquired an influence of her own with the Queen destined to deflect the course of European history.

Abigail was a cousin of Sunderland's. She was at the same time a cousin of Harley's.

Churchill is writing about the third Earl of Sunderland who was not only a Whig but also Marlborough's son-in-law.

The Queen, as much as she loathed them for their irreligious attitudes, needed the Whigs to keep the government and the war going. It was the Whig vote which, in general terms, kept the war funds coming through. So, considering they were important to the Queen's government, they wanted a greater say in Cabinet. They put forward Sunderland and Anne most certainly didn't want him. But the Whigs, by threatening to withdraw their support from the war effort, forced Marlborough and his closest political friend, Godolphin, to insist that Anne should allow him public office. She gave way.

The other relation Churchill mentioned, Harley (him of the Street), had been a Whig, but became a Tory when Anne arrived on the throne and was shortly to become her Chancellor of the Exchequer. Within two years there would be what was called a Whig Junto. Junto comes from the Spanish word junta, which means council. Sunderland was part of that Junto, so was Marlborough, but until the nod came from a not entirely unexpected quarter, Harley wasn't quite sure what to do.

C❖One day a gardener handed him a secret letter from the Queen. She appealed for his help. No greater temptation could have been cast before an eighteenth-century statesman. Moreover it harmonized with Harley's deep political calculations and his innate love of mystery and subterranean intrigue. Forthwith he set himself to plan an alternative Government based on the favour of the Queen, comprising Tories and moderate Whigs and sheltered by the renown and, he hoped, the services of Marlborough. This plan implied the ruin of Godolphin. Harley imagined that this would be no obstacle . . .

Sidney Godolphin had been minister to Charles II, James II and now Queen Anne. He'd been instrumental in getting through the Act of Union with Scotland; but most important to Marlborough, and therefore the Queen, Godolphin was Lord Treasurer, the government's financial manager, the man who could manage the flow of war expenses. So, and even leaving aside their friendship, of course Marlborough would try to protect Godolphin.

Sarah Churchill, the Duchess of Marlborough, was no longer an influence with the Queen and it would only take a poor campaigning season at the war to reduce Marlborough's stock. Which is what happened. On the Rhine, the French commander Marshal Villars took and pillaged large parts of Germany. In Spain, the Alliance generals split their forces. It was a disastrous decision. Everything that had been gained the previous year was now lost.

In the Low Countries Marlborough was stuck simply trying to hold what he'd got. He had allowed many of his forces south for what he'd hoped would be the taking of the French port of Toulon. It failed. Worse still, the British fleet was wrecked off the Scillies and 1500 sailors drowned. And although he made it ashore, the finest of England's admirals, Sir Cloudesley Shovell, died. And, at the same time, one of Robert Harley's clerks passed Harley's correspondence to a French agent. The clerk swung at Tyburn for it and Harley was dropped in an altogether safer manner.

C❖. . . Marlborough demanded Harley's dismissal from his Secretaryship of State. Anne, now completely estranged from Sarah and with Abigail at her elbow, fought a stubborn fight for her favourite Minister. . . . Marlborough refused to sit another day in Cabinet with Harley and tendered his resignation . . . [and] returned to his home at St Albans. When the Cabinet met and Harley rose to read some paper one of the Ministers roughly asked the Queen how they would do business in the absence of the General and the Treasurer. Harley was unconcerned. . . . The news spread far and wide that Marlborough and Godolphin had been dismissed. Both Houses of Parliament decided to conduct no business until they were better informed. . . . Anne's husband, the Prince George, perturbed by what he heard and saw of the public mood, and strengthened by what he felt himself, implored his wife to bow to the storm. Even then it was Harley and not the Queen who gave way. He advised the Queen to accept his resignation. She wept, and he departed.

So Marlborough and Godolphin had won but the real winners were the Whigs. From now on there would be increasing distance between the monarch and the man who had once been her favoured general and friend. With this dismal prospect and in some depression, Marlborough returned to the war.

Yet the nation grew weary of the conflict. 'A fruitless carnage – so much death but no peace.' That was the charge, and Marlborough had to face it. But although the Duke – the greatest commander of all, some have said – was now without royal favour, no politician dared put him down. Many coveted his political influence, but none felt brave enough to challenge his generalship. And for the moment, Marlborough had more pressing matters, soon to be terrible matters. He was with his great friend and fellow campaigner, Eugene of Savoy, preparing once more to fight the French, this time at a bridgehead on the River Scheldt outside the obscure Netherlands town of Oudenarde.

During the next few hours, 20,000 or so men would die. Prince Eugene of Savoy had command of the right, Marlborough of the centre. The Dutch allies behind them would cross the river to their left. Before them was the French army. It was 11 July 1708.

C❖The French had not contemplated the possibility of a battle, and their great army was crossing the river in a leisurely manner at Gavre. By half-past ten, General Cadogan, with the English vanguard, had reached the high ground north of Oudenarde. . . . Behind Cadogan the whole Army, 80,000 strong, came on in a state of extraordinary wrath and enthusiasm. . . . The soldiers hurled all the officers' baggage wagons from the road in eagerness to engage. . . . Vendôme could not at first believe that the Allies were upon the scene in force.

Vendôme was the Duke of Vendôme, the French commander.

C❖He rode out to see for himself, and was drawn into action by degrees. As the Allies poured across the Scheldt, the French army wheeled to their left to face them. . . . The pace of the battle and its changes prevented all set arrangement. The French fought desperately but without any concerted plan, and a large part of their army was never engaged. The shadows of evening had fallen upon a battlefield of hedges, enclosures, villages, woods and watercourses, in which the troops were locked in close, fierce fighting, when the Dutch, under the veteran Overkirk, . . . swung round upon the heights to the north. At the same time, Eugene, with magnificent courage, broke through on the right. The opposite wings of the Allies almost met.

The French army was now utterly confused and divided into two parts. More than 40,000 men were virtually surrounded by the Allies; the other 40,000 stood baffled on the ridge above the battle. It was pitch dark when the fighting stopped. So intermingled were the combatants that orders were given to the Allies to cease firing and lie upon their arms. . . . In furious anger and consternation, Vendôme ordered a retreat on Ghent. A quarter of his army was destroyed or dispersed. Seven thousand prisoners, many high officers, and a wealth of standards and trophies were in Marlborough's hands when on the morning of July 12 he, and his great companion, rode into the fine old square of Oudenarde.

But it wasn't over. Marlborough and Eugene laid siege to the great fortress of Lille. Fifteen thousand Frenchmen defended the city. They held out until December. Then Bruges fell and then Ghent. At the same time, the navy took the Mediterranean island of Minorca, and as a bitter, freezing winter covered Europe, all military sense suggested that the French were beaten. Louis XIV talked peace with the Dutch. Marlborough talked terms, but in great secrecy, with his nephew, the Duke of Berwick. The Duke was the illegitimate Jacobite son of King James II. He was a general, a marshal of the French army and had fought with distinction against Marlborough's armies in Spain and now in the Lowlands. Thus were the families at war in eighteenth-century Europe – and the war would continue for many more winters.

C❖Meanwhile in England, the Whigs had at last achieved their long purpose. They had compelled Marlborough and Godolphin to rest wholly upon them. They overbore the Queen. They drove the remaining Tories from the Cabinet, and installed a single-party administration, above which still sat Marlborough and Godolphin. . . . The Whigs, ardent, efficient masters of the Parliamentary arts, arrived in power at the very moment when their energy and war spirit were least needed. Marlborough and Godolphin, estranged from the Queen, must now conform to the decisions of a Whig Cabinet, while the Tories, sullen and revengeful in their plight, looked forward to their former leaders' downfall. Harley, by his gifts and his craft, by his injuries and his eminence, became their natural leader.

Harley, the Queen's favourite, had been forced to resign after his confrontation with Marlborough.

C❖To [Harley] rallied the elder statesmen, Rochester and Nottingham. Strong in the favour of the Queen, maintained up the backstairs by Abigail [Hill], Harley reached out to Shrewsbury, now back in English politics after a long retirement, and ready to play an ambitious and powerful middle part.

Marlborough's reign was ended. Henceforward, he had but to serve. His paramount position in Europe and with the armies made him indispensable to either party as long as the war continued. . . . His great period, from 1702 to 1708, was over. There still remained three difficult campaigns, upon a scale larger than any yet seen; but he no longer had control of the policy which alone could render fruitful the sombre struggles of the Army.

The reason for the War of the Spanish Succession had not been truly resolved. And there was a reasonable fear that if the war against Spain continued while France was allowed to withdraw quietly, then the French might get back their military breath and once again threaten the Alliance. The French protested that the war was really over and that they would no longer defend Philip Duke of Anjou, Louis XIV's grandson, in his claim to the Spanish throne. They would withdraw from Spain and even give over French fortresses to the Alliance. But what Louis XIV wouldn't, and couldn't be expected to do, was actually go to war against his grandson. And it was on this point that the peace broke down. The combined armies of the Alliance once more gathered their guns and men to face the French south of what would, in the twentieth century, become a notorious battle field, Mons. But this was 1709 and the place was the pretty wooded countryside of Malplaquet.

C❖On September 11 110,000 Allied troops assaulted the entrenchments, defended by about 90,000 French . . . little quarter was asked for or given. Marlborough in the main repeated the tactics of Blenheim. He first attacked both French wings. The Dutch were repelled with frightful slaughter on the left. The right wing, under Eugene, broke through the dense wood, and eventually reached the open country beyond. Under these pressures [the French general] Villars and his second in command, the valiant Boufflers, were forced to thin their centre. . . . Marlborough . . . launched the English corps . . . [and] brought forward his immense cavalry masses, over 30,000 strong, which had been waiting all day close at hand. . . . Villars had been grievously wounded, but the French cavalry came forward in magnificent spirit, and a long series of calvary charges ensued. At length, the French cavalry were mastered. Their infantry were already in retreat.

Marlborough wrote, in seemingly great sadness as well as hope, to Sarah his wife. 'I am,' he said, 'so tired that I have but strength enough to tell you that we have had this day a very bloody battle; the first part of the day we beat their foot, and afterwards their horse. God Almighty be praised, it is now in our powers to have what peace we please.'

But the following year the armies were greater than ever and the war continued. And when a weary Marlborough returned to London it was to find the politicians at their own war and the Queen seeking vicious revenge. She was determined to rid her government of Whig domination. The political order was about to change.

C♣. . . the whole character of the government was altered. First Sunderland was dismissed; then in August, Queen Anne ordered Godolphin to break his staff of office and quit her service, adding 'But I will give you a pension of £4,000 a year.' Godolphin spurned the pension and retired into a straitened private life. The Whig Ministers of less consequence were also relieved of office. Harley formed a predominantly Tory government, and at his side Henry St John became Secretary of State.

Henry St John was the first Viscount Bolingbroke, a Tory, a Jacobite sympathizer, and no stranger to personal scandal. He and Harley had been forced out of government when Marlborough refused to sit with Harley in Cabinet. Now the Queen had them back, nestled to her dull, but political bosom.

C♣The General Election . . . produced a substantial Tory majority in the House of Commons.
    Marlborough returned from his ninth campaign to find England in the control of his political and personal foes. . . . Yet . . . Marlborough remained the most precious possession of the hostile Government and vengeful Queen. [The Tories] thought they could have peace on victorious terms merely by intimating their willingness for it. They now realized that the downfall of Marlborough was also the revival of Louis XIV. . . . All the states of the Grand Alliance saw in bitter remorse that they had missed their chance. In their distress and returning fears they clung to Marlborough. . . . From every quarter therefore, even the most unfriendly, Marlborough was urged, implored, or conjured to serve.

And so, for the tenth year Marlborough returned to the war in Europe, which was exactly what the Queen, Abigail Hill, Harley and St John wanted: Marlborough was out of the way.

C♣. . . they pursued with consistency, craft, and vigour the whole policy of the Tory Party. St John sent a large, ill-managed, ill-starred expedition to take Quebec from the French. Harley, as Chancellor of the Exchequer, was deep in financial plans for the creation of a great South Sea Company, which was to take over a part of the National Debt and add to its revenues by importing slaves and merchandise into South America. From this the South Sea Bubble was later to be blown. But above all, he [Harley] sought peace with

France. By secret channels, unknown to the Allies, he established contact with [the foreign minister, the Marquess de] Torcy. Finding the French painfully stiff, he brought St John into the negotiations, which proceeded throughout 1711 without the knowledge of Parliament, or any of the confederate states. The method was treacherous, but the object reasonable.

Although Harley and St John were political manipulators, both men were important draftsmen in the treaties which would end the war. And unlike Marlborough and Godolphin, or Marlborough and Prince Eugene, both found it difficult to suppress their jealousies. What's more Harley's position, socially, politically and nationally, was about to be boosted in the most unexpected manner. In one moment of silliness, Harley became a national hero. A French refugee stabbed him with a tiny knife. Nothing serious, but the people rose to their Chancellor of the Exchequer – not a common emotion in any century. And the Queen made him Earl of Oxford and Mortimer, and gave him Godolphin's old post as Lord Treasurer.

C❖It was now impossible to conceal any longer the secret peace negotiations . . . They came as a shock to the vehement London world. Harley . . . commanded a solid Tory majority in the Commons, but the Whigs still controlled the House of Lords. The Tory leaders were sure they could carry the peace if Marlborough would support it. To bend him to their will, they had during the campaign set on foot an inquiry into the accounts of the armies, with the object of establishing a charge of peculation against him. If he would join with them in making peace and forcing it upon the Allies, or in making a separate peace, these charges would be dropped . . . If not, they thought they had enough to blacken his character. . . . The two great parties faced one another upon all the issues of the long war. The Whigs used their majority in the Lords. They carried a resolution, hostile to the Government, by a majority of twelve. But Harley, strong in the support of the Commons, and using to the full the favour of the Queen, . . . loosed the charges of peculation upon Marlborough . . . [who] was dismissed from all his offices and exposed to the censure of the House of Commons. . . . He was now charged chiefly with converting to his own use during his ten years' command the 2½% levied upon the pay of all foreign contingents in the Allied army. . . . He declared that all the money – nearly £250,000 – had been expended upon the Secret Service . . . This did not prevent the Tories . . . from impugning his conduct by a majority of 276 against 165.

Marlborough's real allies were the other leaders of the Grand Alliance, the countries he had led to so many victories. The King of Prussia and the Elector of Hanover set out their belief in his innocence in a solemn document in his defence. And some lines from the Elector himself reflected their opinion.

❖We are fully convinced and satisfied that the Prince, Duke of Marlborough, has annually applied these sums to the Secret Service according to their destination and that his wise application of these amounts has forcibly contributed to the gaining of so many battles, to the passing of so many entrenchments and so many lines, successes which, after the blessing of God, are due in great part to the good intelligence and information which the said Prince has had of the movement and condition of the enemy.

Prince Eugene went to London to plead friendship and the cause of Marlborough. The Tory government ignored the princes of Europe. And Eugene returned, downhearted, to the war. The French were not at all downhearted. Apparently beaten, Louis XIV rallied his people at the news of the downfall of the man they had almost believed invincible in any warfare. And the French found another ally, the British government. In 1712, at the siege of Quesnoy, the Tory government sent instructions to the British commander to, in effect, not get involved in the battle.

And so, between 1713 and 1714, a series of nine agreements that came to be known as the Treaties, or more correctly, the Peace, of Utrecht brought the War of Spanish Succession to an end. Europe was carved up, boundaries drawn, territory handed over. From the Spanish empire Britain was given Gibraltar and Minorca. From the French, Hudson Bay, Nova Scotia, Newfoundland and the island of St Christopher. And the British fear that France would invade in support of the Old Pretender, and the French refusal to recognize the Hanoverian succession to the English throne were addressed in Article Four signed at Utrecht.

❖For adding a greater strength to the peace which is restored, and to the faithful friendship which is never to be violated, and for cutting off all occasions of distrust which might at any time arise from the established right and order of the hereditary succession . . . to the Crown of Great Britain . . . That therefore the said succession may remain safe and secure, the most Christian King [Louis XIV] sincerely and solemnly acknowledges the abovesaid limitation of the succession to the kingdom of Great Britain . . . and for adding more ample credit to the said acknowledgment and promises, the most Christian King does engage that whereas the person who, in the lifetime of the late King James II, did take upon him the title of Prince of Wales, and since his decease that of King of Great Britain, is lately gone of his own accord out of the kingdom of France to reside in some other place, he the aforesaid most Christian King, his heirs and successors, will take all possible care that he shall not at any time hereafter, or under any pretence whatsoever, return into the kingdom of France or any of the dominions thereof.

So the war was over and Europe was at some sort of peace with itself. Marlborough, like the Old Pretender, was hounded into exile and in London, the celebration of exile and victory was marked by squalid and spiteful scheming for the power of both throne and government.

CHAPTER THIRTY-TWO

1714–1720

———— ❖ ————

The last months of Queen Anne's reign found Great Britain in a bad-tempered political mood, with the Queen even less capable than before of controlling her government; Harley, by now the Earl of Oxford and Mortimer, and Henry St John were at each other's throats, and the Tories were seeking spiteful revenge over the Whigs they'd displaced.

C❖St John, raised to the peerage as Viscount Bolingbroke, became involved in a mortal quarrel with Harley Earl of Oxford . . . having procured the aid of Abigail [Hill, the Queen's trusted Lady-in-Waiting] by bribes, he supplanted Oxford in the Queen's favour. Anne was now broken with gout and other ailments.

The old Duke of Buckingham, albeit in extravagant language, reflected on the undignified government of the closing weeks and months of Anne's reign.

C❖'Good God! How has this poor nation been governed in my time. During the reign of King Charles II we were governed by a parcel of French whores, in King James II's time by a parcel of Popish priests, in King William's time by a parcel of Dutch footmen, and now we are governed by a dirty chambermaid, a Welsh attorney and profligate wretch that has neither honour nor honesty.'

Now, the government was on its last legs. Bolingbroke, who resented being only a viscount and wanted to be an earl, was bent on getting rid of Harley, the Earl of Oxford. The ruling Tories were split. Some didn't like the terms of the Treaties of Utrecht. Others wouldn't agree the orderly succession of the throne. Some wanted James Edward Stuart, the Old Pretender, the son of James II, to be king. Others wanted George of Hanover. As for Harley, he was in a sad state, he drank too much. He was incapable of managing the government (he'd never been very good at it, drunk or sober) and he was politically and mentally befuddled. Above all, he was showing less and less respect for the Queen. At the Cabinet Council on 27 July, in apparent and terrible distress, she dismissed

Harley as Lord Treasurer and ordered him to surrender his white staff of office.
It looked as though Bolingbroke had won.

C❖[Harley] denounced Bolingbroke to her [the Queen] as a rogue and a thief
. . . Anne . . . was harassed beyond endurance . . . two days later the
afflictions which had hitherto tormented her body, moved towards her
brain. . . . On July 30, . . . the Council pressed upon the deathbed of the
Queen; they urged her to give to Shrewsbury the White Staff of Lord
Treasurer . . . This would make [him] virtually head of the Government.

Charles Talbot, the Earl of Shrewsbury, was, interestingly, one of the seven
signatories of the document inviting William of Orange to come to England in
1688.

The Tory party had also set themselves the task of prosecuting the exiled
Marlborough and making him repay the hundreds of thousands of pounds
which he said he had spent on spies, which the European Princes insisted he had
spent on spies, but which the Tories said he had spent on himself. By the end
of 1712, Marlborough was in Germany. The Whigs, in opposition, kept in
touch with Marlborough who sided with the Hanoverians in the matter of the
succession. They got ready to put the fifty-two-year-old George, the Elector
of Hanover (who had written in defence of Marlborough) on the throne of
England. Elector was the title given to a German Prince entitled to vote for, or
elect, the Emperor. And the reason this Prince, the Elector of Hanover, was
next in line to the throne of Great Britain was that the 1701 Tory-dominated
Parliament had passed the Act of Settlement which proclaimed that no Catholic
could ever be monarch, and, what's more, that no one married to a Catholic
could be monarch. It also stated that if William III and his sister-in-law, Anne,
had no heirs, then the British throne should be inherited by Sophia of Hanover,
the grand-daughter of James I, or her descendants – as long as they were
Protestants.

Queen Anne had been pregnant eighteen times, five children had survived
birth, but none had survived childhood. George, the Elector of Hanover, was
Sophia's son. And, of course, he was a Protestant.

C❖The Whigs, strong in the Act of Succession and in the Protestant resolve
of the nation, prepared openly to take arms against a Jacobite restoration.
The Elector of Hanover, supported by the Dutch and aided by Marlborough,
gathered the forces to repeat the descent of William of Orange.
The closing months of 1714 were laden with forebodings of civil war
. . . Messengers were dispatched in all directions to rally to their duty every
functionary and officer throughout the land. The Fleet was mobilized
under the Whig Earl of Berkeley and ordered to patrol the Channel and

watch the French ports. Ten battalions were recalled from Flanders. The garrisons were put under arms ... The Dutch were reminded of their Treaty obligations. [And] When Queen Anne breathed her last, at half-past seven on August 1, it was certain that there would be no popery, no disputed succession, no French bayonets, no civil war.

No popery: this is important because by these opening years of the eighteenth century, certainly by 1714, the British Isles was a firmly Protestant state. It gave the people a sense of something approaching arrogance. The British were beginning to see themselves as different, as superior to continental Europe. And the economic prosperity which was apparent at this time coincided with this assurance of Protestantism. There was a common sense that Protestantism was the free and obvious religious persuasion of the successful. And the written word had much to do with it: in 1662 Parliament had passed the Licensing Act which banned all publications that didn't conform to official Church teachings. But by 1695, just nineteen years before the death of Anne, that Licensing Act was allowed to lapse and the printing presses were freed.

In Scotland, England and Wales, printing became more than business, it unblocked the political, social and, most important, the religious arteries of the nations. The first London daily newspaper appeared in 1702; provincial papers carried the latest from London and Parliamentary reporting was probably more extensive than it is today. This meant that people began to get an idea that they were part of something much greater than their provincial existence had thus far allowed them to think: Great Britain.

This then was the nation of the new monarch: the beginning of the Hanoverian reign of England, Scotland, Wales and Ireland. There were six Hanoverian monarchs from George I to Queen Victoria and it was a curious dynasty; for example, George I couldn't speak English, didn't much care for England, imprisoned his wife for life and took continuing comfort in at least two mistresses. But on 18 September 1714, George, Elector of Hanover, sailed up the Thames and landed at Greenwich. The people of Britain had what they wanted: a Protestant succession.

In other words, George I became King of Great Britain because it was convenient to the British – or more precisely, because it was convenient to British politicians. He had watched their vicious skirmishing with considerable distaste, especially when they accused his friend Marlborough of misappropriating war funds. He had even written to the British government defending Marlborough. His petition had been ignored with open contempt – even though he was the heir to the throne.

C❖In accepting the throne ... he was conferring, as it seemed to him, a favour upon his new subjects. He was meeting the convenience of English politicians. In return, he expected that British power and wealth would be made serviceable to his domains in Hanover, and to his larger interests on the European scene.

One of the few people who talked to George I at any length (in French) was Edward Wortley Montagu, a Treasury Commissioner. Montagu's wife, Mary, wrote down her impressions of the new King.

❖The King's character may be comprised in very few words. In private life he would have been called an honest blockhead; and fortune, that made him King, added nothing to his happiness, only prejudiced his honesty, and shortened his days. No man was ever more free from ambition; he loved money, but loved to keep his own, without being rapacious of other men's.

He would have grown rich by saving, but was incapable of laying schemes for getting; he was more properly dull than lazy, and would have been so well contented to have remained in his little town of Hanover, that if the ambition of those about him had not been greater than his own, we should never have seen him in England; and the natural honesty of his temper, joined with the narrow notions of a low education, made him look upon his acceptance of the crown as an act of usurption [sic], which was always uneasy to him.

But he was carried by the stream of the people about him, in that, as in every act of his life. He could speak no English, and was past the age of learning it. Our customs and laws were all mysteries to him, which he neither tried to understand, nor was capable of understanding if he had endeavoured it. He was passively good-natured, and wished all mankind enjoyed quiet – if they would let him do so.

But this was also the German Prince who, having married his cousin, then divorced her and locked her up in Ahlden Castle for thirty-two years – the rest of her life. She was guilty of adultery and George, a Lutheran, took this very seriously. But he also took two of his mistresses very seriously. One of them he made the Duchess of Kendal, and the other became the Countess of Darlington.

And while some in politics rose, others fell.

C❖Many holders of office under the previous reign nursed hopes of the new King. Others were filled with well-justified apprehension. Foremost among those now in acute anxiety was Bolingbroke. His fall was relentless and rapid. Upon the death of Anne he was still Secretary of State. But everyone suspected that if the Queen had lived a few weeks longer, Bolingbroke would have laid the train for a Jacobite Restoration. . . . He had played high, and at the critical moment wavered and lost. . . . The first Parliament of the new regime demanded his impeachment.

Bolingbroke's connection with the Jacobites was hardly a secret. The Whigs, once more in the ascendant, wanted blood.

C❖In despair, Bolingbroke turned for advice to Marlborough, now back from exile, whom he had once mercilessly harried and driven from office. At their interview, Marlborough was all urbanity. But he continued to suggest that . . . Bolingbroke alone of the Tory leaders would pay with his blood for their misdeeds. That night, Bolingbroke fled to France disguised as a valet, his jauntiness utterly shattered. A few months later, he took the plunge and became Secretary of State to the Pretender. . . . Eight years of exile lay ahead. But this false, glittering figure has not yet passed out of our story. His great rival, Robert Harley, Earl of Oxford, was meanwhile imprisoned in the Tower of London. No condign punishment was inflicted on him; but when he emerged from the Tower, he was a broken man.

The new King understood little of the political system and held many of its guardians in contempt. And two of the great reformers and political managers were dead: Thomas Wharton, leader of the Whigs, and enthusiastic supporter of the 1688 revolution that led to the removal of James II, and Charles Montagu, First Lord of the Treasury (to this day the Prime Minister's official title is Prime Minister and *First Lord of the Treasury*), the brilliant financier who invented the National Debt and who, in 1694, had set up the Bank of England.

There was also a new Lord Chancellor, William Cowper, who attempted to write down, presumably for translation into his sovereign's tongue, a description of the differences between the political parties and their doctrines.

❖The Tories accuse the others of being inclined to set up a commonwealth, and the Whigs the Tories, of a design to introduce popery, or at least to bring the Church of England nearer to that of Rome. I have sat continually in one or other House of Parliament now about twenty-four years, and observed with as much diligence and indifference as I could the inclinations of both parties, and I will venture to assure your Majesty as what I am very certain of: that the Whigs would venture all to support the Protestant succession in your Majesty's family; on the other hand, that many of the Tories would rejoice to see [the] Pretender restored, as they call it, even by a French power, much more if by any safer means; that the best of them would hazard nothing to keep him out, though probably do nothing hazardous to bring him in; but that if he should ever declare himself a Protestant, with proper circumstances to make his conversion probable, they would greedily swallow the cheat, and endeavour by all means to put in practice again their old notions of divine, hereditary, and indefeasible right, by a restoration of the person in whom by their opinion, that right is lodged.

Cowper then explained to the King that it would be no good trying to be even-handed when it came to choosing a government. There was no question, given these basic differences, of a working, or even a workable coalition.

❖If such a perfect equality was possible to be observed, perhaps it would follow that an equal degree in power, tending at the same time different ways, would render the operations of the government slow and heavy, if not altogether impracticable. It remains therefore, in my humble opinion, for your Majesty to determine which of these shall have the chief share in your Majesty's confidence, as most likely to support your title to the Crown with the greatest zeal and most untainted affection to it.

It is needless to suggest to your Majesty, but for method's sake, it ought just to be touched upon, that whichsoever party shall have the lower degree of your Majesty's trust, it ought nevertheless to be used by those in power with very great tenderness and affection while obedient to your Majesty and the laws, and, as a father would a child whom he dearly loves, though he does not totally approve, and, to be more particular, should in my humble opinion, be admitted to a fair share of such places and employments of trust, according to their several qualifications, as are during the pleasure of the Crown, and not attended by the chief dependences.

This need to painfully suggest political management to the King may seem unnecessary, but the political experiences of the previous year or so had been filled with spite, vengeance and the very real risk that civil war could break out. And then Cowper, with a final caution that it was best to keep an eye on the Church, ends with the most charming of pleas and hopes for an end to the bickering and recriminations.

❖I have nothing further to importune your Majesty with, nor that the good providence which so visibly has placed you on the throne with any thing so earnestly as my hearty prayers that your reign may be long and glorious, and that your posterity to the end of time may rule over an happy and dutiful, and, if it is not too much to ask, an unanimous people.

But the Jacobites, the supporters of the Old Pretender, were not yet done. It was said, by the Jacobites of course, that five out of six people in England supported them. This is doubtful, but certainly there were many who didn't like the idea of a German-speaking King using English resources for Hanoverian ambitions in Europe. And the government's spies were sending in reports of plans for a landing in England, for a general uprising. Then on 1 September Louis XIV died.

Some suggest that this was a blow to the Jacobite cause. Perhaps it was, but the Treaties of Utrecht stated that the French would no longer support the Jacobites. Yet what Treaty was ever signed but to be adjusted at a later date?

C❖On September 6, the Earl of Mar raised the Jacobite standard at Perth. Within a few weeks, 10,000 men were in arms against Hanoverian rule in Scotland. But they had no proper plans and no solid link with the exiles in France. The Government in London acted at once. Parliament passed the Riot Act . . .

Simply put, the Act said that if riotous assemblies of twelve or more people didn't disperse after they been read a royal proclamation to do so, then they'd be guilty of a capital felony. (This is where the expression 'to read the riot act' comes from).

C❖A reward of £100,000 was posted for the Pretender, dead or alive. . . . In the North of England a small band of gentry, led by Lord Derwentwater, rose in support of the Stuarts . . . reinforced with 4000 Scots, they made a rash and forlorn attempt to raise help from the towns and countryside to the south of them. . . . Government forces in Scotland, led by the Whig Duke of Argyll, met the Jacobite army at Sheriffmuir. The battle was indecisive, but was followed by desertion and discouragement in the Jacobite ranks.

The accession of George I had wrecked the political ambitions of the Tories and of the Jacobite sympathizers. The Earl of Mar, who'd called out his Jacobites in Perth, had been in Queen Anne's government, but was sacked by George's advisers. In France, the Old Pretender, James Edward Stuart, had been told what he wanted to hear – that now was the time to strike – but his advisers were wrong. The Fifteen, as the Jacobite rising of 1715 is known, ended with the Old Pretender escaping to France in February the following year and from there to Rome, where he died in 1766 and was buried at St Peter's. But the Fifteen uprising gave the Whigs good reason to strengthen the authority of the government, even to the extent of preventing the King creating new peerages which might have upset the balance of power. And within six years, Robert Walpole, a Norfolk squire, would become the first Prime Minister of Great Britain.

C❖Political power was henceforth founded on influence, in the dispensation of Crown patronage: Stars [a knighthood or a military decoration], sinecures, pensions; the agile use of the Secret Service fund; jobs in the Customs for humble dependants; commissions for Church livings for younger sons. Thus the Whigs established control of the Parliamentary machine. Though they had split among themselves, there was no hope of an organized opposition to the Whig oligarchy. . . . The 1715 rebellion made it even more easy for the Government to brand all Tories as Jacobites and disturbers of the peace.

The Tories were now a broken political force, but although they were branded as Jacobites, and although the 1715 rebellion had signally failed, it would be wrong to suggest that the Jacobites were no longer of any consequence.

In spite of the apparent ease with which the rebellion had been put down, there was a fear in the country that there could just be a chance of a Stuart, a Jacobite, revival and therefore the possibility of yet another confrontation with France. And there was, in any case, more to the Scottish uprising than simply wanting the Stuart line to continue. For example, many – perhaps most – Scots thought little of the Union of England and Scotland. There was little evidence of its benefit to them. The Act of 1707 which had brought England and Scotland together had demolished the Scottish Parliament. Even though that assembly had itself been largely governed from London, it had represented some semblance of a distinctively Scottish voice in the sometimes disparate Scottish nation.

Also when the eleventh Earl of Mar raised the Jacobite standard at Braemar in September 1715, he was doing so as a man who had served the last Stuart, Queen Anne, well, and had, by all accounts, attempted to make the Union work. But his motives were probably not purely those of a Jacobite. If George I had given him a profitable post, he would have stayed with the monarch. Scottish historians may dispute this point, but it's certainly true that having been rejected by George I, Mar was no longer to be counted upon. And Mar believed he could count on the Episcopalian Church in Scotland and the countryside indulgences of what was still a near feudal system based on allegiance to a family.

The Whig revenge against the Fifteen's leaders was fairly mild. The Lords Derwentwater and Kenmure (who had risen in support of the Stuarts) were executed after the Battle of Preston in November 1715, but many others were allowed to escape. Even some who were condemned to death, for example at Carlisle, were never hanged. In fact, two years after the rising, in 1717, the government's Act of Grace gave free pardon to all who'd taken part, except to the Macgregors. The Macgregors didn't expect a free pardon because they didn't exist, at least not officially.

The Macgregors were considered as little more than bloodthirsty criminals and raiders. At the start of the 1600s the Macgregors had been on yet another raid, this time a very bloody one in Glen Fruin. It became known in Scottish history as the Slaughter of Lennox and the then Earl of Argyll was charged with bringing the Macgregors to account. The chief of the clan Macgregor crossed the borders to plead his case to his King, James VI of Scotland and James I of England. But Macgregor never made it. He was arrested, then hanged. And, in 1610, a government commission issued an order of fire and sword against the Macgregors – in other words, an order to hunt them down. In 1617, Parliament abolished the name Macgregor. So no pardon for the Macgregors who continued to oppose authority. Among their number, incidentally, was Rob Roy.

But for the moment, the Whigs were confident of their political power and there was stability at Westminster. There was, however, a little matter of a £50 million debt to be sorted out. The debt was the result of the war and taxes couldn't be raised in sufficient amounts to cover it, so when an apparent sure-fire trading opportunity was presented, even the grandest snouts slurped from the eighteenth-century financial trough.

C❖In 1710, a Tory Ministry had granted a charter to a company trading with the South Seas and had arranged for it to take over part of the National Debt. This connection had rapidly expanded the wealth of the South Sea Company, and in 1720, a group of directors approached the government with a plan to absorb the whole National Debt, then standing at about £30 million. The scheme soon came to stink of dishonesty, but the politicians were too greedy to reject it. There was a chance of wiping out the whole debt in twenty-five years. . . . The Whig Chancellor of the Exchequer, John Aislabie, purchased £27,000 worth of South Sea stock before introducing the project to the House of Commons. The Bank of England, nervous of a growing financial rival, competed for the privilege of undertaking this gigantic transaction. But the South Sea Company outbid the Bank. In April 1720, the Bill sanctioning these proposals was brought before the House. It received a sober and savage attack at the hands of Robert Walpole . . .

Walpole had himself been Chancellor, but had resigned in 1717. He had done so partly because he disliked the internal political jockeying for the position of the minister with most influence over the King, and partly because he disapproved of the government's foreign policy. He was about to return to government but, three months before that occasion, he lambasted the South Sea scheme. This is part of the record of what he said.

❖The scheme countenanced the pernicious practice of stock-jobbing, by diverting the genius of the nation from trade and industry; it held out a dangerous lure for decoying the unwary to their ruin by false prospect of gain, and to part with the gradual profits of their labour for imaginary wealth. . . . The great principle of the project was an evil of the first magnitude; it was to raise artificially the value of the stock, by exciting and keeping up a general infatuation and by promising dividends out of funds which would not be adequate to the purpose.

Walpole was regarded as a bit of an old bore. Here was an opportunity for everyone to get rich. There is a reluctance to give the original promoters of the South Sea Company any credit for honourable behaviour and, perhaps, this is reasonable. But there was a moment surely when the reasoning behind the use of the Company was thought of as sensible, if eighteenth-century speculation ever could be sensible. And it was at this point that Robert Harley, Earl of Oxford and Mortimer, surfaced once more.

It was Harley, the one-time Chancellor and Lord Treasurer, sacked by Queen Anne days before she died, who had started the South Sea Company a decade earlier, partly with the idea that it should deal in the slave trade with the Spanish Americas. But by now the Company had shifted from being a trading organization to becoming a finance house; and that was the root of its problem.

King George I's closest government ministers, the first Earl of Stanhope and the second Earl of Sunderland, promoted the scheme's new purpose. Stanhope had been very good at war – it was he who had captured Minorca for the British; he was a master of diplomacy, but not much of a financial brain. Sunderland was not very bright either; he probably only got into Queen Anne's government because Marlborough was his father-in-law. Stanhope and Sunderland wanted to reduce the taxes which were necessary because of the interest the government had to pay on the National Debt. Any modern budgeteer would recognize the motive – but not necessarily the method: but, at the time, 60% of the National Debt converted into stock sounded good. And it wasn't the only business scheme exciting the investors. In Paris for example, there was great admiration for the promise of profits in the Mississippi Project which, claimed the prospectus, couldn't fail. And there were several other schemes recommended to investors including a scheme for buying Irish bogs; a scheme for the financing of a gun to fire square cannon balls; and the scheme for a company to 'carry on an undertaking of Great Advantage but no one to know what it is'. It may sound ludicrous but £2000 was invested. But then, in London, the South Sea Bubble burst.

C❖The porters and ladies' maids who had bought carriages and fineries found themselves reduced to their former station. Clergy, bishops, poets and gentry found their life savings vanish overnight. There were suicides daily. The gullible mob whose innate greed had lain behind this mass hysteria and mania for wealth called for vengeance. The Post-Master General took poison. His son, a Secretary of State, was snatched from his accusers by opportune smallpox. Stanhope, the Chief Minister, died of strain. The Directors of the Company were arrested and their estates forfeited for the benefit of the huge army of creditors. A secret committee was appointed by the House of Commons to inquire into the nature and origins of these astonishing transactions. The books of the company were mutilated and incomplete. Nevertheless, it was discovered that 462 Members of the Commons and 122 peers were involved. Groups of frantic bankrupts thronged the Parliamentary lobbies. The Riot Act was read.

Almost everyone was involved, even the King's German mistresses who'd never been liked so they were scorned and blamed. Ironically, the man who would save the Court and Government from the full wrath of the people and Parliament, Robert Walpole, had himself been involved in the rush and grab for profit.

CHAPTER THIRTY-THREE

1721–1726

❖

Robert Walpole became Britain's first Prime Minister in 1721. He was short, ruddy-faced, weighed twenty stone and spoke with a Norfolk farmer's accent. But Walpole didn't appear suddenly at Westminster on the day the bubble burst, promising to save court, party and government if they would call him Prime Minister. In fact, Walpole often suggested that he wasn't 'Prime Minister', a term quite new to government. But he most certainly was the person who managed the embarrassment and political position of court, party and government – the three victims of the greed and unwise investments of the moment. He brought political stability to Britain, and he set the style and method of government management for the rest of the eighteenth century.

C❖This Norfolk squire, who hunted five days a week, had risen to prominence as Secretary of War in the days of Marlborough. He had been imprisoned in the Tower after the Whig defeat in 1710, and since his release had been a leading figure of the Whig Party in the House of Commons. He had already been Chancellor of the Exchequer for three years, but he and his brother-in-law, Townshend, had resigned in 1717 in protest at the excessive pliancy of certain Whigs to the Hanoverian foreign policy of the King.

Walpole's father was also Robert Walpole. He was a Whig MP, but better remembered as the country squire of a Norfolk estate. Robert Walpole was the squire's third son, born in 1676, so he was just coming up to his forty-fifth birthday when he became Prime Minister. He went to Eton and then to Cambridge in 1696. He was there for only two years, but would have been aware of the terrible turmoil of the country and the monarchy. In his first year, there was, or it was said that there was, a plot to assassinate King William III. In his second year, the War of the Grand Alliance against France came to an end with signing of the Treaty of Ryswick. That was the accord that, for the moment, set the balance of power in Europe in favour of the Habsburgs of Spain and the Holy Roman Empire.

Walpole left Cambridge after only two years because his brothers died and he, at the age of twenty-two, returned to Norfolk to run the family estate. Two years later, in 1700, his father died, and so Walpole became head of the family, married his first wife, Catherine, and then became the Whig MP for Castle Rising and, in the following year, for King's Lynn – a seat he was to hold for most of the rest of his life.

In 1708 Walpole became Secretary at War and later Treasurer of the Navy. These were important posts: England was leading the Alliance in the War of Spanish Succession. Walpole was, by then, the established leader of the Whig Junto in the Commons. But when Queen Anne came to the throne, Harley was head of the Tory government. He needed to get rid of the outspoken Walpole and through some curious and historically unproven corruption, Walpole was actually expelled from the Commons. It was then (1712) that Walpole was sent to the Tower for six months. But by the time of George I's accession, Walpole was back in favour and, in October 1715, became Chancellor of the Exchequer. That was the year of the Jacobite uprising and Walpole helped put it down.

Walpole's rise to power had much to do with his own authority in managing party affairs and government, but also, in the early years especially, it had a great deal to do with his cousin, who was also his brother-in-law. That man was Townshend, whom Churchill mentions. Charles Townshend, the second Viscount Townshend and in later life known as Turnip Townshend: he too was a Norfolk farmer.

The brothers-in-law were clearly of similar persuasion and neither liked King George's preparations for his adventures in the Baltic (Britain's military power was one of the few attractions for the Hanoverian). Walpole said Britain couldn't afford the costs of personal wars and that the government couldn't be sure of its majority if they went ahead. He and Townshend were forced to resign.

Walpole spent his time out of government getting on good terms with the Prince of Wales (the future George II who didn't like his father anyway – no Hanoverian Prince of Wales ever liked his father) and by 1720 Walpole was back in favour enough to persuade the Prince to make it up with the King. Walpole became Post-Master General. By the following year, he was First Lord of the Treasury and Chancellor of the Exchequer, and sorting out the problems left by the bursting of the South Sea Company's investment bubble. In effect he led the Government, but at this stage – the 1720s – the position of Prime Minister did not exist.

C❖Walpole, on becoming head of the Government, immediately turned to financial reconstruction. . . . The last sections of the National Debt taken over by the South Sea Company were portioned out between the Bank of England and the Treasury. The Sinking Fund he had instituted in 1717 whereby a sum of money was set aside from the revenue each year to pay off the National Debt, was put into operation. Within a few months the situation improved and England settled down again under another edition of Whig rule.

With a business man at the head of affairs, the atmosphere of national politics became increasingly materialistic. Walpole realized that the life of his Government depended on avoiding great issues that might divide the country. He knew that a mass of hostile opinion smouldered in the manor-houses and parsonages of England, and he was determined not to provoke it.

By careful attention to Episcopal appointments, delicately handled by his friend Edmund Gibson, the Whig Bishop of London, Walpole increased the preponderance of his party in the House of Lords. He refused a comprehensive measure of toleration for the Dissenters, for this might have introduced religious strife into the world of politics.

The Dissenters had been persecuted both socially and legally for their disagreement with the Established Church. In the previous century the Test Acts had banned Non-Conformists from holding civil and military office, and even Parliamentary office.

C❖But while unwilling to legislate broadly on grounds of principle, he took care that his Dissenting supporters who accepted office in local government in defiance of the Test Acts were quietly protected by annual Acts of Indemnity. Any sign of Tory activity was greeted by Walpole with the deadly accusation of Jacobitism. . . . He had no illusions about the virtue of his supporters; but he knew there was a point beyond which corruption would not work. There was a limit to the mercenary nature of the men with whom he dealt, and it was plain that in the last resort they would be moved to vote by fear or anger rather than according to their interests. Anything tending to crisis must be avoided as the plague. For the rest, by pensions to the German mistresses and by a liberal Civil List, he could be assured of the continued enjoyment of royal confidence.

Churchill's point about the Acts of Indemnity indicates how far the law was bent for political reasons. But it should not be thought that the Protestant influence, even demand on society, was any less significant. The legal difference, for example, between Catholic and Protestant was distinct. Catholics, for instance, were not allowed to be Members of Parliament nor were they allowed to vote. They were banned from keeping weapons, they were seen as Jacobites, therefore potential traitors. But Catholics shouldn't be confused with, say, Non-Conformists. The 1689 Toleration Act allowed Dissenters, under certain conditions, freedom to worship. They could do all the things Catholics could not do, the Acts of Indemnity allowed them to. An extract from the Act states that no one should be elected to any municipal office unless he has taken or will take the sacrament.

❖All and every member and members of any corporation within this kingdom, that were required to take the sacrament of the Lord's supper according to the rites of the Church of England within one year next before his election, shall be and are hereby confirmed in their several and respective offices, notwithstanding their omission to take the sacrament of the Lord's supper, and shall be indemnified, freed, and discharged of all incapacities, disabilities, forfeitures and penalties arising from such omission; and that none of their acts nor the acts not yet avoided of any who have been members of any corporation shall be questioned or avoided for or by reason of such omission; but that all such acts shall be and are hereby declared and enacted to be as good and effectual as if all and every such person and persons had taken the sacrament of the Lord's supper in the manner aforesaid.

At this stage the Royal court was still a hotchpotch of Hanoverians, although the King was learning to trust his English advisers, especially Walpole, which was wise because the advisers held the purse-strings, almost the only thing of interest to the new royalty. So keeping the King and his mistresses in line was not too difficult particularly because one of the King's mistresses, the Duchess of Kendal, became a little richer every time Walpole needed her to explain a difficult point of (his) view to the King. Communicating with the monarch himself was not easy because George I could not speak English.

It seems that George I and his Prime Minister communicated in Latin. Neither was proficient and their conversations rarely touched the heart of political and economic thought, but the relationship worked well enough and it reflected the apparently bland atmosphere of the Hanoverian court in London.

C❖Walpole's object was to stabilize the Hanoverian regime and the power of the Whig party within a generation. Taxation was low: the land tax, which was anxiously watched by the Tory squires, was reduced by economy to one shilling within each freehold. The National Debt decreased steadily, and an overhaul of the tariff and the reduction of many irksome duties stimulated and expanded trade. By an entente with France and by rigid non-intervention in European politics, Walpole avoided another war. He was the careful nurse of England's recovery after the national effort encouraged under Queen Anne. But men remembered the great age that had passed and scorned the drab days of George I. A policy of security, prosperity, and peace made small appeal to their hearts, and many were ready to attack the degeneration of politics at home and the futility of the English abroad.

Walpole may have solved the needs of the King and his mistresses, but the lives of the vast majority were uncertain. Just as none of Queen Anne's children had survived, so thousands upon thousands of ordinary mothers died in childbirth: as many as 20% of babies died in their first year; one-third died before the age of five. In some parts of London fewer than one-third of the youngsters reached the age of six.

There were then about 6.7 million people living in England, Wales and Scotland. By the end of the century, that figure would be approximately 10.5 million. The increase in population reflected advances in medicine and the general well-being of the people. However, at the beginning of the eighteenth century, of those who survived childhood, life expectancy was thirty-five years. People died in what would now be called ordinary circumstances, not because there was some genetic reason for dying young. It wasn't a characteristic of the human race, especially the British people, to have short lives. Someone who did get through an epidemic or a war might well live to what, even now, would be called old age. It was simply that when people did fall ill they couldn't rely on medicine to cure the simplest of ailments. And so something like measles quickly became an epidemic. Also surgery was crude; there were no anaesthetics and, although alcohol may have helped the symptoms of pain, the results of shock could be death. This meant that more people were dying than were being born.

And in 1720 another, unexpected, epidemic appeared: cheap gin. Low taxes on alcohol and a freedom to distil, encouraged people to abandon beer for the much cheaper gin. It was, among the poor, a killer. And there's evidence to show that the gin epidemic was very much concentrated in London, where perhaps as many as one in ten were dying from drink.

Daniel Defoe claimed that because gin used much corn, the landed classes and the traders benefited from the fashion. Parliament took its time to do something about the problem but the solution was, after all, simple: tax gin out of the poor man or woman's grasp and send them back to ale – which medically, at least, was probably less harmful than the water. Defoe wondered if the traders minded either way, but he was their champion.

❖And by whom have the prodigious taxes been paid, the loans supplied, and money advanced upon all occasions? By whom are the Banks and Companies carried on? And on whom are the Customs and Excises levied? Has not the trade and tradesmen borne the burthen of the war? And do they not still pay four millions a year interest for the publick debts? On whom are the funds levied, and by whom the publick credit supported? Is not trade the inexhausted fund of all funds, and upon which all the rest depend?

And how wealthy are tradesmen in almost all the several parts of England, as well as London? How ordinary it is to see a tradesman go off the stage even from mere shopkeeping, with from £10,000–£40,000 estate to divide among his family? When, on the contrary, take the gentry in England from one end to the other, except a few here and there, what with excessive high living, which is of late grown so much into a disease, and the other circumstances of families, we find few families of the lower gentry, that is to say, from £600–£700 a year downwards, but they are in debt and in necessitous circumstances, and a great many of greater estates also.

The eighteenth-century class system was being reshaped. The trading classes were elevated. Walpole's first wife, Catherine, was the daughter of a timber merchant of Kent. Defoe describes the changes:

❖ The antient [sic] families are worn out by time and family misfortunes, and the estates possessed by a new race of tradesmen, grown up into families of gentry, and establish'd by the immense wealth, gain'd, as I may say, behind the counter; that is, in the shop, the warehouse, and the compting-house. The sons of tradesmen are adorn'd among the prime of the gentry, and the daughters of tradesmen adorned with ducal coronets, and seen riding in the coaches of the best of our nobility. Nay, many of our trading gentlemen refuse to be rated among the richest knighted, and content themselves with being known to be rated among the richest commoners in the nation.

And Defoe was well qualified to write about the changes in the class system. He understood every nuance of the London underclass. His father's name was Foe but Daniel changed it to Defoe in about 1703 – when he was in his early forties. His father was a butcher and he, Daniel Defoe, became a hosiery trader. He was also a Protestant.

Defoe joined Monmouth's rebellion against the Catholic James II and then signed for William of Orange's army in the Glorious Rebellion of 1688. He started pamphleteering and produced a notorious tract entitled, 'The Shortest Way With Dissenters'. But this wasn't just some popular diatribe. Defoe himself was a Dissenter, a Non-Conformist. He was illustrating what he saw as the farce of intolerance, as here:

❖ Trade is so far here from being inconsistent with a Gentleman, that in short trade in England makes Gentlemen, and has peopled this nation with Gentlemen. After a generation or two, the tradesmen's children, or at least their grand-children, come to be as good Gentlemen, Statesmen, Parlia-ment-men, Privy Counsellors, Judges, Bishops and Noblemen, as those of the highest birth and the most antient families. Thus the Earl of Haversham was originally a merchant. The late secretary Craggs was the son of a barber. The present Lord Castlemaine's father was a tradesman. The great grand-father of the present Duke of Bedford, the same.

We see the tradesmen of England, as they grow wealthy, coming everyday to the herald's office, to search for the Coats of Arms of their ancestors in order to paint them upon their coaches. It was said of a certain tradesman in London, that if he could not descend from the antient race of gentlemen, from which he came, he would begin a new race who should be as good Gentlemen as any that went before them.

Centuries earlier the aristocracy had emerged in English society, a class that assumed rights over others by birth. An aristocracy that spread from the family of monarchs. Here Defoe was concerned with a new aristocracy, a mass migration from the bottom up. But he disliked much of what he saw. He travelled about Britain observing the old order of the island. But he did so with the sharp sense of the successful tradesman he was and that his father had been before him. What he saw was the beginning of a new revolution, an industrial revolution. In the 1720s the development of science and a curiosity about things mechanical, coupled with the new opportunities for the trading people, mark the track towards the term 'industrial'. For instance, in agriculture – the largest industry in Britain at the time – until the eighteenth-century farmers scattered seed by hand. In 1701, a man called Jethro Tull invented the wheeled seed drill. And because he did so, corn, for example, began to grow in rows. And the gap between those rows needed to be weeded, so Tull developed a hoe drawn by a horse.

And travelling through Yorkshire – Defoe called it 'frightful country' – in the early 1720s, Defoe described the textile industry. This was possible, he said, because there was coal and fast running water. Even the villages were arranged to dig the coal and to catch the water to produce the cloth that the growing manufacturing masterclass and their markets demanded.

❖Having thus fire and water at every dwelling, there is no need to enquire why they dwell thus dispers'd upon the highest hills, the convenience of the manufacturers requiring it. Among the manufacturers' houses are likewise scattered an infinite number of cottages in which dwell the workmen which are employed, the women and children of whom are always busy carding, spinning, et cetera so that no hands being unemploy'd, all can gain bread, even from the youngest to the antient; hardly anything above four years old, but its hands are sufficient to itself.

If we knocked at the doors of the master manufacturers, we presently saw a house full of lusty fellows, some at the dye vat, some dressing cloths, some in the loom, some one thing, some another, all hard at work, and full employed upon the manufacture, and all seeming to have sufficient business.

Note this use of the word manufacture. It wasn't new. It had developed as a reference to the subject Defoe was describing: cloth making. And the place where all those lusty fellows worked was already called a factory. Originally the term was used for a place where traders worked for overseas markets. But by the 1700s the two words were acceptably joined: manufactory. And while Defoe travelled throughout England watching the ways of the new Hanoverian age, in London its protectors, Walpole and Townshend, were preparing for its next generation. At a distance the Prince of Wales also watched and waited. For the days of George I were now drawing to an end.

By the early 1700s the British monarchy had lost its sparkle. It was no longer the one element by which the nation could be governed. Furthermore, the monarchy had lost its Englishness, its Britishness. The line of kings and queens, albeit with Norman, Angevin, origins, was broken. The carefully developed responsibility of successive monarchs had been kingship – the promise to protect the people from invaders and lawmakers in return for the right to rule. When, in the past, a king or queen talked about 'My People' there was a sense of responsibility but most of all, identity. This essential part of kingship had disappeared. Now there was a German King on the throne who spoke little or no English and who cared little or nothing for his people. He was succeeded by his son who hated him, and who was unpopular with his people too, and who would sooner have been in Hanover.

And as identification with the monarchy waned, the British Protestants saw themselves as favoured, chosen, set aside for greatness by their Protestant ethic. The only people to be feared or scorned were Catholics. The Whigs were determined to stay in power and take every opportunity to denounce the Tories as Jacobites – and therefore promoters of a Catholic monarchy. The Whigs were becoming the ruling aristocracy. Against this background the Prime Minister, Robert Walpole, determined his threefold task of stabilizing the economy, the monarchy and the Whig party.

Old enemies reappeared, or tried to: one of them was Henry Bolingbroke, the Tory plotter against Marlborough who had gone into exile once George I became King. And new and rising politicians nibbled at power such as the arrogant and ambitious John Carteret; the one time ally of Walpole, William Pulteney, and the bland Henry Pelham and his brother, Tom Pelham-Holles, the first Duke of Newcastle. Walpole was careful to exclude from his circle those who threatened, and encourage those who could never do so.

C❖Bolingbroke had offered an alliance, but Walpole had refused to allow him to regain his place in the House of Lords. The younger Whigs, like Pulteney and Carteret, were too clever to be allowed to shine in Walpole's orbit. Nor could they weaken his hold on the House of Commons while he exercised the patronage of the Crown. There was no hope except to undermine his position with the King. A series of appeals to the German ladies [the King's mistresses] by flattery and cash followed. Walpole was always quicker in satisfying their cupidity than his opponents. The Parliamentary Opposition gathered round the Prince of Wales. It was the Hanoverian family tradition that father and son should be on the worst of terms, and the future George II was no exception. The government depended on the King; the Opposition looked to his son. All had an interest in the dynasty. But for the strong support of Caroline, Princess of Wales, Walpole would have been in serious danger.

In 1724, as Walpole dealt with the Cabinet threats to his administration, others found themselves in danger. One of the first to go was Carteret. At the start of the Walpole government, John Carteret had become a secretary of state. Townshend, Walpole's brother-in-law was, with Carteret, responsible for foreign policy – forerunners of the modern Foreign Secretary. But Carteret was a threat to Walpole and Townshend. The solution to the problem of Carteret was simple and hardly original: Ireland. A letter that has survived from Townshend to the Duke of Grafton, himself the Governor of Ireland, tells us a little of the politics of the eighteenth-century Cabinet reshuffle.

❖Your grace is so perfectly acquainted with the factions and divisions that have been for some time past among his Majesty's servants, and have so often lamented the mischiefs arising from such divisions, that you will not be surprised to hear that the King is at last come to some resolution of doing every thing in his power to put an end to them. The first instance his Majesty has given, is by removing Mister Treby from the war office, which he has this day displaced of to Mister Henry Pelham; and I believe the seals will be taken from my Lord Carteret in a day or two, and given to the Duke of New Castle [sic]. In that case, the King intends the Lord Chamberlain's place for your grace, and Ireland for Lord Carteret. As the post his Majesty designs for your grace is of great dignity, so you may depend, that your friends and humble servants will endeavour to render it as advantageous and easy in all respects as your grace can desire.

I send this by express, being desirous to give your grace the first notice of what is doing in these particulars, in which your grace is so much concern'd; but as I write this to yourself alone, must desire this may be an entire secret till the event is determined, of which your grace shall not fail to receive the earliest account possible. I am convinced that your grace is so well convinced of the necessity there was of removing Lord Carteret from the employment he was in, and of the impossibility there was of doing it without giving some considerable equivalent, that you are sensible his having the government of Ireland was in a manner unavoidable. The care his Majesty has taken in placing your grace so near his person will sufficiently convince the world that his taking away the government of Ireland from you at this time does not proceed from any disapprobation of your conduct.

Grafton did not suffer. And the next Duke, forty years on, became Prime Minister. Walpole balanced, as much as he could, the ambitions of the King, the Government and Parliament. The Government needed the King. The King needed the Government. Both needed Parliament. But there were factions even at court. And at the end of 1717 George I banished his son, the Prince of Wales, from St James's Palace. The Prince, with his wife, Caroline of Ansbach, established their own Court. And this wasn't ignored by the politicians: Walpole and Townshend were frequent visitors. This was the period before Walpole's return and his appointment as Prime Minister. But it laid the way for at least a token reconciliation, later, between King and Prince. The King understood that he needed his son to succeed him but most of all, he needed Walpole. And the most obvious sign that George I could, and would, rely on Walpole was the way in which the politician had quietly demonstrated, with all the guile of an elegant courtier, that he would save the embarrassment and the dignity of the court on the occasion of the collapse of the South Sea Company. It is worth going back a few paces in the story to read the letter Walpole sent to the King because its contents explain why George I was encouraged to trust Walpole.

❖A due and compassionate regard is to be shown to the losses of private men, and all that I conceive can be expected is to give some ease and relief to the present unhappy circumstances, in which great numbers are now involved; but it seems to me impossible, so far to repair every man's losses, that a great many will not still remain considerable losers. An attempt to raise the stock to a higher value than it can be supported at would only involve a new set of persons in the misfortunes, that others at present labour under, and expose the publick to the great loss that will be sustained by foreigners selling out at high prices, and exporting our gold and silver. And what I desire your Majesty may be observed thro' this scheme is, that I take everything as I found it, and do nothing to alter any man's circumstances, but by an accession of profit, from the Bank and India Company, and by an impartial distribution of the whole, as it now appears, from the public transactions of the company; and have carefully avoided either to enforce or release any publick or private contract of obligation, or to ease or relieve any one sort of adventurers, at the loss or expense of another.

This was a measured, resourceful and realistic solution. Where others were promising easy ways out, Walpole could be trusted to keep the country, and especially the monarch (in other words his mistresses), from any further embarrassment. And so attempts by Walpole's enemies to distract the King from the Prime Minister's methods of political management were unlikely to succeed. And Walpole's demands that all members of the Cabinet must totally obey him were, for the most part, successful. What he couldn't control were events abroad, although he tried, by distancing the Cabinet from them.

Austria and Spain, once enemies, joined forces under the Treaty of Vienna in the spring of 1725. Spain was demanding the return of Gibraltar from Great Britain, and the Austrian Ostend Company was a direct competitor of the East India Company. Then Russia joined Austria.

There was a strong difference of opinion between Walpole and his trusted, but not always bright, brother-in-law, Townshend, at this point. Townshend quickly organized, too quickly according to Walpole, a new alliance of Britain, Hanover, France and Prussia. To Walpole this was entirely against the delicate balance he was trying to maintain. Parliament didn't want to go to war but here was Townshend bringing together an anti-Austria cabal in the name of the House of Hanover. It never came to war, but it could have.

The ordinary people weren't particularly preoccupied with matters in Europe, but rather more with matters at home, in particular with a new tax. For centuries the nation had grumbled about the burden of taxes and rioted against the levying of them: they were usually imposed to raise money for wars. But now there were riots against local levies, toll taxes. The roads of Britain were in a sad state of repair. The roads that the Romans had built 1300 years earlier were in better condition than roads built much more recently, because those who remained after the Romans were not builders. And, of course, there had been a massive increase in traffic.

The tenant farmers, the most frequent users of the roads, had to pay the road surveyors and, in eighteenth-century England, national attention to road building and repair was in its infancy. So, to build and repair the roads the people had to pay tolls. Daniel Defoe thought the toll taxes worked well.

❖ Turn pikes or toll bars have been set up on the several great roads of England, beginning at London, and proceeding thro' almost all those dirty deep roads in the Midland Counties especially; at which turn pikes all carriages, droves of cattle and travellers on horseback are oblig'd to pay an easy toll; that is to say, a horse a penny, a coach three pence, a cart four pence, at some six to eight pence, a wagon six pence, in some a shilling. Cattle pay by the score, or by the herd, in some places more. But in no place is it thought a burthen that ever I met with, the benefit of a good road abundantly making amends for that little charge the travellers are put to at the turn pikes.

If that sounds like a department of transport leaflet, then it's as well to remember that not everyone agreed with Defoe, especially those who had to pay. And in 1726 the people rioted. It didn't get them very far. The turn pike had first appeared in the 1660s and from now until the end of the eighteenth century it was to be the main means of improving the road system. In the 1700s more than 1000 turn pike acts were passed. Britain was beginning its great industrial journey.

CHAPTER THIRTY-FOUR

1727–1746

❖

At three o'clock in the afternoon on 14 June 1727 a messenger arrived from the Continent at a house in Chelsea with news for the Prime Minister, Robert Walpole. He in turn hurried to Richmond to the King's son, the Prince of Wales, and his wife, Caroline of Ansbach. The news was the news they had all been waiting for: George, the first Hanoverian King of Great Britain and Ireland, was dead. George Augustus, Elector of Hanover, Prince of Wales, became George II. That night the new King made his solemn declaration to his people.

❖The sudden and unexpected death of the King, my dearest father, has filled my heart with so much concern and surprise, that I am at a loss how to express myself upon this great and melancholy occasion; but my love and affection to this country, from my knowledge and experience of you, makes me resolve cheerfully to undergo all difficulties for the sake and good of my people.

In reality the new King detested everything about the British and Britain. And he was not some latter day Prince Hal, impatient for the power the crown would bring. That kind of power no longer existed, and he knew it – which was part of his frustration. By the end of the seventeenth century the power of the monarch had been limited by the laws of a Parliament which was not inclined to surrender those laws. Now the Crown's greatest power was patronage. Some might argue that this had always been so. But this wasn't patronage by brute force; it was the King's constitutional right to control who got what job in Government, in Parliament, and in the Church. Thus the new King continued to need the Government, the Government needed the King, and they both needed Parliament.

And Walpole now had an ally at court in the new Queen, the very clever Caroline of Ansbach. But Walpole was not a favourite of the new King who promptly sacked him and offered his job to Sir Spencer Compton. But only Walpole and his powerful political army of Whigs could maintain the balance of power between monarch, government and Parliament. There was powerful opposition in Parliament, and within days Walpole was back.

But it was the Queen, Caroline, who actually persuaded the King to retreat so quickly. She understood what was happening, and convinced her husband to retrieve Walpole. The new King himself was short-tempered, precise and determined to use the powers he had. He wanted to know who was being appointed to what and made sure that he approved. John Hervey, who for ten years was Vice Chamberlain, described George II and his views.

❖No English or even French cook could dress a dinner; no confectioner set out a dessert; no English player could act; no English coachman could drive or English jockey ride, nor were any English horses fit to be ridden; no Englishman knew how to come into a room, nor any English woman how to dress herself, nor were there any diversions in England, public or private, nor any man or woman in England whose conversation was to be borne – the one as he said, talking of nothing but their dull politics, and the other nothing but their ugly clothes. Whereas at Hanover, all these things were in the utmost perfection.

In truth he hated the English, looked upon them all as King-killers and republicans, grudged them their riches as well as their liberty, thought them all overpaid, and said to Lady Sundon one day as she was waiting at dinner, just after he returned from Germany, that he was forced to distribute his favours here very differently from the manner in which he bestowed them at Hanover; that there he rewarded people for doing their duty and serving him well, but that here he was obliged to enrich people for being rascals, and buy them not to cut his throat.

John Hervey also described the Queen, Caroline of Ansbach.

❖The Queen did not always think in a different style of the English, though she kept her thoughts more to herself than the King, as being more prudent, more sensible, and more mistress of her passions; yet even she could not entirely disguise these sentiments. . . . I have heard her at different times speak with great indignation against assertors of the people's rights; have heard her call the King, not without some despite, the humble servant of Parliament, the pensioner of his people and a puppet of sovereignty, that was forced to go to them for every shilling he wanted, that was obliged to court those who were always abusing him, and could do nothing of himself.

The King was a constitutionally appointed monarch whose first qualification was his Protestantism and his second, an agreement to rule within the boundaries drawn by legislators. For example, the 1689 Bill of Rights that followed the Glorious Revolution may not have controlled the prerogatives of the Crown, but it most certainly set the ideals of so-called Parliamentary supremacy over the sovereign. But the quarrel was not simply between Government, Parliament and Crown. The in-fighting at court was, as Churchill reflects, and as Robert Walpole well knew, nothing compared with that in government. Walpole's policy was to sort out the problems within the nation and avoid the foreign adventures, especially those dear to the King. Those especially would be difficult to get through Parliament.

C❖There had always been a danger that discontented, ambitious members of his Government would play on the King's interest in Hanoverian affairs. They would espouse the causes dear to the royal heart – the ancestral home, the great Continental scene, the Grand Alliance, the wars of Marlborough. This lure of European politics was too much for several of the men around Walpole. He meant to do as little as possible; to keep the peace, to stay in office, to juggle with men, to see the years roll by. But others responded to more lively themes. Walpole was forced to quarrel. His own brother-in-law, Charles Townshend, was dismissed. . . .

Townshend went in 1730. He retreated to his Norfolk farm, developed a new system of root crop rotation and earned himself the nickname 'Turnip' Townshend. He was discarded for being too adventurous in foreign affairs. Walpole took over his portfolio.

C❖[Walpole] then entered into close co-operation with a man of limited intelligence and fussy nature, but of vast territorial and electoral wealth – Thomas Pelham-Holles, Duke of Newcastle. Newcastle became Secretary of State because, as Walpole said, he himself 'had experienced the trouble that a man of parts gave in that office'. By his enemies, Walpole was now mockingly called the 'Prime Minister' – for this honourable title originated [as a term of abuse just as had the terms 'Whigs' and 'Tories']. The chances of a successful Opposition seemed to be gone for ever. With every weapon of wit and satire at their command, the brilliant young men who gathered round Bolingbroke [now returned from exile] and the surviving mistress of George I, the Duchess of Kendal, could make no dint on the dull, corrupt, reasonable solidarity of the administration.

Henry Bolingbroke was to remain a leading figure in the Opposition to Walpole's administration. He got his estates back in 1725, but not a place in government. His home became a gathering point for opposition figures, both political and literary, including Alexander Pope and Jonathan Swift. Swift, the Irish clergyman, pamphleteer, and author of *Gulliver's Travels*, was also a marshal of Irish patriots, a Tory, and therefore against Walpole.

C❖Walpole proposed an excise on wines and tobacco, to be gathered by Revenue officers in place of a duty at the ports. The measure was aimed at the vast smuggling that rotted this source of the revenue. Every weapon at their command was used by the Opposition. Members of Parliament were deluged with letters. Popular ballads and pamphlets were thrust under doors. National petitions and public meetings were organized throughout the land. Doleful images were raised of the tyranny of the Excisemen. . . . The storm swamped the country and alarmed the Government majority in the House of Commons. . . . Walpole's majority dwindled; his supporters deserted him like sheep straying through an open gate. Defeated by one of the most unscrupulous campaigns in English history, Walpole withdrew his Excise reform . . . [but] the Opposition snatched no permanent advantage.

Bolingbroke now despaired of ever achieving political power and, in 1735, he retired once more to France.

A major cause of the Opposition's failure lay in Bolingbroke himself. He had not reformed: he was still the unprincipled rascal so scorned by Harley and Queen Anne. It was discovered that he had been passing political intelligence to the French ambassador, which, considering the popular belief that France could at any time support a Jacobite rising, was unwise. Even worse was to come when it was known that he had taken money from the French to support the Opposition cause against Walpole. But Walpole's skill as a political manager, his pragmatism and shrewdness served him well. Bolingbroke and his friends could never agree among themselves for long enough to sustain the pressure against Walpole and, no matter how much they mocked him as the 'Prime' Minister, that's exactly what Walpole was.

It's generally thought that Caroline of Ansbach, George II's wife, was Walpole's strongest ally. Sometimes she might suggest policy to the King which Walpole couldn't put forward without sparking one of their not infrequent quarrels. George II and his Prime Minister could never agree the constitutional restraints imposed on the monarchy by Parliament. Worse the King often, especially in matters of foreign policy, tried to go against Parliament and always had to give in – which didn't improve his political temper. So Walpole spent much time trying to placate the King, his ultimate patron.

But if the Queen, Walpole's ally, died and the young Prince of Wales, who was no friend to his father and mother, set himself against Walpole and came out for the Opposition, then Walpole's authority might well be weakened.

C❖Those Whigs who were out of office grouped themselves round Frederick, the new Prince of Wales. He in his turn became the hope of the Opposition, but all they could produce was an increased Civil List for this ungifted creature. Their arrogance showed Walpole that people were growing tired of his colourless rule. One of his sharpest critics was a young Cornet of Horse named William Pitt.

In 1736 Pitt was twenty-eight. He was a member of a group known as Cobham's Cubs, the young followers of one of Walpole's critics, Viscount Cobham. He'd become part of the so-called Leicester House set. Leicester House was where the Prince of Wales held court. Walpole, who could not stand any public opposition, made sure Pitt lost his commission in Viscount Cobham's regiment of dragoons. But within a year, Pitt had a salary of £400 a year as the Prince of Wales's Groom of the Bedchamber. Pitt's polemics and his rhetoric excited the nation. Here was a young man to watch and Walpole knew it.

The next year, 1737, the King and Queen once more fell out with their son, Frederick, whom they disliked intensely. This time, Walpole was not able to bring about a royal reconciliation. A few months later his ally, Queen Caroline, died. She had been one of the few who understood the advantages of his tight political management and the importance to the King of maintaining his support.

C❖At long last the Opposition discerned the foundation of Walpole's ascendancy, namely, the avoidance of any controversy which might stir the country as a whole. . . . Supreme in the narrow circle of the Commons and the Court, Walpole's name angered many and inspired no one. The country was bored. It rejected squalid, peaceful prosperity. Commercial wealth advanced rapidly. Trade figures swelled. Still the nation was dissatisfied. . . . All that was keen and adventurous in the English character writhed under this sordid, sleepy Government. Sometimes whole sessions of the House of Commons rolled by without a division.

All that was needed to destroy the mechanism of Walpole's rule was an issue that would stir the country, and which would in its turn stampede the quiescent, half-squared Members of Parliament into a hostile vote against the Minister.

What the British wanted was a fight, but Walpole began his ministry by avoiding confrontation. He had smoothed over the financial scandals of the South Sea Company rather than risking the outcome of a Parliamentary inquiry. He'd withdrawn a patent for making halfpennies to be distributed in Ireland, not because it was a bad idea, but because there was well-organized public resentment of it. And he pulled back from excise on wines and tobaccos.

More recently Captain John Porteous, the Commander of the Edinburgh City Guard, had fired on a crowd watching the public execution of four smugglers. Porteous was sentenced to death, reprieved, and then strung up by the Scottish mob. London called the Scots judges to the bar of the House, humiliated them, and proposed fines on the City. The protest was loud, and not only from Scotland. Walpole backed down, again.

The prosperity of Britain suggests that Walpole's eighteenth-century pragmatism worked. But in foreign relations his belief that all disputes should be settled by negotiation, rather than after hopeless fighting, was perhaps naive. What Walpole, for all his skills, didn't understand was that France did not see things his way. France believed that the differences of France, Spain, Austria, and Britain could be settled only by war. France was right. By the mid-1730s, Austria (Britain's ally) was fighting Spain and France (also Britain's allies). And very shortly Britain too would be at war. By the late 1720s the British who, in 1714, had forced the French and the Spanish to make trading concessions under the Treaties of Utrecht at the end of the War of Spanish Succession, had turned these limited treaty concessions into a complete trading invasion of the Spanish-American colonies. It amounted to economic piracy. But by this time Spain was once again stronger and started to take action.

C❖ . . . when the Spanish Government at last began to reorganize and extend its colonial government, English ships trading unlawfully in the Spanish seas were stopped and searched by the Spanish coastguards. . . . Profits were high, and merchants in London forced Walpole to challenge the right of search.

Walpole had avoided every possibility of overseas confrontation. He saw no future in getting involved in conflicts which would unbalance the British domestic economy and political system. And also, by this point, Britain believed unswervingly in its Protestant right and these were Catholics interrupting British passages on the high seas. In 1731 Walpole decided negotiation was the best way to resolve the matter. But also in 1731 a certain British captain had his ear cut off by a Spaniard. Or so he claimed.

C❖ . . . the Opposition in Parliament had opened a broad attack on the Government's negotiations with Spain. . . . A captain trading with the Spanish possessions, one Jenkins, was brought before the House of Commons to produce his ear in a bottle and to maintain that it had been cut off by Spanish coastguards when his ship was searched. 'What did you do?' he was asked. 'I commended my soul to God and my cause to my country', was the answer put in his mouth by the Opposition. Jenkins's ear caught the popular imagination and became the symbol of agitation. Whether it was in fact his own ear or whether he had lost it in a seaport brawl remains uncertain, but the power of this shrivelled object was immense.

By January 1739, Walpole had achieved at least an outline agreement, the Convention of Prado, but it would not save Britain from war. Nor would it put off the so-called Patriots. They were a Whig Opposition group which included Pulteney, a former ally of Walpole's, as well as Carteret, whom Walpole had dispatched to Ireland, Viscount Cobham, and the young William Pitt.

C❖Without troubling to study the terms of the preliminary agreement with Spain, the Opposition drove their attack home. As one of Walpole's supporters wrote, 'The Patriots were resolved to damn it before they knew a word of it, and to influence the people against it, which they have done with great success.' And as the British envoy in Madrid, Benjamin Keene, put it to Walpole months later, 'The Opposers make the war.' . . . Walpole . . . yielded ground slowly and steadily. On October 19, 1739 war was declared. The bells rang out from the London churches and the crowds thronged the streets shouting. Looking down upon the jubilant mob, the Prime Minister remarked sourly, 'They are ringing their bells now, but soon they will be wringing their hands.' . . . By sure degrees, in the confusion and mismanagement which followed, Walpole's power . . . slipped from him. The operations of the ill-managed Fleet failed. The one success, the capture of Portobello, on the isthmus of Panama, was achieved by Admiral Vernon, the hero of the Opposition.

Incidentally, the 'Hero of the Opposition', Admiral Vernon, was the originator of one of the most famous expressions among British tipplers. Vernon used to wear a boat cloak made from a fabric of mohair and coarse wool stiffened with resin gum. This material was called grogram so Vernon's sailors called him Old Grogram. Old Grogram ordered the sailors' rum to be watered down and after that the rum ration was known as 'Grog'.

And as sailors were raising tots to their admiral and ruling the seas, the people at home were raising their cheap gin pots and singing perhaps the most famous song of all British time. James Thomson had written a masque, called *Alfred* – Alfred the Great, the father of the navy. And the opening lines fitted perfectly the jingoism of the year 1740.

> *When Britain first, at heaven's command,*
> *Arose from out of the azure main,*
> *This was the charter of the land,*
> *And guardian angels sung this strain:*
> *Rule Britannia, rule the waves;*
> *Britons never will be slaves.*

Note that it is not 'Britannia rules the waves' as is sometimes sung in the Albert Hall, but 'Rule Britannia, rule the waves'. It was not a statement, it was a command from heaven that Britain must rule. It was a declaration that Protestant Britons were chosen by heaven to rule. This is a small point, but it should not be ignored.

In spite of Vernon's success at Portobello, the war, now known as the War of Jenkins's Ear, was badly managed by Walpole. He was a manager of peace, not of military conflict, and his Parliamentary support was deserting him. In 1741 the Opposition had rarely felt so sure of itself. On 13 February the MP for Worcester, Samuel Sandys, rose in the Commons to speak for the motion to remove Walpole from office.

❖According to our constitution, we have no sole and prime minister: but it is publicly known that this minister, having obtained sole influence over all our public counsels, has not only assumed the sole direction of all public affairs, but has got every officer of state removed that would not follow his direction. . . . He has made a blind submission to his direction the only ground to hope for any honours or preferments. Has not this minister himself not only confessed it, but boasted of it? Has he not said, and in this House too, that he would be a pitiful fellow of a minister who did not displace any officer that opposed his measure in Parliament?

It was in this same Parliamentary debate that Walpole declared that he was not the 'Prime' Minister.

❖While I unequivocally deny that I am the sole and prime minister, and that to my influence and direction all the measures of government must be attributed, yet I will not shrink from the responsibility which attaches to the post I have the honour to hold. And should, during the long period in which I have sat upon this bench, any one step taken by government be proved to be either disgraceful or disadvantageous to the nation, I am ready to hold myself accountable.

Once again Walpole outwitted his opponents and the House voted for him. But it was his last victory. In February 1742, the first Prime Minister of Britain, Sir Robert Walpole, resigned. In the vanguard of the Opposition to Walpole was the Prince of Wales, the heir to the throne. The Prince had left George II's Court in the summer of 1737 and set up his own Court. Now he and the other political dissenters, including Pitt, attacked.

C❖The Prince of Wales spent lavishly in buying up seats, and his campaign, managed by Thomas Pitt, brother of William, brought twenty-seven

Cornish seats over to the Opposition. The electoral influence of the Scottish earls counted against Walpole, and when the Members returned to Westminster, his Government was defeated on an electoral petition (contested returns were in those days decided by the House on purely Party lines) and resigned. . . . Sir Robert had governed England for twenty-one years. During the last days before his fall he sat for hours on end, alone and silent, brooding over the past in Downing Street. He was the first Chief Minister to reside at Number Ten. . . . He had built up a powerful organization, fed and fattened on Government patronage. He had supervised the day-to-day administration of the country, unhampered by royal interference. The sovereign had ceased, after 1714, to preside in person over the Cabinet, save on exceptional occasions. . . . [But] his [Walpole's] obstinate monopoly of political power in the Commons had put all men of talent against him, and in the end his policy enabled the Opposition to arouse the public opinion he had so assiduously lulled. He was the first great House of Commons man in British history, and if he had resigned before the war with Spain, he might have been called the most successful.

In the record of Parliament produced by William Cobbett there's a passage that gives some insight into Walpole's feelings and those of the King, George II. The Hanoverians had relied on Walpole for sound advice as well as sufficient funds to maintain more than a modest lifestyle. Although the record is compiled some time after the event, it is apparently based on the memories of those who were there. And it certainly supports the notion that Walpole had intended to survive by whatever means he could find.

❖He retired unwillingly and slowly; no shipwrecked pilot ever clung to the rudder of a sinking vessel with greater pertinacity than he did to the helm of state; he did not relinquish his post until he was driven from it by the desertion of his followers and the clamours of the public.

'I must inform you,' he observes in a letter to the Duke of Devonshire, 'that the panic was so great among – what shall I call them? – my own friends, that they all declared that my retiring was become absolutely necessary, as the only means to carry on the public business with honour and success.'

The interview, when he took leave of the King, was highly affecting. On kneeling down to kiss his hand, the King burst into tears, the ex-minister was so moved with that instance of regard, that he continued for some time in that posture; and the King was so touched, that he was unable to raise him from the ground. When at length he rose, the King testified his regret for the loss of so faithful a counsellor, expressed his gratitude for his long services, and his hopes of receiving advice on important occasions.

And certainly Walpole was not finished with politics and the manipulation of power. He was created Earl of Orford and then set about making sure that the Whigs continued to rule and that the weaknesses in the Opposition were exploited. And he had a personal battle to fight. During his two decades of office, Walpole had made his fortune. This point is usually dismissed as unimportant to the story of Britain's first Prime Minister. But when Walpole was accused of making money out of being head of the government, men who had expected reward for their Opposition and didn't get it were the first to demand Walpole's prosecution. The bargaining was hardly for the good of the nation as Cobbett describes.

❖Chesterfield was disappointed that he was not made secretary of state; Waller was irritated at not being chancellor of the exchequer, and thought the situation of a lord of the treasury beneath his acceptance. Cobham, though restored to a regiment and appointed a member of the Cabinet, aspired to a far greater share of power; and the Grenvilles, Lyttleton, Pitt and Doddington were highly dissatisfied that they had no share in the new administration. While the posts remained unfilled, and the members of the opposition conceived hopes that an arrangement might take place in their favour, the great body continued apparently united; but when suspicions began to be formed of a separate negotiation, and the places of secretary of state and chancellor of the exchequer were disposed of, without the general concurrence, murmurs and discontents succeeded and a schism took place.

Most at Westminster were convinced that political patronage, paying off men (and not always the brightest) with high and medium office, was dangerous but nevertheless the best way to stay in power. Everyone did it, and everyone made money out of office, especially the nobility. Walpole wasn't the only one who understood the workings of political corruption. At the time, not many more than 1000 rich people influenced the governance of Britain. Little wonder few would have questioned Henry Fielding's definition of a Nobody as, 'All the people in Britain except about twelve hundred'.

About 25% of the peerage had some form of official office and with them came salaries and pensions. Walpole, for example, had given his son Horace three sinecures. He was one of the Tellers of the Exchequer (that was worth £1200 a year alone); also he was Comptroller of the Pipe and Clerk of Escheats. An escheat was land or property that was supposed to revert to the Crown, and there were profits and percentages to be made from those transactions. A secretary of state could make perhaps £7000–£8000 a year. Walpole had been Paymaster General and had made his fortune from it. Commissions (backhanders might be a twentieth-century description) from contractors and suppliers alone could set up the office-holder for life. One Lord Chancellor, when fined

£30,000 for misappropriating government funds, paid it within six weeks and still made a 60% profit. But many of them, probably all of them, needed the money. For example, it cost Walpole £15 a day in candles to light his home, Houghton Hall. He spent £30 a week on wine.

None of this was the concern of the King. He simply needed a government capable of supporting (that meant with funds) his view that the real dangers lay not in the counting houses of Westminster, but in the ambitions of the new order in Europe. George II's particular concern was with his nephew Frederick, now King of Prussia. Frederick's accession made George II extremely nervous. He was still a Hanoverian and Frederick could well decide to invade the King's estates. And George had no doubts about Frederick's ambitions because he knew him very well.

This then was the atmosphere as Lord Wilmington became Prime Minister instead of the man who would have been a safer choice, Henry Pelham, supported as later he would be, by his wealthy brother, the Duke of Newcastle. Wilmington, now an earl, was the Sir Spencer Compton to whom George II had offered the job of chief minister instead of Walpole and who was immediately opposed in Parliament so that Walpole was almost instantly back in power. Wilmington was quite incompetent.

C❖George II turned for help and advice to the Pelhams' rival, Lord Carteret. Under Walpole, Carteret had shared the fate of all men who were clever enough to be dangerous, and was dismissed to the Lord Lieutenancy of Ireland. Sir Robert's fall restored him to public life at Westminster. By supporting the King's German interests he was able to outbid the Pelhams for the royal favour. Carteret wanted Hanover and England to preserve and promote a balance of power in Europe. He thought he held the clue to the Continental maze. He spoke German and was an intimate of the sovereign. He discerned the growing Prussian menace, and realized that a Franco-Prussian alliance could create measureless dangers for Britain. In 1742 he was appointed a secretary of state. To meet the combination of France, Spain and Frederick the Great, he negotiated a treaty with Maria Theresa. Forty years earlier Britain had supported her father, when he was Archduke Charles, in his attempt to win the throne of Spain. Now the Island was again allied with the House of Austria against France. It was not for the last time.

Carteret may have been called brilliant. Certainly he was the power behind Wilmington. But he was an individualist, he cared little for the detail of political management which was necessary to hold together all factions at Westminster, especially if Britain was once again to enter the larger stage of Continental warfare. But the King, George II, wanted none of the inhibitions of the Parliamentarians he detested. He wanted to be at the war. And during the following year, 1744, he'd mark his place in the history of these islands as the last British monarch to lead his forces into battle. In 1740 the War of the Austrian Succession began.

C❖Britain had expected to fight naval and colonial campaigns in Spanish waters and on the Spanish Main. Instead she found herself engaged in a Continental war. Two royal deaths in 1740 set the conflict in motion. East of the Elbe, the rising kingdom of Prussia acquired a new ruler. Frederick II, later called the Great, ascended his father's throne. He inherited a formidable army which he fretted to use. It was his ambition to expand his scattered territories and weld them into the strongest state in Germany. Military gifts and powers of leadership, a calculating spirit and utter ruthlessness, were his in equal portion. Almost immediately he had the chance to put them to the test. In October the Habsburg Emperor Charles VI died, leaving his broad domains, though not his Imperial title, to his daughter Maria Theresa. The Emperor had extracted solemn guarantees from all the powers of Europe that they would recognize her accession in Austria, Hungary, Bohemia, and the southern Netherlands. But these meant nothing to Frederick. He attacked and seized the Austrian province of Silesia, which lay to the south of his own territories. France, ever jealous of the Habsburgs, encouraged and supported him. Thus Europe was plunged into what is termed the War of the Austrian Succession.

The House of Habsburg was one of the oldest European royal families. The name comes from Habsburg Castle which was built in Switzerland by the Bishop of Strasbourg. That was in the eleventh century at about the same time that the Normans were building in England. By the late thirteenth century, the then Count of Habsburg, one Rodolph, became the Holy Roman Emperor. And the last male in that line was Maria Theresa's father, Charles. However that wasn't the end of the Habsburgs because Maria Theresa and the Duke of Lorraine, her husband, began the modern line of the family, the last of whom (another Charles) abdicated as Emperor in 1918. Britain engaged in the War of the Austrian Succession because it had a treaty with Austria, and the fear that her old enemies, the French, might gain the Austrian Netherlands was worrying for the Hanoverian George II. It would bring the French too close to home.

But monarchs have never had an easy time raising money for wars other than when they were already winning them, or there was about to be an invasion. In the opening months of this one Walpole had resigned, and the not-very-bright Lord Wilmington was nominally Prime Minister. But the leading figure was Lord Carteret, undoubtedly bright, but quite unwilling to involve himself in the detail of policy-making needed to execute foreign and military policy. Carteret wanted power and he felt that, with the King's backing, he could sweep others along with him. Walpole had known all this and had, at one time, got rid of Carteret across the Irish Sea as Lieutenant Governor. But Walpole was gone.

C❖Carteret, to his misfortune, lacked both the personal position and the political following to put his decisions to good effect. He was an individualist, with no gift for party organization, depending essentially and only upon the favour of the Crown. Hostility soon gathered against him in Parliament. Foremost among his critics was William Pitt, Member for the ancient but uninhabited borough of Old Sarum.

Old Sarum was what was called a rotten, or pocket borough. It was nothing more than a bump in the ground. But a landowner who owned one of these so-called boroughs could nominate an MP and, because the deed to the land was in the landowner's pocket, so the MP, or the constituency, was in his pocket. Hence pocket borough. Pitt came from a wealthy family and was of independent means, and mind. Pitt was part of the Prince of Wales's alternative court which consisted, largely, of disaffected Whigs including Viscount Cobham, Lyttleton and the Grenvilles.

C❖In close political association with this group of disaffected Whigs, Pitt began his political career. He played a noisy part in the Opposition campaign for war against Spain, . . . but the main attack fell upon the extension of the war to Europe. The Opposition proclaimed it a disgraceful and irresponsible subservience to Hanoverian influences.

This was always a good tactic. Most people understood that George II, like his father, disliked his people, wished to be in Hanover most of the time (and much of it, was) and saw military power as one of the few advantages to being King of Britain.

C❖Pitt made a withering speech against the subsidies proposed for raising Hanoverian troops, which gained him the lasting displeasure of the King. In another speech, he declared that if Walpole had 'betrayed the interest of his country by his pusillanimity, our present Minister sacrifices it by his quixotism'.

Nevertheless, the war existed and Britain had obligations and George wanted to protect his Hanoverian borders, but the Prussians and the French threatened to invade if he did. George agreed to remain neutral for twelve months so Maria Theresa fought on alone – she had to. She was defending her right to the

Austrian throne which the old Emperor, her father, had stated was hers when he changed the so-called Pragmatic Sanction to favour her right to the throne on his death.

But once the period of neutrality was ended George got his money and his permission from Parliament and, under the guise of being Maria Theresa's auxiliaries (today they'd be called military advisers or assistance) 30,000 British soldiers went to the Continent. Their army was known as the Pragmatic Army. So the King had his way and was soon to make a lasting entry in the history books.

C❖In the spring of 1743 the King himself, accompanied by his younger son the Duke of Cumberland, left England to take part in the campaign. The Allied forces were concentrated upon the River Main, in the hope of separating the French from their German allies. Bavaria too had taken advantage of the turmoil to attack Queen Maria Theresa, and the Bavarian Elector, with French backing, had been declared Holy Roman Emperor.

The elector had already put forward his wife as Queen instead of Maria Theresa and historically the Bavarian case was strong.

C❖In the Empire, this was the first departure from the Habsburg line in 300 years. It proved to be a brief interlude. A superior French army, under Marshal Noailles, lay in the neighbourhood, with the object of cutting off his enemy from their bases in Holland and destroying them in open battle. At the village of Dettingen, near Aschaffenburg, the forces came into conflict. The French cavalry, impatient at delays, charged the Allied left wing. King George [II]'s horse bolted, but, dismounting, and sword in hand, he led the Hanoverian and British infantry into action against the French dragoons. They broke and fled, and many were drowned in trying to cross the Main. The French foot failed to retrieve the day, and after four hours' fighting, the Allies were in possession of the field. They had lost barely 2000 men, the French twice as many. For the last time, an English king had fought at the head of his troops.

This 'English' King's only interest was protecting his Hanoverian interests. Furthermore, the battle was poorly managed. The reason George II's horse bolted was that the inexperienced British troops, who had no idea how far a musket ball would carry, started to open fire before they were supposed to and scared the beast into flight. However the French Army, in spite of its mistakes and sometimes indifferent morale, was considered a formidable opposition and the British Army had not been tried like this for three decades.

C❖The campaign subsided. There was bickering between the English and the Hanoverians and much inactivity. The Battle of Dettingen raised a brief enthusiasm in London, but opinion slowly hardened against the continuance of a major European war. England was again the head and the paymaster of another Grand Alliance. A new Bourbon Family Compact had been signed between France and Spain, and Secret Service agents reported Jacobite intrigues in Paris. There was talk in London of a French invasion. Dutch troops were hastily brought over to Sheerness. At the end of 1744, Carteret, now Lord Granville, was driven from office.

Carteret couldn't have been expected to last much longer. Wilmington, the Prime Minister, had died the previous year and Wilmington had been his patron. But now, in 1745, Britain needed a strong political leader. Henry Pelham became the nation's third Prime Minister. Walpole had liked him and Walpole's first rule of government was to safeguard his own position. This more or less confirms that Pelham was never blatantly ambitious. He was quiet, industrious and efficient. But the King still took a great deal of notice of Carteret and his friend Pulteney, the Earl of Bath, because they supported his military ambitions. And it was very easy for them to undermine Pelham. Pelham was a Walpole man and Walpole had got rid of Carteret. So Pelham was not in complete control when he became Prime Minister.

The nation was still at war and the King had made his third son, the then twenty-four-year-old Duke of Cumberland, captain general of the armies.

C❖This young martinet had created the illusion of military capacity by his bravery at Dettingen. His conduct at the head of the Army was, said one of his officers, 'outrageously and shockingly military'. He had to face the most celebrated soldier of the day, Marshal Saxe. The French Army concentrated against the barrier fortress line, the familiar battleground of Marlborough's wars, now held by the Dutch. Having masked [covered] Tournai, Saxe took up a strong position centring upon the village of Fontenoy, near the Mons road. Cumberland drew up his army in battle order, and marched it under fire to within fifty paces of the French Army. He was outnumbered by nearly two to one. . . . The English advanced, and at thirty paces the French fired. The murderous fusillade did not halt the Allied infantry, and they drove the enemy from their positions. For hours the French cavalry tried to break the Allied columns, and, watching the Irish Brigade of the French Army sweeping into action, Cumberland exclaimed, 'God's curse on the laws that made those men our enemies.' . . . At the fall of darkness, he withdrew in perfect order down the road to Brussels.

Actually this was a retreat. Withdrawal is what generals tell their men and governments they're doing when in fact they're retreating. It was 11 May 1745. The 50,000 Dutch, English, Austrian and Hanoverian troops could not stop the French from taking Tournai and then occupying Flanders within about four months.

C❖The only good news came from across the Atlantic. English colonists, supported by a naval squadron, captured the strongest French fortress in the New World, Louisburg, on Cape Breton. This 'Dunkirk of North America', commanding the mouth of the St Lawrence and protecting communications between Canada and France, had cost the French over £1 million.

In London there were other matters on the minds of the King, Pelham and his Secretary of State brother, the Duke of Newcastle, as they tried to hold together the differing interests of the administration.

C❖Newcastle, 'the impertinent fool' as King George called him, was in confusion. He had no war policy, and having ousted Carteret from the Government had now to 'broaden the bottom of the administration', as they said in the terms of those days. The Pelham regime, built up upon the support of Whig family groups, was artificial, but it had its merits. Henry Pelham was a good administrator, economical and efficient, but. . . . the war dominated everything. For ten years the Pelham brothers made constant and frantic efforts to create a stable Government. The ghost of King William hovered over them. Their foreign policy was a faint and distorted shadow of the previous generation's. Austria and Holland were no longer Great Powers on the Continent. The Grand Alliance was dead.

And then, in 1745 the Pelhams were tested at home. The Jacobites were once more on the march and the Forty-Five, as it became known, was in the making. Legend was also in the making: this was the uprising led by Bonnie Prince Charlie, the Young Pretender, who, in defeat, would be comforted by Flora Macdonald. There had been three Jacobite risings before the Forty-Five in 1708, 1715 and 1719. And they had three things in common: bad timing, bad organization and false hope. The 1708 uprising, which included a French invasion fleet, was scuppered by appalling weather, indifferent navigation and a failure actually to get ashore. The attempt in 1715 stood a better chance. The eleventh Earl of Mar, who led the rising, soon raised support in Scotland. But this time there was no French support for the Jacobites. In 1719, the year of the third Jacobite uprising, raiding parties were sent from Spain to preoccupy the

British and perhaps deter them from taking sides in a European conflict that was going on at the time. It came to nothing other than a skirmish at Glen Shiel.

C❖The Old Pretender was now living in retirement, and his son, Prince Charles Edward, was the darling of the impecunious exiles who clustered around him in Rome and Paris. His handsome presence and gay demeanour fortified the popularity of his cause. . . . he sailed from Nantes in June 1745 with a handful of followers and landed in the Western Isles of Scotland. Thus began one of the most audacious and irresponsible enterprises in British history. Charles had made scarcely any preparations. He could command support only in the Highlands, which contained but a small proportion of the whole population of Scotland. The clans were always ready to fight, but never to be led. Arms and money were short, the Lowlands hostile, and the Highland troops were hated. The commercial classes regarded them as bandits. The cities had long accepted Hanoverian rule.

Twelve hundred men under Lord George Murray raised the Jacobite standard at Glenfinnan. About 3000 Government troops gathered in the Lowlands under Sir John Cope. The rebels marched southwards; Prince Charles entered the palace at Holyrood, and Cope was met and routed on the battlefield of Prestonpans. By the end of September, Charles was ruler of most of Scotland in the name of his father, 'King James VIII'; but his triumph was fleeting.

Some of the important clans had never supported him. The important Hebridean chiefs, Macdonald of Sleat, Macdonald of Clanranald and Macleod of Dunvegan, had refused to come out for him, although the young Clanranald did so. By the time he was at Edinburgh, the Young Pretender could begin to organize his brigade of followers: the Stewarts of Appin, the Robertsons, and the Macphersons. Perhaps Prince Charles's most important ally was Lochiel, the clan chief of the Camerons, although it is said that he joined against his better judgment.

C❖The mass of the Scottish people were apathetic. In London, however, there was panic; a run on the Bank was only met by paying out in sixpences.

Incidentally, it was at this point that the words of a rousing, patriotic song began to be sung in London:

God Save our noble King,
God Save great George our King,
God Save the King.
Send him victorious. . .
et cetera

The irony is that other versions had been used for years by the Jacobites. But now the Hanoverians had commandeered the song which, one day (in the nineteenth century), would be called the national anthem. So with God save noble George ringing to the rafters of London theatres, Prince Charles marched south.

C❖[In September 1745] With 5000 men, the Young Pretender crossed the Border. Three forces were assembled against him. . . . Charles knew of the panic in London, and hoped to profit by it, but he had no control over his followers . . . it was December. The English commanded the sea; there was no hope from France; the Dutch and Hessians [from Hesse] were sending troops to England. . . .

At Derby, Charles gave the signal to retreat. . . . The English forces followed like vultures. [General] Murray showed great skill in the withdrawal, and in rearguard actions his troops were invariably successful. They turned and mauled their pursuers at Falkirk. But with Teutonic thoroughness, the Duke of Cumberland concentrated the English armies for a decision and in April 1746, on Culloden Moor, the last chances of a Stuart restoration were swept into the past for ever.

On that famous moor near Inverness, Cumberland killed 1000 Scots – in not much more than half an hour. And so the legend was made. Bonnie Prince Charlie, the Young Pretender to the English throne, disguised as a woman by Flora Macdonald, escaped in a boat to Skye. But by then he was hardly a princely figure and Flora Macdonald took him to the island with some considerable reluctance. He was torn, hunted, hungry and nibbled by lice and mosquitoes. He was, eventually, rescued and taken to France as the hero of the moment. But the moment did not last long and in later years the once Bonnie Prince ended his days in Italy, as a drunkard. And there is one often-forgotten postscript to the Battle of Culloden: it was the last land battle ever to be fought in Britain. The date was 16 April 1746.

CHAPTER THIRTY-FIVE

1747–1751

❖

After Culloden, the Prime Minister, Henry Pelham and his brother, the Duke of Newcastle, found themselves with a crisis of quite a different sort. The Pelhams wanted to improve their administration by bringing in William Pitt. But the King didn't like the Pelhams and he still fancied he could have Carteret and Lord Bath leading his government so he said no to William Pitt.

Newcastle wrote to Lord Chesterfield, who was then Lord Lieutenant of Ireland.

❖Newcastle House, February 18, 1746
   Private
   My Dear Lord,
      I am now to give you an account of the most surprising scene that has ever happened in this country, or, I believe, in any other.
      Some few days before the meeting of Parliament after Christmas Mr Pitt went to the Duke of Bedford, expressed an inclination to know our foreign scheme, shewed a disposition to come into it, and wished that some of us would go and talk with Lord Cobham, into whose hands they had now entirely committed themselves.

Lord Cobham was Richard Temple, Viscount Cobham, for some time one of Pitt's patrons. His young followers were known as Cobham's Cubs or the Boy Patriots, and had been Walpole's sharpest critics. In fact Cobham himself had been stripped of the command of his own regiment: Cobham's Horse. Newcastle's letter continues:

❖He seemed very desirous to come into us and to bring in his Boys, as he called them, exclusively (as he expressly said) of the Tories, for whom he had nothing to say. The terms were Mr Pitt to be Secretary at War, Lord Barrington in the Admiralty and Mr James Grenville [Pitt's brother-in-law] to have an employment of £1000 a year. Upon this, I opened the budget to the King, which was better received than I expected; and the only objection was to the giving Mr Pitt this particular office of Secretary at War.

> We had several conferences with his Majesty upon it, the King insisting for some time that he would not make him Secretary at War; afterwards that he would use him ill if he had it; and at last that he would give him the office, but would not admit him into his presence to do the business of it.

Two long-time political enemies of the Pelhams, Carteret, since 1744 the Earl of Granville, and William Pulteney, the Earl of Bath, now sided with the King against Pitt and, of course, the wishes of the Pelhams.

❖The King grew very uneasy, and complained extremely of being forced. But, when the difficulty seemed in a way of being removed, my Lord Bath got to the King, represented against the behaviour of his ministers in forcing him in such a manner to take a disagreeable man into a particular office and thereby dishonouring him both at home and abroad and encouraging the King to resist it by offering him, I suppose, the support of his friends in so doing. This strengthened the King in his dislike of the measure, and encouraged, I conclude, his Majesty to think that he had a party behind the curtain would either force his ministers to do what he liked or, if they did not do it, would be able to support his affairs without them.

Tho' Lord Bath was the open transactor of this affair, it is not to be imagined but that my Lord Granville was in the secret. Mr Pitt, very decently and honourably, authorized us immediately to renounce all his pretensions to the Office of Secretary at War.

But it was thought proper, at the same time, to suggest to the King that, after so public an éclat as my Lord Bath had made of this affair, it was thought absolutely necessary that his Majesty should give some publick mark of his resolution to support and place confidence in his then administration; or otherwise we should be at the mercy of our enemies, whenever they were able to take advantage of us, without having it in our power to do the King or the publick any service.

In other words, the Pelhams were demanding a public vote of confidence from the King.

❖His Majesty was extremely irritated, loudly complaining of our conduct both at home and abroad, unwilling to give us any satisfaction of assurance of his countenance or support and plainly shewing a most determined predilection for the other party. Upon this, we thought, in duty to the King and in justice to ourselves, the wisest and honestest part that we could take was to desire leave to resign our employments.

But the King's party, in other words Bath and Granville, simply did not have the Commons support to lead a government so the King backed down at least partly. Pitt was immediately created Joint Vice Treasurer of Ireland and, a couple of months later, Paymaster General of the forces.

C❖By a custom, openly avowed, the Paymaster was permitted to carry his balances to his private account and draw the interest on them. Further, he received commission on the subsidies paid to foreign allies for the maintenance of their troops in the field. Pitt refused to accept a penny beyond his official salary. The effect on public opinion was electric. By instinct rather than calculation, he gained the admiration and confidence of the middle classes, the City, the rising mercantile towns, and the country freeholders. A born actor, by this gesture he caught the eye of the people, and held it as no statesman had held it before him. . . . He . . . [appealed] to the imagination of the country.

But the imagination of the country was more usually reflected at the time by its artists, illustrators and writers. One such was William Hogarth. Hogarth would have been nearly fifty years old at the time of Pitt's appointment as Paymaster. By 1746 he was established as an artist of considerable influence. In the 1730s he'd begun to produce a series of engravings with moral themes. The titles tell all: 'The Harlot's Progress' followed by 'The Rake's Progress', then 'Marriage à la Mode' and later, 'The Election'. One of his most powerful images was called 'The March to Finchley', a picture of part of Cumberland's army before its march north to Culloden. The central figure is a soldier. On one side he is tugged by a dark-cloaked, haggard female with a swinging crucifix who clutches the newspapers of the day. On the other arm is a comely lady, heavily pregnant, a basket on her arm from which peeps a scroll on which we can see the words 'God Save the King'. The soldier is Hogarth's Britain and the two women are fighting for his soul. The dark figure is Catholicism in the form of the Jacobites. The lady in white is for the monarch and the child she carries is Britain's child. Another of Hogarth's drawings, 'Gin Lane', illustrates the commonplace of drunkenness in London, and in a 1740s journal there's a report of a christening in Surrey.

❖The nurse was so intoxicated that after she had undressed the child, instead of laying it in the cradle, she put it behind a large fire, which burned it to death in a few minutes. She was examined before a magistrate, and said she was quite stupid and senseless, so that she took the child for a log of wood; on which she was discharged.

There were about 7000 gin shops in London alone and it was to this city that Hogarth turned for his social commentary. Parliament passed the Gin Act which put up taxes on the spirit and restricted its sale through retailers. The nation continued to drink, but the gin craze was on the wane. The moral crusade of the decade was reflected by Charles Wesley who had been preaching and writing what became a collection of 7000 hymns, and his elder brother, John Wesley, the founder of Methodism, began his open-air evangelical crusade and would eventually preach 40,000 sermons.

Small factories were being built and textile makers were leading what one day would be known as the Industrial Revolution. John Kay invented his flying shuttle for weavers but reaped few rewards. There was still famine in Ireland; witchcraft in England was no longer a crime, and Handel finished his Messiah.

And at the time of the passing of the Gin Act, William Pitt was mourning the passing of his powerful ally, the Prince of Wales, in 1751. The man who would have been King on George II's death would probably have guaranteed Pitt's future. An unexpected interruption to a political career and an even more unexpected cause of death: it is thought that the Prince died as a result of having been struck by a cricket ball.

It was the middle of the eighteenth century and the war in Europe, the War of the Austrian Succession, was about to end. Henry Fielding was finishing his fat bawdy novel, *Tom Jones*. Robert Clive was about to establish his name forever in India. The calendar that is still used today – the Gregorian calendar – was introduced by Henry Pelham. It replaced the Julian calendar and meant that Britain, after a lapse of almost 200 years, was once more using the same calendar as the rest of Continental Europe. Dr Johnson published his dictionary and Pitt eventually became Prime Minister. The Black Hole of Calcutta became notorious; Wolfe set off to fight, and die, at Quebec and, in the sky, the world saw the return of Halley's Comet.

First, the war in Europe. The Austrian Succession had never been Britain's war but a series of unnecessary treaties and the King's belief that his homelands were threatened, especially by Frederick of Prussia, Frederick the Great, had involved the British. But now the war was over chiefly because Frederick the Great had got what he wanted: Silesia, and Britain, preoccupied with the Forty-Five Jacobite rebellion, had once again found it impossible to fight on more than one front. And in London there was more concern for the National Debt than the outcome of the war. The conclusion was yet another peace accord which did little to guarantee peace. It was called the Treaty of Aix-la-Chapelle and dated 18 October 1748. In this treaty the title of George II is King of Great Britain, Ireland and France. The English monarchy had not formally given up its claim to France, the old enemy. However in the treaty the French once more recognized the Hanoverian right to Great Britain, said they would not support the Jacobite claim to the English throne and gave back Madras which had been won from the English East India Company in 1746. But the war had been inconclusive, so the treaty was similarly inconclusive. Within eight years, Britain would be once again at war.

By now Britain fully understood the difficulties of controlling its foreign interests which were stretched from India to the Americas. This was all very new and quite a difficult day-to-day bureaucratic problem for the government. There was no great foreign policy, no great office of state with a century of expertise. Acquiring bits of the world was rather like a general taking a hill from the enemy and then asking: 'Now what do I do with it? How do I hold on to it? What's it for?'

But these were the beginnings of the British Empire. And if there was to be an empire, there was an even greater need for foreign policy based beyond the traditional relations and animosities on the Continent of Europe. However, the monarch's first interest was that he remained a German. Therefore, just as George I had done, George II was inclined to set off for war in Europe if he thought his Hanoverian interests were threatened. And he often believed they were.

John Campbell's European treatise called *The Present State of Europe* covers his principles of foreign policy. He makes distinctions between trade, political and military ambitions. It could have been written at the end of the twentieth century, by what today would be called a Media Don, not in the middle of the eighteenth century.

❖There is a distinction often made, chiefly by foreigners, between the Interest and the Commerce of Great Britain; but in reality this is a Distinction without a Difference; for the Interest and the Commerce of the British Empire are so inseparably united, that they may be very well considered as one and the same. For Commerce is that tie, by which the several, and even the most distant Parts of this Empire, are connected and kept together, so as to be rendered Parts of the same whole, and to receive not only Countenance and Protection, but Warmth and Nourishment from the vital Parts of our Government of which, if I may be indulged so figurative an expression, our Monarchy is the head, and our Liberty the Soul. Whatever therefore assists, promotes, and extends our Commerce, is consistent with our Interest, and whatever weakens, impairs, or circumscribes it, is repugnant thereto.

We may easily, considering things in this light (and if we consider them in any other we shall deceive ourselves) derive from thence a true Notion of the Interest of Great Britain, with respect to the other Powers of Europe; and be able to judge when that Interest is really pursued and when it is either neglected or abandoned.

The first point dictated by our Interest, is the maintaining [of] others in their rights, or to make use of a more known Term, to support the Independency of the Powers of Europe; because the engrossing, subjecting, or subduing [of] several Countries under one Potentate, naturally and even necessarily contributes to lessen the Number of Inhabitants, to extinguish Industry amongst them, and consequently to enfeeble and impoverish them. Another point is the stipulating with foreign Nations proper terms of Security, Indulgence and Respect for our Subjects ... when these kind of Alliances are made, they become sacred ties and we are bound to fulfil them punctually, so that whatever different form appearances may wear, the true Interest of Great Britain is always to comply exactly with her Treaties.

All British alliances and interests in Europe had to be based on an understanding that trade was of fundamental interest to Britain. And even in the eighteenth century, there was the recognition of the importance of maintaining Europe as an alliance of independent states. A common eighteenth-century market, not a federation.

John Campbell's Britain was an age when the number of newspapers and books was growing. The *Gentleman's Magazine* listed more than 400 new publications – plays, novels, cookery books, travel directories, religious tracts etc. In the capital there were half a dozen daily newspapers and there were probably forty or so in the provinces. And for foreign visitors there was the less serious side to the English. For example, the Swedish naturalist Pehr Kalm was in England in 1748 on his way to America. His observations between February and August of that year have survived, including his thoughts on a great English tradition: toast for breakfast.

March 1748
Breakfast was almost everywhere partaken of by those more comfortably off, [and] consisted in drinking tea. They ate at the same time one or more slices of wheat-bread, which they had first toasted at the fire and when it was very hot had spread butter on it. In the summer they do not toast the bread, but only spread the butter on it before they eat it. The cold rooms here in England in the winter – and because the butter is then hard from the cold, and does not easily admit of being spread on the bread – have perhaps given them the idea to thus toast the bread – and then spread the butter on it while it is still hot.

Dinner
The Englishmen understand almost better than any other people the art of properly roasting a joint, which is not be wondered at because the art of cooking as practised by most Englishmen does not extend much beyond roast beef and plum pudding.

Little Gaddesden, April 1748

When English women in the country are going out to pay their compliments to each other, they commonly wear a red cloak. All go laced and use for everyday a sort of manteau made commonly of brownish camlot. The same head-dress as in London. Here it is not unusual to see a farmer's or other small personage's wife clad on Sundays like a lady of quality at other places in the world and her everyday attire in proportion. When they go out they always wear straw hats, which they have made themselves from wheat straw and are pretty enough. On high days they have ruffles.

The duty of the women in this district scarcely consists in anything else but preparing food, which they do uncommonly well, though roast beef and pudding forms nearly all an Englishman's eatables.

In the North Americas, where Pehr Kalm was heading with his notebooks and social observations, the British experiment was manoeuvring towards a dramatic conclusion. But in the other direction, to the east of Greenwich, a young man was preparing for an expedition that would lead to a more famous passage in the history of these islands.

He was hot tempered and he loved fighting. He was a descendant of one of Cromwell's most famous colonels and one day, he would be known as Clive of India. People talk about the British Raj. But most of the stories that feed images of that period were written when the nineteenth-century Raj was either well established or dying. In 1751 a sometime clerk who had attempted suicide, who had volunteered to join the East India Company's army, was about to capture a fortress town called Arcot, sixty miles inland from the south eastern seaport of Madras. It was held by a not very impressive force of Indians and Frenchmen.

The young man's name was Robert Clive; he was twenty-six years old.

In 1600, 150 years earlier, the East India Company had been given a Royal Charter. The Portuguese had been the major European trading nation in South East Asia. But Portuguese influence was declining and the English East India Company believed it could replace the Iberian commercial managers. However, the Dutch were much stronger in what were called the East Indies, and they forced out the British. The British retreated to the Indian subcontinent and, by 1633, the East India Company had established itself in Bengal.

C❖About the year 1700, probably no more than 1500 English people dwelt in India, including wives, children and transient seamen. They lived apart in a handful of factories, as their trading stations were called, little concerned with English politics. . . . The great empire of the Moguls was disintegrating. For two centuries these Moslem descendants of Tamburlaine had gripped and pacified a portion of the world half as large as the present United

States. Centred in Delhi and supported by able proconsuls, they had kept the peace in Oriental fashion and conferred on the eighty million inhabitants of the sub-continent an orderly existence which they were not to know again for another 100 years. Early in the eighteenth century this formidable dynasty was shaken by a disputed succession. Invaders from the North soon poured across its frontiers. Delhi was sacked by the Shah of Persia. The Viceroys of the Moguls revolted and laid claim to the sovereignty of the Imperial provinces. Pretenders rose up to challenge the usurpers. In Central India the fierce fighting tribes of the Mahrattas, bound in a loose confederacy, saw and seized their chance to loot and to raid. The country was swept by anarchy and bloodshed.

The two companies making money out of India were the English East India Company with its centres at Madras, Bombay and Calcutta, and the French Compagnie des Indes. The French had made their base at Pondicherry south of Madras. The two companies were rivals, but commercial ones. And there's little evidence, at this stage, that they were interested in gaining territory. They were trading, not colonial, powers.

C❖About 1740, events forced them to change their tune. The Mahrattas slaughtered the Nawab, or Imperial Governor, of the Carnatic, the 500-mile long province on the south-eastern coast. They threatened Madras and Bombay, and raided the depths of Bengal. It was becoming impossible for the European traders to stand aside. . . . Most of the Dutch had already withdrawn to the rich archipelago of the East Indies; the Portuguese had long since fallen behind in the race; the French and English resolved to stay . . . Joseph Dupleix, [the French] Governor of Pondicherry since 1742, had long foreseen the coming struggle with Britain. He perceived that India awaited a new ruler. The Mogul Empire was at an end, and a Mahratta Empire seemed unlikely to replace it. Why then should not France seize this glittering, fertile prize?

In the past, when England and France had gone to war in Europe, traders in India maintained a neutrality so that their main interest, trade, should not suffer. But with the arrival of a British naval squadron, apparently determined to interrupt French shipping, Dupleix decided to go on the offensive; although even then, there was evidence that the French action was to protect their trading interests rather than simply to conquer territory.

In 1746, two years before the European War of the Austrian Succession ended, the French took Madras. And Clive, then a twenty-one-year-old clerk in the East India Company, was one of the defenders who escaped from the city.

C❖. . . hitherto there had been few signs in his career to mark him as the man who would reverse his country's fortunes and found the rule of the British in India. He was the son of a small squire, and his boyhood had been variegated and unpromising. Clive had attended no fewer than four schools, and been unsuccessful at all. In his Shropshire market town he had organized and led a gang of adolescent ruffians who extorted pennies and apples from tradesmen in return for not breaking their windows. At the age of eighteen he was sent abroad as a junior clerk in the East India Company at a salary of £5 a year and £40 expenses. He was a difficult and unpromising subordinate. He detested the routine and the atmosphere of the counting-house. Twice, it is said, he attempted suicide, and twice the pistol misfired. . . . In 1748, a new upheaval gave him the chance of leadership.

Indian pretenders seized the Mogul viceroyalty of the Deccan and conquered the Carnatic. With a few French soldiers and a couple of thousand Indian troops, Dupleix expelled them and placed his own puppets on the throne. The British candidate, Mahomet Ali, was chased into Trichinopoly and fiercely besieged.

Clive had left his clerking and had travelled on one expedition as the Commissary, the person in charge of victualling the army. This taught him, and very quickly, the need to understand the people of the main force, the Indians, and most important, the logistics of keeping an army on the move and ready to fight. On his return, Clive volunteered for army service with the Company, without pay, but with the rank of captain. With most of the army preoccupied with the siege of Mahomet Ali, Clive's offer was welcome and shortly after he led a detachment to Trichinopoly. It is very likely that he met Mahomet Ali and they talked over the way in which the siege might be lifted. An attack on the French at Trichinopoly would have been foolhardy. The plan was to attack the most important outpost of French and Indian interests because it was all but undefended.

C❖Arcot, capital of the Carnatic, had been stripped of troops; most of them were at Trichinopoly besieging Mahomet Ali. Capture Arcot and they would be forced to come back. With 200 Europeans, 600 Indians, and eight officers, of whom half were former clerks like himself, Clive set forth. The town fell easily to his assault and he and his small handful prepared desperately for the vengeance which was to come. Everything turned out as Clive had foreseen. The Indian potentate, dismayed by the loss of his capital, detached a large portion of his troops from Trichinopoly and attacked Clive in Arcot. The struggle lasted for fifty days. Twenty times outnumbered, and close to starvation, Clive's puny force broke the onslaught in a night attack in which he served a gun himself, and the siege was lifted by the threat of an admiring Mahratta chieftain to come to the aid of the British. This was the end of Dupleix, and of much else besides. By 1752, Clive, in combination with Stringer Lawrence, a regular soldier from England, had defeated the French and the French-sponsored usurpers and placed Mahomet Ali on the throne.

Britain had found a new military genius, although the detail of first the fall and then the defence of Arcot is full of conditions which point to fortune, incompetence, ill, then good, luck. For example, Abdul Codah Khan, the commander of the Indian sepoys, had been the only one to seriously attack Clive. But he was killed and his followers lost heart. If he hadn't been killed the result might well have been different. Clive was also saved from a sniper's musket ball by the quick thinking of a friend, who died for his pains.

But whether it was Clive's fortune, or the enemy's ineptitude, the legend of British invincibility was born. Mahomet Ali gave him the title, Sabit Jang, which means 'steady in war'. And when he was sent on other expeditions to take the French forts at Covelong and Chingleput, the legend grew. At Chingleput, his forces were raw recruits, ill-trained and with little courage under fire. Clive was seen standing in the vanguard of the action, quite exposed to enemy fire in an attempt, a successful one it seems, to shame his soldiers into action.

And Clive would have been inhuman had he not encouraged the myth. However he was never again to have such a celebrated victory, and there is, in Clive's story, a sense that he spent too much time trying to justify his image. There's even evidence that this pressure, on a not always stable character, damaged his health.

Shortly after his celebrated victory, Clive became quite ill. It was probably gallstones, but there are hints of fits of nervous depression, even manic depression. He was prescribed opium as a pain killer and another legend, that he was an opium addict, grew up. The only firm evidence suggests he took opium when he was ill and at no other time.

But the growing fame of Clive brought with it sufficient enemies to encourage such rumours.

Just a few days before sailing for home, Clive had married Margaret Maskelyne; but his departure from India was not the high occasion it might have been because he was later accused of making too much money out of his exploits and of pocketing a percentage of the cost of keeping his soldiers and those he had rescued from French rule, or worse, that he had been generous. But if he was not always popular with the highest in the Madras administration, Clive was popular on his return to England. England needed a hero and Clive would do. But he was a hero to be kept at arm's length.

C❖In England, Clive used part of his fortune in an attempt to enter Parliament for a rotten borough in Cornwall. He was unsuccessful, and, in 1755, he returned to India.

The East India Company had actually asked him to serve as Deputy Governor of Fort St David, which was south of Madras, and had applied for a commission for him as a Lieutenant-Colonel of foot. So he didn't return to India in a fit of rejection.

C❖He was only just in time, for a new struggle was about to open in the North East. Hitherto French, Dutch and English had traded peacefully side by side in the fertile province of Bengal, and its docile, intelligent, and industrious inhabitants had largely escaped the slaughter and anarchy of the South. Calcutta, at the mouth of the Ganges, was earning good dividends. Peace had been kept by a Moslem adventurer from the North West who had seized and held power for fourteen years. But he died in 1756, and the throne passed to his grandson, Surajah Dowlah, young, vicious, violent, and greedy.

The name Siraj-ud-daula was unknown in Britain but soon the consequences of his confrontation would be on the lips of the whole island. In one night, the Black Hole of Calcutta would claim the lives of 123 Europeans.

But more important than the ghastly deed itself was the fact that that single event would destroy any lingering belief that the British could remain in India simply as innocent traders.

CHAPTER THIRTY-SIX

1752–1759

———— ❖ ————

In 1751, while Robert Clive was making a name for himself and the British in India, William Pitt, Pitt the Elder as he became known, was wondering if he would ever become Prime Minister. His patron, the Prince of Wales, had died. The Prince favoured Pitt and the politician fancied that he would replace the Pelhams as leader of the Government. The Prince's father, however, George II, did not like Pitt. He regarded him as an enemy. After all, Pitt had made no secret of his contempt for Hanover and the way British men and finances were being used to protect the Electorate.

There's another aspect to Pitt that's sometimes overlooked. He was often quite ill. In the mid-eighteenth century, that was hardly unusual. A small gripe could easily turn into something far more complicated. Although medicine was advancing, quite rapidly in fact, Pitt and his fellow sufferers were two centuries away from small white cure-all tablets. And it wasn't quite out of the question that, like many great men, Pitt's illnesses were sometimes brought about by stress and personality disorder. At different times, a cocktail of medical symptoms including something described as 'gout of the stomach' baffled his doctors. He suffered fevers, nervous depression, and insomnia. Perhaps, like Clive in India, Pitt was prone to manic depression.

Henry Pelham, the Prime Minister, was quite different. He was solid. Sanity never deserted him, politically nor mentally. Pelham was described as an honest bore, by one observer. And, with his enormously rich brother, the Duke of Newcastle, Pelham balanced the very differing factions in the administration and Parliament. When Henry Pelham died in March 1754 George II is said to have remarked, 'Now I shall have no more peace'. That was because he knew the battle for political leadership would centre on William Pitt.

C❖. . . the King was relentless in his dislike of Pitt, and Cumberland [the third son of George II], who had a political following of his own, succeeded in pushing into the Cabinet Pitt's most dangerous rival, Henry Fox.

Hope of a great political career seemed at an end for William Pitt. . . . Appealing over the heads of petty groups to the nation at large, he was eventually to knock down the fragile structures of contemporary politicians and bring a driving wind of reality into politics. But the arrival of Fox in the Government, an avaricious expert in contemporary political method, made Pitt despair. After a great speech in the Commons, he was dismissed from the Pay Office in November 1755.

Pitt's attack on the Government – his own Government – was an attack on the Duke of Newcastle, who had become Prime Minister on the death of his brother, Henry Pelham. Pitt insisted that Newcastle was neglecting Britain's trade interests overseas, especially those threatened by France. And he returned to his theme that Britain was more interested in defending Hanover than her real interests on the Continent. This was hardly the tactic to endear him to a Hanoverian king.

C❖Two months later, a diplomatic revolution took place towards which the four main Powers of Europe had for some time been groping. A convention was signed between Britain and Prussia, shortly followed by a treaty between the French and the Austrians. Thus there was a complete reversal of alliances.

The changes that influenced these new alliances were, first, the rise of Russia as well as Prussia and, second, the overseas rivalry between Britain and France in India and in North America. The British East India Company and the French Compagnie des Indes knew full well that neutrality would protect their trading interests and thus war had been avoided.

But in North America there had never been a convention, an understanding, to avoid war and the issue was territory, not trade. In 1745 the Governor of Massachusetts and the British military Commander in America was William Shirley. He wrote a letter to the Duke of Newcastle encouraging Britain's control of Canada.

❖Louisburg, October 29

I took the liberty to mention in a former Letter to your Grace, that I thought, if the Expedition against Cape Breton should succeed, a Spirit would be immediately rais'd in the Colonies for pushing the success as far as Canada; which observation I find was not ill grounded; And I trouble your Grace with the repetition of it now, because the Reduction of that Country to the Obedience of his Majesty seems to be the most effectual means of securing to the Crown of Great Britain not only Nova Scotia, and this Acquisition, but the whole Northern Continent as far back as the French settlements on the River Mississippi, which are about 2000 miles distance from Canada, by making all the Indians inhabiting within that Tract (who are now chiefly in the French Interest) dependent upon the

English; the immediate consequence of which would be throwing the whole fur trade, except such part of it as the French Settlements at Mississippi might keep, into the hands of His Majesty's Subjects; breaking up all the French fishing settlements in the Gulph and river of St Lawrence, and even on the bank of Newfoundland, and securing the whole Codfishery to the English . . . which besides the Profits arising from that part which the French lately had of it amounting to near £ 1 million sterling, would be further Beneficial to the British subjects by the great consumption of Rum, and Cloathing [sic] necessary for the Men in carrying on Fishery, and the great quantity of Shipping, small Craft and Fishing Gear of all Sorts necessarily employed in it, which would in such Case be all British.

At this point William Shirley thought ahead to the twentieth century.

❖I may add that from the Healthfulness of the Climates on this Continent and the Surprising growth of its inhabitants within the last Century, it may be expected that in one or two more centuries, there will be such an addition from hence to the Subjects of the Crown of Great Britain, as may make 'em vye for numbers with the subjects of France, and lay a foundation for a superiority of British Power on the Continent of Europe at the same time that it secures that which the Royal Navy of Great Britain has already at Sea; and this is the remarkable Difference between the other acquisitions in America belonging to the several Crowns in Europe and this Continent, that the others diminish the Mother Country's inhabitants, as Jamaica, Barbados, and the other Southern Colonies belonging to Great Britain have done, and the Spanish West Indies have done even to the exhausting of Old Spain.

By the second half of the eighteenth century Britain had more than doubled its overseas trade largely because of exports to the American market that Shirley had been so keen to encourage. And this import and export trade even survived a decade of war. The British had broken France's commercial grip on India and America. The Spanish (exhausted, said Shirley) had lost influence in the West Indies. By the 1750s, the British Merchant Fleet was more than half a million tons. Twenty years later, it was 30% bigger, a measure of the developing trade particularly with the growing population of the 'Northern Continent'.

At the start of the century there were about 300,000 settlers living in America. By the 1770s there were three million. And that increased population generated industry, including those needing imports. America wanted, for example, iron and wool. So the stagnant wool industry in Britain was revived and the young iron industry boomed. Then, in 1756, the uneasy peace in Europe slipped away. The diplomatic revolution that had set new allies against old friends now meant war. It was called the Seven Years' War. Britain and Prussia against France, Russia, Austria, Sweden and Saxony.

In truth, Britain hadn't been at peace for some time. The War of the Austrian Succession ended eight years earlier, but France and Britain had continued their conflicts in India and North America.

During the Seven Years' War France tried to invade Britain; Britain lost Minorca (which resulted in the execution of a British Admiral by the name of Byng), won Martinique, St Lucia, St Vincent, Grenada, Tobago, Havana, Manila (some of which was given back to the French and Spanish). The Black Hole of Calcutta became an infamous entry in British colonial history and General Wolfe died famously at Quebec. But most significantly, this war was the first world war and the beginning of the British Empire.

And so everything should have pointed to a successful period in British Government but it was not. The Duke of Cumberland (or the Butcher as he was known after the Battle of Culloden) was no strategist, and the Duke of Newcastle, in name Prime Minister, demonstrated expected incompetence. This opened the way for William Pitt, Pitt the Elder who, although not Prime Minister, not yet First Lord of the Treasury, became Britain's war leader, an early day Churchill.

C❖The mismanagement of the early years of the struggle, which had been precipitated by the bellicose Cumberland, gave Pitt his chance. The loss of the island of Minorca raised a national outcry. The Government, faced with this national disgrace, lost its nerve. Cumberland's favourite, Henry Fox, bolted into retirement. The Government shifted the blame onto Admiral Byng, whose ill-equipped fleet had failed to relieve the Minorca garrison. By one of the most scandalous evasions of responsibility that an English government has ever perpetrated, Byng was shot for cowardice upon the quarter-deck of his flagship. Pitt pleaded for him with the King.

'The House of Commons, Sir, is inclined to mercy.'

'You have taught me,' the King replied, 'to look for the sense of my people elsewhere than in the House of Commons.'

Minorca was a symbol of British military virility and the feelings of the British at the time were similar to the feelings that would have erupted in Britain more than 200 years later, if the Task Force Commander had backed away from trying to re-take the Falkland Islands after the Argentinian invasion.

Minorca had been British for more than forty years; it was part of the spoils of the War of Spanish Succession. In April 1756, Admiral John Byng had been sent to relieve the English garrison at Fort St Michael which was then besieged by the French Army commanded by the Duc de Richelieu. Byng's fleet was not in best condition and the Admiral himself had a reputation as a commander who could find reasons why a mission was far more difficult than his instructions suggested. But in the case of relieving Minorca, he may well have been correct. He engaged the French Fleet, but little came of it and the siege went on. Byng then left the region without landing British reinforcements and without blockading the French logistics line between Toulon and Minorca.

In the Fleet, as well as in Parliament, there was a sense of hopelessness and injustice. Captain Augustus Hervey, who later became the third Earl of Bristol, supported Byng throughout his trial. Hervey was just one officer who believed that more famous men were protecting themselves and that Byng was to be used as an example. In his journal, Hervey described the naval action in the Mediterranean, the sad state of Byng's squadron, the senseless orders given him to relieve Fort St Philip, patrol the high seas and protect Gibraltar – all at the same time. He also makes it clear that the only real evidence against Byng was supplied not by his colleagues and superiors, but by the French Admiral's account of what happened off Minorca. The first sentence of his record expresses Byng's doubts about the mission.

❖*May 1756*

The morning early the eighteenth [sic], I went on board of Admiral Byng and did lament his not having more force when he told me that Lord Anson sent all the best ships cruising with his favourites, and, all he could do, he could not obtain two or three more, tho' he might with ease have brought them.

And then after the action – which even if the troops had been landed before its start, would not necessarily have changed its outcome – Hervey returned to Gibraltar to find, alongside and ashore, the reinforcements Byng had needed at sea. Hervey knew who to blame.

❖*June 12*

I was ordered to make the best of my way to Gibraltar and get the hospital ready, and stores et cetera; to fit the Fleet with all dispatch. I spoke to a Dutch man-of-war from Cadiz who told me the French had sent express everywhere that we were beat and they had gained a complete victory. I arrived the sixteenth at Gibraltar where I found Commodore Broderick and five sail of the line arrived yesterday from England with a regiment on board. Alas, had these been sent out with Mister Byng, Minorca had been saved, the French Fleet destroyed and the Duke de Richelieu's Army obliged to lay down their arms. Such was the inexcusable error of our wicked Ministers, that detested wretch Lord Holland, and that poor contemptible one Lord Anson . . . I went ashore and dined with the General, gave a faithful account of the engagement, and told them the French were too strong and too good sailors, our Fleet in too shattered a condition to re-engage, and the instruction too peremptory to leave Gibraltar exposed, as they could not hope to relieve Minorca.

We had a council of war next day on board the Commodore, when a ship was proposed to be sent out to look for the Admiral, and I proposed the whole squadron going out to join him, but it was carried against me.

Not only is the sense of the inevitability of Byng's court martial implied here but also the slow motion of eighteenth-century naval warfare. News, claim and counter-claim took days, often weeks, to reach home. So by the time the report of the loss of the Minorca reached London the chattering crowds, the superior officers who had kept back ships and, most of all, the King, all wanted the head of the man who'd failed to bring them Minorca.

This incident in the Seven Years' War is hardly discussed today, but in the mid-eighteenth century it was celebrated in long articles in the growing numbers of newspapers and journals. And one of the most telling quotes of the Byng affair remains common currency. It comes from Voltaire in his novel *Candide*: *'Dans ce pays-ci il est bon de tuer de temps en temps un amiral pour encourager les autres.* (In this country it is thought well to kill an admiral from time to time to encourage the others.)

A scapegoat was needed and so Byng was shot. But the incident, and the other inefficiencies of this war, reinforced the fact that no matter how much the King disliked William Pitt, he needed this man who was capable of marshalling the people, the military, Parliament and Government if the wider war, the coming world war, was to be won.

C❖When Pitt first joined the Ministry as Secretary of State [for War] in November 1756, Frederick the Great declared, 'England has long been in labour, but at last she has brought forth a man'.

Nothing like it had been seen since Marlborough. From his office in Cleveland Row, Pitt designed and won a war which extended from India in the East to America in the West. The whole struggle depended upon the energies of this one man. He gathered all power, financial, administrative, and military, into his own hands. He could work with no one as an equal. His position depended entirely on success in the field. His political enemies were numerous. He would tolerate no interference or even advice from his colleagues in the Cabinet; he made no attempt either to consult or to conciliate, and he irritated Newcastle and the Chancellor of the Exchequer by interfering in finance. But in the execution of his military plans, Pitt had a sure eye for choosing the right man. He broke incompetent generals and admirals and replaced them with younger men upon whom he could rely:

Wolfe, Amherst, Conway, Howe, Keppel, and Rodney. Thus he achieved victory.

But Pitt's success was not immediate. He had opposed the popular clamour for Admiral Byng's court-martial. He was at odds with his colleagues, and the Duke of Cumberland used his powerful and malevolent influence against him. The City merchants were still suspicious of the alliance with Prussia. In April 1757, Pitt was dismissed by the King. Nevertheless, he had already made his mark with the nation. He received from the towns and corporations of England a manifestation of their deep feeling, a 'shower of gold boxes'. For three months there was no effective government, though Pitt gave all the orders and did the day-to-day work. A stable war Ministry was not formed until June, but for the next four years Pitt was supreme.

The people wanted Pitt and so they had him.

C❖By taking the initiative in every quarter of the globe Britain prevented the French from concentrating their forces, confused their plan of campaign, and forced them to dissipate their strength. Pitt had fiercely attacked Carteret for fighting in Europe, but he now realized that a purely naval and colonial war, such as he had advocated in the 1740s, could yield no final decision. Unless France were beaten in Europe as well as in the New World and in the East, she would rise again. Both in North America and in Europe she was in the ascendant. At sea she was a formidable enemy. In India it seemed that if ever a European Power established itself on the ruins of the Mogul Empire its banner would be the lilies and not the cross of St George. War with France would be a world war – the first in history; and the prize would be something more than a rearrangement of frontiers and a redistribution of fortresses and sugar islands.

If Minorca was an affront to the whole nation, the reaction to what became known as the Black Hole of Calcutta can easily be imagined. Until the nineteenth century a black hole was the common name for a military detention cell. The Black Hole of Calcutta was the detention cell in Fort William in Calcutta.

The Indian leader (a man called Siraj-ud-daula) marched on Calcutta - the traditional headquarters of the East India Company. The Governor, Roger Drake, was a weak, arrogant man with few diplomatic talents and an even smaller sense of military appreciation. When the garrison was besieged by Siraj-ud-daula, it was abandoned. The families, women and children, with Drake in the middle of them, took to ships in the river leaving the rest of the garrison to the Nawab's mercy. Many of them were shut up in the Black Hole, a room fourteen feet by eighteen feet wide. John Zephaniah Holwell, one of the survivors, wrote in his official report that out of 146 prisoners, 123 died. Holwell probably got it wrong – deliberately. It is possible that he dramatized the incident to foster the desire for revenge at home. Fewer than half the number Holwell claimed were in the Black Hole and perhaps forty or forty-five perished, suffocated during a hot, airless, Bengal night. But whatever the truth of the matter, as with the incident at Minorca, the British wanted revenge.

C❖Whether Pitt possessed the strategic eye, whether the expeditions he launched were part of a considered combination, may be questioned. Now, as at all times, his policy was a projection on to a vast screen of his own aggressive, dominating personality. In the teeth of disfavour and obstruction he had made his way to the foremost place in Parliament, [the Government Front Bench] and now at last fortune, courage, and the confidence of his countrymen had given him a stage on which his gifts could be displayed and his foibles indulged. To call into life and action the depressed and languid spirit of England; to weld all her resources of wealth and manhood into a single instrument of war which should be felt from the Danube to the Mississippi; to humble the House of Bourbon, to make the Union Jack supreme in every ocean, to conquer, to command, and never to count the cost, whether in blood or gold – this was the spirit of Pitt, and this spirit he infused into every rank of his countrymen, admirals and powder-monkeys, great merchants and little shopkeepers; into the youngest officer of the line, who felt that with Pitt in command failure might be forgiven but hesitation never; into the very Highlanders who had charged at Prestonpans and now were sailing across the Atlantic to win an empire for the Sovereign who had butchered their brethren at Culloden.

A rousing chorus for a national leader perhaps. But to Pitt all this was far from his grand design, a design that was looking the worse for wear during the opening months of the war.

C❖On the Continent Britain had one ally, Frederick of Prussia, facing the combined power of Austria, Russia, and France. Sweden too had old grudges to avenge, old claims to assert against him. Frederick, by a rapid march through Saxony into Bohemia, sought to break through the closing circle. But in 1757 he was driven back into his own dominions; Cumberland, sent to protect Hanover and Brunswick, was defeated by the French and surrendered both. Russia was on the march; Swedish troops were again seen in Pomerania. Minorca had already fallen. From Canada, Montcalm was pressing against the American frontier forts. Never did a war open with darker prospects. Pitt's hour had come. . . . Before the year was out it

seemed as if Fortune, recognizing her masters, was changing sides. Frederick
. . . routed the French at Rossbach and the Austrians at Leuthen.

In 1757, Pitt introduced a Militia Act which laid down who would be called
up, who would be trained, for how long, and when. It was a system that lasted
until the twentieth century and the introduction of the Territorial Army of
1917. For the first time, the militia would be raised by ballot. This meant that
almost anyone, rich or poor, would be trained, county by county, would be
subject to the Mutiny Act, and would, in theory at least, be the Home Guard
or the second line of defence against invasion and – and this is important –
against any rebellion in Britain.

Pitt's attention now turned to America. Lord Loudoun had command of
the British forces in North America but he wasn't much good at it; his planning
was bad, he had poor tactical vision and he had unrealistic expectations. So he
was replaced by General James Abercromby. And Pitt, who was wise enough
to bring the colonial governors into his confidence, wrote to those of
Massachusetts, New Hampshire, Connecticut, Rhode Island, New Jersey and
New York. He had a plan: he was going to invade Canada.

❖Whitehall, December 13, 1757.

His Majesty, having nothing more at heart than to repair the Losses and
Disappointments of the last inactive, and unhappy Campaign; and by the
most vigorous and extensive Efforts, to avert, by the Blessing of God on his
Arms, the Dangers impending in North America; and not doubting, that
all His faithful and brave Subjects there, will cheerfully co-operate with, and
second to the utmost, the large Expence, and extraordinary Succours
supplied by this kingdom for their Preservation and Defence; and His
Majesty considering that their several Provinces, in particular, from
Proximity and accessibility of Situation, more immediately obnoxious to
the main interruptions of the Enemy from Canada, are, of themselves, well
able to furnish, at least, 20,000 men, and join a Body of the King's Forces
for Invading Canada and carrying the War into the Heart of the Enemy's
possessions; And his Majesty not judging it expedient to limit the zeal and
Ardor of any of His Provinces, by making a Repartition of the Force to be
raised by Each respectively, for this most important Service;

I am commanded to signify The King's Pleasure, that you do forthwith
use your utmost endeavours, and Influence with the Council and Assembly
of your Province, to induce Them to raise, with all possible Dispatch, as
large a Body of Men within your Government, as the Number of its
Inhabitants may allow; and forming the same into Regiments, as far as shall
be found convenient, That you do direct them to hold Themselves in
Readiness, as early as may be, to march to the Rendezvous at Albany, or

such other Place as His Majesty's Commander in Chief in America shall appoint, in order to proceed, from thence, in Conjunction with a Body of the King's British Forces, and under the supreme command of His Majesty's said Commander in Chief in America, so as to be in a Situation to begin the Operations of the Campaign, by the first of May, if possible, or as soon after, as shall be in any way practicable, by attempting to make an Interruption into Canada.

This is the start of a campaign which, although not immediately successful, led, eighteen months later, to the conquering of Quebec and, more famously, the death of General James Wolfe and the beginnings of Canada as part of a British Empire.

Pitt wanted to attack on three fronts. It was an ambitious plan. The first thrust would be the St Lawrence River, Louisburg and Quebec; the second through Ticonderoga and the Great Lakes; and the third into Ohio. Louisburg fell in the summer of 1758 and Fort Duquesne in the November. (Incidentally Fort Duquesne was soon renamed Pittsburg.) But the attack on Ticonderoga failed.

While the great and often bloody events were occupying the minds of Pitt and his generals, life in Britain plodded on from one meal to the next. Or, perhaps, from one wedding breakfast to the next. The nation was settling down to married life under a new Marriage Act. This Act was the first to state that marriage was a civil contract in which both Church and State had an interest. The Church, for example, had long said that couples should have published banns of marriage. Now it was law and this meant that for the first time, if those banns weren't published, the marriage was not legal. Nineteen articles of marriage were set down by Parliament and among them, the very important Article Fourteen.

❖And for preventing undue entries and abuses in registers of marriages, the church wardens and chapel wardens of every parish or chapelry shall provide proper books of vellum, or good and durable paper, in which all marriages and banns of marriage respectively, there published or solemnized, shall be registered, and every page thereof shall be marked at the top, with the figure or the number of every such page, beginning at the second leaf with number one; and every leaf or page so numbered, shall be ruled with lines at proper and equal distances from each other, or as near as may be; and all banns and marriages published or celebrated in any church or chapel, or within any such parish or chapelry, shall be respectively entered, registered, printed, or written upon as near as conveniently may be to such ruled lines, and shall be signed by the parson, vicar, minister or curate, or by some other person in his presence . . . and all books provided as aforesaid shall be deemed to belong to every such parish or chapelry respectively, and shall be carefully kept and preserved for publick use.

Meanwhile Pitt plotted his wars on three continents and by 1758, the tide was beginning to turn. One central policy of this war was to keep the enemy – that is, France – occupied. One way to achieve this was to subsidize the Prussian war effort in order to make them more enthusiastic about taking on the French. This allowed British forces to attack the French in India and North America, knowing that the enemy would be stretched on more than one front. It also allowed the Royal Navy to raid the French coast, thereby stretching the French resources even further. However these ideas, which looked good on paper, weren't always successful.

C❖In America Pitt faced a difficult and complex task. The governors of the English colonies had long been aware of the threat beyond their frontiers. The French were moving along the waterways beyond the mountain barrier of the Alleghanies and extending their alliances with the Red Indians in an attempt to link their colony of Louisiana in the South with Canada in the North. Thus the English settlements would be confined to the seaboard and their westward expansion would stop . . . General Braddock was sent from England to re-establish British authority west of the Alleghanies, but his forces were cut to pieces by the French and Indians in Pennsylvania. In this campaign a young Virginian officer named George Washington learnt his first military lessons.

The New England colonies lay open to attack down the easy path of invasion, the Hudson valley. . . . Each of the colonies attempted to repel Red Indian raids and French settlers with their own militias. They were united in distrusting the home Government, but in little else. Although there were now over a million British Americans, vastly outnumbering the French, their quarrels and disunion extinguished this advantage. Only the tactful handling of Pitt secured their co-operation, and even so throughout the war colonial traders continued to supply the French with all their needs in defiance of the Government and the common interest.

Many of the British Americans were by now second, third, and fourth generation Americans. The reasons they left Britain are well documented: poverty, disillusion, adventure and opportunity. The circumstances of life in America were little understood in the Royal Closet and in the halls of Kensington, Westminster and Whitehall. The efforts of British commanders in America had never been impressive, and there was little real reason for these people not be united against the Government in Britain.

C❖At the head of the [Hudson valley] were three small forts: Crown Point, Edward, and William Henry. The French, under the Governor of Canada, Montcalm, and his Red Indian allies, swept over the frontier through the wooded mountains and besieged Fort William Henry. The small colonial garrison held out for five days, but was forced to surrender. Montcalm was unable to restrain his Indians and the prisoners were massacred. The tragedy bit into the minds of the New Englanders. . . . The British were not defending them.

America was more than 3000 miles away and no British leader had ever been asked to execute a war over such vast distances. And, as the Romans had found, the more roads their legions marched along, the more vulnerable they became. Pitt understood this, especially with regard to America. Years later, in his last speech to the House of Commons he would plead for an understanding of the colonists. But he would be ignored.

And as Amherst and James Wolfe prepared their battle plans, Britain was only twenty years away from a war that would result in American Independence. In 1759 Wolfe was dead, killed taking the Heights of Abraham, and, across the other side of the world, a victory of another form was being shaped. This was also the year in which India was won for the British Empire, not by government, but by trading interests, and the private army of the East India Company. Robert Clive was creating the foundations of the British Raj and his own place in history.

The main trading province was Bengal whose new ruler, Siraj-ud-daula, believed that war between France and Britain would engulf his own province. And now, for the British, to remain in India simply as traders was an impossibility. From this point they would have to rule, or perish.

C❖In January 1757, with 900 European and 1500 Indian soldiers, [Clive] recaptured Calcutta and repulsed Surajah Dowlah's army of 40,000 men. The war with France now compelled him to retreat, but only long enough for him to attack Chandernagore, which he dared not leave in French hands, before hastening back to Madras. . . . Then fortune came to Clive's aid. Surajah Dowlah's cruelty was too much, even for his own people. A group of courtiers resolved to depose him and place a new ruler, Mir Jafar, on the throne. Clive agreed to help. On June 23, his army having grown to 3000 men, of whom less than a third were British, he met Surajah Dowlah at Plassey. He was outnumbered seventeen to one.

In fact, the Nabob (a senior official, subordinate to the Nawab), as Siraj-ud-daula was called, in spite of the remarkable array of weapons and men, lost his nerve. He leapt onto a camel and with 2000 horsemen as his bodyguard, fled at 'the utmost pace of the animal'.

C❖Surajah Dowlah, sensing treachery in his own camp, and listening to the counsel of those plotting to betray him, ordered a withdrawal. . . . The enemy dispersed in panic, and a few days later Surajah Dowlah was murdered by Mir Jafar's son. For the loss of thirty-six men Clive had become the master of Bengal and the victor of Plassey.

Much, however, still remained to be accomplished. Mir Jafar, who had taken no part in the so-called battle, was placed on the throne, but the province swarmed with Moslem fighting men from the North and was fertile in pretenders. The neighbouring state of Oudh was hostile; the French were still active; and even the Dutch showed signs of interfering. Clive beat the lot. If the English would not rule the country themselves, they must ensure that a friendly local potentate did so. Indirect control was the order of the day. The alternative was more anarchy and more bloodshed.

But Clive and his masters needed approval from home for building what was, in the next century, to become the British Raj.

C❖Modern generations should not mistake the character of the British expansion in India. The Government was never involved as a principal in the Indian conflict, and while Pitt, who justly appreciated the ability of Clive, supported him with all the resources at his command, his influence on events was small. In any case, he already had a world war on his hands. Faced with the difficulties of communication, the distance, and the complexities of the scene, Pitt left Clive with a free hand, contenting himself with advice and support. The East India Company was a trading organization. Its Directors were men of business. They wanted dividends, not wars, and grudged every penny spent on troops and annexations. But the turmoil in the great sub-continent compelled them against their will and their judgment to take control of more and more territory, till in the end, and almost by accident, they established an empire no less solid and certainly more peaceful than that of their Mogul predecessors. . . . Of India it has been well said that the British Empire was acquired in a fit of absence of mind.

However the British Raj was not established as a benign trading institution. The problem with winning territory is that you have to hang onto it – and that means that some people are suppressed, or think they are. Clive had written to Pitt telling him that a small force of Europeans, a larger force of well paid Indians, and a percentage of profits handed over to the princes would eventually secure, if not the loyalty, then the subservience of the whole of India. Pitt's view of this was that if Clive could keep things under control, then so be it.

Clive wrote to Pitt in January 1759; but it wasn't clear whether Pitt believed that the Indian territories belonged to the East India Company or to the Crown. And it wasn't until eight years later that Pitt decided that India should belong to the Crown and not to the Company. No constructive decisions were taken until the nineteenth century.

C❖The object of the East India Company was to make profits. How the country was ruled they neither knew nor cared, so long as peace was maintained and trade prospered. They deposed the aging Mir Jafar, and, when his puppet-successor became restless, defeated him in a bloody battle and sold the throne of Bengal by auction. The ill-paid servants of the Company were both forced and encouraged to take bribes, presents, and every kind of shameful perquisite from the inhabitants. Tales of corruption and the gaining of vast and illicit private fortunes crept back to England.

Clive returned to England. He'd finally bought his seat in Parliament in 1761, and in the following year he'd been given an Irish peerage. Three years later, he returned to India for the last time. The Directors of the Company made him Commander in Chief and Governor of Bengal, and pleaded with him to establish order.

C❖His reforms were drastic, high-handed and ... far-reaching. ... Their success prompted the Mogul Emperor to invite him to extend a British protectorate to Delhi and all Northern India. Clive refused. He had long doubted the ability of the Company to undertake the larger responsibilities of Empire. ... Meanwhile, in return for a subsidy, the Great Mogul ceded to the company the right to administer the revenues.

But by this time the changes in India were nothing to those in Britain. A couple of years before Clive's return to India, the Seven Years' War reached a watershed in North America.

C❖In September 1760 [Montreal] fell and the huge province of French Canada changed hands. ... Pitt had not only won Canada, with its rich fisheries and Indian trade, but had banished for ever the dream and danger of a French colonial empire stretching from Montreal to New Orleans.

In the autumn of 1760 George II, the last man who could keep Pitt in power, died. He was seventy-seven and for the thirty-three years of his reign, Britain had flourished. As much as George disliked Pitt, he had learned to trust his abilities. And he recognized the wisdom of supporting the combination of Newcastle managing the finances with Pitt managing the war. Political leaders who insist that victories do not remove the dangers of war have never had much of a hearing in any century, including the twentieth. Pitt was no exception and on 5 October he resigned.

CHAPTER THIRTY-SEVEN

1760–1768

❖

T he importance of George II's reign is that during his three decades the system of constitutional monarchy was established: the monarch no longer reigned by divine right. There were rules of succession and the powers of the monarch, although still considerable, were governed by political expediency. The monarch needed the prime minister; the prime minister needed the monarch; both needed Parliament.

Into this, now established, system came the twenty-two-year-old George III, in 1760. He was George II's grandson, the son of Frederick, the Prince of Wales who died. The third Earl Waldegrave observed the young George shortly before he became king and remarked that it would be unfair to decide upon his character in the early stages of his life. But he observed that there was time for improvement.

❖His parts, though not excellent, will be found very tolerable, if ever they are properly exercised. He is strictly honest, but wants that frank and open behaviour which makes honesty appear amiable. When he had a very scanty allowance, it was one of his favourite maxims that men should be just before they are generous: his income is now considerably augmented, but his generosity has not increased in equal proportion.

His religion is free from all hypocrisy, but is not of the most charitable sort; he has rather too much attention to the sins of his neighbour. He has spirit, but not of the active kind; and does not want resolution, but it is mixed with too much obstinacy. He has great command of his passions, and will seldom do wrong, except when he mistakes wrong for right; but as often as this shall happen, it will be difficult to undeceive him, because he is uncommonly indolent, and has strong prejudices.

His want of application and aversion to business would be far less dangerous, was he eager in the pursuit of pleasure; for the transition from pleasure to business is both shorter and easier than from a state of total inaction. He has a kind of temper, which, if it be not conquered before it has taken too deep a root, will be a source of frequent anxiety. Whenever he is displeased, his anger does not break out with heat and violence; but he becomes sullen and silent, and retires to his closet; not to compose his mind by study or contemplation, but merely to indulge the melancholy enjoyment of his own ill humour. Even when the fit is ended unfavourable symptoms very frequently return, which indicate that on certain occasions, His Royal Highness has too correct a memory.

There has indeed been some alteration; the authority of the nursery has gradually declined, and the Earl of Bute, by all assistance of the mother, has now the intire [sic] confidence. But whether this change will be greatly to his Royal Highness's advantage, is a nice question, which cannot hitherto be determined with any certainty.

George III was not bright, perhaps even a little backward. He was nevertheless seen as a conscientious man with ideas (not always his own), who relied on John Stuart Bute for his political education. And at the start of his reign at least, like the first two Hanoverian Kings, he fancied that he could overturn the constitutional contract between Crown and Government. In his fancy, the King was mistaken. It was characteristic of George III that he took some time learning from his mistakes.

C❖He meant to be King, such a king as all his countrymen would follow and revere. Under the long Whig regime the House of Commons had become an irresponsible autocracy. Would not the liberties of the country be safer in the hands of a monarch, young, honourable, virtuous, and appearing thoroughly English, than in a faction governing the land through a packed and corrupt House of Commons? Let him make an end of government by families, choose his own Ministers and stand by them, and end once and for all the corruption of political life. But in such a monarchy what was the place of a man like Pitt, who owed nothing to corruption, nothing to the Crown, and everything to the people and to his personal domination of the House of Commons? . . . His profound reverence for the person and office of George III could not conceal from either of them the fact that Pitt was a very great man and the King a very limited man. Bute, [known as] 'the Minister behind the curtain', was now all-powerful at Court.

John Stuart Bute had joined the royal circle during a downpour at Egham race course. The rain had driven the then heir to the throne, Frederick Prince of Wales, into a sporting marquee. The Prince's party needed a fourth at cards; Bute was their man, and from that moment he became an intimate member of Frederick's set. When the Prince died Bute befriended his widow, Princess Augusta. In fact it was thought they became very close friends indeed. Bute became indispensable to the intellectually immature Prince George – the future king. Bute was a father figure and the new King George relied on him. Bute was George III's political mentor, and would soon succeed the Duke of Newcastle as Prime Minister. But Bute was not a great political plotter or manipulator.

Pitt on the other hand, although not Prime Minister, was the most powerful politician in the land – but not at Court, and it was at this point that he found himself isolated. The Seven Years' War trundled on. Britain's successes against the French in India, in North America and her support for Frederick the Great of Prussia had brought victories and commercial dividends. Now there was, to Pitt and Newcastle, the Prime Minister, a case for declaring war against Spain. The Cabinet said no and Pitt resigned.

C❖Unsupported by the fame of Pitt, the Duke of Newcastle was an easy victim and the administration slid easily into the hands of Lord Bute. His sole qualification for office, apart from great wealth and his command of the Scottish vote, was that he had been Groom of the Stole to the King's mother. For the first time since the assassination of the Duke of Buckingham [Charles I's Chief Minister] the government of England was committed to a man with no political experience, and whose only connection with Parliament was that he had sat as a representative peer of Scotland for a short time twenty years before. . . . Within three months of Pitt's resignation, the Government were compelled to declare war on Spain. This led to further success in the West Indies and elsewhere. The British Fleet seized the port of Havana, which commanded the trade routes of the Spanish Main and the movement of the Treasure Fleets. In the Pacific Ocean an expedition from Madras descended upon the Philippines and captured Manila. At sea and on land England was mistress of the outer world.

The time was right, or so the administration thought, to sign a peace treaty with France. Pitt's reading of history suggested to him that there was a danger, a very real one, of concluding not a peace treaty, but a truce. In other words, he felt that unless France was hobbled and not allowed to regain its possessions, regroup its resources and then its forces, a new war between the two nations would come soon. But Pitt was no longer in command.

C❖Bute sent the Duke of Bedford to Paris to negotiate its terms. The Duke thought his country was taking too much of the globe and would be in perpetual danger from European coalitions and attacks by dissatisfied nations. He believed in the appeasement of France and Spain and the generous return of conquests. Pitt . . . vehemently denounced the treaty as undermining the safety of the realm.

Britain's acquisitions under the terms of the Peace of Paris in 1763 were nevertheless considerable. In America she secured Canada, Nova Scotia,

Cape Breton, and the adjoining islands, and the right to navigate the Mississippi, important to Red Indian trade. In the West Indies Grenada, St Vincent, Dominica, and Tobago were acquired. From Spain she received Florida. In Africa she kept Senegal. In India . . . the East India Company preserved its extensive conquests, and although their trading posts were returned the political ambitions of the French in the sub-continent were finally extinguished. In Europe Minorca was restored to England, and the fortifications of Dunkirk were at long last demolished.

. . . [This treaty] was a perfect exposition of the principles of the Duke of Bedford. The naval power of France had been left untouched. In America she received back the islands of St Pierre and Miquelon in the Gulf of the St Lawrence, with the right to fish upon the shores of Newfoundland.

Bedford gave away a fishing industry that, in 1745, was worth £1 million a year.

C❖In the West Indies the richest prize of the war, the sugar island of Guadeloupe, was also handed back, together with Martinique, Belle Isle, and St Lucia. Guadeloupe was so rich that the English Government even considered keeping it and in exchange returning Canada to the French. These islands were also excellent naval bases for future use against England.

Spain regained the West Indian port of Havana, which controlled the maritime strategy of the Caribbean. She also received back Manila, an important centre for the China trade. If the English had retained them, the fleets of France and Spain would have been permanently at their mercy. . . . Moreover, the treaty took no account of the interests of Frederick the Great.

Frederick was Britain's ally in the Seven Years' War. He had fought France in Europe, thus stretching her resources and in some ways making Britain's task easier in India and North America.

C❖This ally was left to shift for himself. He never forgave Britain for what he regarded as a betrayal, which rankled long afterwards in the minds of the Prussian leaders.

The terms of the Paris peace treaty, together with new and unpopular taxes in the spring of 1763, brought about mob protests on the streets of England and newspaper articles condemned the Government and Bute in particular. Bute was not a political pugilist and within weeks he was heading for a nervous breakdown. He resigned and the new chief minister, the new First Lord of the Treasury, was George Grenville, William Pitt's brother-in-law. But the King still regarded Bute as his Prime Minister. So, effectively, there were two Prime

Ministers: Grenville and, behind the curtain, the Earl of Bute.

Bute was, and remained, George's mentor, his father confessor, his 'dearest friend', and although Grenville might have become a fine office manager for Britain, he was no managing director. He was an isolationist. And he had an ambition to reduce the tax burden. He did so by making the British Americans pay more. In doing so, and in doing so diligently, Grenville may perhaps be accused of hastening the American War of Independence.

The administration of Britain was going through the agony of the King's dislike and mistrust of his Prime Minister, of that Minister's mistrust of the King, and of Parliament's mistrust of both. As Dr Johnson remarked, 'Most schemes of political improvement are very laughable things'. But Johnson's own 'improvements' were helped by political patronage, and by Lord Bute's own hand, which was perhaps why Boswell was able to record Sheridan's dislike of Johnson.

❖Sheridan said he now could not bear him, because he had taken a pension of £300 a year from the Court, by the particular interest of Lord Bute, and yet he still railed against the royal family and the Scots minister [Bute]. I said I imagined he put it upon this: that the pension was not a favour but a reward due to his merit, and therefore he would show still the same principles of opposition freely and openly.

'No Sir,' said he, 'Johnson took it as a favour; waited on Lord Bute, said he could not find an English word to express what he felt, and was therefore obliged to have recourse to the French "I am *pénétré* with his Majesty's goodness".'

Arrangements for £300 a year to Johnson and even the ambivalent expression of gratitude were, perhaps, some light relief for Bute, whose effigy was, by now, being burned in the streets. And the fire raisers could have burned effigies of any number of public figures at the time. In the early 1760s the seven million or so people of England and Wales knew that the ruling society was inevitably corrupt in some of its dealings.

The buying and selling of votes and seats was commonly practised and for all the learned treatises on foreign policy, economic reform and medical advancement, it was a society that had only very recently decided that witchcraft wasn't a crime; a society that treated its poor as outcasts, commonly practised religious and racial bigotry, accepted slavery without question, and treated backhanders and bribes as a way of everyday life and office.

The North Briton, a newspaper started by a man called John Wilkes in 1762, accused those in power.

C❖On April 23, 1763 . . . *The North Briton* attacked Ministers as 'tools of despotism and corruption. . . . They have sent the spirit of discord through the land, and I will prophesy it will never be extinguished but by the extinction of their power.' . . . The writer hinted that the peace treaty with France was not only dishonourably but also dishonestly negotiated, and that the King was a party to it. George was incensed. A week later his Secretary of State issued a warrant commanding that the authors, printers, and publishers of *The North Briton*, Number 45, none of whom was named, should be found and arrested. Searches were made, houses were entered, papers were seized, and nearly fifty suspects were put in prison. Among them was John Wilkes, a rake and a Member of Parliament. He was sent to the Tower. He refused to answer questions. He protested that the warrant was illegal and claimed Parliamentary privilege against the arrest. There was a storm in the country. The legality of 'general' warrants which named no actual offender became a constitutional question of the first importance. Wilkes was charged with seditious libel and outlawed. But his case became a national issue when he returned to fight his Parliamentary seat. The radical-minded Londoners welcomed this rebuff to the Government, and in March 1768 he was elected for Middlesex. The next February he was expelled from the House of Commons and there was a by-election. Wilkes stood again and obtained 1143 votes against his Government opponent, who polled 296. There were bonfires in London. The election was declared void by Parliament, and Wilkes, now once more in prison for printing an obscene parody of Pope's 'Essay on Man', entitled 'Essay on Woman', became the idol of the City. Finally his opponent in Middlesex was declared duly elected. When Wilkes was released from gaol in April 1770, London was illuminated to greet him.

Wilkes was a patriot, a nationalist, and an extremist. He was a member of Sir Francis Dashwood's 'Hell Fire Club', which was devoted to complicated versions of debauchery. Such clubs were not uncommon in the eighteenth century. Wilkes's background was middle class, the son of a malt distiller. He was ugly, with a lazy eye which produced a disconcerting squint, and he was a brilliant self-publicist and radical journalist. Here's part of Wilkes's article from the famous issue Number 45 of *The North Briton* which appeared on St George's Day.

❖This week has given the public the most abandoned instance of ministerial effrontery ever attempted to be imposed on mankind. The Minister's speech of last Tuesday is not [to] be paralleled in the annals of this country. I am in doubt whether the imposition is greater on the Sovereign, or on the nation. Every friend of his country must lament that a prince of so many great and amiable qualities, whom England truly reveres, can be brought to give sanction of his sacred name to the most odious measures, and to the most unjustifiable public declarations, from a throne ever renowned for truth, honour and unsullied virtue.

The Minister's speech of last Tuesday refers to the speech proroguing Parliament in which (Wilkes claimed) there was a lie about the desertion of England's great ally, Frederick of Prussia.

This passage in *The North Briton* was quoted in the information laid in the King's Bench Division against the publisher. Wilkes goes on to say that the *Scottish* Prime Minister, Bute, had deserted England's great ally under the terms of the Paris Peace Treaty which ended the Seven Years' War, and he accused the Court of handing out offices to what he called the Scottish Faction.

❖The prerogative of the Crown is to exert the Constitutional Powers entrusted to it in a way not of blind favour and partiality, but of wisdom and judgment. This is the spirit of our Constitution. The people too have their prerogative, and I hope the fine words of Dryden will be engraven on our hearts: 'Freedom is the English Subject's Prerogative.'

Wilkes represented a growing sense of Nationalism; he felt that the fundamental principles of Englishness, that began with opposition to the Normans, had been abandoned. It was Dr Johnson who said that patriotism is the last refuge of a scoundrel, and Wilkes would surely have been very much in Johnson's mind. But, although it is fashionable to dismiss Wilkes as a rabble-rouser, a rake and a rogue (and probably a scoundrel as well) he undoubtedly caught the public imagination. Besides, there were quite a few senior politicians to whom a similar set of labels might justly have been applied.

And what's often forgotten is that when Wilkes claimed that the Scots were moving into positions of political power, he was correct. Wilkes successfully played on the nervousness of the English nation which felt that, as a result of the creeping influence of outsiders, the Act of Union was somehow likely to remove its very Englishness, its cherished sovereignty. It was a sentiment which today might have earned Wilkes the title Union-Sceptic.

C❖The whole machinery of eighteenth-century corruption was thus exposed to the public eye. By refusing to accept Wilkes [as an MP], the Commons had denied the right of electors to choose their Members, and held themselves out as a closed corporation of privileged beings. Wilkes's cause now found the most powerful champion in England. Pitt himself, now Earl of Chatham, in blistering tones attacked the legality of general warrants and the corruption of politics, claiming that more seats in the counties would increase the electorate and diminish the opportunities for corruption, so easy in the small boroughs. His speeches were indeed the first demands for Parliamentary reform in the eighteenth century.

And there were other forms of corruption. For years, the engravings of Hogarth and others, and the writings of many had shown how badly, at least by twentieth-century standards, children were treated at this time. And although Defoe talks of five-year-olds working at machinery, and praises this as good, industrious order, Jonas Hanway, in 1766, wrote a pamphlet, 'An Earnest Appeal for Mercy to the Children of the Poor'.

❖One may with great truth assert that many children born of poor, idle, or unfortunate parents, though they should have the best constitutions, yet die in great numbers under five years old. Many children, instead of being nourished with care by the fostering hand or breast of a wholesome country nurse, are thrust into the impure air of a workhouse, into the hands of some careless, worthless young female, or decrepid old woman. It is hard to say how many lives these cities have lost, or how many they yet lose annually, by the poverty, filth, and vice of parents, which no public institutions in this land of freedom can save; and though we live on as fine a spot as any of the three Kingdoms can boast of, yet by being closely built, and many living in confined places, and many too much congregated, joined to the sulphurous air created by so vast a number of coal fires, we must not be surprised, that so great a proportion as near 47% die under two years of age.

We ought no more to suffer a child to die for want of the common necessaries of life, though he is born to labor, than one who is the heir to a dukedom. One thousand or 1200 children have annually perished under the direction of parish officers. I say under their direction, not that they ordered them to be killed, but that they did not order such means to be used as are necessary to keep them alive.

Never shall I forget the evidence given at Guildhall, upon occasion of a master of a workhouse of a large parish, who was challenged for forcing a child from the breast of a mother, and sending it to the Foundling Hospital. He alleged this in his defence, 'We send all our children to the Foundling Hospital; we have not saved one alive for fourteen years.'

Jonas Hanway wanted an Act of Parliament that would make London parishes send poor children under the age of six into the country to be nursed. Hanway was not much interested in the Englishness or Scottishness of the infants, only that 47% died before the age of two.

While social pleading depended on debate and Parliament's whim, the industrial upheaval brought added miseries. Take, for example, the plight of hand spinners. In 1765 James Hargreaves, a carpenter and weaver, produced his most famous invention. And he named it after his wife, Jenny. It was to be called the spinning-jenny. By using eight spindles driven by a great wheel, Hargreaves revolutionized the methods of the textile industry. And just like those who, 200 years on, viewed automation with dismay, the spinners understood perfectly that their livelihoods would never be the same again. This was the beginning of what is now called the Industrial Revolution. And inventiveness was not confined to the industrial drawing board: musicians, writers, painters and diarists were prolific, and to be found at every coffee house, salon and studio. Among them were Thomas and then his son, Richard Sheridan, George Steevens, Thomas Tyrwhitt, Joshua Reynolds, Smollett, Boswell, Johnson, Laurence Sterne, and Oliver Goldsmith.

Smollett published *Peregrine Pickle* and *Sir Launcelot Greaves* and then he decided to produce a political magazine. Smollett's *The Briton* was in direct opposition to John Wilkes's *North Briton*. Where Wilkes lambasted the King's closest friend and political mentor, the Earl of Bute, Smollett supported Bute. But it was neither a well- produced journal nor a popular cause and *The Briton* folded. It was Laurence Sterne who called Smollett Smelfungus, and it was now Sterne who achieved a great following through his volumes of *Tristram Shandy*.

But Sterne, like many of his time, was a moralist. Horace Walpole said that the sermon in the third volume of *Tristram Shandy* was the best part of the novel and Voltaire regarded it as required reading. Perhaps William Pitt thought so too – the first two volumes were dedicated to him. Another Irishman (Sterne was born in Clonmel), Oliver Goldsmith, became a friend of Samuel Johnson's. It was Johnson who sold the manuscript of *The Vicar of Wakefield* for Goldsmith. Johnson got £60 for it and probably saved Goldsmith from the debtors' prison by so doing.

But for the King there was a more complicated book balancing to be performed: the sombre business of balancing his own ambitions for government with the reality of eighteenth-century politics was uppermost. In the royal archives, there is a memorandum written by the King which expresses his feelings for his Prime Minister. In it, we find George III's objection to the notion that ministers – especially George Grenville – could insist on conditions before agreeing to serve in his administration.

❖To prove the hight of Mr Greenville's [sic] insolence, he say'd if people presume'd to speak to Me on business without his previous consent, he would not serve an hour; had I given way to my feelings on receiving this account, he would have been instantly dismiss'd; but I thought it detrimental to the business of the Nation to make any alteration during the sitting of Parliament. All the advantage I expect from this account of What has pass'd, is that honest men will feel for Me and will see that it was impossible for me either as King or Man to bear any longer the Usage I met with, and that necessity not choice has made me take several Steps that cut Me to the Soul.

This document, although not dated, was probably written towards the end of 1765. The significance of this is that it was recording the King's feelings and his justification for getting rid of Grenville, which he had done by the summer of that year.

But for the moment Grenville was Prime Minister, and First Lord of the Treasury, with Halifax and Egremont as the two senior secretaries of state. When, after Egremont's death, the King tried to persuade Pitt to become Prime Minister, Pitt said no. Two years later, George III tried once more but the result was the same and Grenville felt himself more secure in office. So much so that he threatened to resign unless the King agreed to get rid of a number of Bute's admirers. He was challenging the monarch, telling him that there could not be two governments of Britain. Most distinctly, he was saying that the King could not have two Prime Ministers. And, for the time being, Grenville won.

Grenville was dedicated to the good of the nation even if he was unimaginative. He was a diligent economist and the arch tax collector of the eighteenth century. And it was a tax that was eventually seen as one of the major contributions to the start of the American War of Independence. By 1765 the Grenville administration had angered the colonists by limiting by law their westward expansion in North America. Now there was to be a new tax: the stamp tax. But the British Americans already regarded themselves as badly treated.

C❖George III was also determined that the colonies should pay their share in the expenses of the Empire and in garrisoning the New World. For this there were strong arguments. England had supplied most of the men and the money in the struggle with France for their protection, and indeed their survival; but the methods used by the British Government were ineffective and imprudent . . . Grenville and his lieutenant Charles Townshend consulted the Law Officers about levying a direct tax on the colonies. Their opinion was favourable, and Grenville proposed that all colonial legal documents should be stamped, for a fee. The colonial agents in London were informed, and discussed the plan by post with the Assemblies in America. There were no protests, although the colonists had always objected to direct taxation, and in 1765 Parliament passed the Stamp Act.

The stamp tax was a duty on newspapers as well as legal documents in the colonies.

C❖The English stamp duty brought in £300,000 a year. Its extension to America was only expected to raise another £50,000. But the Act included newspapers, many of whose journalists were vehement partisans of the extremist party in America, and the colonial merchants were dismayed because the duty had to be paid in bullion already needed for meeting the adverse trade balance with England. The dispute exposed and fortified the more violent elements in America, and gave them a chance to experiment in organized resistance. The future revolutionary leaders appeared from obscurity – Patrick Henry in Virginia, Samuel Adams in Massachusetts, and Christopher Gadsden in South Carolina – and attacked both the legality of the Government's policy and the meekness of most American merchants. A small but well organized radical element began to emerge. But although there was an outcry and protesting delegates convened a Stamp Act Congress there was no unity of opinion in America. . . . The most effective opposition came from English merchants, who realized that the Act imperilled the recovery of their commercial debts and denounced it as contrary to the true commercial interests of the Empire and a danger to colonial resources.

By July 1765 Grenville was gone. George III asked the Marquess of Rockingham, 'a shy well-meaning Whig' as Churchill calls him, to form a government. The King didn't like him but he had to accept him just to get rid of Grenville. Rockingham told the King that the Stamp Act had to go. The King didn't agree but he had to accept Rockingham's decision, and so the Act was repealed.

The King was uneasy among his new politicians. Here is part of a letter from the King to the Earl of Bute, whose own friends were set aside by Rockingham. It is noticeable how the King distinguishes between his friends and his Government.

❖Friday January 10, 1766.
My Dear Friend,
You cannot feel more strongly than I do the situation of those men who have invariably stood by you, and those few besides whose personal conduct to me have made them dear to you; what I now learn from you, concerning the treatment they meet from the present Ministers does not surprise, though it grieves me; for I knew too well from the many cruel scenes I underwent during the formation of them how very personal they are against the men they got remov'd, and their diffidence of those that remain'd; as to their being wrong represented to me that shall never affect me in my opinion; for as I am apprised of the passions that influence those who may try to hurt them with me, they may throw dirt but none of it will stick . . . As to the tallents [sic] or experience necessary to carry on the business of this

nation, we I should imagine, look on the present set with the same eyes; but I owne I should think I had great reason to complain if those of my friends that are still in office try'd to overturn those I employ.

It was not a happy period for the King. Rockingham, in predictable Whig manner, opposed war with the American colonists which some were already suggesting. He forced through legislation that declared British sovereignty over the colonies. By the following summer Rockingham too would be gone but he would return and with him his secretary, who was one of the most influential thinkers in eighteenth-century political history. His name was Edmund Burke.

Rockingham perceived the need for a change in Whig politics. He believed in a proper party programme of government, one that would be supported by a wider electorate, especially among traders. He saw the need for a group that would act on party principle rather than simply do anything to stay in power. And in this the beginnings of a system of party political politics – not just the parties themselves – began to emerge.

But Rockingham, although he was a party and an economic reformer, was not a Parliamentary Reformer. Had he stayed in power, that too might have come. But reformers need energy, and he was probably too lazy. He much preferred horse-racing to the everyday business of governing. Once he actually forgot to attend his own Cabinet Meeting. Add to this the double-dealings of the King and the campaign to persuade Pitt the Elder to return, and it was inevitable that Rockingham would not survive.

C❖Rockingham's Government, which lasted thirteen months, passed three measures that went far to soothe the animosities raised by Grenville on both sides of the Atlantic. They repealed the Stamp Act, and induced the House of Commons to declare general warrants and the seizure of private papers unlawful. At the same time they reaffirmed the powers of Parliament to tax the colonies in a so-called Declaratory Act. But the King was determined to be rid of them, and Pitt, whose mind was clouded by sickness, was seduced by royal flattery and by his own dislike of party [sic] into lending his name to a new administration formed on no political principle whatever. His arrogance remained; his powers were failing; his popularity as the 'Great Commoner' had been dimmed by his sudden acceptance of the Earldom of Chatham. The conduct of affairs slipped into other hands: Charles Townshend, the Duke of Grafton, and Lord Shelburne. In 1767, Townshend, against the opposition of Shelburne, introduced a Bill imposing duties on American imports of paper, glass, lead, and tea. There was a rage in America.

The supply of coin in the colonies would be still more depleted, and any surplus from the new revenue was not, as originally stated, to be used for the upkeep of the British garrisons but to pay British colonial officials. This threatened to make them independent of the colonial assemblies, whose chief weapon against truculent governors had been to withhold their salaries. Even so, revolt was still far from their minds.

Behind this was the right of the British government to tax the American-British. Pitt didn't want to antagonize them. William Mansfield, the Lord Chief Justice (who six years later would be unpopular for declaring slavery illegal in England) now declared that the colonists were subjects of the Crown and therefore liable to the Crown's laws, including taxation. It's fine to decide to tax people, but how do you actually get the money from them if they happen to be 3500 miles away, in many instances disinclined to obey British officials, and inclined to say so in the most forceful manner?

C❖Intelligent men, like Governor Hutchinson of Massachusetts, preferred not to impose taxes at all if they could not be enforced, and declared that another repeal would only 'facilitate the designs of those persons who appear to be aiming at independency'. John Dickinson, of Pennsylvania, in his *Letters from a Farmer*, voiced the opposition in the most widely read pamphlet of the time. It was studiously cautious in tone, and at this stage there were few people who desired secession. The authority of Parliament over the colonies was formally denied, but there was a general loyalty to the King and Empire.

There's a parallel here with the attitude to government in the English Parliament. At Westminister there were more or less three groups. First there were the Royalists who would support the Government if that's what the King wanted. Then there were the squires, the landowners who were not ambitious for public office, and who wouldn't blindly support the Government because the King said so; but they would give it a fair hearing if the monarch did. The third group contained those who were ambitious for public office and who would swing with the prevailing mood and hang upon the Court's coat-tails.

What was missing in Parliament was a formal Opposition. There were opposition groups, but no organized Opposition. Certainly, during the early part of his long reign, it is unlikely that any Opposition would have made much impression on George III.

C❖He was one of the most conscientious sovereigns who ever sat upon the English throne. Simple in his tastes and unpretentious in manner, he had the superficial appearance of a typical yeoman. But his mind was Hanoverian, with an infinite capacity for mastering detail, and limited success in dealing with large issues and main principles. He possessed great moral courage and an inveterate obstinacy, and his stubbornness lent weight to the stiffening attitude of his Government. His responsibility for the final breach [with America] is a high one. He could not understand those who feared the consequences of a policy of coercion. He expressed himself in blunt terms.

'It is with the utmost astonishment that I find any of my subjects capable of encouraging the rebellious disposition which unhappily exists in some of my colonies in America. Having entire confidence in the wisdom of my Parliament, the Great Council of the Nation, I will steadily pursue those measures which they have recommended for the support of the constitutional rights of Great Britain and the protection of the commercial interests of my Kingdom.'

These constitutional and commercial interests raise a matter often ignored when trying to understand why the radicals in America were so successful in setting the colonies on the road to revolution. Pitt the Elder had argued in the Commons that Britain had no right to tax the colonies because although they were supposedly subjects of the Crown, they were not represented in Parliament. In the Lords, the Duke of Grafton (who would soon be Prime Minister and who was said to have a more conciliatory attitude towards America) nevertheless proposed a motion which insisted that Parliament did indeed have the authority to bind the colonies to any laws.

And when, on 10 February 1766, Lord Mansfield got to his feet in that debate, it was clear that the division was not simply about the colonies, but the whole authority of an unwritten constitution. Here's part of what Lord Mansfield had to say.

❖The proposition before your Lordships has unhappily been attended with a difference of opinion in England. I shall therefore use my endeavours, in what I have to offer your Lordships on this occasion, to quiet men's minds upon this subject. In order to do this, I shall first lay down two propositions:

First, That the British legislature, as to the power of making laws, represents the whole British Empire, and has authority to bind every part and every subject without the least distinction, whether such subjects have a right to vote or not, or whether the law binds places within the realm or without.

Second, That the colonists, by the condition on which they migrated, settled and now exist, are more emphatically subjects of Great Britain than those within the realm; and that the British legislature have in every instance exercised their right of legislation over them without any dispute or question till the fourteenth of January last.

As to the first proposition: In every government the legislative power must be lodged somewhere, and the executive must likewise be lodged somewhere. In Great Britain the legislative is in Parliament, the executive in the Crown.

And then he gave the House a constitutional history lesson before concluding his argument.

❖When the Supreme Power abdicates, the Government is dissolved. Take care, my Lords, you do not abdicate your authority. In such an event, your Lordships would leave the worthy and innocent, as well as the unworthy and guilty, to the same confusion and ruin.

Ten years before the American War of Independence, a great deal of Parliamentary time was taken up with discussing whether or not the taxation of Americans was legitimate and the consequences understood. In the early months of 1766 newspapers regarded the future of America as the most important matter of the day. Beneath the headline, 'Political Controversy' on the Letters pages of the *Lloyd's Evening Post* a correspondent claims the colonists' attempt to justify their actions are in vain.

❖But as they are our relations, and fellow-subjects, it is to be hoped and wished that they will endeavour, by their future good behaviour, to endear themselves to their mother country, instead of incurring her displeasure, contempt, or resentment, by an obstinate, despicable, and pitiful withholding of a small contribution towards the public support, and carrying on an illicit trade in prejudice of the mother country, though lately at a very great charge and trouble in defending them against the French and Indians.
                    Philopolites M'Ulader, January 22, 1766.

The American debate may have been ten years in the making, but it held little for a British nation rapidly changing shape. At the start of the eighteenth century England and Wales had a combined population of almost five and a half million. Thanks to illness, a very high child mortality rate and, in London, an adult death rate accelerated by cheap gin until the 1750s, the population grew by only one million in the first half of the century. In the next fifty years, partly due to huge increases in medical science, it had grown by something approaching three million, ending the century at about nine million.

Scotland, over the same period, went from little more than one million to nearly three million by the end of the century and most people expected to live until they were about thirty-one or thirty-two. By the end of the century that expectation had risen to thirty-nine.

But that doesn't mean there weren't any old people – after all the King, George III, was on the throne for almost sixty years.

As the population grew, so, of course, did towns and cities. For example, at the start of the eighteenth century, about 10,000 people lived in Glasgow. By the middle of the century there were 25,000 and 100 years on, there were more than 200,000. Bigger city populations meant bigger, sometimes redesigned, towns. In 1767 Edinburgh's Town Council approved James Craig's plan for the development of new buildings and for what was called feuing. A feu was a perpetual lease at a set rent.

❖Act anent settling the plan of the new buildings and for feuing the grounds on the north of the city, July 29, 1767.

The Committee, after many meetings and consulting with Lord Kaims, Lord Alemour, Commissioner Clerk, and Mr Adams, and other persons of skill in these matters, had reviewed all the former plans with the greatest care and attention, and considered several amendments proposed by Mr Craig; and that Mr Craig, by their direction, had made out a new plan, which plan, signed by the Lord Provost of this date was produced . . . That they were of the opinion:

One:
That the Council should immediately form the principal street of the plot now to be feued in the manner of a turn pike road; and so proceed in the same way with the other plots, as they come to be feued, for the conveniency of the feuars.

Two:
That the pavement on each side of the street should be ten feet broad, not to rise higher than a foot above the level of the street, and that there should be no posts erected betwixt the street and the pavement.

Three:
That the pavement ought to be laid and repaired at the expense of the proprietors of houses, in the same way as is practised in the Old Town.

And so on until the very important matter of the drains is addressed.

Item Eight:
That the Council should execute a common sewer in the middle of the street, to be kept up at the expense of the city; and that the feuars should have liberty to make a communication sewer from their respective houses to the said common sewer, to be kept up at their expense.

So there was no longer any need to empty chamber pots from the upstairs window and good drainage meant better health and therefore the possibility of lower death rates, at least for some.

Back in the South, Pitt, now the Earl of Chatham, was once more in the King's Government but he was not at all well. He suffered from gout and from bouts of desperate depression. By March 1768 he was not really in control. He would take himself into a darkened room and often the only communication with his colleagues would be through his wife Hester. But Ministers didn't rally round the ailing Pitt the Elder (who was no longer Prime Minister, the Duke of Grafton was). And it wasn't until Pitt the Younger became Prime Minister that collective Cabinet responsibility became a reality. But he was, at this point, only a boy.

CHAPTER THIRTY-EIGHT

1768–1770

———— ❖ ————

One of the great adventurers of the eighteenth century was a man whose death was bizarre as well as horrific, and whose legacy survived well into the second half of the twentieth century. Captain James Cook was a navigator, an explorer and an hydrographer. Cook began the first of his three great voyages in 1768, and in a decade he sailed to Tahiti, New Zealand, Australia and Hawaii; plotted the exact positions of the Easter Islands and Tonga, New Caledonia and Norfolk Island; surveyed the North American coast; and charted the extreme coast of Siberia before sailing south again to Hawaii. It was in Hawaii that he was murdered.

On Friday 26 August 1768 Lieutenant James Cook sailed from Plymouth to the Pacific via Cape Horn. He left behind a nation which was hardly at peace with itself and moving inexorably towards war with its American colonies.

C❖Colonial resistance was now being organized on a continental scale and the barriers of provincialism and jealousy were being lowered. Non-importation agreements were concluded and there was a systematic and most successful boycott of English goods. But tempers began to rise. In May 1768 the sloop *Liberty*, belonging to John Hancock, the most prominent Boston merchant, was stopped and searched near the coast by Royal Customs officers. The colonists rescued it by force. By 1769, British exports to America had fallen by one-half. The Cabinet was not seriously apprehensive, but perturbed. It agreed to drop the duties, except on tea. By a majority of one, this was carried. Parliament proclaimed its sovereignty over the colonies by retaining a tax on tea of three pence a pound.

The political atmosphere of 1769 was full of the signs of the beginnings of a dissolution of the then Empire, at least for those who cared to read them. But geographically there was still enormous ignorance of what lay south of the equator. Everyone knew about Europe, something of China, India and North America, but not much about the southern hemisphere.

Two centuries earlier, Columbus, Magellan and, by 1587, Drake, had shown that the world was far larger than most had imagined and that there was plenty of room for other continents. In 1606, a Dutch admiral, William Jansz, had discovered Australia. A few years later Abel Tasman and the Dutch navigator, Visscher, found Tasmania and New Zealand in their search for a commercial route to South America. But very little detail was known, hence Cook's expedition.

The expedition was well planned. It was also highly classified. Cook had two sets of instructions: the first, entirely public, were given him by his masters, the Admiralty, with guidance from the Royal Society. He was to sail via Cape Horn to what was then called King George's Island, what is now called Tahiti. Cook had instructions to observe a transit of Venus in June 1769. It wasn't until this had been done that he was allowed to open his second set of instructions, or Secret Orders. These Orders were not published until as late as 1928.

❖ By the Commissioners for executing the office of the Lord High Admiral of Great Britain. Additional instructions for Lieutenant James Cook, Appointed to Command His Majesty's Bark the *Endeavour*.

Secret

Whereas the making Discoverys of Countries hitherto unknown, and the Attaining a Knowledge of distant Parts which though formerly discover'd have yet been but imperfectly explored, will redound greatly to the Honour of this Nation as a Maritime Power, as well as to the Dignity of the Crown of Great Britain, and may trend [sic] greatly to the advancement of the Trade and Navigation thereof; and Whereas there is reason to imagine that a Continent or Land of great extent, may be found to the Southward of the Tract lately made by Captain Wallis in His Majesty's Ship the *Dolphin* (of which you will herewith receive a Copy) or of the Tract of any former Navigators in Pursuits of the like kind; You are therefore in Pursuance of His Majesty's Pleasure hereby requir'd and directed to put to Sea with the Bark you Command so soon as the Observation of the Transit of the Planet Venus shall be finished. . . . You are to proceed to the southward in order to make discovery of the Continent above-mentioned until you arrive in the Latitude of 40 degrees, unless you sooner fall in with it.

The latitude 40 degrees south runs roughly through Southern Australia and Tasmania and the southern end of New Zealand's North Island. The furthest point north in the Continent mentioned in the Secret Orders, the Continent now known as Antarctica, is more than 60 degrees south.

❖ But not having discover'd it or any Evident signs of it in that Run, you are to proceed in search of it to the Westward between the Latitude before mentioned and the Latitude of 35 degrees until you discover it, or fall in with the Eastern side of the Land discover'd by Tasman and now called New Zeland [sic].

Cook's Secret Orders instructed him that, if and when he discovered the Continent, he must measure it, survey the coastal waters, shoals, currents, tides and harbours, headlands and rocks. He was to look for fish, plants, minerals, precious stones, beasts and fowl and bring examples back to England so, as the Orders stated, 'We may cause proper examination and experiments to be made of them.'

❖ You are likewise to observe the Genius, Temper, Disposition and Number of the Natives, if there be any, and endeavour by all proper means to cultivate a Friendship and Alliance with them, making them presents of such Trifles as they may Value, inviting them to Traffick, and Shewing them every kind of Civility and Regard; taking Care however not to suffer yourself to be surprized by them, but to be always upon your guard against any Accident. . . . You are also with the Consent of the Natives to take possession of Convenient Situations in the Country in the Name of the King of Great Britain.

And after a further list of Orders, this most secret document concludes that the consequences of the voyage should remain secret.

❖ Upon your arrival in England you are immediately to repair to this office in order to lay before us a full account of your Proceedings in the whole Course of your voyage, taking care before you leave your Vessel to demand from your Officers and Petty Officers the Log Books and Journals they may have kept, and to seal them up for our inspection, and enjoining them, and the whole Crew, not to divulge where they have been until they have Permission so to do.

Given under our hands July 30, 1768,

Edward Hawke, Peircy Brett, C. Spencer.

Cook did as he was asked but he didn't find the great southern Continent. However he did experiment with shipboard medicine and it's popularly said that Cook found the cure for scurvy – the fatal disease of many a long-distance sailor. It's said that he gave everyone the juice of lemons and limes and that was that. In fact the Admiralty had already done a great deal of research into keeping sailors healthy and the person who probably did more to cure scurvy was a naval surgeon called James Lind. More than twenty years before Cook sailed Lind had carried out a series of anti-scurvy tests using sailors as guinea pigs, as his medical notes record.

❖On May 20, 1747, I took twelve patients in the scurvy, on board the *Salisbury* at sea. Their cases were as similar as I could have them. They all in general had putrid gums, the spots and lassitude, with weakness of their knees. They lay together in one place, being a proper apartment for the sick in the fore-hold; and had one diet in common to all, viz. water-gruel sweetened with sugar in the morning; fresh mutton-broth often times for dinner; at other times puddings, boiled biscuit with sugar et cetera; and for supper, barley and raisins, rice and currants, sago and wine, or the like. Two of these were ordered each a quart of cyder a-day. Two others took twenty-five gutts of elixir vitriol three times a-day, upon an empty stomach; using a gargle strongly acidulated with it for their mouths.

Two others took two spoonfuls of vinegar three times a-day, upon an empty stomach; having their gruels and their other food well acidulated with it, as also the gargle for their mouths.

On Cook's second voyage, which lasted three years, he recorded the loss of only one man through disease. And in a letter in 1776 he remarked that although lemons had their value, they were impractical to keep on board.

❖The dearness of . . . lemons and of oranges will hinder them from being furnished in large quantities, but I do not think this so necessary; for although they may assist other things, I have no great opinion of them alone. Nor have I a higher opinion of vinegar: my people had it very sparingly during the late voyage; and towards the latter part, none at all; and yet we experienced no ill effects from the want of it. The custom of washing the inside of the ship with vinegar I seldom observed, thinking that fire and smoke answered the purpose much better.

Cook was killed by islanders in Hawaii in 1779. It was not a premeditated act although the manner of his killing and dismemberment was sickening. By the time of his death, Cook had explored the edges of the Antarctic, staked the English flag across islands of the peaceful ocean, disproved the hypothesis of the great southern Continent and developed charting and marine surveying to a level that was barely improved until modern echo and satellite technology. But most of all Cook honoured the central ambition of George III, an ambition contained in those first Secret sailing Orders. He opened a route that would allow English-speaking peoples to one day colonize the South West Pacific.

Meanwhile in the towns and countryside of these islands people believed themselves to be overtaxed. One adjustable form of revenue, the window tax, had existed since 1696. The formula was simple: each house was charged a single sum for the building itself and then so much per window. The idea was to raise millions, and millions were raised – and not a little opposition. It is still possible to see older houses where windows have long ago been bricked up to avoid the tax.

Of course there was nothing new in taxation but at the start of the 1700s, the government was taking £4.3 million a year from the people in taxes. By the end of the century it was nearly £32 million. As the country advanced, someone had to pay. Britain now had organized government and organized government was costly. The National Debt was rising. In 1700 it was about £14 million but by the end of George III's first decade, it was £129 million. By the end of the century it would be £456 million. The interest alone was £9 million a year and taxation had doubled.

And when the population wasn't being taxed, some of it was being robbed in a more traditional manner. The magistrate Sir John Fielding wrote to the Secretary to the Treasury, Charles Jenkinson, to inform him of several recent robberies. If his style seems strange, it was probably because the letter was dictated: Sir John was blind.

❖Bow Street, June 28, 1764

Sir John Fielding presents his respectful compliments to Mr Jenkinson; thought it his indispensable duty to his country to transmit to him the enclosed account of robberies committed since Monday night last, and to acquaint him that in consequence of these repeated informations, he last night sent a foot patrol consisting of a peace officer and three assistants, into the fields near Tyburn and Tottenham Court Roads to search the ditches where footpads have lately infested, that before they got out of the coach which carried them to the spot, they narrowly escaped being murdered by three footpads, who without giving them the least notice fired two pistols immediately into the coach, but thank God without effect; two of them were afterwards taken, though not before one of them was dangerously wounded; all which circumstances might, I am convinced, have been prevented. There is nothing I so sincerely lament as the want of an opportunity of convincing Mr Grenville [the then Prime Minister] of the amazing importance of the police to Government; for notwithstanding his most laudable resolution not to lay any permanent expense on the Crown that can be avoided, yet I am sure that he will never spare any necessary expense where public good is the object. For my part I can only propose and inform, which I shall always do most faithfully.

Your sincere friend and the public's faithful servant,
John Fielding

But, at the time, there wasn't a police force. Sir John's only help came from the Bow Street Runners who were the nearest thing to an organized police force. The Runners, as they became known, were set up in 1748 by Sir John's half brother who was Henry Fielding, now better known as the author of *Tom Jones*. The year before *Tom Jones* was published, Henry Fielding was the Chief Justice of the Peace at Bow Street Magistrates Court.

At the time there was, in government, a considerable debate on what powers existed to maintain law and order. For example, in 1768 there was a mob riot in St George's Fields, part of what is now South London, and the troops were called out. In a debate following the riots, Edmund Burke told the House that liberty was all and a police force must be treated with suspicion, yet must be considered.

❖I am by opinion, by principle, by constitution, an enemy to all violence whatever. There is an innovation from above as well as from below: power can innovate as well as be innovated upon. I premise this, because such an innovation has been, as I conceive, attempted in this country; an innovation tending to subvert, first its liberty, next its order; and to introduce, instead of order and decorum, confusion into this country. Depend on it, Sir, this country will not let go its liberty without a struggle. An attempt has been made to introduce into the administration of our justice a martial police, upon a principle, as I understand, acknowledged, avowed, supported, winked at, by the greatest lawyers in the kingdom. Some of the great men in place, like those in authority, may declare otherwise: but I say they have expressed a desire and a design of incorporating the military with the civil constitution of this country: they teach the magistrate to look to the military power as its first instrument, and not as the final and desperate resource in cases of necessity.

Burke, of course, was right. In an increasingly affluent society, the question of how to maintain law and order brought considerable stress upon the government of the day. At the same time there was a need to reduce the cost of government, a need to find new ways of raising taxes, and the new methods of law and order should not threaten the security and liberty of the people.

The rate of change in the nation in the 1770s was rapid enough to frighten people who were used to the slow rates of change characteristic of previous generations. Perhaps every generation argues that case, but during this period the reasons were, to many of the eight or so million people in England, Wales and Scotland, coming to mean revolutionary rather than evolutionary change. There were technological and scientific innovations and the first tentative steps towards the Industrial Revolution were taken.

In the first decade of the century, twenty-two new patents were registered. By the 1760s the figure was 205. By the last decade of the eighteenth century there would be more than 900 new inventions. In 1769 a one-time barber and wigmaker patented a machine that would make him a famous, rich, dark satanic mill owner. His name was Richard Arkwright and his invention was a spinning frame powered by water.

In the same year, James Watt patented his steam engine and Josiah Wedgwood opened another pottery. The newly formed Royal Academy was now in its first home, Somerset House, and its first president, Joshua Reynolds, gave the first of his Fifteen Discourses, in which he claimed history painting to be the most noble form of art. Tobias Smollett left England for ever, William Smith, the founder of English geology was born and, in the summer of 1769, the men of Hambledon were having a lean season on the cricket field.

But Britain was still almost entirely an agricultural society. Arthur Young, who helped found the Board of Agriculture, produced a series of tables and commentaries at this time which showed exactly how much the nation depended on the land for its living.

❖The soil	£66,000,000
Manufacturers	£27,000,000
Commerce	£10,000,000
Publick revenue	£ 9,000,000
Sums at interest	£ 5,000,000
Law and physick	£ 5,000,000

From this review of agriculture et cetera of this Kingdom, I apprehend there is no slight reason to conclude that England is, at present, in a most rich and flourishing situation; that her agriculture is, upon the whole, good and spirited, and every day improving; that her industrious poor are well fed, clothed, and lodged, and at reasonable rates of expense, the prices of all necessaries of life being moderate; that our population is consequently increasing; that the price of labour is in general high (of itself one of the strongest symptoms of political health, but at the same time not so high as to leave any reason to fear those ill effects which have been prognosticated concerning it); that the wealth of all other ranks of people appear to be very great, from the almost universal manner in which the Kingdom is adorned with stately as well as useful buildings, ornamented parks, lawns, plantations, waters, et cetera, which all speak a wealth and happiness not easily mistaken; that all kinds of public works shew the public to be rich, witness the navigations, roads, and public edifices.

If these circumstances do not combine to prove a Kingdom to be flourishing, I must confess myself to be totally in the dark.

This idea that the public was rich should be treated cautiously. Perhaps Britain was not a poor nation. Certainly the level of gambling suggested that the rich were very rich and that the not-so-rich thought gambling a simple way to become so. But the sums involved were sometimes enormous, even by twentieth-century standards. In the eighteenth century, thousands of pounds were bet on a horse or the turn of a card and, perhaps more surprisingly, bets of around twenty thousand guineas were not uncommon at the more fashionable cricket matches. However, there was still a need for foundling homes, charity schools, parish workhouses, and the burial of those who had died undernourished and badly cared for.

At the same time, the courts were recognizing that new schemes, inventions, or processes were just as much part of a man's property as was his house or livestock. A letter from Matthew Boulton, the owner of a factory in Birmingham, to Lord Dartmouth, the President of the Board of Trade (there had been a Board of Trade since 1696), requests the extension of a patent.

❖I take the liberty of writing to your lordship in favour of my friend Mr James Watt, an engineer, who intends to petition Parliament for a prolongation of the term of an exclusive privilege granted by His Majesty's patent which he has already obtained for certain very capital improvements invented by him in steam or fire engines. I need not point out to your lordship's consideration the great utility of steam or fire engines in collieries, in lead, in tin, and copper mines, and in other great works where great power is required, but I shall beg leave to observe that Mr Watt's intentions, if carried into execution, will very much extend the utility of fire engines by rendering them one fourth of the usual expense, and by adapting them to a great variety of purposes and manufactures to which the present engines cannot be applied. In the year 1769, he took out a patent for the sole use of his invention, but from the many mechanical difficulties that occurred in carrying into execution his newly discovered principles, from bad health, and from his having been employed by the boards of police and other public boards in Scotland, in making surveys, superintending the execution of a navigable canal, and other public works, and from the expense of attending the necessary trials, experiments and models of engines, he has not been able to finish large engines till the latter end of last year.

And then there is a warning to Dartmouth that unless an extension is granted then he, Boulton, may withdraw funding.

❖From the difficulties Mr Watt has met with in the execution of this invention and from those he still saw before him he was discouraged and would have dropped the scheme, had I not assisted him. But as a great part of the time of his patent is elapsed and his own life very precarious and as a large sum of money must yet be expended before any advantage can be gained from it, I think that his abilities and my money may be otherwise better employed, unless Parliament be pleased to grant a prolongation of the term of his exclusive privilege.

The rest is a blatant request to have a word in the Prime Minister's ear and make sure the patent was extended. Boulton knew his man: Dartmouth had a deep fascination for science and technology and this was all very new. In many cases (and Watt's was one) the techniques were revolutionary, as if the Internet had arrived in the early 1940s. Boulton's letter was persuasive enough and for the moment the Boulton and Watt investment was safe.

The industrial changes after the 1760s were even greater than the political events of the day, and went far beyond money-making schemes.

C❖In the last forty years of the eighteenth century exports and imports more than doubled in value and the population increased by over two millions. England was silently undergoing a revolution in industry and agriculture, which was to have more far-reaching effects than the political tumults of the times. Steam engines provided a new source of power in factories and foundries, which rapidly multiplied. A network of canals was constructed which carried coal cheaply to new centres of industry. New methods of smelting brought a tenfold increase in the output of iron. New roads, with a hard and durable surface, reached out over the country and bound it more closely together. An ever expanding and assertive industrial community was coming into being.

The rapid growth of an urban working class, the gradual extinction of small freeholders by enclosures and improved farming methods, the sudden development of manufactures, the appearance of a prosperous middle class for whom a place must be found in the political structure of the realm, made the demands of reformers seem inadequate. A great upheaval was taking place in society, and the monopoly which the landowners had gained in 1688 could not remain.

Churchill is referring to the revolution that chased the Catholic James II from England and began the process to prevent a Roman Catholic ascending to the British throne in the future. The Whigs had organized that revolution and the Protestant succession and, since then, they'd had an unshakable grip on government. Every British Prime Minister but one had been a Whig.

But now as the year 1769 moved to a close, the reign of the Whigs was about to be broken. The political climate was one of radical thinking, public opposition to Crown and government, and growing rebellion in America and in Ireland. Furthermore, in spite of the picture of rich and healthy Britain painted by Arthur Young, and the industrial innovation, there was an increasingly obvious economic depression settling over the management of Britain's affairs.

By 1770 George III had been on the throne for ten years. He was thirty-two years old and his first decade as King had been one of political instability. He wanted to change the political system. He wanted to get back control of political patronage – the key to government.

By the time George III came to the throne, the Whigs had broken into Old Whigs and New Whigs (although that's not a term found in history books). On one side were the Old Whigs, the followers of Pitt, Grenville, and Newcastle, and on the other side the New Whigs who said the King was a tyrant, seeking more political control than was good for the country. They said he corrupted Parliament and ignored the views of the people. They claimed he was trying to return to the age of the Stuarts and absolute power.

It was now that a stout, loud-voiced Earl became Prime Minister. His name was Lord North and his task was to bring about political stability. Frederick North, Baron North and Earl of Guildford, was fat, thick-lipped and had bulging eyes. He had an apparently inexhaustible good humour and the knack of explaining in the simplest terms the most complex matters of national economics. From 1770 until 1782 he was Tory Prime Minister and so ended the Whig domination which had existed since the death of Queen Anne in 1714. The name Tory comes from an Irish word for outlaw, *toraidhe*, given to the Tories when they opposed the Exclusion of the Catholic Duke of York from becoming James II. They were considered outlaws to the cause and so they were called, abusively, Tories. But they liked the name and adopted it. And although they went along with the 1688 Rebellion which eventually got rid of James II, they were seen as supporters of the Catholic Jacobite Pretenders to the throne. But in 1770, there was not so much a Tory revival as a decline in the influence of the Protestant Whigs.

During Lord North's twelve years, attempts were made to reform Parliament; Adam Smith published his great work, *The Wealth of Nations*, and Jeremy Bentham published his *Fragment on Government*. Joseph Priestley discovered and isolated oxygen. The actress Sarah Siddons appeared with Garrick at Drury Lane and became the darling of theatre-goers, and Gainsborough painted her. The Sunday School movement started. Britain lost the American War of Independence, and the first Derby was run at Epsom Racecourse.

Lord North's constituency, Banbury, was owned by his family and thus his family could say who would be MP: it was a 'pocket' or 'rotten' borough. In 1754 North became the MP for Banbury, but although his ministerial career was prompted by family and friends, North was no political charlatan. He was a good debater and he had a sharp and amiable mind which could unravel tangled policy problems. The movement towards Parliamentary reform was partly prompted by growing mistrust of the very system which had made North an MP. And debates in the House were still, officially, secret affairs but, in 1770, William Pitt (later the Elder and by then Earl of Chatham) proposed in the House of Lords an increase in County Members.

❖Whoever understands the theory of the English Constitution, and will compare it with the fact, must see how widely they differ. The Constitution intended that there should be a permanent relation between the constituent and representative body of the people. Will any man affirm that, as the House of Commons is now formed, that relation is in any degree preserved? My Lords, it is not preserved, it is destroyed. The boroughs of this country have properly enough been called the rotten parts of the constitution. But in my judgment, my Lords, these boroughs, corrupt as they are, must be considered as the natural infirmity of the Constitution. Like the infirmities of the body, we must bear them with patience, and submit to carry them about with us. The limb is mortified, but amputation might be death.

Pitt himself had set out on his Parliamentary career by becoming the Member for Old Sarum, a family borough which was nothing more than a mound of earth in Wiltshire. He'd sat for Seaford in Sussex and Aldborough in Yorkshire, both owned by the Duke of Newcastle. He'd also been the Member for Okehampton which was owned by his old school chum George Lyttelton.

❖Since we cannot cure the disorder, let us endeavour to infuse such a portion of new health into the Constitution, as may enable it to support its most inveterate diseases. The infusion of health, which I now allude to, would be to permit every county to elect one Member more, in addition to their present representation.

The knights of the shires approach nearest to the constitutional representation of the country, because they represent the soil. It is not in the little dependent boroughs, it is the great cities and counties that the strength and vigour of the Constitution resides, and by them alone, if an unhappy question should ever arise, will the Constitution be honestly and firmly defended. I would increase that strength, because I think it is the only security we have against the profligacy of the times, the corruption of the people, and the ambition of the Crown.

It was not until 1832, and then only as a result of revolts at Westminster and riots in the streets, that a Reform Bill became law. It was the fourth attempt. Most of the rotten boroughs were then scrapped and the seats given to the counties, almost exactly as Pitt the Elder had suggested sixty or so years earlier. But in 1770, one person who most definitely did not want Parliamentary supremacy was George III. George demanded that Parliament took its cue from him, not from the nation. The way it worked was simple: the King handed out jobs, contracts, offices of state and fat pensions to those who did as they were told, in other words, those who voted for his policies. For those who didn't there were punishments which included loss of pensions and jobs. There was nothing new in this; it was the centuries-old practice of royal patronage and for the first twenty years of his reign, George III followed the path of Parliamentary, and official, corruption.

This didn't mean that Parliament was a dull place in which yes-men said yes, and no-men said very little that was heard. The debating chamber was still a place of occasionally inspired speech-making. Horace Walpole, son of Robert Walpole, the very first prime minister and himself a member for twenty-five years, kept a sketch-writer's pad on the different styles of oratory. This is Walpole on William Pitt before he became the Earl of Chatham.

❖Eloquence as an art was but little studied by Pitt, yet the grace and force of words were so natural to him, that when he avoided them, he almost lost all excellence. As set speeches were no longer in vogue, except on very solemn occasions, the pomp and artful resources of oratory were in a great measure banished. Similes and quotations and metaphors were fallen into disrepute, deservedly: even parallels from old history were exhausted and disregarded. It was not the same case with invectives; in that respect, eloquence was little more chastened. On the whole, the style that prevailed was plain, manly, argumentative.

Walpole tried to be fair and claimed that he didn't want to go into detail about who was and who wasn't a good speaker. However . . .

❖Pitt, illustrious as he was in the House of Commons, would have shone still more in an assembly of inferior capacity: Fox, the boldest and ablest champion, was still more formed to worry: but the keenness of his sabre was blunted by the difficulty with which he drew it from the scabbard; I mean the hesitation and ungracefulness of his delivery took from the force of his arguments. Murray, the brightest genius of the three, had too much and too little of the lawyer: he refined too much and could wrangle too little for a popular assembly.

But the waspish sketch-writer in Walpole was at its best in his descriptions of those he then regarded as the less important figures in the chamber.

❖Northey saw clearly, but it was for a little way. Lord Strange was the most absurd man that ever existed. Nugent's assertions would have made everybody angry, if they had not made everybody laugh. Lord Granville was novelty itself. Doctor Hay seldom said anything new; his speeches were fair editions of the thoughts of other men. Doddington was always searching for wit; and what was surprising, generally found it . . . Lord Dulphin aimed at nothing but understanding business and explaining it . . . George Grenville and Hume Campbell were tragic speakers of very different kinds; the latter far superior . . . Charles Townshend neither caring whether himself or others were in the right, only spoke to show how well he could adorn a bad cause, or demolish a good one. It was frequent with him, as soon as he had done speaking, to run to the opposite side of the House, and laugh with those he had attacked, at those who had defended . . . Townshend had such openness in all his behaviour, that he seemed to think duplicity the simplest conduct.

The second decade of George III's rule, the 1770s, witnessed every wit and radical, every stoic and pragmatist on his feet in both Houses. The National Debt, taxes, and a badly thought-through war inspired even the dullest Parliamentary speaker. But in spite of near calamity the King was safe, if only for one simple reason. In Lord North, he now had a leader who would be the agent of the King's business; in other words, His Majesty's most loyal subject. George III held Parliament, the Cabinet, and policy in his hand. His ambition was fulfilled. Effectively, the King was his own prime minister. However, although power was his, the blessing of all his people was not. And, in 1774, the nation lost a hero: Clive of India committed suicide.

During the days following his death, there were stories that Clive had died from an apoplectic fit, or that he had taken an overdose of opium. Certainly he had taken opium, on his doctor's advice, for the stomach pains from which he'd suffered for so long. But the truth seems to be that on 22 November 1774, he could stand the agonies of his illness no longer and, as one observer has said, 'In a paroxysm of agony, he thrust his penknife into his throat.'

In the late 1760s Clive was attacked, not by the French nor by rebellious Indians, but by the British for whom he had established rule on the sub-continent. He was accused of diverting funds for his own purpose. The charges came a few years after he had been asked to re-organize the workings of the English East India Company. At this stage it was still the Company and not the British Government that administered India.

C❖The Directors of the Company suddenly found that they had lost both their dividends and their good name. They appealed to Clive. . . .

As Churchill described (see page 376) Clive's reforms were drastic, and their success prompted the Mogul Emperor to invite Clive to extend a British protectorate to Delhi and all Northern India. This is a useful reminder that at that time, British interests only covered Bengal. The reason was that when the East India Company established itself in India, Bengal became the capital of its trading interests. (The popular image of the British Raj is a nineteenth-century phenomenon.) So, in the 1760s, Clive had to decide whether to expand the Company administration or to stay put. To expand would require an enormous bureaucracy, complex communications, and a ruthless army – and it would have been a Company army, not a British army. So he refused the Mogul's request.

C❖He had long doubted the ability of the Company to undertake the larger responsibilities of Empire, and five years earlier he had suggested . . . to Pitt that the Crown should assume the sovereignty of the Company's possessions in India. This advice was disregarded for nearly a century.

At the time Britain was fighting yet another war, the Seven Years' War, and had insufficient interest and certainly neither the manpower nor the organization to take over from the Company.

C❖Administration of justice remained with the Indian rulers. Such division of responsibilities could not last, and was soon to create formidable problems, but at least it was a step forward. The British held the purse strings, and 'The power,' wrote Clive, 'is now lodged where it can only be lodged in safety.' In January 1767, [Clive] returned to England. The British public were critical and ill-informed. Clive was assailed in the House of Commons. He defended himself in an eloquent speech. He pointed out that by his exertions the Directors of the East India Company 'had acquired an Empire more extensive than any kingdom in Europe. They had acquired a revenue of £4 million sterling, and trade in proportion.'

Just as an earlier British hero, Marlborough, had been accused of lining his pockets, so Clive was now subject to the same accusations. Clive mounted a counter-offensive as bold as any skirmish he'd led or organized in India. And he reminded Parliament that after the horror of the Black Hole of Calcutta, it was he, Robert Clive, who had defeated Siraj-ud-daula, the man the British held responsible, at the Battle of Plassey. Churchill quotes him:

❖'Am I not rather deserving of praise for the moderation which marked my proceedings? Consider the situation in which the victory at Plassey had placed me. A great prince was dependent on my pleasure; an opulent city lay at my mercy; its richest bankers bid against each other for my smiles; I walked through vaults which were thrown open to me alone, piled on either hand with gold and jewels. Mr Chairman, at this moment I stand astonished at my own moderation.'

This of course was a huge exaggeration, if eloquently put. Clive did do well out of India. But by the end of the Parliamentary Committee's interrogation, it was clear to everyone that although he had received great gifts and had made minor fortunes, his profits were never so great as rumour would have wished. The Commons passed a motion declaring that Clive had 'rendered great and meritorious services' and that as far as Parliament was concerned, the matter was done with. Yet it is doubtful if Clive properly recovered from his inner torments.

Clive's successor was Warren Hastings. Hastings came from a wealthy Worcestershire family that had fallen on hard times. The family home, Daylesford, had been sold many years earlier and Hastings intended to make his fortune and buy it back. At the age of sixteen he went to India, like Clive, to be a clerk in the English East India Company.

C❖Between 1769 and 1770, a third of the population of Bengal died of famine. Throughout these ordeals, Warren Hastings held fast to an austere way of life. He desired fame and power, and enough money to buy back Daylesford. The gathering of private fortunes he left to others. . . . Rich adventurers from the East were making and marring the repute of the new Empire in India. . . . 'India,' declared the aging Chatham, 'teems with iniquities so rank as to smell to heaven and earth.' Jealousy, ignorance, and sentimentality combined in a cry for reform.

But by 1770, the Company itself was close to bankruptcy. North went to Parliament in 1773 with his Regulating Act which left all the commercial operations of the East India Company in the hands of its Directors, but the government of Bengal was to be administered by a Governor General and a four-man council. And Britain was to appoint a Justice of the Supreme Court. Warren Hastings was made the first Governor General, with a salary of £25,000 a year.

C❖. . . in trying to make sure that power was not abused it [the government of Bengal] was made impotent. On paper it was divided between the Nawab of Bengal, the Board of Directors, the Governor General, and a Council appointed to veto and control him.

This was North's idea. His motto for India was 'Shackle the great'.

C❖For years Hastings fought against his shackles. His principal opponent was his new colleague, Philip Francis, the reputed author of the savage 'Letters of Junius' [published in a British newspaper] which had attacked the Government at home during the agitations over Wilkes. Francis never ceased to intrigue against him, openly and behind his back. But Hastings knew what needed to be done, and he was determined to do it. Though naturally a man of quick temper, he learned the virtues of patience and cool persistence. At one moment the Government tried to recall him.

Then the French became involved. France declared war on Britain in 1778 in support of the American rebellion. Hastings was forced to lend his troops to an Indian dictator so that he could crush an uprising, which if it had succeeded, could have threatened Bengal itself. The French Fleet encouraged rebellion against British interests and the French intriguing went on until the end of the American War of Independence.

C❖Hastings could get very little help, financial or material, from England, exhausted and overstrained by the conflict in America, Europe, and on the seas. His only course was to raise it on the spot. The inhabitants of Bengal were wealthy. They were also, thanks to British arms and leadership, comparatively safe. They should pay for their protection, and Hastings had been quite ruthless in making them do so. Thus he gathered the funds to rescue Bombay and the Carnatic and to stop the bloodshed once more engulfing Bengal.

The Carnatic was the long thin region running down the Eastern side of India. Today it's very approximately what is known as Mysore. Then, in the eighteenth century, it surrounded the important coastal capital of Madras which was British.

C❖[Hastings] left India in 1785, not without the gratitude of the inhabitants. . . . In the beginning he was welcomed and honoured in England. His achievements and victories were some compensation for the humiliations and disasters in America . . . Soon after Hastings' return a Parliamentary inquiry into his conduct had been set on foot. No personal charge of corruption could be proved against him, but he was arrogant and tactless in his dealings with the politicians of all parties. Headed by Burke, Fox and Sheridan, Parliament resolved to have his blood. Philip Francis, whom he had wounded in a duel in Calcutta, malignly urged his enemies on. The ancient weapon of impeachment was resurrected and turned against him. The trial opened in Westminster Hall on February 13, 1788.

That trial went on for seven years. In the end, Hastings was acquitted. And in spite of the cost of defending himself, there was still enough left to realize his ambition. He bought back the family home, Daylesford. And at Westminster there was growing support for the proper governing of India. Hastings, certainly no saint, had gone a long way to lessen the corruption and maladministration that had been the Company's way in India. He had effectively laid the ground rules for what became the Indian Civil Service. Above all, he had preserved British rule of one Empire while the wise Councils of Westminster had managed to lose another in America.

CHAPTER THIRTY-NINE

1770–1781

———— ❖ ————

The Boston Tea Party did not start the American War of Independence, but it did inflame an already sore relationship between Britain and her colonial interests in America. At the time there were thirteen colonies in America. Parliament declared that Britain had a right to tax those colonies because they were subjects of the Crown just as much as any county in England. But most, although not all, British taxpayers were represented in Parliament. No colonist was, and so the argument was based upon 'Taxation without representation'.

Furthermore, the money was supposed to provide British troops to protect the colonists. In fact, the money ended up in the pockets of the bureaucracy rather than in the garrisons. And so it was no wonder that taxes, including the stamp tax which covered legal documents and newspapers (for which radical journalists wrote) were, together with the inherent instincts of colonists, enough to inspire outright rebellion.

Many of the taxes were repealed (see below) and, until the 1770s, there was probably no overwhelming support for the idea of breaking away from the Crown. But one tax remained. Parliament wanted to assert its right to levy duty on the colonies, and so kept three pence a pound on tea.

The tea came from the desperately hard up East India Company and by the middle of 1770, with the King becoming more and more his own Prime Minister, the chances of reconciliation seemed possible. But not in Boston.

C❖Here, Samuel Adams, fertile organizer of resistance and advocate of separation, saw that the struggle was now reaching a crucial stage. Hitherto the quarrel had been at bottom a commercial dispute, and neither the American merchants nor the English Ministers had any sympathy for his ideas. Adams feared that the resistance of the colonies would crumble and the British would reassert their authority unless more trouble was stirred up. This he and other Radical leaders proceeded to do.

News that the duties were withdrawn had hardly reached America when the first blood was shed. Most of the British garrison was stationed in Boston. The troops were unpopular with the townsfolk, and Adams spread evil rumours of their conduct. [They] . . . were insulted and jeered at wherever they appeared. In March 1770, the persistent snowballing by Boston urchins of English sentries outside the barracks caused a riot. In the confusion and shouting some of the troops opened fire and there were casualties.

Five colonists were killed and the incident became known as the Boston Massacre. The American who did much to calm feelings was Benjamin Franklin. He was a Bostonian, a scientist, a diplomat and a politician, and he was sent to Britain to lobby for the repeal of the Stamp Act. It was Franklin who put into words what was at stake.

❖There seems to be among us some violent spirits who are for an immediate rupture; but I trust that the general prudence of our country will see that by our growing strength we advance fast to a situation in which our claims must be allowed, that by a premature struggle we may be crippled and kept down, that between governed and governing every mistake in government, every encroachment on right, is not worth a rebellion, remembering withal that this Protestant country (our mother, though lately an unkind one) is worth preserving, and that her weight in the scales of Europe and her safety in a great degree may depend on our union with her.

But Lord North, the Prime Minister, acted unwisely.

C❖The East India Company was nearly bankrupt, and the Government had been forced to come to its rescue. An Act was passed though Parliament, attracting little notice among the Members, authorizing the Company to ship tea, of which it had an enormous surplus, direct to the colonies, without paying import duties, and to sell it through its own agents in America. Thus in effect the Company was granted a monopoly. The outcry across the Atlantic was instantaneous. The extremists denounced it as an invasion of their liberties, and the merchants were threatened with ruin. American shippers who bought tea from the British customs houses and their middle men who sold it would all be thrown out of business. The Act succeeded where Adams had failed: it united colonial opinion against the British.

The Radicals, who began to call themselves 'Patriots', seized their opportunity to force a crisis. In December 1773 the first cargoes arrived in Boston. Rioters disguised as Red Indians boarded the ships and destroyed the cases.

The man who would be a signatory to the Declaration of Independence and become the second President of the United States was John Adams. He was overwhelmed by the tea dumping in Boston harbour:

❖Last night three cargoes of Bohea tea were emptied into the sea. This is the most magnificent movement of all. There is a dignity, a majesty and sublimity in this last effort of the Patriots that I greatly admire. . . . This destruction of the tea is so bold, so daring, so firm, intrepid, and inflexible, and it must have so important consequences, and so lasting, that I cannot but consider it as an epoch in history. This, however, is but an attack upon property.

Another similar exertion of popular power may produce the destruction of lives. Many persons wish that as many dead carcasses were floating in the harbour as there are chests of tea. A much less number of lives, however, would remove the causes of all our calamities.

In London there was an equally strident reaction. The more thoughtful, including the Earl of Chatham (Pitt the Elder), would not join the reactionaries. Instead, he made what was to be his last speech to the House of Lords, calling for reconciliation and efforts to make amends. But none was made and the very title of the legislation against the colonists sums up Parliamentary feeling. The House passed the Intolerable Acts. First the Boston Port Bill closed the harbour (or was supposed to) until the tea owners had been paid compensation. Then an Act to revoke the charter of the Boston territory, Massachusetts, meant that Massachusetts was to be directly governed by the Crown. The Justice Act allowed British officials accused of capital offences to return to England in the hope of a fair trial and under the Quartering Act, the colonists could not object to British troops being billeted in their homes.

On 19 April 1774 Edmund Burke addressed the House of Commons about ways of preserving and managing the British Empire.

❖I look, I say, on the imperial rights of Great Britain, and the privileges which the colonists ought to enjoy under these rights, to be just the most reconcilable things in the world. The Parliament of Great Britain sits at the head of her extensive Empire on two capacities: one as the local legislature of this island, providing for all things at home, immediately, and by no other instruments than the executive power. The other, and I think her nobler capacity, is what I call her imperial character; in which, as from the throne of heaven, she superintends all the several inferior legislatures, and guides and controls them all, without annihilating any. As all these provincial legislatures are only co-ordinate with each other, they ought all to be subordinate to her; else they can neither preserve mutual peace, nor hope for mutual justice, nor effectually afford mutual assistance.

It is necessary to coerce the belligerent, to restrain the violent, and to aid the weak and deficient, by the overruling plenitude of her power. She is never to intrude into the place of others, whilst they are equal to the common ends of their institution. But in order to enable Parliament to answer all these ends of provident and beneficient superintendence, her powers must be boundless. The gentlemen who think the powers of Parliament limited, may please themselves to talk of requisitions. But suppose their requisitions are not obeyed? What! Shall there be no reserved power in the Empire, to supply a deficiency which may weaken, divide, and dissipate the whole?

He then goes on to say that if, for example, there is a war, then everyone should be taxed. If a colony doesn't tax its people for the common cause, then Parliament can do it for them. But taxing must not, says Burke, simply be a way of raising money. He had long believed that the power of Parliament to tax was what he called, 'an instrument of Empire, and not a means of supply'.

❖Such, sir, is my idea of the Constitution of the British Empire, as distinguished from the Constitution of Britain; and on these grounds I think subordination and liberty may be sufficiently reconciled through the whole; whether to serve a refining speculatist, or a factious demagogue, I know not; but enough surely for the ease and happiness of man.

However thoughtful Burke and Chatham, and some of those who campaigned for a hard line towards the colonists were, the legislation that appeared had little calming effect.

C❖In September 1774, the colonial assemblies held a congress at Philadelphia. The extremists were not yet out of hand, and the delegates still concentrated on commercial boycotts. An association was formed to stop all trade with England unless the Coercion Acts [laws designed to put down unrest] were repealed, and the Committees of Correspondence were charged with carrying out the plan. A Declaration of Rights demanded the rescinding of some thirteen commercial Acts passed by the British Parliament since 1763. The tone of this document, which was dispatched to London, was one of respectful moderation. But in London all moderation was cast aside. The 'sugar interest' in the House of Commons, jealous of colonial competition in the West Indies; army officers who despised the colonial troops; the Government, pressed for money and blinded by the doctrine that colonies only existed for the benefit of the Mother Country: all combined to extinguish the last hope for peace. The petition was rejected with contempt.

For eight years, from 1775, England was occupied with what is now seen as the first anti-colonial war in modern history. The American War of Independence began in 1775 and officially ended in 1783. Briefly, war broke out at Concord and Lexington in April 1775, the time of Paul Revere's famous ride to warn the Radicals, or Patriots, that the British were on the march. The Declaration of Independence was published in America on 4 July 1776. Britain lost at the Battle of Saratoga in 1777 and the French joined the war on the American side. Britain surrendered at Yorktown in 1781 and conceded American Independence in the Treaty of Versailles in 1783.

At the very beginning, even before war broke out, the only British stronghold, Boston, suffered a breakdown in law and order.

C❖The Massachusetts Military Governor, General Thomas Gage, tried to enforce martial law, but the task was beyond him. Gage was an able soldier, but he had only 4000 troops and could hold no place outside Boston. The Patriots had about 10,000 men in the colonial militia. In October [1774] they set up a 'Committee for Safety', and most of the colonies started drilling and arming. Collection of military equipment and powder began. Cannon were seized from Government establishments. Agents were sent to Europe to buy weapons. Both France and Spain refused the British Government's request to prohibit the sale of gunpowder to the Americans, and Dutch merchants shipped it in large glass bottles labelled 'Spirits'.

The Patriots began accumulating these warlike stores at Concord, a village twenty miles from Boston, where the Massachusetts Assembly, which Parliament had declared illegal, was now in session. Gage decided to seize their ammunition and arrest Samuel Adams and his colleague John Hancock.

Samuel Adams had long been a separatist and was the second cousin of John Adams who would become the second President of the United States. John Hancock was Boston's most important businessman and a long-time agitator against direct taxation from Westminster. In 1768 it was Hancock's sloop, the *Liberty*, that having been stopped and searched by Customs officers, was grabbed back by rebellious colonists. Adams and Hancock put their rebels on standby. They both knew that confrontation with the British would come. The Patriots were ready.

C❖Every night they patrolled the streets of Boston watching for any move by the English troops. As Gage gathered his men, messengers warned the assembly at Concord. The military supplies were scattered among towns farther north and Adams and Hancock moved to Lexington. On April 18, 1775, 800 British troops set off in darkness along the Concord road. But the secret was out. One of the patrols, Paul Revere, from his post in the steeple of the North Church, warned messengers by lantern signals. He himself . . .

rode hard to Lexington, rousing Adams and Hancock from their beds. . . .

At five o'clock in the morning, the local militia of Lexington, seventy strong, formed up on the village green. As the sun rose the head of the British column, with three officers riding in front, came into view. The leading officer, brandishing his sword, shouted, 'Disperse, you rebels, immediately!' The militia commander ordered his men to disperse. The colonial committees were very anxious not to fire the first shot, and there were strict orders not to provoke open conflict with the British regulars. But in the confusion, someone fired. A volley was returned. The ranks of the militia were thinned . . . Brushing aside the survivors, the British column marched on to Concord. But now the countryside was up in arms and the bulk of the stores had been moved to safety. It was with difficulty that the British straggled back to Boston, with the enemy close at their heels. The town was cut off from the mainland. The news of Lexington and Concord spread to the other colonies, and Governors and British officials were expelled. . . . the War of Independence had begun.

The reaction in Britain was divided. Many who, like Chatham, had pleaded a case for reconciliation still believed full-scale war could be avoided. Others, at the extreme end, expressed contempt for the colonists as fighting men and sent General Sir William Howe across the Atlantic with reinforcements to sort the matter out.

The English newspapers were equally divided but neither camp believed there was an outright anti-colonial sentiment behind the rebellion. It was more to do, they felt, with economics and the original aggravation: taxation without representation. About five weeks after the news from Concord and Lexington had reached London, a correspondent wrote to the *Morning Chronicle*.

❖Sir,

The American rebels are constantly boasting of the prodigious services which they rendered us, in the course of the last war [the Seven Years' War], when it is notoriously known that the last war was entered into for their own immediate protection; and therefore, whatever efforts they made, were entirely made from motives of private interest, and not from generous principle of attachment to their Mother Country: while a foreign enemy, indeed, was at their backs, they affected a prodigious deal of loyalty to the present state; but the moment their fears on that head were removed by the cession of Canada to Great Britain, that moment the dutiful colonies began to change their tone; America was no longer ours, but theirs; the champions for Constitutional Rights would no longer obey the voice of the Constitution; from petitions which we could not grant, they proceeded to acts of outrage which we could not overlook; and, finding at last that we are not to be intimidated by the apprehension of losing their trade, these miracles of political fidelity, these paragons of patience under oppression, fly heroically to their tents, and endeavour (pretty souls) to persuade us, that they are only fighting against a wicked Ministry. The insult offered in this argument, to our national understanding, will, however, be punished as properly as . . . the violence offered to our national honour, in the daring commencement of hostilities. 'Tis neither the cloud of manufactured perjury from the other side of the Atlantick, nor the stupid fabrications of newspaper treachery on this, which can have weight with a thinking Englishman.

That letter was written by the Reverend James Scott. He was chaplain to Lord Sandwich who is remembered for two things: as First Lord of the Admiralty it was he who was responsible for the fact that the navy was not ready for this war – with disastrous results. Second, Sandwich spent much of his time at the gaming tables. To keep him going, he invented the idea of putting titbits between two slices of bread.

There was opposition to the war but it had little effect. On 25 May, General Sir William Howe, with generals Sir Henry Clinton and John Burgoyne, and commanding much needed reinforcements, sailed into Boston harbour. The first plan was to take Breed's Hill and Bunker Hill overlooking Boston. If the Patriots captured those, Boston would be virtually defenceless. But the tactics of General Gage reflected the bellicose sentiments expressed in the chaplain's letter to the *Morning Chronicle* rather than sound military sense. Gage was going to teach these fellows a British lesson.

C❖He decided to make a frontal attack on the hill, so that all Boston, crowded in its windows and upon its roofs, should witness the spectacle of British soldiers marching steadily in line to storm the rebel entrenchments. . . . In three lines the redcoats moved slowly towards the summit of Breed's Hill. There was silence. The whole of Boston was looking on. At 100 yards from the trenches there was still not a sound in front. But at fifty yards a hail of buck-shot and bullets from ancient hunting guns smote the attackers. . . . Howe, his white silk breeches splashed with blood, rallied his men, but they were scattered by another volley. . . . Howe's reputation was at stake and he realized that ammunition was running short on the hill-top. At the third rush, this time in column, the regulars drove the farmers from their line. It was now evening. The village of Charlestown, on the Boston side of the peninsula, was in flames. Over 1000 Englishmen had fallen on the slopes. Of the 3000 farmers who had held the crest, a sixth were killed or wounded. Throughout the night, carriages and chaises bore the English casualties into Boston.

> This sharp and bloody action sent a stir throughout the colonies . . . The rebels had become heroes. . . . The British had captured the hill, but the Americans had won the glory.

Gage was eventually recalled and Howe given his command. And a southerner was chosen to form the first American army. He was a Virginian and his name was Colonel George Washington. He was forty-three.

C❖His immediate task was to provide the ragged band at Boston with discipline and munitions, and to this he devoted the autumn and winter months of 1775. . . . An expedition was dispatched to Canada under Benedict Arnold, who was to be for ever infamous in American history [Arnold much later turned traitor and went over to the British], and Richard Montgomery . . . [who] captured and occupied Montreal, which was undefended. He then joined Arnold, who after desperate hardships had arrived with a ghost of an army before the fortifications of Quebec. In the depth of winter, in driving snow, they flung themselves at the Heights of Abraham defended by Sir Guy Carleton with a few hundred men. Montgomery was killed and Arnold's leg was shattered. The survivors, even after this repulse, hung on in their wind-swept camp across the river. But in the spring, when the ice melted in the St Lawrence, the first reinforcements arrived from England.

However the logistics, the terrain and the seemingly inevitable arrival of the French on the colonists' side always made a British military victory unlikely. In retrospect, the only way the British could have succeeded was if they divided the Americans, probably by tax and commercial reforms in favour of the thirteen colonies. As it was, radical thinkers in America were refusing to obey what they saw as the outrageous demands of a reactionary monarchy in Great Britain. The Patriots simply wanted to break the colonial thread. And there was, in Whitehall and Westminster, a powerful and reactionary group which would, given the opportunity, take a whip to what they saw as the recalcitrant spirit in the New World.

But not all colonists wanted to break away, just as not all British politicians wanted to force the issue. However the issue was forced by the British need for more money to administer its increasing colonial holdings. George III's financial advisers believed that the British people could not be taxed any more than they already were, so it was decided to tax the colonies, with disastrous results.

It was the Congress at Philadelphia that decided to raise a combined American army and, for the first time, to have an overall commander, Colonel George Washington. And while Washington raised and trained an army, the British Commander in Chief, General Sir William Howe, was a good enough soldier to realize that not only was he trapped, but that satisfying Westminster's demand to quickly put down this anti-colonial nonsense was not going to be at all easy.

C❖. . .for at least the first two years of the war he hoped for conciliation. Both he and his generals were Whig Members of Parliament, and they shared the party view that a successful war against the colonists was impossible. . . . He now set himself the task of overawing the Americans. This, however, needed extensive help from England, and as none arrived, and Boston itself was of no strategic importance, he evacuated the town in the spring of 1776 and moved to the only British base on the Atlantic seaboard, Halifax, in Nova Scotia. At the same time a small expedition under General Clinton was sent southwards to the Loyalists in Charleston in the hope of rallying the Middle and Southern colonies. But the Patriot resistance was stiffening, and although the moderate elements in Congress had hitherto opposed any formal Declaration of Independence, the evacuation of Boston roused them to a sterner effort. Until they acquired what would nowadays be called belligerent status they could get no military supplies from abroad, except by smuggling, and supplies were essential. The Conservative politicians were gradually yielding to the Radicals. . . . But it was the British Government which took the next step towards dissolving the tie of allegiance between England and America. Early in 1776, Parliament passed a Prohibitory Act forbidding all intercourse with the rebellious colonies and declaring a blockade of the American coast. At the same time, it being impossible to raise enough British troops, Hessians were hired from Germany and dispatched across the Atlantic.

Even if there had been conscription, the chances were slim of maintaining a supply line of thousands of troops. In a national British population which was still only roughly equivalent to, say, modern-day London, the number of able-bodied men was limited. Besides, there were other commitments. George III could not send all his troops to America if he was still to be able to defend himself elsewhere. Washington had similar difficulties in raising an army. The adult fighting population at his command was, in theory, between 275,000 and 285,000. But Washington never managed to raise and equip more than 25,000 men.

The British need to hire Germans to put down the colonists may have brought a limited military relief to the British commander, but it also helped the cause of the Patriots.

C❖The resulting outcry in America strengthened the hands of the extremists. At Philadelphia on June 7, Richard Henry Lee, of Virginia, moved the following resolution: 'That these united colonies are and of right ought to be free and independent states; that they are absolved from all allegiance to the British Crown, and that all political connection between them and the state of Great Britain is and ought to be totally dissolved.' But six of the thirteen colonies still opposed an immediate Declaration. A large-scale British invasion was feared. No foreign alliances had yet been concluded. Many felt that a formal defiance would wreck their cause and alienate their supporters.

Maintaining support was important for the Patriots. At this stage, they could not be sure how far public opinion would go along with their ideas of breaking away from what many still regarded as the Mother Country. And Congress was a regional seat of government only: in the mid-eighteenth century concepts such as statehood without monarchy were untested. And so the drafting of a declaration became far more than the drafting of a brave pamphlet. The drafting committee was Benjamin Franklin, Roger Sherman, Robert Livingston, John Adams and Thomas Jefferson. But the work was really Jefferson's.

Jefferson was then thirty-three and part of the eighteenth-century Enlightenment. He was a musician, a writer, a painter and a political philosopher. Two years earlier he'd published his *Summary View of the Rights of America*, and when he started work on the Declaration of Independence, he was reflecting not a federalist view of the world, but one more akin to that of the seventeenth-century English philosopher, John Locke. It was Locke who had attacked the divine right of a king to rule; it was Locke who had insisted that monarchs had an obligation to preserve the liberties of their people. The message was clear: George III himself (rather than the tax-imposing British Parliament) took the full broadside of Jefferson's criticism. For the fifty-six members of Congress who signed the Declaration of Independence, Jefferson's document was the beginning of the history of the United Colonies, the United States of America.

❖When in the course of human events, it becomes necessary for one people to dissolve the political bands which have connected them with another, and to assume among the powers of the earth, the separate and equal station to which the Laws of Nature and of Nature's God entitle them, a decent respect to the opinions of mankind requires that they should declare the causes which impel them to the separation. We hold these truths to be self evident, that all men are created equal, that they are endowed by their Creator with certain unalienable Rights, that among these are Life, Liberty and the pursuit of Happiness. That whenever any Form of Government becomes destructive of these ends, it is the Right of the People to alter or to abolish it, and to institute new government, laying its foundation on such principles and organizing its powers in such form as to them shall seem most likely to effect their Safety and Happiness. Prudence, indeed, will dictate that Governments long established should not be changed for light and transient causes. But when a long train of abuses and usurptions evinces a design to reduce them under absolute Despotism, it is their right, it is their duty, to throw off such Government, and to provide new Guards for their future security.

The Declaration of Independence, published on 4 July 1776, was not simply a writ of American anger. It had to encourage other countries to take the American side – particularly the French who would, or suggested that they would, supply weapons. It had, too, to carry the American waverers. The Declaration of Independence could only become a turning point in American history if the American people themselves turned with it. The final paragraph left no doubt of what must follow.

❖We, therefore, the Representatives of the United States of America, in General Congress Assembled, appealing to the Supreme Judge of the world for the rectitude of our intentions, do, in the Name and by the authority of the good People of these Colonies, solemnly publish and declare: That these United Colonies are, and of Right ought to be, Free and Independent States; that they are Absolved from all Allegiance to the British Crown, and that all political connection between them and the State of Great Britain is and ought to be totally dissolved; and that as Free and Independent States, they have full Power to levy War, conclude Peace, contract Alliances, establish Commerce, and to do all other acts and Things which Independent States may of right do. And for the support of this Declaration, with a firm reliance on the Protection of Divine Providence, we mutually pledge to each other our Lives, our Fortunes and our sacred Honor.

For many of the waverers, the uncompromising Declaration was too much. But there was little they could do about it. In July 1776 there was no turning back.

George Washington was moving his army towards New York. It was an army of few well-drilled men and some had deserted, others had caught smallpox. The English Commander in Chief's brother, Admiral Richard Howe, arrived with reinforcements, giving General Sir William Howe the biggest army ever seen in North America: about 25,000 men. His headquarters were on Staten Island and from there he could see Washington's troops encamped on Long Island and Brooklyn Heights. In August, Howe made a dummy assault towards the Long Island positions and then sent in his main force against Washington's rearguard. Washington was forced to withdraw into New York City but the winds were against Howe and he couldn't use his large naval force to follow up his success. Even so, for the Americans this was a huge setback, and they were now vulnerable. Washington knew that to withdraw entirely from New York would leave the Patriots dejected but he must withdraw if the war was not to be lost in one action.

C❖At this juncture victory lay at Howe's fingertips. He was master of New York and of the Hudson River for forty miles above it. If he had pursued Washington . . . he might have captured the whole colonial army. But for nearly a month Washington was unmolested. At the end of October he was again defeated in a sharp fight at White Plains; but once more the English made no attempt to pursue, and Washington waited desperately to see whether Howe would attack up the Hudson or strike through New Jersey at Philadelphia. Howe resolved to move on Philadelphia. . . . Thousands of Americans flocked to the British camp to declare their loyalty.

Washington, meanwhile, now reckoned that the British southern advance on Philadelphia could force him to withdraw further inland and regroup as a guerrilla force.

This wasn't at all what he wanted. But his first concern was Howe's line of advance towards Philadelphia. If Washington failed to stop that advance, then his own retreat would be long and costly.

C❖The British were hard on his heels and began a rapid occupation of New Jersey. The Patriot cause seemed lost. But Washington remained alert and undaunted and fortune rewarded him. With an imprudence which is difficult to understand, and was soon to be punished, outposts from the British Army were flung about in careless fashion through the New Jersey towns. Washington determined to strike at these isolated bodies before Howe could cross the Delaware River. He selected the village of Trenton, held by a force of Hessians. On Christmas night, the Patriot troops fought their way into the lightly guarded village. At the cost of two officers and two privates they killed or wounded 106 Hessians. The survivors were captured and sent to parade the streets of Philadelphia. The effect of the stroke was out of all proportion to its military importance. It was the most critical moment of the war. At Princeton, Lord Cornwallis, a subordinate of Howe's . . . tried to avenge the defeat, but was foiled. Washington marched behind him and threatened his line of communications. The year thus ended with the British in winter quarters in New Jersey, but confined by these two actions to the east of the Delaware. Their officers spent a cheerful season in the society of New York. Meanwhile Benjamin Franklin and Silas Deane, first of American diplomats, crossed the Atlantic to seek help from France.

France was only too pleased to join the American rebellion against the British. In Britain the Prime Minister, Lord North, had Commons' support for the King's war, although North himself was not in overall control because the King insisted upon being, effectively, his own prime minister. But Commons' support did not mean total national support.

Shortly after the conflict began a letter appeared in the *Gentleman's Magazine*, addressed to Lord North. Here is part of it.

❖Did not the Americans before they took up arms in defence of their liberties, present the most humble petition that injured subjects could offer? Did they ask for any thing more than to be put in the same situation they were in at the close of the last war [the Seven Years' War]? They did not: yet even that request was refused them. And what is the consequence? Exactly what was predicted by those illustrious worthies, who protested against and reprobated the measure. Our friends and fellow-subjects, to the inexpressible grief of every good man, are now made desperate with injuries and wrongs; the flame of civil war rages throughout the vast continent of America; and an impolitic Junto are sacrificing the flower of our troops, and exhausting the wealth of the nation, to remedy evils their own misconduct have [sic] occasioned, and which nothing but friendship and good offices can remove. Ask the merchant or the manufacturer what he thinks of the arbitrary proceedings? He will tell thee that they are big with ruin, and that bankruptcy stares him in the face.

The commercial consequences of the war spread throughout the country, to Scotland and later to Ireland, and the military and political doubts were widespread. Lord North might have resigned had it not been for his belief that it was his duty to carry out the King's wishes. As for George III, he had grown stubborn and even more intent.

C❖He closed his ears to moderate counsel and refused to admit into his Government those men of both parties who, like many American Loyalists, foresaw and condemned the disasters into which his policy was tottering and were horrified at the civil war between the Mother Country and her colonies. . . .

Rarely has British strategy fallen into such a multitude of errors. Every maxim and principle of war was either violated or disregarded. . . . Obvious truths were befogged and bedevilled by multiplicity of counsel. Howe was still determined to capture Philadelphia, the seat of the revolutionary Congress . . . Burgoyne . . . was hot for a descent from Canada into the upper reaches of the Hudson valley, and a seizure . . . of the forts which dominated the waterway. Once in control of the Hudson, New England could be isolated and speedily subdued.

What's remarkable about this strategy was that it came about when Burgoyne, Howe's subordinate, went to London and told the King what he planned and got the King's personal approval. And so the Government, knowing full well that Howe was going in the opposite direction, approved a plan which, if it were to work, needed both forces to combine.

C❖Washington, from his winter quarters at Morristown, on the borders of New Jersey, moved hastily south-westwards to screen Philadelphia. Having abandoned New York without a serious fight, he could hardly do the same at the capital of the Congress, but with his ill-disciplined force, fluctuating in numbers, he could only hope to delay the British advance. . . . Howe perceived and exploited the faulty equipment of the army in front of him, its lack of an efficient staff and its inability to get quick information.. . . [His] attack was successful, disorder spread . . . By sunset Washington was in full retreat. . . . But here, as at Long Island, Howe refused to pursue and capture the enemy. He was content. On September 26, his advance-guards entered Philadelphia . . . and soon afterwards the capital fell.

By now however the London plans for the northern theatre were beginning to miscarry. Burgoyne, with a few hundred Indians and 7000 regulars, of whom half were German, was moving through the Canadian forests expecting to join with the British forces from New York. After an arduous march he reached Fort Ticonderoga and found that the Americans had retired, leaving their artillery behind them. He pushed eagerly south-wards. If Howe was moving up to West Point, nothing could prevent an overwhelming success. But where was Howe? On the day that Burgoyne moved upon the next American fort Howe had sailed southwards from New York. All concerned were confident that after capturing Philadelphia, Howe could quickly return to New York and reach out to the expedition from Canada. He failed to do so, and Burgoyne paid the price.

What happened next is a complex story of two forces failing to rendezvous, of poor logistics, of difficult fighting terrain, of reinforcements failing to arrive when needed, of successful raids by the opposing troops, and, as ever in war, of the weather.

C❖. . . as the autumn rains descended, Burgoyne was cornered at Saratoga, and the New Englanders, their strength daily increasing, closed in. He was only fifty miles from Albany, where he should have met the column from New York, but he could make no headway. Days of hard fighting in the woodlands followed. His supplies ran low, and he was heavily outnumbered. The Americans were operating in their own country by their own methods. Each man fighting mostly on his own initiative, hiding behind bushes and in the tops of trees, they inflicted severe casualties upon some of the best regiments that Europe could muster. The precise drill and formations of Burgoyne's men had no effect. . . . The Germans refused to fight any longer, and on October 17, 1777, Burgoyne surrendered to the American Commander, Horatio Gates. The surrender terms were violated by Congress and the main body of his army were kept prisoners until the signing of the peace.

In 1778 France joined the war. The Americans wanted France as an ally for two reasons: first, the French Navy would be able to attack the British supply routes as well as to bring soldiers to the East Coast; and second, as an ally, France could supply the Patriots with much-needed modern weaponry. Here was an opportunity to avenge the defeats suffered in the Seven Years' War, as a result of which Britain had gained so much from France – including territory in America. So, despite misgivings about joining a battle for independence, personal freedom and human rights, something his own government hardly encouraged, on 6 February 1778, Louis XVI agreed to an alliance.

France now said she would supply the Americans with ships, men, and arms. George Washington designed the strategy. Howe, the British Commander who had surrendered a large part of his army at Saratoga, was replaced by Sir Henry Clinton. Clinton changed military tack – or tried to. He wanted to move the campaign from the North to the South. He needed to be where the majority of the Loyalists were, and he needed to control a seaport in the South.

C❖Savannah was 800 miles and fifty days' march from New York. Hitherto Britain had held command of the sea, . . . but all was changed by the intervention of France and the French Fleet. . . .

In April 1778, twelve French ships of the line, mounting, with their attendant frigates, over 800 guns, set sail from Toulon. News of their approach reached Clinton and it became his immediate and vital task to stop them seizing his main base at New York. If they captured the port, or even blockaded the mouth of the Hudson, his whole position on the Continent would be imperilled. On June 18, he abandoned Philadelphia and marched rapidly across New Jersey with 10,000 troops. Washington, his army swollen by spring recruiting to about equal strength, set off in [a] parallel line of pursuit. . . . Clinton beat off the Americans, not without heavy loss, and did not reach New York till the beginning of July. He was only just in time. On the very day of his arrival a French fleet under d'Estaing appeared off the city. They were confronted by a British squadron under Admiral Howe, brother of the superseded military commander, and for weeks the two forces manoeuvred outside the harbour. . . . In the autumn d'Estaing abandoned the struggle and sailed for the West Indies.

Clinton's plans to dominate the South came to little. A combination of French fleets and New England privateers hampered the supply lines from Britain. And in London the fear of French invasion, which had kept back supplies and men, was doubled when, in 1779, Spain was persuaded by France to enter the war. Gibraltar was besieged, and Britain's already doubtful lines of naval communication were weakened further.

C❖In December, Clinton decided to try his hand once more at subduing the South. He resolved to capture Charleston, and in . . . May 1780 the town fell and 5000 Patriot troops surrendered in the biggest disaster yet sustained by American arms. Then fortune began to turn against Clinton. He had gained a valuable base, but he . . . found himself faced, not with a regular army in the field, but with innumerable guerrilla bands which harassed his communications and murdered Loyalists.

But there was the American traitor Benedict Arnold, a Connecticut merchant. He'd fought heroically at Saratoga and he now commanded the fort at West Point. But he'd married a Loyalist, was deep in debt, and appears to have pocketed badly needed Government funds. So he offered to sell West Point to Clinton for £20,000. Clinton sent a young officer, Major John André, to find out what Arnold had to offer. It was nothing less than the layout, strengths and tactical plans of the Patriot Army. On his way back from the meeting, Major André was caught, his intelligence notes discovered, and he was hanged.

Arnold escaped and was made a general in the British Army. For the Patriots, the discovery of Arnold's treachery had saved them from disaster. But there was another aspect to the incident: not all Americans supported this conflict. There were effectively two wars going on: the one between the British and the Franco-American forces, and the one between the American Patriots and Loyalists. But any advantage the British might have gained made little difference to their ultimate misfortunes.

C❖Cornwallis [Clinton's second-in-command] had long chafed under Clinton's instructions, which tethered him to his base at Charleston. . . . Cornwallis . . . was eager to press forward. . . . He held that Virginia was the heart and centre of the Patriot cause and that all efforts should be concentrated on its conquest and occupation. . . . There is no doubt he was wrong. . . . But Cornwallis's military reputation had been in the ascendant [for some time], and he was encouraged by the British Government to proceed with his plans, which largely depended for their success on the Southern Loyalists. . . . Cornwallis resolved to advance. Thus he marched to destruction.

In January 1781, Cornwallis's forward troops met and were beaten by the Americans, largely thanks to the French forces in their ranks. The British Commander headed for the coast, for vital supplies, and eventually the way north to Virginia.

C❖Throughout these months, Clinton lay in New York, and as Cornwallis drew nearer it seemed possible that Clinton might evacuate the Northern base and concentrate the whole British effort on preserving the hold on the Southern colonies. This, if it had succeeded, might have wrecked the Patriot cause, for the Congress was bankrupt and Washington could scarcely keep his army together.

It was the French who saved the Americans, or, rather, the French Navy. Washington was still in White Plains. The French naval commander, De Grasse, told Washington that the French would attack the Virginian coast and that Washington and his French Army ally, Rochambeau, should head South to join the bombardment. Sir Henry Clinton ordered Cornwallis to Yorktown where he could get to the sea and the re-supply routes. But De Grasse had driven the English Navy back to the waters off New York in September and so he commanded these lines.

C❖The Franco-American strategy was a feat of timing, and the convergence of force was carried out over vast distances. Nearly 9000 Americans and 8000 French assembled before Yorktown, while De Grasse blockaded the coast with forty ships of the line. For nearly two months Cornwallis sat and waited. At the end of September . . . the bombardment of the French siege artillery shattered his earth redoubts. Cornwallis planned a desperate sortie as the defences crumbled. At the end one British cannon remained in action.

Cornwallis surrendered the troops under his command as prisoners of war in October 1781. And that was it. There would be other battles, especially at sea and against the French, and it would take another two years for a peace treaty to be signed. But effectively, on 19 October 1781, Britain lost its American colonies for ever.

CHAPTER FORTY

1782–1792

———— ❖ ————

The British were beaten at Yorktown in 1781. The Treaty of Paris, in 1783, officially ended the American War of Independence. Here's part of the document agreed with the new 'United States of America', a document in which the British monarch still called himself 'King of France'.

❖His Britannic Majesty acknowledges the said United States, viz. New Hampshire, Massachusetts Bay, Rhode Island and Providence Plantations, Connecticut, New York, New Jersey, Pennsylvania, Delaware, Maryland, Virginia, North Carolina, South Carolina, and Georgia, to be free, sovereign, and independent states; that he treats them as such; and for himself, his heirs and successors, relinquishes all claims to the government, propriety, and territorial rights of the same, and every part thereof.

Within six years the United States of America, as the new country was already being called, would have its first President, George Washington. The newly united states of America may have been free of Britain but Britain, of course, was not free from the consequences of losing the war. George III talked of giving up his crown, and of retreating to his homelands in Germany. He didn't, but he did become insane, although, under Constitutional law, that was no bar to the throne of Great Britain. The mood in Great Britain generally was one of anger.

C❖The surrender at Yorktown had immediate and decisive effects in England. When the news was brought to Lord North, his amiable composure slid from him. He paced his room, exclaiming in agonized tones, 'Oh, God, it is all over!'

The Opposition gathered strongly in the Commons. There were riotous meetings in London. The Government majority collapsed on a motion censuring the administration of the Navy. . . . In March, North informed the Commons that he would resign. . . . [he] maintained his dignity to the last. After twelve years of service, he left the House of Commons a beaten man.

This was far more than the simple departure of a prime minister. When he went he did so because of something unique in Parliamentary history, up to that point. monarchs had accepted, reluctantly, the mood of the nation. Monarchs had sometimes accepted the decisions of their prime ministers. But now the House of Commons had the voting power to force the resignation of a prime minister and all but a few of his colleagues. And for that reason North's going can be seen as a milestone in Parliamentary history.

There were only two men capable of succeeding him, of rallying support for a new ministry. One was Charles Watson-Wentworth, the second Marquess of Rockingham, who'd already been prime minister for a short spell in the 1760s. The other was the second Earl Shelburne. Both had advocated an end to the war and had even opposed it in the first place, and both were Whigs. However Shelburne couldn't maintain a majority without the help of the Rockingham Whigs, and they were unlikely to give him any support, so George III called for Rockingham. But by July Rockingham was dead and Shelburne became leader. The difference between the two was in the style and composition of their Cabinets. By and large, Rockingham, with Burke, had seen Cabinet government as a group of like-minded individuals who would present a unified front to the King. Shelburne didn't think like that. He was – or posed as – an intellectual and he was politically inept. Most importantly, Shelburne thought little of party government. He gathered together politicians of differing views and supported the King's right to choose his ministers – a concept conveniently dear to the King's heart.

C❖. . . politics were now implacably bitter between three main groups, and none of them was strong enough alone to sustain a Government. Shelburne himself had the support of those who had followed Chatham, including his son, the young William Pitt, who was appointed Chancellor of the Exchequer.

Pitt was twenty-three, and would be Prime Minister by the time he was twenty-four.

C❖But North still commanded a considerable faction, and . . . coveted a renewal of office. The third group was headed by Charles James Fox, vehement critic of North's regime, brilliant, generous-hearted, and inconsistent. . . .

Hostility to Shelburne grew and spread. Nevertheless, . . . the Prime Minister succeeded in bringing the world war to an end on the basis of American independence. . . . Shelburne, like Chatham, dreamt of preserving the Empire by making generous concessions, and he realized that freedom was the only practical policy. In any case, Fox had already committed Britain to this step by making a public announcement in the House of Commons.

Fox and Shelburne never got on. In fact Fox detested Shelburne. Even when Rockingham was alive they'd competed with each other for the right to hand out offices and general patronage. They disagreed over the way in which peace might be negotiated. Fox had long abandoned the illusion that the thirteen colonies were in fact colonies. He and Shelburne even had different envoys in Paris where the talks were taking place.

Closer to home, political animosities were to have a much longer lasting effect. The historical differences between the English and the Irish had not disappeared, or become any less important simply because Britain had been at war across the Atlantic ocean.

For example, Lord Shelburne had criticized the North administration for its attitude to Ireland, especially for its restrictions on trade with the colonies during the war. To be fair, North had attempted to make concessions and it was English merchants who had opposed him. (Which explains something of the political realities of the day and particularly why it is wrong to think in simple terms of Whigs, Tories and the power of political majorities.)

The Speaker of the Irish House of Commons, Edmond Sexton Pery, reported, in 1779, that the restrictions were 'one general Cause of Distress in the economy and the people'. The laws, he believed, were cruel and short-sighted, the interests of the English merchants repressive.

❖That Ireland must continue in a state of poverty, frequently of misery, appears evident not only from reason but experience; it seems to be equally obvious that it is not the interest of Great Britain to keep her in that state, in the view of commerce only. Great Britain must be a loser by it. Little is to be got by trading with a poor country. The benefit of one nation constitutes that of the other.

But several bodies of manufacturing people, more attentive to their own private interest than to that of the public, look upon the progress of improvement in the latter with a jealous eye. The woollen manufacturer requires some particular notice. It is asserted by the drapiers and clothiers in Ireland, that all the wool produced in Ireland is not sufficient to clothe its inhabitants; the price of wool in Ireland being so much higher than in England seems to countenance the assertion, unless it is to be raised by a great Demand for it in France, and the consequent temptation to Smugglers to transport it into that Kingdom.

Pery ended with a note of encouragement that might also be read as a note of warning about Anglo-Irish relations in the future. He wrote of partial laws, that is, laws in favour of the English.

❖At present the people of Ireland are taught by partial laws to consider themselves as separated from the inhabitants of Great Britain. Were that fatal obstacle removed, they would be united as much in affection, as they certainly are in interest; and it would not then be in the power of malice to disturb their harmony. But the seeds of discord are sown, and if suffered to take root, it is to be feared will soon overspread the land.

This may have been wise prophecy, yet the problem was deeper than the constraints of trade. For example, in 1780 Arthur Young published his observations of the people of Ireland.

❖The food of the common Irish, potatoes and milk, have been produced more than once as an instance of the extreme poverty of the country, but this I believe is an opinion embraced with more alacrity than reflection. I have heard it stigmatized as being unhealthy, and not sufficiently nourishing for the support of hard labour, but this opinion is very amazing in a country, many of whose poor people are as athletic in their form, as robust, and as capable of enduring labour as any upon earth. When they are encouraged, or animate themselves, to work hard, it is all by whisky, which though it has a notable effect in giving a perpetual motion with their tongues, can have but little of that invigorating substance which is found in strong beer or porter; probably it has an effect as pernicious, as the other is beneficial.

The common Irish are in general clothed so very indifferently, that it impresses every stranger with a strong idea of universal poverty. Shoes and stockings are scarcely ever found on the feet of children of either sex, and great numbers of men and women are without them. A change, however, is coming in, for there are many more of them with those articles of clothing now than ten years ago.

A long series of oppressions, aided by very many ill-judged laws, have brought landlords into a habit of exerting a very lofty superiority, and their vassals into that of an almost unlimited submission: speaking a language that is despised, professing a religion that is abhorred, and being disarmed, the poor find themselves in many cases slaves even in the bosom of written liberty.

A landlord in Ireland can scarcely invent an order which a servant, labourer, or cottar dares to refuse to execute. [A cottar lived in a cottage owned by the landlord and worked in return.] Disrespect or anything tending towards sauciness he may punish with his cane or his horsewhip with the most perfect security. A poor man would have his bones broke if he offered to lift his hand in his own defence. Landlords of consequence have assured me that many of their cottars would think themselves honoured by having their wives and daughters sent for to the bed of their master; a mark of slavery that proves the oppression under which such people must live.

By 1780 the suffering of Ireland and the Irish, particularly from the restrictions on trade, began to have some political effect, yet solutions were not really obvious. Two Bills went through the Westminster Parliament which allowed the export of woollens and glass, and an expansion of trade with America, the West Indies, and Africa. But not much actually changed. Industry did not attract investors. Both the hard cash necessary to build these industries, and shipping, were in short supply. And so, in spite of the joy with which the new legislation was greeted in Ireland, reality soon descended, and Edmond Pery's hoped-for economic miracle and calming of animosities barely materialized.

In Scotland in the eighteenth century, there was an unprecedentedly strong export trade, especially in sturdy clothing and iron tools and, thanks to the increasing demand for glass, high investment there meant bigger potential export markets, which in turn supported an expanding fleet. And Scottish entrepreneurs appear to have been more imaginative than those trading from or through Ireland.

Yet even in Scotland the effects of the war were catastrophic. Just before the war, the Scottish Tobacco Lords, as they were known, were bringing in some forty-six million pounds of tobacco. More than 90% of it was then re-exported, much of it to France. Halfway through the war, the Scottish import-export trade was down by 40%, but the resilience of the Scottish traders meant they survived. In 1783 Glasgow set up a group to examine potential markets. It became the first Chamber of Commerce in Great Britain and it worked. Within seven years Scottish trade figures had recovered to their pre-war levels.

But it was at the centre of British power where reform was most needed.

C❖The King now seized his chance of regaining popularity . . . In William Pitt, the son of the great Chatham, the King found the man [to assist him]. . . . His reputation was honourable and clear. By what was certainly the most outstanding domestic action of his long reign, in December 1783, the King asked Pitt to form a Government. The old Parliamentary machine had failed, and as it broke down a new combination took its place whose efforts were vindicated by the events of the next twenty years.

Between 1782 and 1783 Britain had five administrations and ministers still owed their loyalty first and foremost to the monarch, not to their party. In fact there probably wasn't a Whig or a Tory party political position on many major matters at the time. An instinct, yes, but not a manifesto in the way they exist today. And the Cabinet was not single minded, it was a coalition. The King had the right, which he exercised, to appoint his ministers but George didn't like political parties. To him a party meant a faction and therefore a danger. Sometimes that faction imposed its will: Rockingham's administration did. So did the coalition of Fox and North.

The political thinking of the early 1780s helps to explain the consequences of the changes taking place in a society that tended to think in terms of tinkering with the system rather than putting in place new political and social machinery. Churchill, for example, says that the system had contributed to the American colonists' decision to break away. But new ideas, publicly debated, had crossed the Atlantic long before Thomas Jefferson had drafted his Declaration of Independence. Indeed, much of that Declaration was based on thinking that been aired in late seventeenth-, not eighteenth-century England.

C❖The revolt of the American colonies had shattered the complacency of eighteenth-century England. Men began to study the root causes of the disaster and the word 'reform' was in the air. The defects of the political system had plainly contributed to the secession, and the arguments used by the American colonists against the Mother Country lingered in the minds of all Englishmen who questioned the perfection of the Constitution. Demand for some reform of the representation in Parliament began to stir; but the agitation was now mild and respectable. The main aim of the reformers was to increase the number of boroughs which elected Members of Parliament, and thus reduce the possibilities of Government corruption. There was even talk of universal suffrage and other novel theories of democratic representation. But . . . the movement in governing circles was neither radical nor comprehensive. It found expression in Burke's Economic Reform Act of 1782, disenfranchising certain classes of Government officials who had hitherto played some part in managing elections. This was a tepid version of the scheme Burke had meant to introduce. No general reform of the franchise was attempted, and when people talked about the rights of Englishmen they meant the sturdy class of yeomen vaunted as the backbone of the country, whose weight in the counties it was desired to increase. Many of the early reform schemes were academic attempts to preserve the political power and balance of the rural interest.

In May 1782 William Pitt (the Younger) had spoken in the House on Parliamentary Reform. But he didn't suggest which was the best way forward.

Yet he pointed out that there wasn't a Member of Parliament who wouldn't, as he put it, agree with him 'that the representation, as it now stood, was incomplete'. (In fact he was wrong on that. Many would disagree with him.) He concluded that there should be a committee to 'enquire into the present state of the Representation of the Commons of Great Britain in Parliament'.

Pitt's proposal was rejected, but only by twenty votes. In that same debate, Edmund Burke spoke against Pitt. Burke wasn't necessarily against reform, he simply recognized that this was not the way towards it. On 7 May Burke reflected on the difference between what people thought to be the rights of men and what was a Constitutional question.

❖There are two parties who proceed on two grounds, in my opinion, as they state them, utterly irreconcilable. The one is juridicial, the other political. The one is in the nature of a claim of right, on the supposed rights of man as man; this party desire the decision of a suit. The other ground, as far as I can divine what it directly means, is that the representation is not so politically framed as to answer the theory of its institution. . . . The language of the first party is plain and intelligible; they who plead an absolute right cannot be satisfied with anything short of personal representation, because all *natural* rights must be the rights of the individual; as by nature there is no such thing as politic or corporate personality; all these ideas are mere fictions of law, they are creatures of voluntary institution; men as men are individuals, nothing else. They, therefore, who reject the principle of natural and personal representation, are essentially and eternally at variance with those who claim it.

As to the first sort of reformers, it is ridiculous to talk to them of the British Constitution upon any or upon all of its bases; for they lay it down that every man ought to govern himself, and that where he cannot go himself he must send his representative; that all other government is usurpation; and is so far from having a claim to our obedience, it is not only our right, but our duty, to resist it. Nine-tenths of the reformers argue thus, that is, on the natural right. It is impossible not to make some reflection on the nature of this claim, or avoid a comparison between the extent of the principle and the present object of the demand. If this claim be founded, it is clear to what it goes. The House of Commons, in that light, undoubtedly is no representative of the people, as a collection of individuals. Nobody pretends it, nobody can justify such an assertion. When you come to examine into this claim of right, founded on the right of self-government in each individual, you find the thing demanded infinitely short of the principle of demand.

And Burke is quite precise when describing the shallowness of some of the arguments for reform. Here are some of his closing remarks made to the House of Commons in the late spring, 1782.

❖On what basis do we go to restore our Constitution to what it has been at some given period, or to reform and reconstruct it upon principles more comfortable to a sound theory of government? A prescriptive government, such as ours, never was the work of any legislator, never was made upon any foregone theory. It seems to me a preposterous way of reasoning, and a perfect confusion of ideas, to take the theories which learned and speculative men have made from the Government, and then, supposing it made on those theories which were made from it, to accuse the Government as not corresponding with them . . .

It is to this humour, and it is to the measures growing out of it, that I set myself (I hope not alone) in the most determined opposition. Never before did we at any time in this country meet upon the theory of our frame of government, to sit in judgment on the Constitution of our country, to call it as a delinquent before us, and to accuse it of every defect and every vice; to see whether it, an object of our veneration, even our adoration, did or did not accord with a preconceived scheme in the minds of certain gentlemen. . . . I look with filial reverence on the Constitution of my country, and never will cut it to pieces, and put it into the kettle of any magician, in order to boil it, with the puddle of their compounds, into youth and vigour. On the contrary, I will drive away such pretenders; I will nurse its venerable age, and with lenient arts extend a parent's breath.

This was the atmosphere in 1783 when the youngest Prime Minister of all time (Pitt was just twenty-four) combined with the most experienced surviving politician of the day: George III. By then George III had reigned for twenty-three years, and had been through, and often suffered from, almost every form of political intrigue. He had watched, fought and compromised at every opportunity to keep control of his administrations and, in some cases, to lead them. Furthermore, his reputation, once the immediate loss of the colonies was out of the way, was high enough for this Hanoverian to be called Good King George by his people. His reputation was helped by the low public esteem in which politicians were held, and by the antics of the Prince of Wales.

George III's position in politics was so important that when, in 1788, the middle-aged King became ill, there was the greatest concern by outsiders for his safety and by insiders for their futures. After all, if the King died there was not simply the matter of the succession, but the political manipulation of that succession. Fox and his friends would be on one side; the Pittites on the other. However the King didn't die and when Pitt the Younger became his Prime

Minister, George III embarked on a remarkable decade in England's political and social history. The Norfolk pamphleteer, Tom Paine, was writing *The Rights of Man*, Gibbon was finishing *The Decline and Fall of the Roman Empire* and the working environment was radically changing.

If the changes were radical, it was because industrial society was shifting and not because there was deep anxiety about the ways and circumstances of people's lives. Furthermore, here was a period which demonstrated that events elsewhere and not at home, might excite the society in which radical thought germinates. For example, Tom Paine's ideas were about England, yet the understanding of what Paine was trying to say was triggered by the American revolt and then the French Revolution. In fact Paine's history as a Sussex excise man (even though he was dismissed for agitation) still doesn't contain anything that would lead an observer to suspect that he would eventually produce such lasting anti-establishment political thought. It was not until he went to live in America in 1774 – with its environment of social and political change – that Paine began to express in print much of what he had been thinking for some years.

C❖The American Revolution had thrown the English back upon themselves, and a mental stocktaking exposed complacencies and anomalies which could ill stand the public gaze. The religious revival of John Wesley had broken the stony surface of the Age of Reason. The enthusiasm generated by the Methodist movement and its mission to the poor and humble accelerated the general dissolution of the eighteenth-century world. The Dissenters, who had long supported the Whig Party, increased in wealth and importance, and renewed their attack on the religious monopoly of the Established Church. . . . Such, in brief, were the turmoils and problems which confronted William Pitt when he became Prime Minister of Britain at the age of twenty-four.

There had been a coalition administration led by Lord North and Charles James Fox so, when the election came in 1784, there was a political confrontation between these two on one side and the King and Pitt on the other. The result represented a show of support for George III's decision to send North and Fox packing and to appoint Pitt as his Prime Minister. And because Pitt never had more than fifty MPs supporting him he was compelled to rely on the King and those who supported the King. One consequence of this was that most of his Ministers also owed more allegiance to the Crown than to the Prime Minister.

But Pitt had advantages of his own. First, he was a Pitt and he carried the family name with ease. He was conscientious, honourable and, considering his age and the fact that he had already been Chancellor of the Exchequer, formidably bright. Above all, he was not associated with the old group of politicians and so it followed that although he had supporters he had no close cronies.

C❖But two men were to play a decisive part in his life, Henry Dundas and William Wilberforce. Dundas, a good-humoured, easy-going materialist, embodied the spirit of eighteenth-century politics, with its buying up of seats, its full-blooded enjoyment of office, its secret influences, and its polished scepticism. He was an indispensable ally, for he commanded both the electoral power of Scotland and the political allegiance of the East India Company, and it was he who kept the new majority together. For Pitt, although personally incorruptible, leant heavily upon the eighteenth-century machinery of government for support.

William Wilberforce, on the other hand, was the friend of Pitt's Cambridge days, and the only person who enjoyed his confidence. Deeply religious and sustained by a high idealism, Wilberforce became the keeper of the young Minister's conscience. He belonged to the new generation which questioned the cheerful complacency of the eighteenth century. The group who gathered round him were known not unkindly as 'the Saints'. They formed a compact body in the House of Commons, and their prime political aim was the abolition of the slave trade. . . . The variety of his following, however, limited the scope of his work. A multitude of interests stifled his early hopes. He failed to legislate against the slave trade. Wilberforce and his 'Saints' were consistently thwarted by the Bristol and Liverpool merchants, who were political supporters of the Ministry and whom Pitt refused to alienate. Such was the meagreness of Pitt's efforts that many doubted his sincerity as a reformer. . . . His supporters were stubborn, jealous, and at times rebellious. . . . [and] from the outset, Pitt was overcome by the dead hand of eighteenth-century politics. He failed to abolish the slave trade. He failed to make a settlement in Ireland. He failed to make Parliament more representative of the nation, and the one achievement in these early months was his India Act, which increased rather than limited the opportunities for political corruption. He saw quite clearly the need and justification for reform, but preferred always to compromise with the forces of resistance.

Pitt recognized that he had to accept political change, and even defeat, rather than risk causing more damage by open confrontation. He was a man who could take stock to analyse, after success, why he had been successful and, after failure, how to avoid repeating the experience. If there existed an advantage in defeat, or an unrecognized one in success, Pitt knew how to make that advantage work for him. One advantage was his understanding with the King. They were never friends in the social sense but their relationship worked. Pitt needed the King and the King needed Pitt – particularly in matters of finance and economic reform.

C❖The antiquated and involved system of customs barriers was now for the first time systematically revised. There were sixty-eight different kinds of customs duties, and some articles were subject to many separate and cumulative imposts [duties]. A pound of nutmegs paid, or ought to have paid, nine different duties. . . . Pitt was able to bring a degree of order into this chaos, and the first visible effect of his wide-ranging revision of tariffs was a considerable drop in smuggling.

Further reform consolidated the revenue. It is to Pitt that we owe the modern machinery of the 'Budget'. . . . The Audit Office was established, and numerous sinecures at the Treasury were abolished. . . . At the end of 1783 over £40 million which had been voted by Parliament for war purposes had not been accounted for. . . . The National Debt stood at £250 million, more than two-and-a-half times as great as in the days of Walpole. Pitt resolved to acquire a surplus in the revenue and apply it to the reduction of this swollen burden.

In 1786 he brought in a Bill for this purpose. Each year £1 million would be set aside to buy stock, and the interest would be used to reduce the National Debt. Here was the famous oft-criticized Sinking Fund.

In the autumn of 1788, the King showed the first visible signs of insanity. Fox and his friends had taken up with the Prince of Wales. There was no chance, after the antagonisms of the Fox–North coalition, that George III would ever admit Fox as his first minister; but the heir to the throne might. Fox was an opportunist and he was older than Pitt, so he felt his chances of becoming prime minister were fading. There were rumours that the King might die. This was good news to Fox's ears. A new King would get rid of Pitt and give his post to Fox. He could hardly have guessed that, ill or not, George III would outlive the lot of them.

And when, in the following year, the Revolution started in France, Fox once again misjudged the mood of the country. It is easy to see why.

C❖It is remarkable to witness the peaceful triteness of English politics, operating almost as if in a vacuum, during the years 1789 to 1793, when the terrible and world-shaking upheavals in Paris and in the provinces of France convulsed men's minds. . . . Pitt was determined to stand clear of the impending European conflict. He was convinced that if the French revolutionaries were left alone to put their house in order as they chose, England could avoid being dragged into war. He watched, unmoved, the passion of the Opposition for an armed crusade against unenlightened despotism. . . . Led by Fox, they saw in war a hope of breaking Pitt's monopoly of political power. But Burke was closer to the general feeling of the country when he remarked that 'the effect of liberty to individuals is that they may do as they please: we ought to see what it will please them to do before we risk congratulations'. The sympathies of the Court were not unmoved by the plight of the French monarchy, and if intervention became inevitable the Court was naturally in favour of supporting Louis XVI. Pitt maintained an even course of neutrality, and with characteristic obstinacy held to it for over three tumultuous years.

In 1789 there was a buoyant mood in England. The King had recovered, and he was pleased at the way in which Pitt had held the administration during his illness. The country at large imagined that the absolutist Bourbon monarchy might be on the verge of reform. And what better way to gauge the mood of the nation than to note that the Marylebone Cricket Club, the MCC, was celebrating its second birthday and one Thomas Lord had established a cricket ground. The national game, no longer a pastime, had still to undergo the revolutions of overarm bowling, the cowardly fashion of wearing pads and allowing bowlers three instead of two stumps as a target. In the drinking houses, these were, truthfully, matters of some importance. But across the Channel a much greater event was to replace the doings of Lumpy Stevens, Nyren and the other men of Hambledon.

C❖The convulsion which shook France in 1789 was totally different from the revolutions that the world had seen before. England in the seventeenth century had witnessed a violent shift in power between the Crown and the People; but the basic institutions of State had been left untouched, or at any rate had soon been restored. Nor as yet had there been in England any broadening of popular sovereignty in the direction of universal suffrage. . . . America in her Revolution had proclaimed the wider rights of mankind.

Americans had rebelled against being ruled and taxed by another nation; theirs was an anti-colonial rebellion. The English Revolution of 1688 had not been against monarchy and nobility, but against a particular monarch, James II, and Roman Catholicism. No one had tried to return to the Cromwellian model, to a republic. But in France, almost without warning to those preoccupied with their own political, commercial and colonial ambitions, that was what was happening.

In eighteenth-century France the King governed from Versailles, surrounded by his courtiers. However the courtiers, the French nobility, had been stripped of power. They were landlords who simply took revenues from their distant estates and as a class, or, more accurately, as a caste, did nothing to help govern the country. They certainly weren't as powerful as the Church, nor were they as powerful as the peasants. The French peasantry was a European phenomenon: peasantry with power. They were depressed by high rates of taxation but they also owned half the land in France and their lot was getting better. They were potentially dangerous.

There was also in France an influential group of extraordinary people not to be under-rated. They carried no guns, received no patronage, and had no crude plans for the downfall of the monarch. Nevertheless, their names have survived longer than many of the revolutionaries themselves. They were the philosophers: Diderot, Rousseau, Voltaire.

C❖The Government of France had long been bankrupt. . . . Many men had laboured, but without success, to make France solvent. The obstacles were formidable. . . . The heaviest fiscal burden lay upon the peasants. Their plight must not be exaggerated . . . Nevertheless their grievances were substantial. . . . The winter of 1788 was very severe. Many died of starvation. Yet it has been well said that revolutions are not made by starving people. The peasants were no worse off and probably slightly more comfortable than a century before. . . . They desired only freedom from oppressive landlords and antiquated taxes. The revolutionary impulse came from elsewhere. The nobles had lost their energy and their faith in themselves. The clergy were divided. The Army was unreliable. The King and his Court lacked both the will and the ability to govern. Only the bourgeois possessed the appetite for power and the determination and self-confidence to seize it. . . . They distrusted the crowd, the mob, and with some reason, but they were nevertheless prepared to incite and use it against the 'privileged' nobility, and, if necessary, in the assertion of their own status, against the monarchy itself.

On 14 July the royal prison in Paris, the Bastille, fell. It held only a handful of prisoners, one of them mad, but it represented the absolute rule of the French monarch. The revolution was well under way. At the start, Britain appears to have assumed that the outcome would be an English-style Constitutional monarchy. Pitt quietly welcomed this idea: he believed a reformed French throne would be less of a military threat.

Fox and the so-called Whig opposition were excited by the prospect of change. But there was no fear that the revolutionary ideas would spread to Britain. Perhaps this short-sightedness had a lot to do with the fact that few people anywhere in Europe, perhaps even in France, understood the implications of what had been started. In Britain in particular, judging the French Revolution's effects was probably influenced by the satisfactory outcome of the nation's own revolution, the centenary of which was being celebrated. It was

100 years since the English Bill of Rights was published. The Glorious Revolution of 1688 could have been mistakenly assumed similar to what was going on in France.

Fox got up in Parliament and sang French praises. Edmund Burke, however, was pessimistic. He supported the idea of change, but he thought that what was actually happening was potentially dangerous.

Furthermore, Burke, a devout Christian, believed the outcome would be, at least, civil war on a scale more ferocious than the old wars of religion. He could not accept that the French were merely shuffling their society. Burke saw the Revolution as a prelude to something quite frightening: a creeping threat to the institutions of Christian Europe. For that reason, Burke wanted Pitt to make troops ready for war against the French. But it's doubtful if he expected Pitt to do as he advised. He thought the Prime Minister was a man of no imagination and little vision.

Pitt did nothing, Burke wanted intervention, and a few Whigs, if not exactly in agreement, took serious note of what Burke was saying; and Fox (even though he understood the instinctive British mistrust of the French) supported the Revolution. But the differences between Fox and Burke were so great that the two men quarrelled in public (in the House of Commons, ironically during the Canada Debate), and Burke broke from the party.

And, by the late summer of 1792, the French Revolution had spread beyond the French borders. The French monarchy was no more. News of mass murders of the aristocracy crossed the Channel. What had been seen as Constitutional reform was turning into bloody dictatorship. And dictatorship was turning into war.

British radicals, poets, writers, and, in some cases, the constituents of the new Working Men's Clubs, were all in touch with the French extremists, the Jacobins (the Jacobin Club existed between 1790 and 1794 and was a club for those with radical ideas). The Jacobins shouldn't be confused with the Jacobites, the old supporters of a Stuart pretender to the English throne. Jacobinism in Britain was strong enough for the French to believe they had support for the export of the Revolution. They turned out to be wrong, but at the end of January, the French announced the annexation of the Austrian Netherlands. The next day, 1 February 1793, they declared war on Holland and on Britain. And so now, with the declaration of war, Pitt, his policy of do-nothing shredded, expressed his misery to the Commons.

❖The contempt which the French have shown for a neutrality on our part most strictly observed; the violations of their solemn and plighted faith; their presumptuous attempts to interfere in the government of this country and to arm our subjects against ourselves, to vilify a monarch, the object of our gratitude, reverence, and affection, and to separate the Court from the people; does not this become, on our part, a war of honour, a war necessary to assert the spirit of the nation and the dignity of the British name? We are at war with those who would destroy the whole fabric of our Constitution. In such a cause as that in which we are now engaged, I trust that our exertions will terminate only with our lives.

So Britain was once more at war with France.

CHAPTER FORTY-ONE

1793–1799

———— ❖ ————

In 1793 a young artillery lieutenant was responsible for the capture of the Royalist fortress sea-port of Toulon. In Paris, Robespierre took note of this young Corsican officer whose name was Napoleon Bonaparte. France would need an imaginative commander. An alliance of Europeans against France was set up. It was called the First Coalition and consisted of Britain, Holland, Spain, Austria and Prussia. But it was not a success because each member was too busy looking after its own interests.

C❖In England the Government had been forced to take repressive measures of a sternness unknown for generations. Republican lecturers were swept into prison. The Habeas Corpus Act was suspended. Distinguished writers were put on trial for treason; but juries could not be prevailed on to convict. The mildest criticism of the Constitution brought the speaker under danger from a new Treason Act. Ireland, governed since 1782 by a Protestant Parliament independent of Westminster, was now on the verge of open rebellion, which, as Pitt saw, could only be averted by liberal concessions to the Irish Catholics. Henry Grattan, the eloquent Irish leader, who had done so much to win more freedom for his country, urged that Catholics should be given both the vote and the right to sit in Parliament and hold office. They got the vote, but seats in Parliament were still denied them.

And the partners in the First Coalition against France were in disarray. The Low Countries, with one British ally, the Prussians, were more interested in sharing the partition of Poland with the Russians. The Prussians then made a peace agreement (to consolidate their Polish gains) and sat out the war in selfish neutrality. The Austrians followed to pick over the Polish bones while the French armies drove into Spain and Holland, which became known as the Batavian Republic. The Spanish, sensing the course of the war, deserted the First Coalition, and, as if all this wasn't enough, the British Royal Navy failed to dominate the sea-lanes. And the navy mutinied twice.

In April 1797, conditions of service in the navy were so bad that the Channel Fleet, at Spithead, refused to put to sea. Within a few days, many of the demands of the ratings were granted. This encouraged the North Sea Fleet to mutiny at the Nore, and so, for weeks, it was the Royal Navy and not the French that virtually blockaded the Thames. The conditions in which ratings lived on the lower decks in the eighteenth century were appalling. Here's part of the petition sent to the Board of Admiralty by the Spithead mutineers.

❖The first grievance which we have to complain of is that our wages are too low and ought to be raised, that we might be better able to support our wives and families in a manner comfortable, whom we are in duty bound to support as far as our wages will allow.

    We beg that your Lordships will take into consideration the grievances of which we complain, and now lay before you: that our provisions be raised to the weight of sixteen ounces to the pound and of better quality. There might be granted a sufficient quantity of vegetables of such kind as may be the most plentiful in the ports to which we go; that your Lordships will be pleased seriously to look into the state of the sick on board His Majesty's ships, that they may be better attended to, and that they may have the use of such necessaries as allowed for them in time of their sickness, and that these necessaries be not on any account embezzled; that we may be looked upon as a number of men standing in defence of our country, and that we may in some wise have grant and opportunity to taste the sweets of liberty on the shore, when in any harbour, and when we have completed the duty of our ship, after our return from sea; that if any man is wounded in action, his pay be continued until he is cured and discharged; and if any ship has any real grievances to complain of, we hope your Lordships will readily redress them, as far as is in your power, to prevent any disturbances.

The French were in the Channel and a squadron was heading for Ireland, so the Admiralty Board responded quickly in order 'that the Fleet should speedily put to sea to meet the enemy of the country'. The Board said that it understood the grievances and wages were raised to four shillings a month extra for petty officers and able seamen, three shillings a month extra for ordinary seamen and two shillings a month for landmen. Wounded sailors would continue to be paid. But the Spithead sailors weren't satisfied. They pushed once more at the Board's eagerness to reach agreement with the Fleet before there was another disagreement with the French.

❖We received your Lordships' answer to our Petition, and, in order to convince your Lordships and the nation in general of our moderation, beg leave to offer the following remarks for your consideration:
    There never has existed but two orders of men in the navy – able and ordinary; therefore the distinction between ordinary and landmen is totally

new. We therefore humbly propose to your Lordships that the old regulations be adhered to; that the wages of seamen be raised to one shilling a day, and that of petty officers and the ordinary in the usual proportion; and, as further proof of our moderation, and that we are actuated by a true spirit of benevolence towards our brethren, the marines, who are not noticed in your Lordships' answer, we humbly propose that their pay be augmented while serving on board, in the same proportion as ordinary seamen; this we hope and trust will be convincing proof to your Lordships that we are not actuated by a spirit of contradiction, but that we earnestly wish to put a speedy end to the present affair.

Then, very gently, they pushed for more payment for pensioners, plus rises for sailors in the East India Company's navy.

The demands of the Spithead sailors were coped with but those of the North Sea Fleet were not settled so easily. The Nore mutineers, as they were known, did not surrender for four weeks. When they finally put to sea, they won the Battle of Camperdown and stopped the Dutch invasion of England.

But for one man in particular, the Nore and Spithead were of little immediate interest. Commodore Horatio Nelson had just been promoted to Rear Admiral, was about to be knighted and, within months, he, the nation, and the wife of Sir William Hamilton would be celebrating his destruction of the French Fleet at the mouth of the river Nile.

By the last three years of the eighteenth century the Bank of England had run into trouble. A bad harvest meant increased imports which had to be paid for in gold, and rumour of a French invasion at Fishguard led to a panic run on the country banks, which turned to the Bank of England. The Bank suspended payments; the war dragged on.

The ambition of the Prime Minister, Pitt the Younger, put simply, was to keep the map of Europe the same as it was before the French Revolution, to avoid the possibility of a French Revolutionary empire stretching from the Atlantic to the Urals. But the French were showing they could dictate the course of the fighting: the so-called Allies weren't really allies at all, and the French were beating their own countrymen, the Royalists, the *ancien régime*. Then they crossed borders and played by their own rules of warfare, and very successfully.

C❖On the Continent the French were everywhere triumphant. Bonaparte, having reduced Northern Italy, was preparing to strike at Austria through the Alpine passes. . . . Belgium was annexed . . . the Republic of Venice, with a glorious history reaching into the Dark Ages, became an Austrian province. Milan, Piedmont, and the little principalities of Northern Italy were welded into a new Cisalpine Republic. France, dominant in Western Europe, firmly planted in the Mediterranean, safeguarded against attack from Germany by a secret understanding with Austria, had only to consider what she would conquer next. A sober judgment might have said England, by way of Ireland. Bonaparte thought he saw his destiny in a larger field. In the spring of 1798 he sailed for Egypt. Nelson sailed after him.

Horatio Nelson was born in Norfolk in 1758, two years after the Black Hole of Calcutta and in the same year as Halley's comet was seen. Nelson was twelve when he joined his first ship, the *Raisonnable*, a ship captured from the French in the days when the Royal Navy rarely changed ships' names. She was a fine ship for Nelson and for her captain, Maurice Suckling. Suckling just happened to be Nelson's uncle, otherwise Nelson, who was a feeble child, might never have been taken into the navy at all.

In the summer of that year, 1771, Nelson transferred to the *Triumph*, and then to a merchant ship which took him to the West Indies. When England went to war with the American colonies, so did Nelson. By 1787, he had commanded four ships and had married Frances Nisbet. But the following year he was unemployed. In those days, if an officer didn't have a ship, then the best he could hope for was to go ashore on half pay. It wasn't until January 1793, only four weeks before France declared war, that the Admiralty called Nelson back. He took command of the *Agamemnon*, the ship he loved more than any other, including *Victory*. The following year he was wounded in his right eye in the Corsican campaign at Calvi, and eventually lost its sight. In 1797 he became a rear admiral, a knight of the Bath and, at Santa Cruz, lost his right arm. And so now, in 1798, it was a half-sighted, one-armed, diminutive, glory-seeking, prone-to-sea-sickness junior admiral who hoisted his pennant in the *Vanguard* and started searching the Mediterranean for the French Fleet.

C❖During the afternoon of August 1, a scouting vessel from Nelson's fleet signalled that a number of French battleships were anchored in Aboukir Bay, to the east of Alexandria. In a line nearly two miles long the thirteen French 'seventy-fours' [vessels, each with seventy-four guns] lay close in to the shallow water, headed west, with dangerous shoals to port. The French Admiral Brueys was convinced that not even an English admiral would risk sailing his ship between the shoals and the French line. But Nelson knew his captains. As evening drew near, the *Goliath*, followed by the *Zealous*, cautiously crept to landward of the French van, and came into action a few minutes before sundown. Five British ships passed in succession on the land side of the enemy, while Nelson, in the *Vanguard*, led the rest of his fleet to lie to on the starboard of the French line.

The French sailors were many of them on shore and the decks of their vessels were encumbered with gear. They had not thought it necessary to clear the gun ports on their landward side. In the rapidly falling darkness confusion seized their fleet. Relentlessly the English ships, distinguished by four lanterns hoisted in a horizontal pattern, battered the enemy van, passing from one disabled foe to the next down the line. At ten o'clock Brueys' flagship, the *Orient*, blew up. The five ships ahead of her had already surrendered; the rest, their cables cut by shot, or frantically attempting to avoid the inferno of the burning *Orient*, drifted helplessly. In the morning hours three ran ashore and surrendered, and a fourth was burned by her officers. Of the great fleet that had convoyed Napoleon's army to the adventure in Egypt, only two ships of the line and two frigates escaped.

It was a grand and an awful spectacle. The French Commander, Admiral Brueys, was seen flopped in a chair, both legs shot off, still trying to direct operations. A further salvo saved him further pain. His captain refused to leave the deck. His ten-year-old son was trapped below in the fire. As Nelson wrote in his dispatch, 'My Lord, Almighty God has blessed His Majesty's Arms in the late Battle by a great victory over the Fleet of the Enemy.' The importance of this battle was that it stopped Napoleon building a communications line between France and Asia. And the Royal Navy was now in Malta, and so could stay in the Mediterranean all year round instead of returning the Fleet to home waters every winter.

C❖But still the British Government could conceive no co-ordinated military plan upon the scale demanded by European strategy. Their own resources were few and their allies seldom dependable. Minor expeditions were dispatched to points around the circumference of the Continent. Descents were made on Brittany, in Spain, and later in Southern Italy. These harassed the local enemy commanders, but scarcely affected the larger conduct of the war. Meanwhile Napoleon again took charge of the French armies in Italy. In June 1800 he beat the Austrians at Marengo, in Piedmont, and France was once more mistress of Europe. The main contribution of the Island to the war at this time was the vigilance of her fleets and the payments of subsidies to allies. Napoleon's taunt of 'a nation of shopkeepers' had some foundation.

It was a problem for the Government that many of those shopkeepers, their customers and suppliers, landlords and tenants, were not making a big enough contribution. Money had been raised by barons from their peasantry, by counties from the landowners, and even windows had been taxed. Pitt had already tried to raise money by trebling the taxes on luxuries – for example, on hair powder, horses, and servants. But now, Pitt – a politician, not a monarch

– proposed the most obvious and universal means of raising money for war. On 3 December 1798, William Pitt gave the House news of the first graduated income tax.

> ❖It is my intention to propose that a general tax shall be imposed upon all the leading branches of income. I trust that all who value the national honour and the national safety will co-operate in obtaining, by an efficient and comprehensive tax upon real ability, every advantage which flourishing and invigorated resources can confer upon national efforts. It is my intention to propose that no income under £60 a year shall be called upon to contribute and that the scale of modification up to £200 a year shall be introduced.

Pitt then went into the sort of detail which would be recognized even today during a Budget Speech, when everyone wants to know 'How Much', but instead gets Treasuryspeak. But several of Pitt's statistics reveal quite a lot about Britain at the close of the century.

> ❖Examinations state the cultivated land of the country amount to little less than forty millions of acres. Many persons most conversant on the subject believe the average value to be fifteen shillings per acre . . . The value of income from land which belongs to the tenant I take at nineteen millions; the income to the landlord at twenty-five millions. I shall propose with respect to the tenant to deduct two-thirds, leaving five millions as the taxable property.
>
> Another species of rent is that received from houses. I shall take the rent of houses at no more than six millions. The profits gained by the professors of law are estimated at one million and a half. Allowing, besides, for all the branches of the medical professions, I conceive that two millions is a very small sum as the amount of incomes arising from the professions.

And so it went on until he had shown that all those who should be taxed must be taxed.

> ❖I felt it materially important to follow some durable, some apparent and sensible criterion, by which to apportion the burden.

Income Tax had arrived at two shillings in the pound. Pitt wanted 10% from everyone earning more than £60 a year. And at the end of the eighteenth century there was a larger population to be taxed.

The century began with a population of less than six million, but by the end of the century it was more than ten million. And by 1800 the National Debt, which had been about £19 million at the beginning of the century, was closer to £500 million. However there had been a 400% increase in cotton output and a four-fold increase in coal mining; the steam engine was invented, the Royal Academy and the first canal opened and the first edition of *The Times* was printed. And it was the century of the Georges, the third of whom became insane but, as the century turned, he outlived all his critics.

CHAPTER FORTY-TWO
1800–1805

———— ❖ ————

Ａnd now to the nineteenth century, which begins with Britain at war: the French Revolutionary War. But closer to home there is a conundrum of greater complexity and one which will live with not just this, but successive governments, for 200 years. Ireland.

C❖In 1800 the political situation in Britain was dominated by the passing of the Act of Union with Ireland. The shocks and alarums of the previous years determined Pitt to attempt some final settlement in that troubled island. The concessions already won by the Irish from British Governments in difficulty had whetted their appetite for more. At the same time Irish Catholics and Protestants were at each other's throats. In Ulster the Protestants founded the Orange Society for the defence of their religion. In the South the party of United Irishmen under Wolfe Tone had come more and more in their desperation to look to France.

The members of the Society of United Irishmen weren't Catholics, they were Protestant radicals. Tone had helped set up the United Irishmen in 1791, in Belfast. They wanted an independent Ireland. Tone was outlawed and fled to France. Inspired with French Revolutionary zeal, he and his radicals organized a rebellion. Tone, who in fact had arrived too late for the fighting, was captured and sentenced to death. He committed suicide.

C❖Rebellion, French attempts at invasion, and brutal civil war darkened the scene. The hopes that had once been pinned in the independent Parliament at Dublin faded away. . . . Pitt decided that the complete union of the two kingdoms was the only solution. Union with Scotland had been a success. Why not with Ireland too? But the prime requisite for any agreement must be the emanci-pation of Irish Catholics from the disabilities of the penal laws. Here Pitt was to stumble upon the rock of the conscience of a monarch now halfcrazy. Unscrupulous backstairs influences, false colleagues within the Cabinet Council, pressed George III to stand by his coronation oath, which he was assured was involved. Pitt had committed himself to the cause of Catholic freedom without extracting a written agreement from the King.

The English conquest of Ireland began with Henry II in 1155. His son, John, was called Lord of Ireland. During the next 150 years or so, the Irish took back some of their land, while the descendants of the invaders merged into Irish society. By the sixteenth century, England had no real control beyond a small area round Dublin called the Pale. Beyond it was considered ungovernable, bandit country. Hence the expression, 'Beyond the Pale'. Even so, Henry VIII took the title King of Ireland.

Elizabethan Ireland became a military threat and it wasn't until the end of the 1500s that some sort of English rule was established. Land was confiscated and given to the so-called new-English aristocracy which, of course, was Protestant. In Ulster, the Lowland Scottish Presbyterians arrived to take the confiscated lands.

In 1641 there was an awful rebellion and it took the ruthless mind of Cromwell to once again bring order. Cromwellian terror added to the legend of English brutality. And so to 1654 and the Act for the Settlement of Ireland. Two-thirds of landed property was taken and given to Protestants. The dispossessed were transported to the far west of the island. In the Revolution of 1688, James II escaped to Ireland. He held a council to restore property. William of Orange then defeated him at the Battle of the Boyne, and the property changed hands once more. James's supporters had their land confiscated and handed over to personal friends of William.

In 1707, the year of the Union with Scotland, the Irish House of Commons, in their loyal address to the then Queen, Anne, prayed, 'May God put into your royal heart to add greater strength and lustre to your crown by yet a more comprehensive union.' But by the 1770s and 1780s, political and economic stability had sent the Irish in completely the opposite direction, and there was an increasing demand for independence. But ideas of independence were Protestant ideas. The Roman Catholics were stripped of almost every chance to prosper. They could not vote, couldn't become lawyers, or join the army. They weren't even allowed to own a horse of any value. And if they had property it could only be left to the eldest son if he became a Protestant.

In 1782, Ireland received a new Constitution but the King could veto anything he didn't like. And in London there was always the fear that a truly independent Ireland might endanger England's security; might even give too many concessions to the Catholics whose peasantry in the South was considered one of the two dangerous groups in Ireland. The other being the Protestants in the North. The Scottish settlers from Stuart times were the ancestors of the Ulster Protestants, and it was in Ulster that Wolfe Tone and his fraternity of United Irishmen campaigned for independence.

This then is the briefest of backgrounds to the troubles at the turn of the century, and perhaps to others that followed. By 1800 Pitt had pushed through the Act of Union with Ireland. On 1 January 1801 it became law.

❖Whereas in pursuance of His Majesty's most gracious recommendation to the two Houses of Parliament in Great Britain and Ireland respectively, to consider of such measures as might best tend to strengthen and consolidate the connection between the two Kingdoms, the two Houses of the Parliament of Great Britain and the two Houses of the Parliament of Ireland have severally agreed and resolved that, in order to promote and secure the essential interests of Great Britain and Ireland, and to consolidate the strength, power and resource of the British Empire, it will be advisable to concur in such measures as may best tend to unite the two Kingdoms of Great Britain and Ireland into one Kingdom, in such manner, and on such terms and conditions as may be established by the Acts of the respective Parliaments of Great Britain and Ireland.

The first and obvious contention was not in the first Article of the Act, but one that was to be found in the body of the text.

❖*Article Fifth*
That the Churches of England and Ireland, as now by law established, be united into one Protestant Episcopal Church, to be called The United Church of England and Ireland; and that the doctrine, worship, discipline and government of the said United Church shall be, and shall remain, in full force for ever, as the same are now by law established for the Church of England; and that the continuance and preservation of the said United Church, as the Established Church of England and Ireland, shall be deemed and taken to be an essential and fundamental part of the Union; and that in like manner the doctrine, worship, discipline and government of the Church of Scotland shall remain and be preserved as the same are now established by law, and by the Acts of the Union of the two Kingdoms of England and Scotland.

This was an endorsement of the Established Church, no one would have expected anything else. But where was the Article for Catholic emancipation? George III believed it unthinkable. 'I shall reckon any man my personal enemy who proposes any such measure,' he said.

So this Act of the Union with Ireland immediately alienated the Catholics. But it did more than that. The wording that describes the United Church as 'an essential and fundamental part of the Union' meant that the Irish would have to pay dues to what they saw as some Established Heretical Institution. (See *A*

Documentary History of England, Vol. 2, by EN Williams, Penguin Books, 1965.)
Furthermore, the Catholic priests would have to rely on their parishioners for
money. So any radical, in almost any parish, had simply to encourage anti-
British feeling on the most fundamental of grounds – religion.

There is little evidence that the people of England supported Catholic
emancipation. In fact the previous decades had seen a decline in Catholicism in
Britain. A priest by the name of Joseph Berington observed that Catholics –
from all walks of life – were giving up their religion and, in some counties, there
were hardly any at all.

❖In the West, in South Wales, and in some of the Midland counties, there
is scarcely a Catholic to be found. After London, by far the greatest number
is in Lancashire. In Staffordshire [Berington had been a parish priest in
Staffordshire] are a good many also. In a few towns, particularly at
Coventry, their number, I find, is increased; but this by no means in
proportion of the general increase of population in the same places.
Excepting in the towns, and out of Lancashire, the chief situation of
Catholics is in the neighbourhood of the old families of that persuasion.
They are the servants, or the children of servants, who have married from
those families, and who chuse [sic] to remain round the old mansion, for
the conveniency of prayers, and because they hope to receive favour and
assistance from their former master.

We have, at this day, but eight peers, nineteen baronets, and about 150
Gentlemen of landed property. Among the first, the Duke of Norfolk, the
Earl of Shrewsbury, and the Lords Arundel and Petre, are in possession of
considerable estates. But the Earl of Surrey, the eldest and only son to the
Duke, having lately conformed, the large possessions of that noble and
ancient family will soon fall onto Protestant hands. The eldest son of Lord
Teynham has also left the religion of his father. Among the baronets are not
more than three great estates. Sir Thomas Gascoigne has this year also taken
the oaths . . . Where one cause can be discovered tending to their increase,
there will be twenty found to work their diminution. Among those
principal are, loss of families by death, or by conforming to the Established
Church; the marrying with Protestants; and that general indifference about
religion, which gains so perceptibly on all ranks of Christians.

The issue of Catholicism would never be far from Pitt's mind. His failure to
bring it forcibly to the minds of others over the Irish question had the inevitable
consequence. Pitt the Younger resigned as Prime Minister.

William Pitt was now forty-two. For half his life he had been an MP and
for most of that time he had been Prime Minister. And now his stamina was
almost gone. For nearly twenty years Pitt had struggled with the Irish problem.

When the Irish Parliament was given apparent independence in 1782, there were those in power in London who believed, or said they believed, that the Constitutional conflict was now settled but it was not. The French Revolution had inspired radical Irish opinion into believing that non-sectarian, independent government was a possibility. A rebellion in 1798 had been put down.

But what Pitt saw as the fundamental challenge went unanswered: he had argued for Catholic emancipation; he wanted to give Catholic freeholders the vote, but this was unacceptable to King George. Irish Catholics were seen as a threat to the security and the social and political structure of Ireland and England. Pitt fully understood that his liberal ideas could not survive the legislative process at Westminster. The waverers, so necessary to Pitt's ambition, would not challenge the King.

Pitt must have been at a low mental and physical ebb. It is very possible that he was already suffering from the cancer from which he would perish five years later. And he was up against the most experienced politician in England – the King. Pitt must have known that there was little chance of creating legislation that would satisfy Dublin, London, and, most important of all, the Court.

C❖. . . Pitt felt bound to resign. Catholic emancipation was delayed for nearly thirty years. The Act of Union had meanwhile been carried through the Irish Parliament by wholesale patronage and bribery against vehement opposition. . . . Westminster absorbed the Irish Members. Bitter fruits were to follow from this in the later nineteenth century.

The fact that Pitt could not rely on his Cabinet did not signify disloyalty in the way it would today. The administration – the Government Ministers – had a clear understanding of Constitutional duty. Ministers would probably accept what would now be called collective responsibility on defence, foreign, and economic policy, but on other matters they would expect to make their own judgments. Catholic emancipation was as much a matter of conscience as of politics. Furthermore, George III's victory over Pitt (and that's what it was) reinforced his belief that he had the right to appoint and dismiss anyone he wished. Most politicians of the time accepted this right to some extent. So, at the start of the nineteenth century, the monarch remained an essential part of the institution of government.

The month after Pitt's resignation a most bloody battle in the continuing war with France took place, and the Government could not turn a blind eye. It took place on 2 April 1801 and it was the battle from which the expression to 'turn a blind eye' comes: the Battle of Copenhagen.

The British Government wanted a negotiated settlement to end the war. Nelson had other ideas. 'A fleet of British ships are the best negotiators in Europe,' he wrote to Lady Hamilton. There was, at the time, something known as armed neutrality. In this neutral group were Denmark, Sweden, Russia, and Prussia. Diplomatic attempts were being made to persuade the Danes in particular to abandon the group: they could control the entrance and the exit to the Baltic. The immensely cautious Admiral Sir Hyde Parker wanted the Fleet to remain in the Kattegat and simply blockade the Baltic. Having heard his Commander in Chief's cautious plan, his Subordinate Commander wrote his objections and had them rowed over to the flagship. His Subordinate Commander was Nelson.

❖The more I have reflected, the more I am confirmed in my opinion that not a moment should be lost in attacking the enemy. They will every day and hour be stronger; we shall never be so good a match for them as at this moment. You are with almost the safety, certainly with the honour, of England more entrusted to you than ever yet fell to any British Officer. On your decision depends whether our country shall be degraded in the eyes of Europe, or whether she shall rear her head higher than ever. Again I do repeat, never did our Country depend so much on the success of any Fleet as on this. I am of the opinion the boldest measures are the safest; and our Country demands a most vigorous exertion of her force directed with judgment. In supporting you, my dear Sir Hyde, through the arduous and important task you have undertaken, no exertion of head or heart shall be wanting from your most obedient and faithful servant, Nelson.

Nelson clearly wanted to get on with the job. One report talks of ice floating past the Fleet. This would suggest that the Russian Fleet, further into the Baltic, could soon be free to sail. Parker, who would have felt safer ashore with his new nineteen-year-old bride, relented and gave orders for the Fleet to sail for the strait between Kristianstad and Elsinore. The Danish shore defences were considerable. There was also a line of vessels including floating batteries: the British Fleet would be outgunned. Nelson conceded as much, but believed he could and would, as he put it, 'annihilate them'. But the difficulty came from the shallows as well as from the guns. Nelson's vessels had some skippers from merchantmen, but they were in no hurry to get their heads shot off. Captain Hardy, who would be at Nelson's side at Trafalgar, was sent in a long boat to take soundings. At last all was set, and a very grisly prospect it must have appeared to those less confident than Nelson.

Here's one paragraph from a midshipman's book. He had seen the ship's doctors making ready.

❖The table was covered with instruments of all shapes and sizes. Another, of more than usual strength, was placed in the middle of the cockpit. As I had never seen this before, I could not help asking the use of it, and received for answer 'that it was to cut off arms and wings upon'. One of the surgeon's men, called loblolly boys, [loblolly was a gruesome navy gruel] was spreading yards and yards of bandages about six inches wide, which he told me was to clap on my back.

The battle started with such overwhelming firepower from the Danish positions, and British ships running aground, that from his position at the rear Admiral Parker told his signaller to send up the flags for Signal Number 39. Signal 39 meant 'Discontinue Action', but Nelson, with shot and cannonballs striking his own ship, had other ideas. 'This day may be the last for us at any moment,' he said, 'but, mark you, I would not be elsewhere for thousands.'

It was then that his Signal Lieutenant spied, through his telescope, the Admiral's instruction. Nelson raised his own spyglass to his right eye, the one he'd lost at Calvi. He then turned to his Flag Captain, Thomas Foley.

❖To leave off action. Now damn me if I do. You know, Foley, I have only one eye. I have a right eye to be blind some time. I really do not see the signal.

And so the fighting continued. By two o'clock the firing had become less intense, but that was mainly because both sides were fighting to a standstill. Bodies floated alongside and Nelson knew the time had come to call a halt. But each time his sailors went alongside apparently dead ships, they'd once again be shot at. Nelson wrote a letter to the Danish Commander saying that he was willing to cease firing, but if the Danes would not, then he would destroy them. He sent a sailor to fetch sealing wax. When the sailor did not immediately return, Nelson asked why. He was told the rating's head had been blown off. Then send another sailor, was Nelson's reply.

Nearly 2000 were killed and maimed at Copenhagen that Maundy Thursday. Nelson and England believed it a victory. It most certainly stopped the French from getting the Danish fleet on their side. It also confirmed that, for the moment, the Royal Navy commanded the sea campaign. But what was needed was formal peace and with Pitt gone, there was no obvious negotiator.

C❖Pitt was succeeded by a pinchbeck coalition of King's friends and rebels from his own party. Masquerading as a Government of National Unity, they blundered on for over three years. Their leader was Henry Addington, an amiable former Speaker of the House of Commons, whom no one regarded as a statesman.

Because the war was a matter of foreign policy, the Prime Minister could expect collective responsibility in the Cabinet. But how to bring the war to an end split the Cabinet. At that time, Henry Dundas was Pitt's closest colleague in government and, in a memorandum, Dundas set out the reason for the Cabinet division: on one side there were those who wanted to restore the Bourbons; on the other were the realists who were saying that however much the British disliked what was happening in France, they had to accept that the new French administration was in control of the country.

❖Some of us are of the opinion that the response to Europe and the security of Great Britain are only to be obtained by the restoration of the ancient royal family of France, and that every operation of war and every step to negotiation which does not keep that object in view is mischievous and will ultimately prove to be illusory. Some of us are of the opinion that although we ought not to consider the restoration of the ancient royal family as a *sine qua non*, we ought not to treat with a revolutionary Government, and that the present Government of France is of that description. Some of us are of the opinion that whatever has been the foundation of the present Government, it has established within its power the whole authority, civil and military, of the country, and that we are not warranted to reject the negotiations with a Government so constituted and *de facto* existing. Some of us are of the opinion that although we ought to negotiate with the present rulers of France, we ought only to do it in conjunction with our Allies, particularly the Emperor of Germany, it being the interest of this country closely to connect our interests with his. Some of us are of the opinion that if ever it was practicable to influence by force of arms the interior Government of France, that time is past.

Dundas's conclusion shows how very much the solution to the war worried every Cabinet member and touched on issues other than foreign policy.

❖If this difference of sentiment could be considered as so many abstract theories, it would be of no moment to examine them minutely, but they daily enter into every separate discussion which occurs on the subject of either peace or war. It is natural for every man to be partial to his own view of a subject, but neither that partiality nor the sincere personal respect or reciprocal good opinion we may entertain of each other can blind us so far as not to perceive that amidst such jarring opinions the essential interests of the country must daily suffer.

When Pitt went, so did Dundas, and the following year he was created the first Viscount Melville. Henry Addington (Pitt's successor who would become the first Viscount Sidmouth) was not a great inspiration in politics. In fact Dundas had thought Addington so lightweight that he could never expect him to hold together a Cabinet, whatever its Constitutional loyalties. Here's part of a letter from Dundas to Pitt.

❖It is impossible for me not to whisper into your ear my conviction that no arrangement can be formed under him as its head that will not crumble to pieces almost as soon as formed. Our friends, who, as an act of friendship and attachment to you, agree to remain in office, do it with the utmost chagrin and unwillingness, and the feeling that they are embarking in an Administration under a head totally incapable to carry it on, and which must of course soon be an object of ridicule, is uppermost in all their minds. Add to this, that although they will not certainly enter into faction and oppose him, all the aristocracy of the country at present cordially connected with Government and part of it under you, feel a degradation in the First Minister of the country being selected from a person of the description of Mr Addington, without the smallest pretensions to justify it and destitute of abilities to carry it on.

This was strong stuff indeed, even allowing for the fact that Dundas was writing to his friend, and that Addington's appointment would mean his own departure from the Cabinet. However Addington, who had been Speaker of the House of Commons for the previous two years, did become Prime Minister.

C❖In March 1802, Addington's Government made terms with Napoleon by the Treaty of Amiens, and for a time there was a pause in the fighting. Pitt supported the Government over the peace in spite of the arguments of some of his own followers. English tourists flocked to France, Fox among them, all eager to gaze upon the scenes of Revolution and to see at first hand the formidable First Consul, as he now was. But the tourist season was short. In May of the following year war was renewed, and once more misman-aged. The administration had failed entirely to use the breathing-space for improving the defences. Napoleon was now assembling his forces at Boulogne, intent upon the invasion of England. Pitt was in retirement at Walmer, in Kent. The strain of the past years had broken his health. He was prematurely aged. He had lived a lonely, artificial life, cheered by few friendships. The only time that he ever came in contact with the people was during his brief interval from office, when as Warden of the Cinque Ports he organized the local militia against the threat of invasion. Few things in England's history are more remarkable than this picture of an ex-Prime Minister, riding his horse at the head of a motley company of yokels, drilling on the fields of the South Coast, while a bare twenty miles away across the Channel the Grand Army of Napoleon waited only for a fair wind and a clear passage.

Pitt's resignation had not meant a sweeping change in the administration of British political life. This was not a collective Cabinet dismissal, rather what would now be called a Cabinet re-shuffle. True, Dundas, Grenville, Castlereagh, Cornwallis, and Canning all went with him but the Cabinet didn't owe him their jobs: their allegiance was to the Sovereign. In the spring of 1803 Dundas, or Viscount Melville as he was by then, reflected on Pitt's views on the role of the Prime Minister, a title which, since it had been levelled at Robert Walpole in accusation (of his assumption of too much authority), had never been politically defined. Melville wrote to Addington, who was having every imaginable difficulty holding together his administration. In his letter, Melville wrote down the first political definition of the position of British Prime Minister – and it's one that would be recognized today. Melville also told Addington that he'd told Pitt that he was wanted back in the Cabinet and that Lord Chatham (Pitt's eldest brother) could become the figurehead Prime Minister.

❖He stated his sentiments with regard to any position founded on such basis. He stated his sentiments with regard to the absolute necessity there is in the conduct of the affairs of this country that there should be an avowed and real Minister, possessing the chief weight in the Council and the principal place in the confidence of the King. In that respect there can be no rivalry [sic] or division of power. That power must rest in the person generally called the First Minister, and that Minister ought, he thinks, to be the person at the head of the finances . . . He knows to [sic] his own experience, that notwithstanding the abstract truth of that general proposition, it is nowadays incompatible with the most cordial concern and mutual exchange of advice and intercourse among the different branches of Executive Departments; but still, if it should come unfortunately to such a radical difference of opinion that no spirit of conciliation or concession can reconcile, the sentiments of the Minister must be allowed and understood to prevail, leaving the other members of Administration to act as they may conceive themselves conscientiously called upon to act under such circumstances.

It was a debate that would shape the structure of British politics and the eventual administration of the nation.

However, while doors in the corridors of Westminister and Whitehall opened and slammed on the hypothesis of a newly emerging political science, there were danker alleys and closets rarely if ever seen by the Addingtons, Melvilles, and Pitts. They ran through that nineteenth-century institution of horror, the workhouse. Perhaps there is a connection. Here are a few lines from the rule book of a workhouse. (There are some more on page 463.)

❖That the master keep peace and good order in the house; and permit none to fight, quarrel, or give abusive or rude language without punishment; nor suffer any strong liquors to be drunk, nor tobacco to be smoked, except in the working-rooms. That if any get drunk, they are to be severely punished by the master; and that care is to be taken to avoid all contentions and quarrels among themselves, that there be no cursing or swearing, nor revilings or bitterness amongst them, but they are to live in love and unity together, as become Christians.

Addington, Dundas, Pitt, and their political friends may not have recognized the conditions these rules were meant to maintain, but the disciplinarians of the workhouses may have recognized what it would take to maintain law and order at Westminster during the coming decade.

It was now the year 1805 and one of the most celebrated battles of the nineteenth century, the Battle of Trafalgar, was about to take place. To the Royal Navy, it was, and is still, its finest moment. The enemy was vanquished and Nelson was killed, and became a national hero for ever. The significance of what happened on 21 September 1805 has continued to this very day.

The peace treaty that was signed to end the French Revolutionary War, the Treaty of Amiens, was, in military and indeed political terms, not a peace agreement but a truce. Another war with France was inevitable. The Treaty was signed on 27 March 1802 but it was simply a recognition that France controlled the land and Britain the seas. Napoleon did not withdraw his troops from the Italian regions. He appeared determined to renew his ambitions in Egypt and what is now called the Middle East. And so Britain did not withdraw her troops from Malta, the pivotal point of Mediterranean power. It was, to paraphrase a future prime minister, George Canning, the peace everyone wanted and of which no one was proud. Incidentally, in the wording of the document, for the first time in hundreds of years, an English king was not described as King of France. That point of principle had finally been abandoned.

War broke out again in 1803 and about 10,000 British tourists, those who had travelled to 'gaze upon the scenes of Revolution', were interned, accused of spying. In Paris in the following year Napoleon had the Pope crown him Emperor of the French.

In London, the hapless Prime Minister Addington, who had reduced the navy while restructuring the army, must have recognized that his administration lived on borrowed time. On 26 April he told the King that he was resigning. The King was persuaded that Pitt should be brought back. But Pitt believed Fox should be in his administration if there were to be an all-Party Government to manage the war. The King refused to accept Fox.

On 2 May 1804, Pitt wrote to the Lord Chancellor, Eldon. In effect he was writing to the King. Here's part of that letter.

❖The present critical situation of this country, connected with that of Europe in general, and with the state of political parties at home, renders it more important and essential than perhaps at any other period that ever existed, to endeavour to give the greatest possible strength and energy to His Majesty's Government, by endeavouring to unite in his service as large a proportion as possible of the weight of talents and connections, drawn without exception from parties of all descriptions, and without reference to former differences and divisions. There seems the greatest reason to hope that the circumstances of the present moment are peculiarly favourable to such an union, and that it might now be possible (with His Majesty's gracious approbation) to bring all persons of leading influence either in Parliament or in the country to concur heartily in a general system formed for the purpose of extricating this country from its present difficulties, and endeavouring if possible to rescue Europe from the state to which it is reduced.

The King didn't like that tone at all. Three days later, Pitt got his reply.

❖The whole tenor of Mr Fox's conduct and more particularly at the Whig Club and other factious meetings, rendered his expulsion from the Privy Council indispensable and obliges the King to express his astonishment that Mister Pitt should one moment harbour the thought of bringing such a man before his royal notice. To prevent the repetition of it, the King declares if Mister Pitt persists in such an idea . . . His Majesty will have to deplore that he cannot avail himself of the ability of Mister Pitt with necessary restrictions. These points being understood, His Majesty does not object to Mister Pitt's forming such a plan for conducting the public business as may under all circumstances appear eligible . . . but should Mister Pitt, unfortunately, find himself unable to undertake what is here proposed, the King will in that case call for assistance of such men as are truly attached to our happy Constitution, and not seekers of improvements which, to all dispassionate men, must appear to tend to the destruction of that noble fabric which is the pride of all thinking minds and the envy of all foreign nations.

The King and his advisers were not being so unreasonable given Fox's objections to any further war, together with his open dislike of Addington. Furthermore, Fox appears to have been tired of the whole affair and told his friends that they should join the administration without him. So Pitt, in spite of his belief that the Prime Minister should be able to choose his own Cabinet, respected the King's wishes and returned.

C❖Feverishly he flung himself into the work of reorganizing England's war effort. . . . The French had . . . cowed the Continent into a passive acceptance of their mastery. . . . An enormous army was organized and concentrated at the Channel ports for the invasion of England. A fleet of flat-bottomed boats was built to bring 200,000 men across the Channel to what seemed inevitable success.

Napoleon planned to invade southern England; Nelson was in the Mediterranean trying to find the French southern Commander, Villeneuve, but he was already in the Atlantic, joined by six Spanish ships, and was sailing westward across the Atlantic. By the middle of May, Villeneuve was at Martinique. Three weeks later Nelson reached Barbados. Villeneuve heard of this and set sail: he was seen heading towards the Bay of Biscay. The French were then intercepted, not by Nelson, but by another squadron which forced them south.

The campaign was spread over thousands and thousands of square miles of ocean, and conducted without the benefit of modern technology: it was an extraordinary feat.

Nelson reached the eastern Atlantic, discovered Villeneuve was to the north and so, on 23 July, he sailed for England. On the same day Napoleon arrived at Boulogne. By the middle of August Nelson was in Portsmouth. Villeneuve was trying to meet up with Ganteaume and break into the Channel, but the latter was boxed in by Britain's southern squadron and so Villeneuve turned back, heading for Cadiz.

On 15 September, Nelson sailed south from Portsmouth in his flagship, the *Victory*. At dawn on 21 October, Nelson stood on his quarter-deck and watched as the Spanish advance squadron of twelve ships, under Admiral Gravina, and twenty-one Frenchmen under Villeneuve hove into sight. The war had started two years earlier, but this was the first time that Nelson had seen the enemy. It was to be the only time.

C❖The British Fleet lay about ten miles west of the enemy, to the windward, and at six in the morning Nelson signalled his ships to steer east-north-east for the attack in two columns he had planned. The enemy turned northwards on seeing the advancing squadrons, and Nelson pressed on with every sail set. The clumsy seamanship of his men convinced Villeneuve that flight was impossible, and he hove to in a long sagging line to await Nelson's attack. . . . Nelson signalled to Collingwood, who was at the head of the southern column in the *Royal Sovereign*, 'I intend to pass through the van of the enemy's line, to prevent him getting to Cadiz.' . . . The fleets were drawing nearer and nearer. Another signal was run up upon the *Victory*, 'England expects every man will do his duty.' . . . A deathly silence fell upon the Fleet as the ships drew nearer. Each captain marked down his adversary, and within a few minutes the two English columns thundered into action. . . . The *Victory* smashed through between Villeneuve's flagship, the *Bucentaure*, and the *Redoutable*. The three ships remained locked together, raking each other with broadsides. Nelson was pacing as if on parade on his quarter-deck when at one-fifteen p.m. he was shot from the mast-head of the *Redoutable* by a bullet in the shoulder. His backbone was broken, and he was carried below amid the thunder of the *Victory's* guns. . . . By the afternoon of October 21, 1805, eighteen of the enemy ships had surrendered and the remainder were in full retreat. Eleven entered Cadiz, but four more were captured off the coast of Spain. In the log of the *Victory* occurs the passage, 'Partial firing continued until four-thirty, when a victory having been reported to the Right Hon. Lord Viscount Nelson, KB and Commander in Chief, he then died of his wound.'

It took time for the news to reach London. On 7 November *The Times,* in an understandably conflicting account of the action, concluded with a reflection of the nation's grief.

❖No ebullitions of popular transport, no demonstrations of public joy, marked this great and important event. The honest and manly feeling of the people appeared as it should have done: they felt an inward satisfaction at the triumph of their favourite arms; they mourned with all the sincerity and poignancy of domestic grief; their HERO slain.

If ever there was a man who deserved to be praised, wept [over] and honoured by his country, it is Lord Nelson. His three great naval achievements have eclipsed the brilliancy of the most dazzling victories in the annals of English daring. If ever there was a hero who merited the honours of a public funeral, and a public mourning, it is the pious, the modest, and the gallant Nelson, the darling of the British Navy, whose death has plunged a whole nation into the deepest grief; and to whose talents and bravery, even the enemy he has conquered will bear testimony. . . . There was a partial illumination throughout the Metropolis last night. A general one will take place this evening.

Nelson had confirmed what Napoleon now had to accept: Britain really did rule the sea-lanes. But the war did not stop at Trafalgar.

CHAPTER FORTY-THREE

1806–1808

❖

Napoleon planned to invade Southern England. Thousands and thousands of French soldiers were moved to Boulogne in 1805. In the summer of that year the Emperor himself arrived at the Channel port. Napoleon looked at the Channel and said, 'It is nothing but a ditch.' He believed he needed only twenty-four hours to launch his invasion and begin his conquest. But the Royal Navy, or 'Nelson's Navy', blockaded the Western approaches to the English Channel, and the French Fleet could not get through. This meant that Napoleon could not protect his invasion force. The invasion was abandoned and Napoleon headed inland.

C❖He determined to strike at the European coalition raised against him by Pitt's diplomacy and subsidies. In August 1805 the camp at Boulogne broke up, and the French troops set out on their long march to the Danube.

The campaign that followed wrecked Pitt's hopes and schemes. In the month of Trafalgar, the Austrian General Mack surrendered at Ulm. Austria and Russia were broken at the Battle of Austerlitz. Napoleon's star had once more triumphed, and for England all was to do again. . . .

A personal sorrow now darkened Pitt's life. The House of Commons, by the casting vote of the Speaker, resolved to impeach his close colleague and lifelong companion, Henry Dundas, now Lord Melville, for maladministration in the Admiralty and for the peculations of certain of his subordinates.

There was far more to this than a minister's maladministration. And the Melville case gives a good insight into the political animosities of the time. Pitt had to submit to the King's right to appoint ministers, and Addington had been returned to Government, this time as Lord President. It was claimed by Addington and his colleagues that Melville, who had been treasurer to the Navy for six years, was guilty of malversation, that's to say, corrupt practice or behaviour in public office. Melville most probably was guilty of negligence – but nothing much more. This difficulty might have been overcome if it hadn't been for the third grouping in politics: the Foxites, the people Pitt had wanted in government; the people the King had turned away. If Fox and his followers could fuel the charges against Melville, then the fight between Addington and Pitt would be noisier, and the Foxites could claim that they displayed the unity the country so much needed. The charge was made and Melville was impeached. Pitt wept openly; some said that he was overcome for his old friend, particularly as their other friend, Wilberforce, spoke against him. But also Pitt was, by then, terribly ill. He was dying of cancer and his stamina, his resourcefulness, and his emotions were all stretched to breaking point. Melville was found not guilty but he was politically ruined.

A few years later, in a letter to his son, Melville wrote of the need for responsibility in government and particularly for party unity. But he maintained that a man must not be sucked into wrong decisions under the guise of unity. Melville was writing about the issue of Constitutional law and precedence during the Regency Crisis – the crisis that was provoked by the further madness of King George III.

❖Considering the present difficult state of the country, it is impossible to disguise from oneself that the Crisis is most embarrassing, and the anxiety of the country for the attainment of a strong and vigorous Government will revive with multiplied force. I trust and pray that there may be found enough honourable and independent men who will look solely to the safety and prosperity of the Empire, without regard to selfish objects or party views. Being in the King's Cabinet, it is your duty to concur with your colleagues in every measure which they may deem necessary for the quiet, safety, ease, happiness, and security of the rights of the Monarch in whose service they are, but I must guard you against every idea of embarking with your colleagues on the footing of a party man. They have no claims of any kind upon you to form such connection with them, and I think that if you were to place yourself in so unnatural a predicament, you would soon find yourself insulated, and destitute of that honorable and natural connection in politics which circumstances have prepared for you, and which seems to be almost within your grasp.

That letter refers to a different time, but the sentiments might have applied to Melville's own case.

The pressures from Napoleon and Westminster remained on Pitt's increasingly frail shoulders and, by the end of 1805, the Austrians and the Russians were beaten at the 'Battle of the Emperors' at Austerlitz. Austria immediately sued for peace and gave Napoleon her Adriatic lands and Venice. By the following year, Napoleon had created the Confederation of the Rhine from the small Western States of Germany.

Pitt heard about Austerlitz but, by the time of the Confederation, he was dead. He was just forty-six. He had spent more or less his whole adult life in Parliament. It is said that his last words were, 'Oh, my country! How I leave my country.' It is this consuming concern for public duty that was remembered by his friend Wilberforce.

❖The time and circumstances of his death were peculiarly affecting. I really never remember any event producing so much apparent feeling. For a clear and comprehensive view of the most complicated subject in all its relations; for the fairness of mind which disposes a man to follow out and, when overtaken, to recognize the truth; for magnanimity which made him ready to change his measures when he thought the good of the country required it, though he knew he should be charged with inconsistency on account of the change; for willingness to give a fair hearing to all that could be urged against his own opinions, and to listen to the suggestions of men whose understanding he knew to be inferior to his own; for personal purity, disinterestedness, integrity, and love of his country, I have never known his equal.

Charles James Fox, Pitt's great political rival, observed that death 'was a poor way of getting rid of one's enemy'. And although he voted against a Commons motion for a Pitt memorial in Westminster Abbey, Fox readily agreed that Pitt's debts should be met by the Exchequer. Fox, just eleven years older than Pitt, would not survive him by many months.

In addition to seeing the death of two English statesmen, 1806 was another year spent at war. It saw the British taking the Cape of Good Hope, but for those in other circumstances perhaps none of this meant much, especially in the more wretched reaches of British life. Hard by Westminster, in the Parish of St James's, a perfect illustration of these extremes could be found in an official Government document.

General State of Poor Children under the care and management of the Governors and Directors of the Poor of the Parish of St James's, Westminster.

Number of children transferred from preceding years:	650
Born and received this year:	565
Of whom have died in the workhouse:	56
Removed and discharged:	273
Above age six, apprenticed out:	113
Left in the care of the Parish:	712

This workhouse was considered for its day to have been neat and even 'commodious'. Here are a few entries from its rule book, which reveal a regime far more unforgiving than any Pitt and his colleagues lived by.

❖That no person go out of the prescribed bounds without leave from the master or mistress, return in good order at the time appointed, or be denied going out for a considerable time afterwards. That all the able Poor be kept to such work as they are fit for, and call them to it by ring [sic] of a bell, in summer, from six in the morning till eight in the evening, allowing proper time for breakfast and dinner, and the children sufficient time to learn to read; and if any grown person refuse to work, such person to be kept on bread and water in the dungeon till he is willing to work. Children to be corrected by the master. That the slothful and idle, who pretend ailments to excuse themselves from work, be properly examined; and if it appears that they have been impostors, and have made false excuses, then they shall be punished, by restricting their allowance of diet, or by confinement in the dungeon. Persons convicted of lying, to be set on stools, in the most public place of the dining-room, while the rest are at dinner, and have papers fixed on their breasts, with these words written thereon, INFAMOUS LYAR [sic], and shall lose that meal.

Far beyond the workhouse, the war with France continued. By 1807 Napoleon was probably at the height of his powers. An agreement with the Tsar of Russia had divided Europe between them, and never again would Napoleon have so much control over the future of the Continent. And George III was faced with a limited choice of politicians from whom to form the next administration. He sent for William Wyndham, Lord Grenville. Grenville was Pitt's cousin, but his political alliance with Charles James Fox had led to a break with Pitt two years earlier. By calling on Grenville to form the next administration, the King was tacitly accepting Fox.

Fox was one of the most fascinating political figures in England in the latter part of the eighteenth century. His great-grandfather was the first Duke of Lennox, who was the son of Louise de Kérouaille, the mistress of Charles II. So the Stuart King Charles was Fox's great-great-grandfather. Fox was very aware of his Stuart origins and the Hanoverian George III cannot have been unaware of them. And should anyone have forgotten, Fox's Christian names were obvious reminders. Fox's father was the first Baron Holland who, as Postmaster General, made a fortune by siphoning funds. With this background, it is hardly surprising that Charles James Fox was a far from ordinary figure. He was a rebel, a gambler, a piercing critic of what he saw as George III's political and fiscal oppression of the American colonists, a supporter of the French Revolution and, when the King suffered temporary insanity, a leader of the movement to have him replaced by the Prince of Wales. Fox was also Great Britain's first Foreign Secretary.

C❖William Pitt's successors were staunch in the prosecution of war, but even less adept at it than he. The three years between the death of Pitt . . . and the rise of Wellington in 1809 were uncheered by fortune. England's military strength was wasted in unfruitful expeditions to the fringes of the Mediterranean coastline. One small victory was won at Maida, in the Kingdom of Naples. . . . But Maida was of no strategic consequence. An ambitious plan to gain a permanent foothold in the Spanish colonies of South America led to the temporary occupation of Buenos Aires and the ultimate loss of valuable forces. Thanks to the Fleet, the sea-lanes of the world remained open, and in Europe the important islands of Sicily and Sardinia were kept from Napoleon's grasp.

In 1806 and 1807, there was a brief Ministry of 'All the Talents' under Lord Grenville. The talent was largely provided by the Whigs, now in office for the first time since 1783, and the last until 1830. . . . The renewal of the European conflict quenched hopes of Parliamentary Reform, upon which they had taken their stand in the early 1790s.

Ministry of 'All the Talents' was an ambitious description. The close supporters of the late William Pitt knew they could never be part of the administration. Addington (now created Lord Sidmouth) was Lord Privy Seal, and Lord Henry Petty was Chancellor of the Exchequer. Charles Grey, a friend of Fox, was his successor as Foreign Secretary, and was later to become Prime Minister; but for the moment he was Grenville's First Lord of the Admiralty. The Pittites, Hawkesbury, Castlereagh and Canning, were left to fume on the back benches. And there was little vision in the British approach to ending the war. It is probable that there could be no end until the French wanted it, or had been beaten, but when Fox died, in September 1806, there was no one left with his political agility to negotiate the peace.

Fox's personality, perhaps more than his political instincts, shaped opinion during this period. Here's part of what the Earl of Carlisle wrote about him.

❖No character I believe was ever more mistaken. He has been generally considered as a man devoted to desperate ambition, capable of seizing on power by any means, even to the excitement of revolutionary commotion.

A reference to Fox's support for the French Revolution, and for those groups in Britain that believed it should have been imported.

❖In truth ambition was not his ruling passion. Pleasure, in all its most extravagant gratifications, held a stronger dominion over him. For pleasure, ambition was perpetually sacrificed. For the sake of sensual indulgences, he himself helped to bar all the avenues to pre-eminence and to those high situations of State, which his rare abilities had so widely opened to him.

For pleasure, he had cast aside the opinion of the world, and taken so little care to fling a veil over the incorrect habits of his general conduct, that the public felt itself affronted by his barefaced exhibitions of failings, which, had he but attempted to have concealed, would possibly have met with pardon.

At length, feeling that by gaming, wine, women, and loss of fortune, the respect of the public was difficult to retrieve, he became so callous to what was said or thought of him, that he almost seemed to take puerile delight in outraging the world. . . . He could have little valued the opinions of those who composed his audience at the Whig Club.

Carlisle had an open affection for Fox. He felt for his friend when a group of scallywags set up Fox with a story that a West Indian heiress wanted to marry him. That Fox became the object of ridicule distressed Carlisle, who then wrote another view of him.

❖His strong and manly eloquence has never been excelled, and his fair and generous manner of grappling with the strongest points of his opponents' argument ought to be a lesson to the many, who, won by the flowers of oratory, forget the irresistible force of simple logic.

This amiable and yielding disposition rendered him unfitted to be a leader of a party, and he maintained too little authority over those who ought to have been on many occasions governed by him. He was unfortunately surrounded by those whose violent courses called for perpetual restraint.

During Fox's last months in office there was a move towards the abolition of the slave trade. The following year, 1807, the Slave Trade Act became law. Slavery itself was not abolished until 1833, but the 1807 Act did reveal that there were, by one estimate presented to the Commons, perhaps one million British subjects living in slavery.

❖Whereas the two Houses of Parliament did, by their resolutions of the 10th and 24th days of June 1806, severally resolve that they would, with all practicable expedition, take effectual measures for the abolition of the African slave trade, be it therefore enacted: that from and after the 1st day of May 1807, the African slave trade, and all manner of dealing and trading in the purchase, sale, barter or transfer of slaves, or of persons intended to be sold, transferred, used or dealt with as slaves, practised or carried on in, at, to or from any part of the coast or countries of Africa, shall be utterly abolished, prohibited and declared to be unlawful.

But within a year of this Act, the Government was gone. It fell not because of the war with Napoleon, but as a result of a poorly managed attempt to return to the matter of Catholic emancipation – the issue that had brought down Pitt the Younger. Grenville's administration had wanted to put through a bill to allow Catholics to become senior officers in the army. But the Parliamentary draftsmanship was poor; the Commons said so, and the King became suspicious that his government was on the road to Catholic emancipation without telling him. Yet little or none of this was political manipulation; it's simply that the Ministry of 'All the Talents' was not actually very talented at all and it fell in 1807.

The new Prime Minister was the elderly third Duke of Portland. He'd been a member of the coalition government of Fox and North in the 1780s and later, for seven years, Pitt the Younger's Home Secretary. At sixty-nine, he was the same age as George III and neither man was at the height of his powers. However Portland's Cabinet did include four men with undoubted and sometimes explosive talent. The Home Secretary was Lord Hawkesbury, Spencer Perceval was Chancellor, Viscount Castlereagh, War Secretary and George Canning, Foreign Secretary.

Towards the end of 1807 Britain was about to embark on another conflict and by the following year, 1808, the Peninsular War had begun. The Peninsula was the Iberian Peninsula – Spain and Portugal – and the Peninsular campaign is significant because it meant a change in tactics and, eventually, in strategy in Britain's determination that Europe should not be controlled by Napoleon. In an age of innovation, of commercial and industrial development, absolute control over Europe could bring about the political and economic domination of Britain by foreign interests.

C❖The Emperor of Austria was a cowed and obsequious satellite. The King of Prussia and his handsome Queen were beggars, and almost captives in his train. Napoleon's brothers reigned as Kings at The Hague, at Naples, and in Westphalia. His step-son ruled Northern Italy in his name. Spain lent itself to his system, trusting that worse might not befall. Denmark and Scandinavia made haste to obey. Russia, the great counterpoise, had swung over to his side. Only Britannia remained, unreconciled, unconquered, implacable. . . .

Secure throughout the rest of Europe, Napoleon turned his attention to the Spanish Peninsula. Powerless at sea, he realized that to destroy his one outstanding rival he must turn the weapon of blockade against the Island. English goods must be kept out of the markets of Europe by an iron ring of customs guards stretching from the borders of Russia round the coasts of Northern Europe and Western France and sealing the whole of the Mediterranean coastline as far as the Dardanelles. . . . It was a land blockade of seapower. The weakest link in the immense barrier of French troops and customs officers was the Peninsula of Spain. To complete this amazing plan it was essential to control not only Spain, but also Portugal, the traditional ally of Britain, whose capital, Lisbon, was an important potential base for the British Fleet. . . . Canning, in charge at the Foreign Office, displayed the energy of youth. An English squadron sailed to the Tagus, collected the Portuguese ships, and packed off the Portuguese royal family, Government, and society to the safety of Brazil. A few days later Marshal Junot entered the Portuguese capital, and the following day Napoleon declared war on the country he had just occupied.

The Peninsular War continued until 1813 but sending Junot to Lisbon was perhaps Napoleon's first and major mistake. An extra display of the Emperor's arrogance (and miscalculation) was to put his brother, Joseph Bonaparte, on the Spanish throne. Spanish pride was outraged and they fought back in what they called little wars and, incidentally, caused to enter the language a word which is used to this day: the Spanish word for little war is guerrilla.

The Spanish cut off Marshal Junot in Lisbon. In Britain Canning sent the man he believed to be Britain's finest general, Sir Arthur Wellesley, to Portugal. Wellesley, or Wellington as the nation would ever remember him, beat Junot at the Battle of Vimiero in 1808. Junot started to negotiate for his withdrawal and the result, the Convention of Cintra, was a military and public scandal for the British.

C❖The Convention of Cintra was signed, and punctiliously executed by the British. Junot and 26,000 Frenchmen were landed from British transports at Rochefort. Wellesley in dudgeon remarked to his officers, 'We can now go and shoot red-legged partridges.' There was a loud and not unnatural outcry in England at Junot being freed. A military court of inquiry in London exonerated the three British commanders [Wellesley, Sir Hew Dalrymple and Sir Harry Burrard], but only one of them was ever employed again. . . .

Napoleon had intended to court-martial Junot, but as the English were trying their own generals he declared himself glad not to have proceeded against an old friend. . . . Napoleon now moved 250,000 of his best troops into Spain. . . . An avalanche of fire and steel broke upon the Spanish Juntas, who, with 90,000 raw but ardent volunteers, had nursed a brief illusion of freedom regained. The Emperor advanced upon Madrid, driving the Spanish Army before him in a series of routs, in which the French cavalry took pitiless vengeance. . . .

A new British general of high quality had succeeded the commanders involved in the Convention of Cintra. Sir John Moore advanced from

Lisbon through Salamanca to Valladolid. He had been lured by promises of powerful Spanish assistance, and he tried by running great risks to turn Spanish hopes into reality. His daring thrust cut or threatened the communications of all the French armies, and immediately prevented any French action in the south of Spain or against Portugal. But Napoleon, watching from Madrid, saw him as prey.

At Christmas, 1808, Napoleon marched through the snows to cut off Sir John Moore's army. Moore saw what was happening and began his withdrawal. He arranged to be rescued by the Fleet at Corunna, on the North West Spanish Coast. Napoleon, who realized by now that his army could not cut off Moore, only pursue him, had been warned of a plot against him. He returned to Paris and left his army to Soult, his Commander.

C❖The retreat of the British through the rugged, snow-bound hill country was arduous. The French pressed heavily. Scenes of mass drunkenness where wine stores were found, pillage, stragglers dying of cold and hunger, and the Army chest of gold flung down a precipice to baffle capture, darkened the British track. But when, at Lugo, Moore turned and offered battle his army showed so firm a posture that for two days Soult, although already superior, awaited reinforcements. It was now resolved to slip away in the night to Corunna, where the army arrived on January 14, 1809. But the harbour was empty. Contrary winds had delayed the Fleet and transports. There would be a battle after all. On the sixteenth, Soult assaulted Moore with 20,000 against 14,000. He was everywhere repulsed, and indeed counter-attacked. When darkness fell the pursuers had had enough. But both Sir John Moore and his second in command, Sir David Baird, had fallen on the field.

One of those wounded at Corunna was Sir Charles Napier. He was witness to Moore's death.

❖From the spot where he fell, the General was carried to the town by a party of soldiers. The blood flowed fast, and the torture of his wound increased; but such was the unshaken firmness of his mind that those about him, judging from the resolution of his countenance that his hurt was not mortal, expressed a hope of his recovery. Hearing this, he looked steadfastly at the injury for a moment, and then said, 'No, I feel that to be impossible.' Several times he caused his attendants to stop and turn him round, that he might behold the field of battle, and when the firing indicated the advance of the British he discovered his satisfaction and permitted the bearers to proceed. . . . [Later, when he] asked if the enemy were defeated, and being told they were, observed, 'It is a great satisfaction to me to know we have beaten the

French.' . . . Soult, with a noble feeling of respect for his valour, raised a monument to his memory.

In London, the Government of Portland was going through difficult times. A certain Mrs Anne Clarke published allegations of corruption in army administration and directly implicated the Duke of York – the King's son and Commander in Chief of the army. The Duke was not a very good soldier (it was this Duke of York who marched them up and down again) but he was a conscientious administrator and had tried to improve the soldiers' lot. Perhaps the fact that Mrs Clarke had been, but no longer was, the Duke's mistress coloured her allegations.

The Duke of York was forced to resign as Commander in Chief although Mrs Clarke was later discredited. But the real importance of this event is that it allowed the Opposition to revive charges of corruption in high places. It also provided the right atmosphere for an independent MP named Curwen to bring forward a Bill to stop the sale of parliamentary seats. Until this Bill, selling and buying a seat in the House was quite common practice and few thought it a dishonourable way in which to get a Commoner or a peer into the House.

Elliot, the Irish Secretary to the then Prime Minister, Grenville, wrote a letter in 1806 which insists that the money for a seat be paid in English money and not Irish, which was very important because the Irish pound was worth less.

❖November 4, 1806.

> Parnell states that he believes Lord Portarlington will let us have his seat for £4000 *British*, provided he is given to understand that he is to have the support of Government for the representative peerage on the second vacancy after Lord Charlemont's election.

The Bill that became known as Curwen's Act eventually restricted the influence of the Crown as well. So it was at this point that something close to the way MPs are elected today began to evolve.

Curwen's Act wasn't Parliamentary Reform but it was one layer of it. And for some, it wasn't the actual buying of seats in the House that angered them, but the way they were bought.

There's a revealing page from the diary of a man who wanted a seat. His name was Sir Samuel Romilly.

❖April 27, 1807

> I shall procure myself a seat in the new Parliament unless I find that it will cost so large a sum, as would be very imprudent for me, which I find is very likely to be the case. Tierney, who manages this business for the

friends of the late Administration, assures me that he can hear of no seats to be disposed of. After a Parliament which has lived little more than four months, one would naturally suppose that those seats which are regularly sold would be very cheap; they are, however, in fact, sold now at a higher price than was ever given for them before. Tierney tells me that he has offered £10,000 for the two seats of Westbury, and has met with a refusal. Six thousand [pounds] and £5500 have been given for seats against the event of a speedy dissolution by the King's death, or by any change of Administration. The truth is, that the new Ministers have bought up all the seats that were disposed of, and at any prices.

The bulk buying-up of seats meant that ministers controlled votes and individuals. One of the seat brokers, Sir Christopher Hawkings, cleared his entire stock to ministers and there was a well-founded suspicion that the money for them came out of the Privy Purse, in other words was financed by the King himself.

A peer who owned a seat would put someone like Romilly into Parliament and then tell him how to vote. So to be independent, a would-be MP had to have money of his own – but even then there was no telling how safe that seat might be, as another of Romilly's diary entries testifies.

❖May 9
After almost despairing, my friend Piggott has at last procured me one, and the Duke of Norfolk has consented to bring me in for Horsham. It is however but a precarious seat. I shall be returned, as I shall have a majority of votes, which the late Committee of the House of Commons decided to be good ones.

But a majority of votes didn't guarantee Romilly his seat. A petition was raised against him in spite of his having paid £2000. By the following year, Romilly had another chance, in Dorset, but before the seat was safely his he discovered that a fund existed, 'formed as I understand, by the most distinguished persons in Opposition, to answer extraordinary occasions'. This fund offered to pay a further £1000 to secure Romilly's seat for him, but Romilly could not persuade himself 'to accept a seat upon these terms; and accordingly, in the evening, I wrote . . . a note in these words: "I feel a very great reluctance to consent to let the matter be arranged in the way that has been proposed. I am afraid that, after the matter is settled, I shall feel uncomfortable about it; and I had rather be at all the expense myself". ' The matter was settled. Romilly apparently paid the whole £3000 and so took his seat, at least feeling independent of the system which he detested.

CHAPTER FORTY-FOUR

1809–1819

❖

While Parliamentarians discussed the price of representation, the war rumbled on. In one battle alone 40,000 died. Another battle was staged for political rather than military reasons and, as a result, two Cabinet Ministers duelled and the Prime Minister suffered a stroke. And, at the end of the first decade of the nineteenth century, a famous general was, for the moment, giving up his political ambitions.

Sir Arthur Wellesley was the son of an Irish peer. After service in India he had become a Tory MP. By 1809 he was back in command of the British forces in Portugal and, at the Battle of Talavera, he earned his first title, Viscount Wellington. (He wasn't created Duke of Wellington until 1814.)

Elsewhere in Europe, one British expedition ended in disaster. The British tried to send its army up the River Scheldt to take Antwerp. When the French reinforced Antwerp, the British Commander left a garrison on an island called Walcheren. The British were destroyed, not by French muskets, but by malaria. Behind this story lies the ambition of the Foreign Secretary, George Canning, to replace the then Prime Minister, Portland, with the Earl of Chatham. Chatham was Pitt's elder brother, and the British Commander in question. Canning thought a famous victory would inspire the change. Against Canning was Lord Castlereagh, the energetic Minister of War. The feud had started the previous year, after the Convention of Cintra, when, having beaten the French in Portugal, a Convention was agreed between the three British commanders and the French Marshal Junot. The British public wanted French blood. What they got, as a result of the Convention, was a group of British transports ferrying more than 25,000 Frenchmen to freedom in France, ready to fight another day.

C❖The close connection between political developments at home and the fortunes of the generals at the front is a remarkable feature of the history of these years. Each military reverse led to a crisis in the personal relations of the Cabinet Ministers in London. The disgrace of the Convention of Cintra had sharpened the rivalry and mutual dislike of Canning and Castlereagh. The former had been anxious to dismiss all the generals involved. . . . the two Ministers were at loggerheads over the disaster that threatened the expedition to Walcheren. Tempers were sharpened by the ill-defined and over-lapping functions of the Foreign Secretary and the Secretary for War. The failing health of the Duke of Portland, the titular head of the Government, increased the rivalry of the two younger statesmen for the succession to the Premiership. A duel was fought between them, in which Canning was wounded. Both resigned office, and so did Portland. Spencer Perceval, hitherto Chancellor of the Exchequer, took over the Government. He was an unassuming figure but an adroit debater, and in the conduct of war a man of considerable resolution. Wellington's cause in Spain was favoured by the new administration. Perceval appointed as his Foreign Secretary the Marquess Wellesley, who steadfastly stood up for his younger brother [Wellington] in the Cabinet. The new War Minister, Lord Liverpool, was also well disposed. The Government did their best to satisfy Wellington's requirements, but, faced with the Whig Opposition and the Tory rebels in the Commons, they were continually obstructed by petty issues.

Wellington also needed a well-disciplined army; something he could not take for granted in 1809, as he complained in a letter to Castlereagh.

❖Coimbra, May 31, 1809
The army behave terribly ill. They are a rabble who cannot bear success any more than Sir John Moore's army could bear failure. I am endeavouring to tame them; but, if I should not succeed, I must make an official complaint about them, and send one or two corps home in disgrace. They plunder in all directions.

By 1810, Wellington had mauled the French Army at Busaco and then allowed them to follow him to the seemingly impregnable lines of Torres Vedras, the lines of fortification he'd built to protect Lisbon. If they had the strength and imagination, the French might attack. The British were vulnerable. But the great chain of Torres Vedras, and the prospect of a bleak winter with few resources, were too much. Come the spring, and leaving behind thousands of their dead, the French retreated from Portugal and into Spain.

C❖Portugal was now free, and Wellington's successes strengthened the position of the Government at home. Rejoicing in London and Lisbon, however, was mingled with a certain impatience. The British Commander had eager critics, even within his own army . . .

Wellington took his time. He refused to hurry for those who demanded spectacular victories. He wanted to take the war to France itself. In 1811 the

British held the enemy at Fuentes d'Oñoro and Albuera but still Wellington waited; the waiting paid off. The French generals began to quarrel. Troops were withdrawn for the campaign in Russia. Wellington advanced on the frontier strongholds of Ciudad Rodrigo and Badajoz and prepared to face the French Marshal Marmont.

C❖Amid the snows of January 1812 [Wellington] was at last able to seize Ciudad Rodrigo. Four months later Badajoz fell to a bloody assault. The cost in life was heavy, but the way was opened for an overpowering thrust into Spain. Wellington and Marmont manoeuvred . . . each watching for the other to make a mistake. It was Marmont who erred, and at Salamanca Wellington achieved his first victory on the offensive in the Peninsular War. King Joseph Bonaparte fled from Madrid, and the British occupied the capital amid the pealing of bells and popular rejoicing.

But the war was far from over. The other French Army under Marshal Soult who had fought Sir John Moore at Corunna was already on the march. Wellington was forced back to the Portuguese frontier.

In London, the Government and the Court were forced to address George III's illness. In 1810 the King became permanently insane. As long ago as 1788 his sanity had been questioned and Pitt had said that Parliament should provide legislation for a limited Regency. In 1810 the Prince of Wales, Prince George, became Regent, but his powers were restricted for one year. There were limitations on what appointments he could make. He couldn't, for example, create new peerages – often done for political reasons.

The King was placed in the care of the Queen, Charlotte, and a council of advisers. And, in 1811, to make it very clear that this was Parliament's doing and therefore the Regent was bound by it, a Regency Act became law.

❖Whereas by reason of the severe indisposition with which it hath pleased God to afflict the King's most excellent Majesty, the personal exercise of royal authority by His Majesty is for the present, so far interrupted, that it becomes necessary to make provision for assisting His Majesty in the administration and exercise of the royal authority, and also for the care of his royal person during the continuance of His Majesty's indisposition and for the resumption of the exercise of the royal authority by His Majesty; Be it therefore enacted that his Royal Highness George Augustus Frederick, Prince of Wales, shall have full power and authority, in the name and on behalf of His Majesty, and under the style and title of Regent of the United Kingdom of Great Britain and Ireland.

The Act was the answer to the constitutional question. For the politicians, the question was would the Prince bring his Whig friends, into government, particularly Grey and Grenville, and discard the Tories? Grey and Grenville had gone four years earlier when the King had refused what was called 'a measure of Catholic relief'. The gossip and speculation spread from Westminster to the Peninsula. In the Windsor Archives there's a letter from the then Quarter-Master General, Colonel JW Gordon, to one Colonel McMahon.

❖November 15, 1811

> The text of every conversation in every company is the question 'What will the Prince do when he has full power? Will he change the Government? Will he abandon his old friends, and will he concede anything to the Catholics?' This I need not tell you is the substance of every conference, at every table et cetera in every society at this moment in the metropolis and probably in the Kingdom.

Gordon's reputation was that he knew every leading person of the day – even if they didn't always know him.

❖The present Ministers with Mr Perceval at their head, owe their situations solely to the undivided support of the King, arising from His Majesty's conscientious opposition to the Catholic Petition. You know also that this Administration is the remains of the Pitt school, of which school, however, two most important members are schismatic, Canning and Castlereagh, each of whom may be considered as possessed of a large share of the confidence and respects of the House of Commons and of the country: the other party (of this school also) is the Sidmouth [the former Prime Minister Henry Addington] party and they also have their share of power in the House. The opposite party, those hitherto distinguished by the appellation of the Prince's friends, are the remains of the Fox school, the head of which may be considered Earl Grey, uniting the whole Grenville family and followers, and having as their organs in the Commons, Messrs Whitbread, Ponsonby and Tierney.

> As the Fox Administration in fact dissolved itself upon the Catholic question, it may be fairly considered . . . indisputably pledged and committed to carry it when in power, and if taken into power as a party, they would not have an alternative, but must effect it or resign their seats as ill-judging and incompetent men.

The Prince had no reason to change government policy or to be seen to do so. Furthermore the quiet and, in many ways, unremarkable Perceval now had his Cabinet under control. But then, in May 1812 Perceval was murdered. It was not an assassination in the political sense. A man, a bankrupt businessman called John Bellingham, armed with a grievance and a gun, shot him dead in the House of Commons lobby. So Perceval, who had achieved more than most recognized, went into the history books as the only British Prime Minister to be assassinated.

As if all this wasn't enough for the new Prime Minister, Lord Liverpool, Britain now found herself at war with the United States. It became known as the War of 1812. It started because the Royal Navy seized American ships trying to run the blockade against Napoleon, and because the British presence in Canada still annoyed the Americans. A plan to avert war was agreed, but it had to be carried more than 3000 miles across the Atlantic by sailing ship, and then across land to the Americans and then, if agreed, to all the waiting commanders. Very simply, the plan didn't arrive in time and the war began, and continued until January 1815.

At sea, Britain was in control. But ashore it was another matter, although the British did burn the White House to the ground. Peace, in this unnecessary war, was signed on Christmas Eve 1814, but perhaps its most famous battle took place a fortnight later: the Battle of New Orleans. In just thirty minutes the Americans, commanded by Andrew Jackson, killed or wounded 2000 British troops and lost just thirteen of their own. Jackson was a hero (and a future President) and a new legend grew up: the War of 1812 was the second War of Independence.

The war with the Americans was, in European terms, a diversion. Napoleon had been pulling back his troops from across Europe for a great assault on Russia. The Tsar, once Napoleon's admirer, now believed that peace in Europe was impossible while Bonaparte marched. And in June, 1812, he marched for Moscow.

C❖He was confronted by two main Russian armies totalling 200,000 men. His plan was to overwhelm them separately and snatch at the old Russian capital. He confidently expected that the Tsar would then treat for peace. All the other sovereigns of Europe in similar circumstances had hastened to bow the knee. But Russia proved a different proposition. . . . Before Napoleon the Russian armies fell back, avoiding the traps he set for them and devastating the countryside through which the French had to pass. At Borodino, some sixty miles west of the capital, the Russians turned at bay. There in the bloodiest battle of the nineteenth century, General Kutusov inflicted a terrible mauling on Napoleon. Both the armies engaged, each of about 120,000 men, [and each] lost a third of their strength. Kutusov withdrew once more, and Moscow fell to the French. But the Russians declined to sue for peace. As winter drew near it was forced on Napoleon's mind that Moscow, burnt to a shell by accident or by design, was untenable by his starving troops. There was nothing for it but retreat through the gathering snows – the most celebrated and disastrous retreat in history. Winter now took its dreadful toll. Rearguard actions, however gallant, sapped the remaining French strength. Out of the huge Grand Army launched upon Russia, only 20,000 straggled back to Warsaw. . . .

On December 5, Napoleon abandoned the remnant of his armies on the Russian frontier and set out by sleigh for Paris.

By the spring of 1814, Wellington had driven the French out of Spain and was in Bordeaux. Napoleon's allies had abandoned him and some were now opposing him. In April that year, Napoleon abdicated and went to Elba. A Bourbon, Louis XVIII, brother of the beheaded king, was on the throne. From his Mediterranean island, Napoleon saw the differences among the allies. Also, his friends brought news that the King of France did not really command the respect of the people. On 26 February 1815, Napoleon sailed for France. Three weeks later he was back in Paris and the Bourbons were running.

Meanwhile the Allies decided the time had come to destroy Napoleon. They prepared to invade France but Napoleon didn't wait for their invasion. He moved on Belgium where Wellington now commanded his own, and Dutch, German and Belgian troops. The Prussian Army under Marshal Blücher was defeated at Lugny on 16 June. Wellington withdrew to Waterloo.

The Battle of Waterloo lasted one day. Wellington had 68,000 troops but Napoleon had 72,000 and attacked three times between the late morning and late afternoon of 18 June. Blücher arrived in the early evening with a further 45,000 troops to support Wellington, and a last French attack at about seven o'clock failed. Napoleon's army retreated, leaving 25,000 dead and 9000 captured. Wellington is thought to have lost 10,000.

Napoleon escaped to Paris; he had visions of making a great stand on French soil but none shared his enthusiasm. On 22 June he abdicated and by the end of the month he had escaped to Rochefort on the Biscay coast.

C❖He had thoughts of sailing for America, and he ordered a set of travel books . . . Perhaps a new Empire might be forged in Mexico, Peru, or Brazil. The alternative was to throw himself on the mercy of his most inveterate foe. This is what happened. . . . Newspapers clamoured that Napoleon should be put on trial. The Government, acting for the Allies, decided on exile in St Helena . . . Escape from it was impossible. On July 26, the Emperor sailed to his sunset in the South Atlantic.

Throughout the long campaign, Waterloo was the only time Napoleon and Wellington met in battle and both would be remembered for this one day, although neither thought it their finest. Now all that remained was to draw up a treaty of Europe that would manage the peace as successfully as Wellington had managed the last days of the war. There was now the chance of a long-lasting peace with France for the first time since the days of the Normans.

C❖The task took three months. The Prussians pressed for harsh terms. Castlereagh, representing Britain, saw that mildness would create the least grievance and guard best against a renewal of war. In this he had the hearty support of Wellington, who now exerted a unique authority throughout Europe. . . . Together with the loss of certain small territories, France was to pay an indemnity of 700,000,000 francs, and to submit to an Allied army of occupation for three years. Yet no intolerable humiliations were involved. In the moderation of the settlement with France the treaty had its greatest success. Wellington took command of the occupying army. For the next three years he was practically a Great European Power in himself. Castlereagh, with his sombre cast of mind, thought the treaty would be justified if it kept the peace for seven years. He had built better than he knew. . . .

The treaties drawn up in 1815 were the last great European settlements until 1919–1920.

Meanwhile the style of early nineteenth-century clothes, furniture, and buildings, the style of Regency Britain, began to establish itself. This was the period of Jane Austen, of the construction of, appropriately, Regent Street in London, of gas lighting in fashionable places, and of Davy's safety lamps in the coalmines. It was also the period of continuous unrest among the newly named working class.

In 1799 a Leicester youth called Ned Ludd is said to have smashed machinery that had been installed by a stocking maker, because the machinery did the jobs of many who had worked by hand. Then, in 1811, organized machine smashing occurred in the textile factories of the Midlands and Yorkshire. In 1813 Luddites, who took their name from Ned Ludd, were executed at York.

The end of the Napoleonic Wars meant peace in Europe, but in England there was now no need for huge numbers of sailors and soldiers: 300,000 servicemen were discharged from the war at a time when the combined British population was perhaps no more than thirteen million. And the labour market was already overcrowded, inflation was high, perhaps artificially so, and taxation was at wartime levels.

Manufacturers who thought that the war's end would bring increased export markets were wrong: there was now no war from which to make profits. Iron production is just one useful indicator: the price of iron was now £8 a ton, whereas during the war it had been £20. Thousands of iron and coal workers lost their jobs and many of them took to the streets. A year after the war ended there was considerable evidence that the Government could lose control of the country.

A secret committee of MPs was set up and, in February 1817, it presented its report, in secret, to the Commons.

❖It appears to your Committee that attempts have been made, in various parts of the country, as well as in the metropolis, to take advantage of the distress in which the labouring and manufacturing classes of the community are at present involved, to induce them to look for immediate relief, not only in a reform of Parliament on the plan of universal suffrage and annual election, but in a total overthrow of all existing establishments, and in a division of the landed, and extinction of the funded property of the country. . . . This hope and prospect of spoliation have been actively and industriously propagated by several Societies, openly existing in the metropolis. The doctrines have been systematically and industriously disseminated among mechanics and manufacturers, discharged soldiers and sailors, and labourers of all descriptions: they have been inculcated at frequent appointed meetings, and they have been circulated, with incredible activity and perseverance, in cheap and often gratuitous publications. It has been proved, to the entire satisfaction of your Committee that some members of these Societies, acting by delegated and assumed authority as an executive Committee of the whole, endeavoured to prepare the means of raising an insurrection, so formidable from numbers, as by dint of physical strength to overpower all resistance.

Here is one of the advertisements prepared by the alleged agitators.

❖*Britons To Arms!*
The whole country waits the signal from London to fly to arms! Haste, break open gunsmiths and other likely places to find arms! Run [see off] all constables who touch a man of us; no rise of bread; no Regent; no Castlereagh, off with their heads; no placemen [those appointed to office regardless of their suitability], tithes or enclosures; no taxes, no bishops, useless lumber! Stand true, or be slaves for ever!

The secret committee of MPs had exactly this sort of uprising in mind when it issued this warning.

❖The intended insurrection assumed the symbols of the French Revolution; a committee of public safety of twenty-four was agreed upon, including the names of several persons extremely unlikely to lend themselves to such a cause. A tri-colour flag and cockades were actually prepared. Your Committee cannot contemplate the activity and arts of the leaders in this conspiracy – the objects of which are not only the overthrow of all the political institutions of the Kingdom, but also such a subversion of the rights and principles of property as must necessarily lead to general confusion, plunder, and bloodshed – without submitting to the most serious attention of the House the dangers which exist, and which the utmost vigilance of Government, under existing laws, has been found inadequate to prevent.

An Act was passed to suspend Habeas Corpus; another reinforced the old Seditious Meetings Act. Here are three Articles:

❖*Article One*

Meetings of more than fifty persons not to be held without notice being published in some newspaper at least five days before the meetings, and signed by seven householders.

Article Ten

Persons not dispersing after one hour to be arrested; and if such persons are killed or maimed by reason of their resistance, the Justices et cetera are indemnified.

Article Eleven

Persons obstructing the Justices in attending meetings or making the Proclamation [preventing the Justices from reading the Riot Act] to suffer death.

This was the atmosphere in Britain on 16 August 1819 when between 60,000–80,000 people attended a meeting in St Peter's Fields in Manchester. The speaker was Henry Hunt, known as Orator Hunt, and described as one of the extremist leaders. The local yeomanry was sent in by magistrates to arrest him but they failed so the magistrates, instead of sending in the army, ordered the hussars to do the job. There was panic and hundreds in the crowd received sabre wounds; eleven died.

The name given to this massacre was Peterloo – a popular irony derived from the British success at Waterloo. The rights and wrongs of that day are debated still. However, in spite of the threat of sedition, treason, and uprising, the increasingly prosperous British had more confidence than ever in the very institutions that had been threatened. And the governing caste was just as confident of its right to govern. Perhaps it was a sign of this confidence, and of a faith in future prosperity, that in the year of Peterloo the East India Company was arranging to buy a tiny area of Asia called Singapore.

CHAPTER FORTY-FIVE

1820–1823

———— ❖ ————

George III died in 1820 and Britain's fourth Hanoverian monarch was another George. George IV, although intelligent, was given to pleasures rather than statesmanship and, as Prince of Wales, he had been incautious in some of his friendships. For example he had been very much under the influence of the best-remembered dandy of early nineteenth-century England, Beau Brummell.

C❖The atmosphere of the Court was like that of a minor German principality. All was stiff, narrow, fusty. The spirited lad who was to be George IV soon rebelled against his decorous mother and parsimonious father. A gift for facile friendship, often with dubious personages, alienated him still further from the home circle. He was early deprived of the companionship of his brothers, who were dispatched to Germany, there to receive a thorough Teutonic grounding. George, as heir to the throne, had to have an English background; and in the circle of his more intimate friends, Charles James Fox, Richard Sheridan, and Beau Brummell, he soon acquired the attributes of the eighteenth-century English gentleman – the arts of acquiring debts, of wearing fine clothes, and making good conversation.

Beau Brummell and the Prince of Wales parted company not long after George III was declared insane and incapable of ruling. By 1820 Brummell was hiding from his creditors in France and later perished in an institution for the insane.

However, before the Prince of Wales assumed the responsibilities of Regent, he took easily to the fashion of drinking and whoremongering, often, it is said, at Carlton House, close by Pall Mall. He attracted an odd baggage of creditors, debtors, madams, officers on half pay, bucks and society wits, and the likes of Letitia Lade, once the mistress of the highwayman Sixteen-String Jack, who was hanged. And then, in 1784, the young Prince lost his heart.

C❖Maria Fitzherbert was not only a commoner of obscure family, but also a Roman Catholic. Her morals were impeccable and she would be content with nothing less than marriage. The Prince's Whig friends were alarmed when the heir to the most Protestant throne in Europe insisted on marrying a Roman Catholic widow who had already survived two husbands.

The Whigs were banking on getting back into power once the Prince became King: marriage to a Roman Catholic could ruin all their chances.

C❖Under the Royal Marriages Act the union was illegal, and George's behaviour was neither creditable to himself nor to his position. The clandestine beginnings of this relationship and the volatile temperament of George did their work. Mrs Fitzherbert, prim and quiet, was not the woman to hold him for long. The relationship slid back into the secrecy from which it had unwillingly emerged.

It may have been an illegal marriage, but a ceremony did take place in Mrs Fitzherbert's Mayfair drawing room. Robert Burt, an Anglican clergyman officiated. In the last decade of the eighteenth century, Mrs Fitzherbert was the love of the Prince's life and the embarrassment of the Court's. And so, as seemed best in the circumstances, a royal wedding was arranged – to a royal princess.

C❖At the bidding of his parents in 1795, he was wedded to Caroline of Brunswick, a noisy, flighty, and unattractive German princess. George was so appalled at the sight of his bride that he was drunk for the first twenty-four hours of his married life.

The only child of this unhappy union, Princess Charlotte, was born the following year. But that young Princess died when giving birth to her own child, who was still born. If either of them had survived, one or other of them would have become Queen and there would have been no William IV, and perhaps no Queen Victoria and perhaps no Elizabeth II.

George and Caroline's marriage was made in Brunswick and St James's, not in heaven. George called the Princess of Wales, 'the vilest wretch this world was ever cursed with'. He absolved her of all marital obligations, which was a nice way of saying that she was to be kicked out of his life – or so he thought. In 1806 a committee of the Privy Council began what was called the 'Delicate Investigation'. It certainly was. Its brief was to examine rumours that the Princess of Wales had given birth to an illegitimate child. If this was true, there would be a Constitutional crisis. After all, she was the wife of the heir to the throne. Nothing was proved although, considering her lifestyle, there was good reason why such a rumour might have gripped the Privy Council's imagination.

In 1814, George banned her from Court, and eventually she left England for the Continent – but still as Princess of Wales, and as the darling of the people. As in other times, the nation took sides. The Prince of Wales was only a few years away from being King or, to put it another way, the Princess of Wales was only a few years away from being Queen.

The Prince wanted a divorce.

C❖But Liverpool's Government were apprehensive. The Prince's extravagance, his lavish architectural experiments at Brighton and Windsor, were already causing them anxiety and giving rise to hostile speeches in Parliament. The Lord Chancellor, bluest of Tories, was vehemently opposed to any idea of divorce. The bench of bishops adopted a similar and suitable attitude. But George was persistent. He got a commission appointed to inquire into the Princess's conduct. It posted to Italy to collect evidence from the unsavoury entourage of Caroline. In July 1819 the Government received a report producing considerable circumstantial evidence against her.

She had been having an affair with a former member of her household, Bartolomeo Pergami, and adultery by the Princess of Wales, the future Queen, was a treasonable offence.

C❖. . . in January 1820 the mad old King died, and the position of the new sovereign's consort had to be determined. George IV . . . insisted upon her name being struck from the Church liturgy. The Cabinet presented him with a nervous note pointing out the difficulties of action. But now he was King. He warned them he would dismiss the lot, and threatened to retire to Hanover. The Whigs were as much alarmed as the Tories by the King's determination. They too feared the effect on public opinion. . . . Whatever happened, there would be a scandal which would bring the monarchy into dangerous disrepute.

Caroline now showed her hand.

A letter from Caroline to George found its way into *The Times*. The Princess of Wales, by now of course uncrowned Queen, had not written the letter. It had been composed for her by those who knew that publication would harm George and bring the people even more to her side. It did both. Not that she needed much in the way of a public relations exercise.

For example, when she returned to England her carriage was spontaneously hauled by exuberant supporters. Crowds gathered outside her London house. Her every public appearance was followed, whereas George was seen as the wrongdoer. In July 1820, a hearing was opened in Westminster Hall to examine the case against the Princess of Wales, accused of adultery. It all fell apart. The witnesses for the Government were unreliable. Parliament was split. Earl Grey, the leader of the Whigs, declared that Caroline was innocent of adultery. The Cabinet was forced to drop the matter.

C❖The London mob rioted in joy; the whole city was illuminated. The windows of the Ministers' houses were broken. . . . But the bubbling effervescence of the masses quickly subsided. Caroline was granted an annuity of £50,000 which she was not too proud to accept. One political result of the crisis was the resignation of George Canning, who had been on friendly terms with the Queen. This gifted pupil of Pitt had rejoined the administration in 1816 as President of the Board of Control, which supervised the Government of India. . . . His departure was a serious loss to the Cabinet.

But even now the matter was not done with. The final scene for Caroline came on 19 July 1821. The stage was the coronation of her husband as George IV at Westminster Abbey. She went to the Abbey and was refused entry. 'Let me pass; I am your Queen,' she cried. The pages slammed the doors on her. Her cause was finished. As Sir Walter Scott wrote, it was 'a fire of straw burnt to the very embers'. And then, the next month, she died. Of what, it is uncertain. She was fifty-three and for the Government, the embarrassment of Caroline of Brunswick, Princess of Wales, and their newly crowned monarch, was over.

In the political arena George IV's Prime Minister, the conservatively natured Lord Liverpool, remained determined, perhaps repressively so, that if change was to come it would be later rather than sooner. And so for the decade of transition from war to peace, Britain was governed by the thoughts of three determined men: Liverpool, Lord Castlereagh and latterly, the hero of Waterloo, the Duke of Wellington.

C❖Castlereagh had served his political apprenticeship as Chief Secretary for Ireland [twenty years earlier]. In the difficult days of the negotiation for Union with Ireland, when the powers of patronage were extensively used, he had seen eighteenth-century jobbery at its worst. He had joined the wartime Cabinet as Secretary for War, but was obliged to resign after a celebrated quarrel with his colleague Canning, which led to a duel between them on Putney Heath. In 1812 Castlereagh had returned to the Government and had been appointed to the Foreign Office. He was the architect of the coalition which gained the final victory and one of the principal authors of the treaties of peace. For home affairs he cared little, and he was unable to expound his far-sighted foreign policy with the eloquence that it deserved. Castlereagh was no orator. His cool, collected temperament was stiffened with disdain; he thought it beneath him to inform the public frankly of the Government's plans and measures. Nevertheless he was

Leader of the House of Commons. Seldom has that office been filled by a man with fewer natural qualifications for it.

Arthur Wellesley, first Duke of Wellington, had once been a member of the Irish Parliament. He left Parliament to fight the wars of the new empire but after India, he laid up his sword for a while and became a Tory MP at Westminster and Chief Secretary for Ireland. After Waterloo, Wellington commanded the occupying army in France and was British ambassador to Paris. Once France had paid the financial and political fines imposed under the Treaty of Paris – it took three years – the Allied forces withdrew and Wellington with them. It was only then, in 1819, that he re-entered Government.

C❖The rest of the Cabinet were Tories of the deepest dye, such as the Lord Chancellor, Eldon; Addington, now Viscount Sidmouth, once Prime Minister and now at the Home Office; and Earl Bathurst, Colonial Secretary, whom Lord Rosebery has described as 'one of those strange children of our political system who fill the most dazzling offices with the most complete obscurity'. These men had begun their political life under the threat of world revolution. Their sole aim in politics was an unyielding defence of the system they had always known. Their minds were rigid, and scarcely capable of grasping the changes pending in English society. They were the upholders of the landed interest in Government, of the Protestant ascendancy in Ireland, and of Anglicanism at home. Castlereagh was a specialist in foreign and Wellington in military affairs. The others were plain Tory politicians resolved to do as little as possible as well as they could.
    . . . The dislocation caused by the end of the war and the novel problems posed by the advance of industry were beyond the power of these men to remedy or solve. . . . They concentrated upon the one issue they understood, the defence of property. In a society which was rapidly becoming industrial most of them represented the abiding landed interest. They were incapable of carrying out even moderate reforms because of their obsessive fears of bloody revolution. . . . It was a misfortune for Britain in these years that the Parliamentary Opposition was at its weakest. A generation in the wilderness had demoralized the Whig Party . . . The Radicals who found their way into Parliament were too few to form an effective Opposition . . . The violence of language used by the Radicals frightened Tories and Whigs alike. It stiffened the resistance of the upper-middle classes, both industrial and landed, to all proposals for change.

At this stage in British politics, collective Party responsibility was still confined to military, foreign and, sometimes, economic affairs. And apart from the fact that Parliamentary systems and collective responsibilities were still developing,

Wellington was not simply a run of the mill politician-turned-soldier-turned-politician. Wellington, like many of his colleagues at the head of the governing classes, was an exceptional personality. He was someone who regarded his own counsel as the correct one. He watched, waited, planned and was cautious. In other words, his instinct was that of the conservative thinker. In a letter to the Prime Minister, Lord Liverpool, Wellington outlined very clearly his idea of how Government should perform without what he called factious opposition.

❖November 1, 1818

I don't doubt that the party of which the present Government are the head will give me credit for being sincerely attached to them and to their interests, but I hope that in case any circumstance should occur to remove them from power they will allow me to consider myself at liberty to take any line I may at the time think proper. The experience which I have acquired during my long service abroad has convinced me that a factious opposition to the Government is highly injurious to the interests of the country; and thinking as I do now I could not become a party to such an opposition, and I wish that this may be clearly understood by those persons with whom I am now about to engage as a colleague in Government.

I can easily conceive that this feeling of mine in the opinion of some render[s] me less eligible as a colleague, and I beg that, if this should be the case, the offer you have so kindly made to me may be considered as not made, and I can only assure you that you will ever find me equally disposed as you have always found me to render you every service and assistance in my power.

This is the Commander in Chief making it clear that he is loyal, but equally, he remains his own man. Within a week, Liverpool was telling Wellington that he understood and accepted the conditions for Wellington's return. After all, Liverpool could hardly afford to lose the nation's one hero.

❖Fife House, November 9

I should certainly not think of proposing to any person to become a member of the Government upon any condition or understanding that he was necessarily to adopt the course of conduct which the party of which the Government was composed might be inclined to pursue in the event of their being removed from office; but, strongly as I should be impressed with this sentiment with respect to any other individual, I feel it more peculiarly in your case, as it is impossible not to be sensible that there are many special circumstances in your situation which render it of the utmost importance, in the event to which you refer, that you should be at full liberty to adopt the line of conduct which you may at the time judge most proper and advisable, with a view to the country and to yourself.

And so Wellington joined Liverpool's Cabinet with the simple ambition of a political system united in preserving the order of things.

Not everyone went along with this view. In 1820, the threat of insurrection was considered very real. Twenty radicals led by a middle-aged man called Arthur Thistlewood met in a hayloft in Cato Street in Marylebone. Their plan, or so it was said, was to assassinate the Cabinet and take over Government. It came to nothing and they were arrested. Five of them, including Thistlewood, were hanged.

The immediate result was the Parliamentary Statutes, known as the Six Acts which, among other things, banned gatherings of more than fifty people at a time; these Statutes further developed the measures laid down in the Acts described on page 479. And a heavy stamp duty was imposed on newspapers, the idea being that the Radicals wouldn't be able to afford to print their own.

The Acts weren't much more than political gestures, in theory to strengthen the authority of the magistrates. Nevertheless, confidence in the Government's ability to cope with civil disorder appears to have been restored, although there is some evidence to suggest that Radicalism was not as threatening as was supposed. But it is important to remember that this was a society which didn't have an organized police force and much of the information came from paid spies. Spying was a lucrative occupation. Here's a bill for spying services sent to the Home Office from the Bolton magistrate.

Mr C and his agents:	£ 71
Mr W and his agents:	£122.11s.3d.
LF and his agent B:	£ 34.17s.
Postage and various expenses:	£ 6. 1s.
Total:	£234. 9s.3d.

At these rates, spies were on to a good thing. So a lot of the intelligence about radicals might have been spiced to keep their paymasters happy.

While the greased palm of domestic bureaucracy kept regular hours, the oil lamps burned nightly in Castlereagh's understaffed and overstretched Foreign Office. Castlereagh became overworked. He had guided the nation's foreign policy through seven dangerous years which had included the re-writing of the political and diplomatic laws of Europe after the defeat of Napoleon. He had hoped for a safer Europe. But much militated against that: revolutions in Portugal and Spain and the two Sicilies; suspicions of Russian ambitions; threats from Austria to existing treaties; the Greek War of Independence and the threat to Turkey. Castlereagh became deranged, and on 13 August 1822 he went into his dressing room and cut his own throat. Some have suggested that on top of these professional stresses, Castlereagh was being blackmailed. Here's part of a letter from Tom Creevey, the famous gossip and Whig MP, to a friend.

❖What an extraordinary event! I take for granted his self-destruction has been one of the common cases of pressure upon the brain which produces irritability, ending in derangement. Taylor will have it, and Ferguson also believes in the nonsense, that Bonaparte's charge against him of his having bagged part of Nap's money has something to do with it.

Do you remember my telling you of a conversation Castlereagh forced upon Tavistock in the park in the spring – about his anxiety to quit office and politicks and Parliament? He did the same thing to Ferguson one of the last nights at Almack's, stating his great fatigue and exhaustion and anxiety to be done with the concern altogether – just as poor Whitbread did to me both by letter and conversation two years before his death. It is a curious thing to recollect that one night in Paris in 1815, when I was [at] a ball at the Beau's, Castlereagh came up to me and asked if I had not been greatly surprised at Whitbread's death, and the manner of it, and then we had a good deal of conversation on the subject.

And the Whig knife is then turned in the still-warm reputation of the late Foreign Secretary.

❖Death settles a fellow's reputation in no time, and now that Castlereagh is dead, I defy any human being to discover a single feature of his character that can stand a moment's criticism. By experience, good manners and great courage, he managed a corrupt House of Commons pretty well. This is the whole of his intellectual merit. He had a limited understanding and no knowledge, and his whole life was spent in an avowed, cold-blooded contempt of every honest public principle. A worse, or, if he had had talent and ambition for it, a more dangerous, public man never existed.

Creevey's sympathies were with the late Queen, so he was unlikely to be objective about Castlereagh. In the same mood comes a letter, this time to Creevey from another Whig MP, Henry Brougham. It was Brougham (after whom the fashionable carriage was named) who had very ably defended the Queen at her trial.

❖Carlisle, August 19

Well! this is really a considerable event in point of size. Put all their other men together in one scale, and poor Castlereagh in the other – single, he plainly weighed them down. One can't help feeling a little for him, after being pitted against him for several years pretty regularly. It is like losing a connection suddenly. Also, he was a gentleman. But there are material advantages; and among them I reckon not the least that our excellent friends are gone, and those for whom we felt so bitterly, are, as it were, revenged. I mean Whitbread and Romilly. I cannot describe to you how this idea has filled my mind these last twenty-four hours. No mortal will now presume to whisper a word against these great and good men – I mean in our time; for there was never any chance of their doing so in after time. All we wanted was a gag for the present, and God knows here we have it in absolute perfection. As for the question of his successor – who cares one farthing about it? We know the enemy is incalculably damaged anyhow. He has left behind him the choice between the Merry Andrew and the Spinning Jenny [nicknames for George Canning and the Duke of Wellington] and the Court – the vile, stupid, absurd, superannuated Court – may make its election and welcome. I think I should prefer the very vulnerable Canning to remain at home.

Brougham had his wish. George Canning was about to go to India as Governor General. He had been friendly with the late Queen and had resigned over the Government's handling of her affairs. (In fact it may be that the King thought Canning was one of the people who had been more than friendly with Queen Caroline.) But now Liverpool, the Prime Minister, needed him in Government.

C❖Canning's presence in the Government was now essential: he was appointed Foreign Secretary . . . The Ministry was reconstructed to include Peel at the Home Office and Huskisson at the Board of Trade.

Peel was Robert Peel, the criminal law reformer and later Prime Minister. William Huskisson, a supporter of Canning, may only be remembered as the politician who was run over and killed at the opening of the Manchester and Liverpool Railway.

C❖The following years saw a more enlightened period of Tory rule. Canning, Peel, and Huskisson pursued bold policies which in many respects were in advance of those propounded by the Whigs. The penal code was reformed by Peel . . . Huskisson overhauled the tariff system, and continued Pitt's work in abolishing uneconomic taxes and revising the customs duties. Canning urged a scaling down of the duty on corn as the price rose at home. This was bound to bring conflict in the Tory ranks. He realized the distress and the political danger it would cause in the country, and declared on one occasion, 'We are on the brink of a great struggle between property and population . . . Such a struggle is only to be averted by the mildest and most liberal legislation.'

For decades there'd been agitation for prison reforms. Here's an extract from a House of Commons Committee inquiry into the state of the gaols in the City of London. The year was 1814.

❖Your Committee finds the gaol of Newgate, as at present regulated, is able to conveniently hold 110 debtors, and 317 criminal prisoners; and it is the opinion of the surgeon that when the whole number exceeds 500, great danger of infectious disorder is to be apprehended. In January last, the whole number amounted to 822. The rooms are generally about fifteen feet wide, and from twenty-three to thirty-six feet in length, and contain in each of them, day and night, from ten to fifteen men, when the prison is not crowded; but double that number have occasionally been placed in them. No bedding is provided: the poorer description of prisoners sleep on the boards, between two rugs given by the city; those who can afford it hire beds at six pence the night, from persons who carry on this traffic with the prison. The allowance of food to debtors is fourteen ounces of bread a day. To the debtors no coals or candles, no mops or pails are given. Wine and beer are sold at the bar of the prison, at the same price as in the public houses, and no one within the gaol is entitled to any profit on their sale. The quantity which each prisoner is allowed to purchase is not otherwise limited than that he shall not have, at one time, more than one bottle of wine, or one quart of ale; a regulation which little tends to preserve sobriety and order. The Act of Parliament against the introduction of spirituous liquors is conspicuously hung up, and all pains are taken, though sometimes ineffectually, to see that it is enforced.

Peel was more concerned with the means of capturing criminals and what to do with them once captured. Peel believed that law and order could easily get beyond the control of government and he set about organizing a police force. Sir Robert's policemen inspired a new slang word: Bobby.

CHAPTER FORTY-SIX

1824–1827

❖

The 1820s began and ended with George IV on the throne. It was a decade of change, a decade of four prime ministers: Liverpool, Canning, very briefly Lord Goderich, and the Duke of Wellington. This was the decade of the opening of the Stockton and Darlington Railway, of the bridge over the Menai Strait, of the death of Lord Byron who had gone to fight in the Greek War of Independence. It was a period in which the term 'reform' was being taken more seriously.

The Reform Acts were three nineteenth-century Bills designed to allow more people to vote, and to change the voting method. The First Reform Act was in 1832, the second in 1867, and the third in 1884. But back in the 1820s there were other reforms: reforms of laws that allowed freer trade and tariffs; reforms that moved towards active trades unions and changed attitudes to the way, and the conditions in which, people worked. For example, in 1823, the Combination Acts were repealed: these Acts made it illegal for two or more people to combine in trying to get better conditions at work and more money. Without the Combination Laws the passage towards active trades unionism is clear – at least with the benefit of hindsight. And there actually was an attempt – an unsuccessful one – to establish something called the Grand National Consolidated Trades Union.

But reform was needed in other more pressing areas of society. For example Robert Peel, the new Home Secretary in 1822, began work to change the criminal law and prisons. Here's an account of an earlier Parliamentary debate. MPs were discussing a particularly grisly form of specifically female execution.

❖Sir Benjamin Hammet rose to make a motion relative to the sentence of burning women convicted of certain crimes. He stated that, it having been his official duty to attend on the melancholy occasion of seeing the dreadful sentence put in execution, he then designed to move for leave to bring in a Bill to make some alteration. The judgment of burning alive, applied to women for certain crimes, was the savage remains of Norman policy, and disgraced our Statutes. At this moment a woman was in Newgate convicted of coining. It had been proved by experience that the shocking punishment did not prevent the crime. Formerly the men were sentenced to be quartered, in addition to their other punishment, and he supposed it arose from this delicacy that the women were to be burnt; but now, the sentence of quartering was not the judgment, and all he contended was that women should not receive a more dreadful punishment than the men, who might influence them to the commission of the crime.

Hanging instead of burning may have been seen as an advance. In 1817 a debate in the Commons elicited the latest liberal thinking from one of the House's Gallant Members.

❖General Thornton moved for leave to bring in a Bill to abolish the public whipping of females. He had been more especially led to this by an article which had appeared in the *Inverness Journal* which stated that a woman, young and beautiful, had been whipped in the public streets – that she was in a state of intoxication, seemed lost to every sense of her situation, and shortly returned to her old courses. Spectacles such as this were not likely to improve the public morals. The punishment had been partly abolished in England, and he proposed to abolish it entirely by commuting the punishment to hard labour in a workhouse for a period not exceeding three months. The motion was agreed to.

Punishment of a less violent kind was abolished also, and the grounds for the arguments would not be unfamiliar today.

❖Mr MA Taylor rose to move for leave to bring in a Bill to abolish the punishment of the pillory. The main ground upon which he rested his dislike to the punishment of the pillory was that it was a punishment which could not be measured or dealt out by a court of justice, but was apportioned solely by the caprice of the multitude. He did not think that such exhibitions were productive of moral good; but, on the contrary, tended to increase the vice that it was meant to suppress. Sir Robert Heron said that the improved and mild morality of the present times had been disadvantageous so far as it was too lenient to crimes. Certain offences had of late much increased owing, he feared, too much to the prevailing mildness and indulgence.

The more violent crimes were punishable by hanging. And although no one questioned the actual punishment, some did question the almost macabre treatment of those in the condemned cells.

❖By the rule of the prison, the prisoners are locked up in their cells from two in the afternoon till nine in the morning. Two prisoners are generally, for the sake of society, and in some cases to prevent suicide, put into each cell. The chaplain attends them every Tuesday and Thursday after sentence; and, after the order for execution, every day. Such as are Dissenters are permitted to see ministers of their own tenets; and a Roman Catholic clergyman is very properly paid by the city for attending on such as are of his persuasion. On the Sunday before the execution, all the prisoners under sentence of death, and who are of the Church of England, are obliged to attend divine service; they are placed in an open pew in the centre of the chapel, and a black coffin is placed on the table before them. Your Committee feel this to be cruel and unnecessary. It is consequently stated to have this bad effect: that it induces many to profess dissenting tenets, to avoid their being thus held up to public view in this last and awful situation; and in general only the most hardened consent so to appear.

If they were to be executed in the Port of London area, then the wretches were placed on a particularly gruesome form of display. There the bodies of hanged villains were left for all to see. It was called gibbeting. The idea was that the sight of these remains should act as a crime deterrent. But there's no evidence that it did. One William Sykes was moved to write to Robert Peel.

❖I am sure you will overlook the intrusion of a letter from a private individual calling your notice to the continuance of the revolting spectacle exhibited on the bank of the Thames, and which excites feelings of disgust in the breasts of numerous voyagers to Ramsgate, Margate, France, the Netherlands, et cetera, et cetera. I allude to the scare-crow remains of the poor wretches who, long since expired by death for their crimes, now hang upon gibbets. It is said that 'Persecution ceases in the grave'. Let these poor remains find a grave, and the remembrance of their offences pass away . . . Tyburn, Kennington, Hounslow, Wimbledon are all freed from the sad practice: why should it be perpetuated to the disgrace and nuisance of the Port of London?

Peel may have been impressed with the plea from Sykes but the practice of gibbeting continued in London until 1834. But those like Peel who wanted criminal law reform were not liberals, in modern terms, although it was at this time that the distinctions between political ministries were beginning to become clearer. And during this time of experiment with reform perhaps the most important change was the evolution of political positions at Westminster. There wasn't yet a clear ideological distinction between those who claimed party labels, but Parliament was definitely moving towards what would now be called the party system, and an official Opposition.

When Lord Liverpool had a stroke in 1827, he had been Prime Minister for fifteen years. Some say that Liverpool was a nonentity but he had governed during the final years of the Napoleonic Wars; the considerable economic and social changes that followed; evidence of rebellion; scandals in the royal household at a time when the monarch's credibility was essential to the political stability of the administration; and the suicide of his Foreign Secretary. And through all this, he had little direct control of the House of Commons because he sat in the Lords.

And the system under which Liverpool governed in the 1820s, although moving slowly towards the two party system, was far removed from what now exists where two main parties lay out their promises and then the nation votes for one lot or the other.

In the 1820s an election was the time when the King and his Government (which the King chose) asked for a vote of confidence. And so a general election wasn't much fought by an Opposition trying to replace the Government, indeed most seats weren't even contested. The biggest influence on the outcome of the election might well turn out to be a public display of confidence not by the people, but by the monarch, in the Government.

From this it is easy to see how Liverpool could be judged as someone who had done little more than keep apart the two powerful government factions of George Canning and the Duke of Wellington, while clinging to the memory of Pitt the Younger. That judgment would be too simple and would not acknowledge the way in which ministers set their own agendas, even if this meant ignoring those of their own government. For instance, there had long been a debate on the extent of Catholic Emancipation. Some of Liverpool's Ministers were as much opposed to this idea as others were in favour. Therefore the chances of success were almost nil. There was no way in which Liverpool could simply say, 'This is Government policy, therefore I insist everyone agrees.' Especially as the King wouldn't have agreed with him anyway. The best he could hope for was an agreeable Parliament, rather than an agreeing one. Every time there was a new idea, his job was to reassure many of his colleagues that it was an evolutionary concept, rather than a radical departure.

Thus Liverpool ruled for fifteen years (probably longer than most had expected him to), but he couldn't have survived without the support of the Regent, the Prince of Wales (the future George IV). Second, the way in which government worked meant that it couldn't be judged in the way that government is judged today, by its legislative programmes.

When, in 1827, Liverpool went (he was to die the following year), the King, reluctantly, appointed his successor: George Canning. Canning had been Foreign Secretary during the previous five years. That period is important to the understanding of many of the animosities in the post-Liverpool governments.

C❖A crisis in Spain confronted Canning with his first task as Foreign Secretary. The popular elements which had led the struggle against Napoleon now revolted against the autocratic Bourbon Government, formed a revolutionary Junta, and proclaimed a constitution on the model of that set up in France in 1815. Canning had backed the Spanish national rising in 1808, and was naturally sympathetic, but Metternich [Prince von Metternich, the Austrian foreign minister who opposed so-called democratic movements] and the Holy Alliance saw the revolt . . . as a threat to the principle of monarchy and to the entire European system. . . . the whole tradition of British foreign politics was against intervention in the domestic affairs of other states. But Austria and Russia were determined to act. An instrument lay ready to their hand. The ex-enemy, France, coveted respectability. Her restored Bourbon Government feared the revolutionaries and offered to send a military expedition to Spain to recover for King Ferdinand his absolutist powers.

An absolutist monarch was one who claimed and attempted to exercise absolute power. That is, with little regard for any democratic process.

C❖Canning would have nothing to do with it. There was great excitement in London. English volunteers went to Spain to serve in the defence forces of the Spanish 'Liberals', a name which entered English politics from this Spanish revolt. . . . But Canning was equally against official intervention on the side of 'Spanish Liberalism', and it was upon this that the Whigs attacked him. These heart-searchings in Britain made little difference to the outcome in Spain. The French expedition met with no serious resistance, and the Spanish Liberals retired to Cadiz and gave in.

The political thoughts of Canning now grew in a direction that would have been recognized during and after the 1939–1945 World War, when plans were laid for a transatlantic Alliance.

The interests of the Europeans in the early nineteenth century turned to Latin America. The Spanish had colonies, the Portuguese were in Brazil and the British traded there. While the Spanish had been distracted by the Napoleonic Wars, many of their South American colonies had gone their own ways – or tried to. The Spanish were now keen to re-establish control. There was every chance of a series of colonial wars. Canning wanted the Americans to help Britain oppose European intervention. This was in the American interest: it didn't want wars on its continent, no matter how far south they were fought. But the then President, James Monroe, was persuaded not to involve America in unworkable alliances. On 2 December 1823, the fifth President of the United States addressed Congress. His speech has become known as the Monroe Doctrine and remains the basis of American foreign policy. A summary of what he said might be that the United States would see any European attempt to politically influence the 'Western hemisphere' as 'dangerous to our peace and safety'. In 1917, it was President Wilson who, during the First World War, declared, 'I am proposing that the nations should adopt the doctrine of President Monroe as the doctrine of the world: that no nation should seek to extend its policy over any other nation or people, but that every people should be left free to determine its own policy, its own way.'

The consequences of the Napoleonic Wars, the ideas of a British foreign secretary and the consequent reservations of a young United States, produced a doctrine that survived into the twentieth century and perhaps beyond.

C❖Monroe's famous message conveyed a warning to Britain as well as to the authoritarian Powers. Canning understood the risks of competition and dispute with the United States upon the continent in which the Americans now claimed predominance. He was determined to avert all conflicts which might embarrass Britain and harm her own proper interests. . . .

Soon afterwards Britain officially recognized the independence of the South American states. King George IV, who bore no love for republics, and many of Canning's colleagues in the Government, had strenuously opposed this step. Even now the King refused to read the Royal Speech containing the announcement. It was read for him by a reluctant Lord Chancellor. So Canning's view prevailed. His stroke over South America may probably be judged his greatest triumph in foreign policy.

Apart from the Hanoverian aversion to republics, George IV had never much trusted Canning. And Canning didn't trust the King. He didn't accept the way in which he interfered in foreign policy. In a letter to his wife after a Cabinet meeting, Canning gives some idea of the way in which foreign ambassadors, especially Lievan the Russian and the Austrian Prince Esterhazy, had direct access to the King and tried to persuade him to countermand the policy over South America. Canning was ready to resign over the worrying interference, or tracasserie, as he called it.

❖January 28, 1825

I shall talk to Lievan and Esterhazy when I next see them, in a manner that will check their meddling in future. I told Cabinet that I knew the whole of this tracasserie to be the work of foreign interference, of which (as Liverpool would vouch) I had warned him six weeks ago that it was concocted in Vienna and that the object was to force the King to change his policy by changing part of his Government.

Will the Duke of Wellington tell all that has passed to Madame Lievan tonight? If this sort of work goes on I shall be obliged to remind His Majesty that constitutionally he has no right to see Foreign Ministers at all except in my presence, and that his father never thought of such co-joberations [sic]. I really hope that we shall all go on the better for this last attempt, and that the ultras among us will now see that they have nothing for it but to submit . . .

Now you shall know what I would have done if this intrigue had gone on, and if, fortunately, the intemperance or miscalculation of the King had not brought it to a premature dénouement and so been obliged to give in, I would have resigned upon the South American question, and I would have declared openly, in the House of Commons, taking care to keep safe my sources of intelligence, that I was driven from office by the Holy Alliance, and further, that the system which I found established of personal communication between the Sovereign and the Foreign Ministers, was one under which no English Minister could do his duty. If after such a denunciation and the debates which would have followed it, the Lievans and Esterhazy did not find London too hot for them, I know nothing of the present temper of the English nation.

Canning had resigned once before – on the Government's treatment of his friend, the King's wife, Caroline of Brunswick. That had not made him a favourite of the King who suspected that Canning had had an affair with her. But if George IV had sleepless nights, they were few in number. Within a few months, George Canning too was dead.

However, when Canning was appointed, seven Cabinet Ministers re-signed, including the Home Secretary Sir Robert Peel, the Duke of Wellington, and the Lord Chancellor, the Earl of Eldon. Canning tried to get support from the Whigs. Some of them, like Lord Lansdowne, were powerful enough to make Government unworkable.

Here's a memorandum written by Canning to Lansdowne more or less promising that the new administration's policies would reward his support. Canning also made it clear that while there was room for negotiation on the main issue, Catholic Emancipation (which he himself supported), he, Canning, demanded loyalty far more akin to what a present day Prime Minister would expect.

❖April 23, 1827
 One:
    The Catholic question is to remain, as in Lord Liverpool's Govern-
    ment, an open question, upon which each member of the Cabinet is at
    perfect liberty to exercise his own judgment, in supporting that question if
    brought forward by others, or in propounding it, either in the Cabinet or
    to Parliament.

But if any member of the Cabinet should deem it an indispensable duty to bring forward individually the Catholic question in Parliament, he is distinctly to state that he does so in his individual capacity.

Two:

The inconvenience (now unavoidable) of having one open question in the Cabinet, makes it more necessary to agree that there should be no other. All the existing members of the Cabinet are united in opposing the question of Parliamentary Reform, and could not acquiesce in its being brought forward or supported by any member of the Cabinet.

Three:

The present members of the Cabinet are also united in opposition to the motion for the repeal of the Test Act, of which notice stands on the books of the House of Commons. They see great inexpediency in now stirring a question which has slept for upwards of thirty years, and they could not consent to a divided vote by the members of the Cabinet upon it.

There were three Test Acts, each dating from the seventeenth century, and each centred on the question of religion in Britain. They were called the Test Acts because they made legal tests of a person's faith. If anyone wanted to hold public office, then he had to be an Anglican communicant, denounce the Roman Catholic doctrine of the Eucharist, and accept that the monarch was head of the Church of England. In two years' time they would be gone.

At this point, British society was dominated by laws which restricted the social, educational, and political movement of large numbers of the population. For example, there was a fundamental discrimination against most people other than male members of the Church of England. Only they had the right to university education and to hold political office. Jews, Roman Catholics, Dissenters and women were excluded. It was also a society that was only slowly relinquishing its hold on eighteenth-century ideas and politics.

In the early nineteenth-century political climate men believed that change would come, that great changes had to be made, but that they had to be evolutionary, rather than revolutionary. The instinct to preserve the institutions of politics meant that for the moment the government of the nation remained a matter of reacting to events rather than deliberately instigating them. This then was the political climate in the Britain over which Canning was to be Prime Minister for just one summer.

C❖Canning's Ministry signalled the coming dissolution of the eighteenth-century political system. . . . the Opposition Tories and the die-hard Whigs harassed the new Government. Had Canning been granted a longer spell of life the group he led might have founded a new political allegiance. But on August 8, after a short illness, Canning died. He was killed, like Castlereagh, by overwork.

Canning had played a decisive part in the shaping of the new century. In war and peace he had proved himself a man of large views and active determination. His quick mind and hasty temper made him an uneasy party colleague. As his friend Sir Walter Scott said of him, he wanted prudence. Through Canning, however, the better side of the Pitt tradition was handed on to the future. In many ways he was in sympathy with the new movements stirring in English life. He was also in close touch with the Press and knew how to use publicity in the conduct of government. As with Chatham [Pitt the Elder], his political power was largely based on public opinion and on a popular foreign policy. Belief in Catholic Emancipation marked him as more advanced in view than most of his Tory colleagues. His opposition to Parliamentary Reform was part of the curse which lay upon all English politicians who had had contact with the French Revolution. On this perhaps he might have changed his mind. At any rate, after his death his followers amid the ruins of the Tory Party were converted to the cause. Disraeli bore witness to this striking man. 'I never saw Canning but once. I remember as if it were but yesterday the tumult of that ethereal brow. Still lingers in my ear the melody of that voice.'

Disraeli would have been about twenty-three when Canning died, and not yet in the House. Thomas Creevey, who seemed to know everyone and wrote gossipy letters to them all, was for once less than waspish when he heard the news of Canning's death.

❖Low Gosforth, August 9

Well, and so goes another man killed by publick life. His constitution, it is true, was not a good one, but the knock-down blow has been his possession of supreme power, his means of getting it, and the personal abuse it brought down upon his head. And now what comes next? As far as the present Cabinet is concerned, I should think they would willingly consent to Lansdowne succeeding Canning; but what says George IV to this? Again, if such was the case, Brougham must lead the House of Commons as a Cabinet Minister, and what would the King and the Church and Tories say to that?

Brougham, the Whig MP and lawyer, was not a favourite with the King because of his successful defence of Caroline of Brunswick, so Canning's Chancellor of the Exchequer, FJ Robinson, Viscount Goderich, became the new Prime Minister in August 1827. But he couldn't hold the Cabinet together, and he was gone by January 1828. The domestic problems of Government remained however, and so did the crises in foreign policy, especially in the Eastern Mediterranean where the War of Greek Independence was reaching its climax.

The twentieth-century differences between Turkey and Greece are not of recent origin. For 2000 years Greece had been passed from one ruler to another. From the fifteenth century she had been ruled by Turkey. In 1821, inspired by the French Revolution, the Greeks rebelled. The Russians joined in against the Turks because the Greek Catholic Church was also the Russian State Church, and the Russians assumed the role of Defender of the Greek Christian faith. The Greek War of Independence from Turkey became a nineteenth-century Crusade. France and Britain joined the Russians, and modern Crusaders from Britain, among them the poet Byron, sailed to fight and die for the cause, in much the same way that, a century later, the Spanish Civil War attracted volunteers. The British wanted to see the Greeks freed, but didn't want to see the Turks beaten by the Russians. In other words, British foreign policy was, to say the least, ambivalent. Goderich tried and failed to make something of the political mess.

C❖More than half the Tory Party, under Peel and Wellington, was in opposition. Quarrels among Whig and Tory members of the Government ruptured its unity. There had been a hitch in carrying out Canning's policy of non-intervention in Greece . . . Admiral Codrington, one of Nelson's captains, who had fought at Trafalgar and was now in command of the Allied squadron in Greek waters, had on his own initiative destroyed the entire Turkish fleet in the Bay of Navarino.

That was in October 1827. Navarino was the last full-scale naval battle under sail.

C❖There was alarm in England in case the Russians should take undue advantage of this victory. The battle, which meant much to the Greeks, was disapprovingly described in the King's Speech as an 'untoward incident', and the victor narrowly escaped court-martial. The Government, rent by Whig intrigues, abruptly disappeared. . . . Wellington and Peel were instructed to form an administration. This they did. Wellington became Prime Minister, with Peel as Home Secretary and Leader of the House of Commons.

Now attention was focused on the new Prime Minister, a man with an immense sense of duty, the hero of Waterloo, Arthur Wellesley, first Duke of Wellington.

CHAPTER FORTY-SEVEN

1828–1832

❖

It was January 1828 when the Duke of Wellington became Prime Minister of Great Britain. In theory he was another Tory leader but Wellington had little notion of party politics. His political conviction was that of duty, of public service, and he became Prime Minister, perhaps reluctantly, and largely because he saw it as his duty to carry on the Government of the monarch. His Cabinet colleagues did not share this philosophy, and the mixture was soon to boil over. Someone said that the first Cabinet meeting had a sense of gentlemen who had just fought a duel. Wellington complained that too much of his time was taken with smoothing feelings.

In its first year, the Cabinet was forced to accept the repeal of the Test Act – the law by which anyone wanting to hold public office had to demonstrate his allegiance to the Church of England and the monarch's leadership of that Church. Peel, Palmerston and Huskisson opposed the repeal, but changed their minds when they saw that the Commons would have it anyway. Dissenters and Non-Conformists had for ages been able to claim indemnity from the Act's punishments, but for many it was an important symbol of something else: Catholic Emancipation.

But the first serious Cabinet split came when two boroughs – Penryn and East Retford – were found guilty of corruption. The High Tories wanted to merge the towns into adjoining constituencies. Huskisson wanted the seats transferred to unenfranchised towns; he said it was a resigning matter. Wellington, probably to Huskisson's surprise, accepted Huskisson's resignation although the Duke could not have imagined the result. With another Canningite gone, the old Tory party began to crumble, and what happened in Ireland hastened their decline.

C❖The greatest failure of British Government was in Ireland. . . . The social and political monopoly of a Protestant minority, which had oppressed Irish life since the days of Cromwell, would not be tolerated indefinitely. British governments were perpetually threatened with revolution in Ireland. A main dividing line in politics after 1815 was upon this issue of Catholic Emancipation. . . . A decision had been postponed from year to year by 'gentlemen's agreements' among the English politicians. But the patience of the Irish was coming to its end. They were organizing under Daniel O'Connell for vehement agitation against England. O'Connell was a landlord and a lawyer. He believed in what later came to be called Home Rule for Ireland under the British Crown.

At that time, anyone appointed to a government office had to go through a by-election. The man who was now given one of the vacant government jobs, at the Board of Trade, was an Irish Protestant called Vesey Fitzgerald. The election was to be in County Clare. Daniel O'Connell, who five years earlier had formed the Catholic Association in Ireland, decided to stand in the by-election. But the law said that as a Catholic he couldn't hold office, couldn't be an MP. But he won the election.

C❖Here was a test case. If the English Government refused to enfranchise the Catholics there would be revolution in Ireland, and political disaster at home.

Peel, whose political career had been built up in Ireland, had long been the symbol of opposition to any concessions to the Catholics . . . His attitude in the growing crisis was unavoidably delicate. Wellington's position was happier. He was less committed and more able to take without qualm the line of expediency. The position in Ireland was simple. An independent association of the Irish people had sabotaged the official administration. The choice was either Catholic Emancipation or the systematic reconquest of Ireland. . . .

As a general, Wellington knew the hopelessness of attempting to repress a national rising. He had seen civil war at close quarters in Spain. He himself came from an Irish family and was familiar with the turbulent island.

The only opponents of Emancipation were the English Bishops, the old-fashioned Tories, and the King. The Bishops and the Tories could be outvoted; but the King was a more serious obstacle.

It is very possible that Peel would have resigned from the Cabinet if Wellington hadn't made it clear that he was absolutely vital to the administration's survival. And so Peel left the safety of High-Tory Oxford and bought himself a seat in Wiltshire. It was this act of loyalty to Wellington, together with the King's horror of the Whigs in power, that persuaded George to agree to a Bill for Catholic Emancipation. And Peel steered it through the House the following year, in April 1829. What this meant practically for Irish Catholics was that all the Irish offices, other than the posts of Viceroy and Chancellor, could now be held by Catholics. For those in Ireland who wanted to repeal the union with England, there was a long way to go. Any agitation for Home Rule was viewed with great suspicion, even by some of the senior clergy of the Roman Catholic church. And not all Irishmen who wanted a degree of autonomy fancied the idea of an Irish parliament dominated by O'Connell. The differences within the island itself were stark – of a kind recognizable today.

In the South West of Ireland, the Catholics wanted more freedom from England. In the most northerly of the five ancient Kingdoms of Ireland, the people of Ulster (descended from English settlers) had little desire to seek independence – even though it had been the Protestant community who attempted to get Home Rule in the eighteenth century, long before Catholics were powerful enough to try.

And in England itself there was little political satisfaction at the outcome of the Bill. The Tories were split three ways into what today is called the right, who had voted against the Bill; the followers of the late George Canning, who were no longer in Government; and, in the middle, the supporters of Wellington and Peel. The Whigs were also divided because some of them had been Canning's supporters, and had therefore voted for the legislation; other Whigs had opposed it.

A further complication arose when some Tories started campaigning for Parliamentary Reform precisely because they thought a more balanced Parliament would not have let the Bill through. This impossible political confusion encouraged a writer in the *Quarterly Review* to suggest that the time had come to forget the political labels Whig and Tory. He believed that the political conflict was not between two parties trying to control government, 'but between the mob and the government . . . the conservative and subversive principles'.

Meanwhile Robert Peel had other matters on his mind – law and order. He wanted to organize the 'thief takers' who had existed since the first half of the 1500s into a police force. Thief-taking was a business, and the money came from the reward for every thief. In the countryside, local villains were known and the system worked. In the towns and cities, unpaid constables and thief-takers might work for a parish or a ward.

But many people, law-abiding people, didn't want an organized police force. There was a very real fear that it could, and would, be used to usurp public liberty. The Parliamentary view at the start of the nineteenth century was that public morality was the best form of protection. However, in London, although constables and watchmen were commonplace, they did most of their work in the daytime. They were often reluctant to seek out footpads and muggers once it was dark. Peel, as Home Secretary, decided to change all this. Here's part of a letter he wrote to the MP Henry Hobhouse.

❖December 12, 1828

I have under my consideration at present very extensive changes in the Police of the metropolis. My plan is shortly this – to appoint some authority which shall take charge of the night police of the metropolis, connecting the force employed by night with the existing police establishments now under the Home Office and Bow Street, to act under the immediate superintendence of the Home Office, and in daily communication with it. I propose that charge of the night police should be taken gradually. I mean that my system of police should be substituted for the parochial system, not by a single leap, but by degrees. I will first organize a force which shall be sufficient to take charge of a district surrounding Charing Cross, composed, we will say, of four or five parishes.

Peel's metropolis police – or Metropolitan Police as it would become known – did not include the jealously guarded jurisdiction of the City of London.

❖In the same way, as a little experience shall enable us to manage a more numerous force of nightly police, I propose to signify to other parishes from time to time that the police will take charge of them. Their present watch will continue to act until such signification be made, and will cease when it is made. The present amount of money issued from the public funds for maintaining horse patrol, foot patrol, magistrates, et cetera, shall continue to be issued, but the surplus that may be requisite to maintain the night police, or to improve and extend the existing patrols, shall be levied from the district within which that night police may act. A Police Rate will be levied instead of the Watch Rate.

Hence the term Police Watch Committee, still used by local authorities. London at this time was a comparatively small city. Peel had also thought of what would happen in the areas beyond its boundaries but influenced by what went on inside them.

❖Now the out-parishes – such places as Brentford, Twickenham, Isleworth, Hounslow, and so forth – in all of which the lack of police at present is scandalous, will feel, and very justly, that if the new police system succeeds in London, it will injure them, by driving a fresh stock of thieves from the heart of the metropolis into the environs, and it will be a great object to me, as well as to them, to devise some mode of improving their police.

And so here are the beginnings of the Metropolitan Police Force, which, in 1829, Robert Peel set up with a Commissioner of Police and his Assistant

Commissioner, in an office in Scotland Yard. The policemen became known as Peelers, or Bobbies.

Peel's recognition that thieves would simply cross boundaries was well founded. Ten years later a Royal Commission said there should be wider police areas, but many people didn't want to pay a national tax for policemen. Others insisted that policing was an entirely local matter. And so county justices were allowed to appoint men who would organize local forces; these men were to be known as Chief Constables.

The need to protect society reflected the social and economic changes in Britain. But they were nothing to those about to take place in France where, in 1830, the July Revolution would bring Louis Philippe to the throne. In the same year Britain too had a new monarch. In June 1830, George IV died with a miniature of Mrs Fitzherbert round his neck. Maria Fitzherbert, the Roman Catholic widow whom the King had married illegally, was his first love.

C❖'The first gentleman of Europe' was not long mourned by his people. During his last illness his mistress, Lady Conyngham, was busy collecting her perquisites. This once handsome man had grown so gross and corpulent that he was ashamed to show himself in public. [His nickname was the Prince of Whales.] His extravagance had become a mania, and his natural abilities were clouded by years of self-indulgence. No tyrant by nature, he yet enjoyed fancying himself as an autocrat. But with thrones tottering on the Continent he realized that the less said on this subject the better.

The new King, William IV, was not another Prince of Wales, but the Duke of Clarence, the late King's brother.

C❖. . . the Duke of Clarence [was] the most eccentric and least obnoxious of the sons of George III. . . . had been brought up in the Navy, and had passed a life of total obscurity, except for a brief and ludicrous interval when Canning had made him Lord High Admiral in 1827. For many years he had lived with an actress at Bushey Park.

The actress's stage name was Dorothy, or Dora, Jordan. Her real name was Dorothy Bland and she was accepted in London society. They lived as man and wife and had ten children but the Royal Marriages Act of 1772, which said that the monarch's approval was necessary for a prince (or a princess), under the age of twenty-five, to marry a commoner, prevented their marriage: the King had made it clear that approval would be refused. Occasionally William found pleasures in other women, but as he said, 'Mrs Jordan is a very good creature, very domestic and careful of the children. To be sure she is absurd sometimes and has her humours. But there are such things, more or less, in all families.' But money (or the lack of it), boredom perhaps, and the prospect of a younger wife meant separation. Dorothy Jordan was given £4400 a year, and she moved from Bushey House. She died alone, hiding from her creditors, just outside Paris.

William had been a naval officer for more than thirty years. He understood strategy and the need for lines of defence. He was a friend and supporter of Nelson and he was the first monarch to have had a career in the Royal Navy, the first sailor-King. But he remained the Duke of Clarence, all but obscure on the royal list, until the death of Princess Charlotte (George and Caroline's only child) in childbirth in 1817. Next in line was his older brother, the Duke of York, but he was in uncertain health, and so the hunt was on for a bride for this naval duke who might one day be King.

Courtiers found Princess Amelia Adelaide Louisa Theresa Caroline, the unmarried daughter of the Duke of Saxe-Meiningen who was twenty-five years old and not particularly pretty. But then the Duke of Clarence was fifty-two and even less pretty. It must have been a daunting prospect for her. In 1818, she arrived in London to be greeted by the grossly fat Prince Regent, the news that her future father-in-law (the insane George III) was locked in Windsor Castle, and the expectation that she would sort out William's finances. But the marriage worked.

C❖She proved to be a generous-hearted and acceptable Queen. Good nature and simplicity of mind were William IV's in equal measure. The gravest embarrassments he caused his Ministers sprang from his garrulity. It was difficult to restrain his tactlessness at public functions. . . .

But the royal pair were popular . . . Her quiet homeliness was a welcome change after the domestic life of George IV.

Thomas Creevey, the Whig MP and political gossip, left a record of the scene when the news came of the King's death, and the appearance of William in the Palace. He referred affectionately, as many did, to the late King as 'Prinny' and to the new King as 'Billy'. Creevey was writing to his step-daughter from his club in St James's.

❖Brooks's, June 26

So poor Prinny is really dead. I have just met our great Privy Councillors coming from the Palace (Warrender and Bob Adair included). I learnt from the former that the only observation he heard from his Sovereign was upon his going to write his name on parchment, when he said: 'You've damned bad pens here!' Here also is Tankerville, who was at the Palace likewise. He says the difference in manner between the late and present sovereign upon the occasion of swearing in the Privy Council was very striking. Poor Prinny put on a dramatic, royal, distant dignity to all;

Billy, who in addition to living out of the world, has become rather blind, was doing his best in a very natural way to make out the face of every Privy Councillor as each kneeled down to kiss his hand. In Tankerville's own case, Billy put one hand over his eyes and at last said in a most familiar tone: 'Oh, Lord Tankerville, is it you? I am very glad to see you. How d'ye do?' It seemed quite a restraint to him not to shake hands with people. He said to Mr Chancellor of the Exchequer – the cock-eyed Goulbourne – 'D'ye know I'm grown so near-sighted that I can't make out who you are. You must tell me your name, if you please.' He read his declaration to the Council, which is said to be very favourable to the present Ministry [the Government of Wellington].

After reading this production of the Government, he treated the Council with a little impromptu of his own, and great was the fear of Wellington, as they say visibly expressed on his face, lest Billy should take too excursive a view of things; instead of which it was merely a little natural and pretty funeral oration over Prinny, who, he said, had always been the best and most affectionate of brothers.

Wellington may have organized the approval of the new King. But he could not control the sentiments of the electorate and now the Constitutional law of the land took over. On the death of the Sovereign the Government was obliged to offer itself for election. At this period the total population was about twenty million people, but only 435,000 were allowed to vote, and many of the Parliamentary seats were controlled by patrons who could more or less appoint a candidate at will – rather like a patron offering the living of a parish to a favoured clergyman.

And it was a big Parliament: 685 Members from the forty English counties and 179 English boroughs, twenty-four Welsh counties and boroughs, the two universities, the twenty-four cities, and the Scottish and Irish constituencies. But there was an imbalance between population and Members. Cornwall, for example, had a population of only 300,000 but had forty-two MPs. Lancashire had one million more people, but only fourteen Members. And for all of them, the prospect of a new Parliament was complicated by a further distraction: a rebellion in Paris.

C❖The July revolution in France set up a constitutional monarchy under the house of Orleans. The new King, Louis Philippe, was the son of the Revolutionary Philippe Égalité, who had voted for the death of his cousin, Louis XVI, and had himself been guillotined later. Louis Philippe was a wiser and more honourable man than his father. He was to keep his uneasy throne for eighteen years, and he also kept his head. Encouraged by events in Paris, the Belgians rebelled against the Kingdom of the Netherlands, in which they had been incorporated by the peace treaties of 1815 signed at the end of the Napoleonic Wars. . . . A wave of revolts spread across Germany into Poland. . . . These agitations on the European continent, largely orderly in character and democratic in purpose, were much acclaimed in England, and their progress was closely and excitedly studied. The Tory Government and the Duke of Wellington alone seemed suspicious and hostile. With some reason the Government feared that France might annex Belgium or establish a French prince in Brussels upon a new throne. Wellington was even suspected of intending to restore the Kingdom of the Netherlands by armed force. This was not true. The preservation of peace was his chief care. But Opposition speakers were pleased to attribute to him an aim he did not profess, and the rumour was enough to inflame the hot tempers of the times.

It was said that these events influenced the outcome of the British general election. They certainly had an effect on what happened in Britain *after* the election.

Wellington's Ministry was defeated and the man asked to form the new government was the Whig leader, Earl Grey. The Revolution in France had aroused his interest. He had campaigned, unsuccessfully, for changes in Parliament since the 1790s and now he saw his chance. He agreed to be Prime Minister only if Parliament would accept a Reform Bill. It did.

It is often said that the Industrial Revolution created inequalities among the peoples of Britain. But the Industrial Revolution simply made the existing inequalities more obvious. In the 1830s almost everything in society was unequal. There were restrictions on the economic, social, educational, religious and democratic development of the people that made sure that one group remained in charge and another remained almost entirely without influence.

Charles Grey began his programme of reform by getting rid of the so-called rotten or pocket boroughs – the constituencies owned, and therefore controlled, by the wealthy. And then he gave the vote to more people. Grey was the natural leader of the Whigs. He was an aristocrat, to the right of the Whig party and he respected the old institutions. And although he was a Reformer, his instinct was to balance the relationship between the governing aristocracy and the general public. He believed reform was the way to stop the Radicals getting their hands on government.

C❖It is given to few men to carry out late in life a great measure of reform which they have advocated without success for forty years. Such was to be Grey's achievement. He had held office briefly under Fox in the Ministry of 1806. For the rest, since the early years of the younger Pitt he had been not only continuously out of office, but almost without expectation or desire of ever winning it. Now his hour was at hand. Grey was a landowner who regarded politics as a social duty, and much preferred his country estates to the lobbies of Westminster. He had, however, made careful study of the insurrections on the Continent, and realized that they were not as sinister as Wellington thought. His judgment on home affairs was also well directed. He and his colleagues perceived that the agitation which had shaken England since Waterloo issued from two quite separate sources – the middle classes, unrepresented, prosperous, respectable, influenced by the democratic ideas of the French Revolution, but deeply law-abiding in their hunger for political power; and on the other side a bitter and more revolutionary section of working men, smitten by the economic dislocation of war and its aftermath, prepared to talk of violence and perhaps even to use it. . . . [Grey] had the support of Lord John Russell, son of the Duke of Bedford, who was a man of impulsive mind, with a high devotion to the cause of liberty in the abstract, whatever the practical consequences might be. With them stood Henry Brougham, expectant of office, an advanced politician who had made his name as the defender of Queen Caroline.

It was November 1830 and Wellington's hopes that the Whigs were too poorly organized to form a government had been dashed. And some of his own party now supported the Whigs.

C❖ King William IV asked Grey to form a Government. With one brief interval the Whigs had been out of office for nearly fifty years. Now at a bound they were at the summit of power and influence.

They were confronted with an ugly scene. French threats to intervene in Belgium made it imperative but unpopular to increase the military estimates. The Chancellor of the Exchequer failed to provide an effective Budget. Law and order were breaking down in the south-eastern counties, and Lord Melbourne, the new Home Secretary, acted decidedly. Over 400 farm workers were sentenced to transportation. The Radicals were indignant and disillusioned. Only Parliamentary Reform could save the Government, and to this they now addressed themselves.

. . . in March 1831, Lord John Russell rose in the House of Commons to move the first Reform Bill. Amid shouting and scornful laughter he read out to their holders a list of over 100 'rotten' and 'pocket' boroughs which it was proposed to abolish and replace with new constituencies for the unrepresented areas of the Metropolis, the industrial North, and the Midlands. To the Tories this was a violation of all they stood for, an affront to their deepest political convictions, a gross attack on the rights of property. A seat was a thing to be bought or sold like a house or an estate, and a more uniform franchise savoured of an arithmetical conception of politics dangerously akin to French democracy. Many Whigs, too, who had expected a milder measure were at first dumbfounded by the breadth of Russell's proposals. They soon rallied to the Government when they saw the enthusiasm of the country, for the Whigs believed that Reform would forestall revolution. The Tories, on the other hand, feared that it was the first step on the road to cataclysm. To them, and indeed to many Whigs . . . wider franchise would mean the beginning of the end of the old system of administration by influence and patronage.

Perhaps the puzzle for the casual observer of the times is the structure of the Government that was pushing through this Reform Bill. It was the most aristocratic Cabinet of the century. However, the Reform Bill didn't make it through the Lords first time. But thanks to the Irish Members, the Bill received its second reading on 23 March at three in the morning. But in April the Tories (who held the balance of power) defeated the Government at the committee stage and the King dissolved Parliament.

This meant another election and, this time, the Reformers achieved a big majority. A new Reform Bill was presented in June with an important amendment: voting would be given to certain tenants in the counties. This allowed the landlords to control the votes on their estates: tenants would be unlikely to vote against their landlords' wishes. It got through the Commons in September but, in spite of the best efforts of the aristocratic Cabinet, not the Lords. In October they defeated the motion when twenty-one bishops voted against it. If they hadn't, Reform would have been on the Statute Book by one vote.

C❖Next morning the newspapers, bordered in black, proclaimed the news. Rioting broke out in the Midlands; houses and property were burned; there was wild disorder in Bristol. . . . In December Russell introduced the Bill for the third time, and the Commons carried it by a majority of two to one. In the following May it came again before the Lords. It was rejected by thirty-five votes. There was now no question of another dissolution and Grey realized that only extreme remedies would serve. He accordingly drove to Windsor and asked the King to create enough new peers to carry the Bill. The King refused and the Cabinet resigned. William IV asked Wellington and Peel to form an administration to carry Reform as they had carried Catholic Emancipation, and thus avoid swamping the Lords. But Peel would not comply; he was not prepared to assume Ministerial responsibility for a measure of which he disapproved. Feeling in the country became menacing. Plans were made for strikes and a general refusal of taxes. Banners and placards appeared in the London streets with the caption 'To Stop the Duke Go for Gold', and there was a run on the Bank of England.

Radical leaders declared they would paralyse any Tory Government which came to power, and after a week the Duke admitted defeat. On the afternoon of May 18, Grey and Brougham called at St James's Palace. The King authorized them to draw up a list of persons who would be made peers and could be counted on to vote for the Whigs. At the same time he sent his private secretary to tell the leading Tories of his decision and suggest that they could avoid such extremities by abstaining. When the Bill was again introduced the Opposition benches were practically empty. It was carried by an overwhelming majority, and became law on June 7, 1832.

The Act abolished many boroughs and handed over seats to the shires and, to a lesser extent, to the cities. But there were anomalies: 56% of the electorate lived in counties but they had only 31% of the seats, fifty-six boroughs were told they could no longer have Members, thirty boroughs were allowed just one Member each and twenty-two new boroughs could have two Members each.

The vote was given to men who were freeholders of property that was worth forty shillings a year, or those with land worth £10 annually, or who were leasing £50 properties.

In truth, the Reform Act didn't change people's lives and rights to the extent some had feared and others had hoped. Yet the preamble to the Act summed up the mood that had driven on Grey and his supporters.

❖Whereas it is expedient to take effectual measures for correcting divers abuses that have long prevailed in the choice of Members to serve in the Commons House of Parliament, to deprive many inconsiderable places of the right of returning Members, to grant such privilege at large, populous and wealthy towns, to increase the numbers of Knights of the Shires, to extend the elective franchise to many of His Majesty's subjects who have not heretofore enjoyed the same, and to diminish the expense of elections; it is therefore enacted . . .

Whatever the argument about the worth of those effectual measures one thing was certain: in 1832 the way the people of Britain would be governed in future had changed.

CHAPTER FORTY-EIGHT

1833–1837

❖

In 1834 the twenty-five-year-old Charles Darwin was sailing with Captain Robert Fitzroy in the *Beagle* on the voyage that would visit the Galapagos Islands. Charles Dickens was twenty-two and about to become Parliamentary reporter for the Whig journal, the *Morning Chronicle*, and in two years' time, the first episode of *The Posthumous Papers of the Pickwick Club* would appear.

Grey was Prime Minister, Palmerston was Foreign Secretary, but by the summer of 1834 Melbourne would replace Grey.

C❖. . . the legislation and the commissions of these years were by no means unfruitful. The slaves in the West Indies were finally emancipated in 1833. For the first time in English history the Government made educational grants to religious societies. The Poor Law was reformed on lines that were considered highly advanced in administrative and intellectual circles, though they did not prove popular among those they were supposed to benefit. The first effective Factory Act was passed, though the long hours of work it permitted would horrify the twentieth century and did not satisfy the humanitarians of the time. The whole system of local government was reconstructed and the old oligarchies abolished.

The Poor Law may have been considered an improvement by some, but it defied the evidence of a desperate need for something more liberal and less dogmatic. There had been a Poor Law since the 1530s; money came from voluntary payments in the parishes. By the end of the sixteenth century magistrates were allowed to raise money – in other words, funding poor relief was now compulsory.

By the eighteenth century, the impoverished who weren't able-bodied had to go to the workhouses. The parishes had to provide jobs outside the workhouses for the sound of limb. But agricultural workers in particular were more and more falling on harder times (England was very much a rural society) and the parishes couldn't, or wouldn't, support the poor.

And so, when the Poor Law Act was amended in 1834, boards of guardians were appointed to administer it. In theory, this was an improvement to the system; in practice, its effects were not necessarily seen that way. Instead of putting the able-bodied to work in the parishes and tending the less able in the workhouses, now all paupers were forced into the workhouses in which conditions were to be wretched – as a matter of policy. As one government commissioner put it: 'Our intention is to make workhouses as like prisons as possible.' This was the nineteenth-century version of the short, sharp shock treatment. The idea was that the poor would do anything to avoid the workhouse.

Consider this extract from the Royal Commission of Inquiry into the Administration and Practical Operation of the Poor Laws. It was written more than 160 years ago.

❖Throughout the evidence it is shown, that in proportion as the condition of any pauper class is elevated above the condition of independent labourers, the condition of the independent class is depressed; their industry is impaired, their employment becomes unsteady, and its remuneration in wages is diminished. Such persons, therefore, are under the strongest inducements to quit the less eligible class of labourers, and enter the more eligible class of paupers.

The converse is the effect when the pauper class is placed in its proper position, below the condition of the independent labourer. Every penny bestowed, that tends to render the position of the pauper more eligible than that of the independent labourer, is a bounty to indolence and vice. We have found, that as the poor's rates are at present administered, they operate as bounties for this description, to the amount of several millions annually.

The standard, therefore, to which reference must be made in fixing the condition of those who are to be maintained by the public, is the condition of those who are maintained by their own exertions.

The cost of looking after the poor was about £8 million a year. Parliament had let through an inadequate piece of legislation and given those who would administer it overwhelming authority. The proposed legislation was never properly scrutinized and the Commissioners presented their evidence in a less than objective way. But MPs were simply glad to get rid of the problem by voting it into law. The Secretary of the Poor Law Commissioners was Edwin Chadwick. He was unbending, domineering, arrogant and unpopular but, apparently, unassailable for nearly two decades.

But in 1834 there were other pressing matters to attend to. In particular, a changing of the order in Downing Street. Grey had gone.

C❖The new leaders were Lord Melbourne and Lord John Russell. Russell was a Whig of the old school, sensitive to any invasion of political liberty and rights. He saw the need for further reforms in the sphere of government, but the broadening paths of democracy did not beckon him. Melbourne in his youth had held advanced opinions, but his lack of any guiding aim and motive, his want of conviction, his cautious scepticism, denied him and his party any theme or inspiration. Personal friendships and agreeable conversation mattered more to him than political issues. He accepted the office of Prime Minister with reluctance, genuinely wondering whether the honour was worth while. Once in power his bland qualities helped to keep his divided team together. But his administration wore an eighteenth-century air in the midst of nineteenth-century stress.

One of Melbourne's ablest colleagues was Lord Palmerston, who held the Foreign Office for nearly eleven years. . . . Under Melbourne Palmerston did much as he pleased in foreign affairs. His leading beliefs were two: that British interests must everywhere be stoutly upheld, if necessary by a show of force, and that Liberal movements in the countries of Europe should be encouraged whenever it was within Britain's power to extend them sympathy or even aid. . . . his imperturbable spirit gradually won the admiration of the mass of his fellow countrymen. He was in these years building up the popularity which later made him appear the embodiment of mid-Victorian confidence.

This was of little interest to those in the 1830s who believed they had few benefits to gain from a dashing approach to foreign affairs, a reform of the Poor Laws and an extension of political franchise. At the start of the nineteenth century the Combination Acts were passed. These said, in simple terms, that two or more people weren't allowed to 'combine' to get better working conditions and higher wages. In 1824, the Combination Acts of 1800 were repealed which meant that there were now people trying to form area and even national trades unions – in other words broadening the authority of organized labour. This movement took trades unionism from groups who wanted better conditions to groups who had an ideological, a social, a political, agenda.

And just as there was something akin to a fear of the poor, so there was a fear of organized labour. The Whigs, for example, appeared so afraid of some union movements that they were reluctant to allow Parliament to confront them for fear of rousing what some saw as a sleeping giant. Where they could act quickly, and sometimes unfairly, they did. Six labourers in Tolpuddle in Dorset administered oaths of trades unionism. They were transported. It was a tactical mistake. The story of the Tolpuddle Martyrs was to be remembered more for its symbolism, than for their punishment.

If any had wished for a sign of disapproval of the way the six labourers were treated, then it might have come in the autumn of 1834. On 16 October the Houses of Parliament burned down. By the following morning, the forum of the first prime minister, Walpole, of Charles James Fox, of the Pitts, of Edmund Burke, was little but dust and ashes. But this was no act of revolution. A janitor in the House was burning bundles of wooden tallies, sticks that for centuries had been used for accounting in the Treasury. He got carried away and the Palace of Westminster overheated and the ultimate result was the neo-Gothic building that exists today. That this inferno happened in the year of the Tolpuddle Martyrs, of the enactment of inadequate Poor Law reform, of an unsuccessful experiment in national trades unionism, and of three prime ministers, is coincidental; however, it's not hard to imagine the stir it caused in William IV's England.

William was not one of the nation's finest monarchs. As Duke of Clarence, he had been considered a comical figure, often tiresome, oddly-shaped – but a loving father to his ten children by his actress mistress of twenty years. As a royal duke he had been a harmless enough figure; on the throne, he was a liability. He'd wanted to be King so much that he took to gargling to keep away infection and any disease that might take him before his royal time was come. His habit of spitting out of the window of his coach, of wandering about London until rescued, and of making less than regal public statements, didn't endear him to his ministers. And he knew it.

But once he was on the throne, which it turned out he didn't like nearly as much as the thought of being on it, William imagined revolution, the rising of the people, the importing of the principles settled by the guillotine in France. He was comforted by his Home Secretary, Viscount Melbourne. But he didn't much like Melbourne, he found him too aristocratic.

Melbourne was a Whig, and the Hanoverians never quite trusted the stylish confidence of the Whigs. William had wanted to be King; Melbourne had never quite wanted to be Prime Minister. That was difficult for William to understand. As Melbourne remarked: 'He hasn't the feelings of a gentleman; he knows what they are, but he hasn't them'. However politicians in the 1830s could not ignore their monarch whatever they thought of him.

When Grey retired in 1834 and Melbourne became Prime Minister, he lasted only a few months, but by the following spring he was back in Number Ten. The change-about presented an interesting Constitutional decision. Towards the end of 1834, the Earl Spencer died. His heir, Lord Althorp, was the Whig leader in the Commons. But now he, the most important Whig in the Commons, had gone to the Lords and Melbourne didn't want to carry on. But he thought it best for the party that he should. The King had other ideas. Even though the Commons was against him doing so, he sacked Melbourne and so, for a few months, Peel was Prime Minister. William IV was the last King to appoint a Prime Minister against the wishes of the Commons.

Melbourne and the King had one thing in common, a wariness, of the growing trades union movement. Melbourne said that employers shouldn't sack men just because they were trades unionists, the danger lay in the taking of secret oaths. He, and William IV, believed that the move from simple bargaining for wages and conditions could lead to political, ideological and social groupings. The mass demonstration against the sentencing of the six Dorset labourers was not in principle wrong to Melbourne but it was the size that he could not accept. To bow to an argument was reasonable, to a crowd was unthinkable. However it was Melbourne's Government which, two years later, did pardon the six.

Melbourne was a member of what was generally called the Whig ruling class: a world of people who could, and did, take for granted their mansions in London and the country, their right to provide ambassadors abroad and political leaders at home, and the ease with which they achieved their purpose in life.

Melbourne's family name was Lamb. The Lambs revolved about his mother Elizabeth, Lady Melbourne, whose lover was the very influential George Wyndham, the third Lord Egremont. In fact, Egremont was probably Melbourne's father. Certainly Melbourne's brother George was fathered by the Prince of Wales.

If Melbourne's elder brother Peniston hadn't died of consumption Melbourne would probably have become a writer rather than a statesman. But as heir to the title, his life took a different route. He became an MP and married Caroline Ponsonby. She, now Lady Caroline Lamb, was erratic, capricious and often unbalanced. She fell in and out of love. And then, most famously and then destructively, she fell in love with Byron – or perhaps in love with the idea of being in love with him. By 1825, Melbourne and Caroline were separated. She was dead by 1828.

By 1835 Melbourne was Prime Minister for the second time. It was hardly an ideal time to be leader. The Whigs were, as ever, split among themselves. They were disliked by the Lords and there never had been a Hanoverian who really trusted them. In Parliament they were more or less a minority and needed the Radical and Irish benches' support in the lobbies.

But important legislation did go through, including, in 1835, the Municipal Corporations Act. This set out to be the first reform of city and urban government. Councillors would be elected and therefore, indirectly, so would mayors and the city and town aldermen. But the biggest change in Melbourne's rule came not with political reform, but with the death of the King. William IV died in 1837.

In his journals Charles Greville left an uncompromising portrait of the King.

❖ King William IV, if he had been born in a private station, would have passed unobserved through life like millions of other men, looked upon as possessing a good natured and affectionate disposition, but without either elevation of mind or brightness of intellect. During many years of his life the Duke of Clarence was an obscure individual, without consideration, moving in a limited circle, and altogether forgotten by the great world . . . The King seemed to be more occupied with the pleasing novelty of his situation, providing for his children, and actively discharging the duties of his high function, than in giving effect to any political opinions . . . the roar of the mighty conflict which the Reform Bill brought on filled him with dismay, and very soon with detestation of the principles of which he had unwittingly permitted himself to be the professor and the promoter.

Greville believed the King's name was used without his understanding in the promotion of the Reform Bill.

❖But although King William was sometimes weak, sometimes obstinate, and miserably deficient in penetration and judgment, he was manly, sincere, honest, and straightforward. . . . The most remarkable foible of the late King was his passion for speechifying . . . he had considerable facility in expressing himself, but what he said was generally useless or improper. He never received the homage of a bishop without giving him a lecture; and the custom he introduced of giving toasts and making speeches at all his dinners was more suitable to a tavern than to a palace.

He was totally deficient in dignity or refinement, and neither his elevation to the throne nor his association with people of the most distinguished manners could give him any tincture of the one or the other.

Twenty years earlier, the Duke of Kent (the fourth son of George III) had married simply because any child of the marriage was likely to be the future monarch. The Duke married a widow, Princess Mary Louisa Victoria of Saxe-Coburg-Gotha. In 1819, a daughter, Alexandrina Victoria, was born. She became fifth in line to the throne, after her father and her uncles, and in the early hours of 20 June 1837, she became Queen Victoria.

CHAPTER FORTY-NINE

1837–1841

❖

At nine o'clock on the morning of 20 June 1837, Viscount Melbourne the Prime Minister, wearing the dress uniform of a Privy Councillor, was ushered into Kensington Palace. He was escorted to a small receiving room. In it, quite alone, stood a blue-eyed girl, not five feet tall, dressed in mourning black. Melbourne bowed, and kissed her hand. She was eighteen years old, her name was Alexandrina Victoria, and she was now Queen of Great Britain. Melbourne would be her mentor.

That same morning, her Privy Council stood in a horseshoe and listened to her speech of declaration which had been written for her by Melbourne. Late in the evening, he returned to Kensington Palace and for an hour or so, the two talked. That night she noted in her diary, 'I had a very important and very comfortable conversation with him.'

C❖[King William]. . . . humorous, tactless, pleasant, and unrespected, had played his part in lowering esteem for the monarchy, and indeed the vices and eccentricities of the sons of George III had by this time almost destroyed its hold upon the hearts of the people. An assault on the institution which had played so great a part in the history of England appeared imminent, and there seemed few to defend it. The new sovereign . . . had been brought up by a dutiful mother, who was shocked at the language and habits of the royal uncles, and had secluded her in Kensington Palace from both the Court and the nation. Her education was supervised by a German governess, with occasional examinations by Church dignitaries, and a correspondence course on her future duties with her maternal uncle, King Leopold of Belgium. The country knew nothing of either her character or her virtues. 'Few people', wrote Palmerston, 'have had opportunities of forming a correct judgment of the Princess; but I incline to think that she will turn out to be a remarkable person, and gifted with a great deal of strength of character.' He was right.

Her mother, the Duchess of Kent, and her private secretary Sir John Conroy (who appears to have been more than private secretary), had longed for her succession and hoped either for an earlier death of William IV or for an extension – a delay – of Victoria's coming of age. Both would have raised the question of a Regency, and thus the chance of even more power for Victoria's mother and for Conroy. Victoria was defended from this prospect by her governess, the Baroness Lehzen. In the journals of Charles Greville, there's a note which tells us how the new Queen dealt with Conroy.

❖It is not easy to ascertain the exact cause of her antipathy to him, but it has probably grown with her growth, and results from divers causes. The person in the world she loves best is the Baroness Lehzen, and Lehzen and Conroy were enemies. Her manner to the Duchess is, however, irreproachable, and they appear to be on cordial and affectionate terms.

Once Victoria was Queen, the dubious ambitions of her mother and of Conroy were defeated.

Victoria's coronation was a blaze of diamonds, encrusted scabbards and elderly burnished breastplates earned in some of the bloodiest wars Europe had witnessed. It was a pageant of British triumphalism, but for organization it would hardly have won a skirmish because, as Greville noted, few, including the Queen, knew what was going on.

❖The different actors in the ceremonial were very imperfect in their parts, and had neglected to rehearse them. Lord John Thynne, who officiated for the Dean of Westminster, told me that nobody knew what was to be done except the Archbishop and himself, and the Queen never knew what she was to do next. She said to John Thynne, 'Pray tell me what I am to do, for they don't know;' and at the end, when the orb was put into her hand, she said to him, 'What am I to do with it?' 'Your Majesty is to carry it, if you please, in your hand.' 'Am I?' she said. 'It is very heavy.' The ruby ring was made for her little finger instead of the fourth, on which the rubric prescribes that it should be put. She said it was too small, and she could not get it on. He said it was right to put it there, and he insisted, she yielded, but had first to take off her other rings, and then this was forced on.

It was said that one million people watched the procession but the real business of royalty was not the business of pageantry. More important to the young Queen was that she understood what was expected of her, and for others to understand what she expected. The Baroness Lehzen had been Princess Victoria's confidante, but Queen Victoria now needed more than a trusted governess. Melbourne was wary of letting anyone become the power behind the throne of the young Queen, and so he took on that role himself. This meant that he was with her for hours at a time, every day. They wrote to each other, sometimes three or four times a day. At royal dinners, the guest of honour would be at the Queen's right hand. But Melbourne was always at her left. As they came to know more of each other it became obvious that this was no ordinary relationship between monarch and Prime Minister.

Melbourne and Victoria were so close that London joked of a romance – although all knew there could be none. The Prime Minister was undoubtedly attracted to the young Queen and she to him. But this was no affair of the heart. Victoria needed someone she could trust and Melbourne was also her friend. And for the moment, while Melbourne was there, Victoria believed, as she wrote to Prince Albert, that 'The Whigs are the only safe and loyal people.' But the Whigs would not be in power for long, even though Melbourne would continue to be an influence at Court.

C❖By the time Queen Victoria came to the throne the Whigs had shot their bolt. The Court and the governing circles were isolated and unpopular; the middle classes were fearful of unrest and beginning to vote for the Tories. Meanwhile Lord Melbourne, who had little faith in law-making, with grace and pleasantness was doing nothing. On top of all this there appeared towards the end of the year the first signs of a great economic depression. Conditions in the industrial North soon became as bad as after Waterloo, and in May 1838 a group of working-class leaders published a 'People's Charter'. Chartism, as it was called, in which some historians discern the beginnings of socialism, was the last despairing cry of poverty against the Machine Age. The Chartists, believing, like the agitators for Reform before 1832, that an extension of the franchise would cure all their miseries, demanded annual Parliaments, universal male suffrage, equal electoral districts, the removal of the property qualification for Membership of Parliament, the secret ballot, and the payment of Members. Their only hope of success was to secure, as the Radicals had done, the backing of a Parliamentary party and of the progressive middle classes. But they deliberately refused to bid for middle-class support. Their leaders quarrelled among themselves and affronted respectable people by threatening and irresponsible speeches. They had no funds, and no organization such as the Catholic Association had found in the parishes of the Irish clergy, or the Labour Party was to find later in the trades unions. For a time England was flooded with petitions and pamphlets, but the ferment varied in warmth from one part of the country to another. Whenever conditions improved the popular temper cooled, and no united national movement emerged as a permanent force.

Churchill's Machine Age was only one catalyst for the Chartists. Others were the depression which started towards the end of 1836; the insensitive administration of the Poor Laws; and the division of haves and have-nots that inspired Disraeli to give his novel *Sybil* the subtitle, *Or, The Two Nations*. And although Chartism may not have achieved its ambition for political and social reform, its ideas influenced Britain for decades to come.

Victoria had been Queen for just two years when she faced her first major political crisis. In May 1839 a motion to suspend the Jamaican Constitution was carried by just five votes. (Jamaica had refused to implement the 1833 anti-slavery legislation and had defied British instructions to change its prison laws.) Melbourne regarded such a tiny majority as a confidence issue and resigned. Victoria was faced with a Tory Government led by Sir Robert Peel. She disliked Tories and Peel knew this, so he wanted some sign that he had her confidence. The way he went about trying to get it was a little clumsy; he said that she should sack some of her Ladies of the Bedchamber, who were the wives of Whig Ministers. The Queen was nervous and she immediately turned to Melbourne for advice. Melbourne wrote to Victoria, telling her not to worry and not to be put off by Peel's cold manner.

❖Lord Melbourne earnestly entreats Your Majesty not to suffer yourself to be affected by any faultiness of manner which you may observe. Depend upon it, there is no personal hostility to Lord Melbourne nor any bitter feelings against him. Sir Robert is the most cautious and reserved of mankind. Nobody seems to Lord Melbourne to know him, but he is therefore not deceitful or dishonest.

But the Queen would have none of this. Besides, if Peel stuck to his demands then wouldn't she be justified in having a faithful and trusted Melbourne at her side once more? Within hours of her meeting with Peel, Victoria was again writing to Melbourne.

❖The Queen writes one line to prepare Lord Melbourne for what may happen in a very few hours. Sir Robert Peel has behaved very ill, and has insisted on my giving up my Ladies, to which I replied that I never would consent, and I never saw a man so frightened. He said he must go to the Duke of Wellington and consult with him, when both would return, and he said this must suspend all further proceedings, and he asked whether I should be ready to receive a decision, which I said I should; he was quite perturbed — but this is infamous. I said, besides many other things, that if he or the Duke of Wellington had been at the head of the Government when I came to the Throne, perhaps there might have been a few more Tory Ladies, but that then if you had come into Office you would never have dreamt of changing them. I was calm but very decided, and I think you would have been pleased to see my composure and great firmness; the

Queen of England will not submit to such trickery. Keep yourself in readiness, for you may soon be wanted.

Not at all the reserved style of a monarch to her Prime Minister. This was a letter to a dear and trusted friend. But Melbourne's position was surely difficult. Firstly he could not see how the Whigs could last in power for very long. Returning to government would probably mean a collapse in political confidence over one of the many issues of the day, and the disgrace of being swept from power. Secondly, Melbourne believed Peel could provide the political stability that Britain needed. Thirdly, he must have known that at this point in her reign, Victoria should not be seen as a monarch under the spell of the Whigs – or any other political group.

Melbourne told his Cabinet what the Queen had said and written to him and, to a man, they appear to have fallen under the spell of the new monarch and instructed Melbourne that she must be supported. Melbourne told the Queen that he would stay. Undoubtedly, it was this promise that encouraged Victoria to stand out against Peel. And this she did in a short letter (he called it a note) to him. (Incidentally, note the address. Victoria was the first monarch to live there full time.)

❖Buckingham Palace, May 10, 1839

The Queen, having considered the proposal made to her yesterday by Sir Robert Peel, to remove the Ladies of her Bedchamber, cannot consent to adopt a course which she conceives to be contrary to usage, and which is repugnant to her feelings.

Within three hours Peel was writing to the Queen making out his case and telling her that he couldn't be her Prime Minister – which is what she wanted to hear anyway. Here's part of what he wrote and it's an opportunity to see the etiquette and protocol a Prime Minister used when writing on a matter of great importance to his Sovereign. Sir Robert practically bows at each comma.

❖Whitehall, May 10, 1839

Sir Robert Peel presents his humble duty to your Majesty, and has had the honour of receiving your Majesty's note of this morning. In respectfully submitting to your Majesty's pleasure, and humbly returning into your Majesty's hands the important trust which your Majesty had been graciously pleased to commit to . . . Robert Peel trusts that your Majesty will permit him to state to your Majesty his impression with respect to the circumstances which have led to the termination of his attempt to form an administration for the conduct of your Majesty's service.

In the interview with which your Majesty honoured Sir Robert Peel yesterday morning, after he had submitted to your Majesty the names of those whom he proposed to recommend to your Majesty for the principal executive appointments, he mentioned to your Majesty his earnest wish to be enabled, with your Majesty's sanction, so to constitute your Majesty's household that your Majesty's confidential servants might have the advantage of a public demonstration of your Majesty's full support and confidence; and that at the same time, as far as possible consistently with that demonstration, each individual appointment in the household should be entirely acceptable to your Majesty's personal feelings.

At this point the Queen had apparently said that she wanted the Earl of Liverpool to have an office and Peel had agreed.

❖Sir Robert Peel then observed, that he should have every wish to apply a similar principle to the chief appointments which are filled by the Ladies of your Majesty's household; upon which your Majesty was pleased to remark, that you must reserve the whole of those appointments, and that it was your Majesty's pleasure that the whole should continue as at present, without any change . . .

Having had the opportunity, through your Majesty's gracious consideration of reflecting upon this point, he humbly submits to your Majesty that he is reluctantly compelled, by a sense of public duty, and of the interest of your Majesty's service, to adhere to the opinion which he ventured to express to your Majesty.

It all seemed quite simple to the Queen; Peel had assumed too much and she would call Melbourne with whom she felt safe. But Melbourne was far from happy, particularly when the true story of Victoria's confrontation with Peel became known. Peel had not, as Melbourne had imagined and as the Queen had implied, demanded the removal of all her Ladies of the Bedchamber – only some. But it was too late to change the appointment and anyway Peel would not hear of it.

Melbourne's first task was to take the blame for the crisis. He could not possibly allow the country to believe that the Queen had behaved wrongly. In the House of Lords he accepted criticism that he had manipulated the matter in order to stay in office. That was far from the truth, but to protect her he made no attempt to deny the political accusations. And so Melbourne reluctantly returned to Downing Street.

Peel was not dissatisfied with the outcome. He hadn't really wanted to lead another minority government, and he sensed it wouldn't be long before he could rouse a greater number of seats. For the Whigs, there was little to gain but the satisfaction of demonstrating their loyalty to their Queen who was only nineteen and may have felt vulnerable without the Ladies of the Bedchamber whom she'd learned to trust.

Just five days after the exchange of letters between Peel and the Queen, the Hansard Parliamentary Report of 15 May 1839 records that the Chartism debate was going on in Parliament. There was no mention of the differences between Melbourne, Peel and Victoria.

❖Mr William Wynn could not help expressing his surprise that so long an adjournment of the House should be proposed while the internal state of the country was so agitated. Six months had now elapsed since certain parties had recommended the people generally to procure arms. They knew that in different parts of the country those recommendations had been carried into effect, that fire arms had been provided, and that pikes had been made to a very great extent. Up to the present moment, they were being publicly sold, and no steps had been taken to put an end to it . . . Deadly weapons had been provided by a large number of people in the country, and it was no wonder that special constables should shew some reluctance in the discharge of their duties . . . He was not afraid of the ultimate success of the parties who were misleading the people. What he was afraid of was, that if this arming continued unchecked, it would lead to a lamentable degree of bloodshed.

The new Queen's Kingdom was less than satisfied with its lot. And Melbourne himself was tired. He was sixty and was sometimes forgetful. His party, the Whigs, had survived for as long as they had perhaps because they were simply the most acceptable alternative to the strengthened Radical movement on the one hand, and the Tories on the other. The Whigs were good at giving ground when the governing of the country required compromise, but Melbourne knew that this could not go on. Melbourne's instinct was simply to avoid the disagreeable, but that policy could not be maintained when the country faced so many difficulties. For example, there was a general recognition that the Poor Laws were not working properly or, more accurately, the Poor Laws were too harshly administered.

But attention was increasingly focused far away from the welfare of the poorhouse tenants towards Afghanistan and China: the First Afghan War and the Opium War. Afghanistan was a land of some 245,000 square miles. In the nineteenth century it was a large and often inhospitable buffer between British interests in India and the Russians, and perhaps the Persians. Whoever controlled Afghanistan could threaten or defend their interests with some assurance.

C❖The Russian threat to India had begun to overhang the minds of English-men. It was in fact a gross exaggeration to suppose that Russian armies could have crossed the ranges of the Hindu-Kush in force and arrived in the Indus valley. But the menace seemed real at the time. When it was learnt that a small body of Russians had penetrated into the fringes of Afghanistan, a British expedition was dispatched, in 1839, to Kabul and a British candidate placed on the Afghan throne.

The Russians supported the claims to the Afghan throne of a man called Dost Muhammad. The British candidate was the very unpopular Shah Shuja.

C❖The result was disaster. The country rose up in arms. In December 1841, under promise of safe conduct, the British garrison of some 4000 troops, accompanied by nearly three times as many women, children, and Afghan camp-followers, began to withdraw through the snow and the mountain passes. The safe conduct was violated, and nearly all were murdered or taken prisoner. Only a handful of survivors reached India in the following January. A second expedition avenged the treachery in the following year, but the repute of European arms was deeply smitten and the massacre resounded throughout the peninsula.

Reputations counted for little when it came to profit and loss sheets in the British counting houses. And so it was with the commercial events which led to what became known as the Opium Wars. Opium farming was a profitable business for the English East India Company and although, officially, the Chinese banned opium imports, some of their officials in Canton were corrupt, and opium was stored in large warehouses. A senior Chinese official was sent to Canton to have the millions of pounds' worth of opium destroyed. The British sent troops and the Opium War began. It went on until the summer of 1842 when the heat was so intense that many of the troops died from sunstroke. In August of that year a truce was signed, the Treaty of Nanking, and the greatest prize was not actually opium, but the ceding by the Chinese to Britain of Hong Kong.

Meanwhile in London, in October 1839, Queen Victoria's two cousins, Ernest and Albert Saxe-Coburg-Gotha, arrived in England. In 1836, the year before Victoria became Queen, her uncle, King Leopold of the Belgians, had been determined that she should marry his nephew Albert. They had met and, although she liked Albert, she was not overly impressed. Then in 1837, when Victoria became Queen, she made it clear to Leopold that although Albert might be a decent enough prince, she was after all Queen. Albert was given a tutor, Baron Stockmar, who had instructions to 'bring on' the young man – as a trainer might a yearling.

And so it was that when Albert and Ernest arrived in 1839, and the Queen looked him over, she recorded in her diary: 'It was with some emotion that I beheld Albert – who is *beautiful*!' On 13 October 1839, Victoria told Melbourne that she meant to marry her cousin. On 10 February 1840, Queen Victoria and Prince Albert were married. Charles Greville, in his worldly way, thought it not quite a splendid occasion. Not enough pomp for such circumstances and very, very damp indeed. But then this was no June bride.

❖The wedding on Monday went off tolerably well. The week before was fine, and Albert drove about the town with a mob shouting at his heels. Monday, as if by a malignant influence, was a dreadful day – torrents of rain, and violent gusts of wind. Nevertheless a countless multitude thronged the park, and was scattered over the town. I never beheld such a congregation as there was, in spite of the weather. The Queen proceeded in state from Buckingham House [as some called it] to St James's without any cheering, but then it was raining enough to damp warmer loyalty than that of a London mob. The procession in the Palace [Westminster] was pretty enough and she went through the ceremony with much grace and propriety, not without emotion, though sufficiently subdued, and her manner to her family was very pretty and becoming. Upon leaving the Palace for Windsor she and her young husband were pretty well received; but they went off in a very poor and shabby style. Instead of the new chariot in which most married people are accustomed to dash along, they were in one of the old travelling coaches, the postilions in undress liveries, and with a small escort, three other carriages with post-horses. The crowds on the road were so great that they did not reach the Castle till eight o'clock.

Prince Albert was not the most educated prince in Europe. He had had eighteen months at the University of Bonn and a little travelling under the guidance of Stockmar who commented that Albert did not concentrate very long on any one subject. And the Opposition had much fun pointing out that nowhere in official documentation was it written that Albert was a Protestant – which all British monarchs and their spouses had to be by law. Victoria had no intention of sharing her Constitutional responsibilities with her husband; however, she did want Albert to have a degree of precedence and privilege which Parliament (in fact the Lords) was not willing to grant. He would not be King but Victoria said her husband should have first place in the land after herself. Her royal uncles objected and they were supported by many in the Tory Opposition.

A Bill was put to Parliament that would have given Victoria what she wanted for her husband. But Melbourne, perhaps showing his growing infirmity, handled it badly and it had to be withdrawn. Greville tells us something of the backstairs opposition, which Melbourne should have anticipated.

❖*February 12*

The Government resolved to withdraw the clause, and they did so, thus leaving the Prince without any specific place assigned by Parliament, and it remains with the Queen to do what she can for him, or for courtesy, tacit consent, and deference for her Consort to give him the precedence virtually which the House of Lords refuses to bestow formally.

February 13

The discussion about the Precedence question induced me to look into the authorities and the ancient practice, and to give the subject some consideration. I came to the conclusion that she has the power to give him precedence everywhere but in Parliament and in Council, and on the whole that her husband ought to have precedence. So I wrote a pamphlet upon it, setting forth the results of my enquiry and my opinion. I have been in many minds about publishing it, and I believe I shall, it is certainly not worth much.

The interesting point here is that Greville's pamphlet was worth more than he thought.

❖Lord Melbourne said to me, 'What is to be done about this Precedence?' I said, 'Have you sent my pamphlet to the Queen?' 'I have sent it to her, and desired her to show it to Prince Albert; and I have sent it to the Chancellor, and desired him to give me his opinion on the law, as it requires great consideration and great care'. . . So thus it stands and if the Chancellor [the chief law officer, the Lord Chancellor] sees no objection, my plan will be adopted, and I shall have settled for them, having no earthly thing to do with it, what they ought to have settled for themselves long ago, and have avoided all the squabbling and bad blood which have been the result of their unlucky Bill.

February 21

On Thursday morning I got a note from Arbuthnot [Charles Arbuthnot, a diplomatist, who was living in Wellington's house] desiring I would call at Apsley House [Wellington's house]. When I got there, he told me that the Duke of Cambridge had sent for Lord Lyndhurst to consult him . . . they were invited to meet the Queen on Friday . . . and he wanted to know what he was to do about giving precedence to Albert. Lord Lyndhurst came to Apsley House and saw the Duke about it, and they agreed to report to the Duke of Cambridge their joint opinion that the Queen had an unquestionable right to give him any precedence she pleased, and that he had better concede it without making any difficulty . . :

I heard from Arbuthnot this morning that the Duke has set his face resolutely against any Bill in the House of Lords to settle the Privilege question; and that Lyndhurst, though not so strong in his opinions as the Duke, is resolved to abide by his determination, and to go with him. The Duke, in fact, goes as far as any of the opponents of Privilege, for he not only thinks that the dicta of the Judges are not to be questioned, but that the House of Commons ought not to have the Privilege at all . . . the strong opinion of his renders the question exceedingly difficult and embarrassing, for it was become very clear that nothing but the intervention of the House of Lords could untie so ravelled a knot.

The importance of Greville and his opinion is two-fold: although the precedent he explained could be questioned by Constitutional lawyers, at the time, he was right. Second, this matter was not thought through.

Albert himself never quite knew what his Constitutional position was, but what he did do, successfully, was replace Melbourne as Victoria's closest adviser. And even when he was dead, the Queen often considered what he would have advised before taking decisions.

C❖The Prince was an upright, conscientious man with far-ranging interests and high ideals. He and the Queen enjoyed for twenty-one years, until his early death, a happy family life, which held up an example much in accord with the desires of her subjects. After the excesses of George IV and his brothers the dignity and repute of the monarchy stood in need of restoration, and this was Victoria and Albert's achievement. . . . They would not let him take a seat in the House of Lords, they cut down his annual allowance, and he was not granted even the title of Prince Consort until 1857. Nevertheless the patronage which he earnestly extended to science, industry, and the arts, and to good causes of many kinds, gradually won him a wide measure of public respect. As permanent adviser to the Queen, on all issues laid before her, he played a scrupulous, disinterested part. Wise counsels from his uncle, King Leopold, and his former tutor, Baron Stockmar, taught him the role and duties of a constitutional sovereign. Eventually the party leaders in England learnt to value his advice, especially on foreign affairs, though they did not always pay heed to it. The Queen was a woman of strong mind, who had begun her reign as a vehement partisan of the Whigs. Under Albert's influence she came to perceive that in public at least she must be impartial and place her trust in whichever Minister could command a majority in the House of Commons.

Prince Albert shouldn't get all the credit for teaching Victoria that the Tories could be just as loyal as she believed Melbourne's Whigs to have been.

Melbourne devoted much time to trying to make Victoria a bipartisan monarch but the country had turned against the Whigs. In 1841 they lost four by-elections, one after the other. In May they lost a budget motion in the House. On 4 June, there was a motion of no-confidence in the government: Melbourne lost it by one vote. On 28 August there was another defeat and Melbourne rose in the Lords to announce that the Whig government would resign.

The end had come and in his letter to the Queen, Melbourne allowed his emotions to show through. 'Lord Melbourne,' he wrote, 'will ever consider the time during which Your Majesty is good enough to think that he has been of service to Her Majesty the proudest as well as the happiest part of his life.'

CHAPTER FIFTY

1841–1853

———— ❖ ————

In September 1841, the year after the penny postage stamp was introduced, Sir Robert Peel once more became Prime Minister. Peel's Cabinet was a conservative group with a small 'c'; some in his Administration had resigned from Government in 1834 over Catholic Emancipation – and that was a Whig Administration – but, although care must still be taken when labelling political parties, it was at about this time that the Tories began to be thought of as Conservative with a capital 'C'.

It was also at this point that a new cast stepped onto the Westminster stage: almost all the great names of the rest of the century had now taken their places and one by one they came forward: Derby the protectionist Conservative; Palmerston who started the Opium War and would become the first Liberal Prime Minister; Gladstone, soon to be President of the Board of Trade, and Prime Minister four times. And Disraeli, Victoria's favourite Prime Minister.

But for the next five years Robert Peel, the man who first organized the Metropolitan Police, would preside with considerable purpose over all his departments. That may now sound pretty obvious but the role of Prime Minister was little more than 100 years old and the authority of the office was still developing. Peel's predecessor, Melbourne, was regarded by the Tories as someone who gave the Government no central control; he just allowed the various departments to get on with it. The importance given to the office of a twentieth-century Prime Minister hadn't really been approached until towards the end of Lord Liverpool's premiership in the 1820s. Liverpool had believed that the Cabinet should be a body for collective decision making not, as it had been, a number of departments and individuals who simply did what they wanted to do.

And there was another aspect of premiership which a modern-day Prime Minister doesn't have to worry about: the monarchy. Although the sovereign's powers were decreasing, he or she was still a considerable political force and often forcibly expressed fear or distaste for one or other of the political parties, as Victoria had during her first couple of years on the throne, for the Tories – especially Peel and his Tories.

Peel recognized the vulnerability of government to royal whim, and the often-sensed Parliamentary politicians' indifference to the authority of almost any government leader. However the Victorian constitutional historian, Walter Bagehot, described Sir Robert Peel as the best leader of the Commons of his (Bagehot's) time. Victoria thought him a cold fish and so he was, in public at least. He was the son of a very wealthy cotton spinner (also called Robert), retained a trace of his earlier Lancastrian accent, recognized his own superb abilities and was sometimes over-aware that he was at the head of a Tory institution founded not on trade, but supposedly upper-class values.

C❖Peel, unlike Melbourne, had given the Queen an impression of awkwardness and coldness of manner; but at last in 1841 a General Election brought him to power. Before long he had won her confidence. His abilities now came into full play. He had absolute control of his Cabinet, himself introduced his Government's more important Budgets, and supervised the work of all departments, including that of William Gladstone at the Board of Trade. Tariffs were once again reformed, customs duties greatly reduced, and income tax was re-imposed. These measures soon bore fruit. In 1843 trade began to revive, prosperity returned, and the demand for political reform was stilled. Once again the sky seemed clear at Westminster. But a storm was gathering in Ireland.

The immediate issue was the price of bread. To promote foreign commerce Peel had reduced the import duties on everything except corn. Dear bread, however, meant either high wages or misery for the masses, and Peel gradually realized that cheap imported food could alone sustain the continued prosperity of the nation.

The question of the Corn Laws had been around for generations; they'd existed in one form or another since the Middle Ages. They were protectionist laws that imposed duties on cheap corn imports to protect British grain prices. In 1815 a Corn Law banned imports until British grain had reached a certain price, indeed an artificially high price. It was unworkable, and a sliding scale was introduced, but not for a decade. But the significance of that law had nothing to do with whether it worked or not.

The Whigs controlled the interests of the majority of political decision makers and the one interest the Whigs had in common was that they were landowners. It wouldn't matter how many times the Corn Laws became an issue, the Whigs would never repeal them. Nor would Peel's own landowning Tories. And so when the 1815 Corn Law was pushed through the House, it was, perhaps, the last time the landowning class in England actually controlled a political decision.

The Anti-Corn Law League was founded in 1839. Its platform was simple: the League accused the protectionist system of having nothing to do with keeping down the price of bread but allowing landowners to get the best prices.

But in Charles Greville's journal for the year the League was established, there is a short note which suggests that the politicians at least thought the matter had once again been side-tracked.

❖The Corn Law question, which appeared so formidable before Parliament met, has lost much of its terrors; and an error committed by one of its champions, Mr Wood of Preston, greatly assisted to damage it. Peel turned against him certain admissions which he had made of the prosperity of the trade, with extraordinary dexterity and effect.

The Anti-Corn-Lawites were so enraged and mortified that they punished their blundering advocate by dismissing him from his post as President of the Manchester Chamber of Commerce; and his constituents invited him to resign. This, and the strong demonstration in favour of the existing system the first night, the divided opinions and indifferences of the Government, and the division made by the Chartists, have placed the Corn Laws in perfect security for this session at least.

Cheap food meant a contented people and, in some ways, really did suppress the need for wage demands. There was also the possibility of counter protection laws in other countries – that is export markets. This did not cheer the landowners, which was something of a dilemma for Peel who had a reputation for doing nothing until he had to. But the Anti-Corn Law League wouldn't go away until the Corn Laws had gone.

C❖It soon exerted a powerful influence on public opinion, and produced two remarkable leaders and organizers who became the Free Trade prophets of nineteenth-century England, Richard Cobden, a calico printer, and John Bright, a Quaker mill-owner. . . . The new penny postage . . . carried circulars and pamphlets cheaply all over the country.

Meetings were held throughout the land. The propaganda was effective and novel: a few simple ideas hammered into the minds of audiences by picked lecturers and speakers. Never had there been such a shrewdly conducted agitation. Monster petitions were sent to Parliament. Cobden persuaded prosperous townspeople to buy forty-shilling freeholds in the county constituencies and thus secure a double vote.

Under the Reform Act, a man who had a freehold worth forty shillings was allowed to vote in the General Election.

C❖This so increased the number of Anti-Corn-Law electors that, instead of only petitioning Parliament from outside, the League started influencing it from within.

The League was far from unopposed outside government. The Chartists, for example, who are sometimes called the forerunners of socialism, were agitating for political and social reform. They were not on the side of the League because they, along with many others, saw the League as a tool of the industrialists who were no friends of Chartism. In fact this threat of something more than legislative reform may have directly encouraged Peel to agree to get rid of the Corn Laws.

C❖England's trade and prosperity demanded the abolition of the Corn Laws, but at least half [Peel's] supporters were landowners, and such a step would wreck the Conservative Party. By 1843, however, Peel was determined to act. His position was very difficult, for some of his followers felt he had betrayed them once already over Catholic Emancipation. But he was sure of himself. Perhaps he believed that his personal ascendancy would carry the majority with him; but he needed time to convince his party, and time was denied him.

In August 1845, the potato crop failed in Ireland. Famine was imminent and Peel could wait no longer, but when he put his proposals to the Cabinet several of his colleagues revolted and in December he had to resign. The Whig leader, Russell, refused to form an administration, and Peel returned to office to face and conquer the onslaught of the Tory Protectionists.

His own party was now turning on him. The fight to stop the repeal of the Corn Laws would strip the Tories of any cohesion Peel had hoped to preserve. And the man who led the Tory Protectionists and attacked Peel was the son of a Spanish Jew who had only been an MP for nine years. His name was Benjamin Disraeli.

Chartists, Protectionists, landowners and industrialists clashed in the furious debate over the repeal of the Corn Laws. The landowners said the League was backed by industrialists who wanted cheap corn, and therefore cheap bread, so that workers had one less good reason to demand higher wages.

The Chartists who wanted social and political reform were against the League, saying that if prices collapsed then agricultural workers would be sacked and they'd flood the already overcrowded labour market.

The labourers were suspicious of the League because it was run by the middle classes.

Peel, who knew that lifting the tariffs was inevitable, was opposed by the Whigs, and by people in his own party – the new Tories, the Protectionists. And there was Disraeli.

Disraeli had become a member of a group called Young England. They opposed Robert Peel and saw themselves as the future of Tory politics. The then Home Secretary, Sir James Graham, believed that Young England was nothing, but that somehow Disraeli made it appear important.

❖With respect to Young England, the puppets are moved by Disraeli, who is the ablest man among them: I consider him unprincipled and disappointed, and in despair he has tried the effect of bullying. I think with you that they will return to the crib and prancing, capering and snorting; but a crack or two of the whip may hasten and insure their return. Disraeli alone is mischievous; and with him I have no desire to keep terms. It would be better for the party if he were driven into the ranks of our open enemies.

Graham and Peel had no doubts about Disraeli's character and motives when the latter had the cheek to write to Graham asking for a sinecure for James Disraeli, his brother. Graham was hardly likely to say yes and told Peel what had happened. Peel's response says everything about his distaste for Disraeli.

❖I am very glad Mr Disraeli has asked for an office for his brother. It is a good thing when such a man puts his shabbiness on record. He asked me for an office for himself, and I was not surprised that being refused he became independent and a patriot. But to ask favours after his conduct last session is too bad. However, it is a bridle in his mouth.

But the Party was indeed changing as Disraeli had warned. And it is from about this time that the Conservatives, in a group which might be recognizable today, began to emerge. In 1843 the whole structure of British society was under stress. There was violence in the towns and people were killed, including two policemen. In Ireland, Daniel O'Connell and a young Irish Protestant group called Young Ireland were pushing for independence (although O'Connell, a pacifist, broke with them when they advocated what would now be called terrorist tactics).

And on 20 January Drummond, Peel's secretary, was assassinated because the murderer thought he was the Prime Minister himself.

It was against this background, and supported by the editor of *The Times*, John Walter, that Disraeli saw his chance to show the public that he was wise enough to warn that the repeal of the Corn Laws would split the Party, and that he was the man to speak for the landowning and agricultural interests of the people.

In a speech to his constituents, Disraeli told them that they must understand that it was the landed, not the manufacturing, gentry who had made the nation.

❖It is an immense element of political power and stability. . . . And this, gentlemen, is the reason why you have seen an outcry raised against your Corn Laws. Your Corn Laws are merely the outwork of a great system fixed and established upon your territorial property, and the only object the Leaguers have in making themselves masters of the outwork is that they may easily overcome the citadel.

Disraeli now had the confidence of all the Protectionists, particularly as they sensed victory. His own party was shambling from one internal crisis to another, but the Protectionists refused to reduce hostilities.

Peel was in an impossible position. He believed the economic situation demanded the repeal of the Corn Laws. It followed, to his way of thinking, that the Party must therefore support these arguments otherwise it would be done for. He judged also that Protectionism would prove so unworkable that the Protectionists themselves would abandon their campaign. In this he was correct, but he never saw it happen. And so it was now Disraeli's moment to lead the attack on the Prime Minister.

C❖[Disraeli] denounced him not so much for seeking to abolish the Corn Laws as for betraying his position as head of a great party. If Peel, he declared, believed in the measure he should resign, as a large section of his party was traditionally pledged to oppose it. The wilful destruction of a great party by its leader was a political crime, for the true working of English politics depended on the balance of parties and if a leader could not convince his colleagues he should withdraw. Thus Disraeli. But Peel maintained that his duty to the nation was higher than his duty to his party, and he believed it was his mission to carry the abolition of the Corn Laws.

And Peel explained that this was far more than a confrontation over what should or should not be on the statute books. In a letter, Peel wrote:

❖Protectionists indeed! To close their eyes to the result of every commercial experiment that has been made, to find every one of their predictions falsified, to disregard the state of public opinion, to call the Corn Laws a labourer's question, and yet listen to the appalling facts as to the condition for years past of the labourers of Dorsetshire . . . to be willing to encounter the tremendous risks of two bad harvests and recurrence of such a state of things in Paisley and Stockport as was witnessed in the winters of 1841 and 1842; not to see that the Corn Laws would . . . be swept away with dishonour on the demand of the starving population – this is to be a Protectionist!

And the Bill went forward. Its sentiment was unambiguous. It would cut all import tariffs on grain – barley, oats and wheat – to a peppercorn sum: one shilling. On 25 June 1846 the Corn Laws were repealed. But on the same night as the Bill went through Disraeli and his friends, with no regard for the Party, turned on Peel. This was simple, bitter, revenge.

The subject was Ireland. Peel understood the so-called Irish Question better than most. In his twenties, he had, for six years, been in Liverpool's government as Secretary for Ireland. As Prime Minister, he accepted the enormity of his task. This is how he described it.

❖The problem of peaceably governing seven millions of people, and maintaining intact the Protestant Church Establishment for the religious instruction and consolation of one million. Great and comprehensive interests, apart from those immediately connected with religion, are involved with the maintenance of that establishment.

It was a sentiment recognized by successive generations of ministers and prime ministers. But the extent of that problem would claim him as it did later politicians. In 1846 the island of Ireland was almost destitute. The Corn Laws could do little for the people. There was a grain famine in Ireland and England which imports could hardly replace. Then in a few months there was a new disaster.

The potato famine began in the spring and the blight had spread across Ireland by the summer. Four million people in Ireland lived almost entirely on potatoes and relief work couldn't cope. Where it might have succeeded there was corruption. More than 100,000 Irish people migrated to America in 1846 alone, and in the following five years perhaps one million died. And from all this, understandably, came violence. Violence from the disaffected, the poor, and from the people who capitalized on it all.

It was this situation that faced Peel at the same time as the Corn Law debate in London. He was determined to act quickly and so he asked for what would now be called Emergency Powers to deal with the agrarian violence in Ireland. The legislation to get these powers was called a Coercion Act. It was reasonable to ask for such a Bill to go through the House. It should have had a bi-partisan passage.

The Protectionists had never opposed the idea. But on the night that Peel got his Corn Laws repeal through, Disraeli and his friends wanted revenge. They voted against the Coercion Bill and Peel lost it by seventy-three votes. Disraeli and the Protectionists were delighted. Four days later, on 29 June 1846, Peel was forced to resign.

C❖Peel had been the dominating force and personality in English politics since the passing of the great Reform Bill. Whether in Opposition or in office, he had towered above the scene. He was not a man of broad and ranging modes of thought, but he understood better than any of his contemporaries the needs of the country, and he had the outstanding courage to change his views in order to meet them. It is true that he split his party, but there are greater crimes than that. The age over which he presided was one of formidable industrial advance. It was the Railway Age. By 1848 some 5000 miles of railroads had been built in the United Kingdom. Speed of transport and increasing output were the words of the day. Coal and iron production had doubled. Engineering was making great, though as yet hesitating, strides. All the steps were being taken, not by Government, but by enterprisers [sic] throughout the country, which were to make Britain the greatest industrial Power of the nineteenth-century world. Peel had a practical sense of these vast developments. Free trade, he knew, was no cure-all for the pangs and anguish of a changing society. But the days of the land owning predominance were doomed. Free trade seemed essential to manufacture, and in manufacture Britain was entering upon her supremacy. All this Peel grasped. . . . Of his own methods of government he once said, 'The fact is, people like a certain degree of obstinacy and presumption in a Minister. They abuse him for dictation and arrogance, but they like being governed.' High words perhaps, but they fitted the time.

Peel never became the elder statesman which he, and the nation, deserved. Four years later, in 1850, he was riding in Green Park in London, when he fell from his horse and died. Disraeli heard the news and thought it a great event. Yet it was Gladstone who later remarked that Peel had died at peace with mankind, even with Disraeli. 'The last thing he did,' said Gladstone, 'was to cheer Disraeli. It was not a very loud cheer, but it *was* a cheer.'

But the Tories – the Conservatives – were so split among themselves that there was no way they could hope to form a government. And so the new Prime Minister was a Whig – Lord John Russell. He was to be the last Whig Prime Minister because at this point a new, important, homogeneous political group began to emerge. It was a mixture of the disciples of Robert Peel (Peelites), of Whigs, and of Radicals, all of whom, in the 1840s and 1850s, came to feel politically homeless. They coalesced into one of the two major parties in British politics between the 1860s and the 1920s – the Liberals. The Liberals didn't come into being on one particular day at Westminster, but it was then that people began talking about Liberals, particularly the disaffected Whigs, Radicals and Conservatives.

By now, Queen Victoria had reigned for a decade. She and Prince Albert already had five children, and now, after Peel's resignation, she had a new Prime Minister.

C❖The Whigs were in power under Lord John Russell, whose family had served the State since the days of Henry VII. After three and a half centuries of generally smiling fortune the Russells and their friends and connections had acquired an assurance that they knew best how to govern the country in its true interests. Whatever novel agitations might spread among working men in the industrial towns, who as yet enjoyed few votes, the Whig leaders pursued their reasonable, moderate, and undemocratic courses. Lord John's Government, with a few upsets, survived for six years. It achieved little of lasting note, but it piloted Britain through a restless period when elsewhere in Europe thrones were being overturned and revolutions multiplied.

The Tories for their part were irreconcilably split. The faithful followers of Peel and Free trade . . . were content to let the Whigs bear the heat of the day. . . . The opponents of the Peelites, the old Tories, were led by Lord Stanley, soon to be Lord Derby . . . Derby was increasingly assisted in the House of Commons by his lieutenant, Disraeli, whose reputation for brilliance was growing faster than his capacity for inspiring trust. It was Disraeli's gradual task over these years to persuade the Tories to abandon their fidelity to the Corn Law tariff and to work out a new and more broadly based Conservative policy.

This was a period of widespread social, political and Constitutional reform, which went far beyond the personal and political ambitions of men like Disraeli, Palmerston, Gladstone and Russell. This was a Britain which was changing the way it earned its living, expanding its interests abroad and expanding its social and religious consciousness. It was a Britain that was building railways, outposts of empire and neo-Gothic churches. It was a period when men were rejoicing in progressive ideas and technologies, and when some of the worst iniquities of the nineteenth century were being questioned.

In the 1840s, it was commonplace to find children down the pits. In Leicestershire for example, for every 1000 males employed in coal mining, more than 400 were described as children and young persons. The figure was the same in Derbyshire, and in Yorkshire and Pembrokeshire the ratio of children to adults employed was higher. This is an extract from the Commission on the Labour of Women and Children in Mines.

❖From the whole of the evidence which has been collected, and of which we have thus endeavoured to give a digest, we find, in regard to Coal Mines:

That instances occur in which Children are taken into these mines to work as early as four years of age . . . while from eight to nine is the ordinary age at which employment in these mines commences.

That a very large proportion of the persons employed in carrying on the work of these mines is under thirteen years of age.

That in several districts female Children begin to work in these mines at the same early ages as the males.

That the nature of the employment which is assigned to the youngest children, generally that of trapping, requires that they should be in the pit as soon as the work of the day commences, and according to the present system, that they should not leave the pit before the work of the day is at an end. . . .

That in the districts in which females are taken down into the coal mines both sexes are employed together in precisely the same kind of labour, and work for the same number of hours; that the girls and the boys, and the young men and the young women, and even married women and women with child, commonly work almost naked, and the men, in many mines, quite naked; . . .

That, in the East of Scotland, a much larger proportion of Children and Young Persons are employed in these mines than in other districts, many of whom are girls; and that the chief part of their labour consists in carrying coals on their backs up steep ladders.

And although there is a feeling in this report that the mine owners were unthinking and exploitative, there is too a line which suggests that sometimes the society itself was cruel.

❖The younger Children are roughly used by their older companions; while in many mines the conduct of the adult colliers to the Children who assist them is harsh and cruel; the persons in authority in these mines, who must be cognizant of this ill-usage, never interfering to prevent it, and some of them distinctly stating that they do not conceive that they have any right to do so.

And, to add to all this, fatal accidents were frequent. A Mines Act was passed which, in theory, stopped females going underground and said that boys under the age of ten shouldn't be employed. But the one group who might have helped the wider cause of children, did not. The move to give factory children better education (its proposers had the lucrative textile industries in mind) was opposed by a petition of two million signatures from the Non-Conformist churches. They believed that education would be a chance for the Established Church to influence youngsters. The Bill that did get through the House did little more than limit the working day of eight to thirteen-year-olds to six and a half hours. Nothing was done to remove the dreadful conditions in the factory schools.

The ambition of reformers was to make sure that children and females didn't have to work more than ten hours a day. But for the moment, this couldn't be allowed through because industry relied so much on these two groups that restricting their hours to ten would mean that no machinery would operate for longer than that.

But, by 1847, a Ten Hour Bill got through. Ironically, one reason it did so was that Robert Peel opposed it. The Protectionists, who had fought Peel to his political death with the Corn Laws, simply voted for it because Peel was against it. Also, by 1847, many mills were running for less than ten hours a day anyway. And people who worked fewer hours were healthier and suffered less stress; the result was greater efficiencies from the labour force and the fears of lost production weren't realized. And, in 1851, the Royal School of Mines was set up to train men as inspectors to monitor and enforce the industrial reform that was now irrevocably under way.

Throughout Europe in the late 1840s there was a change in social as well as constitutional attitudes. There were revolutions in France, Germany, Austria and Italy (although Italy was still a collection of states and would not be a country as it is now until the 1860s).

In Britain Charles Dickens published *Dombey and Son*, William Thackeray *Vanity Fair*, Macaulay his *History of England* and Charlotte Brontë her *Jane Eyre*. And in November 1847 two men were commissioned, at a secret meeting in London, to write 'A detailed theoretical and practical programme of the Party'. The document was written in German and translated into English by Miss Helen Macfarlane. That done, it was ready to be published in London in 1850. The two men were Karl Marx and Friedrich Engels, and the document was called 'The Manifesto of the Communist Party'.

C❖The turmoil in Europe was viewed in England with sympathetic interest, but it went unmatched by any comparable disturbance. The Chartist movement, for some time languishing, took fresh courage from the Republican example in France. It was also stirred by a new economic crisis at home. There was half-hearted talk of revolution, but in the end it was decided to present a new petition to Parliament, reiterating all the old Chartist demands. . . . Such was the measure of revolutionary feeling in London in 1848.

In the same year . . . Macaulay [in his *History of England*] . . . set out to show that the story of England since the Whig Revolution of 1688 was one of perpetual and limitless [physical, moral and intellectual] advance. . . . This was a heartening note, much appreciated by contemporary readers. Optimism reigned throughout the land.

Not everyone shared this optimism, certainly an Irishman called William Hamilton didn't. In May, 1849, Hamilton took a pistol and fired at Queen Victoria as she was driving in Hyde Park. The Queen was in no danger, the gun wasn't loaded, but Hamilton was deported to Australia for seven years. Hamilton wasn't the first would-be assassin of Victoria. There were seven attempts on her life.

The first came one evening in 1840, when she and Prince Albert were driving to Belgrave Square to see her mother. Edward Oxford, 'an impudent, horrid little vermin of a man' as Viscount Melbourne called him, fired two pistols. Oxford was charged and found guilty but insane, and sent to a lunatic asylum. What was never established was his motive. There was some evidence that he had been put up to it by agents of Ernest, King of Hanover. Certainly if Oxford had succeeded, then Ernest would have become king.

Two years later, John Francis, the son of a stage carpenter at Covent Garden, tried. His pistol misfired. He was condemned to be hanged but was, instead, deported. Two days after Francis's reprieve from execution, a hunchback by the name of John Bean fired a pistol loaded with paper and tobacco. He got eighteen months. In 1850, a one-time Hussar, Robert Pate, attacked Victoria with his walking stick. She was knocked unconscious. He appears to have been unbalanced and was, like Hamilton, deported. Victoria later wrote that this was the worst of all attacks. 'It is very hard and very horrid that I, a woman, should . . . be unable to go out quietly for a drive.'

In 1831 cholera attacked the people of Britain and, for the first time, health boards were set up, and although they fell away once the cholera epidemic died down, the Poor Law commissioners, under their often criticized secretary Edwin Chadwick, later produced a report on sanitary conditions. It showed a nation gravely threatened by a simple lack of sanitary engineering. Another commission in 1844 reported that out of fifty town water supplies, thirty-one were impure. In some towns – Newcastle, for example – fewer than 10% of the houses had their own water supply. The 1848 Public Health Act created a central health board to 'clean up' Britain, but, as predicted, cholera returned. And Chadwick, by now a member of the new health board, was extremely critical of the opposition, or, at best, the inaction of vested interests, and official indifference, to the health board's proposed solutions to most of the nation's ills. One of their reports records that, in some instances, there was organized opposition to their recommendations for a healthier Britain.

The health board recommended the provision of clean water, the setting up of a proper drainage and sewerage system, the introduction of refuse collections and building regulations for air and space in housing. In one building alone, Chadwick and his colleagues had found forty Irishmen and their families living as best they could. Deaths from diseases caused by dirty and overcrowded housing conditions in England were, at that time, greater than those caused by war.

But in spite of the departments set up and the intentions announced, nothing much was actually done until another outbreak of cholera in 1865. And it wasn't until the 1870s, more than twenty years after Chadwick's report, that a local government board was established to oversee the implementing of his original ideas.

But it was possible for such terrible conditions to be ignored in a society where there was also so much progress. When the half century turned, the sense of achievement was greater than the sense of hopelessness. And it was now that Prince Albert turned to Henry Cole, the man who had helped Rowland Hill bring in the penny post. Incidentally, in the 1840s, the penny post opened communications more than anything else in Britain. When it was introduced, about seventy-six million letters went by post. Within just a quarter of a century, that figure had risen to more than 640 million.

Henry Cole was a doer. He made the penny post happen when others didn't want it. He helped set up the Public Record Office and published the first Christmas card.

Now Henry Cole would help Prince Albert set up the Great Exhibition.

C❖In 1849, after opening the new Albert Dock in Liverpool, the Prince had been so much impressed by the surging vigour of British industry, and its maritime cause and consequence, that he adopted with enthusiasm a plan for an exhibition on a far larger scale than had ever been seen before. It would display to the country and the world the progress achieved in every field. It would also be international, proclaiming the benefits of free trade between nations and looking forward to the universal peace which it was then supposed must inevitably result from the unhampered traffic in goods.

Britain was hardly a bringer of universal peace. Her soldiers had been, and still were, fighting – and would continue to fight – as far away as China, and in both hemispheres of the globe. In India, the First Sikh War had been fought three years earlier, the Second Sikh War was just finishing. The First Maori War had just finished after five years, and the conditions were being laid for the Burma Campaign. The First Afghan War had not ended until 1842, and the Crimean War would start within five years. In Africa, there were eleven wars to come in the remaining half of the nineteenth century.

C❖For two years, against considerable opposition, the Prince headed a committee to further his project. In 1851 the Great Exhibition was opened in Hyde Park. Nineteen acres were devoted to the principal building, the Crystal Palace, designed by an expert glass-house gardener, Joseph Paxton. Housing most of the exhibits, and enclosing whole trees within its glass and iron structure, it was to be the marvel of the decade. In spite of prophecies of failure, the Exhibition was a triumphant success. Over a million people a month visited it during the six months of its opening. Nearly 14,000 exhibits of industrial skill and craft were shown, of which half were British.

By the middle of the nineteenth century there were more than twenty-seven million people living in these islands. The nation, or some of it, had gas lighting, photography, Davy's safety lamp, penny postage stamps, and, for the first time, Christmas cards. By the second decade of the century all Jane Austen's novels were published. Malta had been annexed, the Cape of Good Hope taken and

Sir Thomas Raffles had bought Singapore and founded the Zoological Society.

In the 1820s Napoleon died, so did Byron. The Stockton and Darlington Railway opened, Telford's Menai bridge was built, so was Stephenson's Rocket. London University opened in 1828, the same year that Thomas Arnold became headmaster of Rugby School. The Test Acts were abolished and Peel established the Metropolitan Police.

In the 1830s, Cobbett published his *Rural Rides*, Darwin voyaged to the Galapagos Islands, the First Reform Act became law, slavery was abolished, Parliament was burned to the ground and the Tolpuddle Martyrs were transported to Australia. Dickens published his *Sketches by Boz*, the Public Record Office was opened, Fox Talbot showed his first photographs, the Chartist Movement was founded. In 1843 Wordsworth became Poet Laureate. And in 1844 the first ever Co-op was opened (in Rochdale), and the first telegraph line in England was laid. There was much to celebrate at the Great Exhibition. But across Europe the clouds of revolution that had hung over the Continent for half a decade and more burst above France and Italy.

C❖While party affairs at Westminster dwelt gently in flux, Europe succumbed to an anguished spasm. In February 1848 the French monarchy fell. The rule of King Louis Philippe had given prosperity to France, or at least to her middle classes, but it had never been accepted by the adherents of the elder Bourbon line, and it appealed neither to staunch Republicans nor to the Bonapartists, who were still dazzled by the remembered glories of the Empire. A few days of rioting sufficed to eject Louis Philippe, and a government of romantic outlook and Socialist complexion briefly took control. This in turn collapsed, and by the end of the year a Bonaparte had been elected President of France by an overwhelming majority. Thus, after half a lifetime spent in plotting, exile, and obscurity, Prince Louis Napoleon, nephew of the great Emperor, came to power. He owed his position to the name he bore, to the ineptitude of his rivals, and to the fondness of the French for constitutional experiment. . . .

The peoples of Italy had also broken into revolt against both their own rulers and the Austrian occupiers of Lombardy and Venetia.

Italy was still a collection of states and not a single country. Since the middle ages popes and kings of Naples and dukes of Milan had talked of restoring Italy as a kingdom. But France and Spain had fought over her and after the French Revolution, Austria had become the controlling power, directly ruling Lombardy and Venetia. It was Metternich, the Austrian Chancellor, who described Italy as 'only a geographical expression'. It would be another decade before Victor Emmanuel II, the leader of Sardinia-Piedmont, became the first king of a united Italy.

C❖In the Italian provinces enthusiastic conspirators soon found that they could not hold their own against the organized forces of Austria and her allies. . . . The Italian revolt ended in failure, but not without arousing a widespread sympathy in Britain, which was benevolently exercised when the next attempt at unity was made.

North of the Alps revolutionary nationalism was also stirring in Germany, Austria, and Poland. The Austrian Chancellor, Metternich, who had dominated Central Europe for forty years, was forced to resign by a revolution in Vienna. This aged pillar of Continental absolutism found refuge in an obscure hotel in the England of the Whigs. The Emperor was obliged to abdicate, leaving the Habsburg throne to a young Archduke, Francis Joseph, destined to live through many tribulations and witness the opening years of the First World War. Czechs, Poles, and Hungarians in turn all took up arms, and their gallant risings were eventually suppressed only with the cordial help of the Tsar of Russia. In Germany itself the minor monarchs were thrown into disarray, and some into exile, by rebellions and demonstrations.

In Britain the Prime Minister Lord John Russell tried to preserve what was effectively the last Whig Government Britain would ever see. And this uncertainty, together with what was happening in Europe, especially Eastern Europe, would lead to Britain going to war with Russia.

The Queen was jealous of her Constitutional position in the government of her Kingdom. This extended to foreign policy and for five years now, Victoria had been angry with the man who would soon be her Prime Minister, Lord Palmerston. Palmerston did not consult the Queen on foreign affairs as she thought he should. Victoria wrote to Lord John Russell.

❖With reference to the conversation which the Queen had with Lord John Russell the other day, and Lord Palmerston's disavowal that he ever intended any disrespect to her by the various neglects of which she has had so long and so often to complain, she thinks it right, in order to prevent any mistake for the future, shortly to explain what it is she expects from her Foreign Secretary. She requires,

One: That he will distinctly state what he proposes in a given case, in order that the Queen may know as distinctly to what she has given her Royal sanction;

Two: Having once given her sanction to a measure, that it be not arbitrarily altered or modified by the Minister; such an act she must consider as failing in sincerity towards the Crown, and justly to be visited by the exercise of her Constitutional right of dismissing that Minister.

She expects to be kept informed of what passes between him and the

Foreign Ministers before important decisions are taken, based upon that intercourse; to receive the Foreign Despatches in good time, and to have the drafts for her approval sent to her in sufficient time to make herself acquainted with their contents before they must be sent off. The Queen thinks it best that Lord John Russell should show this letter to Palmerston.

Of course he did and Palmerston agreed to his Queen's wishes. That might have been the end of the matter had Palmerston not gone his own, sometimes undiplomatic, way once again. In December 1851 there was a *coup d'état* in Paris and the Queen made it clear that Britain should express no opinion of the event and that the ambassador to Paris, Lord Normamby, should understand this.

❖Osborne, December 4, 1851
To Lord John Russell,
The Queen has learnt with surprise and concern the events which have taken place in Paris. She thinks it is of great importance that Lord Normamby should be instructed to remain entirely passive, and take no part whatsoever in what is passing. Any word from him might be misconstrued at such a moment.

The Prime Minister's response was prompt.

❖Downing Street, December 4, 6pm
Lord John Russell presents his humble duty to your Majesty. Your Majesty's directions respecting the state of affairs in Paris shall be followed.

The French President dissolved the Assembly. Palmerston, who believed that increasing antagonism between President and Assembly made this inevitable, approved of the action. The embarrassment was that he told the French representative that he approved and this got back, of course, to Paris, and Normamby. And, via Paris, to the Queen.

❖To Lord John Russell
Osborne, December 13
The Queen sends the enclosed despatch from Lord Normamby to Lord John Russell from which it appears that the French Government pretend to have received the entire approval of the late *coup d'état* by the British Government as conveyed by Lord Palmerston ... The Queen cannot believe in the truth of this assertion, as such an approval given by Lord Palmerston would have been in complete contradiction to the line of strict neutrality and passiveness which the Queen expressed her desire to see

followed with regard to the late convulsion at Paris, and which was approved of by Cabinet.

Palmerston wrote to the Prime Minister admitting his indiscretion. The Prime Minister wrote to the Queen telling her that Palmerston was, as everyone already knew, guilty. And then, just before Christmas 1851, he wrote once more to Palmerston.

❖Woburn Abbey, December 19

My Dear Palmerston,

I have just received your letter of yesterday. No other course is left to me than to submit the correspondence to the Queen, and to ask Her Majesty to appoint a successor to you in the Foreign Office. Although I have often had the misfortune to differ from you in minor questions, I am deeply convinced that the policy which has been pursued has maintained the interests and the honour of the country.

I remain, yours truly, J. Russell

And so Palmerston went and Russell lost his Foreign Secretary. And Britain was once more on the road to battle: an icy, chaotic confrontation of useless heroism and unnecessary suffering. It was called the Crimean War.

CHAPTER FIFTY-ONE

1854–1856

———— ❖ ————

In the late 1840s and early 1850s, the British believed implicitly in their military invincibility and in their ability to put down uprisings in far-off lands. In the 1840s, British troops had fought the First and Second Sikh Wars in India, the First Afghan War, and the First Opium War in China. And now, in 1854, the Crimean War began. The Russians had moved into an area of Eastern Europe which included what is now called Romania and was then part of the Ottoman Empire.

The Ottomans were the Turks. The Russians moved in on the pretext that they were the protectors of Slav Christians. The French and the British saw this Russian action as a portent of Russian designs on the rest of Europe. And the British were still convinced that Russian expansionism could move eastwards and threaten British interests in India.

The Ottoman Empire was huge and rickety, and the Victorians feared the instability that might follow its collapse should Russian adventurism prove irresistible to the Tsar.

C❖The urgency and imminence of such questions were sharpened by the evident determination of Russia to seize the Danubian lands, Constantinople, and the Black Sea. England could not ignore the threat: the shadow of Russia, already a formidable Asiatic Power, appeared to be creeping over India. . . . British diplomacy was confused . . . For it was also necessary to keep an eye on the French, who had ambitions for extending their influence in the Levant.

The most influential policy adviser to the government was Stratford Canning, a cousin of the one-time Prime Minister George Canning, whose understanding of what could happen had been obvious two decades earlier.

C❖[George] Canning had planned to head Russia off from South-East Europe, not by direct opposition, but by founding on the ruins of the Turkish Empire a *bloc* of small independent states who would stand firm and if necessary fight for the sake of their own survival. With such a programme of emancipation he had hoped to associate not only France, but Russia herself. The creation of the kingdom of Greece was the first and only result of his efforts. But twenty years had gone by and the ruling politicians of England . . . reversed the policy of Canning, and now attempted to check Russian expansion by the opposite method of propping up the decaying system of Turkish rule in South-East Europe. In the execution of this plan the Government was much assisted by Stratford Canning . . . Proud, difficult, quick-tempered, he enjoyed immense authority with the Turks.

Canning had come to the conclusion that persuading the Turks to reform the administration of the Ottoman Empire would simply delay its collapse. But other events would hasten what Canning called 'the evil hour'. And the Russian Orthodox belief that it should protect Christian Orthodox Serbs exacerbated the situation.

C❖. . . the Tsar sent his envoy, Menschikoff, to Constantinople to revive his claims for a general protectorate over the Christians in the Turkish Empire. This, if granted, would have given Russia authority over the many millions of Romanians, Serbs, Bulgarians, Greeks and Armenians within the Ottoman domains. The balance of power, for which the British Government always sought in the Near East, as elsewhere, would have been destroyed.

Menschikoff was tactless and his demands angered the Turks. The electric telegraph, recently invented, only reached to Belgrade. [Stratford] was the man on the spot, with considerable freedom from Cabinet control and with strong views on the Russian danger and the need to support Turkey.

Now the political situation in England was in some state of change and difficulty. In 1852, Lord John Russell's Whig government collapsed. In February, the Earl of Derby became Prime Minister. By the end of the year, he too had gone and the Earl of Aberdeen had formed the first Coalition Government in English political history. Lord John was his new Foreign Secretary, but only for a couple of months, although he did stay in the Cabinet as Minister without Portfolio.

The new foreign secretary was *not* the one man who would have made more sense of foreign policy, Palmerston, but another earl, Lord Clarendon. However, Palmerston was influential. Canning relied on his help and on the general anti-Russian feeling in Britain. The Turks, knowing they had Canning's support and believing that any British Government idea of appeasement would fall away if the Russians attacked, rejected all demands from the Tsar. And so, on 2 June 1853, the Government ordered the British Fleet to sail for the Dardanelles.

But the Cabinet could not make up its mind what it really wanted to do next. And although at that point war might have been avoided, what the Turks did next made that impossible.

C❖On October 4 the Sultan declared war on Russia, and soon afterwards attacked the Russians beyond the Danube. Such efforts as Aberdeen and Stratford [Canning had been created the first Viscount Stratford de Redcliffe] could still make for peace were extinguished by a Russian onslaught against the Turkish fleet of Sinope, in the Black Sea. Indignation flared in England, where the action was denounced as a massacre. . . . Aberdeen was accused of cowardice. . . . In February 1854 [Tsar] Nicholas recalled his ambassadors from London and Paris, and at the end of March the Crimean War began, with Britain and France as allies of the Turks. To the last, Aberdeen vacillated. 'I still say that war is not inevitable,' he futilely wrote to Clarendon in February, 'unless indeed, we are determined to have it; which, for all I know may be the case.'

The operations were ill-planned and ill-conducted on both sides. With the exception of two minor naval expeditions to the Baltic and the White Sea, fighting was confined to Southern Russia, where the great naval fort of Sebastopol, in the Black Sea, was selected as the main Allied objective. The necessity for this enterprise was questionable: the Turks had already driven the Russians out of the Danube valley, there was little danger of an attack upon Constantinople, and it was folly to suppose that the capture of Sebastopol would make much impression on the vast resources of Russia. However, the British expeditionary force was encamped in Turkish territory and some use had to be made of it. Orders from London dispatched it to the Crimea against the wishes of its commander, Lord Raglan.

Raglan was sixty-six years old. He had fought, and was wounded, at Waterloo in 1815. He was not a distinguished general and for some reason persisted in calling the enemy the French. However he may be remembered for his style of coat and raglan sleeve. Many of his commanders were about the same age and older, with the exception of his Cavalry Commander, Lord Cardigan, who, apart from leading the charge of the Light Brigade, had the woollen jacket, the cardigan, named after him.

C❖At Balaclava in October, the British cavalry distinguished themselves by two astonishing charges against overwhelming odds. The second of these was the celebrated charge of the Light Brigade, in which 673 horsemen . . . rode up the valley under heavy fire, imperturbably, as if taking part in a review, to attack the Russian batteries. They captured the guns, but only a third of the Brigade answered the first muster after the charge. Lord

Cardigan calmly returned to the yacht on which he lived, had a bath, dined, drank a bottle of champagne, and went to bed. His brigade had performed an inspiring feat of gallantry. But it was due, like much else in this war, to the blunders of commanders. Lord Raglan's orders had been badly expressed and were misunderstood by his subordinates. The Light Brigade had charged the wrong guns.

The Commander who misread the orders was later promoted to Field Marshal. His name was Lord Lucan. As William Howard Russell, the famous correspondent of *The Times,* reported, 'At twenty-five to twelve not a British soldier, except the dead and dying, was left in front of those bloody Muscovite guns.'

It was all a fine nineteenth-century example of useless military heroism. Of the 673 cavalry in that charge, 113 were killed, and 134 wounded. Nearly 500 horses were left for dead in what Tennyson would call 'The Valley of Death'. After the charge, the British and their allies were still determined to take Sebastopol, the great Russian fort on the Black Sea.

But before that could be achieved, the two sides met again, this time at the Battle of Inkerman. On the eve of the battle, a British force of 3600 men faced 15,000 Russians.

C❖It was a desperate infantry action, in which the British soldier proved his courage and endurance. Russian casualties were nearly five times as many as those of the Allies. But Inkerman was not decisive . . . it became plain there was no hope of taking Sebastopol before the spring of 1855.

Dreadful weather took command of the campaign. The soldiers were still in their summer clothes and many had lost their kit altogether.

C❖Amid storms and blizzards the British Army lay, without tents, huts, food, warm clothes, or the most elementary medical care. Cholera, dysentery, and malarial fever took their dreadful toll. Raglan's men had neither transport nor ambulances, and thousands were lost through cold and starvation because it did not occur to the Government of the greatest engineering country in the world to ease the movement of supplies from the port of Balaclava to the camp by laying down five miles of light railway.

The hospital ships running between the Crimea and Constantinople (Istanbul, as it is now called) were hardly safe havens for the wounded. One in ten died on that voyage and in February, half the patients in one died – and by no means all of them from their wounds. And then conditions started to improve, and lives began to be saved. The Government finally woke up to the disaster that would eventually bring them down, and Florence Nightingale and her nurses had arrived in the Crimea. But the scandal of the Crimea could no longer be hidden from the British public. A Commission of Inquiry was set up although its report was not published until the worst was over.

❖Lord Aberdeen has significantly observed that the Government was left in ignorance of the real state of matters in the East. The Ministers, he says, were informed of the condition of the army from public papers and private sources long before they heard it officially, and, not hearing it officially, they discredited the rumours around them. Thus, whilst the whole country was dismayed by the reports, and was eagerly looking for some gleam of official intelligence, the Cabinet was in darkness. ... Mr Sidney Herbert, as Secretary-at-War, had no power to originate anything, but from praiseworthy motives ... undertook to do a great deal which was not the business of his office. Thus, in December, having learnt, from private sources, the deplorable conditions of the hospitals, he wrote to the Commandant, to the Chief Medical Officer, and to the Purveyor, urging and authorizing them to procure whatever might be wanted – assistants, supplies, or additional buildings – promising them his approbation for such outlay, and placing unlimited funds at their disposal.

The Secretary-at-War, Sidney Herbert, wrote to Florence Nightingale and gave her his backing for the actions she believed necessary to relieve the suffering of the soldiers. And the evidence of neglect which faced Miss Nightingale was an equally damning example of bad planning and buckpassing.

❖Your Committee inquired why ships for the conveyance of the sick and wounded had not been prepared at an early period of the war. The unnecessary sufferings of the soldiers, directly referable to this neglect, form one of the most painful portions of the evidence; but on what department responsibility should rest, whether on the office of the Commander in Chief, or of the Secretary-at-War, or the Secretary of State for War, your Committee are unable to decide. Sir James Graham said that the naval Commander in Chief, Vice Admiral Dundas, had authority over the whole of the transports. Lord Raglan had a concurrent authority over this service. Vice Admiral Dundas, on the contrary, alleged that he had nothing to do with the transports. According to his assertions, they were entirely under the management of Lord Raglan, Rear Admiral Boxer, and Captain Christie.

The message was clear: no one would accept responsibility. But the lessons were learned, and the effects of Miss Nightingale and her staff are best summed up in the report's conclusions.

❖Your Committee, in conclusion, cannot but remark that the first real improvements in the lamentable condition of the hospitals at Scutari are to be attributed to private suggestions, private exertions, and private benevolence. Miss Nightingale, at the suggestion of the Secretary-at-War, with admirable devotion, organized a band of nurses, and undertook the care of the sick and wounded. A fund, raised by public subscription, was administered by the proprietors of *The Times* newspaper. By these means much suffering was alleviated, the spirits of the men were raised, and many lives were saved.

Raglan resigned and then, ten days later, died, and in September 1855, Sebastopol at last fell. In March 1856, yet another Paris Peace Treaty was signed. The war was over and Britain, under its new Prime Minister, Lord Palmerston, got on with the business of industrial and economic expansion and, as she expanded her trading interests abroad, there were extra mouths to feed at home.

The population of England and Wales had grown from less than fourteen million at the 1831 census, to nearly eighteen million in 1851. In the same period, Scotland's population grew from 2.2 million to 2.8 million. In Ireland, the population had fallen from 7.8 million in 1831 to 6.5 million at the eve of the Crimean War – and, for the moment, that downward trend continued. The famine had had its effect, but emigration now contributed greatly. In Scotland alone, more than 10% of the population was Irish born. Famously, the biggest movement was to America. But those seeking a new life in the New World weren't all Irish. In 1850, the number of Americans who'd been born in Great Britain was reckoned to be 1.3 million.

The 1851 census provides a picture of the nation, and of what the people of Britain were doing for a living halfway through the century. The biggest single group was still agricultural workers – nearly one and a half million of them. Then came domestic servants – about one million. Here, in extracts from a report in the 1851 census, is a simplified picture of the nation's workers.

Cotton calico, manufacture, printing and dyeing:	501,565
Boot and shoe makers:	more than 274,000
Hat and dress makers:	268,000
Coal miners:	219,000
Washerwomen, manglers and laundry keepers:	146,091
Errand boys, porters and messengers:	101,000
Grocers:	86,000
Gardeners:	81,000
Engine and machine makers:	48,000
Railway labourers:	34,306

Pedlars:	30,500
Horsekeepers, grooms and jockeys:	29,000
Nurses:	25,500
Straw hat and bonnet makers:	22,000
Anglican clergymen:	18,587
Policemen:	18,348
Surgeons and apothecaries:	15,163
Stay makers:	13,700
Hair dressers and wig makers:	more than 12,000

The census also reveals something about one class that was expanding rapidly in Victorian society: civil servants. There were now 31,000 of them. In 1853 a commission reported to the Government that there was a need to improve the upper echelons of the Civil Service. Its principal authors, Sir Stafford Northcote and Sir Charles Trevelyan, put forward the idea of recruiting by examination. They recognized that just as a man expected results if he paid any professional – a lawyer, for example – then the tax payer had the right to a similar professional expectation from the Civil Service. The nineteenth-century Civil Service mandarins pointed out that setting an examination didn't necessarily test a man's character. And surely the best people would not care to sit for a public examination. But Northcote and Trevelyan had identified a widely recognized weakness in the nation's bureaucracy.

Reform too was under way in another area of English life associated with scandal, corruption and privilege – the Established Church. By the 1850s, the Church had undergone administrative and constitutional reform in rather the same public manner as had the Civil Service. The Roman Catholics remained in a minority with restricted civil rights and there was a larger minority group, the Dissenters, or Non-Conformists: those who chose not to conform to the Established Church.

What people actually believed is hard to judge but there is a perception that, in most rural areas, superstition was a greater influence on lower-class country-men and women than the parson's promises of heaven or his threats of hell. However, contemporary opinion suggests that by the 1850s the Church and the people were well pleased with each other.

C❖Many millions, more than half the total population, were regular attenders at church and chapel, though church-goers were fewer among the very poor. Religious debate was earnest, sometimes acrimonious, but the contests it bred were verbal. Civil strife for the sake of religion was a thing of the past. . . . When the Roman Catholic Church re-established its hierarchy of bishops in England there was vehement commotion and protest in London, but nothing amounting to riot.

And while High and Low Churches may have striven for men's souls, the liberal wing of the Church strove for reform. This was the age of reform of almost any institution and the anomalies in church administration made it an obvious target. Bishops had done very well from endowments, some making tens of thousands of pounds a year. One archbishop is said to have died with an estate in excess of £1 million.

Liberal churchmen wanted to wipe clean the Black Book of financial management which suggested that the church revenues in England were greater than those in the whole of Europe. And there were those who wanted reform because they believed the Church had lost its religious way. Yet it took government-sponsored commissions and legislation to make basic changes, such as those forbidding a clergyman to hold more than two livings.

The number of pews and churches needed for these reformed characters to preach salvation or damnation in were contained in the 1851 census.

❖Various computations have been made respecting the number of sittings proper to be furnished for a given population. With respect to towns, it has been thought by some that accommodation for 50% would be sufficient; while others have considered that provision for not less than 75% should be afforded. The maximum for rural districts is put lower than for towns; the distance of the church from people's residences operating as an unavoidable check upon attendance. But . . . the rural population will consist of only those who live remote as well from villages containing churches as from towns, in fact, of only those who are remoter from any place of worship, the proportion deemed to be sufficient for a town may be applied, with very slight reduction, to the whole of England . . . and, according to the best authorities, this proportion seems to lie between 50% and 60% of the entire community.

Which pleased not only the church, but the building trade. In the twenty years up to 1851, more than 2000 new churches were built. The nineteenth-century desire to erect what would eventually become nationwide neo-Gothic memorials to God and, of course, the Victorians was under way.

In 1855 the Coalition Government of George Gordon, the fourth Earl of Aberdeen, collapsed. It did so over an issue of principle: its management, or rather mismanagement, of the Crimean War. The Cabinet refused to accept the motion in the House for a Commission of Inquiry into the 'condition of the army and the supply services'. Lord John Russell, the former Prime Minister who was, by then, Lord President of the Council, protested and resigned. The House voted against the Government by more than 150 votes. And so Aberdeen's Cabinet, which had included Gladstone as Chancellor of the Exchequer and Palmerston, out of place as Home Secretary, had to go.

The Queen was unhappy. She liked Aberdeen and it was thanks to him that the royal family came by Balmoral Castle. Aberdeen had inherited the lease from his brother and the Castle was said to sit in one of the driest areas of Scotland – something to do with the rain clouds breaking to the west. This attracted the Queen. Without seeing anything more than water colours of the castle, the Queen bought the lease from Aberdeen in the late 1840s. 'It was,' she wrote in her journal on first seeing it, 'so calm, so solitary, it did one good as one gazed around; and the pure mountain air was most refreshing. All seemed to breathe freedom and peace, and to make one forget the world and its sad turmoils.'

The most obvious man to be Prime Minister was Palmerston but the Queen didn't much care for that. The Conservatives held a majority in the House and so she called on the Earl of Derby. The fourteenth Earl was then in his later fifties. He'd entered Parliament as a Whig in the 1820s, served as Secretary for Ireland, worked for the abolition of slavery, and then had joined Disraeli and the ranks of the Protectionists, the Conservative group who'd brought down the Peel government. Briefly in 1852, Derby had become Prime Minister. If there had to be a change, then it would have to be Derby. Disraeli was delighted. This was a chance of office. He, Disraeli, even threatened to break up the party if Derby didn't accept the challenge. But Derby knew that any government he formed wouldn't last long if it was without Gladstone, Sidney Herbert and most important of all Palmerston. Derby couldn't count on Gladstone. He detested Disraeli (he actually said Disraeli inspired in him a sense of revulsion) and would never sit in Cabinet with him. He and Herbert could not forgive the way in which Disraeli had brought about Peel's downfall. That left Palmerston who wouldn't serve under Derby.

So with Derby failing to get the three men he needed, the Queen tried Lord John Russell. Although well regarded, there wasn't enough support for him. And so, the first and obvious choice, Palmerston, at the age of seventy-one became Prime Minister. Disraeli was very Disraeli about the whole affair. He described Palmerston as an imposter, an old painted pantaloon. A man utterly exhausted. But not everyone shared this sense of spite. Sidney Herbert pointed out that people may criticize and dislike Palmerston but he was, said Herbert, 'the only public man in England who has a name'.

Palmerston's peerage was Irish. At twenty-two he'd become a Tory MP and by the age of twenty-five, a junior minister. By 1830 he was in charge of foreign policy. He was Lord Grey's foreign secretary and then Melbourne's. After the fall of the Peel government, Palmerston was back as Lord John Russell's foreign secretary. But he lost his job because he simply disregarded the wishes of the Queen and therefore the government. Now, four years after forcing Lord John Russell to sack him, the Queen had Palmerston as her Prime Minister.

How would she get on with this man she called 'Pilgerstein'? The answer was, very well indeed. Palmerston took charge of the war and proved to be a good war leader. Victoria recognized this. He, in turn, recognized her intellect and her careful enthusiasm. Furthermore, Palmerston changed his mind about Prince Albert. Until this point, he hadn't held Albert in much regard. Now he saw him as a thoughtful adviser. 'How fortunate,' Palmerston once remarked, 'it has been for the country that the Queen married such a prince'.

And by the end of Palmerston's first year as Prime Minister, and the end of the Crimean War, Victoria had completely changed her attitude towards the man she had dismissed for going his own, and not her, way. 'Of all the prime ministers we have had,' said Victoria, 'Lord Palmerston is the one who gives the least trouble, and is most amenable to reason and most ready to adopt suggestions.' What her once beloved Melbourne (by now seven years dead) would have thought of such praise, can only be guessed at.

Palmerston was now favoured statesman. And to prove so publicly, Victoria raised her former, and recalcitrant, foreign secretary to the Garter. But his practical approach to government was disliked by many of the younger Members of the House of Commons.

C❖Disraeli, chafing on the Opposition benches, vented his scorn and irritation on this last of the eighteenth-century politicians. . . . Peel's disciples and followers were no less despairing and powerless. So long as leadership remained in the hands of Palmerston, Russell, and the Whig nobility, there could be little hope of advance towards the Liberalism of which they dreamed.

The Whigs were truly a well bred but dying breed. It was Sidney Herbert who had written the first of many drafts of their obituary.

❖The Whigs are incurable in their superstitions about ducal houses. I see no prospect of the formation of an efficient party, let alone Government, out of the chaos of the Opposition benches. No one reigns over or in it but discord and antipathy. The aristocratic Whigs seem to be nearly used up, and the Party produces no new men, but at the same time complains of the old ones. Middle-aged merchants, shrewd men of business, feel their vanity hurt that they have not the [chance of] refusal of office

As for the Tories:

C❖Disraeli had become the leader of his party in the House of Commons. His struggle for power was hard and uphill. A Jew at the head of a phalanx of country gentlemen was an unusual sight in English politics. After the repeal of the Corn Laws, protection was not only dead, but, as Disraeli himself said, damned, and he and Derby had agreed to discard it as a party principle. But the search for a new theme was long, painful, and frustrating.

Palmerston was the man of the moment, the man who sensed that the country wanted an Inquiry into the mismanagement of the Crimean War and who risked the resignation of two of his Cabinet Ministers – Gladstone and Herbert – in the process. A more innovative Prime Minister might have suffered, but Palmerston was at the pinnacle of his public popularity. And no matter how talented the Peelites (who included Gladstone and Herbert) were, they had no great numbers to support them. And Palmerston had, as Disraeli pointed out, a war, the supreme test of foreign policy and domestic political diversion. Furthermore, Palmerston understood how to exploit the authority of his office. The nineteenth-century constitutional analyst, Walter Bagehot, once described the office of Prime Minister as that of the nation's head master, a person with influence, an authority, a facility in giving a great tone to discussion, or a mean tone, which no other person had. He saw Palmerston as a head master who applied not a mean, but a light tone to the proceedings of Parliament.

Palmerston was twice Prime Minister, and when he won the 1858 General Election, he won it on his personality rather than his policies. Equally, the Party really did accept Palmerston's opinion that no new legislation was necessary. On one occasion he was asked what new ideas he would bring before the House. 'Oh', he said, 'there is really nothing to be done. We cannot go on adding to the Statute Book *ad infinitum* . . . we cannot go on legislating for ever.'

Within a year of bringing the war with Russia in the Crimea to an end, Palmerston, his Government, and most of all, his far-flung soldiers, were about to face a test of great and long-lasting consequence – the Indian Mutiny.

CHAPTER FIFTY-TWO

1857–1863

———— ❖ ————

The British had been in India since 1663 when the East India Company set up in Bengal, having been chased from their other holdings in South East Asia by the Dutch. Bengal had been ruled by the Moguls since 1576. About halfway through the eighteenth century, Clive of India defeated the ruler of Bengal at the Battle of Plassey and the Moguls ceded Bengal to the East India Company. The Company nominated an Indian prince to the throne, but in truth ruled through a British governor – whom, of course, they appointed.

The Indian Mutiny started in 1857. For about twelve months Indians had rebelled against British rule – rule not by the British Government, but by the East India Company. The Company had its own governor, princes in its pocket, its own bureaucracy and, most important, its own army.

C❖The East India Company's Army of Bengal had long been of ill-repute. Recruited mainly in the North, it was largely composed of high-caste Hindus. This was bad for discipline. Brahmin privates would question the orders of officers and NCOs of less exalted caste. [And] . . . the Company's British officers were often of poor quality. . . . By the 1850s, railways, roads, posts, telegraphs, and schools were beginning to push and agitate their way across the countryside, and were thought by many Indians to threaten an ancient society whose inmost structure and spirit sprang from a rigid and unalterable caste system. If everyone used the same trains and the same schools, or even the same roads, it was argued, how could caste survive? . . . Unfounded stories spread that the Government intended to convert India forcibly to Christianity. . . . the introduction of a new type of ammunition provided a spark and focus for the mass of discontent.

. . . rumours began to flow that the cartridges for the new Enfield rifle were greased with the fat of pigs and cows, animals which Moslem and Hindu respectively were forbidden to eat. The cartridges had to be bitten before they could be inserted in the breech. Thus sepoys of both religions would be defiled. There was some truth in the story, for beef-fat had been used in the London arsenal at Woolwich, though it was never used at the Indian factory at Dum-Dum, [where the dum-dum bullet, the soft-nosed cartridge that expands when it enters the target, gets its name from], and as soon as the complaints began no tainted missiles were issued. Nevertheless the tale ran through the regiments in the spring of 1857 and there was much unrest. In April, some cavalry troopers at Meerut were court-martialled and imprisoned for refusing to touch the cartridges, and on May 9 they were publicly stripped of their uniforms. . . . Next night three regiments mutinied, captured the prison, killed their British officers, and marched on Delhi.

Every British family that could be found was killed by the Indians. Now they went to the palace of the aged Bahadur Shah, the retired King of Delhi. He was taken from his home and proclaimed Mogul Emperor. But the people did not rush to his side. For three weeks there was stalemate. But then, and probably too late, the mutiny spread.

C❖At Lucknow, the capital, Henry Lawrence prepared the Residency for what was to be a long and glorious defence. Meanwhile, rightly perceiving that the key to the revolt lay in Delhi, the British mustered such forces as they could and seized the ridge overlooking the city. They were too few to make an assault, and for weeks in the height of summer 3000 troops, most of whom were British, held the fifty-foot eminence against an enemy twenty or thirty times their number. Early in August . . . reinforcements arrived from the Punjab, having marched nearly thirty miles a day for three weeks. Thus animated, the British attacked on September 14 and after six days' street fighting . . . the city fell.

There was a terrible massacre of British and loyal Indians at Cawnpore, and of the survivors – who had been granted safe conduct – all the men were subsequently killed and the women and children were imprisoned and then assassinated.

C❖. . . the British troops took horrible vengeance. Mutineers were blown from the mouths of cannon, sometimes alive, or their bodies sewn up in the skins of cows and swine.

    . . . The recapture of Delhi destroyed all semblance and pretence that the mutiny was a national revolt. Fighting, sporadic but often fierce, continued in the Central Provinces until the end of 1858, but on November 1, the Governor General, 'Clemency' Canning, derisively so called for his mercifulness, proclaimed with truth that Queen Victoria was now Sovereign of all India.

An Act of Parliament took away the East India Company's territories and their soldiers, and gave them to the Crown. A council was established, with a principal Secretary of State, and this took over full government. And to show that it was now Victoria and not the East India Company who ruled, it was at this point that the title Viceroy of India first appeared. People in Britain were encouraged to go to India, to become planters. The railways were extended. Forestry commissions were set up, the judicial system overhauled, canals were dug, irrigation improved. And so a new order was established, a new era in colonial living founded.

The 1850s saw a distinct change in the needs of British political leadership. The old guard still believed that government was best left in the hands of the ruling classes. Government and the House were not places to discuss wage demands and working practices, but grand strategy, and the exercise of sovereign authority. And the middle classes, the nub of the electorate, appeared still to prefer to be ruled by their betters rather than by their peers.

C❖Standing apart both from the Whigs and Derby's Tories were the Peelites, of whom the most notable was William Gladstone. Having started his Parliamentary career in 1832 as a strict Tory, he was to make a long pilgrimage into the Liberal camp. The death of Peel had destroyed his allegiance to Toryism and he too was in search of a new theme. The son of a rich Liverpool merchant with slave-owning interests in the West Indies, Gladstone came from the same class as his old leader, and believed, like him, in the new arguments for Free Trade.

Gladstone was no friend of the slave traders nor owners. In fact his first major speech in the House was made during the debate to do away with slavery. But because his father owned slaves, Gladstone had (to be exceptionally charitable) seen both sides of the argument. In that first speech, he seemed to contradict the much stronger position he would take later in life.

C❖Though admired as an administrator and an orator, his contemporaries considered him wanting in judgment and principle, but in fact, as Palmerston perceived, he was awaking to the political potentialities of the English middle class. 'He might,' he said, 'be called one of the people; he wished to identify himself with them; he possessed religious enthusiasm, and made it powerful over others from the force of his own intellect.' . . . Long years of waiting made Gladstone sure of himself.

It was in this atmosphere that Gladstone became Chancellor of the Exchequer in Aberdeen's coalition government of 1852. Gladstone, who would be remembered as the great Liberal prime minister, entered Parliament as a Tory in 1832. With the exception of a few months, he remained an MP for sixty-three years.

Now, at the age of forty-three, standing in the Commons Chamber, he gave the country his ideas of an economy which would move towards Free Trade, a fairer taxation system and, he hoped, within seven years, the abolition of Income Tax. Here's a fragment of his Budget speech. Gladstone was talking about Income Tax.

❖The Committee will recollect that I said we thought it our duty to look the whole breadth of this difficulty in the face – not to endeavour to escape it, not to endeavour to attenuate, or to understate it, but to face and to settle ... the whole question of the income tax. We propose then to re-enact it for two years, from April 1853 to April 1855 at the rate of seven pence in the pound. From April 1855 to enact it for two more years at six pence in the pound; and then for three more years – I cannot wonder at the smile which I perceive that my words provoke – for three more years, from April 1867 at five pence. Under this proposal, on April 5, 1860, the income tax will expire.

Of course, income tax never was allowed, as Gladstone put it, to expire. By the following year, the Crimean War had started, and just as Kings and Queens had done for centuries, the Government turned to the people to finance the war. Instead of seven pence, then six pence and then five pence, income tax was doubled. Someone had to pay for the Government's miscalculations, particularly in wartime.

The Arrow War – the Second Opium War – began in 1856. A Chinese magistrate ordered the torture and execution of a French missionary in Kwangsi Province, then, in October, the Chinese boarded the *Arrow*. The *Arrow* was a small vessel, owned by a Chinaman, who, because he lived in Hong Kong, had registered the vessel in the colony – it was an early example of the use of flags of convenience.

Some of the ships (they were called Lorchas) were used for piracy and smuggling. The Chinese took twelve of the men who had been aboard the *Arrow* and threw them into prison. The Arrow War was under way and the French and British, perhaps bolder after their defeat of Russia in the Crimea, joined forces to defeat the Chinese – which they did. British gunboats bombarded the Chinese on the banks of the Canton river. The Chinese declared every Englishman an outlaw. In Parliament the Prime Minister, Palmerston, was attacked, called an election and won it with a manifesto of pure jingoism. The British and French, supported diplomatically but not militarily by the Americans and Russians, demanded the right to set up embassies in Peking. Peking was a closed city and the Allies, instead of pretending the opium trade didn't exist, legitimized it and the Chinese could do nothing about it.

In 1860, faced with an Anglo-French army, the Chinese called for a truce but then broke it. A delegation led by Sir Harry Smith Parkes was captured. He was humiliated and starved, others were murdered. In revenge, the British burned down the Emperor's revered Summer Palace. As the *Daily News,* one of the eleven daily papers then printing in London, reported in its 'Foreign Intelligence' column, the best thing the Chinese could do was to learn the lesson that, emperor or no emperor, the British were not to be trifled with. It was a sentiment that the Chinese have continued to ignore.

The new decade (the 1860s) was to be one of continuous upheaval in Europe, religious and moral disturbance in Britain in the aftermath of Darwin's *Origin of Species,* personal tragedy for the monarch when her Consort, Prince Albert, died, and carnage in the United States.

In 1861 the Civil War between the Confederate and Union forces began in America. In the same year, Italy became one nation and Victor Emmanuel II its first King. The two events aren't linked, but they made a powerful contrast that wasn't lost on Europeans. Here was a Europe able at last to celebrate the unity of long-divided peoples, while in America – which seemed to represent everything that was possible for a nation: a truly new world, a land of opportunity – all that seemed about to be destroyed by the very people who had created it.

C❖. . . the prospects of the United States filled America with hope and Europe with envious admiration. The continent had been conquered and nourished. Exports, imports, and, most of all, internal trade, had been more than doubled in a decade. The American mercantile marine outnumbered the ships under the British flag. Nearly £50 million in gold was added to the coinage each year. More than 30,000 miles of railway overcame the vast distances, and added economic cohesion to political unity. Here democracy, shielded by the oceans . . . from European dangers, founded upon English institutions and the Common Law, stimulated by the impulse of the French Revolution, seemed at last to have achieved both prosperity and power. . . . In all material affairs the American people surpassed anything that history had known before.

Yet thoughtful men and travellers had for some years observed the approach of a convulsion which would grip not only the body but the soul of the United States. Of the three races who dwelt in North America, the Whites towered overwhelming and supreme. The Red Men, the original inhabitants . . . were ousted and eclipsed. . . . Almost all the four million negroes were slaves . . . It was said that over 660,000 slaves were held by ministers of the Gospel and members of different Protestant Churches. Five thousand Methodist Ministers owned 219,000 slaves; 6500 Baptists owned 125,000; . . . and so on.

In the 1830s the British Parliament had banned slave owning. The effect of this Act was to reduce the profits of the British planters in the West Indies. Their life style wasn't so unlike those in the American South. Little wonder that the Southerners saw what had happened in the West Indies and became determined that no Federal anti-slavery legislation would go uncontested. In England, the political and moral oppositions to American slavery were inflamed by the publication, in 1852, of Harriet Beecher Stowe's book, *Uncle Tom's Cabin*. That book is not always today seen for what it was in mid-nineteenth century Britain: it was a polemic against slavery. More than one million copies of *Uncle Tom's Cabin* were sold in that first year of publication in England. The only other book to sell more copies was the Bible.

When the intractable Abraham Lincoln was sworn in as President of the United States on 4 March 1861, war was inevitable. The Southern states decided to secede from the Union. The united states were no longer.

In England there were mixed feelings. If the war had been entirely about slavery, then the British would probably have supported the North. But Lincoln had said publicly that he wouldn't interfere in the slavery policies of the Southern states. And so, in Britain, there was a notion that if the issue was not simply slavery, then the Southern states had the right to go their own way. In fact in May 1861, the British officially declared neutrality and made it illegal for British subjects to fight on either side or help supply weapons. Lord John Russell and Gladstone even considered that Britain might have a role as mediator, although there wasn't much Cabinet support for the idea.

And so the war began, with Lincoln's Federal Army expected to quickly bring the Southerners to heel. But Jefferson Davis and his two generals, Robert E. Lee and Stonewall Jackson, were determined and clever soldiers.

C❖. . . opinion in England was curiously divided. The upper classes, Conservative and Liberal alike, generally looked with favour upon the South, and in this view Gladstone concurred. Disraeli, the Conservative leader, was neutral. The Radicals and the unenfranchised mass of the working classes were solid against slavery . . . . The arrest on a British ship, the *Trent,* of the Confederate agents, Mason and Slidell, by a United States cruiser roused a storm. The Foreign Secretary, Lord John Russell, penned a hard dispatch which the Prince Consort persuaded the Prime Minister, Lord Palmerston, to modify. A clause was inserted which enabled the Federal Government without loss of honour to declare their cruiser's action unauthorized. President Lincoln took some persuading, but in the end he sagely remarked 'One war at a time', liberated the captives, and all remained in sullen suspense. Blockade-running, both in cotton outwards and arms inwards, developed on a large scale; but not a single European government received the envoys of the Confederate states. No one in Europe imagined the drama of terrific war which the year 1862 would unfold. None appraised truly the implacable rage of the antagonists. None understood the strength of Abraham Lincoln or the resources of the United States. Few outside the Confederacy had ever heard of Lee or Jackson.

Britain's interest in what was going on in America was more than strategic and political. It was already touching the British where they were most vulnerable – in the economy. The cotton blockade was not taken lightly in Britain. In peacetime, something like 80% of Britain's supply of raw cotton came from the United States. Probably 600,000 of Britain's workers directly and indirectly depended for their livelihoods on the cotton industry. At first, there was little shortage. The record American crop of 1860 had reached Britain before the war started. But eighteen months later, the industry in Lancashire was all but closed down. And the war looked like being a long drawn out business.

What might have been an uprising easily put down became a protracted war, until the resources and resourcefulness of the Federal Armies told. General George Meade beat Lee at Gettysburg in 1863 and the Confederates were forced to surrender at Richmond. Americans fought each other until more than 620,000 soldiers and about 50,000 civilians were killed.

1861 was to be the most miserable year for Queen Victoria. On the morning of 16 March her mother, the Duchess of Kent, died at Frogmore with Victoria at her bedside. The Queen had never before witnessed the death of another human being. The deep distress was overwhelming and for six months the Queen struggled with her grief. Some of her closest friends believed that she was 'determined to cherish her grief'.

And Victoria still saw her husband as the handsome prince she had married twenty-one years earlier, yet, by 1861, he was portly, his hair was going and his dull complexion reflected the anxieties and workload he took so seriously as Prince Consort. He was obviously ill. He suffered bouts of vomiting and high temperatures, his gums were inflamed and his glands swollen. In November, after a visit to Sandhurst to see the new Staff College, he returned to Windsor soaked through, full of rheumatic pains and quite unable to sleep for nights on end. One of the Queen's doctors explained that the Prince was suffering from 'gastric fever'. This was not true, however the reason for telling him this was more than poor diagnosis. They actually believed that the Prince had typhoid, but they well knew his terrible fear of the disease and the seriousness of his illness was hidden from him. Also, the royal physicians, for all their standing, were not particularly celebrated for their accuracy in diagnosing serious illness. It is even possible that Albert had bowel cancer.

But just a week before his death, Queen Victoria's optimism (or was it blindness?) is reflected in a letter to the King of the Belgians.

❖Windsor Castle, December 4, 1861

My Dearest Uncle,

I have many excuses to make for not writing yesterday, but I had a good deal to do, as my poor Albert's rheumatism has turned out to be a regular influenza, which has pulled and lowered him very much. Since Monday he has been confined to his room. It affects his appetite and sleep, which is very disagreeable, and you know he is always so depressed when anything is the matter with him. However, he is decidedly better today, and I hope in two or three days he will be quite himself again. It is extremely vexatious, as he was so particularly well till he caught these colds, which came upon worries of various kinds. . . . Ever your devoted Niece,

Victoria R

Two days before the Prince died, Victoria once again wrote to her uncle, and seemed to believe that Albert was getting better.

❖My Beloved Uncle,

I can again report favourably of our most precious invalid. He maintains his ground well – had another very good night – takes plenty of nourishment, and shows surprising strength. I am constantly in and out of his room, but since the first four dreadful nights, last week, before they had declared it to be gastric fever – I do not sit up with him at night as I could be of no use; and there is nothing to cause alarm. I go out twice a day for about an hour. It is a very trying time, for a fever with its despondency, weakness, and occasional and invariable wandering, is most painful to witness – but we have never had one unfavourable symptom.

That was 12 December. In the evening of 14 December, Prince Albert's breathing quickened and his doctors understood the pneumonia they could not control was with him. At some time shortly before eleven o'clock that same night, his breathing eased and then ceased. The Queen, kneeling by her husband's bed, holding his hand, waited and then whispered, 'Oh, yes, this is death; I know it. I have seen it before.'

Her father had died when she was eight months old, and with her mother dying just nine months before Albert, Victoria now experienced absolute loneliness. She went into the deepest mourning, from which she never quite emerged. And she went to the place she dearly loved, her retreat, Osborne House on the Isle of Wight. It was from Osborne, less than a week after Albert's death, that she wrote to her uncle King Leopold of the Belgians.

❖My Own Dearest, Kindest Father – For as such have I ever loved you! The poor fatherless baby of eight months is now the utterly broken-hearted and crushed widow of forty-two! My life as a happy one is ended! The world is gone for me! If I must live on, his spirit will guide and inspire me! But oh! to be cut off in the prime of life when I had hoped with such instinctive certainty that God never would part us, and would let us grow old together is too awful, too cruel! . . . I am also anxious to repeat one thing, and that one is my firm resolve, my irrevocable decision, namely that his wishes – his plans – about everything, his views about everything are to be my law! And no human power will make me swerve from what he decided and wished. . . . And I live on with him, for him; in fact I am only outwardly separated from him, and only for a time.

God bless and preserve you,

Ever your wretched but devoted Child,

Victoria R

Some of those very close to her wondered for her sanity. At first she would see no one, not even her Prime Minister, Palmerston – perhaps especially Palmerston, whom she had hardly trusted throughout her reign. The scene at her first and much delayed Privy Council meeting only added to the bizarre stories. Ministers stood in the traditional three-quarter circle, but instead of being with them, the Queen hid in an adjacent room and they had to shout to her through the door that was left just ajar.

At night she cried herself to sleep cuddling his red dressing gown. Wherever she went, she was never without his watch and red handkerchief. She even carried his keys. She grew thin, became abnormally weak and sometimes could scarcely walk. On occasions, she couldn't speak. The Queen may have been suffering from a nervous breakdown without her staff realizing what was happening. She was to write later that year, 'For me my very misery is now a necessity and I could not exist without it.'

Gradually the sympathy of her people and her ministers turned against the Queen. Her self-imposed seclusion became too trying. People like to see their monarch. They could not. She shied away from the noise and the ceremonials that were part of her expected duties, especially those in London. She became a stranger in her own capital. In 1864, a notice was tied to Buckingham Palace railings: 'These commanding premises to be let or sold, in consequence of the late occupants' declining business.'

Many of her people were experiencing a misery of their own. 1861 was the year of the new census. In the mid-1860s, there were about twenty-one million people living in England and Wales, more than three million in Scotland, and in Ireland about five and a half million. The 1861 census shows that of those twenty-one million English and Welsh, more than two and a quarter million were agricultural workers or domestic servants – still the two commonest occupations.

The Britain of the 1860s was prosperous but it was also a land in which there was squalor, poverty, and sometimes little hope. Many believed the future was far away from the British Isles: the nineteenth century was the century of the great migration of peoples. In the 1860s alone, 1.7 million would leave. Some would return, but most would have left for good.

C❖Famine drove at least a million Irishmen to the United States and elsewhere. Gold lured hardy fortune hunters to Australia, and to the bleak recesses of Canada, where they discovered a more practical if less respectable El Dorado than had dazzled the Elizabethan adventurers. Hunger for land and for the profits of the wool trade beckoned the more sober and well-to-do. All this was largely accomplished in the face of official indifference and sometimes hostility. The American War of Independence had convinced most of the ruling classes in Britain that colonies were undesirable possessions. They did not even have a departmental Secretary of State of their own until 1854. The Government was interested in strategic bases, but if ordinary people wanted to settle in the new lands then let them do so. It might cure unemployment and provide posts for penniless noblemen, but the sooner these communities became completely independent the better and cheaper for the tax-payer in England.

Shortly before Christmas 1860, the South of England was covered by rains, then frosts and snow. The terrible weather stopped all work on the Thames waterfront and in the docks. Britain was by then a great ship-owning nation. There were, for example, about 160,000 seamen in England and Wales; more than 30,000 bargemen and lightermen; about the same number of dock-workers. London was one of the busiest ports in the world. Newspapers of the time report that the frost froze the London docks on 17 December and didn't ease until 19 January. And if the docks couldn't work, then neither could the hauliers nor the markets. Thousands were laid off. The Poor Laws were supposed to help but, in many cases, they failed to do so.

❖For five weeks, the pauperism was raised from the average of 96,752 to 135,389. Mr Howard, Chairman of the Bethnal-green Board of Guardians, is of the opinion that but for charitable subscriptions, 'there would have been fearful loss of life from starvation'. Mr Selfe, the police magistrate, adds, 'I think the distress was terrible; the amount to which the pawnshops were filled with the absolute necessities of the home, and the way in which it was stripped to support bare life, was terrible.' . . . The workhouse test, or the labour test, which no doubt was properly applied in the case of the sturdy vagrant or the idle, was wholly unfit to be applied to a vast number of those who were destitute. In the eastern district of the Metropolis there were numbers of the most deserving poor who would never go near the poorhouse; they would sooner die.

This was a period when the advances of the age outstripped the social needs of the people. Many of those freezing London dockers would have started their working lives loading and unloading sailing ships. Now there were vessels with steam engines (although sail was by no means finished – the famous *Cutty Sark* wasn't launched until 1869).

The railways now criss-crossed the country and, as transport spread, so did housing. The suburbs were created, with small houses, one in five of which often contained two families. In industry, Whitworth had patented his standard sizes in threads and screws. The Bessemer converter, and then Siemens with his steel-making process, accelerated the change from iron to steel. And although most of British industry relied on small firms, new systems meant factories were expanding and therefore changing the shape and skyline of towns that were now becoming cities.

CHAPTER FIFTY-THREE

1864–1870

———— ❖ ————

L ess than a year after Prince Albert's death in 1861, Palmerston was ready to concede that he needed the late Prince Consort's advice. Albert would have known what was going on in Germany.

C❖. . . William I of Prussia ascended the throne of Frederick the Great, and marked the first years of his reign with three public appointments whose impact on European history and modern events is incalculable. Count von Moltke became Chief of the General Staff, Count von Roon Minister of War, and – most important of all – Count Otto von Bismarck was recalled from the Embassy in Paris to become Minister-President of Prussia. First as Chancellor of the North German Federation, and finally of the German Empire, this singular genius presided with a cold passion over the unification and Prussianization of Germany, the elimination of Prussia's nearest European rivals, and the elevation of William to the German Emperor's throne in 1871. He was to serve, or dominate, William and his two successors uninterruptedly until his clashes with the young Emperor William II finally and acrimoniously ended his tenure in 1890.

There's another connection, a more immediate one. The Queen's daughter, Vicky, was married to William's son, Frederick, or Fritz as he was always known. And, albeit briefly, Fritz became Emperor. It was their son who became known in Britain, especially in the First World War, as Kaiser Bill.

Palmerston did not understand what Bismarck was up to, and nor did Russell. They should have done. During Palmerston's time at the Foreign Office, he had doubled the number of dispatches coming into Whitehall from the embassies and he had read them. But then, Bismarck was simply a Prussian ambassador to St Petersburg and Paris who was now in a position of some power. What they would soon discover was that to Bismarck, power, absolute power, was everything.

When the Poles rose against the Russians, Bismarck supported the Russians. He'd never cared for the idea of Polish independence and he looked to the future when he, in turn, might need Russian support. Britain could do little about it. Public opinion supported the Polish rebels, to too did Palmerston, but he didn't want to go to war with her. Worse still, neither Palmerston nor Russell seemed to remember the strategic axiom of never making threats unless you can, if necessary, carry them out. Militarily, Britain couldn't help the Poles.

And as for the confrontation with Denmark, in 1864, during which the Duchies of Schleswig and Holstein were attached to Prussia, Palmerston ought to have been better prepared. And once more there was a royal family connection: Bertie, the Prince of Wales, married in March 1863. His bride was Princess Alexandra of Denmark so it was no wonder that the Danes thought it reasonable for the British to side with them – which they did, but then they didn't. It was that sort of affair. The Schleswig-Holstein Question was so complicated that it became a euphemism for any subject to which there was no conclusive and textual answer in every political examination paper for the next 100 years. It was said at the time that only three people understood it: one was insane, the second was a Prussian and had got it wrong and the third was Palmerston who knew nothing about it. But he was not alone, the question had remained unanswered since mediaeval times.

C❖With the death of the King of Denmark, without a direct heir, an old dispute about the succession to the Duchies of Schleswig and Holstein came to a head. For centuries the Danish kings had ruled these Duchies as fiefs of the Holy Roman Empire. The Empire had vanished [in 1806] but the Duchies remained an ill-defined part of the loose German Confederation created at the Congress of Vienna [concluded in 1815 after Napoleon's defeat at Waterloo]. Schleswig was half Danish in population and the Danes wished to incorporate it into their Kingdom. Holstein was wholly German. The conflict of national feeling was inflamed by dynastic issues. Was the Danish King of the new line entitled to succeed to the Duchies? There was a rival claimant in the field. Mounting German patriotism was determined to prevent the parting of the Duchies from the German fatherland.

Bismarck knew well how to cast his line in the troubled waters. The German Confederation had already clashed with the Danes on the issue, and when the new Danish King assumed sovereignty over the Duchies, Hanoverians and Saxons united in a Federal Army and occupied Holstein. At this point Bismarck intervened, dragging with him Austria. . . . In January 1864 an Austro-Prussian ultimatum was dispatched to Copenhagen, and by July Denmark was defeated and over-run and Schleswig was occupied. That superb weapon, the new Prussian Army, had hardly been extended, and its future victims were scarcely made aware of its power.

Britain did nothing much, even though she had a treaty with Denmark, and even though Palmerston had told the Commons that if Denmark were attacked, then Britain would not stand aside. More important, Palmerston, the man so interested in foreign affairs, completely misread Bismarck's determination and ability. He called him 'crazy'. He believed the French could become involved (a lasting fear of his generation), and he believed his military advisers who said the Prussian Army was not very good. Bismarck had outmanoeuvred everybody, as he would continue to do. He had Austria and Russia on his side and a certain belief that France and Britain would not hold together as allies to do anything to stop him.

C❖An ominous precedent was thus set for what the Germans politely called *Realpolitik*, while Britain and France looked on. *Realpolitik* meant that standards of morality in international affairs could be ignored whenever material advantage might be gained. In this instance Denmark, the small victim, was not extinguished, nor were the peace terms unduly onerous.

In London Palmerston and Russell were attacked in the House and in the Press. Lord Derby described the government's foreign policy as 'a policy of meddle and muddle'. But it is doubtful if the country would have wanted to go to war. Even if they had, it wasn't realistic. Britain was probably incapable of sustaining an intervention without the support of its naval power and the assurances of an equally powerful allied army.

Within a few months, and while Bismarck's Prussians plotted their next moves (against Austria and then France), Palmerston had grown physically weak. This old Irish peer was in his eighties, and although, in the General Election of 1865 Palmerston's continuing ability to appeal to the middle-class voters (and therefore the vast majority of those allowed to vote) won him another majority, by October of that year, he was dead.

Victoria, who never settled to him, saw his death as a sad state of affairs for the nation. Palmerston reflected a sometimes over-confident nation by his style, language, and prejudices, and especially his notion that all foreigners could do with a good dose of English advice. But Palmerston took his own decisions based on his own readings of any subject. His prejudices tended to be arrived at rather than instinctive. Palmerston was not a party man, he was simply Palmerston and when he was gone, so too was a remarkable age of English politicians.

Palmerston's Foreign Secretary, Lord Russell (the grandfather of the philosopher Bertrand Russell), once again became Prime Minister in 1865, and once more most people expected Russell to bring a new Reform Bill to the House.

Since 1832, the population pattern had changed – there were now new industries, new towns, and bigger boroughs, but the distribution of seats was the same. Russell's Cabinet decided to take one issue at a time, but without having thought it through. The Bill was defeated in the House and Russell offered his resignation. The Queen refused to accept it, but a week later, she was forced to. Derby became Prime Minister, and Disraeli his Chancellor of the Exchequer.

So with Disraeli, the Conservative, in Government and with Gladstone, the Liberal, in Opposition, the battle line was drawn for the debate on what would become the Second Reform Act. Disraeli took the lead. Derby was Prime Minister, but he was in the Lords; Disraeli was leader of the Commons. The Conservatives had just as much of a problem drafting their own Bill as Russell's government had had. Three ministers resigned, but eventually it went through.

The Reform Act was a political success, although it could never be said to have righted all the thirty-five-year-old legislation it replaced. The urban working class man (as long as he was a householder) was now allowed to vote, but the working class man in rural areas was not. There was still no such thing as a secret ballot. Nor were the women allowed to vote. Forty-five new parliamentary seats were created. The electoral boundaries were reshaped on the advice of a Commission, which Disraeli made sure was loaded with Conservatives. But, as might have been expected, working-class voters found few working-class men to send to Westminster.

Disraeli, not so much interested in the detail as in the result, was triumphant. There was just one further step needed and he hadn't long to wait. In February 1868 Lord Derby, who had been Prime Minister for less than two years, was too ill to carry on and so Disraeli, at the age of sixty-four, took over the Conservative leadership.

His letter to the Queen accepting the Premiership quite properly offered his devotion. But Disraeli immediately played on her vanity and her undoubted experience, coloured as it was by her assumption of what Prince Albert would have done in almost any circumstance.

❖Your Majesty's life has been passed in constant communication with great men, and the acknowledgment and management of important transactions. Even if your Majesty were not gifted with those great abilities, which all now acknowledge, this rare and choice experience must give your Majesty an advantage in judgment which few living persons, and probably no living prince, can rival.

Victoria rather cared for that letter and, for the moment, Disraeli was where he'd long wanted to be – in Number Ten. But by December, the Conservatives would be out and Gladstone and his Liberals would be in.

C❖These two great Parliamentarians in alternation ruled the land from 1868 to 1885. For nearly twenty years no one effectively disputed their leadership, and until Disraeli died in 1881 the political scene was dominated by a personal duel on a grand scale. Both men were at the height of their powers, and their skill and oratory in debate gripped and focused public attention on the proceedings of the House of Commons. . . . The political differences between them were no wider than is usual in a two-party system, but what gave the conflict its edge and produced a deep-rooted antagonism was their utter dissimilarity in character and temperament.

The arrival of these two at the political pinnacle coincided with the emergence of two distinct political parties, as opposed to vague labels beneath which various small groups congregated.

C❖Thus they faced each other across the dispatch-boxes of the House of Commons: Gladstone's commanding voice, his hawk-like eyes, his great power to move the emotions, against Disraeli's romantic air and polished, flexible eloquence. . . . To face Gladstone, Disraeli needed all the courage and quickness of wit with which he had been so generously endowed. Many Tories disliked and distrusted his reforming views, but he handled his colleagues with a rare skill. . . . In all his attitudes there was a degree of cynicism; in his make-up there was not a trace of moral fervour. Large sections of the working classes were held to Church, Crown, Empire, and aristocracy by practical interests which could be turned to party advantage. Or so he saw it. He never became wholly assimilated to English ways of life, and preserved to his death the detachment which had led him as a young man to make his own analysis of English society. It was this which probably enabled him to diagnose and assess the deeper political currents of his age.

Disraeli was a novelist before he became a politician. His father, Isaac D'Israeli, had written or edited collections of literary and historical anecdotes. Disraeli's literary education began among his father's books and he never went to university. But, when he was twenty-two, he published his first novel *Vivian Grey*. By the time he'd become an MP, in 1837, Disraeli had published nine books. In the 1840s, his political novels *Coningsby* and *Sybil* were published. It is in the first that Disraeli wrote his definition of what Conservatism was then.

He attacked something called the Tamworth Manifesto – a speech made in Tamworth, by the then Conservative Prime Minister Robert Peel, Disraeli's leader. It was always considered to be the speech that distinguished the new Conservatives from the old Tories.

❖The Tamworth Manifesto was an attempt to construct a party without principles . . . its inevitable consequence has been Political Infidelity. . . . There was indeed a considerable shouting about what they called Conservative Principles; but the awkward question naturally arose, what will you conserve? The prerogatives of the Crown, provided they are not exercised; the independence of the House of Lords, provided it is not asserted; the Ecclesiastical state, provided it is regulated by a commission of laymen. Everything, in short, that is established, as long as it is a phrase and not a fact. . . . Conservatism discards Prescription, shrinks from Principle, disavows Progress; having rejected all respect for Antiquity, it offers no redress for the Present, and makes no preparation for the Future.

And in *Sybil, or The Two Nations* Disraeli wrote:

❖Two nations; between whom there is no intercourse and no sympathy; who are as ignorant of each other's habits, thought and feelings, as if they were dwellers in different zones, or inhabitants of different planets; who are formed by different breeding, are fed by a different food, are ordered by different manners, and are not governed by the same laws. . . . The rich and the poor.

That appeared in the 1840s. There was no first hand experience of the two nations, the rich and the poor, in Disraeli's life, although in his early years he was strapped for cash – but never really poor. His research came from articles, official reports and surveys. *Sybil* is a more cumbersome book than *Coningsby*, but its message survived deep into the twentieth century.

As for Gladstone, he disliked, or rather, felt bitter towards, Disraeli. Yet perhaps his sharpest feeling against him was the way in which he had kidnapped the Queen – politically that is. Gladstone was convinced that Disraeli had blatantly and unscrupulously brought Victoria into the Conservative fold. Disraeli certainly left nothing to chance, although any explanation to be found in his own writings doesn't go that far.

❖The principles of the English Constitution do not contemplate the absence of personal influence on the part of the Sovereign; and, if they did, the principles of human nature would prevent the fulfilment of such a theory.

Which was all still true. But before the end of 1868 it was William Ewart Gladstone, not Disraeli, who was Prime Minister. And for the next half decade, Disraeli, the Queen's most devoted servant, would, once more, be on what he saw as the wrong side of the House. Gladstone became leader of the Liberals at the start of 1868 and so, for the first time, the leaders of the two main parties were men born in the nineteenth, not the eighteenth, century.

1868 was the year in which flogging was banned in the army. Sailors weren't so lucky: it would take the Admiralty another three years to be convinced of the wisdom of sparing the lash – and then only in peacetime. Transportation of criminals to the colonies was also banned. Work began on a draft Bill to abolish debtors' prisons and this was the year in which the Trades Union Congress (the TUC) was founded. It was also a year of three Prime Ministers: Derby, Gladstone and Disraeli.

Disraeli had no great intellect, but enormous and ill-disciplined style. He lacked the depth, or perhaps the real interest, to offer a way along which social injustice might be overcome. Napoleon III, the French leader of the day, said Disraeli was ignorant of the world. Disraeli's ambition was greatly inspired by his sense of being an outsider desperate to be accepted.

This then was the man who, despite Victoria's deepest reservations, would be accepted by the monarch as one of, if not the, most favoured prime minister of her time. For all his faults, Disraeli was a man of great courage and honourable emotions – which the Queen understood even if his political enemies, and friends, refused to contemplate them. It was the Oxford historian, Llewellyn Woodward, who wrote that Disraeli 'brought politics nearer to poetry, or, at all events, to poetical prose, than any English politician since Burke'.

However in November 1868, Disraeli's Conservatives lost the General Election. They did so because they were outwitted by Gladstone on the question of Ireland. Earlier in the year, Disraeli had hoped to shelve the Irish debate by referring the questions of education and land to a commission of inquiry. What couldn't be hidden, even by a Royal Commission, was the question of the disestablishment of the Anglican Church in Ireland. Gladstone put down a motion in the House to rid the state of the church he called a 'hideous blot'. This meant that the Catholics went over to Gladstone.

On the first vote, Disraeli was defeated, but adjourned the House for Easter. After Easter, he was again defeated, but had anticipated that. His plan was not to resign but to dissolve Parliament. This would delay the end of the Government, and give him the chance (which the Queen supported) of winning an election and staying in power. And when the Government went to the country, it was defeated. Gladstone and his Liberals had a majority of more than 100 seats.

For Disraeli, there were but three consolations. First, Gladstone lost his seat (but would have another, of course). Second, he asked the Queen for, and got, a title for his wife Mary Anne (she became Viscountess Beaconsfield. He became the Earl of Beaconsfield on his retirement eight years later). Third, and most important to Disraeli, he kept the friendship of the Queen.

None of this impressed Gladstone who was now Prime Minister of a Liberal Government. In the first Cabinet sat eight peers and seven commoners (including Gladstone himself). John Bright, the great orator and reformer at the Board of Trade, George Villiers, the fourth Earl of Clarendon, at the Foreign Office. Robert Lowe at the Treasury, Edward Cardwell, who was to reform the army. They were a mixture of reformers, small 'c' conservatives, radicals and Whigs.

Gladstone's first task was Ireland and when the Queen's telegram arrived asking him to form the next government, he is said to have remarked, 'My mission is to pacify Ireland.' Ireland had long preoccupied Gladstone. Here is part of a letter to his wife, Catherine, written more than twenty years earlier.

❖Ireland, Ireland! that cloud in the west, that coming storm, the minister of God's retribution upon cruel and inveterate and but half-atoned injustice! Ireland forces upon us those great social and great religious questions – God grant that we may have courage to look them in the face, and to work them through.

On 1 March 1869, Gladstone introduced his Irish Church Bill (to disestablish the Church of Ireland) in the Commons. It went through on the second reading by 118 votes. On the third, by 114. But the real battle came in the Lords. It was more than a battle for a Bill, this was a Constitutional matter. The Government was telling the Lords to send back its Bill without blemish, but the Lords might well vote against it on the second reading. At this point, the Queen intervened. As much as she preferred Disraeli to Gladstone, up with a Constitutional crisis, the monarch would not put. And so before the damage might be done, she wrote to the former Prime Minister, Lord Derby, a Conservative.

❖Balmoral, June 7, 1869

The Queen writes to Lord Derby today upon a subject which causes her the deepest anxiety, and, she must add, considerable surprise. She hears that it is proposed to throw out the Irish Church Bill by opposing the second reading.

The Queen has never concealed her opinion as to this measure – which remains unaltered; but, after the Dissolution last autumn, and the large majorities with which the Bill has been passed in the House of Commons, for the House of Lords to throw it out, and thus place itself in collision with the House of Commons, would be most dangerous, if not disastrous.

The Queen knows only too well how loyal, and how devoted to her person and Throne, Lord Derby is; and she cannot therefore doubt, that he will pause before he concurs in pursuing a course fraught with such danger to the country and constitution. If the House of Lords does not oppose the second reading, it will be in his power to make important and useful amendments, which it is hoped the House of Commons may be disposed to adopt.

This would raise the House of Lords in the country; but to put itself into collision with the other House would – above all at this moment when alas! the aristocracy is lowered by the conduct of so many who bear the oldest, proudest names – she must repeat it, lead to most disastrous results.

Most earnestly does the Queen appeal to Lord Derby to try to prevent this dangerous course from being pursued.

Two days later, Lord Derby replied – at some length.

❖St James' Square, June 9

Lord Derby, with his humble duty, submits to your Majesty the expression of his deep regret at finding by the letter with which he was honoured yesterday evening, that the course which he has felt himself bound to take with regard to the Irish Church Bill, has caused your Majesty the deepest anxiety and even surprise . . . He ventures to tell your Majesty that there is no sacrifice that he would not be prepared to make for your Majesty's ease and comfort, except that of his own personal honour and character, which would be involved in his abstaining from opposing such a measure as has been brought forward by your Majesty's Ministers.

So it was a matter of honour. And after all Derby had, for most of his political life, been set against the ideas behind the Bill. But he also saw the danger ahead.

❖Lord Derby does not affect to conceal from himself the serious peril of a collision with the House of Commons, especially under the guidance of the present head of your Majesty's administration; but on the other hand he sees in the passing of this measure consequences so infinitely more serious, that he will not venture to contemplate them, still less to hint at them to your Majesty. . . . Having, however, submitted to your Majesty, with that frankness which your Majesty has always graciously allowed him to use, his own individual opinion, he may add . . . that there is a great probability that a majority of the House of Lords may support the Second Reading of the Bill, in hopes that some substantial amendments may be introduced in Committee; and that this probability would be greatly increased if any assurances were given by your Majesty's Ministers that such amendments would be favourably, or even fairly considered. But the House of Lords have at present no reason to anticipate such a conclusion. Every amendment proposed in the Commons tending to mitigate the severity of the enact-ment has been summarily, and even contemptuously rejected by Mr Gladstone, and the majority which blindly follows him; and the organs of the Government in the Press have not hesitated to say that any amendment of importance would be tantamount to a rejection of the Bill, and to menace the House of Lords with the most serious consequences, to which they venture to assume your Majesty's consent.

And now, the irreconcilable Constitutional difference.

❖Lord Derby is bound to say that no amendments would remove his individual objections to the whole principle of the Bill; but he ventures to add that if there be one more certain than another to ensure its rejection, it is the language of menace and coercion which is sought to be applied to the House of Lords; and to which if they were to submit, their influence in the State would be for ever and deservedly lost.

The Bill went through. The Conservative peers had, for the first time in twenty years, been defeated on an important piece of legislation. But the intervention of the Queen, and the long reply of Lord Derby, is a reminder that the twentieth-century debate over the power of the House of Lords has been heard many times. In the nineteenth century, a prime minister could still live in the Lords – but the real power, and *the monarch's concern for that power*, rested in the Commons.

Certainly for hundreds of years, the Lower House had nursed its right to take decisions, with the 'advice and consent' of the Upper House. In June 1869, the Commons, the Prime Minister and the monarch reminded their Lordships of their duty to give that advice, but above all, that consent, when the Commons so demanded. And so they did. But that, of course, was not the end of the debate. However, Gladstone's Government was not a set-piece government, not the sort that had almost casually ruled Britain in the 1850s. It was a government full of imagination, an intelligent administration, a government of ideas.

C❖The Civil Service, the Army, the universities, and the law were all attacked and the grip of the old landed interest began to crumble. The power of what James Mill [the political philosopher whose writings had influenced, among others, Karl Marx] had called the 'sinister interests' shrivelled bit by bit as the public service was gradually but remorselessly thrown open to talent and industry. Freedom was the keynote, *laissez-faire* [the policy of government not interfering with economic matters] the method; no undue extension of Government authority was needed; and the middle class at last acquired a share in the political sphere equal to their economic power. Gladstone came in on the flood; a decisive electoral victory and a country ready for reform gave him his opportunity . . . in spite of bitter opposition and in defiance of his own early principles, which had been to defend property and the Anglican faith, he [Gladstone] carried, in 1869, the disestablishment of the Protestant Church of Ireland. This was followed next year by a Land Act which attempted to protect tenants from unfair eviction . . . the extension of the franchise and the general Liberal belief in the value of education led to the launching of a national system of primary schools. This was achieved by WE Forster's Education Act of 1870, blurred though it was, like all education measures for some decades to come, by sectarian passion and controversy. At the same time patronage was finally destroyed in the home Civil Service.

The judicial system was simplified and modernized and university teaching posts were now thrown open to men of any religious persuasion. And next came the overhaul of the army, the role for Edward Cardwell. The army hated this. In truth, the army had been left to itself since Waterloo, more than half a century ago. Flogging was abolished (in peacetime anyway). And a man could now join up for as little as six years and then go on reserve for six years. But the biggest shock to the military system came when, in 1871, officers found they could no longer buy commissions and the Commander in Chief was, for the first time, made subordinate to the Secretary of War. The county infantry regiments were created and soldiers were gradually armed with the new Martini-Henry breech-loading rifle.

C❖All this was achieved in the space of six brilliant, crowded years, and then, as so often happens in English history, the pendulum swung back. Great reforms offend great interests. The Anglicans were hit by several measures; the Non-Conformists found little to please them in the Education Act. The Army and Court resented Cardwell's onslaught. . . . An unsuccessful Licensing Bill, prompted by the Temperance wing of the Liberal Party, estranged the drink interest and founded an alliance between the brewer and the Conservative Party. Gladstone was soon to complain that he had been borne down from power 'in a torrent of gin and beer'.

There was another question of power under discussion: the monarchy. In October, a plot to kidnap the Queen was discovered. And shortly before Christmas, the Government thought there would be a Fenian (Irish Republican) attempt to capture her at Osborne on the Isle of Wight. Nothing happened and Victoria suspected that the plots were imaginary anyway (although there had, by this time, been five attempts on her life). But since Prince Albert's death in 1861, Queen Victoria rarely visited London and she thought this was a ruse to get her to leave the places she loved, Osborne and Balmoral, and return to her public duties. To many, Victoria had become the invisible queen.

And when, in 1870, the Third French Republic was declared in Paris, Republican ideas spread, albeit momentarily, to England. A rally in Trafalgar Square demanded that the Queen should step aside. In 1871, some Radical MPs began to question the Civil List. They wanted to know why the people paid for the royal children. In Parliament, they wanted to know the reason for handing out money to Prince Arthur, the 'princely pauper' as they called him. In November 1871 the Radical MP for Chelsea, Sir Charles Dilke, said the royal family cost too much and weren't worth it. *The Times*, while condemning what Dilke had said, also noted that his definition of royalty as a 'cumbersome fiction' was, in fact, received with 'great enthusiasm'.

Five months later, Dilke got up in the House to move a motion that there 'be laid before the House certain returns relating to the Civil List'. This was nothing but a way of getting a Republican debate. Dilke got his motion listened to, but only two MPs supported him. Dilke (whose father, incidentally had been a friend of Prince Albert's) was not really much of a Republican at heart. And by the time he spoke, the mood of the nation had shifted back to the Crown. 'A certain sympathy', it was called.

And when, in December 1871, Bertie, the Prince of Wales, was struck down with typhoid – exactly ten years, almost to the day, after his father's death from the same illness, the nation waited anxiously for news. So serious was the Prince's illness that the bell ringers of St Paul's were gathered to toll another royal mourning. The Prince recovered, but the Republican cause did not.

CHAPTER FIFTY-FOUR

1870–1885

———— ❖ ————

In the 1860s the Industrial Revolution put to sea. For shipping, it was necessary to have high-quality steel, not so much to build the ships themselves, but to make boilers that could stand enormous pressures, and which wouldn't be too big. The secret which engineers needed to unlock was a technique to use the steam not once, but twice – and that could only be done if the steam was pushed through under enormous pressure.

In 1865, a Liverpool engineer-turned-shipowner called Alfred Holt built three ships fitted with engines that met the criteria, and could carry 3000 tons of cargo – twice as much as the big clippers – as well as plenty of coal, and could steam, at ten knots, for more than 8000 miles without stopping. This meant that one of these new steam ships could get to China and back in about two months. Even in good weather conditions the clippers would take three months, and carry nowhere near that amount of cargo.

And then, in the year that the *Cutty Sark* was built, 1869, the Suez Canal was opened. This gave the new steam ships an advantage. By the end of the 1870s only the smaller ships were built of wood. A centuries-old tradition had died. Also about to die was one of Britain's most famous writers, Charles Dickens. In 1868 he returned from a series of gruelling public readings in America. He was in poor health but two years later he began work on his final novel, *Edwin Drood*. He did not live to finish it. One of the last people to see him was Lord Redesdale.

❖One night towards the end of May [1870], I was at the theatre with Charles Dickens and old Lady Molesworth. Just we three in a private box. Between the acts we had great fun. Dickens was in high spirits, brim-full of the *joie de vivre*. His talk had all the sparkle of champagne, and he himself kept laughing at the majesty of his own absurdities, as one droll thought followed another. He was not always in such vein, for if he thought he was being lionized he would sit mumchance; but he really liked the old lady and of course I did not count; so he was at his ease and at his very best, so bright, so merry and – like his books – so human.

During the evening Lady Molesworth insisted on his naming a night to go and dine with her. The date was fixed and on the following day the invitations came out for a day in June. Alas! That dinner never came off, for on June 9, two or three days before the night agreed upon, the whole English-speaking world was stricken with grief. Dickens was lying dead at his beloved Gad's Hill. It seemed impossible. He had been so brilliant that night. He was only fifty-eight years of age, and though we knew that he suffered terribly from exhaustion after his readings, which seemed to sap all his energy, undermined as it had been by the strain of many troubles, added to hard and incessant work, he was at times still so young and almost boyish in his gaiety that it was an unspeakable shock.

Dickens was an optimist who believed that human nature would eventually over-ride the power of the institutions in which he had so little trust. The extent to which he was mourned by the vast middle class suggests that he was far from alone in his belief.

One of the first demonstrations of a change in social policy came in the same year Dickens died – in education. The Minister who introduced the new Education Act was William Edward Forster. His Bill was an important advance. Its purpose was to provide more schools, good and active schools inspectors, and religious freedom – a controversial subject if ever there was one. The Church schools could and did carry on, with increased grants, but no local authority money. Most important, this was to be the first time that local authorities had money for education. Local education boards could now put education on the rates. For the first time, children would not be denied elementary education because they came from impoverished families. It was a beginning.

The imaginative reforms of the Gladstone government are said to have drawn the template for the twentieth-century state: Education, the Law, the Civil Service. But the very brilliance of the Gladstonian changes helped bring about his government's downfall. Real reform means the reform of the institutions that make up the Establishment, and thorough reform creates enemies within the Establishment. So perhaps Gladstone tried to do too much. Certainly the reform of the army came too late to have an effect on the implementation of foreign policy. An illustration of this came in the summer of 1870.

France had declared war on Prussia. There was plenty of diplomatic posturing, but with a run-down army, there really was little that Britain could have done, and so Britain did nothing. No one supported the French, who lost, and the Emperor, Napoleon III, was captured. The Empress escaped to Britain where she made their home at Camden House in Chislehurst, south of London. But the astonishing military efficiency of the Prussian Army reinforced the Gladstone Cabinet's belief that the British Army had to be re-structured and re-equipped as a matter of national urgency. And of equal long-term importance, as a result of the armistice treaty negotiations it was decided that all nations should now recognize William of Prussia as the German Emperor.

C❖. . . gradually the Powers of Europe drifted into two separate camps, with Britain as an uneasy and uncommitted spectator. From this division, growing into an unbridgeable chasm, the eruptions of the twentieth century arose. . . . Nevertheless, so long as Bismarck led Germany, he was careful to do nothing to arouse British hostility. . . . Not until Kaiser William II had dismissed the great Chancellor and plunged into provocative policies did Britain fully awake to the Teutonic menace.

At home, one of the reforms of the Liberal Government was about to work against Gladstone. In 1872 he had introduced the Ballot Act. For the first time in British history, men would vote in secret. In theory at any rate, they would not be pressured by lords or masters, landlords or employers. The Conservatives saw the advantage of good party organization, and Conservative Associations began to appear across Britain. The Liberals began to lose by-elections.

In 1873 Gladstone was defeated in the Commons when he tried to introduce a Bill to set up a new Dublin University at which Roman Catholics and Protestants could study side by side. In January 1874, Gladstone called an election and ran on the platform not simply of tax cuts, but of the abolition of Income Tax altogether. The voters were not fooled. And so, perhaps thanks to the secret ballot which the Liberals had introduced, the Conservatives came back to majority government for the first time since the collapse of the Tories almost thirty years earlier – which, of course, Disraeli had helped bring about.

C❖While his great adversary devoted his leisure to felling trees at Hawarden [the Gladstone home in Flintshire] and writing articles about Homer, Disraeli seized his chance. . . . For twenty-five years he had been the leader of the Conservative Party in the House of Commons and now he was over seventy. His physique had never been robust, and his last years, made lonely by the death of his wife, were plagued by gout and other ailments. . . . [He] succeeded in persuading much of the Conservative Party not only that the real needs of the electorate included healthier conditions of life, better homes, and freedom to organize in the world of industry, but also that the Conservative Party was perfectly well fitted to provide them. Well might Alexander Macdonald, the miners' leader, declare later that 'The Conservative Party have done more for the working classes in five years than the Liberals have in fifty.' Gladstone had provided the administrative basis for these great developments, but Disraeli took the first considerable steps in promoting social welfare.

The second part of the new Conservative programme, Imperialism, had also been launched before Disraeli came to power. Gladstone's passion for economy in all things military, his caution in Europe, and his indifference to the Empire jarred on a public which was growing ever more conscious of British Imperial glory. . . . At first Disraeli was brilliantly successful. The Suez Canal had been open for six years, and had transformed the strategic position of Great Britain. No longer was the Cape of Good Hope the key to the route to India and the Far East. The Foreign Office had been curiously slow to appreciate this obvious fact and had missed more than one opportunity to control the waterway. In 1875 Disraeli, on behalf of the British Government, bought, for £4 million, the shares of the Egyptian, Khedive Ismail, in the Canal. . . . [He] was bankrupt and glad to sell; his holding amounted to nearly half the total issue. The route to India was safeguarded, a possible threat to British naval supremacy was removed, and – of fateful importance for the future – Britain was inexorably drawn into Egyptian politics.

In the mid-nineteenth century there was a rise in nationalism, especially in South Eastern Europe. The main area of contention was the Balkan Peninsula: Serbia, Montenegro, Albania, Greece, Bulgaria, Romania, Turkey, and the Austrian-controlled districts of Dalmatia, Bosnia, and Herzegovina. The Christians in the region began to rebel against the Islamic rule of the Ottoman Empire.

The Russian Christian Orthodox Tsars defended the rights of the Christians – at least that was the reason they gave for becoming involved against Turkey. The British supported the Turks because they feared the Russians might get control of the Mediterranean and Indian trading routes. Meanwhile, the Russians had made it clear that they wanted control of the waterway between Asia and Europe: the Bosphorus. The first major confrontation came in 1830 with the Greek War of Independence, but more particularly in 1854 when Russia went to war with Turkey. In this war, the Crimean War, Turkey was supported by the British and French.

In 1874, there was a bad harvest in Herzegovina. In the following year, Slav peasants in Herzegovina revolted against the tax collectors, and Serbian volunteers came to help them. The fighting spread through Bosnia. In the late spring of 1876, the Bulgarians joined the rebellion. The Turks sent in troops.

C❖The Crimean War had been mismanaged by the soldiers, and at the peace the diplomats had done no better. Most of the Balkans still remained under Turkish rule, and all attempts to improve the Ottoman administration of Christian provinces had foundered on the obstinacy of the Sultan and the magnitude of the task. Slavs, Romanians, and Greeks were united in their detestation of the Turk. Revolt offered little hope of permanent success, and they had long looked to the Tsar of Russia as their potential liberator. Here was a fine dilemma for the British Government. The possibility of creating independent Balkan states . . . was not yet seriously contemplated. The nice choice appeared to lie between bolstering Turkish power and allowing Russian influence to move through the Balkans and into the Mediterranean by way of Constantinople. The threat had long been present, and the insurrection which now occurred confronted Disraeli with the most difficult and dangerous situation for Great Britain since the Napoleonic Wars.

Disraeli, now in his seventies, was tired, gouty and asthmatic, and had wondered aloud to the Queen whether or not he should retire. She persuaded him to stay, but sent him to the Lords as the first Earl of Beaconsfield, which she believed to be a less strenuous place, but from which Disraeli could, as she put it, 'direct everything'. But he could not direct the news of terrible Turkish atrocities in Bulgaria.

C❖Disraeli, handicapped by faulty reports from his ambassador at Constantinople, who was an admirer of the Turks, failed to measure the deep stir in public opinion. In reply to a Parliamentary question in July he took leave to doubt whether 'torture has been practised on a great scale among an Oriental people who seldom, I believe, resort to torture, but generally terminate their connection with culprits in a more expeditious manner'. This tone of persiflage fanned into fierce and furious activity the profound moral feeling which was always simmering just below the surface of Gladstone's mind.

What happened after the Bulgars joined the rebellion and the Turkish irregular troops, the Bashi-Bazouks, arrived, was indeed massacre. It's been estimated that 12,000 Christian Bulgarians were massacred. The exact figure was never known.

Gladstone had been in semi-retirement for nearly two years – since his general election defeat. When the massacre reports began to circulate he was at Hawarden, contemplating the writings of Thomas Aquinas. He was working on the question of religious and philosophical retribution. Bulgaria called him away from his studies and in three days he wrote what was to become his famous pamphlet, 'Bulgarian Horrors and the Question of the East'. It was this document, or rather the events which prompted him to write it, that brought Gladstone back to Front Bench politics.

❖I entreat my countrymen, upon whom far more than perhaps any other people in Europe it depends, to require, and to insist, that our Government, which has been working in one direction, shall work in the other, and shall apply all its vigour to concur with the other States of Europe in obtaining the extinction of the Turkish executive power in Bulgaria. Let the Turks now carry away their abuses in the only possible manner, namely by carrying off themselves. Their Zaptiehs, and their Mudirs, their Bimbashis and their Yuzbachis, their Kaimakams and their Pashas, one and all, bag and baggage, shall, I hope, clear out from the provinces they have desolated and profaned. This thorough riddance, this most blessed deliverance, is the only reparation we can make to the memory of those heaps on heaps of dead; to the violated purity alike of matron, of maiden, and of child; to the civilization which has been affronted and shamed; to the laws of God or if you like of Allah; to the moral sense of mankind at large.

The uncompromising accusations, the finger pointing at criminal acts and unquestionable sin, could never have been made by Disraeli. This was Gladstone at his most outraged.

❖There is not a criminal in a European gaol, there is not a cannibal in the South Sea Islands, whose indignation would not arise and overboil at the recital of that which has been done, which has too late been examined, but which remains unavenged; which has left behind all the foul and all the fierce passions that produced it, and which may again spring up in another more murderous harvest, from the soil soaked and reeking with blood, and in the air tainted with every imaginable deed of crime and shame. . . . No Government ever has so sinned.

Curiously, Gladstone was not directly identified with this pamphlet until the following year. Disraeli, or the Earl of Beaconsfield as by then he was, was overwhelmed with anger. After all, Gladstone's insistence that the Government had done nothing suggested a guilt that was not quite fairly cast. To Disraeli, Gladstone was no better than the Bulgarians (see below) – and he said so.

At the end of 1876, a conference was held at Constantinople which agreed Russian proposals for Turkish reform. The problem was the Turks didn't agree to them. The Sultan, persuaded by the Young Ottoman leader, Midhat Pasha, appears to have believed that recent history would repeat itself – that there'd be another Crimean War. Then, in the spring of 1877, the Austrians, ever mindful of the rich pickings of the Balkans, agreed to remain neutral in the inevitable war between Turkey and Russia, as long as she would be given Bosnia and Herzegovina, and that the Russians would promise not to set up a Slav state at the end of the war. So, the war began. The Russians went into the Balkans – the graveyard of so many strategic ambitions. The advance should have been swift but it wasn't. At a place called Plevnia in Bulgaria, the Turks held out until starved into submission.

Gradually, the mood in Britain changed. The nasty Turks who'd massacred 12,000 innocent Bulgar Christians were now the heroic defenders. It became, for some, a weekend sport to go along to Gladstone's London house and shout at his windows. By the third week of January 1877, the Russians had reached the gates of Constantinople.

The British people resorted to jingoism. In the streets and in the music halls, the strident verses rang out.

We don't want to fight, but by jingo, if we do,
We've got the men, we've got the ships, we've got the money too.

The Royal Navy was ordered to Constantinople and Disraeli's Government asked for an extra £6 million as a war fund.

C❖In February . . . a fleet of British ironclads steamed into the Golden Horn. They lay in the Sea of Marmora, opposite the Russian Army, for six uneasy months of truce; the whale, as Bismarck said, facing the elephant.

In March Turkey and Russia signed the Treaty of San Stefano. Andrassy, the Austrian Foreign Minister, in anger called it 'an orthodox Slavic sermon'. It gave Russia effective control of the Balkans, and was obviously unacceptable to the other Great Powers [Britain, Prussia, Austria and France].

At the Congress of Berlin, a conference of the Great Powers, the area was carved up between them. Russian territory now extended to the mouth of the Danube. Bulgaria received her autonomy. Montenegro, Romania and Serbia were designated principalities. Austria was allowed to occupy Bosnia and Herzegovina, as she'd originally demanded. And in a separate piece of diplomatic trading with Turkey, Britain was given charge of a Mediterranean island called Cyprus.

When Disraeli returned from the Congress of Berlin, he claimed he had brought 'peace with honour', and there was one aspect to the settlement which was to have far-reaching consequences in British history. The Russians believed they had been defeated by Bismarck manipulating the other European partners against the Tsar. Gradually, the friendship between Russia and Germany cooled. Not many years into the future this led to an alliance of France, Britain and Russia – but not Germany.

If Disraeli had gone to the country after the Congress of Berlin, he would probably have secured a huge Commons majority. But he didn't because other matters were pressing. And when he did, almost inevitably, the nation forgot Disraeli, the preserver of peace, and Gladstone triumphed. However Disraeli earned himself a secure place in the affections of the sometimes very affectionate Queen. Disraeli had presented Victoria with the most sumptuous jewel in her crown.

C❖. . . Queen Victoria, to her great pleasure, was proclaimed Empress of India. Such a stroke would never have occurred to Gladstone, or, indeed, to the next generation of Imperialists. But Disraeli's oriental, almost mystical, approach to Empire, his emphasis on Imperial symbols, his belief in the importance of outward display, gave his policy an imaginative colour never achieved by his successors. His purpose was to make those colonies which he had once condemned as 'millstones round our necks' sparkle like diamonds.

On 1 January 1877, Victoria made a note in her journal that for the first time she had signed herself as Queen and Empress. The Imperial Raj was confirmed. In India, it was an occasion akin to the blessing and recognition of a high priestess. The Earl of Lytton, the new Viceroy, applied all the literary talents inherited from his novelist father in his telegram of loyal greeting.

> ❖Her Majesty's title as Empress of India was proclaimed at noon this day upon the Plain of Delhi, with the most impressive pomp and splendour in an assemblage attended by fifty ruling Chiefs with their followers; a vast concourse of native Princes and nobles from all parts of India; the Khan and Sirdars of Khelat; the Ambassadors of Nepaul, Yarkand, Siam, and Muscat; the envoys of Chitral and Yassin; the Governor-General of Goa and Consular body; all the Governors, Lieutenant Governors, and chief authorities, military, civil, and judicial, of British India, besides an immense gathering of Her Majesty's unofficial subjects of all classes, European and native. The flower of her Majesty's Indian Army was drawn up on the Plain, and made a splendid appearance.

If the language, and references to natives, jars in the late-twentieth century, at the time, it did not. The Maharajah of Cashmere, for example, believed it was indeed an auspicious day and the Empire really would be seen as a protective cloak for the people, whatever their caste. Disraeli considered the colonial impression important for Britain's world standing. Most of all, he loved the pomp of the whole affair and delighted in the pleasure his huge sweet-scented imperial bouquet gave his Queen.

Yet Imperial triumphs could not hide the need for further reform in Britain. Disraeli's Conservative Cabinet spent much thought on it, and continued the reforms others had started. But, just as Disraeli hadn't been able to find a solution to the problem of the two nations, the haves and the have-nots, in his fiction, nor could he truly find one in real life.

And then, once more, war erupted on two fronts: Afghanistan and Africa, and in one year, Disraeli's popularity had more or less evaporated. There's some evidence to suggest that, even by the 1870s, with their Queen Empress of India, the British were not necessarily well tuned to the idea of Imperialism. Perhaps there was too much depressing news at home. The economy was in a more or less terrible state, and there were continuing unsolved difficulties, especially Ireland. When the election came in 1880, the result was clear enough: Conservatives: 240 seats; Liberals: 347. The Queen didn't want Gladstone as her Prime Minister. She didn't want anyone but Disraeli and she all but ignored the result of the election. She said that Gladstone would 'ruin the country'. Gladstone had declared that he was loyal to the Queen, that he was devoted, but the Queen didn't for one moment believe that. And so it was with enormous reluctance, on St George's Day 1880, that Victoria accepted the inevitable.

Gladstone's fight was against what he called Beaconsfieldism. He wanted to undo everything that Disraeli stood for. Disraeli could do little but watch in growing anger. He still directed his Party's campaign against Gladstone in Parliament, and there were those who believed that this was the old Disraeli, but the cold white winter of 1880 and his asthma were killing him.

On 29 March he told his friend, Philip Rose, 'I shall never survive this attack. I feel it is quite impossible . . . this is the last of it.' On 29 April 1881, the body of Benjamin Disraeli was entombed in the churchyard vault close by his country home, Hughenden, in Buckinghamshire. Three princes – including the Prince of Wales – six dukes, and a crammed bench of lesser nobles mourned him, as the crimson cushion, on which rested his coronet and his insignia of the Garter, was carried before the coffin on which had been placed wild primroses – flowers sent by the Queen. She was distraught. The man she had once loathed had become her closest confidant. 'The terrible void makes the heart sick,' she said.

Sir Edward Hamilton, Gladstone's private secretary, hardly an admirer of Disraeli, reflected in his journals on the passing of an extraordinary statesman.

❖Thus ends one of the most remarkable and eventful careers in English history. One cannot help feeling that by his death a prodigious blank is made in politics. They will be now denuded of half their brilliancy, interest, and excitement. One of 'the two great gladiators' in the nineteenth century is gone, and the remaining one will, I know, greatly feel the disappearance of the other. Most conspicuous of all the qualities of Lord Beaconsfield comes his courage. Next to his courage would probably come his extraordinary dexterity and ingenuity, and after that his sagacity and knowledge of character.

C❖He made the Conservatives a great force in democratic politics. The large-scale two-party system with its 'swing of the pendulum' begins with him. Tory democracy – working men by hundreds of thousands who voted

Conservative – became the dominant factor. The extension of the franchise, which had hitherto threatened to engulf the past, bore it proudly forward. . . . Such was the work of Disraeli, for which his name will be duly honoured.

In 1881 scarcely remembered men were also dying, for their country in Africa. This was the First Boer War – or, as it's sometimes known, the Transvaal Revolt. British troops arrived in the Cape in 1795. After some diplomatic juggling, the British began to assume the government of the area early in the new century. They were largely ignored by the Dutch settlers, who wished simply to get on with their own lives. Then in 1828, Britain declared that English had to be the official language. That was bad enough, but when, five years later, the British passed a law freeing all slaves, it was too much for the Boers. As a result, more than 50% of the Boers trekked, with their Bibles in one hand and rifles in the other, away from the coastal regions towards the interior. This Great Trek welded the Boers into a nation with all the fervour of a chosen people.

In 1867, diamonds were discovered and the British declared the area around the mines as their territory. And then came the annexation of the Transvaal. On 16 December 1880, the Boer flag was raised over Heidelberg. In February 1881, two months before the death of Disraeli, the Boers cut to pieces the British Army at the Battle of Majuba Hill. In Britain, hardly anyone had expected the revolt of the Boers to be so decisive.

C❖Gladstone had denounced the annexation of the Transvaal . . . He himself was convinced that federation was the only solution for the South African puzzle, and . . . continued with the negotiations that had already been under way at the time of Majuba. The outcome was the Pretoria Convention of 1881, which, modified in 1884, gave virtual independence to the Transvaal.

It remained a colony, and so it was not wholly independent, as the Boers wanted.

C❖All might have gone more smoothly in the future but for two developments. Immensely rich gold fields were discovered on the Rand and a large, bustling cosmopolitan mining community was suddenly planted in the midst of the Boer farmers' Republic. Meanwhile at Cape Town, Cecil Rhodes had entered politics, resolved to create a vast, all-embracing South African dominion, and [was] endowed by nature with the energy that often makes dreams come true.

More immediately, Gladstone's Liberal Government was faced with a stiffer problem – Ireland. The terrible storms that had swept the summer pastures and arable crops of these islands at the end of the 1870s and the early 1880s had sent the economy into further decline. Irish tenant farmers were destitute. In one year alone, there were 10,000 evictions. Fury translated into violence. The Irish Land League, formed in 1879 to campaign for the security of tenants and for Home Rule, had, as its President, Charles Parnell.

Parnell was an Anglo-Irish Protestant, who since 1875 had been an MP at Westminster. The strength of the Irish lobby, the 'Home Rulers' as they're sometimes known, was great enough to force the Government to agree to put through legislation for compensation for the evicted tenants. But the Bill, at best a half-hearted piece of Parliamentary draftsmanship, was thrown out by the Lords. The Irish reacted with violence. There were burnings and beatings, and Parnell invented a tactic whose description has remained in the English language:

❖When a man takes a farm from which another has been evicted, you must show him on the roadside, you must show him in the streets of the town, you must show him at the shop counter, you must show him in the fair and in the market place, and even in the house of worship, by leaving him severely alone, by putting him into moral Coventry, by isolating him from the rest of his kind as if he were a leper of old – you must show him your detestation of the crime he has committed, and you may depend on it, that there will be no man so full of avarice, so lost of shame, as to dare to transgress your unwritten code of laws.

In other words, ostracize him. A few days after Parnell's speech, such a man was used as an example. No one would work for him, he couldn't get his horses shod, and no shop would serve him. And when he and his family escaped to the Harman Hotel in Dublin, the manager made them leave. Because of all this his name has lodged itself in the English language. His name was Captain Boycott.

The Home Rule movement wanted to repeal the Act of Union and bring back an Irish Parliament which at least had responsibility for internal government. After the election of 1874, there were nearly sixty Irish MPs sitting at Westminster. After the 1886 election, they held the balance of power at Westminster. There was, for Gladstone at least, another strand to this. It was the realization that unless some constitutional solution could be found, independence might come about by violent means. The origin of that fear was found not in London, nor in Dublin, but in New York.

In the late 1850s, James Stephens formed the Fenian Society in New York. Its aim was Irish independence from Britain. In 1867 the Fenians moved their campaign to Britain. They murdered a policeman and three Fenians were hanged. They then blew a hole in the wall of Clerkenwell gaol. Twelve people were killed. The Fenians – or the Irish Republican Brotherhood as they became – eventually faded, but only because they were replaced in 1916 by a new organization – the IRA, the Irish Republican Army.

By this time, terrorism, as it is now known, was rife. There was still in Ireland a viceroy, just as there was in India. In March 1881 a Coercion Act was passed to give him absolute power – including what was called, in the later-twentieth-century in Belfast, the power of internment.

C❖. . . Parnell, driven by Irish-American extremists and by his belief that even greater concessions could be extracted from Gladstone, set out to obstruct the working of the new land courts. The Government had no alternative, under the Coercion Act, but to arrest him. . . . what was called the 'Kilmainham Treaty' [after the Kilmainham Gaol in which Parnell was imprisoned] was concluded, based on the understanding that Parnell would use his influence to end crime and terror in return for an Arrears Bill which would aid those tenants who, because they owed rent, had been unable to take advantage of the Land Act. WE Forster, Chief Secretary for Ireland and advocate of coercion, and the Viceroy, Lord Cowper, resigned. They were replaced by Lord Frederick Cavendish and Lord Spencer. Parnell and two of his henchmen were released on May 2, and it seemed that at last there was some likelihood of peace. But these bright prospects were destroyed by a terrible event.

Within hours of Cavendish arriving in Dublin, he and his under-secretary went for a walk in Phoenix Park. They were set upon by a group calling themselves the Invincibles and stabbed to death with surgical knives. Another Coercion Act quickly followed. The Phoenix Park assassins were captured and five were hanged.

Gladstone still believed that Parnell remained the key to peace. The majority of the Cabinet believed this was akin to supping with the Irish devil. There were allegations that Parnell had been involved in – or at least approved – the assassinations, but in truth there is little evidence to say that he was. For the next couple of years there was a period of calm, but not for Gladstone. He presided over a Britain trying to recover from economic depression. In 1885, he was defeated on a budget amendment, and resigned. He then lost the 1885 election, partly because his Liberal Party was split.

C❖In the new House of Commons the Liberal majority over the Conservatives was eighty-six. But Parnell had realized his dream. His followers, their ranks swollen by the operation of the Reform Act in the Irish counties, also numbered eighty-six.

In other words, the Irish held the balance of power.

The most significant point in all this was that, very quietly, Gladstone had taken one of the most important decisions in nineteenth-century politics. He had become a convert to Home Rule for Ireland. He realized that for Home Rule to come to anything, supporting the Conservatives was more likely to bring it about than attempting to drag his own people through the lobby. What actually happened was a fiasco of political mismanagement. A new Coercion Bill was introduced, and defeated. Salisbury was forced to resign and Gladstone became Prime Minister again. Within months his Home Rule Bill was before the House. Within days it had been thrown out and so was he. Salisbury was back. The Irish Question was still on the table .

Unanswered also, was what to do about Britain's foreign policy in the Middle East.

CHAPTER FIFTY-FIVE

1886–1901

———— ❖ ————

Britain and France had set up joint rule in Egypt. Since the previous century, Britain and France had vied for control over the country. Now, after an uprising by Colonel Arabi Pasha, there was every possibility of a nationalist rebellion in Egypt.

C❖On June 11, 1882, fifty Europeans were killed in riots in Alexandria. . . . the Cabinet decided to dispatch an army under Sir Garnet Wolseley to Egypt. The decision was crowned by military success, and Arabi's army was decisively defeated . . . The Liberal instinct was now to withdraw, but Egypt could not be left a vacuum.

British advisers had tried to help in Sudan, but had not been able to prevent what happened in 1881. There was a fanatical leader called Muhammad Ahmad. He was known as the Mahdi, or 'the guided one'. Very quickly the Mahdi had control of most of the Sudan. Gladstone saw the Sudanese rebellion as a 'struggle for freedom'. He decided that it was only right to leave the country, and the Egyptians were forced to agree with him.

To make the decision was easy; to carry it out more difficult. But on 14 January 1884, General Charles Gordon, who had achieved fame in the Chinese Wars of 1859-1860 and 1863-1864 when he commanded the Chinese Army against the Taipings, left London charged by the Cabinet with the task of evacuation. He arrived in Khartoum in February, and once there he judged that it would be wrong to withdraw the garrisons and abandon the country to the mercy of the Mahdi's Dervishes. He accordingly asked for reinforcements and put forward plans for counter-attack. He was resolved to remain in Khartoum until his self-imposed mission was accomplished. By May of that year, 1884, Gordon was trapped in Khartoum. Public opinion demanded that he should be rescued. The Government, with other matters on its mind and obviously dithering, did nothing until it was too late. At last, Gordon's dilemma became a Cabinet crisis. Gladstone gave in and General Wolseley was ordered to Cairo.

C❖In October he set out from the borders of Egypt upon the 800-mile advance
to Khartoum. . . . Wolseley was aware that time was fatally short. . . . On
January 21 steamers arrived from Khartoum, sent down river by Gordon.
. . . On the 28th they reached Khartoum. It was too late. Gordon's flag no
longer flew over the Residency. He was dead; the city had fallen two days
before . . . Gordon became a national martyr.

That was in 1885. In the twelve months between June 1885 and June 1886 Britain
had four leadership changes. The obvious reason was Ireland, but there was also
a lack of cohesion in Gladstone's Liberal Party; the unpopularity of his handling
of the crisis in Sudan which led to the death of General Gordon, and the
emergence of another generation of political thinkers in the Commons – among
them the thirty-six-year-old Lord Randolph Churchill, the leader of the younger
Conservatives, and, on the other side of the House, the Liberal rebel, Joseph
Chamberlain. Salisbury was Conservative leader in the Lords, and was the man
who became Prime Minister. But he was wise enough to understand that the
chances of remaining in office were slim. He was right. By January 1886 Gladstone
was back in power, armed with his now public crusade for Irish Home Rule. But
he needed support and too many in the Liberal Party refused to support him.

Gladstone wanted an Irish Parliament in Dublin. An Irish governing
executive was to have control over internal affairs leaving, among other things,
foreign policy, defence, and custom duties to London. Ireland would keep the
vast majority of her own revenues, would have her own judges, and a loan fund
was to be set up to buy out the landlords. When the Bill was sent to the House,
Joseph Chamberlain attacked it, inflicting mortal wounds on Gladstone's
Parliamentary draftsmanship. The Bill was thrown out by thirty votes and
Gladstone failed. And when the General Election came, the people voted
against him.

The final figures show that the Conservatives had 316 MPs, Gladstone's
Liberals had 191, and Parnell 85 Irish MPs. But there were also 78 Liberal-
Unionists; they were Liberals who stood for the continuation of the Union with
Ireland and who had pulled away from Gladstone over this single issue. What
had happened was this: led by Chamberlain, the Liberal-Unionists, who might
well have attracted votes from the growing working-class movement, instead
started aligning themselves with the Conservatives. The result was that the
working-class vote had no natural home, and this meant there was a very real
electoral opportunity for a third British political party. It would be called the
Labour Party.

But if Gladstone had little to celebrate, the nation had. It was 1887, a year
of great celebration: Victoria had been on the throne for fifty years. The editor
of *The Times,* writing on the morning after the anniversary celebrations, was
quite overwhelmed.

❖No scene was ever depicted on canvas, narrated by historian, or conjured up by a poet's fancy, more pathetic, or more august than the spectacle of Victoria, Queen and Empress, kneeling yesterday at the foot of the throne to thank Heaven for her reign, with all its joys and all its griefs, of fifty marvellous years. The eye wandered over groups of statesmen, writers, orators, famous soldiers and sailors, ermine-clad judges, divines in rarely-worn vestments, Asiatic princes gleaming with jewels, forms and faces as fair as they were royal and noble, a bench crowded with Kings and the heirs of Kings. The centre to which the gaze constantly returned as the reason and interpretation of the whole was the figure seated, solitary [still dressed in mourning for her husband], in all that sunshine of splendour, on her chair of state. On her account alone, the rest were there, whatever their degree. They were met together to attest the judgment of Great Britain and the world that Queen Victoria had redeemed the pledge she accepted on that throne, beside the altar, half a century ago.

The party over, the business of government and the closing century beckoned. And Ireland nagged at every political manifesto, partly because positions on Ireland could decide real political support in the House. Salisbury's government, for example, depended on Liberal Unionists who didn't support Home Rule and had broken from Gladstone to say so. And Salisbury's Cabinet was hardly a place of calm and cheerfulness. One of the sources of anguish was Lord Randolph Churchill, the father of the twentieth-century Prime Minister. He was just thirty-seven and was the youngest Chancellor of the Exchequer and leader of the House since William Pitt. He had been one of the founders, and then the leader, of the radical Conservative group of younger MPs known as the Fourth Party. It talked about Tory Democracy. This was a programme of party reform. Churchill stirred the fears of the Tory managers.

In December 1886, he presented his Budget to Cabinet. He wanted to reduce taxation and, so that he could, he said death duties would rise, and so would estate duties on private houses; and £8 million would come out of the army and navy budget. Unsurprisingly, the War Minister refused to accept the cuts. Salisbury didn't want either to leave, but wouldn't go so far as to over-rule his War Minister.

C❖He [Churchill] resigned . . . at the wrong time, on the wrong issue, and he made no attempt to rally support. He lived for another nine years, enduring much ill-health, but already his career lay in ruins.

This dramatic fall came as the finale to a year of political sensations. It was the equivalent on the Conservative side to the Whig defection from Gladstone. Salisbury made George Goschen, a Liberal Unionist of impeccable Whig views, his Chancellor of the Exchequer, thus proclaiming that

Tory Democracy was now deemed an unnecessary encumbrance. There-after his Government's record in law-making was meagre in the extreme. The main measure was the Local Government Act of 1888, which created county councils and laid the basis for further advance. Three years later school fees were abolished in elementary schools, and a Factory Act made some further attempt to regulate evils in the employment of women and children. It was not an impressive achievement. Even these minor measures were largely carried out as concessions to [Joseph] Chamberlain.

For most of the century, local government was overseen by Justices of the Peace. They were mainly members of the landed gentry. Social, as well as political, evolution demanded local government reform, and, despite the fact that County Councillors still came from the wealthier classes, this was a real attempt to introduce democratic reform at grass-roots level.

And, while this was happening, there was a wider, more aggressive movement for social and political reform.

C❖The lull which followed the collapse of the Chartist movement had already been broken . . . by an outburst of Socialist propaganda and a wave of Trades Union activity. The first manifestation was the founding in 1881 of the Democratic Federation, which was converted to Marxism by the energy and money of a wealthy exponent of the principles of class warfare and revolution, HM Hyndman. But the working class found Marxism unattractive even when expounded by a rich man, and the movement had little success.

Of far greater importance in England was the emergence about the same time of the Fabian Society, run by a group of young and obscure but highly gifted men, Sidney Webb and George Bernard Shaw among them. They damned all revolutionary theory and set about the propagation of a practical Socialist doctrine. They were not interested in the organization of a new political party. Socialist aims could be achieved by 'permeating' the existing political parties. . . . But in 1889 the dockers of London, a miserably underpaid group, struck for a wage of six pence an hour. John Burns, one of the organizers of the strike, reminded the dockers of the relief of Lucknow.

This took place in 1858 when, during the Indian Mutiny, the British garrison was besieged, but after terrible consequences, rescued.

C❖'This, lads,' [Burns] said, 'is the Lucknow of Labour, and I myself, looking to the horizon, can see a silver gleam – not of bayonets to be imbrued in a brother's blood, but the gleam of the full round orb of the dockers' tanner.'

It was indeed the Lucknow of Labour. The dockers' victory, made possible by much public sympathy and support, was followed by a rapid expansion of Trades Union organization among the unskilled workers.

Throughout the country small groups of Socialists began to form, but they were politically very weak. Their sole electoral success had been the return for West Ham in 1892 of Keir Hardie.

Keir Hardie was a Scot. At the age of ten, he had become a coal miner in Lanarkshire. He stayed in the pits for twelve years until he was sacked. He was an agitator they said, and so he was. By 1886 he had become the secretary of the Scottish Miners' Federation. That was the year that Gladstone was defeated and the Liberal Unionists broke away to side with the Conservatives. Working-class voters saw the popular Liberal Radicals, like Joseph Chamberlain, even though they sat on the Liberal side of the House, as Conservatives. Which is why Keir Hardie had so much support when he encouraged the idea of creating a third political party, the Labour Party, instead of relying on the Liberals. And in 1892, Hardie was elected Independent Labour MP for West Ham and arrived to take his seat wearing a cap and supported by a brass band. But there was still a long way to go for the movement.

C❖Keir Hardie patiently toiled to woo the Unions away from the Liberal connection. He had some success with the new Unions which had expanded after the dock strike and were willing to support political action. He was greatly aided in his task by the reluctance of the Liberal Party to sponsor working-class candidates for Parliament, apart from a handful known as 'Lib-Labs', most of whom were miners.

The outcome was a meeting sponsored by the Socialist societies and a number of Trades Unions which was held in the Memorial Hall, Farringdon Street, London, on February 27, 1900. It was there decided to set up a Labour Representation Committee, with Ramsay MacDonald as its secretary. The aim of the committee was defined as the establishment of a 'distinct Labour group in Parliament who shall have their own Whips and agree upon policy'. The Labour Party had been founded.

The political face of Britain was indeed changing. When the final decade of the nineteenth century opened, the Conservative Leader, Lord Salisbury, had been in power for more than four years. His government lacked the sparkle of the Disraeli and Gladstone Parliaments, yet there were achievements including the Local Government Act and the Factory Act (see Churchill extract on page 593). And because the Conservatives thought that some future Liberal administration would make all schooling free, thus destroying the position of the Church Schools, they introduced a Bill to make all elementary schooling free. Some

Conservative back-benchers denounced that Bill as a 'surrender of Conservative principles'. Yet 83% of schoolchildren would now get free education, paid for by the people, the taxpayers.

It would, in the wording of the Act, be 'a grant in aid of the cost of elementary education in England and Wales at the rate of ten shillings a year for each child of the number of children over three and under fifteen years of age'. Yet Britain was falling behind other nations, and its own ambitions, by not providing a comprehensive secondary education. Here's a section from a Royal Commission report published in the middle of the 1890s.

❖Elementary education is among the first needs of a people. . . . But it is by those who have received a further and superior kind of instruction that the intellectual progress of a nation is maintained. It is they who provide its literature, who advance its science, who direct its government.

  In England, those classes which have been wont to resort to the universities have, during the last sixty or seventy years, fared well. Those who could afford to pay the very high charges made at some of the great endowed schools have had an education which, if somewhat one-sided, has been highly stimulative to certain types of mind. But the great body of the commercial and professional classes were long forced to content themselves with a teaching which was usually limited in range and often poor in quality, and whose defects had become so familiar that they had ceased to be felt as defects.

There had been improvements, of sorts. During the previous quarter of a century there were more schools. But there wasn't a central government watchdog and certainly no yardstick for standards. And the new free elementary education was really concerned with overcoming illiteracy, and it wasn't until progress had been made here that secondary education became more imaginative. By 1889, the new County Councils were told to provide technical education. This meant new colleges and they became grant maintained from central government. However, the Royal Commission report stated that the 'educational opportunities offered . . . to boys and girls who . . . leave school . . . are still far behind the requirements of our times'.

The importance of this Royal Commission report is not that it directly achieved a great deal, but that it led to later reform. This was because one of the Commissioners, Robert Morant, was the draftsman of the great Education Act of 1902. He made sure many of the Commission's recommendations appeared in that legislation, the architecture of which survived until the Butler Education Act forty years later. And so at the beginning of the decade, the Conservatives had introduced worthy but uninspiring legislative programmes. The party managers had wanted trusty Conservative, not Radical Conservative, government and that was what they got.

Gladstone's party seemed full of ideas, but little cohesion. So there was not much of a choice for the British people at the election of 1892.

C❖Liberal prospects, which had been so bright in 1889, were now badly clouded. They were not improved by the adoption of the comprehensive 'Newcastle Programme' of 1891.

The Newcastle Programme was named after the Liberal Party conference which took place in Newcastle in October 1891. It promised Home Rule for Ireland (Gladstone's last ambition), disestablishment of the Scottish and Welsh Churches, rural government, Parliaments every three years and industrial accident compensation for workers.

C❖In trying to meet the demands of every section of the party this programme gave far more offence than satisfaction. When the election came in the summer of the following year the result was a Home Rule majority of only forty, dependent on the Irish Members. . . . The majority was too thin for Gladstone's purposes, but he formed a Cabinet which included men as gifted as Harcourt, Rosebery, Morley, and Campbell-Bannerman. The brightest star of them all was HH Asquith, the most able Home Secretary of the century.

Three of them, Rosebery, Asquith and Campbell-Bannerman, were in turn to be the last three Prime Ministers of a wholly Liberal government.

C❖Gladstone was resolute. Work began immediately on a second Home Rule Bill, and in February 1893, he introduced it himself. At the age of eighty-four he piloted the Bill through eighty-five sittings against an Opposition led by debaters as formidable as Chamberlain and Balfour. There have been few more remarkable achievements in the whole history of Parliament. It was all in vain. Passing through the Commons by small majorities, the Bill was rejected on the second reading in the Lords by 419 votes to forty-one. Thus perished all hope of a united, self-governing Ireland, loyal to the British Crown. A generation later civil war, partition, and the separation of the South from the main stream of world events were to be Ireland's lot. The immediate reaction in England was one of indifference. Encouraged by their victory, the Lords hampered the Government incessantly. Only one major issue was successful, a new Local Government Act . . .

This was the Act of Parliament which led to the creation of urban and district councils, and elections to parish councils. But it wasn't the Act the Government had wanted; the Lords had wrecked it.

Gladstone fought hard against the Queen and the House of Lords, both unelected institutions, when they tried to spoil legislation he thought best for the country.

And on 1 March 1894, Gladstone rose in the House to make a speech which, in effect, marked the end for him as a Parliamentarian. His speech accepted the Lords' amendments to the new Local Government Act, but it gave him the opportunity to wonder at the differences between the centuries-old question of balance between Lords and Commoners.

❖The question is whether the work of the House of Lords is not merely to modify, but to annihilate the whole work of the House of Commons, work which has been performed at an amount of sacrifice – of time, of labour, of convenience, and perhaps of health – but at any rate an amount of sacrifice totally unknown to the House of Lords?

Well Sir, we have not been anxious – I believe I speak for my colleagues, I know I speak my own convictions – we . . . have been desirous to save something from the wreck of the Session's work. We feel that this Bill is a Bill of such value that, upon the whole, great as we admit the objections to be to the acceptance of these amendments, the objections are still greater and weightier to a course which would lead to the rejection of the Bill.

We are compelled to accompany that acceptance with the sorrowful declaration that the differences, not of a temporary or casual nature merely, but differences of conviction, differences of prepossession, differences of mental habit, and differences of fundamental tendency, between the House of Lords and the House of Commons, appear to have reached a development in the present year such as to create a state of things of which we are compelled to say that, in our judgment, it cannot continue.

It wasn't until the Parliament Act of 1911 that any government had the courage to deal with that issue, and curb the wrecking powers of their unelected lordships.

Gladstone had already decided to resign before he made that speech. It wasn't the issue of local government that made him go. He was perhaps angrier with his Cabinet's determination to support a building programme for new battleships. Gladstone the Radical, in old age hard of hearing, short of sight, retreated to his Liberal instincts that money to be spent on weapons was better spent elsewhere.

But Gladstone was a totally committed European. His was the template for modern Liberal European commitment, and perhaps because of this vision, he never fully believed that the Bismarckian policy of armed peace could usurp the greater ambition of a united Continent of Europe of which, he believed, Britain had to be part.

On 3 March 1894, two days after that speech, he went to see the Queen and resigned. She cared little for him, and was not much bothered. Four years later, William Ewart Gladstone, 'the greatest popular leader of his age', was dead.

Lord Rosebery was reluctant to be Prime Minister. He didn't really believe a Liberal could lead the country from the Lords but the Queen thought this was nonsense. She liked him, perhaps because he was instrumental in the creation of the Scottish Office (of which she much approved), but more probably because he was very careful to take her advice and explain everything to her.

C❖Rosebery had the good luck to win the Derby twice during his sixteen months in office. Not much other fortune befell him. . . . When the Government was defeated on a snap vote in June 1895, it took the opportunity to resign. . . . At the General Election, the Conservative-Liberal Unionist alliance won a decisive victory.

The Liberal-Unionists – who broke away from Gladstone over Home Rule for Ireland – had, by 1912, officially merged with the Conservatives to become the Conservative and Unionist Party, which is how the Tories got their present-day name.

C❖Lord Salisbury . . . formed a powerful administration. . . . His methods of dispatching business were by now unorthodox. It is said that he sometimes failed to recognize members of his Cabinet when he met them on rare social occasions.

But the man who, in the public eye, dominated the Government was the Liberal Unionist leader, Joseph Chamberlain, now at the height of his powers. By his own choice Chamberlain became Colonial Secretary. The excitement of politics lay in the clash of Imperial forces in the continents of Africa and Asia. And this meant wars, major and minor. The first expedition was against the Ashantis whom Britain saw as insufferable slave-raiders of the Gold Coast. By January 1896 they'd been brought to heel. In the same year, Kitchener, the British Commander in Egypt, set about the reconquest of Sudan and, at the same time, the campaign to avenge the death of Gordon.

C❖After two and a half years the Dervish Army was finally confronted and destroyed outside Khartoum at the Battle of Omdurman on September 2, 1898. This, as described at the time by a young Hussar who took part in the battle, was 'the most signal triumph ever gained by the arms of science over barbarians'.

But hardly were the victory bells silent, when others rang out, this time in alarm. For Britain was once more at war and it was a war which would take her into the twentieth century. This war was the Boer War.

It was one of those conflicts of which most have heard, yet can't quite place in the historical calendar and most certainly can't remember why British troops were fighting in Africa. Yet a half a million men fought in the Boer War. One in ten were killed or wounded. This war was the second war between the British and the Afrikaners, or Boers. Boer is the Dutch word for farmer and the Afrikaners were farmers of Dutch origin.

There are three particular characters in the story of Africa and Britain and the Boer War: Cecil Rhodes, Paul Kruger and Dr Leander Starr Jameson. Cecil Rhodes was the man who founded the De Beers diamond company and after whom Rhodesia (now Zimbabwe) was named. He was a parson's son who, as a child, was ill and so went to South Africa because it had a healthier climate. He made his money out of diamond mining and, in 1889, set up the British South Africa Company to develop the northern neighbouring territories of the Transvaal – which became Rhodesia.

Paul Kruger was an Afrikaner. He was the President of the Transvaal. His battle wasn't directly with the British Government, but the so-called Uitlanders, the non-Dutch Afrikaner settlers. They had grievances which he refused to acknowledge.

Jameson is perhaps the least known of the three. He was Cecil Rhodes's friend and the colonial administrator. He succeeded Rhodes as leader of his Progressive Party and, in 1904, became Prime Minister of the Cape Colony. In summary, Jameson, on behalf of Cecil Rhodes, led a raid on the Transvaal in an attempt to overthrow the President, Paul Kruger. This invasion failed, but it worsened relations between Britain and the Afrikaners and the eventual result was the Boer War.

C❖When Joseph Chamberlain became Colonial Secretary in 1895 he was confronted by a situation of great complexity. The Transvaal had been transformed by the exploitation of the extremely rich gold fields on the Witwatersrand. This was the work of foreign capital and labour, most of it British. . . . The Uitlanders – or Outlanders, as foreigners were called – equalled the native Boers in number, but the Transvaal Government refused to grant them political rights, even though they contributed all but one-twentieth of the country's taxation. Paul Kruger, the President of the Republic, who had taken part in the Great Trek and was now past his seventieth year, determined to preserve the character and independence of his country. He headed the recalcitrant Dutch, unwilling to make common cause with the British, and opposed to the advance of industry, though ready to feed on its profits. The threat of a cosmopolitan gold field to a close community of Bible-reading farmers was obvious to him. But his fears were intensified by the encircling motions of Rhodes' British South Africa Company, which already controlled the territories to the north that were to become the Rhodesias, and was now trying to acquire Bechuanaland to the west. [Bechuanaland is now Botswana.] Rhodes, who had large financial interests on the Rand, dreamt of a United South Africa and a Cape-to-Cairo railway running through British territory all the way.

Jameson took 500 men when he invaded the Transvaal. But the uprising had been postponed although Jameson didn't know that until too late. He and his men were captured by the Boer army, and Rhodes was forced to resign as Prime Minister of the Cape Colony.

The Boers now believed that their whole way of life was threatened by Britain and, under Kruger, they began to arm themselves for war. But it didn't come immediately. In London, Chamberlain believed war could be avoided in spite of the best advice he was getting from South Africa. The weakness in Chamberlain's, and to a similar extent, Rhodes's, reading of the situation, was that they both failed to understand the determination and grit of Kruger and the Boers. By autumn 1899, all negotiations were meaningless. Furthermore, both sides had so armed themselves, that the threat of war had a momentum of its own.

C❖At the outbreak of the war the Boers put 35,000 men, or twice the British number, in the field, and a much superior artillery derived from German sources. They crossed the frontiers in several directions . . . Within a few weeks they had invested Ladysmith to the east, and Mafeking and Kimberley to the west. At Ladysmith, on the Natal border, 10,000 men, under Sir George White, were surrounded and besieged after two British battalions had been trapped and forced to surrender their guns at Nicholson's Nek. At Mafeking a small force commanded by Colonel Baden-Powell was encircled by many times its number under Piet Cronje. At Kimberley, Cecil Rhodes himself and a large civilian population were beset. . . . Meanwhile a British army corps of three divisions was on the way as reinforcement, under the command of Sir Redvers Buller, and volunteer contingents from the Dominions were offered or were forthcoming. [But] . . . within a single December week each of them advanced against the rifle and artillery fire of the Boers, and was decisively defeated with, for those days, severe losses in men and guns.

In Britain, there was something close to bewilderment and disbelief at the defeats. For example, at Magersfontein there were more than 1000 casualties. Some of the Scottish units lost as many as six out of every ten officers. The bleak seven days for the British army became known as Black Week and Buller, who at one point panicked and ordered the besieged soldiers at Ladysmith to surrender (which they didn't), was sacked and replaced by Lord Roberts with the hero of Omdurman, Lord Kitchener, as his Chief of Staff. Perhaps, if the Boers had been content with keeping the three towns of Ladysmith, Kimberley and Mafeking under siege, they might have beaten the British. Instead they tried to capture the towns, thus using resources they could ill-afford and tactics they little understood.

The Boers were good at mounted, hit and gallop warfare and at holding onto defensive positions – they literally retreated into laagers. And now with Roberts and Kitchener running the war, with Buller sent off to Natal and with reinforcements in place, the campaign began to take on a new shape. The objectives were Bloemfontein and Pretoria, the Boer capitals. Cronje moved many of his troops from Mafeking to protect Kimberley but he was outwitted and surrendered his 4000 men to Kitchener.

C❖Thereafter all went with a rush. . . . Buller relieved Ladysmith; on March 13 Roberts reached Bloemfontein, on May 31, Johannesburg, and on June 5, Pretoria fell. Mafeking was liberated . . . and its relief provoked unseemly celebrations in London. Kruger fled. The Orange Free State and the Transvaal were annexed, and in the autumn of 1900 Roberts went home to England. After almost exactly a year of lively fighting, and with both the rebel capitals occupied, it seemed to the British people that the Boer War was finished, and won.

But the war was not won. The Boers now embarked on what they were best at – a guerrilla campaign. It began in autumn 1900, and it went on until spring 1902. It was the most vicious part of the war. Kitchener dealt with what was, in effect, a resistance movement, by setting up concentration camps. In fourteen months, more than 20,000 inmates of these camps died – mostly as a result of the conditions in them. This tragedy appears to have been due to mismanagement rather than barbarism although, at the time, there were those who didn't see it that way. When the peace came, the terms were generous and led to the final agreement in 1906. Within a few days of the war ending, Cecil Rhodes died. Salisbury resigned, and his nephew, Balfour, became Prime Minister.

At the dark point of the conflict, the so-called Black Week, the Queen had stiffened the resolve of her government. 'Please understand,' she had said, 'that there is no one depressed in *this* house. We are not interested in the possibilities of defeat. They do not exist.' But when the news of final surrender was brought to the monarch, it was brought not to Victoria. The Queen who had come to the throne in the first half of the nineteenth century was dead.

A young Welsh lawyer, by the name of David Lloyd George, joined the minority of radicals who saw the war as an indictment of Britain's Imperialist policies. Six thousand troops had died in action, and 16,000 had died from diseases. More than £220 million had been spent. But there was little to suggest that the public at large supported his view. For example the leaders of the Independent Labour Party, and the trades unions, opposed the war. But they had to accept that predictably, the working class they represented was swept up in the general patriotic atmosphere, especially over Mafeking.

When, for example, the Queen visited Wellington College, news had just arrived that the siege had been lifted. Over the college arch was the slogan, 'Welcome to the Queen of Mafeking'. For Victoria, this was a time to be seen. She wanted the people to see her take her daily drives in her coach. Gone was the reclusive Queen who refused to be the people's Queen for so many years after the death of 'Dearest Albert'. And she made clear that she wanted every dispatch, every military and political report of the war, to be on her desk. It was soon known that although now eighty, her eyesight failing and a tendency to nod off after lunch, Victoria read piles of war reports, questioned her Ministers, wept for her 'dear brave soldiers', knitted them scarves and, in 1899, sent her troops a personal Christmas present – 100,000 tins of chocolate, many of which remained unopened and more prized than any campaign medal.

In October 1900, the British Commanders appeared to believe the war was all but over but Victoria did not believe this. She told Lord Salisbury, her Prime Minister, as much. And she said that in the light of her 'great experience' she knew that the British always withdrew too soon and ended up having to send in more troops to sort out the mess.

But Lord Salisbury, encouraged by the advice of the Commander in Chief himself, Lord Roberts, decided to exploit the good news of war and called what became known as the Khaki Election. His Conservative Government was returned with a big majority – the Boer War factor had done for the Conservatives what another conflict was to do for them eighty years later. But by the end of that year it was clear that the old Queen's health was dramatically failing.

The first page of Queen Victoria's journal for 1901 makes sad reading.

❖Another year begun and I am feeling so weak and unwell that I enter upon it sadly.

Victoria had kept a daily journal since the age of fourteen. The last entry is dated 13 January 1901. She refers to two of her children, Princess Beatrice and Princess Helena, whom the family called Lenchen.

❖Had a fair night, but was a little wakeful. Got up earlier and had some milk. Lenchen came in and read some papers. Out before one, in the garden chair,

Lenchen and Beatrice going with me. Rested a little, had some food, and took a short drive with Lenchen and Beatrice. Rested when I came in, and at five-thirty went down to the drawing room, where a short service was held by Mr Clement Smith, who performed it so well, and it was a great comfort to me. Rested again afterwards, then did some signing, and dictated to Lenchen.

There is, after this last entry, a simple postscript.

❖Here on Sunday, January 13, the Queen's Journal, kept for nearly seventy years, ends. On the Monday Her Majesty saw Lord Roberts again for a short while; but within a few days the illness assumed a critical character; and on Saturday [January 19], a bulletin was published, giving her people the first intimation of the impending calamity. It said: 'The Queen has not lately been in her usual health, and is unable for the present to take her customary drives. The Queen during the past year has had a great strain upon her powers, which has rather told upon Her Majesty's nervous system. It has, therefore, been thought advisable by Her Majesty's physicians that the Queen should be kept perfectly quiet in the house, and should abstain for the present from transacting business.' The last phase was mercifully short; and at six-thirty pm on Tuesday, January 22, 1901, Queen Victoria, in the words of the final bulletin, 'breathed her last, surrounded by her children and grandchildren'.

She died at Osborne, the country home on the Isle of Wight which had remained just as it was when Albert died in 1861. Victoria had given specific instructions: hers would be a military funeral. Also, the Queen who wore widows' weeds for forty years wanted a white funeral. This was probably an idea she took from Tennyson, who once told her that all funerals should be white. And there were instructions that certain precious articles should be placed in her coffin: Prince Albert's dressing gown, a plaster moulded from his hand, family photographs. But there was one item that few ever knew existed. She had told Sir James Reid, her private physician – and no one else – that he was to place a particular photograph in her hand. Not Albert's, but that of her Scottish retainer John Brown. Reid did so, and then, being a man of great discretion and mindful that some believed Brown and Victoria had been secretly married, placed flowers on top of the photograph.

Her coffin was taken by ship, the *Alberta*, to the mainland and, close by Nelson's *Victory*, was borne ashore and thence by train to London and finally to Windsor for the funeral ceremony. The following afternoon she was buried in the mausoleum at Frogmore alongside Albert, for whom she had been in mourning for forty years.

C❖She had determined to conduct her life according to the pattern set by the Prince; nor did she waver from her resolution. Nevertheless a great change had gradually overtaken the monarchy. The Sovereign had become the symbol of Empire. At the Queen's Jubilees in 1887 and 1897 India and the colonies had been vividly represented in the State celebrations. The Crown was providing the link between the growing family of nations and races which the former Prime Minister, Lord Rosebery, had with foresight christened the Commonwealth. . . . The Queen herself was seized with the greatness of her role. She sent her sons and grandsons on official tours of her ever-increasing dominions, where they were heartily welcomed. . . . She appointed Indian servants to her household, and from them learned Hindustani. Thus she sought by every means within her power to bind her diverse peoples together in loyalty to the British Crown, and her endeavours chimed with the Imperial spirit of the age. One of her last public acts, when she was over eighty years of age, was to visit Ireland. She had never believed in Irish Home Rule, which seemed to her a danger to the unity of the Empire. Prompted by a desire to recognize the gallantry of her Irish soldiers in South Africa, she travelled to Dublin in April 1900, wearing the shamrock on her bonnet and jacket. Her Irish subjects, even the Nationalists among them, gave her a rousing reception. In Ireland a fund of goodwill still flowed for the Throne, on which English Governments sadly failed to draw. . . . When she died she had reigned for nearly sixty-four years. Few of her subjects could remember a time when she had not been their Sovereign.

And so the Victorian age closed. The population of England, Wales, Scotland and Ireland was forty-one million. There were six and a half million people living in London and more than 160,000 living in Cardiff. The population of Bolton was 168,000 and in Glasgow, 900,000. When Victoria died there were more than six million registered voters and more than 1300 unions with over two million members.

Victoria died a Queen and an Empress, the last Hanoverian, and monarch of the most prosperous nation on earth. But before the new decade was out, Edward VII would be dead and the road to the First World War would be opened.